COMPUTER ARCHITECTURE AND LOGIC DESIGN

Also Available from McGraw-Hill

Schaum's Outline Series in Computers

Most outlines include basic theory, definitions, and hundreds of solved problems and supplementary problems with answers.

Titles on the Current List Include:

Advanced Structured Cobol
Boolean Algebra
Computer Graphics
Computer Science
Computers and Business
Computers and Programming
Data Processing
Data Structures
Digital Principles, 2d edition
Discrete Mathematics
Essential Computer Mathematics
Linear Algebra, 2d edition
Mathematical Handbook of Formulas & Tables
Matrix Operations
Microprocessor Fundamentals, 2d edition
Programming with Advanced Structured Cobol
Programming with Assembly Language
Programming with Basic, 3d edition
Programming with C
Programming with Fortran
Programming with Pascal
Programming with Structured Cobol

Schaum's Solved Problems Books

Each title in this series is a complete and expert source of solved problems containing thousands of problems with worked out solutions.

Related Titles on the Current List Include:

3000 Solved Problems in Calculus
2500 Solved Problems in Differential Equations
2000 Solved Problems in Discrete Mathematics
3000 Solved Problems in Linear Algebra
2000 Solved Problems in Numerical Analysis

Available at your College Bookstore. A complete listing of Schaum titles may be obtained by writing to: Schaum Division
McGraw-Hill, Inc.
Princeton Road, S-1
Hightstown, NJ 08520

COMPUTER ARCHITECTURE AND LOGIC DESIGN

Thomas C. Bartee

Harvard University

McGraw-Hill, Inc.

New York   St. Louis   San Francisco   Auckland   Bogotá   Caracas
Hamburg   Lisbon   London   Madrid   Mexico   Milan   Montreal
New Delhi   Paris   San Juan   São Paulo   Singapore   Sydney   Tokyo   Toronto

To my mother and father

This book was set in Times Roman by Publication Services.
The editor was David M. Shapiro;
the production supervisor was Kathryn Porzio.
The cover was designed by Joseph Gillians.
Project supervision was done by Publication Services.
R. R. Donnelley & Sons Company was printer and binder.

COMPUTER ARCHITECTURE AND LOGIC DESIGN

1 2 3 4 5 6 7 8 9 0   DOC   DOC   9 5 4 3 2 1 0

ISBN 0-07-003909-7

Library of Congress Cataloging-in-Publication Data

Bartee, Thomas C.
    Computer architecture and logic design / Thomas C. Bartee.
      p.   cm.
    ISBN 0-07-003909-7
    1. Computer architecture.   2. Logic design.   I. Title.
QA76.9.A73B374   1991
004.2'2—dc20   90-42808

2. *Symbolic referencing of storage addresses.* One of the greatest facilities offered the programmer is the ability to name the different pieces of data used in the program and to have the assembler automatically assign an address to each name.

For the algebraic expression $y = ax^3 + bx^2 + cx + d$, the program can appear as shown in Table 1.7. Notice that the address of the first instruction was given the name FST, consisting of three letters, and that no further addresses in memory were specified. If we tell the assembler that FST = 1, the assembler will see that the instructions are placed memory as in Table 1.4. Notice also that the operands were simply given the variable names X, A, B, C, and D, as in the equation, instead of being assigned addresses in memory. The assembly program will assign addresses to these names of variables, and if it assigns A to 22, B to 23, C to 24, etc., the final program will look as in Table 1.4.

The assembler will also see that actual arithmetic values for X, A, B, C, and D are placed in the correct locations in memory when the data are read into the computer.

3. *Convenient data representation.* This simply means that the programmer can write input data as, for instance, decimal numbers or letters, or in some other form specific to the problem, and the assembly program will convert the data to the form required for machine computation.

4. *Program listings.* An important feature of most assemblers is their ability to print for the programmer a listing of the source program and the object program, which is in machine language. A study of these listings can greatly help the programmer to detect any errors made in writing the program and to modify the program when this is required.

5. *Error detection.* An assembler program will notify the programmer if an error has been made in the usage of the assembly language. For example, the programmer may use the same variable name (for instance, X) twice and give X two different values; or the programmer may write illegal operation codes. This sort of diagnosis of a program's errors is very useful during the checking of a new program.

Assemblers provide many other facilities to the programmer, such as the ability to use programs that have already been written as part of a new program and the ability to use routines from these programs as part of a new program. Often a programmer will

TABLE 1.7

Address in memory	Instruction word	
	Operation	Operand
FST	CLA	A
	MUL	X
	ADD	B
	MUL	X
	ADD	C
	MUL	X
	ADD	D
	STO	Y
	HLT	

have a set of different programs that are run together in different combinations. This is done simply by specifying to the assembler the variable names to be repeated in the different programs, the entry and exit points for the programs, and so on. Programs written in an assembly language can thus be linked together in various ways.

Let us consider the short program in Table 1.6, which sums even integers from 0 to 100. This will illustrate the use of symbolic names for addresses when a BRANCH instruction is used. The assembly-language program is shown in Table 1.8.

Notice that the values of the variables were specified before the program was begun; DEC indicates that the values given for A, B, C, D, and E are decimal. This enables the assembler to locate the variables in the memory and assign values to them.[4] Also note that the transfer instruction BRM was to the symbolic address N.

If the assembler were told to start the program at address 1 in the memory, conversion to object or machine language would make it look similar to the one in Table 1.6, provided the assembler decided to store A, B, C, D, and E in locations 39 through 43.

1.8   HIGH-LEVEL LANGUAGES

More advanced types of programming languages are called *compiler languages*, *high-level languages*, or *problem-oriented languages*. These are the simplest languages to use for most problems and are the simplest to learn. These languages often reveal very little about the digital machines on which they are run, however. The designer of the language generally concentrates on specifying a programming language that is simple enough for the casual user of a digital computer and yet has enough facilities to make it and its associated compiler valuable to professional programmers. In fact,

---

[4] In a sense, the operation code DEC says "assign the decimal value in the operand column to the variable name in the address column."

TABLE 1.8

Address	Operation	Operand	Comments
	Instruction word		
A	DEC	0	
B	DEC	−50	
C	DEC	2	
D	DEC	1	
E	DEC	0	
N	CLA	A	Last value of integer
	ADD	C	
	STO	A	Stores sum for next time
	ADD	E	
	STO	E	
	CLA	B	
	ADD	D	
	STO	B	
	BRM	N	
	HLT		

many languages are almost completely computer-independent; programs written in one of these languages may be run on any computer that has a compiler or translator for the language in its program library.

Certain languages have been very successful and have found extremely wide usage in the computer industry. The best-known are Fortran, Ada, Pascal, BASIC, C, and Cobol. A program written in these languages can be run on most computers that have a memory size large enough to accommodate a compiler, because most manufacturers prepare a compiler for each of these languages for their computer.

The following is a section of program written in Pascal. It shows the difference between high-level language programs and assembly language programs. This program could easily be converted into an Ada program, a C program, a BASIC program, or a Fortran program, although the languages differ considerably in their details.

```
READ (A,B,D,X);
C := 0;
Y := 0;
WHILE Y <= 2000 DO
   BEGIN
      C := C + 1;
      Y := A * X * X * X + B * X * X + C * X + D;
   END;
WRITE (C,Y);
```

QUESTIONS

1.1. Discuss possible applications of microprocessors in real-time control systems.

1.2. The computer's ability to translate languages such as Pascal and Fortran greatly simplifies programming. Comment on the difficulty a computer might have in translating English. What about ambiguities? Must programming languages avoid them?

1.3. Sometimes the same computer is used by several different companies during the day, and the computer is timeshared between these companies. Discuss problems that might arise in billing the companies for the computer's services.

1.4. Discuss interactive computer systems, and give examples of businesses and industries that might use interactive systems.

1.5. Discuss batch processing, and give several examples of businesses and industries that might use it.

1.6. Give examples of industries that might use real-time control systems for manufacturing.

1.7. Values for X, Y, and Z are stored at memory addresses 40, 41, and 42, respectively. Using the instructions for the generalized single-address computer described in Sec. 1.6, write a program that will form the sum $X + Y + Z$ and store it at memory address 43.

1.8. Explain the difference between the address of a word in memory and the word itself.

1.9. Given that values for X, Y, and Z are stored in locations 20, 21, and 22, respectively, develop assembly-language instructions to write a program that will form $X^2 + Y^2 + Z^2$ and store this at memory address 40.

1.10. Discuss the disadvantages of storing both programs and data in the same memory. In what kind of systems might it be desirable to store programs and data in different memories?

1.11. What are the functions performed by each of the following?
(*a*) CPU   (*b*) Memory   (*c*) Editor
(*d*) Operating system   (*e*) Compiler

1.12. What are some of the functions performed by a loader?

1.13. Explain how directives differ from other assembly-language instructions.

1.14. Why might a programmer use macros instead of subroutines in a program?

1.15. A computer that has separate program and data memories is often called a *Harvard* machine, after the Harvard Mark I computer. A computer that has a single memory for program and data storage is called a *Von Neumann* computer, after the IAS machine. Most personal computers belong to one of these classes. Which class, and why?

1.16. If the program in Table 1.4 is started with location 22 containing 4, location 23 containing 4, location 24 containing 4, location 25 containing 1, and location 26 containing 2, what number will be stored in location 27 after the program is run?

1.17. Write a program that will store $X^5 + X$ in register 40, using assembly language, given that X is in register 20. Use fewer than 20 instructions.

1.18. For the program in Table 1.6, if the number at address 40 were -30 instead of -50 when the program started, the number at address 43 would be the sum of all even integers from 2 to ____.

1.19. Given that a value for X is stored at address 39, write an assembly-language program that will form X^4 and store it at address 42.

1.20. Draw a flowchart showing how to find the largest number in a set of five numbers stored at locations 30, 31, 32, 33, and 34 in memory.

1.21. Given three different numbers, determine whether they are in ascending or descending order. Draw a flowchart for the problem, and write a program in assembly language. Assume that the numbers are stored in memory locations 30, 31, and 32.

1.22. Values for X and Y are stored at addresses 30 and 31. Write a program that will store the larger of the two values at address 40, using assembly language.

1.23. A value for Y is stored at location 55 and a value for A at location 59. Write an assembly-language program to store AY^3 at location 40.

1.24. Write a program to find $ax^2 + by + cz^2$, with A in location 20, B in location 21, C in location 22, X in location 23, Y in location 24, and Z in location 25. Store your result in location 40.

1.25. Using assembly language, write a program that will branch to location 300 if the number stored in memory register 25 is larger than the number stored in register 26, and that will transfer or branch to location 400 if the number at address 26 is equal to or larger than the number at address 25.

1.26. A value for X is stored at address 40. Write a program that will store X^9 at address 45, using fewer than 10 instruction words.

1.27. Calculate the largest of the three numbers A, B, and C and assign the largest of the numbers to the variable X. Write the program using the assembly language described.

1.28. Write a program, using the assembly language described, that will rearrange five numbers stored in addresses 200 through 204 so that they are in descending order (for example, 10, 3, 0, -5, -7).

1.29. Thirty numbers are stored in successive memory registers, starting at location 300. Write a program that will convert any negative numbers in the 30 to positive form. That is, write a program that will take the 30 numbers, convert each number to its positive value without changing its magnitude, and restore in it the same location. Use assembly language.

CHAPTER

2

NUMBER SYSTEMS

Since hands are the most convenient tools nature has provided, human beings have always tended to use them in counting. The decimal number system followed naturally from this usage.

An even simpler system, the binary computer system, has proven the most natural and efficient system for computer use. This chapter develops this number system along with other systems used in computer technology.

2.1 DECIMAL SYSTEM

Our present system of numbers has 10 separate symbols, 0, 1, 2, 3, . . . , 9, which are called arabic numerals. We would be forced to stop at 9 or to invent more symbols if it were not for the use of *positional notation*. An example of earlier types of notation can be found in roman numerals, which are essentially additive: III $= I + I + I$, XXV $= X + X + V$. New symbols (X, C, M, etc.) were used as the numbers increased in value: thus, V rather than IIIII is equal to 5. The only importance of position in roman numerals lies in whether a symbol precedes or follows another symbol (IV $= 4$, VI $= 6$). The clumsiness of this system can be seen easily if we try to multiply XII by XIV. Calculating with roman numerals was so difficult that early mathematicians were forced to perform arithmetic operations almost entirely on abaci, or counting boards, translating their results back to roman numeral form. Pencil-and-paper computations are unbelievably intricate and difficult in such systems. In fact, the ability to perform such operations as addition and multiplication was considered a great accomplishment in earlier civilizations.

Now the great beauty and simplicity of our number system can be seen. It is necessary to learn only the 10 basic numerals and the positional notational system to count to any desired figure. After memorizing the addition and multiplication tables and learning a few simple rules, we can perform all arithmetic operations. Notice the simplicity of multiplying 12×14 using the present system:

$$
\begin{array}{r}
14 \\
12 \\
\hline
28 \\
14 \\
\hline
168
\end{array}
$$

The actual meaning of the number 168 can be seen more clearly if it is spoken as "one hundred and sixty-eight." Basically, the number is a contraction of $1 \times 100 + 6 \times 10 + 8$. The important point is that the value of each digit is determined by its position. For example, the 2 in 2000 has a different value than the 2 in 20. We indicate this verbally by saying "two thousand" versus "twenty." Different verbal representations have been invented for numbers from 10 to 20 (eleven, twelve, . . .), but from 20 upward we break only at powers of 10 (hundreds, thousands, millions, billions). Written numbers are always contracted, however, and only the basic 10 numerals are used, regardless of the size of the integer written. The general rule for representing numbers in the decimal system using positional notation is as follows: $a_{n-1}10^{n-1} + a_{n-2}10^{n-2} + \cdots + a_0$ is expressed as $a_{n-1}a_{n-2} \cdots a_0$, where n is the number of digits to the left of the decimal point.

The *base*, or *radix*, of a number system is defined as the number of different digits that can occur in each position in the number system. The decimal number system has a base, or radix, of 10; that is, the system has 10 different digits (0, 1, 2, . . . , 9), any of which may be used in each position in a number. History records the use of several other number systems. The quinary system, which has 5 for its base, was prevalent among Eskimos and North American Indians. Examples of the duodecimal system (base 12) may be seen in clocks, inches and feet, and dozens or grosses.

2.2 BISTABLE DEVICES

The basic elements in early computers were relays and switches. The operation of a switch or relay is essentially *bistable*, or binary in nature; that is, the switch is either on (1) or off (0). The principal circuit elements in more modern computers are semiconductor devices. The desire for reliability led designers to use these devices so that they were always in one of two states, fully conducting or nonconducting. A simple analogy may be made between this type of circuit and an electric light. At any given time the light (or semiconductor) is either on (conducting) or off (not conducting).

Because of the large number of electronic parts used in computers, it is highly desirable to utilize them in such a manner that slight changes in their characteristics will not affect their performance. The best way of accomplishing this is to use circuits that are basically bistable (having two possible states).

2.3 COUNTING IN THE BINARY SYSTEM

The same type of positional notation is used in the binary number system as in the decimal system. Table 2.1 lists the first 20 binary numbers.

TABLE 2.1

Decimal		Binary	Decimal		Binary
1	=	1	11	=	1011
2	=	10	12	=	1100
3	=	11	13	=	1101
4	=	100	14	=	1110
5	=	101	15	=	1111
6	=	110	16	=	10000
7	=	111	17	=	10001
8	=	1000	18	=	10010
9	=	1001	19	=	10011
10	=	1010	20	=	10100

Although the same positional notation system is used, the decimal system uses powers of 10 and the binary system powers of 2. As was previously explained, the number 125 actually means $1 \times 10^2 + 2 \times 10^1 + 5 \times 10^0$. In the binary system, the same number (125) is represented as 1111101, meaning $1 \times 2^6 + 1 \times 2^5 + 1 \times 2^4 + 1 \times 2^3 + 1 \times 2^2 + 0 \times 2^1 + 1 \times 2^0$.

To express the value of a binary number, therefore, $a_{n-1}2^{n-1} + a_{n-2}2^{n-2} + \cdots + a_0$ is represented as $a_{n-1}a_{n-2} \cdots a_0$, where a_i is either 1 or 0 and n is the number of digits to the left of the binary (radix) point.

The following examples illustrate the conversion of binary numbers to the decimal system:

$$101 = 1 \times 2^{3-1} + 0 \times 2^{3-2} + 1 \times 2^{3-3}$$
$$= 1 \times 2^2 + 0 \times 2^1 + 1 \times 2^0$$
$$= 4 + 1 = 5$$

$$1001 = 1 \times 2^{4-1} + 0 \times 2^{4-2} + 0 \times 2^{4-3} + 1 \times 2^{4-4}$$
$$= 1 \times 2^3 + 0 \times 2^2 + 0 \times 2^1 + 1 \times 2^0$$
$$= 8 + 1 = 9$$

$$11.011 = 1 \times 2^{2-1} + 1 \times 2^{2-2} + 0 \times 2^{2-3} + 1 \times 2^{2-4} + 1 \times 2^{2-5}$$
$$= 1 \times 2^1 + 1 \times 2^0 + 0 \times 2^{-1} + 1 \times 2^{-2} + 1 \times 2^{-3}$$
$$= 2 + 1 + \frac{1}{4} + \frac{1}{8}$$
$$= 3\frac{3}{8}$$

Note that fractional numbers are formed in the same general way as in the decimal system. Just as

$$0.123 = 1 \times 10^{-1} + 2 \times 10^{-2} + 3 \times 10^{-3}$$

in the decimal system,

$$0.101 = 1 \times 2^{-1} + 0 \times 2^{-2} + 1 \times 2^{-3}$$

in the binary system.

2.4 BINARY ADDITION AND SUBTRACTION

Binary addition is performed in the same manner as decimal addition. Actually, binary arithmetic is much simpler to learn. The complete table for binary addition is as follows:

$$0 + 0 = 0$$

$$0 + 1 = 1$$

$$1 + 0 = 1$$

$$1 + 1 = 0 \qquad \text{plus a carry-over of 1}$$

Carry-overs are performed in the same manner as in decimal arithmetic. Since 1 is the largest digit in the binary system, any sum greater than 1 requires that a digit be carried over. For instance, 100 plus 100 binary requires the addition of the two 1s in the third position to the left, with a carry-over. Since $1 + 1 = 0$ plus a carry-over of 1, the sum of 100 and 100 is 1000. Here are three more examples of binary addition:

DECIMAL	BINARY	DECIMAL	BINARY	DECIMAL	BINARY
5	101	15	1111	$3\frac{1}{4}$	11.01
6	110	20	10100	$5\frac{3}{4}$	101.11
11	1011	35	100011	9	1001.00

Subtraction is the inverse operation of addition. In binary arithmetic, as for decimal, it is necessary to establish a procedure for subtracting a larger from a smaller digit. The only case in which this occurs with binary numbers in when 1 is subtracted from 0. The remainder is 1, but it is necessary to borrow 1 from the next column to the left. Following is the binary subtraction table.

$$0 - 0 = 0$$

$$1 - 0 = 1$$

$$1 - 1 = 0$$

$$0 - 1 = 1 \qquad \text{with a borrow of 1}$$

A few examples will make the procedure for binary subtraction clear:

DECIMAL	BINARY	DECIMAL	BINARY	DECIMAL	BINARY
9	1001	16	10000	$6\frac{1}{4}$	110.01
-6	-110	-3	-11	$-4\frac{1}{2}$	-100.1
4	100	13	1101	$1\frac{3}{4}$	1.11

2.5 BINARY MULTIPLICATION AND DIVISION

The table for binary multiplication is also very short, with only four entries instead of the 100 necessary for decimal multiplication:

$$0 \times 0 = 0$$

$$1 \times 0 = 0$$

$$0 \times 1 = 0$$

$$1 \times 1 = 1$$

The following three examples of binary multiplication illustrate the simplicity of each operation. It is necessary only to copy the multiplicand if the digit in the multiplier is a 1 and to copy all 0s if the digit in the multiplier is a 0. The ease with which each step of the operation is performed is apparent.

DECIMAL	BINARY	DECIMAL	BINARY	DECIMAL	BINARY
12	1100	102	1100110	1.25	1.01
×10	×1010	×8	×1000	×2.5	×10.1
120	0000	816	1100110000	625	101
	1100			250	1010
	0000			3.125	11.001
	1100				
	1111000				

Binary division is, like multiplication, very simple. As in the decimal system (or in any other), division by zero is meaningless. The complete table is

$$0 \div 1 = 0$$

$$1 \div 1 = 1$$

Here are two examples of division:

```
            DECIMAL              BINARY
               5                  101
           5) 25             101) 11001
                                  101
                                   101
                                   101
```

```
    DECIMAL                        BINARY
    2.416 · · ·              10.011010101 · · ·
12) 29.0000              1100) 11101.00
    24                          1100
    50                          10100
    48                           1100
    20                          10000
    12                           1100
    80                          10000
    72                           1100
     8                           · · ·
```

To convert the quotient obtained in the second example form binary to decimal, we would proceed as follows:

$$10.011010101 = 1 \times 2^1 \quad = 2.0$$
$$0 \times 2^0 \quad = 0.0$$
$$0 \times 2^{-1} = 0.0$$
$$1 \times 2^{-2} = 0.25$$
$$1 \times 2^{-3} = 0.125$$
$$0 \times 2^{-4} = 0.0$$
$$1 \times 2^{-5} = 0.03125$$
$$0 \times 2^{-6} = 0.0$$
$$1 \times 2^{-7} = 0.0078125$$
$$0 \times 2^{-8} = 0.0$$
$$1 \times 2^{-9} = \underline{0.001953125}$$
$$2.416015625$$

Therefore, 10.011010101 binary equals approximately 2.416 decimal.

2.6   CONVERTING DECIMAL NUMBERS TO BINARY

There are several methods for converting a decimal number to a binary number. The first and most obvious method is simply to subtract all powers of 2 that can be subtracted from the decimal number until nothing remains. The highest power of 2 is subtracted first, then the second highest, and so on. To convert the decimal integer 25 to the binary number system, first the highest power of 2 that can be subtracted from 25 is found. This is $2^4 = 16$. Then $25 - 16 = 9$. The highest power of 2 that can be subtracted from 9 is 2^3, or 8. The remainder after subtraction is 1, or 2^0. The binary representation for 25 is therefore 11001.

This is a laborious method for converting numbers. It is convenient for small numbers, when it can be performed mentally, but is less used for larger numbers. Instead, the decimal number is repeatedly divided by 2, and the remainder after each division is used to indicate the coefficients of the binary number to be formed. Notice that the binary number derived is written from the bottom up.

$$125 \div 2 = 62 + \text{remainder of } 1$$
$$62 \div 2 = 31 + \text{remainder of } 0$$
$$31 \div 2 = 15 + \text{remainder of } 1$$
$$15 \div 2 = 7 + \text{remainder of } 1$$
$$7 \div 2 = 3 + \text{remainder of } 1$$
$$3 \div 2 = 1 + \text{remainder of } 1$$
$$1 \div 2 = 0 + \text{remainder of } 1$$

The binary representation of 125 is, therefore, 1111101. Checking this result gives

$$1 \times 2^6 = 64$$
$$1 \times 2^5 = 32$$
$$1 \times 2^4 = 16$$
$$1 \times 2^3 = 8$$
$$1 \times 2^2 = 4$$
$$0 \times 2^1 = 0$$
$$1 \times 2^0 = \underline{1}$$
$$125$$

This method will not work for mixed numbers. To convert a mixed decimal number, first it is necessary to divide the number into its whole and fractional parts; that is, 102.247 would be divided into 102 and 0.247. The binary representation for each part is found, and then the two parts are added.

The conversion of decimal fractions to binary fractions may be accomplished using various techniques. Again, the most obvious method is to subtract the highest negative power of 2 that can be subtracted from the decimal fraction. Then the next highest negative power of 2 is subtracted from the remainder of the first subtraction, and this process is continued until there is no remainder, or until the desired precision level is reached:

$$0.875 - 1 \times 2^{-1} = 0.875 - 0.5 = 0.375$$
$$0.375 - 1 \times 2^{-2} = 0.375 - 0.25 = 0.125$$
$$0.125 - 1 \times 2^{-3} = 0.125 - 0.125 = 0$$

Therefore, 0.875 decimal is represented by 0.111 binary. A much simpler method for longer fractions consists of repeatedly "doubling" the decimal fraction. If a 1 appears to the left of the decimal point after a multiplication by 2 is performed, a 1 is added to the right of the binary fraction being formed. If, after a multiplication by 2, a 0 remains to the left of the decimal point of the decimal number, a 0 is added to the right of the binary number. The following example illustrates the use of this technique in converting 0.4375 decimal to the binary system.

	BINARY REPRESENTATION
$2 \times 0.4375 = 0.8750$	0.0
$2 \times 0.875 = 1.750$	0.01
$2 \times 0.75 = 1.50$	0.011
$2 \times 0.5 = 1.0$	0.0111

The binary representation 0.4375 is therefore 0.0111.

2.7 NEGATIVE NUMBERS

A standard convention adopted for writing negative numbers consists of placing a sign symbol before a number that is negative. For instance, negative 39 is written as -39. If -39 is to be added to $+70$, we write

$$+70 + (-39) = 31$$

When a negative number is subtracted from a positive number, we write $+70 - (-39) = +70 + 39 = 109$. The rules for handling negative numbers are well known and are not repeated here, but since negative numbers constitute an important part of our number system, the techniques used to represent negative numbers in digital machines will be described.

In binary machines, numbers are represented by a set of bistable storage devices, each of which represents one binary digit. For example, given a set of five switches, any number from 00000 to 11111 may be represented if we define a switch with its contacts closed as representing a 1 and a switch with open contacts as representing a 0. To increase the total range of numbers that we can represent to include the negative numbers from 00000 to -11111, a sixth bit (or switch) is required. We then treat this bit as a *sign bit* and place it before the magnitude of the number to be represented.

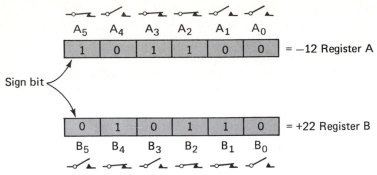

FIGURE 2.1
Example of negative number representation.

The convention is that when the sign bit is a 0, the number represented is positive; when the sign bit is a 1, the number is negative. In the previous situation, when the contacts of the sign bit switch are open, the number will be a positive number equal to the magnitude of the number stored in the other five switches; if the switch for the sign bit is closed, the number represented by the six switches will be a negative number with a magnitude determined by the other five switches. An example is shown in Fig. 2.1.

Sets of storage devices that represent a single number or are handled as an entity are referred to as *registers*; they are given names such as register A, register B, register C, etc. We can then state that register A contains -12 and register B contains $+22$. In writing a signed number in binary form, the sign bit is set apart from the magnitude of the number by means of an underscore; thus, $\underline{0}0111$ represents $+0111$, or positive 7 decimal, and $\underline{1}0111$ represents -0111, or negative 7 decimal.

The use of an underscore to mark the sign bit does not indicate any difference between this bit and the other bits, as the number is stored in a computer. Every binary bit is simply stored in a separate bistable device. A symbol other than the underscore could be used to distinguish the sign and magnitude bits, such as a hyphen, period, or a star. Then, -1011 (negative 11 decimal) could be written 1-1011, or 1*1011 or 1.1011; and $+1100$ could be written as 0-1100, 0*1100, or 0.1100. In fact, no marking whatever could be used, but it is felt that some indication makes for easier reading of numbers that use a sign bit.

2.8 USE OF COMPLEMENTS TO REPRESENT NEGATIVE NUMBERS

The convention of using a sign bit to indicate whether a stored number is negative or positive has been described. The magnitude of the number stored is not always represented in normal form, however. Quite often negative numbers are stored in *complemented* form. By using this technique, a machine can be made to both add and subtract using only the circuitry for adding. The actual technique is described in Chap. 5.

There are two basic types of complements that are useful in the binary and decimal number systems. In the decimal system, the two types are referred to as the *10s complement* and the *9s complement*.

The 10s complement of any number may be formed by subtracting each digit of the number from 9 and then adding 1 to the least significant digit of the number thus formed. For instance, the 10s complement of 87 is 13, and the 10s complement of 23 is 77.

To subtract one positive number (the minuend) from another (the subtrahend), the 10s complement of the subtrahend is formed, and this 10s complement is added to the minuend.[1] If there is a carry from the addition of the most significant digits, then it is discarded, the difference is positive, and the result is correct. If there is no carry, the difference is negative, the 10s complement of this number is formed, and a minus sign is placed before the result.

Here are some examples:

NORMAL SUBTRACTION	10s COMPLEMENT SUBTRACTION

```
NORMAL SUBTRACTION        10s COMPLEMENT SUBTRACTION
        89                   89          89
       -23                  -23   =    +77
        66                            ┌  166
                                      └→ the carry is dropped

        98                   98          98
       -87                  -87   =    +13
        11                            ┌  111
                                      └→ the carry is dropped

        49                   49
       -62                  +38
       -13                   87      no carry, so result is negative
                                     10s complement, or -13

        54                   54
       -81                  +19
       -27                   73      no carry, so result is negative
                                     10s complement, or -27
```

The 9s complement of a decimal number is formed by subtracting each digit of the number from 9. For instance, the 9s complement of 23 is 76, and the 9s complement of 87 is 12. When subtraction is performed by using the 9s complement, the complement of the subtrahend is added, as in 10s complement subtraction, but any carry generated must be added to the rightmost digit of the result. As is the case with 10s complement subtraction, if no carry is generated for the addition of the most significant digits, then the result is negative, the 9s complement of the result is formed, and a minus sign is placed before it.

---

[1] The number of digits in each number must be the same. If one number has fewer digits than the other, then 0s can be added to the left until the number of digits is the same. The same holds true for the 9s complement.

NORMAL SUBTRACTION   9s COMPLEMENT SUBTRACTION

```
        89           89            89
       −23          −23 =         +76
        66                        165
                             ┌─     1
                             └→   166
```

```
        98           98            98
       −87          −87 =         +12
        11                        110
                             ┌─     1
                             └→   111
```

```
        15           15            15
       −37          −37 =         +62
       −22                         77   no carry, so difference is negative
                                        9s complement, which is −22
```

```
        27           27            27
       −44          −44 =         +55
       −17                         82   no carry, so difference is negative
                                        9s complement, which is −17
```

Complete rules for handling signs during the subtraction process and for handling all combinations of positive and negative numbers are explained later. This may seem to be an unwieldy technique, but the majority of computers now being constructed subtract by using a complemented number.

Complements in Other Number Systems

There are two types of complements for each number system. Since now only binary and Binary Coded Decimal machines are being constructed in quantity, only these number systems will be explained in any detail. The two types of complements and the rules for obtaining them are as follows:

1. *True complement.* The true complement is formed by subtracting each digit of the number from the radix minus one of the number system and then adding 1 to the least significant digit. The true complement of a number in the decimal system is referred to as the 10s complement and in the binary system as the 2s complement.

   In binary, there is a short-cut technique for forming 2s complement numbers: Leave the rightmost 0s as they are and also the rightmost 1; then change the remaining 1s to 0s and 0s to 1s.

2. *Radix-minus-one complement.* The radix minus one is 9 for the decimal system and 1 for the binary system. The complement in each system is formed by subtracting each digit of the number from the radix minus one. For instance, the radix-minus-one complement of decimal 72 is 27.

As just stated, the 2s complement of a binary number is formed by simply subtracting each digit (bit) of the number from the radix minus one and adding a 1 to the least significant bit. Since the radix in the binary number system is 2, each bit of the binary number is subtracted from a 1. The application of this rule is actually very simple: Every 1 in the number is changed to a 0 and every 0 to a 1; then a 1 is added to the least significant bit of the number formed. For instance, the 2s complement of 10110 is 01010, and the 2s complement of 11010 is 00110.

Subtraction using the 2s complement system involves forming the 2s complement of the subtrahend and then adding this true complement to the minuend. For instance,

$$\begin{array}{r} 11011 \\ -10100 \\ \hline 00111 \end{array} = \begin{array}{r} 11011 \\ +01100 \\ \hline 1\ 00111 \end{array} \qquad \text{and} \qquad \begin{array}{r} 11100 \\ -00100 \\ \hline 11000 \end{array} = \begin{array}{r} 11100 \\ +11100 \\ \hline 1\ 11000 \end{array}$$

$$\text{carry is dropped} \qquad\qquad \text{dropped}$$

Subtraction using the 1s complement system is also straightforward. The 1s complement of a binary number is formed by changing each 1 in the number to a 0 and each 0 in the number to a 1. For instance, the 1s complement of 10111 is 01000, and the 1s complement of 11000 is 00111.

When subtraction is performed using the 1s complement system, any end-around carry is added to the least significant bit. For instance,

$$\begin{array}{r} 11001 \\ -10110 \\ \hline 00011 \end{array} = \begin{array}{r} 11001 \\ +01001 \\ \hline 1\ 00010 \\ \qquad 1 \\ \hline 00011 \end{array} \qquad \text{and} \qquad \begin{array}{r} 11110 \\ -01101 \\ \hline 10001 \end{array} = \begin{array}{r} 11110 \\ +10010 \\ \hline 1\ 10000 \\ \qquad 1 \\ \hline 10001 \end{array}$$

Addition and Subtraction in the 1s Complement System

The 1s complement system for representing negative numbers was the most common method used in early computers because of the ease with which the 1s complement of a binary number is formed. It is still widely used in communication systems. Following are descriptions of the four basic situations that arise in adding combinations of positive and negative numbers using the 1s complement system.

1. When a positive number is added to another positive number, the addition of all bits, including the sign bit, is straightforward. Since both sign bits will be 0, no sum or carry will be generated in the sign-bit and the output will remain 0. Here is an example of the addition of two 4-bit positive numbers.[2]

$$\begin{array}{cc} \text{NORMAL NOTATION} & \text{COMPUTER WORD} \\ +0011 & \underline{0}0011 \\ +0100 & \underline{0}0100 \\ \hline +0111 & \underline{0}0111 \end{array}$$

2. When a positive and a negative number are added, the sum may be either positive or negative. If the positive number has a greater magnitude, the sum will be positive; if the negative number is greater in magnitude, the sum will be nega-

---

[2] In this, and in all discussions that follow, we assume that the result (sum) does not exceed the capacity of the number of digits being used. This is discussed later.

tive. In the 1s complement system, the answer will be correct as is if the sum of the two numbers is negative in value. In this case no overflow will be generated when the numbers are added. For instance,

$$
\begin{array}{rr}
+0011 & \underline{0}0011 \\
-1100 & \underline{1}0011 \\
\hline
-1001 & \underline{1}0110
\end{array}
$$

In this case, the output of the adder will be 10110, the last 4 bits of which are the 1s complement of 1001, the correct magnitude of the sum. The 1 in the sign bit indicates a negative number.

3. If the positive number is larger than the negative number, the addition of the end-around carry to the least significant bit will produce the correct sum. There will be a 0 in the sign bit, indicating that the sum is positive.

$$
\begin{array}{rr}
+1001 = \underline{0}1001 & +0011 = \underline{0}00011 \\
-0100 = \underline{1}1011 & -0010 = \underline{1}1101 \\
\hline
+0101 \quad \underline{0}0100 & +0001 \quad \underline{0}0000 \\
 \quad \longrightarrow 1 & \quad \longrightarrow 1 \\
\hline
\underline{0}0101 & \underline{0}0001
\end{array}
$$

Notice what happens when two numbers of equal magnitude but opposite signs are added:

$$
\begin{array}{rr}
+1011 = \underline{0}1011 & +0000 = \underline{0}0000 \\
-1011 = \underline{1}0100 & -0000 = \underline{1}1111 \\
\hline
+0000 \quad \underline{1}1111 & 0000 \quad \underline{1}1111
\end{array}
$$

The result in these cases will be a negative zero, which is correct.

4. When two negative numbers are added, an end-around carry will always be generated. This will place a 1 in the sign bit.

$$
\begin{array}{rr}
-0011 = \underline{1}1100 & -0100 = \underline{1}1011 \\
-1011 = \underline{1}0100 & -0111 = \underline{1}1000 \\
\hline
-1110 \quad \underline{1}0000 & -1011 \quad \underline{1}0011 \\
 \quad \longrightarrow 1 & \quad \longrightarrow 1 \\
\hline
\underline{1}0001 & \underline{1}0100
\end{array}
$$

The output will be in 1s complement form in each case, with a 1 in the sign-bit position.

Addition and Subtraction in the 2s Complement System

When negative numbers are represented in the 2s complement system, the operation of addition is very similar to that in the 1s complement system. The 2s complement of a number may be formed by first 1s complementing the register and then adding 1 to the least significant bit. This process requires two steps and so is more time-consuming than the 1s complement system.[3] However, the 2s complement system has

---

[3] Generally this 1 is "sneaked in" during calculation, as will be shown.

the advantage of not requiring an end-around carry during addition and it is now the most-used system.

Four situations may occur in adding two numbers when the 2s complement system is used:

1. When both numbers are positive, the situation is completely identical to case 1 in the 1s complement system.

2. When one number is positive and the other negative, and the positive number has the greater magnitude, a carry will be generated through the sign bit. This carry may be discarded, as shown below:

$$+0111 = \underline{0}0111 \qquad\qquad +1000 = \underline{0}1000$$
$$-0011 = \underline{1}1101 \qquad\qquad -0111 = \underline{1}1001$$
$$+0100 \quad \underline{0}0100 \qquad\qquad +0001 \quad \underline{0}0001$$
$$\qquad \text{carry is discarded} \qquad\qquad \text{carry is discarded}$$

3. When a positive and negative number are added, and the negative number has the larger magnitude, no carry will result in the sign bit, and the answer will again be correct as it stands:

$$+0011 = \underline{0}0011 \qquad +0100 = \underline{0}0100$$
$$-0100 = \underline{1}1100 \qquad -1000 = \underline{1}1000$$
$$-0001 \quad \underline{1}1111 \qquad -0100 \quad \underline{1}1100$$

Note: A 1 must be added to the least significant bit of a 2s complement negative number in converting it to a magnitude. For example,

$$\underline{1}0011 = \quad 1100 \qquad \text{form the 1s complement}$$
$$\qquad\qquad \underline{0001} \qquad \text{add 1}$$
$$\qquad\qquad -1101$$

When both numbers are of the same magnitude but the opposite signs, the result is as follows:

$$+0011 = \underline{0}0011$$
$$-0011 = \underline{1}1101$$
$$0000 \quad \underline{0}0000$$

Thus, when a positive and a negative number of the same magnitude are added, the result will be a positive zero.

4. When two negative numbers are added, a carry will be generated in the sign bit and also in the bit to the right of the sign bit. This will cause a 1 to be placed in the sign bit, which is correct, and the carry from the sign bit may be discarded.

$$-0011 = \underline{1}1101 \qquad\qquad -0011 = \underline{1}1101$$
$$-0100 = \underline{1}1100 \qquad\qquad -1011 = \underline{1}0101$$
$$-0111 \quad \underline{1}1001 \qquad\qquad -1110 \quad \underline{1}0010$$
$$\qquad \text{carry is discarded} \qquad\qquad \text{carry is discarded}$$

2.9 BINARY-CODED-DECIMAL NUMBER REPRESENTATION

Since most electronic circuit elements used to construct digital computers are inherently binary in operation, the binary number system is the most natural number system for a computer. Also, computers constructed with the binary number system require a smaller amount of circuitry and so are more efficient than machines operating in other number systems. However, the decimal system has been used for a long time, and there is a natural resistance to performing calculations using the binary number system. Also, since checks, bills, tax rates, prices, and so forth are all figured in the decimal system, the values of most things must be converted from decimal to binary before computations can begin. For these and other reasons, most of the early machines used binary-coded-decimal number systems. In such systems, a coded group of binary bits is used to represent each of the 10 decimal digits. An obvious and natural code is a simple *weighted binary code*, which is shown in Table 2.2.

This is known as a *binary-coded-decimal 8,4,2,1 code*, or simply BCD. Notice that 4 bits are required for each decimal digit, and each bit is assigned a weight; for instance, the rightmost bit has a weight of 1, and the leftmost bit in each code group has a weight of 8. By adding the weights of the positions in which 1s appear, the decimal digit represented by a code group may be derived. This is somewhat uneconomical since $2^4 = 16$, and, thus, the 4 bits could actually represent 15 different values. But the next lesser choice, 3 bits, gives only 2^3, or 8, values, which are insufficient. If the decimal number 214 is to be represented in this type of code, 12 binary bits are required as follows: 0010 0001 0100. For the decimal number 1246 to be represented, 16 bits are required: 0001 0010 0100 0110.

This is a very useful code and is the most used. The only difficulty with the code lies in forming the complements of numbers. It is common practice to perform subtraction in a computer by adding the complement of the subtrahend; however, when the BCD system is used, the most natural complement of the number stored is not useful. The most direct way for a computer to complement a number is simply to change each 0 to a 1 and each 1 to a 0. However, the natural complement of 0010 (2 decimal) is 1101, which is 13, and not an acceptable BCD character. To get around this difficulty, several other codes have been used in computers and in instruments.

A weighted code in which the 9s complement is formed by complementing each binary digit is the *2,4,2,1 code* (see Table 2.3). If each bit of a code group

TABLE 2.2

Binary code	Decimal digit
0000	0
0001	1
0010	2
0011	3
0100	4
0101	5
0110	6
0111	7
1000	8
1001	9

TABLE 2.3
2, 4, 2, 1 Code

Decimal	Coded binary weight of bit 2421
0	0000
1	0001
2	0010
3	0011
4	0100
5	1011
6	1100
7	1101
8	1110
9	1111

TABLE 2.4
2, 4, 2, 1 Code Complements

Decimal	2421	9s complement
0	0000	1111
1	0001	1110
2	0010	1101
3	0011	1100
4	0100	1011
5	1011	0100
6	1100	0011
7	1101	0010
8	1110	0001
9	1111	0000

TABLE 2.5

Decimal	2, 4, 2, 1 representation			
2436	0 0 1 0	0 1 0 0	0 0 1 1	1 1 0 0
359	0 0 1 1	1 0 1 1	1 1 1 1	
726	1 1 0 1	0 0 1 0	1 1 0 0	
83	1 1 1 0	0 0 1 1		

is complemented, the 9s complement of the decimal digit represented results. For instance, 0010 (2 decimal) complemented is 1101 (7 decimal), and 1011 (5 decimal) complemented is 0100 (4 decimal). This is shown in Table 2.4. Table 2.5 shows several decimal numbers as written in 2,4,2,1 code. This code is widely used in instruments and electronic calculators.

The following convention is generally adopted to distinguish binary from decimal. A binary number is identified by a subscript of 2 placed at the end of the number (00110_2) and a decimal number by the subscript 10 (for instance, decimal 948 may be written 948_{10}). So we may write 0111_2 as 7_{10}. We will use this convention when necessary.

2.10 OCTAL AND HEXADECIMAL NUMBER SYSTEMS

Two other number systems are very useful in the computer industry: the octal number system and the hexadecimal number system.

The octal number system has a base, or radix, of 8; eight different symbols are used to represent numbers. These symbols are commonly 0, 1, 2, 3, 4, 5, 6, and 7. We show the first 18 octal numbers and their decimal equivalents in Table 2.6.

To convert an octal number to a decimal number, we use the same sort of polynomial as was used in the binary case, except that we now have a radix of 8 instead of 2. Therefore, 1213 in octal is $1 \times 8^3 + 2 \times 8^2 + 1 \times 8^1 + 3 \times 8^0 = 512 + 128 + 8 + 3 = 651$ in decimal. Also, 1.123 in octal is $1 \times 8^0 + 1 \times 8^{-1} + 2 \times 8^{-2} + 3 \times 8^{-3}$, or $1 + \frac{1}{8} + \frac{2}{64} + \frac{3}{512} = 1\frac{83}{512}$ in decimal.

TABLE 2.6

Octal	Decimal	Octal	Decimal
0	0	11	9
1	1	12	10
2	2	13	11
3	3	14	12
4	4	15	13
5	5	16	14
6	6	17	15
7	7	20	16
10	8	21	17

TABLE 2.7

Binary	Octal
000	0
001	1
010	2
011	3
100	4
101	5
110	6
111	7

There is a simple trick for converting a binary number to an octal number. Simply group the binary digits into groups of 3, starting at the binary point, and read each set of three binary digits according to Table 2.7.

Let us convert the binary number 011101. First, we break it into groups of three (011 101). Then, converting each group of three binary digits, we get 35 in octal. Therefore, 011101 binary = 35 octal. Here are several more examples:

$$111110111_2 = 767_8$$
$$110110101_2 = 665_8$$
$$11011_2 = 33_8$$
$$1001_2 = 11_8$$
$$10101.11_2 = 25.6_8$$
$$1100.111_2 = 14.7_8$$
$$1011.1111_2 = 13.74_8$$

Conversion from decimal to octal can be performed by repeatedly dividing the decimal number by 8 and using each remainder as a digit in the octal number being formed. For instance, to convert 200_{10} to an octal representation, we divide as follows:

$$200 \div 8 = 25 \qquad \text{remainder is } 0$$
$$25 \div 8 = 3 \qquad \text{remainder is } 1$$
$$3 \div 8 = 0 \qquad \text{remainder is } 3$$

Therefore, $200_{10} = 310_8$.

Notice that when the number to be divided is less than 8, we use 0 as the quotient and the number as the remainder. Let us check this:

$$310_8 = 3_{10} \times 8_{10}^2 + 1_{10} \times 8_{10}^1 + 0_{10} \times 8_{10}^0 = 192_{10} + 8_{10} = 200_{10}$$

Here is another example. To convert 3964_{10} to octal:

$$3964 \div 8 = 495 \qquad \text{with a remainder of } 4$$
$$495 \div 8 = 61 \qquad \text{with a remainder of } 7$$
$$61 \div 8 = 7 \qquad \text{with a remainder of } 5$$
$$7 \div 8 = 0 \qquad \text{with a remainder of } 7$$

Therefore, $7574_8 = 3964_{10}$. Checking, we find

$$7574_8 = 7_{10} \times 8_{10}^3 + 5_{10} \times 8_{10}^2 + 7_{10} \times 8_{10} + 4_{10}$$
$$= 7_{10} \times 512_{10} + 5_{10} \times 64_{10} + 7_{10} \times 8_{10} + 4_{10} \times 1_{10}$$
$$= 3584_{10} + 320_{10} + 56_{10} + 4_{10}$$
$$= 3964_{10}$$

There are several other techniques for converting octal to decimal and decimal to octal, but they are seldom used manually, and tables have proven to be of value in this process. Octal-to-decimal and decimal-to-octal tables are readily available from a number of sources, including the manuals distributed by manufacturers of computers.

An important use for octal is in listings of programs and in memory "dumps" for binary machines, thus making the printouts more compact. The manuals for several of the largest manufacturers use octal numbers to represent binary numbers because of the ease of conversion and compactness.

The hexadecimal number system is useful for the same reasons. Most minicomputers and microcomputers have their memories organized into sets of *bytes*, each consisting of eight binary digits. Each byte either is used as a single entity to represent a single alphanumeric character or is broken into two 4-bit pieces. (We examine the coding of alphanumeric characters later.) When the bytes are handled in two 4-bit pieces, the programmer is given the option of declaring each 4-bit character as a piece of a binary number or as two BCD numbers. For instance, the byte 00011000 can be declared a binary number, in which case it is equal to 24 decimal, or as two BCD characters, in which case it represents the decimal number 18.

When the machine is handling numbers in binary but in groups of four digits, it is convenient to have a code for representing each of these sets of four digits. Since 16 different numbers must be represented, the digits 0 through 9 will not suffice; the letters A, B, C, D, E, and F are used also (see Table 2.8).

To convert binary to hexadecimal, simply break a binary number into groups of four digits and convert each group of four digits according to the code. Thus,

TABLE 2.8

Binary	Hexadecimal	Decimal
0000	0	0
0001	1	1
0010	2	2
0011	3	3
0100	4	4
0101	5	5
0110	6	6
0111	7	7
1000	8	8
1001	9	9
1010	A	10
1011	B	11
1100	C	12
1101	D	13
1110	E	14
1111	F	15

$10111011_2 = BB_{16}$, $10010101_2 = 95_{16}$, $11000111_2 = C7_{16}$, and $10001011_2 = 8B_{16}$. The mixture of letters and decimal digits may seem strange at first, but these are simply convenient symbols, just as decimal digits are.

The conversion of hexadecimal to decimal is straightforward but time-consuming. For instance, BB represents $B \times 16^1 + B \times 16^0 = 11 \times 16 + 11 \times 1 = 176 + 11 = 187$. Similarly,

$$
\begin{aligned}
AB6_{16} &= 10_{10} \times 16_{10}^2 + 11_{10} \times 16_{10} + 6_{10} \\
&= 10_{10} \times 256_{10} + 176_{10} + 6_{10} \\
&= 2560_{10} + 176_{10} + 6_{10} \\
&= 2742_{10}
\end{aligned}
$$

To convert $3A6_{16}$ to decimal:

$$
\begin{aligned}
3A6_{16} &= 3_{10} \times 16_{10}^2 + 10_{10} \times 16_{10} + 6_{10} \\
&= 3_{10} \times 256_{10} + 10_{10} \times 16_{10} + 6_{10} \\
&= 768_{10} + 160_{10} + 6_{10} \\
&= 934_{10}
\end{aligned}
$$

Again, tables are convenient for converting hexadecimal to decimal and decimal to hexadecimal. Table 2.9 is useful for converting in either direction.

The chief use of the hexadecimal system is in connection with byte-organized machines. And since most computers are now byte-organized, a knowledge of hexadecimal is essential to using manufacturers' manuals and to reading the current literature.

Quite a large number of questions have been included for this chapter. For those desiring to study octal and hexadecimal number systems further, Questions 2.58 through 2.67 contain information and exercises on octal addition and multiplication, and Questions 2.68 through 2.72 can be used to supplement the study of the hexadecimal system.

2.11 FLOATING-POINT NUMBER SYSTEMS

Earlier we described number representation systems in which positive and negative integers are stored in binary form. In this representation system, the binary point is "fixed" in that it lies at the end of each word, so each value represented is an integer. When computers calculate with binary numbers in this format, the operations are called *fixed-point arithmetic*.

In science it is often necessary to calculate with very large or very large or very small numbers, so scientists have adopted a convenient notation in which a *mantissa* and an *exponent* represent a number. For instance, 4,900,000 may be written as 0.49×10^7, where 0.49 is the mantissa and 7 is the value of the exponent. Similarly, 0.00023 may be written as 0.23×10^{-3}. The notation is based on the relation $y = a \times r^p$, where y is the number to be represented, a is the mantissa, r is the base of the number system ($r = 10$ for decimal and $r = 2$ for binary), and p is the power to which the base is raised.

It is possible to calculate using this representation system. To multiply $a \times 10^n$ and $b \times 10^m$, we form $a \times b \times 10^{m+n}$. To divide $a \times 10^m$ by $b \times 10^n$, we form

TABLE 2.9
Hexadecimal-to-Decimal Conversion

Integer conversion

Hex	Decimal	Hex	Decimal	Hex	Decimal	Hex	Decimal	
0000	0	000	0	00	0	0	0	Example: 2322_{16} is
1000	4,096	100	256	10	16	1	1	$8192_{10} + 768_{10} + 32_{10}$
2000	8,192	200	512	20	32	2	2	$+ 2_{10} = 8994.0$
3000	12,288	300	768	30	48	3	3	
4000	16,384	400	1024	40	64	4	4	
5000	20,480	500	1280	50	80	5	5	
6000	24,576	600	1536	60	96	6	6	
7000	28,672	700	1792	70	112	7	7	
8000	32,768	800	2048	80	128	8	8	
9000	36,864	900	2304	90	144	9	9	
A000	40,960	A00	2560	A0	160	A	10	
B000	45,056	B00	2816	B0	176	B	11	
C000	49,152	C00	3072	C0	192	C	12	
D000	53,248	D00	3328	D0	208	D	13	
E000	57,344	E00	3584	E0	224	E	14	
F000	61,440	F00	3840	F0	240	F	15	

| Hexadecimal positions | 4 | | 3 | | 2 | | 1 | |

Fractional conversion

Hex	Decimal	Hex	Decimal		Hex	Decimal			Hex	Decimal			
.0	.0000	.00	.0000	0000	.000	.0000	0000	0000	.0000	.0000	0000	0000	0000
.1	.0625	.01	.0039	0625	.001	.0002	4414	0625	.0001	.0000	1525	8789	0625
.2	.1250	.02	.0078	1250	.002	.0004	8828	1250	.0002	.0000	3051	7578	1250
.3	.1875	.03	.0117	1875	.003	.0007	3242	1875	.0003	.0000	4577	6367	1875
.4	.2500	.04	.0156	2500	.004	.0009	7656	2500	.0004	.0000	6103	5156	2500
.5	.3125	.05	.0195	3125	.005	.0012	2070	3125	.0005	.0000	7629	3945	3125
.6	.3750	.06	.0234	3750	.006	.0014	6484	3750	.0006	.0000	9155	2734	3750
.7	.4375	.07	.0273	4375	.007	.0017	0898	4375	.0007	.0001	0681	1523	4375
.8	.5000	.08	.0312	5000	.008	.0019	5312	5000	.0008	.0001	2207	0312	5000
.9	.5625	.09	.0351	5625	.009	.0021	9726	5625	.0009	.0001	3732	9101	5625
.A	.6250	.0A	.0390	6250	.00A	.0024	4140	6250	.000A	.0001	5258	7890	6250
.B	.6875	.0B	.0429	6875	.00B	.0026	8554	6875	.000B	.0001	6784	6679	6875
.C	.7500	.0C	.0468	7500	.00C	.0029	2968	7500	.000C	.0001	8310	5468	7500
.D	.8125	.0D	.0507	8125	.00D	.0031	7382	8125	.000D	.0001	9836	4257	8125
.E	.8750	.0E	.0546	8750	.00E	.0034	1796	8750	.000E	.0002	1362	3046	8750
.F	.9375	.0F	.0585	9375	.00F	.0036	6210	9375	.000F	.0002	2888	1835	9375

| Hexadecimal positions | 1 | | 2 | | | 3 | | | | 4 | | | |

$a/b \times 10^{m-n}$. To add $a \times 10^m$ to $b \times 10^n$, we must first make m equal to n. If $m = n$, then $a \times 10^m + b \times 10^n = a + b \times 10^m$. The process of making m equal to n is called *scaling* the numbers.

Considerable bookkeeping can be involved in scaling numbers, and it can be difficult to maintain precision during computations when numbers vary over a very wide range of magnitudes. For computer usage these problems are alleviated by means of two techniques whereby the computer (not the programmer) keeps track of the radix (decimal) point, automatically scaling the numbers. In the first, programmed *floating-point routines* automatically scale the numbers used during the computations while maintaining the precision of the results and keeping track of the scale factors. These routines are used with small computers having only fixed-point operations. A second technique lies in building what are called *floating-point operations* into the computer's hardware. The logic circuitry of the computer is then used to perform the scaling automatically and to keep track of the exponents when calculations are performed. To effect this, a number representation system called the *floating-point system* is used.

A floating-point number in a computer uses the exponential notation system described. During calculations, the computer keeps track of the exponent as well as the mantissa. A computer number in a floating-point system may be divided into three pieces; the first is the sign bit, indicating whether the number is negative or positive; the second part contains the exponent for the number to be represented; and the third part is the mantissa.

As an example, let us consider a computer with a 12-bit word length. Figure 2.2 shows a floating-point word for such a computer. It is common practice to call the exponent part of the word the *characteristic* and the mantissa section the *integer part*.

The integer part of the floating-point word represents its value in signed-magnitude form (rather than 2s complement, although this has been used). The characteristic is also in signed-magnitude form. The value of the number expressed is $I \times 2^C$, where I is the value of the integer part and C is the value of the characteristic.

Figure 2.3 shows several values of floating-point numbers, both in binary form and after conversion to decimal. Since the characteristic has 5 bits and is in signed-magnitude form, C can have values from -15 to $+15$. The value of I is a sign-plus-magnitude binary integer of 7 bits, and so I can have a value from -63 to $+63$. The largest number represented by this system is thus 63×2^{15}. This shows the use of a floating-point number representation system to store "real" numbers of considerable range in a binary word.

Another widely followed practice is to express the mantissa of the word as a fraction instead of as an integer. This is in accord with common scientific usage, since 0.93×10^4 is the normal form for exponential notation (and not 93×10^2). In this

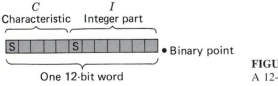

FIGURE 2.2
A 12-bit floating-point word.

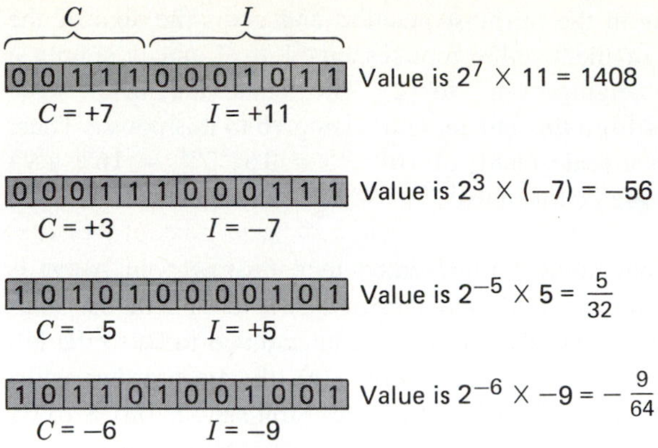

$$\underbrace{\boxed{0\,0\,1\,1\,1}}_{C}\,\underbrace{\boxed{0\,0\,0\,1\,0\,1\,1}}_{I}$$ Value is $2^7 \times 11 = 1408$

$C = +7$ $I = +11$

$\boxed{0\,0\,0\,1\,1\,1\,0\,0\,0\,1\,1\,1}$ Value is $2^3 \times (-7) = -56$

$C = +3$ $I = -7$

$\boxed{1\,0\,1\,0\,1\,0\,0\,0\,0\,1\,0\,1}$ Value is $2^{-5} \times 5 = \dfrac{5}{32}$

$C = -5$ $I = +5$

$\boxed{1\,0\,1\,1\,0\,1\,0\,0\,1\,0\,0\,1}$ Value is $2^{-6} \times -9 = -\dfrac{9}{64}$

$C = -6$ $I = -9$

FIGURE 2.3
Values of floating-point numbers in 12-bit all-integer system.

usage a mantissa in decimal normally has a value from 0.1 to 0.999. Similarly, a binary mantissa in normal form would have a value from 0.5 (decimal) to less than 1. Most computers maintain their mantissa sections in normal form, continually adjusting words so that a significant (1) bit is always in the leftmost mantissa position.

When the mantissa is in fraction form, this section is called the *fraction*. For our 12-bit example, we can express floating-point numbers with characteristic and fraction by simply supposing the binary point is to the left of the magnitude (and not to the right, as in integer representation). In this system, a number to be represented has value $F \times 2^C$, where F is the binary fraction and C is the characteristic.

For the 12-bit word considered before, fractions would have values from $1 - 2^{-6}$, which is 0111111, to $-(1 - 2^{-6})$, which is 1111111, where the leftmost bit in each number is the sign bit. Thus, numbers from $(1 - 2^{-6}) \times 2^{15}$ to $-(1 - 2^{-6}) \times 2^{15}$, or about $+32,000$ to $-32,000$, can be represented. The smallest value the fraction part could have is 01000000, which is 2^{-1}, and the smallest characteristic is 2^{-15}, so the smallest positive number representable is $2^{-1} \times 2^{-15}$, or 2^{-16}. Most computers use this fractional system for the mantissa, although Burroughs and NCR use the integer system.

An example of computers with internal circuitry that performs floating-point operations is the IBM series. IBM calls the exponent part the *characteristic* and the mantissa part the *fraction*. In the IBM series, floating-point data words can be either 32 or 64 bits in length. The basic format for a short or single-word floating-point number is:

S	characteristic	fraction
0	$1 \rightarrow 7$	$8 \rightarrow 31$

The format for a long or double-word floating-point number is:

S	characteristic	fraction
0	$1 \rightarrow 7$	$8 \rightarrow 63$

In both cases, the sign bit, S, is in the leftmost position and gives the sign of the number. The characteristic part of the word comprises bits 1 to 7 and is simply a binary integer, which we call C, ranging from 0 to 127. The actual value of the scale factor is formed by subtracting 64 from this integer and raising 16 to this power. Thus, the value 64 in bits 1 to 7 gives a scale factor of $16^{C-64} = 16^{64-64} = 16^0$; a 93 (decimal) in bits 1 to 7 gives a scale factor of $16^{C-64} = 16^{93-64}$, which is 16^{29}; and a 24 in bits 1 to 7 gives 16^{-40}.

The magnitude of the actual number represented in a floating-point word is equal to this scale factor times the fraction contained in bits 8 to 31 (for the short number) or 8 to 63 (for a long number). The radix point is assumed to be to the left of bit 8 in either case. So if bits 8 to 31 contain 1000...00, the fraction has value $\frac{1}{2}$ (decimal); that is, the fraction is .1000...000 in binary. Similarly, if bits 8 to 31 contain 11000...000, the fraction value is $\frac{3}{4}$ decimal, or .11000...000 binary.

The number represented then had magnitude equal to the value of the fraction times the value determined by the characteristic. Consider a short number:

	sign	characteristic	fraction
Floating-point number:	0	1 0 0 0 0 0 1	1 1 1 0 0 ... 0
Bit position:	0	1 2 3 4 5 6 7	8 9 10 11 12 ... 31

The sign bit is a 0, so the number represented is positive. The characteristic has binary value 1000001, which is 65 decimal, so the scale factor is 16^1. The fraction part has value .111 binary, or $\frac{7}{8}$ decimal, so the number represented is $\frac{7}{8} \times 16$, or 14 decimal.
Consider the following number:

	sign	characteristic	fraction
Floating-point number:	1	1 0 0 0 0 0 1	1 1 1 0 0 ... 0
Bit position:	0	1 2 3 4 5 6 7	8 9 10 11 12 ... 31

This has value -14, since every bit is the same as before, except for the sign bit.
As further examples:

sign	characteristic	fraction	
0	1 0 0 0 0 1 1	1 1 0 ... 0	$16^3 \times \frac{3}{4} = 3072$
0	0 1 1 1 1 1 1	1 1 0 ... 0	$16^{-1} \times \frac{3}{4} = \frac{3}{64}$

Most PCs (and microprocessors) now use the IEEE Standard for Binary Floating-Point Arithmetic. This standard is the result of work by several organizations (not just IEEE) and is widely supported.

The principal feature of the standard is the *hidden 1* principle. Floating-point numbers generally have their fraction (magnitude) part stored with a leading 1 in the leftmost position. This is called *normalized form;* it ensures that the maximum number of significant bits is carried in the number. The reasoning behind the *hidden 1* principle is that if the leftmost bit in the fraction (magnitude) section is always a 1, why carry it? Instead, this section of the floating-point number is shifted left one more bit, and the 1 is discarded. However, in any reconstruction of the number for external use or during calculations, the 1 is replaced.

There is a single format and a double format. The single format is:

1	←8 →	←23 bits→
S	E	F

where S is the sign bit, E is a binary integer, and F is a binary fraction of length 23. However, the value of F is formed by adding 1 to this fraction. Thus, if F in this format is stored as 11000...00, the value of F is 1.11000...00, which is $1\frac{3}{4}$ in decimal. The value of a floating-point number in this system is

$$V = (-1)^S \times 2^{E-127} \times 1.F$$

Notice that this system uses an offset of 127 for the exponent (characteristic) value.
Here are three examples of the single-format system:

Floating-point format (hexadecimal)	$(-1)^S \times 2^{E-127} \times 1.F$	Decimal value
3F800000	$1 \times 2^0 \times 1.0$	$+1$
BF800000	$-1 \times 2^0 \times 1.0$	-1
40400000	$1 \times 2^0 \times 1.5$	$+3$

Note that fraction values for F range from 1 to slightly less than $2 (1 \le F < 2)$.
The double format is:

1	←11 →	←52 bits→
S	E	F

where S is the sign bit, E is an 11-bit binary integer, and F is a 52-bit binary fraction with the binary point to the far left. However, as before, the value for F is formed by adding 1 to the left of this fraction. So if F is stored as 101000...00, then the value of F is 1.10100...00, or $1\frac{5}{8}$ decimal. The value of the number stored is then

$$V = (-1)^S \times 2^{E-1023} \times F$$

Here are examples:

Floating-point format (hexadecimal)	$(-1)^S \times 2^{E-1023} \times 1.F$	Decimal value
3DF0000 . . . 00	$1 \times 2^2 \times 1.0$	0.25
C03E000 . . . 00	$-1 \times 2^4 \times 1.875$	-30
401C000 . . . 00	$1 \times 2^2 \times 1.75$	7

There is also a single extended format, with $E \ge 11$ bits and $F \ge 31$ bits, and a double extended format, with $E \ge 15$ bits and $F \ge 63$ bits. These are used only in particular implementations.
Since a 1 is assumed to be "invisibly" stored with each number, the representation for 0 must be special. The standard 0 is represented by all 0s in the E and F

sections (there is a $+0$ and a -0). Furthermore, infinity is represented by all 1s in the E section and all 0s in the F section. There is, therefore, also a $+\infty$ and a $-\infty$.

When numbers are so small that they cannot be represented in normalized form, because E would need to be less than 1, the F part is handled in denormalized form, and the 1 is not added when the numbers are evaluated.

The results of invalid operations are signaled as follows: E is all 0s; S can be anything; and if F is nonzero, the 1s in F signal an illegal operation.

Performing Arithmetic Operations with Floating-Point Numbers

A computer obviously requires additional circuitry to handle floating-point numbers automatically. Some machines come equipped with floating-point instructions and sometimes circutiry must be added.

To handle the floating-point numbers, the machine must be capable of extensive shifting and comparing operations. The rules for multiplying and dividing are

$$(a \times r^p) \times (b \times r^q) = ab \times r^{p+q}$$

$$(a \times r^p) \div (b \times r^q) = \frac{a}{b} \times r^{p-q}$$

The computer must be able to add or subtract the exponent sections of the floating-point numbers and to perform the multiplication or division operations on the mantissa sections of the numbers. In addition, precision is generally maintained by shifting the numbers stored until significant digits are in the leftmost sections of the word. With each shift, the exponent must be changed. If the machine is shifting the mantissa section left, for each left shift the exponent must be decreased.

For instance, in a computer that can do BCD floating-point operations consider the word

0	10	0064
sign	exponent	mantissa

To attain precision, the computer shifts the mantissa section left until the 6 is in the most significant position. Since two shifts are required, the exponent must be decreased by 2, and the resulting word is 0.08 6400. If all numbers to be used are scaled in this manner, maximum precision may be maintained throughout the calculations.

For addition and subtraction the exponent values must agree. For instance, to add 0.24×10^5 to 0.25×10^6, we must scale the numbers so that the exponents match. Thus,

$$0.024 \times 10^6 + 0.25 \times 10^6 = 0.274 \times 10^6$$

The machine must also follow this procedure. The numbers are scaled as described, so that the most significant digit of the computer mantissa section of each word contains the most significant digit of the number stored. Then the larger of the two exponents for the operands is selected, and the other number's mantissa is shifted and its exponent adjusted until the exponents for both numbers match. The numbers may then be added or subtracted according to these rules:

$$a \times r^p + b \times r^p = (a + b) \times r^p$$
$$a \times r^p - b \times r^p = (a - b) \times r^p$$

Often floating-point calculations are not exact since numbers are approximated in many cases. However, floating-point number systems are almost always used for large scientific computations and by higher-level languages for "real" numbers.

2.12 ALPHANUMERIC CODES

Data and programs are almost invariably entered in alphanumeric form, and the internal operation of computers, particularly those that involve business records, makes extensive use of alphanumeric codes. Because of the diversity of applications and the many viewpoints on codes and code construction, many different alphanumeric codes have been suggested and used.

Fortunately, there has been an attempt to standardize an alphanumeric code that will be agreeable to both manufacturers and users. The American National Standards Institute has published an American Standard Code for Information Interchange (ASCII). This code is now the most widely used, and major manufacturers are using the code so that their equipment will be compatible with that of other manufacturers. This code is shown in Fig. 2.4. Notice that the decimal digits are represented by

	000	001	010	011	100	101	110	111
0000	NUL	DLE	SP	0	@	P		p
0001	SOH	DC1	!	1	A	Q	a	q
0010	STX	DC2	"	2	B	R	b	r
0011	ETX	DC3	#	3	C	S	c	s
0100	EOT	DC4 (Stop)	$	4	D	T	d	t
0101	ENQ	NAK	%	5	E	U	e	u
0110	ACK	SYN	&	6	F	V	f	v
0111	BEL	ETB		7	G	W	g	w
1000	BS	CAN	(	8	H	X	h	x
1001	HT	EM	)	9	I	Y	i	y
1010	LF	SUB	*	:	J	Z	j	z
1011	VT	ESC	+	;	K	[	k	{
1100	FF	FS	(Comma) ,	<	L	\	l	'
1101	CR	GS	—	=	M	]	m	}
1110	SO	RS	*	>	N	↑	n	~
1111	SI	US	/	?	O	←	o	DEL

Example: 100 0001 = A

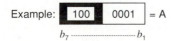

$b_7 \text{-----------} b_1$

FIGURE 2.4
American Standard Code for Information Interchange (ASCII).

NUL	Null	DLE	Data link escape
SOH	Start of heading	DC1	Device control 1
STX	Start of text	DC2	Device control 2
ETX	End of text	DC3	Device control 3
EOT	End of tape	DC4	Device control 4
ENQ	Enquiry	NAK	Negative acknowledge
ACK	Acknowledge	SYN	Synchronize
BEL	Bell	ETB	End of transmitted block
BS	Backspace	CAN	Cancel
HT	Horizontal tab	EM	End of medium
LF	Line feed	SUB	Substitute
VT	Vertical tab	ESC	Escape
FF	Form feed	FS	File separator
CR	Carriage return	GS	Group separator
SO	Shift out	RS	Record separator
SI	Shift in	US	Unit separator
SP	Space	DEL	Delete

FIGURE 2.5
Special characters in ASCII.

the normal 8,4,2,1 code preceded by the three binary digits 011. Thus, decimal 1 is 0110001, decimal 2 is 0110010, and decimal 7 is 0110111. To expand the code, the letter A is 1000001, B is 1000010, and so on. There are various codes, such as "end of text," "backspace," and "carriage return," which are very useful in communications systems and in editing data processes in computers. These are shown in Fig. 2.5.

Many IBM computers, and a number of other manufacturers' computer systems, use the extended BCD interchange code (EBCDIC) shown in Fig. 2.6. This code is the second most used code after the ASCII.

QUESTIONS

2.1. Convert the following decimal numbers to equivalent binary numbers:

(a) 43	(b) 64	(c) 4096
(d) 0.375	(e) 27/32	(f) 0.4375
(g) 512.5	(h) 131.5625	(i) 2048.0625

2.2. Convert the following numbers to the equivalent binary numbers:

(a) 14	(b) 0.25	(c) 2 1/8
(d) 6.25	(e) 2 3/8	(f) 0.625

2.3. Convert the following binary numbers to equivalent decimal numbers:

(a) 1101	(b) 11011	(c) 1011
(d) 0.1011	(e) 0.001101	(f) 0.001101101
(g) 111011.1011	(h) 1011011.001101	(i) 10110.0101011101

2.4. Convert the following binary numbers to equivalent decimal numbers:

(a) 1011	(b) 11000	(c) 100011
(d) 11011	(e) 111001	(f) 1011010

2.5. Convert the following binary numbers to equivalent decimal numbers:

(a) 1011	(b) 100100	(c) 10011
(d) 0.1101	(e) 0.1001	(f) 0.0101
(g) 1011.0011	(h) 1001.1001	(i) 101.011

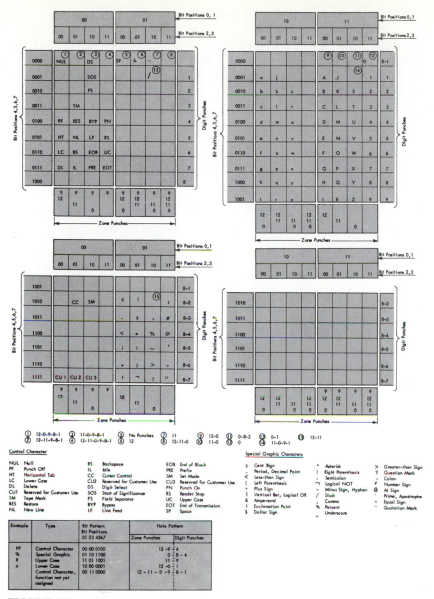

FIGURE 2.6
Extended BCD Interchange Code (EBCDIC).

2.6. Convert the following binary numbers to equivalent decimal numbers:
(a) 0.111   (b) 0.11011   (c) 1.011
(d) 111.1011   (e) 0110.0101   (f) 101.101011

2.7. Perform the following additions and check by converting the binary numbers to decimal:
(a) 1001.1 + 1011.01   (b) 100101 + 100101   (c) 0.1011 + 0.1101
(d) 1011.01 + 1001.11

2.8. Perform the following additions and check by converting the binary numbers to decimal and adding:

(a) 1011 + 1110   (b) 1010 + 1111   (c) 10.11 + 10.011
(d) 1101.11 + 1.11   (e) 11111.1 + 10010.1 (f) 101.1 + 111.11

2.9. Perform the following additions and check by converting the binary numbers to decimal:

(a) 1101.1 + 1011.1
(b) 101101 + 1101101
(c) 0.0011 + 0.1110
(d) 1100.011 + 1011.011

2.10. Perform the following subtractions in binary and check by converting the numbers to decimal and subtracting:

(a) 1101 − 1000   (b) 1101 − 1001   (c) 1011.1 − 101.1
(d) 1101.01 − 1011.1   (e) 111.11 − 101.1   (f) 1101.1 − 1010.01

2.11. Perform the following subtractions in the binary number system:

(a) 64 − 32   (b) 127 − 63   (c) 93.5 − 42.75
(d) 84 9/32 − 48 5/16

2.12. Perform the following subractions in the binary number system:

(a) 128 − 32   (b) 1/8 − 1/16   (c) 2 1/8 − 4 3/32
(d) 31 − 5/8   (e) 62 − 31 1/16   (f) 129 − 35

2.13. Perform the following subtractions in the binary number system:

(a) 37 − 35   (b) 128 − 64   (c) 94.5 − 43.75
(d) 255 − 127

2.14. Perform the following multiplications and divisions in the binary number system:

(a) 16 × 8   (b) 31 × 14   (c) 23 × 3.525
(d) 15 × 8.625   (e) 6 ÷ 2   (f) 16 ÷ 8

2.15. Perform the following multiplications and divisions in the binary number system:

(a) 24 × 12   (b) 18 × 14   (c) 32 ÷ 8
(d) 27 ÷ 18   (e) 49.5 × 51.75   (f) 58.75 ÷ 23.5

2.16. Perform the following multiplications and divisions in the binary number system:

(a) 16 × 2.75   (b) 19 ÷ 6   (c) 256 1/2 ÷ 128 1/4
(d) 31.5 ÷ 15.75   (e) 3 ÷ 5/8   (f) 2 5/8 × 1 5/8

2.17. Perform the following multiplications and divisions in the binary number system:

(a) 15 × 13   (b) 10 × 15   (c) 44 ÷ 11
(d) 42 ÷ 12   (e) 7.75 × 2.5   (f) 22.5 × 4.75

2.18. Convert the following decimal numbers to both their 9s and 10s complements:

(a) 9   (b) 19   (c) 8
(d) 24   (e) 25   (d) 99

2.19. Convert the following decimal numbers into both their 9s and 10s complements:

(a) 5436   (b) 1932   (c) 45.15
(d) 18.293

2.20. Convert the following decimal numbers into both their 9s and 10s complements:

(a) 95   (b) 79   (c) 0.83
(d) 0.16   (e) 298.64   (f) 332.52

2.21. Convert the following decimal numbers to both their 9s and 10s complements:

(a) 3654   (b) 2122   (c) 54.19
(d) 37.263

2.22. Convert the following binary numbers to both their 1s and 2s complements:

(*a*) 1101	(*b*) 1010	(*c*) 1111
(*d*) 1110	(*e*) 1011	(*f*) 1011

2.23. Convert the following binary numbers to both their 1s and 2s complements:

(*a*) 1011	(*b*) 11011	(*c*) 1011.01
(*d*) 11011.01		

2.24. Convert the following binary numbers to both their 1s and 2s complements:

(*a*) 1011	(*b*) 1101	(*c*) 0.0111
(*d*) 0.101	(*e*) 11.101	(*f*) 101.011

2.25. Convert the following binary numbers to both their 1s and 2s complements:

(*a*) 101111	(*b*) 100100	(*c*) 10111.10
(*d*) 10011.11		

2.26. Perform the following subtractions, using both 9s and 10s complements:

(*a*) $8 - 4$	(*b*) $16 - 8$	(*c*) $198 - 124$
(*d*) $28.5 - 23.4$	(*e*) $27.6 - 23.4$	(*f*) $0.55 - 0.42$

2.27. Perform the following subtractions, using both 9s and 10s complements:

(*a*) $948 - 234$	(*b*) $347 - 263$	(*c*) $349.5 - 245.3$
(*d*) $412.7 - 409.2$		

2.28. Perform the following subtractions, using both 9s and 10s complements:

(*a*) $14 - 9$	(*b*) $15 - 9$	(*c*) $0.5 - 40.24$
(*d*) $0.41 - 0.4$	(*e*) $0.434 - 0.33$	(*f*) $1.2 - 0.34$

2.29. Perform the following subtractions, using both 9s and 10s complements:

(*a*) $1024 - 913$	(*b*) $249 - 137$	(*c*) $24.1 - 13.4$
(*d*) $239.3 - 119.4$		

2.30. Perform the following subtractions of binary numbers, using both 1s and 2s complements:

(*a*) $1010 - 1011$	(*b*) $110 - 10$	(*c*) $110 - 0.111$
(*d*) $0.111 - 0.1001$	(*e*) $0.1111 - 0.101$	(*f*) $11.11 - 10.111$

2.31. Perform the following subtractions, using both 1s and 2s complements:

(*a*) $1011 - 101$	(*b*) $11011 - 11001$	(*c*) $10111.1 - 10011.1$
(*d*) $11011 - 10011.11$		

2.32. How many different numbers can be stored in a set of four switches, each having three different positions (four three-position switches)?

2.33. How many different binary numbers can be stored in a register consisting of six switches?

2.34. How many different BCD numbers can be stored in a register of 12 switches? (Assume two-position, on/off, switches.)

2.35. How many different BCD numbers can be stored in a register containing 12 switches using an 8,4,2,1 code?

2.36. Write the first 12 numbers in the base 4 (or *quaternary*) number system.

2.37. Write the first 10 numbers in the quaternary number system, which has a base, or radix, of 4. Use the digits 0, 1, 2, and 3 to express these numbers.

2.38. Write the first 20 numbers in the base 12 (or *duodecimal*) number system. Use A for 10 and B for 11.

2.39. Write the first 25 numbers in the base 11 number system, using the digits 0, 1, 2, 3, 4, 5, 6, 7, 8, 9, and A to express the 25 numbers that you write. (Decimal 10 = A, for instance.)

2.40. Perform the following subtractions in the binary number system, using 1s complements:

(*a*) 1111 − 1001   (*b*) 1110 − 1011   (*c*) 101.11 − 101.01
(*d*) 111.1 − 100.1

2.41. Using the 1s complement number system, perform the following subtractions:
(*a*) 0.1001 − 0.0110   (*b*) 0.1110 − 0.0110   (*c*) 0.01111 − 0.01001
(*d*) 11011 − 11001   (*e*) 1110101 − 1010010

2.42. Perform the following subtractions in the binary number system, using 2s complements:
(*a*) 1111 − 110   (*b*) 1110 − 1100   (*c*) 1011.11 − 101.001
(*d*) 111.1 − 110.1

2.43. Using the 2s complement number system, perform the following subtractions and represent the answers as decimal fractions:
(*a*) 0.101010 − 0.010101
(*b*) 0.11001 − 0.00100
(*c*) 0.111000 = 0.000111
(*d*) 0.101100 − 0.010011

2.44. Convert the following hexadecimal numbers to decimal numbers:
(*a*) 15   (*b*) B8   (*c*) AB4
(*d*) 9.B   (*e*) 9.1A

2.45. Convert the following hexadecimal numbers to decimal:
(*a*) B6C7   (*b*) 64AC   (*c*) A492
(*d*) D2763

2.46. Convert the following octal numbers to decimal:
(*a*) 15   (*b*) 125   (*c*) 115
(*d*) 124   (*e*) 156   (*f*) 15.6

2.47. Convert the following octal numbers to decimal:
(*a*) 2376   (*b*) 2473   (*c*) 276431
(*d*) 22632

2.48. Convert the following binary numbers to octal:
(*a*) 110   (*b*) 111001   (*c*) 111.111
(*d*) 0.11111   (*e*) 10.11   (*f*) 1111.1101

2.49. Convert the following binary numbers to octal:
(*a*) 101101   (*b*) 101101110   (*c*) 10110111
(*d*) 110110.011   (*e*) 011.1011011

2.50. Convert the following octal numbers to binary:
(*a*) 54   (*b*) 44   (*c*) 232.2
(*d*) 232.4   (*e*) 453.45   (*f*) 31.234

2.51. Convert the following octal numbers to binary:
(*a*) 7423   (*b*) 3364   (*c*) 33762
(*d*) 3232.14   (*e*) 3146.52

2.52. Convert the following decimal numbers to octal:
(*a*) 17   (*b*) 8   (*c*) 19
(*d*) 0.55   (*e*) 0.625   (*f*) 2.125

2.53. Convert the following decimal numbers to octal:
(*a*) 932   (*b*) 332   (*c*) 545.375
(*d*) 632.97   (*e*) 4429.625

2.54. Convert the following hexadecimal numbers to binary:
(*a*) 9   (*b*) 1B   (*c*) 0.A1
(*d*) 0.AB   (*e*) AB   (*f*) 12.B

2.55. Convert the following hexadecimal numbers to binary:

    (*a*) CD   (*b*) 6A9   (*c*) A14

    (*d*) AA.1A   (*e*) AB2.234

2.56. Convert the following binary numbers to hexadecimal:

    (*a*) 1101.0110   (*b*) 11011110   (*c*) 1111

    (*d*) 11101   (*e*) 11110.01011   (*f*) 1011.11010

2.57. Convert the following binary numbers to hexadecimal:

    (*a*) 10110111   (*b*) 10011100   (*c*) 1001111

    (*d*) 0.01111110   (*e*) 101101111010

2.58. A simple rule for multiplyng two digits in any radix is to multiply the two digits in decimal. If the product is less than the radix, use it; if it is greater, divide (in decimal) by the radix and use the remainder as the first (least significant) digit and the quotient as the carry (most significant) digit. In base 6, $2 \times 2 = 4$, and $3 \times 1 = 3$; however, $2 \times 4 = 8$, and

$$\begin{array}{r} 1 \\ 6\overline{)\ 8} \\ \underline{6} \\ 2 \end{array}$$

So $2_6 \times 4_6 - 12_6$. Similarly, in base 7, $3 \times 4 = 12$, and

$$\begin{array}{r} 1 \\ 7\overline{)\ 12} \\ \underline{7} \\ 5 \end{array}$$

So $3_7 \times 4_7 = 15\ _7$. Using this rule, perform, in base 7, the following multiplications:

    (*a*) $2_7 \times 3_7$ (*b*) $2_7 \times 2_7$ (*c*) $4_7 \times 4_7$

    (*d*) $4_7 \times 3_7$

2.59. Using the rule in Question 2.58, perform:

    (*a*) $3_6 \times 4_6$ (*b*) $3_6 \times 3_6$ (*c*) $3_9 \times 4_9$

    (*d*) $4_9 \times 5_9$ (*e*) $5_9 \times 15_9$

2.60. An addition table for octal is as follows:

+	0	1	2	3	4	5	6	7
0	0	1	2	3	4	5	6	7
1	1	2	3	4	5	6	7	10
2	2	3	4	5	6	7	10	11
3	3	4	5	6	7	10	11	12
4	4	5	6	7	10	11	12	13
5	5	6	7	10	11	12	13	14
6	6	7	10	11	12	13	14	15
7	7	10	11	12	13	14	15	16

Using this table, we add in octal:

$$11 \longleftarrow \text{carries}$$
$$126$$
$$357$$
$$\overline{505}$$

Perform the following additions:

(a) $7_8 + 7_8$ (b) $6_8 + 5_8$ (c) $7_8 + 16_8$

(d) $5_8 + 4_8$ (e) $5_8 + 14_8$

2.61. Using the table in Question 2.60, perform:

(a) $15_8 + 14_8$ (b) $24_8 + 36_8$ (c) $126_8 + 347_8$

(d) $67_8 + 45_8$ (e) $136_8 + 636_8$

2.62. Make up a hexadecimal addition table.

2.63. Using the table from Question 2.62, perform:

(a) $6_{16} + A1_{16}$ (b) $7_{16} + 17_{16}$ (c) $8_{16} + 28_{16}$

(d) $A16A_{16} + B16A_{16}$ (e) $A84_{16} + A83_{16}$

2.64. Perform the additions in Question 2.63 in binary and convert back to hexadecimal.

2.65. Perform the additions in Question 2.61 in binary and convert back to octal.

2.66. To multiply two numbers in octal, we use the rule given in Question 2.58 and then proceed as follows:

$$6 \times 27 = 6 \times 20 + 6 \times 7$$
$$= 140 + 52 = 212$$

Multiply the following in octal:

(a) 6×7 (b) 6×10 (c) 5×14

2.67. To multiply numbers of more than one digit, proceed as in Question 2.66 and then add in octal. Multiply the following octal numbers:

(a) 3×14 (b) 23×2 (c) 11×22

(d) 22×44 (e) 13×13 (f) 14×15

2.68. Perform the following multiplications of hexadecimal numbers:

(a) $A \times 8$ (b) 9×14 (c) $A1 \times 8$

(d) $A11 \times 9$ (e) $A12 \times 6$ (f) $A13 \times 2B$

2.69. Using the rule in Question 2.58, perform the following multiplications of hexadecimal numbers:

(a) $15 \times B$ (b) $14 \times B$ (c) $11 \times A$

(d) $142 \times A$ (e) 13×14

2.70. Perform the multiplications in Question 2.68 in binary, then convert back to hexadecimal.

2.71. Perform the multiplications in Question 2.69 in binary, then convert back to hexadecimal.

2.72. In converting decimal numbers to hexadecimal, it is convenient to go first to octal, then to binary, then to hexadecimal. For instance, to convert 412_{10} to hexadecimal, we go first to octal:

$$\begin{array}{r} 51 \\ 8)\overline{412} \\ 40 \\ \hline 12 \\ 8 \\ \hline 4 \end{array} \leftarrow \text{3d digit}$$

$$\begin{array}{r} 6 \leftarrow \text{1st digit} \\ 8)\overline{51} \\ 48 \\ \hline 3 \leftarrow \text{2d digit} \end{array}$$

Thus, $412_{10} = 634_8$; converting this to binary gives

$$634_8 = \underbrace{110}_{6} \; \underbrace{011}_{3} \; \underbrace{100}_{4}$$

Regrouping yields

$$\underbrace{1}_{1} \; \underbrace{1001}_{9} \; \underbrace{1100}_{C}$$

So

$$412_{10} = 19C$$

Convert the following decimal numbers to hexadecimal:

(a) 24 (b) 397 (c) 1343
(d) 513 (e) 262

2.73. (a) Give the IBM floating-point representations for decimal 27.25 and -27.25.
(b) Give the IEEE standard format representations for $+12$ and -12.

2.74. (a) Give the IBM floating-point representations for decimal 55.4 and -53.4.
(b) Give the IEEE standard single-precision floating-point representations for $+29$ and -29.
(c) Compare the ranges, accuracy, and other system design considerations for the preceding two floating-point number systems.

2.75. If numbers are represented in a 2s complement, 7-bit magnitude plus 1 sign-bit integer system, and we ignore overflow (that is, any result will be stored, even if it requires more magnitude bits), then the largest positive integer that can result from the addition of two numbers is _____, and the largest positive integer that can result from the subtraction of one number from another is _____. The smallest negative numbers that can result from an addition and subtraction are _____ and _____. As a result, any sum or difference can be stored in _____ bits.

2.76. Write all 4-bit 2s complement numbers (that is, sign plus 3-bit numbers) and their decimal values. Show that negative numbers exceed positive numbers by one. Consider 0 to be neither negative or positive.

2.77. When addition is performed in a binary machine using the 2s complement number system to represent negative numbers, an overflow may occur in a register only when two positive or two negative numbers are added. Show that the addition of a positive number and a negative number cannot result in an overflow condition.

2.78. Show that there are as many negative as positive numbers in a 1s complement system.

2.79. Show how to represent $+6$ in the 12-bit floating-point word in Fig 2.3.

2.80. Show how to represent -14 in the 12-bit floating-point word in Fig 2.3.

2.81. (a) Give the IBM floating-point representations for 57.5 and 54.5.
(b) Give the IEEE standard format floating-point representations for $+25.0$ and -25.0.
(c) Compare the ranges, accuracy, and other system design considerations for the preceding two computer floating-point number systems.

2.82. Show two decimal numbers that, when converted to the IBM floating-point number system, will have .0011 in bits 9, 10, 11, and 12.

2.83. Can you suggest any reasons behind the decision of the systems architects at IBM to use hexadecimal as the base for the IBM series floating-point number system instead of conventional base 2? That is, in system 370 a floating-point full word of 32 bits has as characteristic a 7-bit integer with value C and as fraction a binary signed-magnitude 25-bit number with value F. The value of the number represented is then $(16^{C-64})F$. Why 16^{C-64} rather than 2^{C-64}? Give system design considerations.

2.84. Give the value of a positive nonzero *integer* less than 16^{62} that cannot be represented in the IBM floating-point number system (using a single 32-bit word). Do not be afraid to use an expression such as $2^{16} + 3$ for your answer, but explain why you think your answer is correct.

2.85. A hexadecimal odometer displays F34B. What are the next six readings?

2.86. The reading on a hexadecimal odometer is 34FA. What is the next reading? Miles later, you see a reading of 8AFC. How far have you gone (give the answer in decimal and hex). What are the next six readings?

2.87. List some advantages and disadvantages of sign-magnitude and 2s complement number systems in representing the mantissas of floating-point numbers.

2.88. For the 64-bit IEEE floating-point number format, determine the largest positive number, the smallest nonzero negative number, and the negative number with the largest magnitude that can be represented.

2.89. For the 64-bit IBM floating-point number format, find the largest and smallest nonzero numbers that can be represented.

2.90. The IBM 32-bit floating-point was described in this chapter. Represent the following decimal numbers in this format.

(*a*) 0   (*b*) -15 (*c*) 0.55
(*d*) 102   (*e*) 4096   (*f*) 43.92×10^2
(*g*) -0.000125 (*h*) 2500   (*i*) -1.0×10^5
(*j*) 0.1×10^{-4}

CHAPTER
3

BOOLEAN ALGEBRA AND GATE NETWORKS

Modern digital computers are designed and maintained, and their operation analyzed, by using techniques and symbology from a field of mathematics called *modern algebra*. Algebraists have studied for over one hundred years mathematical systems called *boolean algebras*. Nothing could be more simple and representative of human reasoning than the rules of boolean algebra, for these originated in studies of how we reason, what lines of reasoning are valid, what constitutes proof, and other, allied subjects.

The name *boolean algebra* honors a fascinating English mathematician, George Boole, who in 1854 published a classic book, *An Investigation of the Laws of Thought, on Which Are Founded the Mathematical Theories of Logic and Probabilities*.[1] Boole's stated intention was to perform a mathematical analysis of logic.

Starting with his investigation of the laws of thought, Boole constructed a "logical algebra." This investigation into the nature of logic and ultimately of mathematics led subsequent mathematicians and logicians into several new fields of mathematics. Two of these, known as the *calculus of propositions* and the *algebra of sets*, were based principally on Boole's work. In this book we designate the algebra now used in the design and maintenance of logical circuitry as *boolean algebra*.[2]

---

[1] George Boole was the son of a shoemaker. His formal education ended in the third grade. Despite this, he was a brilliant scholar, teaching Greek and Latin in his own school, and an accepted mathematician who made lasting contributions in the areas of differential and difference equations as well as algebra.

[2] This algebra is sometimes called *switching algebra*. It is, in fact, only one of several realizations of what modern algebraists call boolean algebra.

There are several advantages to having a mathematical technique for the description of the internal workings of a computer. For one thing, it is often far more convenient to calculate using expressions that represent switching circuits than it is to use schematic or even logical diagrams. Further, just as an ordinary algebraic expression may be simplified by means of basic theorems, the expression describing a given switching circuit network may be reduced or simplified. This enables the designer to simplify the circuitry used, achieving economy of construction and reliability of operation. Boolean algebra also provides an economical and straightforward way of describing the circuitry used in computers. In all, a knowledge of boolean algebra is indispensable in the computing field.

3.1 FUNDAMENTAL CONCEPTS OF BOOLEAN ALGEBRA

When a variable is used in an algebraic formula, it is generally assumed that the variable may take any numerical value. For instance, in the formula $2X - 5Y = Z$, we assume that X, Y, and Z may range through the entire field of real numbers.

A variable used in boolean equations has a unique characteristic, however: it may assume only one of two possible values. These two values may be represented by the symbols 0 and 1.[3] For instance, in the logic equation $X + Y = Z$, each of the variables X, Y, and Z may have only the values 0 or 1.

This concept will become clearer once the + symbol is defined. Since each of two variables, X and Y, can take only the value 0 or 1, we can define the + symbol by listing all possible combinations for X and Y and the resulting values of $X + Y$. The possible input and output combinations may be arranged as follows:

$$0 + 0 = 0$$
$$0 + 1 = 1$$
$$1 + 0 = 1$$
$$1 + 1 = 1$$

This is a *logical addition* table and could represent a standard binary addition table except for the last entry. When both X and Y represent 1s, the value of $X + Y$ is 1. The + symbol, therefore, does not have the normal meaning but is a logical addition, or *logical OR*, symbol. The equation $X + Y = Z$ can be read "X or Y equals Z" or "X plus Y equals Z." This concept may be extended to any number of variables. For instance, in the equation $A + B + C + D = E$, even if A, B, C, and D all had values of 1, E would represent only a 1.

To avoid ambiguity, a number of other symbols have been recommended as replacements for the + sign, for example, $\cup$ and $\vee$.[4] Computer people still use the + sign, however, which was the symbol originally proposed by Boole.

---

[3] Or T and F, + and $-$, or some other symbology for opposite states. However, 0 and 1 are almost universally used in computer work.

[4] The preceding equation might then be written as $A \cup B \cup C \cup D = E$.

Logical Multiplication

A second important operation in boolean algebra is *logical multiplication* or the *logical AND operation*.[5] The rules for this operation can be given by simply listing all values that might occur:

$$0 \cdot 0 = 0$$

$$0 \cdot 1 = 0$$

$$1 \cdot 0 = 0$$

$$1 \cdot 1 = 1$$

Thus, if we write $Z = X \cdot Y$ and find $X = 0$ and $Y = 1$, then $Z = 0$. Only when X and Y are both 1s would Z be a 1.

Both $+$ and $\cdot$ obey a mathematical rule called the *associative law*. This law says, for $+$, that $(X + Y) + Z = X + (Y + Z)$ and, for $\cdot$, that $X \cdot (Y \cdot Z) = (X \cdot Y) \cdot Z$. This means that we can write $X + Y + Z$ without ambiguity; no matter in what order the operation is performed, the result is the same. That is, ORing X and Y and then ORing Z gives the same result as ORing Y and Z and then ORing X. We can test this for both $+$ and $\cdot$ by trying all combinations.

Note that although either $+$ or $\cdot$ can be used freely, the two cannot be mixed without ambiguity in the absence of further rules. For instance, does $A \cdot B + C$ mean $(A \cdot B) + C$ or $A \cdot (B + C)$? The two form different values for $A = 0$, $B = 0$, and $C = 1$: $(0 \cdot 0) + 1 = 1$ and $0 \cdot (0 + 1) = 0$. (Always operating from left to right will alleviate this. This technique is used in some programming languages, but not usually by algebraists or computer designers or maintenance personnel.) The rule that is used is that $\cdot$ is always performed before $+$. Thus, $X \cdot Y + Z$ is the same as $(X \cdot Y) + Z$, and $X \cdot Y + X \cdot Z$ means the same as $(X \cdot Y) + (X \cdot Z)$.

3.2   AND GATES AND OR GATES

The $+$ and $\cdot$ operations are physically realized by two types of electronic circuits, called *OR gates* and *AND gates*. We will treat these as "black boxes," deferring until later any discussion on how the actual circuitry operates.

A *gate* is simply an electronic circuit that operates on one or more input signals to produce an output signal. One of the simplest and most frequently used gates is the OR gate. The block diagram symbol for the OR gate is shown in Fig. 3.1, as is the table of combinations for the inputs and outputs for the OR gate. Since the inputs, X and Y, are signals with values of 0 or 1 at any given time, the output signal, Z, can be described simply by listing all values for X and Y and the resulting value for Z. A study of the table in Fig. 3.1 indicates that the OR gate ORs, or logically adds, its inputs.

---

[5] It is necessary to know both the terms *logical addition* and *OR operation* for the $+$ symbol and both the terms *logical multiplication* and *AND operation* for the $\cdot$ symbol, since all these terms are actively used in computer manuals, technical journals, and trade magazines. The term $X + Y$ is called either a *sum term* or an *OR term* in computer literature, for example.

X

Y

OR ──── Z

INPUT		OUTPUT
X	Y	Z
0	0	0
0	1	1
1	0	1
1	1	1

FIGURE 3.1
OR gate.

Similarly, the AND gate in Fig. 3.2 ANDs, or logically multiplies, input values, yielding an output, Z, with value $X \cdot Y$. Z is a 1 only when both X and Y are 1s.

Just as the $+$ and $\cdot$ operations can be extended to several variables by using the associative law, OR gates and AND gates can have more than two inputs. Figure 3.3 shows three-input OR and AND gates and the table of all input combinations for each. As might be hoped, the OR gate with inputs X, Y and Z has a 1 output if X or Y or Z is a 1, so that we can write $X + Y + Z$ for its output. Also, the output of the AND gate with inputs X, Y and Z is a 1 only when all three of the inputs are 1s, so that we can write the output as $X \cdot Y \cdot Z$.

These rules can be extended to any number of inputs. For example, a four-input OR gate has a 1 output when any of its inputs is a 1, and a four-input AND gate has a 1 output only when all four inputs are 1s.

It is often convenient to shorten $X \cdot Y \cdot Z$ to XYZ, and we sometimes use this convention.

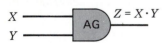

X

Y

AG $Z = X \cdot Y$

INPUT		OUTPUT	
X	Y	Z	
0	0	0	$0 \cdot 0 = 0$
0	1	0	$0 \cdot 1 = 0$
1	0	0	$1 \cdot 0 = 0$
1	1	1	$1 \cdot 1 = 1$

FIGURE 3.2
AND gate.

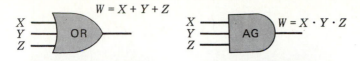

| INPUT | OUTPUT |
X Y Z	W
0 0 0	0
0 0 1	1
0 1 0	1
0 1 1	1
1 0 0	1
1 0 1	1
1 1 0	1
1 1 1	1

| INPUT | OUTPUT |
X Y Z	W
0 0 0	0
0 0 1	0
0 1 0	0
0 1 1	0
1 0 0	0
1 0 1	0
1 1 0	0
1 1 1	1

FIGURE 3.3
Three-input OR and AND gates.

3.3 COMPLEMENTATION AND INVERTERS

The two operations defined so far are what algebraists call *binary operations*, in that they define an operation on two variables. There are also *singular* or *unary operations*, which define an operation on a single variable. A familiar example of a unary operation is $-$, as in -5, -10, or $-X$, meaning that we are to take the negative of these values. (The $-$ is also used as a binary operation symbol for subtraction, which makes it a familiar but ambiguous example.)

Boolean algebra uses an operation called *complementation*, and the *symbol* for this is $^-$. Thus, $\overline{X}$ means "take the complement of X," and $\overline{(X + Y)}$ means "take the complement of $X + Y$." The complement operation can be defined quite simply:

$$\overline{0} = 1$$
$$\overline{1} = 0$$

The complement of a value can be taken repeatedly. For instance, we can find $\overline{\overline{\overline{X}}}$: for $X = 0$ it is $\overline{\overline{\overline{0}}} = \overline{\overline{1}} = \overline{0} = 1$, and for $X = 1$ it is $\overline{\overline{\overline{1}}} = \overline{\overline{0}} = \overline{1} = 0$. A useful rule is based on the fact that $\overline{\overline{X}} = X$. Checking, we find that $\overline{\overline{0}} = \overline{1} = 0$ and $\overline{\overline{1}} = \overline{0} = 1$. [This rule—that double complementation gives the original value—is an important characteristic of a boolean algebra that does not hold for most unary operations. For instance, the rule does not hold for the operation of squaring a real number: $(3^2)^2 = 81$, not 3.]

The complementation operation is physically realized by a gate or circuit called an *inverter*. Figure 3.4(*a*) shows an inverter and the table of combinations for its input and output. Figure 3.4(*b*) shows also that connecting two inverters in series gives an output equal to the input; this is the gating counterpart to the law of double complementation, $\overline{\overline{X}} = X$.

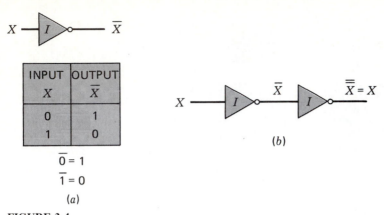

FIGURE 3.4
(*a*) Block diagram of an inverter. (*b*) Two inverters in series.

Several other symbols have been used to denote complementation. For instance, $\sim$ is often used by logicians; $\sim X$ is read as "the negation of X." The symbol $\prime$ has been used by mathematicians and computer people; thus, $X\prime$ is the complement of X in these systems. The overbar symbol is now used by the American National Standards Institute and in military standards, as well as by most journals and manufacturers, so we use it here.

3.4   EVALUATION OF LOGICAL EXPRESSIONS

The tables of values for the three operations just explained are sometimes called *truth tables* or *tables of combinations*. To study a logical expression, it is very useful to construct a table of values for the variables and then evaluate the expression for each possible combination of variables. Consider the expression $X + Y\overline{Z}$. There are three variables in this expression, X, Y, and Z, each of which can assume the value 0 or 1. The possible combinations of values may be arranged in ascending order, as in Table 3.1.[6] One of the variables, Z, is complemented in the expression, so a column is added to the table listing values of $\overline{Z}$ (see Table 3.2).

Next, a column is added listing the values that $Y\overline{Z}$ assumes for each value of X, Y, and Z. This column will contain the value 1 only when both Y is a 1 and $\overline{Z}$ is a 1 (see Table 3.3).

Finally, the ORing, or logical addition, of each value of X to each of the values calculated for $Y\overline{Z}$ is listed in a fifth column (see Table 3.4). This column contains

---

[6] Note that the variables in each row of this table may be combined into a binary number. The binary numbers will then count from 000 to 111, or from 0 to 7 decimal. Sometimes each row is numbered in decimal according to the number represented. Then reference may be made to the row by using the decimal number. For instance, row 0 has values of 0, 0, 0, for X, Y, and Z; row 6 has values of 1, 1, 0; and row 7 has values of 1, 1, 1.

TABLE 3.1

X	Y	Z
0	0	0
0	0	1
0	1	0
0	1	1
1	0	0
1	0	1
1	1	0
1	1	1

TABLE 3.2

X	Y	Z	$\overline{Z}$
0	0	0	1
0	0	1	0
0	1	0	1
0	1	1	0
1	0	0	1
1	0	1	0
1	1	0	1
1	1	1	0

TABLE 3.3

X	Y	Z	$\overline{Z}$	$Y\overline{Z}$
0	0	0	1	0
0	0	1	0	0
0	1	0	1	1
0	1	1	0	0
1	0	0	1	0
1	0	1	0	0
1	1	0	1	1
1	1	1	0	0

the value of $X + Y\overline{Z}$ for each set of input values X, Y, and Z may take. For instance, when $X = 1$, $Y = 0$, and $Z = 1$, the expression has the value of 1.

Evaluation of an Expression Containing Parentheses

The following example illustrates the procedure for constructing a truth table for the expression $X + Y(\overline{X} + \overline{Y})$.

There are only two variables in the expression, X and Y. First, a table of the values that X and Y may assume is constructed (see Table 3.5). Since the expression contains both $\overline{X}$ and $\overline{Y}$, two columns are added listing complements of the original values of the variables (see Table 3.6). Next, the various values of $\overline{X} + \overline{Y}$ are calculated (see Table 3.7). The values for $\overline{X} + \overline{Y}$ are now multiplied (ANDed) by the values of Y in the table, forming another column representing $Y(\overline{X} + \overline{Y})$ (see Table 3.8). Finally, the values for $Y(\overline{X} + \overline{Y})$ are added (ORed) to the values for X listed, forming another column and completing the table (see Table 3.9).

Inspection of the final column of the table indicates that the values taken by the function $X + Y(\overline{X} + \overline{Y})$ are identical to the values found in the table for ORing X and Y. This indicates that the function $X + Y(\overline{X} + \overline{Y})$ is equivalent to the function $X + Y$. This equivalence has been established by trying each possible combination of values for the variables and noting that the resulting expressions have the same value. This is called a *proof by perfect induction*. If a logic circuit were constructed for each of the two expressions, both circuits would perform the same function, yielding identical outputs for each combination of inputs.

TABLE 3.4

X	Y	Z	$\overline{Z}$	$Y\overline{Z}$	$X + Y\overline{Z}$
0	0	0	1	0	0
0	0	1	0	0	0
0	1	0	1	1	1
0	1	1	0	0	0
1	0	0	1	0	1
1	0	1	0	0	1
1	1	0	1	1	1
1	1	1	0	0	1

TABLE 3.5

X	Y
0	0
0	1
1	0
1	1

TABLE 3.6

X	Y	$\overline{X}$	$\overline{Y}$
0	0	1	1
0	1	1	0
1	0	0	1
1	1	0	0

TABLE 3.7

X	Y	$\overline{X}$	$\overline{Y}$	$\overline{X} + \overline{Y}$
0	0	1	1	1
0	1	1	0	1
1	0	0	1	1
1	1	0	0	0

TABLE 3.8

X	Y	$\overline{X}$	$\overline{Y}$	$\overline{X} + \overline{Y}$	$Y(\overline{X} + \overline{Y})$
0	0	1	1	1	0
0	1	1	0	1	1
1	0	0	1	1	0
1	1	0	0	0	0

TABLE 3.9

X	Y	$\overline{X}$	$\overline{Y}$	$\overline{X} + \overline{Y}$	$Y(\overline{X} + \overline{Y})$	$X + Y(\overline{X} + \overline{Y})$
0	0	1	1	1	0	0
0	1	1	0	1	1	1
1	0	0	1	1	0	1
1	1	0	0	0	0	1

3.5 BASIC LAWS OF BOOLEAN ALGEBRA

Some fundamental relations of boolean algebra have been presented. A complete set of the basic operations follows.[7] Although simple in appearance, these rules may be used to construct a boolean algebra,[8] determining all the relations that follow:

$$\text{If } X \neq 0, \text{ then } X = 1$$

and

$$\text{If } X \neq 1, \text{ then } X = 0$$

OR OPERATION (LOGICAL ADDITION)	AND OPERATION (LOGICAL MULTIPLICATION)	COMPLEMENT RULES
$0 + 0 = 0$	$0 \cdot 0 = 0$	$\overline{0} = 1$
$0 + 1 = 1$	$0 \cdot 0 = 0$	$\overline{1} = 0$
$1 + 0 = 1$	$1 \cdot 0 = 0$	
$1 + 1 = 1$	$1 \cdot 1 = 1$	

A list of useful relations is presented in Table 3.10. Most of the basic rules by which boolean algebra expressions may be manipulated are contained in this table.

---

[7] Actually, a number of possible sets of postulates may be used to define the algebra. The particular treatment of boolean algebra given here is derived from that of E. V. Huntington and M. H. Stone. The author would also like to acknowledge the influence of I. S. Reed and S. H. Caldwell on this development of the concepts of the algebra.

[8] These rules are used to construct an *example*, or *realization*, of a boolean algebra. We note that, strictly speaking, this boolean algebra consists of a set B of two elements, which we call 0 and 1, an addition operation (+), a multiplication operation ($\cdot$), and a complement operation ($\overline{}$). There are other boolean algebras (an infinite number), but this was Boole's original algebra. This algebra is sometimes called *switching algebra* to identify it more closely, but it is the same as propositional calculus, for instance.

TABLE 3.10
Boolean algebra rules

1. $0 + X = X$	11. $X \cdot Y = Y \cdot X$
2. $1 + X = 1$	12. $X + (Y + Z) = (X + Y) + Z$
3. $X + X = X$	13. $X(YZ) = (XY)Z$
4. $X + \overline{X} = 1$	14. $X(Y + Z) = XY + XZ$
5. $0 \cdot X = 0$	15. $X + XZ = X$
6. $1 \cdot X = X$	16. $X(X + Y) = X$
7. $X \cdot X = X$	17. $(X + Y)(X + Z) = X + YZ$
8. $X \cdot \overline{X} = 0$	18. $X + \overline{X}Y = X + Y$
9. $\overline{\overline{X}} = X$	19. $XY + YZ + \overline{Y}Z = XY + Z$
10. $X + Y = Y + X$	

Each rule may be proved using the proof by perfect induction. An example of this proof for rule 3 in Table 3.10 is as follows: The variable X can have only the value 0 or 1. If X has the value 0, then $0 + 0 = 0$; if X has the value 1, then $1 + 1 = 1$. Therefore, $X + X = X$.

The same basic technique may be used to prove the other rules. For example, rule 9 states that double complementation of a variable results in the original variable. If X equals 0, then the first complement is a 1 and the second is 0, the original value. If the original value for X is 1, then the first complement will be 0 and the second 1, again, the original value. Therefore, $X = \overline{\overline{X}}$.

Rules 10 and 11, which are known as the *commutative laws*, express the fact that the order in which a combination of terms is operated on does not affect the result of the combination. Rule 10 is the commutative law of addition, which states that the order of addition, or ORing, does not affect the sum $(X + Y = Y + X)$. Rule 11 is the commutative law of multiplication $(XY = YX)$, which states that the order of multiplication, or ANDing, does not affect the product.

Rules 12 and 13, as discussed earlier, are the *associative laws*. Rule 12 states that in the logical addition of several terms, the sum obtained if the first term is added to the second and then the third term is added will be the same as the sum obtained if the second term is added to the third and then the first term is added $[X + (Y + Z) = (X + Y) + Z]$. Rule 13 is the associative law of logical multiplication, stating that in a product with three factors, any two may be multiplied, followed by the third $[X(YZ) = (XY)Z]$.

Rule 14, the *distributive law*, states that the product of a variable (X) times a sum $(Y + Z)$ is equal to the sum of the products of the variable multiplied by each term of the original sum $[X(Y + Z) = XY + XZ]$.

The three laws—commutative, associative, and distributive—may be extended to include any number of terms. For instance, the commutative law for logical addition may be extended to

$$X + Y + Z + A = A + Y + Z + X$$

The commutative law for logical multiplication also may be extended: $XYZ = YZX$. These two laws are useful in rearranging the terms of an equation.

The terms also may be recombined:

$$(X + Y) + (Z + A) = (A + Y) + (X + Z)$$

and $(XY)(ZA) = (XA)(ZY)$. These two laws are useful in regrouping the terms of an equation.

The distributive law may be extended in several ways:

$$X(Y + Z + A) = XY + XZ + XA$$

If two sums, $W + X$ and $Y + Z$, are to be multiplied, then one of the sums is treated as a single term and multiplied by the individual terms of the other sum. The results are then multiplied according to the distributive law:

$$(W + X)(Y + Z) = W(Y + Z) + X(Y + Z) = WY + WZ + XY + XZ$$

Proof by Perfect Induction

Notice that rule 17, among others, does not apply to normal algebra. The rule may be obtained from the preceding rules as follows:

$$
\begin{aligned}
(X + Y)(X + Z) &= XX + XZ + XY + YZ & &\text{where } XX = X \text{ (rule 7)}\\
&= X + XZ + XY + YZ\\
&= X + XY + XZ + YZ\\
&= X(1 + Y) + Z(X + Y) & &\text{where } 1 + Y = 1 \text{ (rule 2)}\\
&= X + Z(X + Y)\\
&= X + XZ + YZ\\
&= X(1 + Z) + YZ & &\text{where } 1 + Z = 1 \text{ (rule 2)}\\
&= X + YZ
\end{aligned}
$$

Therefore,

$$(X + Y)(X + Z) = X + YZ$$

Since rule 17 does not apply to normal algebra, it is interesting to test the rule by using the proof by perfect induction. It will be necessary to construct truth tables for the right-hand $(X + YZ)$ and left-hand $[(X + Y)(X + Z)]$ members of the equation and compare the results (see Tables 3.11 and 3.12). The last column of the table for the function $X + YZ$ is identical to the last column of the table for $(X + Y)(X + Z)$. This proves (by means of the proof by perfect induction) that the expressions are equivalent.

Rules 15 and 16 are also not valid in normal algebra. The following is a proof of rule 15 using preceding rules:

TABLE 3.11

X	Y	Z	YZ	X + YZ
0	0	0	0	0
0	0	1	0	0
0	1	0	0	0
0	1	1	1	1
1	0	0	0	1
1	0	1	0	1
1	1	0	0	1
1	1	1	1	1

TABLE 3.12

X	Y	Z	X + Y	X + $\underline{Z}$	(X + Y)(X + Z)
0	0	0	0	0	0
0	0	1	0	1	0
0	1	0	1	0	0
0	1	1	1	1	1
1	0	0	1	1	1
1	0	1	1	1	1
1	1	0	1	1	1
1	1	1	1	1	1

$$X + XZ = X(1 + Z) \qquad \text{by the distributive law}$$

Since $1 + Z = 1$, by rule 2,

$$X + XZ = X(1) \qquad \text{and} \qquad X(1) = X \qquad \text{by rule 6}$$

Therefore,

$$X + XZ = X$$

It is worthwhile to try to prove rule 15 using the proof by perfect induction at this point.

Here is a proof of rule 16 using rules that precede it:

$$
\begin{aligned}
X(X + Y) &= XX + XY && \text{distributive law} \\
&= X + XY && \text{since } XX = X \\
&= X(1 + Y) && \text{where } 1 + Y = 1, \text{ by rule 2} \\
&= X
\end{aligned}
$$

It is instructive to prove this rule also by perfect induction at this point.

Simplification of Expressions

The rules given may be used to simplify boolean expressions, just as the rules of normal algebra may be used to simplify expressions. Consider the expression

$$(X + Y)(X + \overline{Y})(\overline{X} + Z)$$

The first two terms consist of $X + Y$ and $X + \overline{Y}$; these terms may be multiplied and, since $X + X\overline{Y} + XY = X$ and $Y\overline{Y} = 0$, reduced to X.

The expression has been reduced now to $X(\overline{X} + Z)$, which may be expressed as $X\overline{X} + XZ$ (rule 14). And since $X\overline{X}$ is equal to 0, the entire expression $(X + Y)(X + \overline{Y})(\overline{X} + Z)$ may be reduced to XZ.

Another expression that may be simplified is $XYZ + X\overline{Y}Z + XY\overline{Z}$. First, the expression may be written $X(YZ + \overline{Y}Z + Y\overline{Z})$, by rule 14. Then, by using rule 14 again, we may simplify to $X[Y(Z + \overline{Z}) + \overline{Y}Z]$; and since $Z + \overline{Z}$ equals 1, we have $X(Y + \overline{Y}Z)$.

The expression $X(Y + \overline{Y}Z)$ may be further reduced to $X(Y + Z)$, by using rule 18. The final expression can be written in two ways: $X(Y + Z)$ or $XY + XZ$. The first expression is generally preferable if the equation is to be constructed as an electronic circuit, because it requires only one AND circuit and one OR circuit.

3.6 DE MORGAN'S THEOREM

The following two rules constitute De Morgan's theorem:

$$\overline{(X + Y)} = \overline{X} \cdot \overline{Y}$$

$$\overline{(X \cdot Y)} = \overline{X} + \overline{Y}$$

The complement of any boolean expression, or a part of any expression, may be found by means of this theorem. Using these rules, two steps are used to form a complement:

1. The $+$ symbols are replaced with $\cdot$ symbols and $\cdot$ symbols with $+$ symbols.

2. Each of the terms in the expression is complemented.

The use of De Morgan's theorem may be demonstrated by finding the complement of the expression $X + YZ$. First, note that a multiplication sign has been omitted, and the expression could be written $X + (Y \cdot Z)$. To complement this, the addition symbol is replaced with a multiplication symbol, and the two terms are complemented, giving $\overline{X} \cdot \overline{(Y \cdot Z)}$; then the remaining term is complemented: $\overline{X}(\overline{Y} + \overline{Z})$. The following equivalence has been found: $\overline{(X + YZ)} = \overline{X}(\overline{Y} + \overline{Z})$.

The complement of $\overline{W}X + Y\overline{Z}$ may be formed by two steps:

1. The addition symbol is changed.

2. The complement of each term is formed:
$$(\overline{\overline{W} \cdot X})(\overline{Y \cdot \overline{Z}})$$

This becomes $(W + \overline{X})(\overline{Y} + Z)$.

Since W and Z were already complemented, they become uncomplemented by the theorem $\overline{\overline{X}} = X$.

It is sometimes necessary to complement both sides of an equation. This may be done in the same way as before:
$$WX + YZ = 0$$

Complementing both sides gives
$$\overline{(WX + YZ)} = \overline{0}$$
$$(\overline{W} + \overline{X})(\overline{Y} + \overline{Z}) = 1$$

Basic Duality of Boolean Algebra

De Morgan's theorem expresses a basic duality that underlies all boolean algebra. The postulates and theorems presented can be divided into pairs. For example, $(X + Y) + Z = X + (Y + Z)$ is the *dual* of $(XY)Z = X(YZ)$, and $X + 0 = X$ is the dual of $X \cdot 1 = X$.

Often the rules or theorems are listed in an order that illustrates the duality of the algebra. In proving the rules of the algebra, it is necessary to prove only one theorem, and the dual of the theorem follows necessarily. For instance, if you prove $X + XY = X$, you can immediately add $X(X + Y) = X$ to the list of theorems as the dual of the first expression.[9] In effect, all boolean algebra is predicated on this two-for-one basis.

3.7   DERIVATION OF A BOOLEAN EXPRESSION

When designing a logical circuit, the designer works from two sets of known values: (1) the various states that the inputs to the logical network can take and (2) the desired

---

[9] When the first expression, $X + XY = X$, is complemented, $\overline{X}(\overline{X} + \overline{Y}) = \overline{X}$ is obtained. Then uncomplemented variables may be substituted on both sides of the equation without changing the basic equivalence of the expression.

outputs for each input condition. The logical expression is derived from these sets of values.

Consider a specific problem. A logical network has two inputs, X and Y, and an output, Z. The relationship between inputs and outputs is to be as follows:

1. When both X and Y are 0s, Z is to be 1.
2. When X is 0 and Y is 1, Z is to be 0.
3. When X is 1 and Y is 0, Z is to be 1.
4. When X is 1 and Y is 1, Z is to be 1.

These relations may be expressed in tabular form, as shown in Table 3.13.

It is now necessary to add another column to the table. This column will consist of the *product terms* obtained from the values of the input variables. The new column will contain each of the input variables for each row, with the letter complemented when the input value for the variable is 0 and not complemented when the input value is 1 (see Table 3.14).

When Z is equal to 1, the product term from the same row is removed and used as a *sum-of-products* expression. Therefore, the product terms from the first, third, and fourth rows, $\overline{X}\,\overline{Y}$, $X\overline{Y}$, and XY, are selected.

There are now three terms, each the product of two variables. The logical sum of these products constitutes the expression desired. This type of expression is often referred to as a *canonical expansion* for the function. The complete expression in normal form is

$$\overline{X}\,\overline{Y} + X\overline{Y} + XY = Z$$

The left-hand side of the expression may be simplified as follows:

$$\overline{X}\,\overline{Y} + X\overline{Y} + XY = Z$$
$$\overline{X}\,\overline{Y} + X(\overline{Y} + Y) = Z$$
$$\overline{X}\,\overline{Y} + X = Z$$

Finally, by rule 18 in Table 3.10, $X + \overline{Y} = Z$.

The truth table may be constructed to check the function that has been derived (see Table 3.15). The last column of this table agrees with the column for the output of the desired function in Table 3.14, showing that the expressions are equivalent.

The expression $X + Y$ may be realized in one of two ways. If only the inputs X and Y are available, as might be the case if the inputs to the circuit were from another logical network or from certain types of storage devices, an inverter would be required to form Y. Then the circuit would require an inverter plus an OR gate.

TABLE 3.13

Inputs		Output,
X	Y	Z
0	0	1
0	1	0
1	0	1
1	1	1

TABLE 3.14

Inputs		Output,	Product
X	Y	Z	terms
0	0	1	$\overline{X}\,\overline{Y}$
0	1	0	$\overline{X}Y$
1	0	1	$X\overline{Y}$
1	1	1	XY

TABLE 3.15

X	Y	$\overline{Y}$	$X + \overline{Y}$
0	0	1	1
0	1	0	0
1	0	1	1
1	1	0	1

Generally, the complement of the Y input would be available, however, and only an OR gate would be required.

Another expression, with three inputs (designated X, Y, and Z), will be derived next. Assume that the desired relationships between the inputs and the output is as shown in Table 3.16. The procedure for deriving the logic circuit is:

1. A truth table is formed (see Table 3.17).

2. A column is added listing the inputs, X, Y, and Z, according to their values in the input columns (see Table 3.18). These are the product terms.

3. The product terms from all rows in which the output is 1 are collected ($\overline{X}\,\overline{Y}\,\overline{Z}$, $\overline{X}Y\overline{Z}$, $X\overline{Y}\,\overline{Z}$, and $XY\overline{Z}$); the desired expression is the sum of these products ($\overline{X}\,\overline{Y}\,\overline{Z} + \overline{X}Y\overline{Z} + X\overline{Y}\,\overline{Z} + XY\overline{Z}$). Therefore, the complete expression in standard form for the desired network is

$$\overline{X}\,\overline{Y}\,\overline{Z} + \overline{X}Y\overline{Z} + X\overline{Y}\,\overline{Z} + XY\overline{Z} = A$$

This expression may be simplified as shown below:

$$\overline{X}\,\overline{Y}\,\overline{Z} + \overline{X}Y\overline{Z} + X\overline{Y}\,\overline{Z} + XY\overline{Z} = A$$

$$\overline{X}(\overline{Y}\,\overline{Z} + Y\overline{Z}) + X(\overline{Y}\,\overline{Z} + Y\overline{Z}) = A$$

$$\overline{X}[\overline{Z}(\overline{Y} + Y)] + X[\overline{Z}(\overline{Y} + Y)] = A$$

TABLE 3.16

Inputs			
X	Y	Z	Output
0	0	0	1
0	0	1	0
0	1	0	1
0	1	1	0
1	0	0	1
1	0	1	0
1	1	0	1
1	1	1	0

TABLE 3.17

Inputs			Output,
X	Y	Z	A
0	0	0	1
0	0	1	0
0	1	0	1
0	1	1	0
1	0	0	1
1	0	1	0
1	1	0	1
1	1	1	0

TABLE 3.18

Inputs			Output,	Product
X	Y	Z	A	terms
0	0	0	1	$\overline{X}\,\overline{Y}\,\overline{Z}$
0	0	1	0	$\overline{X}\,\overline{Y}Z$
0	1	0	1	$\overline{X}Y\overline{Z}$
0	1	1	0	$\overline{X}YZ$
1	0	0	1	$X\overline{Y}\,\overline{Z}$
1	0	1	0	$X\overline{Y}Z$
1	1	0	1	$XY\overline{Z}$
1	1	1	0	XYZ

$$\overline{X}\,\overline{Z} + X\overline{Z} = A$$

$$\overline{Z} = A$$

Thus, the function can be performed by a single inverter connected to the Z input. Inspection of the truth table will indicate that the output, A, is always equal to the complement of the input variable Z.

3.8 INTERCONNECTING GATES

The OR gates, AND gates, and inverters can be interconnected to form *gating* or *logic networks*. (Those who study switching theory would also call these *combinational networks*.) The boolean algebra expression corresponding to a given gating network can be derived by systematically progressing from input to output on the gates. Figure 3.5(a) shows a gating network with three inputs, X, Y, and Z, and an output expression

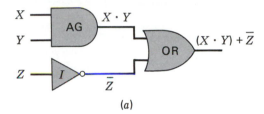

(a)

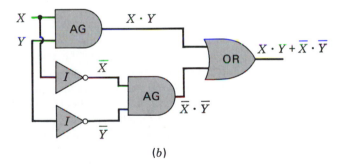

(b)

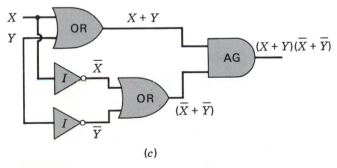

(c)

FIGURE 3.5
Three gating networks.

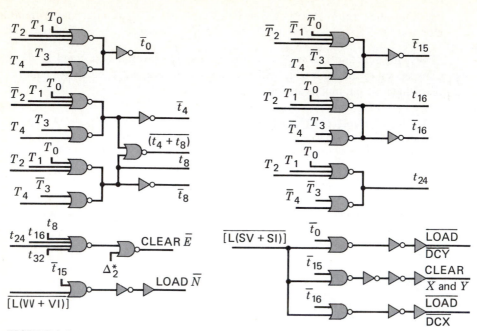

FIGURE 3.6
Block diagram from a computer.

$(X \cdot Y) + \overline{Z}$. A network that forms $(X \cdot Y) + (\overline{X} \cdot \overline{Y})$ and another network that forms $(X + Y) \cdot (\overline{X} + \overline{Y})$ are shown in Fig. 3.5(b) and (c).

We can analyze the operation of these gating networks by using the boolean algebra expressions. For instance, in troubleshooting a computer, we can determine which gates have failed by examining the inputs to the gating network and the outputs and seeing whether the boolean operations are properly performed. The bookkeeping for computer circuitry is done by means of block diagrams such as the one in Fig. 3.6. The use of boolean algebra is widespread throughout the computer industry.

3.9 SUM OF PRODUCTS AND PRODUCT OF SUMS

An important consideration in dealing with gating circuits and their algebraic counterparts is the form of the boolean algebra expression and the resulting form of the gating network. Certain types of boolean algebra expressions lead to gating networks that are more desirable from most implementation viewpoints. We now define the two most used forms for boolean expressions.

First, let us define terms:

1. *Product term.* A product term is a single variable or the logical product of several variables. The variables may or may not be complemented.
2. *Sum term.* A sum term is a single variable or the sum of several variables. The variables may or may not be complemented.

For example, the term $X \cdot Y \cdot Z$ is a product term; $X + Y$ is a sum term; X is both a product term and a sum term; $X + Y \cdot Z$ is neither a product term nor a sum term; $X + \overline{Y}$ is a sum term; $X \cdot \overline{Y} \cdot Z$ is a product term; and $\overline{Y}$ is both a sum term and a product term. (*Comment:* Calling a single variable a sum term and a product term is disagreeable but necessary. Since we must suffer with it, remember that some apples are red, round, and shiny, that is, more than one thing.)

We now define two most important types of expressions.

1. *Sum-of-products expression.* A sum-of-products expression is a product term or several product terms logically added.
2. *Product-of-sums expression.* A product-of-sums expression is a sum term or several sum terms logically multiplied.

For example, the expression $\overline{X} \cdot Y + X \cdot \overline{Y}$ is a sum-of-products expression and $(X + Y)(\overline{X} + \overline{Y})$ is a product-of-sums expression. The following are all sum-of-products expressions:

$$X$$

$$X \cdot Y + Z$$

$$\overline{X \cdot Y} + X \cdot Y \cdot Z$$

$$X + Y$$

The following are all product-of-sums expressions:

$$(X + Y) \cdot (X + \overline{Y}) \cdot (\overline{X} + \overline{Y})$$

$$(X + Y + Z) \cdot (X + \overline{Y}) \cdot (\overline{X} + \overline{Y})$$

$$\overline{X}$$

$$(X + Y)X$$

A primary reason for favoring sum-of-products or product-of-sums expressions is their straightforward conversion to simple gating networks. Their purest form is represented by *two-level networks*, which are networks whose longest signal path from input to output is two gates.

Note: In the following discussion we assume that when a variable X is available, its complement, $\overline{X}$, is also available; that is, no inverters are required to complement inputs. This is quite important and quite realistic, since most signals come from flip-flops, which we study later and which provide both an output and its complement.

Figure 3.7 shows several gating networks. Figure 3.7(a) shows sum-of-products networks, and Fig. 3.7(b) shows product-of-sums networks. The gating networks for sum-of-products expressions in "conventional" form—that is, expressions with at least two product terms and with at least two variables in each product term—are AND-to-OR gate networks. Conventional product-of-sums expressions are realized by OR-to-AND gate networks, as shown in the figure.

Derivation of Product-of-Sums Expressions

Section 3.7 described the sequence of steps for deriving a sum-of-products expression for a given circuit. Another technique, really a dual of the first, forms the required expression as a product of sums. The expression derived in this manner is made up,

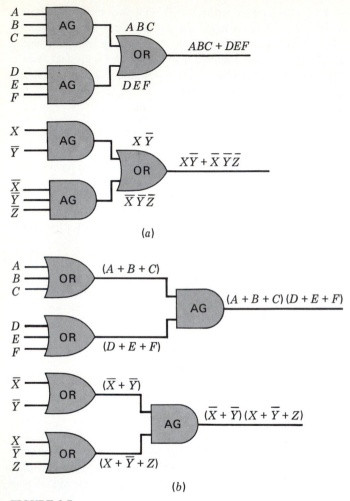

FIGURE 3.7
(*a*) AND-to-OR gate networks. (*b*) OR-to-AND gate networks.

before simplification, of terms consisting of sums of variables, such as $(X + Y + Z)\cdots$. The final expression is the product of these sum terms and has the form $(X + Y + Z)(X + Y + \overline{Z})\cdots(\overline{X} + \overline{Y} + \overline{Z})$.

The method for arriving at the desired expression is as follows:

1. Construct a table of the input and output values.
2. Construct an additional column of sum terms containing complemented and uncomplemented variables (depending on the values in the input columns) for each row of the table. However, in this case, if the input value for a given variable is 1, the variable will be complemented; if it is 0, it is not complemented.
3. The desired expression is the product of the sum terms from the rows in which the output is 0.

The use of these rules is illustrated by the examples in this and the following sections.

TABLE 3.19

Inputs		Output,
X	Y	Z
0	0	1
0	1	0
1	0	0
1	1	1

TABLE 3.20

Inputs		Output,	Sum
X	Y	Z	terms
0	0	1	$X + Y$
0	1	0	$X + \overline{Y}$
1	0	0	$\overline{X} + Y$
1	1	1	$\overline{X} + \overline{Y}$

Table 3.19 contains the input and output values that describe a function to be realized by a logical network. A column containing the input variables in sum-term form is now added. A given variable is complemented if the input value for the variable is 1 in the same row and is not complemented if the value is 0 (see Table 3.20). Each sum term is, therefore, simply the complement of the product term for the same row in Table 3.14, for sum-of-products expressions. For example, the sum term $\overline{X} + Y$ in the third row of Table 3.20 is the complement of the product term $X\overline{Y}$ used in the sum-of-products derivation.

A product-of-sums expression is now formed by selecting those sum terms for which the output is 0 and multiplying them. In this case, 0s appear in the second and third rows, so the desired expression is $(X + \overline{Y})(\overline{X} + Y)$. A sum-of-products expression may be found by multiplying the two terms of this expression, yielding $XY + \overline{X}\,\overline{Y}$. In this case, the same number of gates would be required to construct circuits corresponding to the sum-of-products and the product-of-sums expressions.

3.10 DERIVATION OF A THREE-INPUT-VARIABLE EXPRESSION

Consider Table 3.21, expressing an input-to-output relationship for which an expression is to be derived. Two columns will be added this time, one containing the sum-of-products terms and the other the product-of-sums terms (see Table 3.22). The two expressions may be written in the following ways:

SUM OF PRODUCTS
$$\overline{X}Y\overline{Z} + \overline{X}YZ + XY\overline{Z} = A$$

TABLE 3.21

Inputs			Output,
X	Y	Z	A
0	0	0	0
0	0	1	0
0	1	0	1
0	1	1	1
1	0	0	0
1	0	1	0
1	1	0	1
1	1	1	0

TABLE 3.22

Inputs			Output,	Product	Sum terms
X	Y	Z	A	terms	
0	0	0	0	$\overline{X}\,\overline{Y}\,\overline{Z}$	$X + Y + Z$
0	0	1	0	$\overline{X}\,\overline{Y}Z$	$X + Y + \overline{Z}$
0	1	0	1	$\overline{X}Y\overline{Z}$	$X + \overline{Y} + Z$
0	1	1	1	$\overline{X}YZ$	$X + \overline{Y} + \overline{Z}$
1	0	0	0	$X\overline{Y}\,\overline{Z}$	$\overline{X} + Y + Z$
1	0	1	0	$X\overline{Y}Z$	$\overline{X} + Y + \overline{Z}$
1	1	0	1	$XY\overline{Z}$	$\overline{X} + \overline{Y} + Z$
1	1	1	0	XYZ	$\overline{X} + \overline{Y} + \overline{Z}$

PRODUCT OF SUMS
$$(X + Y + Z)(X + Y + \overline{Z})(\overline{X} + Y + Z)(\overline{X} + Y + \overline{Z})(\overline{X} + \overline{Y} + \overline{Z}) = A$$

The two expressions may be simplified as shown:

SUM OF PRODUCTS
$$(\overline{X}Y\overline{Z}) + (\overline{X}YZ) + (XY\overline{Z}) = A$$

$$\overline{X}(Y\overline{Z} + YZ) + (XY\overline{Z}) = A$$

$$\overline{X}Y + XY\overline{Z} = A$$

$$Y(\overline{X} + X\overline{Z}) = A$$

$$\overline{X}Y + Y\overline{Z} = A$$

PRODUCT OF SUMS
$$(X + Y + Z)(X + Y + \overline{Z})(\overline{X} + Y + Z)(\overline{X} + Y + \overline{Z})(\overline{X} + \overline{Y} + \overline{Z}) = A$$

$$(X + Y)(\overline{X} + Y)(\overline{X} + \overline{Z}) = A$$

$$Y(\overline{X} + \overline{Z}) = A$$

The two final expressions are clearly equivalent. Notice, however, that the shortest sum-of-products expression, $\overline{X}Y + Y\overline{Z}$, requires two AND gates and an OR gate (Fig. 3.8), whereas the shortest product-of-sums expressions, $Y(\overline{X} + \overline{Z})$, requires only a single AND gate and a single OR gate. In some cases the minimal sum-of-products expression will require fewer logical elements to construct, and in other instances the construction of the minimal product of sums will require fewer elements. If the sole criterion is the number of logical elements, it is necessary to obtain both a minimal sum-of-products expression and a minimal product-of-sums expression and compare the two. It is possible first to derive the canonical expansion expression for the network to be designed in one of the forms—for instance, product of sums—to simplify the expression, and then to convert the simplified expression to the other form, by using the distributive laws. Then any additional simplification required can be performed. In this way, minimal expressions in each form may be obtained without deriving both canonical expansions, although this may be desirable.

The simplification techniques that have been described are algebraic and depend on judicious use of the theorems presented. The problem of simplifying boolean

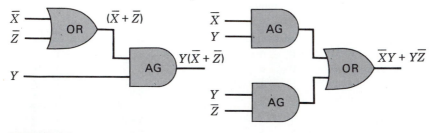

FIGURE 3.8
Networks for $Y(\overline{X} + \overline{Z})$ and $\overline{X}Y + Y\overline{Z}$.

expressions so that the shortest expression always results is quite complex. However, it is possible, by means of the repeated use of certain algorithms, to derive minimal sum-of-products and product-of-sums expressions. We examine this problem in following sections.

3.11   NAND GATES AND NOR GATES

Two other types of gates, NAND gates and NOR gates, are often used in computers. Fortunately, the boolean algebra that has been described can be easily used to analyze the operation of these gates.

   A NAND gate is shown in Fig. 3.9. The inputs are A, B, and C, and the output from the gate is written $\overline{A} + \overline{B} + \overline{C}$. The output will be a 1 if A is a 0 or B is a 0 or C is a 0, and the output will be a 0 only if A and B and C are all 1s. The operation of the gate can be analyzed using the equivalent block diagram circuit, which is an AND gate followed by an inverter. If the inputs are A, B, and C, the output of the AND gate will be $A \cdot B \cdot C$, and the complement of this is $(\overline{A \cdot B \cdot C}) = \overline{A} + \overline{B} + \overline{C}$, as shown in the figure.

   The NOR gate can be analyzed in a similar manner. Figure 3.10 shows the NOR gate block diagram symbol with inputs, A, B, C and output $\overline{A}\,\overline{B}\,\overline{C}$. As shown, the NOR gate's output will be a 1 only when all three inputs are 0s. If any input represents a 1, the output of a NOR gate will be a 0.

   Below the NOR gate block diagram symbol in Fig. 3.10 is an equivalent circuit showing an OR gate and an inverter.[10] The inputs A, B, and C are ORed by the OR gate, giving $A + B + C$, which is complemented by the inverter, yielding $(\overline{A + B + C}) = \overline{A}\,\overline{B}\,\overline{C}$.

   Multiple-input NAND gates can be analyzed similarly. A four-input NAND gate with inputs, A, B, C, and D has an output $\overline{A} + \overline{B} + \overline{C} + \overline{D}$, which means that the output will be a 1 if any one of the inputs is a 0 and will be a 0 only when all four inputs are 1s.

   Similar reasoning will show that the output of a four-input NOR gate with inputs A, B, C, and D can be represented by the boolean algebra expression $\overline{A}\,\overline{B}\,\overline{C}\,\overline{D}$, which will be equal to 1 only when A, B, C, and D are all 0s.

---

[10] The "bubble," or small circle, on the output of the NAND or NOR gate represents complementation. The NAND can be seen as an AND symbol followed by a complementer, and the NOR can be analyzed similarly.

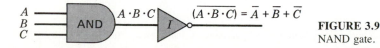

FIGURE 3.9
NAND gate.

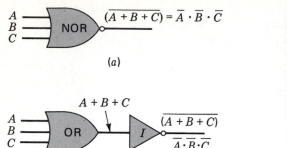

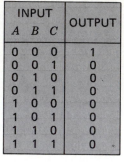

INPUT			OUTPUT
A	B	C	
0	0	0	1
0	0	1	0
0	1	0	0
0	1	1	0
1	0	0	0
1	0	1	0
1	1	0	0
1	1	1	0

FIGURE 3.10
(*a*) Block diagram symbol for a NOR gate. (*b*) OR gate and inverter equivalent circuit to NOR gate.

If one of the input lines to a two-input NAND gate contains the input $A + B$ and the other contains $C + D$, as shown in Fig. 3.11(*a*), the output from the NAND gate will be

$$\overline{[(A + B)(C + D)]} = \overline{A}\,\overline{B} + \overline{C}\,\overline{D}$$

We can show this by noting that the NAND gate first ANDs the inputs (in this case $A + B$ and $C + D$) and then complements this value.

If one of the input lines to a two-input NOR gate contains the signal $A{\cdot}B$ and the other input line contains the signal $C{\cdot}D$, the output from the NOR gate will be $\overline{(A{\cdot}B + C{\cdot}D)} = (\overline{A} + \overline{B})(\overline{C} + \overline{D})$, as shown in Fig. 3.11(*b*).

Notice that we can make an AND gate from two NAND gates, using the trick shown in Fig. 3.12, and a two-input OR gate from three NAND gates, as also shown

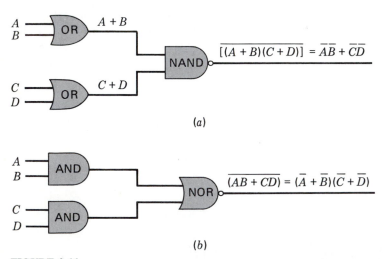

FIGURE 3.11
Two types of gating networks. (*a*) OR-to-NAND gate network. (*b*) AND-to-NOR gate network.

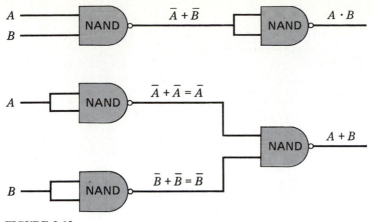

FIGURE 3.12
AND or OR operations from NAND gates.

in the figure. A set of NAND gates can thus be used to make any combinational network by substituting the block diagrams shown in Fig. 3.12 for the AND and OR blocks. (Complementation of a variable, when needed, can be obtained from a single NAND gate by connecting the variable to all inputs.)

The NOR gate also can be used to form any boolean function desired; the fundamental tricks are shown in Fig. 3.13.

Actually, it is not necessary to use the boxes shown in Figs. 3.12 and 3.13 to replace AND and OR gates singly, since a two-level NAND gate network yields the same function as a two-level AND-to-OR gate network, and a two-level NOR gate network yields the same function as a two-level OR-to-AND gate network. This is shown in Fig. 3.14. Compare the output of the NAND gate network with that in Fig. 3.7, for example. In later sections, design procedures for NAND and NOR gate networks are given.

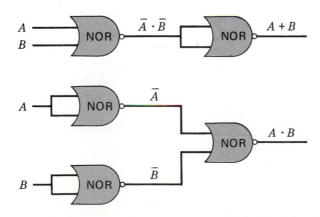

FIGURE 3.13
AND and OR gates from NOR gates.

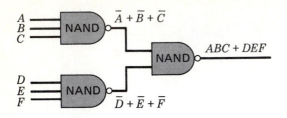

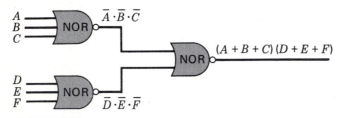

FIGURE 3.14
NAND or NOR gates in two-level networks.

3.12 MAP METHOD FOR SIMPLIFYING EXPRESSIONS*[11]

We have examined the derivation of a boolean algebra expression for a given function by using a table of combinations to list desired function values. To derive a sum-of-products expression for the function, a set of product terms is listed, and those terms for which the function is to have a 1 value are selected and logically added.

The table of combinations provides a natural way to list all values of a boolean function. There are several other ways to represent or list function values. The use of certain kinds of maps also permits minimization of the expression. The particular type of map we will use is called the *Karnaugh map* after its originator.[12] Figure 3.15 shows the layouts for Karnaugh maps of two to four variables. Each diagram lists the 2^n different product terms that can be formed from n variables, each in a different square. A product term in these n variables is called a *minterm*. Thus, for three variables X, Y, and Z there are 2^3, or 8, different minterms: $\overline{X}\,\overline{Y}\,\overline{Z}$, $\overline{X}\,\overline{Y}Z$, $\overline{X}Y\overline{Z}$, $\overline{X}YZ$, $X\overline{Y}\,\overline{Z}$, $X\overline{Y}Z$, $XY\overline{Z}$, and XYZ. For four variables there are 2^4, or 16, terms; for five variables there are 32 terms; etc. A map of n variables will have 2^n squares, each representing a single minterm. The minterm in each box or cell of the map is the product of the variables listed at the abscissa and ordinate of the cell. Thus, $\overline{X}YZ$ is at the intersection of $\overline{X}Y$ and Z.

A Karnaugh map is filled in by placing 1s in the cells for terms that lead to a 1 output. As an example, consider a function of three variables for which the following input values are to produce an output of 1:

---

[11] Sections marked with asterisks can be omitted in a first reading without loss of continuity.

[12] Similar maps are sometimes called *Veitch diagrams*.

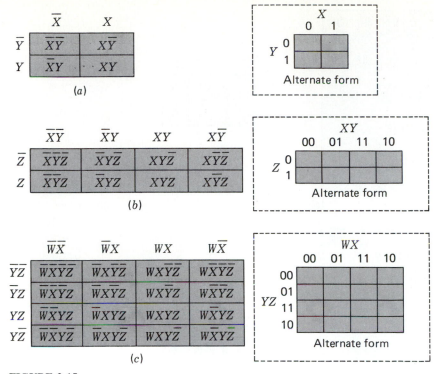

FIGURE 3.15
Karnaugh maps for (a) two, (b) three, and (c) four variables.

$$X = 0, \ Y = 1, \ Z = 0$$
$$X = 0, \ Y = 1, \ Z = 1$$
$$X = 1, \ Y = 1, \ Z = 0$$
$$X = 1, \ Y = 1, \ Z = 1$$

This function is shown in Fig. 3.16(a) in both combinations table form and Karnaugh map form. Another function of four variables is shown in Fig. 3.16(b).

As a means for displaying the values of a function, the Karnaugh map is convenient and provides some "feel" for the function because of its graphic presentation. However, its usefulness is due chiefly to the arrangement of cells. Each cell differs from the adjacent cell by having exactly one variable complemented in the minterm. As an example, consider the four-variable map in Fig. 3.16 and the minterm $\overline{W}X\overline{Y}Z$. There are four cells adjacent to the cell containing $\overline{W}X\overline{Y}Z$. These contain (1) $WX\overline{Y}Z$, which differs in the variable W; (2) $\overline{W}\,\overline{X}\,\overline{Y}Z$, which differs in X; (3) $\overline{W}XYZ$, which differs in Y; and (4) $\overline{W}X\overline{Y}\,\overline{Z}$, which differs in Z.

One feature should be noted at this point. The maps are considered to be "rolled," or continuous, so that top and bottom edges or left and right edges are touching. For the three-variable map, consider the left edge and the right edge to be touching so that

$X \cdot Y \ Z$	FUNCTION VALUES
0 0 0	0
0 0 1	0
0 1 0	1
0 1 1	1
1 0 0	0
1 0 1	0
1 1 0	1
1 1 1	1

$$\overline{X}\,\overline{Y} \quad \overline{X}Y \quad XY \quad X\overline{Y}$$

	$\overline{X}\,\overline{Y}$	$\overline{X}Y$	XY	$X\overline{Y}$
$\overline{Z}$	0	1	1	0
Z	0	1	1	0

(a)

W X Y Z	FUNCTION VALUES
0 0 0 0	1
0 0 0 1	1
0 0 1 0	0
0 0 1 1	0
0 1 0 0	0
0 1 0 1	1
0 1 1 0	1
0 1 1 1	0
1 0 0 0	0
1 0 0 1	1
1 0 1 0	1
1 0 1 1	0
1 1 0 0	0
1 1 0 1	0
1 1 1 0	0
1 1 1 1	1

$$\overline{W}\,\overline{X} \quad \overline{W}X \quad WX \quad W\overline{X}$$

	$\overline{W}\,\overline{X}$	$\overline{W}X$	WX	$W\overline{X}$
$\overline{Y}\,\overline{Z}$	1	0	0	0
$\overline{Y}Z$	1	1	0	1
YZ	0	0	1	0
$Y\overline{Z}$	0	1	0	1

(b)

FIGURE 3.16
Two Karnaugh maps. (a) Map of boolean expression $\overline{X}Y\overline{Z} + \overline{X}YZ + XY\overline{Z} + XYZ$. (b) Map of four-variable function.

the map is rolled like a hoop horizontally on the page. This places the cell containing $\overline{X}\,\overline{Y}\,\overline{Z}$ next to $X\overline{Y}\,\overline{Z}$. Also, for this map it places $\overline{X}\,\overline{Y}Z$ next to $X\overline{Y}Z$.

For the four-variable map, the map is considered to be rolled so that the top edge touches the bottom edge, and the left side touches the right side. The touching of top and bottom places $\overline{W}X\overline{Y}\,\overline{Z}$ next to $\overline{W}XYZ$, and the touching of the left to the right edges places $W\overline{X}YZ$ next to $\overline{W}\,\overline{X}YZ$.

A good rule to remember is that there are two minterms adjacent to a given minterm in a two-variable map; there are three minterms next to a given minterm in a three-variable map; there are four minterms next to a given minterm in a four-variable map; and so on.

3.13 SUBCUBES AND COVERING

A *subcube* is a set of exactly 2^m adjacent cells containing 1s. For $m = 0$ the subcube consists of a single cell (and, thus, a single minterm). For $m = 1$ a subcube consists of two adjacent cells; for instance, the cells containing $\overline{X}\,\overline{Y}Z$ and $\overline{X}YZ$ form a subcube in the upper map in Fig. 3.17(a), as do the cells for $X\overline{Y}\,\overline{Z}$ and $\overline{X}\,\overline{Y}\,\overline{Z}$ in the lower map (since the map is rolled).

For $m = 2$ a subcube has four adjacent cells; several such subcubes are shown in Fig. 3.17(b) and 3.17(c). Notice that here we have omitted 0s for clarity and filled in only the 1s for the function. This policy will be continued.

Finally, subcubes containing eight cells (for $m = 3$) are shown in Fig. 3.17(d). (It is sometimes convenient to call a subcube containing two cells a 2 cube, a subcube of four cells a 4 cube, a subcube of eight cells an 8 cube, etc., and this is done often.)

To demonstrate the use of maps and subcubes in minimizing boolean algebra expressions, we need to examine a rule of boolean algebra:

$$AX + A\overline{X} = A$$

In this equation, A can stand for more than one variable. For instance, if $A = WY$, we have

$$(WY)X + (WY)\overline{X} = WY$$

Or let $A = W\overline{Y}\,\overline{Z}$; then we have

$$W\overline{Y}\,\overline{Z}X + W\overline{Y}\,\overline{Z}\overline{X} = W\overline{Y}\,\overline{Z}$$

The basic rule can be proved by factoring

$$AX + A\overline{X} = A(X + \overline{X})$$

Then, since $X + \overline{X} = 1$, we have

$$AX + A\overline{X} = A(X + \overline{X}) = A\cdot 1 = A$$

Each of the examples given can be checked similarly; for instance,

$$W\overline{Y}\,\overline{Z}X + W\overline{Y}\,\overline{Z}\overline{X} = W\overline{Y}\,\overline{Z}(\overline{X} + X) = W\overline{Y}\,\overline{Z}\cdot 1 = W\overline{Y}\,\overline{Z}$$

This rule can be extended. Consider

$$WX\overline{Y}\,\overline{Z} + WX\overline{Y}Z + WXY\overline{Z} + WXYZ$$

There are four terms here, each with two variables, WX, constant while the other two variables Y and Z take all possible values. The term WX is equal to the sum of the other terms:

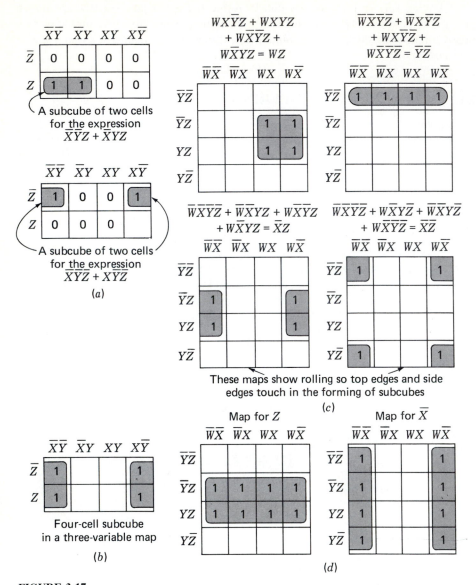

FIGURE 3.17
Subcubes with two, four, and eight cells. Blank cells are assumed to contain 0s.

$$WX\overline{Y}\,\overline{Z} + WX\overline{Y}Z + WXY\overline{Z} + WXYZ = WX\overline{Y}(\overline{Z} + Z) + WXY(Z + \overline{Z})$$
$$= WX\overline{Y} + WXY$$
$$= WX(\overline{Y} + Y)$$
$$= WX$$

Thus, WX could be substituted for the four terms in the expression, that is, $WX = WX\overline{Y}\,\overline{Z} + WX\overline{Y}Z + WXY\overline{Z} + WXYZ$.

On a map such algebraic moves may be performed easily. Since a subcube of two cells has only a single variable differing, a product term in just those variables that do not differ will cover (can be substituted for) the minterms in the two cells.

Consider the subcube of two cells for $\overline{X}\,\overline{Y}Z$ and $\overline{X}YZ$ on the upper three-variable map in Fig. 3.17(a). The single product term $\overline{X}Z$ is equal to the sum of these two minterms; that is,

$$\overline{X}\,\overline{Y}Z + \overline{X}YZ = \overline{X}Z$$

Likewise, the two cells containing minterms $X\overline{Y}\,\overline{Z}$ and $X\overline{Y}\,\overline{Z}$ form a subcube of two cells in the lower map in Fig. 3.17(a), from which we form $\overline{Y}\,\overline{Z}$, which can be substituted for $\overline{X}\,\overline{Y}\,\overline{Z} + X\overline{Y}\,\overline{Z}$ in an expression.

Similarly, the subcube of four cells in a three-variable map [Fig. 3.17(b)] with terms $\overline{X}\,\overline{Y}\,\overline{Z}, \overline{X}\,\overline{Y}Z, X\overline{Y}\,\overline{Z}, X\overline{Y}Z$ has a single-variable constant, $\overline{Y}$. Therefore, we have $\overline{Y} = \overline{X}\,\overline{Y}\,\overline{Z} + \overline{X}\,\overline{Y}Z + X\overline{Y}\,\overline{Z} + X\overline{Y}Z$.

In general, a subcube with 2^m cells in an n-variable map will have $n - m$ variables that are the same in all the minterms, and m variables that take all possible combinations of complementation and noncomplementation. Thus, for a four-variable map for $m = 3$, any eight adjacent cells that form a subcube will have $4 - 3 = 1$ variable constant and three variables that change complementation from cell to cell. Therefore, a subcube of eight cells in a four-variable map can be used to determine a single variable that can be substituted for the sum of the minterm in all eight cells. For example, Fig. 3.17(d) shows a subcube of eight cells with the minterms $\overline{W}\,\overline{X}\,\overline{Y}Z$, $\overline{W}\,\overline{X}YZ$, $\overline{W}X\overline{Y}Z$, $\overline{W}XYZ$, $W\overline{X}\,\overline{Y}Z$, $W\overline{X}YZ$, $WX\overline{Y}Z$, and $WXYZ$. The sum of these will be found to be equivalent to Z.

The set of minterms in an expression does not necessarily form a single subcube, however. A *maximal subcube* is the largest subcube that can be found around a given minterm. There are two cases to be dealt with:

1. All maximal subcubes are nonintersecting; that is, no cell in a maximal subcube is a part of another maximal subcube. Several examples are shown in Fig. 3.18.

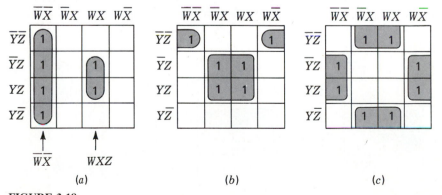

(a) (b) (c)

FIGURE 3.18
Maps with disjoint subcubes. (a) Map for $\overline{W}\,\overline{X} + WXZ$. ($b$) Map for $XZ + \overline{X}\,\overline{Y}\,\overline{Z}$. ($c$) Map for $X\overline{Z} + \overline{X}Z$.

2. The maximal subcubes intersect; that is, cells in one maximal subcube are also in other maximal subcubes. Figure 3.19 shows examples of this.

Case 1 is more easily dealt with. In this case, the product terms corresponding to the maximal subcubes are selected, and the sum of these forms a minimal sum-of-products expression. (In switching theory, the product term corresponding to a maximal subcube is called a *prime implicant*.)

Figure 3.18(a) shows an example of this in four variables. There is a subcube of two cells containing $WXYZ$ and $WX\overline{Y}Z$ that can be covered by the product term WXZ. There is also a subcube of four cells containing $\overline{W}\,\overline{X}\,\overline{Y}\,\overline{Z}$, $\overline{W}\,\overline{X}\,\overline{Y}Z$, $\overline{W}\,\overline{X}Y\overline{Z}$, and $\overline{W}\,\overline{X}YZ$, which can be covered by $\overline{W}\,\overline{X}$. The minimal expression is therefore $\overline{W}\,\overline{X} + WXZ$.

Two other examples are shown in Fig. 3.18(b) and (c). In each case, the sub-cubes do not share cells, so the product term (prime implicant) corresponding to a given maximal subcube can be readily derived, and the sum of these for a given map forms the minimal expression.

When the subcubes intersect, the situation can be more complicated. The first principle to note is: *Each cell containing a 1 must be contained in some subcube that is selected.*

Figure 3.19(a) shows a map with an intersecting pair of subcubes plus another subcube. The minimal expression is, in this case, formed simply by adding the three product terms associated with the three maximal subcubes. Notice that a single term, $\overline{W}X\overline{Y}\overline{Z}$, is shared between two subcubes and, because of this, is effectively included in the minimal expression twice. This is permissible because of the idem-potent rule of boolean algebra, $A + A = A$, which states that repetition of terms does not change functional equivalence.

As long as the maximal subcubes can be readily found and there are no options in subcube selection, minimization is straightforward. In some cases, however, the problem is more complicated. Figure 3.20 shows an expression with a subcube of four cells in the center of the map, which is maximal. Selection of this maximal subcube does not lead to a minimal expression, however, because the four cells with 1s around this subcube must be covered also. Each of these 1 cells has a single adjacent cell and so is part of a maximal subcube consisting of two cells. In Fig.

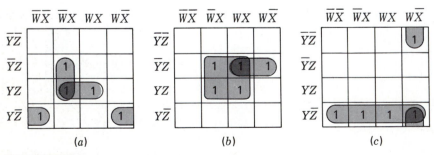

FIGURE 3.19
Intersecting subcubes. (a) $\overline{W}XZ + XYZ + \overline{X}Y\overline{Z}$. ($b$) $XZ + W\overline{Y}Z$. (c) $Y\overline{Z} + W\overline{X}\,\overline{Z}$.

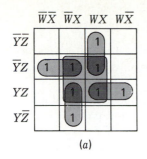
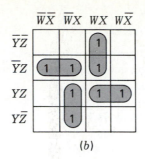

FIGURE 3.20
Intersecting subcubes and solution.
(a) $XZ + WYZ + \overline{W}\,\overline{Y}Z + \overline{W}XY + WX\overline{Y}$. (b) $WX\overline{Y} + WYZ + \overline{W}XY + \overline{W}\,\overline{Y}Z$.

3.20(a), $\overline{W}\,\overline{X}\,\overline{Y}Z$ is in a cell adjacent to only $\overline{W}X\overline{Y}Z$ and so forms part of a two-cell subcube. Figure 3.20(b) shows another way to form subcubes for the map, and this leads to the minimal expression $WX\overline{Y} + WYZ + \overline{W}XY + \overline{W}\,\overline{Y}Z$.

The derivation of minimal expressions for such maps is not direct, but these rules should be followed:

1. Begin with cells that are adjacent to no other cells. The minterms in these cells cannot be shortened and must be used as they are.

2. Find all cells that are adjacent to only one other cell. These form subcubes of two cells each.

3. Find those cells that lead to maximal subcubes of four cells. Then find subcubes of eight cells, and so on.

4. The minimal expression is formed from a collection of as few cubes as possible, each of which is as large as possible, that is, each of which is a maximal subcube.

Figure 3.21 shows a difficult map. The maximal subcubes can be selected in several ways so that all cells are covered. The figure shows three maps, only one of which leads to a minimal expression. Practice with various maps will lead to skill in finding minimal expressions.

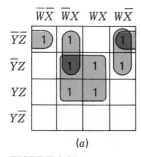
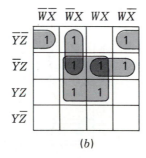
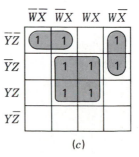

FIGURE 3.21
Three coverings of the same map. (a) $XZ + \overline{X}\,\overline{Y}\,\overline{Z} + W\overline{X}\,\overline{Y} + \overline{W}X\overline{Y}$. (b) $XZ + \overline{X}\,\overline{Y}\,\overline{Z} + \overline{W}X\overline{Y} + W\overline{Y}Z$.
(c) $XZ + \overline{W}\,\overline{Y}\,\overline{Z} + W\overline{X}\,\overline{Y}$.

3.14 PRODUCT-OF-SUMS EXPRESSIONS—DON'T-CARES

The technique for product-of-sums expressions is almost identical to the design procedure using sum-of-products expression. The basic rule can be stated quite simply: *Solve for 0s, then complement the resulting expression.*

Let us take an example. Figure 3.22 shows a table of combinations and a Karnaugh map for a four-variable problem. In Fig. 3.22(a) the sum-of-products expression is derived whose minimal form is found to be $\overline{X}\,\overline{Y} + YZ + WY$.

In Fig. 3.22(b) the same problem is solved for the 0s, which gives $X\overline{Y} + \overline{W}Y\overline{Z}$. Since we have solved for 0s, we have solved for the complement of the desired problem. That is, if the output is called F, then we have solved for $\overline{F}$. We then write $\overline{F} = X\overline{Y} + \overline{W}Y\overline{Z}$. What is wanted is F, so both sides of this expression are complemented:

$$F = (\overline{X} + Y)(W + \overline{Y} + Z)$$

This expression is in product-of-sums form and is somewhat simpler than the sum-of-products expression.

If sum-of-products and product-of-sums expressions are equally easy to implement, then a given problem must be solved in both forms and the simpler solution chosen. There is no way to determine which will be simpler other than completely working the problem.

Another frequently encountered situation is one in which certain outputs are not specified in a problem. Such outputs are called *don't-cares*, for the designer does not

INPUTS				FUNCTION VALUES
W	X	Y	Z	
0	0	0	0	1
0	0	0	1	1
0	0	1	0	0
0	0	1	1	1
0	1	0	0	0
0	1	0	1	0
0	1	1	0	0
0	1	1	1	1
1	0	0	0	1
1	0	0	1	1
1	0	1	0	1
1	0	1	1	1
1	1	0	0	0
1	1	0	1	0
1	1	1	0	1
1	1	1	1	1

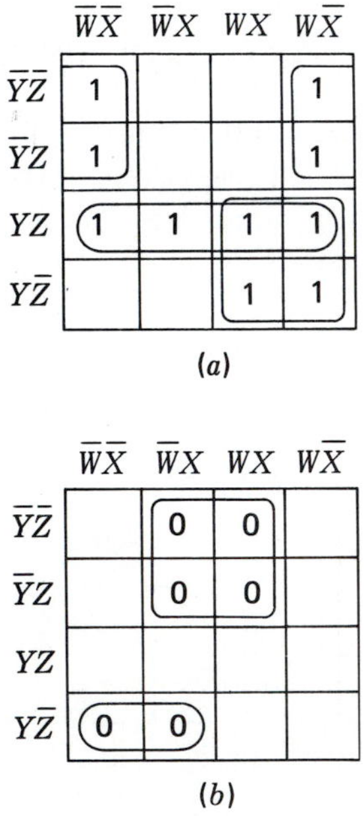

Map (a):

	$\overline{W}\,\overline{X}$	$\overline{W}X$	WX	$W\overline{X}$
$\overline{Y}\,\overline{Z}$	1			1
$\overline{Y}Z$	1			1
YZ	1	1	1	1
$Y\overline{Z}$			1	1

(a)

Map (b):

	$\overline{W}\,\overline{X}$	$\overline{W}X$	WX	$W\overline{X}$
$\overline{Y}\,\overline{Z}$		0	0	
$\overline{Y}Z$		0	0	
YZ				
$Y\overline{Z}$	0	0		

(b)

FIGURE 3.22
Solving for product of sums. (a) $\overline{X}\,\overline{Y} + YZ + WY$. ($b$) $(\overline{X} + Y)(W + \overline{Y} + Z)$.

care what the outputs are for these particular inputs. The table in Figure 3.23 shows such a problem, with 6 of the possible 16 output values listed as d's (don't-cares). This is a part of a BCD translator, so these particular input combinations are never used.

Since don't-care output values are of no importance, they may be filled in with 1s and 0s in any way that is advantageous. Figure 3.23(a) shows a Karnaugh map of the table of combinations in the figure, with d's in the appropriate places. In solving this table, a d may be used as either a 1 or a 0, so the d's are used to enlarge or complete a subcube whenever possible but otherwise are ignored (that is, made 0). *The d's need not be covered by the subcubes selected, but are used only to enlarge subcubes containing 1s, which must be covered.*

In Fig 3.23(a), the vertical string of four d's in the WX column is of use twice, once in completing the top row of 1s and once in completing the third row. These subcubes specify the terms $\overline{Y}\,\overline{Z}$ and YZ, so the minimal sum-of-products expression is $\overline{Y}\,\overline{Z} + YZ$. Notice that if all the d's were made 0s, the solution would require more terms.

Another problem is worked in Fig. 3.23(b). For this problem, the solution is $W\overline{Z} + W\overline{Y}$. Notice that two of the d's are made 0s. In effect, the d's are chosen so that they lead to the best solution.

As the number of variables in a boolean algebra expression increases, the difficulty in using maps also increases. Problems using five and six variables are included in the exercises.

The Quine-McCluskey Minimization Technique

It is also possible to minimize using algorithms. The following discussion explains how to use the Quine-McCluskey technique. The minimization principles are the same

W	X	Y	Z	
0	0	0	0	1
0	0	0	1	0
0	0	1	0	0
0	0	1	1	1
0	1	0	0	1
0	1	0	1	0
0	1	1	0	0
0	1	1	1	1
1	0	0	0	1
1	0	0	1	0
1	0	1	0	d
1	0	0	1	d
1	1	0	0	d
1	1	0	1	d
1	1	1	0	d
1	1	1	1	d

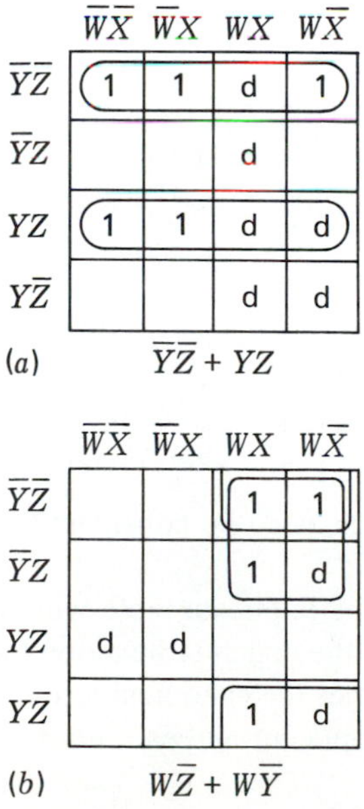

(a)

	$\overline{W}\,\overline{X}$	$\overline{W}X$	WX	$W\overline{X}$
$\overline{Y}\,\overline{Z}$	1	1	d	1
$\overline{Y}Z$			d	
YZ	1	1	d	d
$Y\overline{Z}$			d	d

$\overline{Y}\,\overline{Z} + YZ$

(b)

	$\overline{W}\,\overline{X}$	$\overline{W}X$	WX	$W\overline{X}$
$\overline{Y}\,\overline{Z}$			1	1
$\overline{Y}Z$			1	d
YZ	d	d		
$Y\overline{Z}$			1	d

$W\overline{Z} + W\overline{Y}$

FIGURE 3.23
Don't-care conditions.
(a) Map for table with don't-cares. (b) Solving another map with don't-cares.

as for maps, and, also as for maps, as the number of variables increases, the difficulty in solving problems manually (without errors) also increases. However, careful work insures correct results. Computer programs implementing the Quine-McCluskey algorithm have been written and are useful for large problems.

Step 1. Convert the expression to binary form as follows:

$$W\overline{X}\,\overline{Y}\,\overline{Z} + WX\overline{Y}\,\overline{Z} + \overline{W}XY\overline{Z} + WX\overline{Y}Z + \overline{W}\,\overline{X}YZ + W\overline{X}\,\overline{Y}Z + \overline{W}\,\overline{X}\,\overline{Y}Z + \overline{W}\,\overline{X}\,\overline{Y}\,\overline{Z}$$

becomes

$$1000 + 1100 + 0110 + 1101 + 0011 + 1001 + 0001 + 0000$$

Step 2. Arrange the binary representations in a table with a different number of 1s in each section:

$$
\begin{array}{c}
\underline{0000} \\
\underline{0001} \\
\underline{1000} \\
\underline{1100} \\
0110 \\
\underline{0011} \\
\underline{1001} \\
1101
\end{array}
$$

Step 3. Perform matches between table entries. Two terms match if they differ in exactly one position. A new term is then formed with a dash (–) substituted in the position where the two binary values differ. The new terms are then arranged according to step 2. Of these new terms, a match occurs if two terms differ in exactly one position and have a – in the same position. Again, a – is substituted in the position where the terms differ, and this procedure is repeated until no more matches are found. Terms involving a match are checked. All possible matches must be considered. Repeated term need not be copied.

✔ 0000		
✔ 0001	✔ 000–	
✔ 1000	✔ –000	–00–
✔ 1100	00–1	1–0–
0110	✔ –001	
✔ 0011	✔ 1–00	
✔ 1001	✔ 100–	
✔ 1101	✔ 110–	
	✔ 1–01	

Only terms in different sections need be considered. The unchecked terms are called *prime implicants*, or PIs.

Step 4. Construct a prime implicant table with all minterms listed at the bottom and all prime implicants from the match table along the side. Place Xs at intersections where a prime implicant matches the canonical term in each binary value (treat dashes as don't-cares). If a prime implicant agrees with a minterm in each binary position, the PI *covers* the minterm.

	0000	0001	1000	1100	0110	0011	1001	1101
0 1 1 0					X			
0 0 –1		X				X		
–0 0–	X	X	X				X	
1 –0 –			X	X			X	X

Step 5. Choose a minimal set of prime implicants so that each minterm is covered. The logical sum of these is the minimal expression.

$$00\text{--}1 + \text{--}00\text{--} + 1\text{--}0\text{--} + 0110$$

or

$$\overline{W}\,\overline{X}Z + \overline{X}\,\overline{Y} + W\overline{Y} + \overline{W}XY\overline{Z}$$

As another example, consider:

$$f(W,\ X,\ Y,\ Z) = \overline{W}\,\overline{X}\,\overline{Y}\,\overline{Z} + \overline{W}\,\overline{X}\,\overline{Y}Z + \overline{W}\,\overline{X}Y\overline{Z} + W\overline{X}YZ + WX\overline{Y}\,\overline{Z} + \overline{W}X\overline{Y}Z$$
$$+ \overline{W}\,\overline{X}YZ + WX\overline{Y}Z + WXY\overline{Z}$$

or

$$0000 + 0001 + 0010 + 1011 + 1100 + 0101 + 0011 + 1101 + 1110$$

✔ 0000	✔ 000–	
✔ 0001	✔ 00–0	00– –
✔ 0010	✔ 00–1	
✔ 0011	0–01	
✔ 0101	✔ 001–	
✔ 1100	–011	
✔ 1011	–101	
✔ 1101	110–	
✔ 1110	11–0	

	0000	0001	0010	0011	0101	1100	1011	1101	1110
0 –0 1		X			X				
–0 1 1				X			X		
–1 0 1					X			X	
1 1 0 –						X		X	
1 1 –0						X			X
0 0 ––	X	X	X	X					

Choose

$$00\text{--} + \text{--}011 + 11\text{--}0 + \text{--}101$$

or

$$\overline{W}\,\overline{X} + \overline{X}YZ + WX\overline{Z} + X\overline{Y}Z$$

To minimize a product of sums, first complement the expression, then minimize, then complement the result.

$$f(a, b, c) = (a + \overline{b} + \overline{c})(\overline{a} + \overline{b} + c)(\overline{a} + b + c)(a + b + \overline{c})(\overline{a} + \overline{b} + \overline{c})$$

$$\overline{f} = \overline{a}bc + ab\overline{c} + a\overline{b}\,\overline{c} + \overline{a}\,bc + abc$$

or

$$011 + 110 + 100 + 001 + 111$$

✔	100	
✔	001	1–0
✔	011	0–1
✔	110	–11
✔	111	11–

	100	001	011	110	111
1–0	X			X	
0–1		X	X		
–11			X		X
11–				X	X

There is a choice of two minimal expressions:

$$1\text{--}0 + 0\text{--}1 + \text{--}11 \quad \text{or} \quad 1\text{--}0 + 0\text{--}1 + 11\text{--}$$

So

$$\overline{f} = a\overline{c} + \overline{a}c + bc \quad \text{or} \quad \overline{f} = a\overline{c} + \overline{a}c + ab$$

Therefore,

$$f = (\bar{a} + c)(a + \bar{c})(\bar{b} + \bar{c})$$

or

$$f = (\bar{a} + c)(a + \bar{c})(\bar{a} + \bar{b})$$

3.15 DESIGN USING NAND GATES

Section 3.11 introduced NAND gates and showed the block diagram symbol for the NAND gate. NAND gates are widely used in modern computers, and an understanding of their use is invaluable.

Any NAND gate network can be analyzed by using boolean algebra, as previously indicated. Sometimes it is convenient, however, to substitute a functionally equivalent block diagram symbol for the conventional NAND gate symbol in order to analyze a block diagram. Figure 3.24 shows a gate symbol that consists of an OR gate symbol with "bubbles" (inverters) at each input. The two block diagram symbols in Fig. 3.24 perform the same function on inputs, as shown. The NAND gate yields $\bar{A} + \bar{B} + \bar{C}$ given the inputs A, B, and C, as does the functionally equivalent gate.

As an example of the use of an equivalent symbol to simplify the analysis of a NAND gate network, examine Fig. 3.25(a). This shows a two-level NAND-to-NAND gate network with inputs A, B, C, D, E, and F. Figure 3.25(b) shows the same network, but with the rightmost NAND gate replaced by the functionally equivalent block diagram symbol. Notice that the output function is the same for Fig. 3.25(b) as for Fig. 3.25(a), as it should be. Finally, recognition of the fact that the bubbles in Fig. 3.25(b) always occur in pairs, and so can be eliminated from a functional viewpoint (since $\bar{\bar{X}} = X$), leads to Fig. 3.25(c), which is an AND-to-OR gate network. This shows that the NAND-to-NAND gate network in Fig. 3.25(a) yields the same function as the AND-to-OR gate network in Fig. 3.25(c).

The substitution of the equivalent symbols followed by the removal of the "double bubbles" in Fig. 3.25 is a visual presentation of the following use of De Morgan's theorem, which should be compared with the transformation in the figure:

$$\overline{(A{\cdot}B){\cdot}(C{\cdot}D){\cdot}(E{\cdot}F)} = \overline{(A{\cdot}B)} + \overline{(C{\cdot}D)} + \overline{(E{\cdot}F)} = A{\cdot}B + C{\cdot}D + E{\cdot}F$$

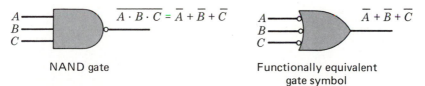

NAND gate   Functionally equivalent gate symbol

FIGURE 3.24
NAND gate and functionally equivalent gate.

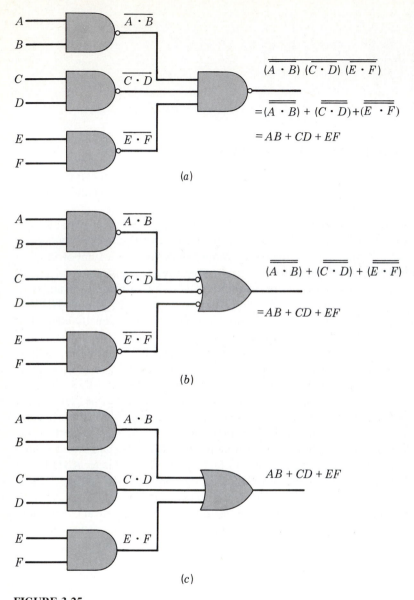

FIGURE 3.25
NAND-to-NAND gate analysis. (*a*) NAND gate network. (*b*) Network in (*a*) with equivalent gates. (*c*) AND-to-OR gate network.

Further study will show that the same principle applies to NAND-to-NAND gates in general. As a further example, Fig. 3.26 shows another NAND-to-NAND gate network and the transformation to an AND-to-OR gate network. The algebraic moves equivalent to the symbology substitutions also are shown.

A question may arise as to why drawings of NAND gate networks in compu- ter diagrams do not use either the equivalent symbol (as in Fig. 3.24) or even the AND-to-OR gate symbols in Figs. 3.25 and 3.26. There are several reasons. First, the industrial and military specifications call for gate symbols that reflect the actual circuit operation. Therefore, if a circuit ANDs the inputs and then complements the result, the circuit is a NAND gate and, strictly speaking, the original NAND gate symbol should be used. Also, if the circuits used are contained in integrated-circuit packages and the computer drawing calls out the part number for the IC packages, an examination of the manufacturer's IC package drawings will show NAND gate symbols (if NAND gates are in the IC package). In the next chapter we show such packages and clarify this. In any case, substitution of symbols might easily lead to

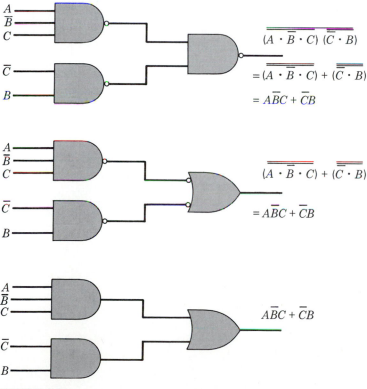

FIGURE 3.26
NAND-to-NAND and AND-to-OR gate transformation.

confusion, so it seems best to use the NAND gate symbol when NAND gates are used.

The preceding analysis of two-level NAND gate networks leads to a direct procedure for designing a NAND-to-NAND gate network.

DESIGN RULE

To design a two-level NAND-to-NAND gate network, use the table-of-combinations procedure for deriving a sum-of-products expression. Simplify this sum-of-products expression by using maps as has been shown. Finally, draw a NAND-to-NAND gate network in the two-level form, and write the same inputs as would have been used in an AND-to-OR gate network, except use NAND gates in place of the AND and OR gates.

For example, let us design a NAND-to-NAND gate network for a problem with three inputs, A, B, and C, and the problem definition in Table 3.23. The table of combinations for this function, the map, the simplified expression, and the NAND-to-NAND gate network are shown in Fig. 3.27. (It would be possible to go directly to the map from the specification. The table of combinations is shown for completeness.)

An adjustment is necessary if the simplified expression contains a single variable as a product term. For instance, if the simplified expression is $A + BC + \overline{B}\,\overline{C}$, the "natural" network is as shown in Fig. 3.28(a). Notice, however, that the NAND gate at the A input is unnecessary if A is available, and this leads to the form shown in Fig. 3.28(b), which eliminates this gate. [The same simplification can be repeated if several single variables occur (as product terms) in the simplified expression.]

TABLE 3.23

Inputs			
A	B	C	Output
0	0	0	1
0	0	1	1
0	1	0	0
0	1	1	1
1	0	0	0
1	0	1	0
1	1	0	1
1	1	1	1

Inputs A	B	C	Output	Product terms		
0	0	0	1	$\overline{A}$	$\overline{B}$	$\overline{C}$
0	0	1	1	$\overline{A}$	$\overline{B}$	C
0	1	0	0	$\overline{A}$	B	$\overline{C}$
0	1	1	1	$\overline{A}$	B	C
1	0	0	0	A	$\overline{B}$	$\overline{C}$
1	0	1	0	A	$\overline{B}$	C
1	1	0	1	A	B	$\overline{C}$
1	1	1	1	A	B	C

$$\overline{A}\,\overline{B}\,\overline{C} + \overline{A}\,\overline{B}C + \overline{A}BC + AB\overline{C} + ABC$$

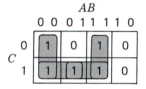

A simplified expression is $\overline{A}\,\overline{B} + \overline{A}\,C + AB$

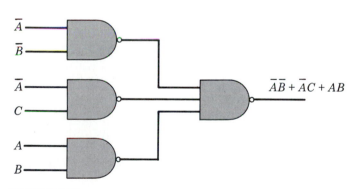

$\overline{A}\,\overline{B} + \overline{A}\,C + AB$

FIGURE 3.27
Design of two-level NAND-to-NAND gate.

3.16 DESIGN USING NOR GATES

Nor gates are used often in computers because current IC technology yields NOR gates in efficient, fast-circuit designs. Fortunately, the design of a NOR-to-NOR gate network, which is the fastest form in which all functions can be realized using only NOR gates, follows naturally from previous design techniques, as will be shown.

First, note the symbol functionally equivalent to the NOR gate, which is shown in Fig. 3.29. The change of the block design symbols mirrors De Morgan's rule:

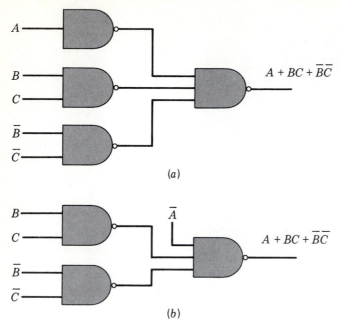

(a)

(b)

FIGURE 3.28
Equivalent NAND-to-NAND gate designs. (*a*) Natural NAND-to-NAND gate design. (*b*) Equivalent NAND-to-NAND gate network.

$$\overline{A + B + C} = \overline{A} \cdot \overline{B} \cdot \overline{C}$$

Figure 3.30(*a*) shows a NOR-to-NOR gate network with the output function $(A + B)(C + D)(E + F)$. To analyze this network, we substitute the functionally equivalent symbol for the rightmost NOR gate, as shown in Fig. 3.30(*b*). This yields the same function, but examination of Fig. 3.30(*b*) shows that the bubbles occur in pairs. Since $\overline{\overline{X}} = X$, these can be eliminated, as shown in Fig. 3.30(*c*), which shows an OR-to-AND gate network.

The transformation in the block diagrams of Fig. 3.30 from (*a*) to (*b*) to (*c*) mirrors the following boolean algebra moves:

$$\overline{\overline{(A + B)} + \overline{(C + D)} + \overline{(E + F)}} = \overline{\overline{(A + B)}} \, \overline{\overline{(C + D)}} \, \overline{\overline{(E + F)}}$$
$$= (A + B)(C + D)(E + F)$$

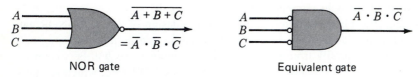

NOR gate   Equivalent gate

FIGURE 3.29
NOR gate symbol and equivalent gate.

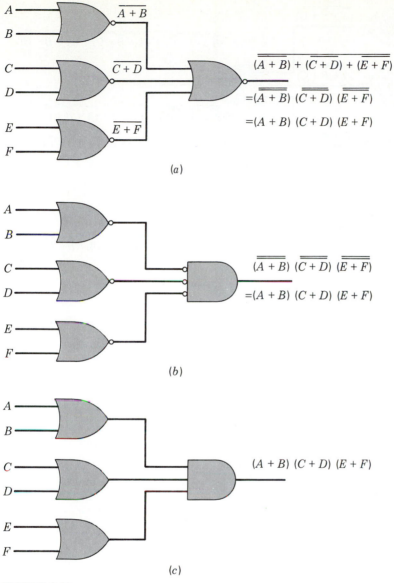

FIGURE 3.30
NOR-to-NOR gate network analysis.

This shows that a NOR-to-NOR gate network is functionally equivalent to an OR-to-AND gate network. Figure 3.31 shows another example of this. The corresponding algebraic transformations are also shown.

Examination of the preceding transformation leads to a rule for the design of a NOR-to-NOR gate network, given the input-output specifications.

Figure 3.32 shows two examples of NOR-to-NOR gate designs, including the simplification of a network where a single variable occurs as a sum term.

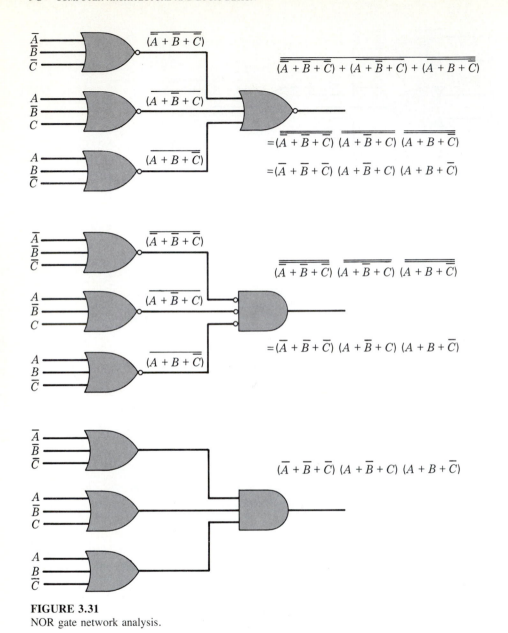

FIGURE 3.31
NOR gate network analysis.

DESIGN RULE

To design a NOR-to-NOR gate network, use the procedures for designing an OR-to-AND gate network. Simplify as for the OR-to-AND gate networks. Finally, draw the block diagram in the same form as for the OR-to-AND gate network, but substitute NOR gates for the OR and AND gates.

A	B	C	OUTPUT	SUM TERMS
0	0	0	1	$A + B + C$
0	0	1	0	$A + B + \bar{C}$
0	1	0	1	$A + \bar{B} + C$
0	1	1	0	$A + \bar{B} + \bar{C}$
1	0	0	0	$\bar{A} + B + C$
1	0	1	1	$\bar{A} + B + \bar{C}$
1	1	0	0	$\bar{A} + \bar{B} + C$
1	1	1	1	$\bar{A} + \bar{B} + \bar{C}$

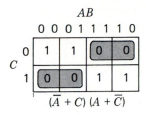

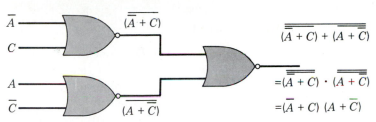

$$\overline{\overline{(\bar{A} + C)} + \overline{(A + \bar{C})}}$$
$$= \overline{\overline{(\bar{A} + C)}} \cdot \overline{\overline{(A + \bar{C})}}$$
$$= (\bar{A} + C)(A + \bar{C})$$

A	B	C	OUTPUT	SUM TERMS
0	0	0	0	$A + B + C$
0	0	1	0	$A + B + \bar{C}$
0	1	0	0	$A + \bar{B} + C$
0	1	1	0	$A + \bar{B} + \bar{C}$
1	0	0	1	$\bar{A} + B + C$
1	0	1	1	$\bar{A} + B + \bar{C}$
1	1	0	0	$\bar{A} + \bar{B} + C$
1	1	1	1	$\bar{A} + \bar{B} + \bar{C}$

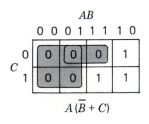

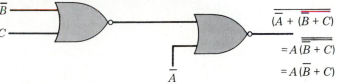

$$\overline{\overline{(\bar{A} + \overline{(B + C)})}}$$
$$= A \overline{(\bar{B} + C)}$$
$$= A(\bar{B} + C)$$

FIGURE 3.32
Two NOR gate designs.

3.17 NAND-TO-AND AND NOR-TO-OR GATE NETWORKS

In the preceding sections, we showed how to analyze and design networks using NAND and NOR gates in NAND-to-NAND and NOR-to-NOR forms. Two other forms are in common usage: the NAND-to-AND and the NOR-to-OR forms.

Since NAND gates are quite popular, and since the outputs from NAND gates sometimes can be ANDed by a simple connection, as we show later, we first present the analysis and design procedures for NAND-to-AND gate networks.

Figure 3.33(a) shows a NAND-to-AND gate network with inputs A, B, C, D, and E. Figure 3.33(b) shows the same configuration but with the NAND gates replaced by the equivalent symbol from Fig. 3.24. This shows that a NAND-to-AND network functions like an OR-to-AND network with each input complemented and leads to this design rule:

DESIGN RULE

To design a NAND-to-AND gate network, use the procedure for deriving a simplified expression in product-of-sums form for an OR-to-AND gate network. Then draw the block diagram, using a NAND-to-AND form, with a NAND gate for each sum term in the simplified expression. To form inputs to the NAND gates, complement each variable in the simplified product-of-sums expression.

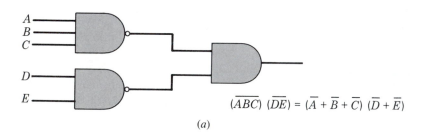

$$(\overline{ABC})\,(\overline{DE}) = (\overline{A} + \overline{B} + \overline{C})\,(\overline{D} + \overline{E})$$

(a)

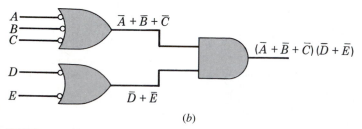

(b)

FIGURE 3.33
NAND-to-AND gate network. (a) Conventional NAND-to-AND gate network. (b) NAND-to-AND with equivalent gates substituted.

TABLE 3.24

A	B	C	Output
0	0	0	1
0	0	1	0
0	1	0	0
0	1	1	1
1	0	0	0
1	0	1	0
1	1	0	1
1	1	1	1

TABLE 3.25

A	B	C	Output	Sum term
0	0	0	1	$A + B + C$
0	0	1	0	$A + B + \overline{C}$
0	1	0	0	$A + \overline{B} + C$
0	1	1	1	$A + \overline{B} + \overline{C}$
1	0	0	0	$\overline{A} + B + C$
1	0	1	0	$\overline{A} + B + \overline{C}$
1	1	0	1	$\overline{A} + \overline{B} + C$
1	1	1	1	$\overline{A} + \overline{B} + \overline{C}$

Example

Design a NAND-to-AND gate network for the input-output values in Table 3.24. First, add a sum term column (Table 3.25), and then AND the sum terms where 0s appear as output values. Our product-of-sums expression is thus $(A + B + \overline{C})(A + \overline{B} + C)(\overline{A} + B + C)(\overline{A} + B + \overline{C})$. This must be simplified. The simplified expression is $(A + \overline{B} + C)(\overline{A} + B)(B + \overline{C})$. The rule states that we must now form a NAND-to-AND gate network, but each input should be complemented. This means each variable in $(A + \overline{B} + C)(\overline{A} + B)(B + \overline{C})$ must be complemented. The inputs for one NAND gate thus will be A, B, and $\overline{C}$, which are from the first sum term, $(A + \overline{B} + C)$. The inputs to the second NAND gate will be A and $\overline{B}$, from the term $(\overline{A} + B)$, and the third NAND gate will have as inputs B and C, from the sum term $(B + \overline{C})$. The resulting block diagram is shown in Fig. 3.34.

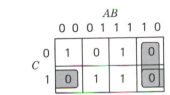

$$(A + \overline{B} + C)\ (\overline{A} + B)\ (B + \overline{C})\ \text{is simplified expression}$$

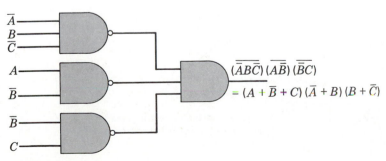

FIGURE 3.34
Design of a NAND-to-AND network.

NOR-to-OR gate networks are also widely used because NORs are the natural gates for emitter-coupled logic (ECL) circuits, a major circuit line. Figure 3.35(a) shows a NOR-to-OR gate network with four inputs and the output boolean algebra expressions. Figure 3.35(b) shows the same configuration with equivalent gates substituted for the NOR gates. This shows that the basic form for the boolean expression realized is AND-to-OR but with each input variable complemented. Thus, the design rule for a NOR-to-OR gate network is as follows:

DESIGN RULE

To design a NOR-to-OR gate network, develop and simplify the sum-of-products expression for the described function. Then draw a NOR-to-OR gate network with a NOR gate for each product term, but complement each input in the sum-of-products expression to form the inputs to the NOR gates.

Table 3.26 shows a table of combinations to be realized as a NOR-to-OR gate network. The product terms are added to the table, and then the boolean algebra expression is derived for the problem: $\overline{A}\,\overline{B}\,\overline{C} + \overline{A}B\overline{C} + A\overline{B}C + AB\overline{C} + ABC$. This expression is then simplified, giving $AB + BC + \overline{A}\,C$.

The design rule says that to realize a NOR-to-OR gate network, we use the above expression but complement each input. This means that the first NOR gate will

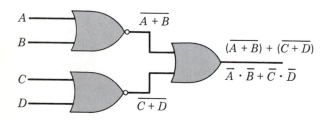

$$A \quad \overline{A + B}$$
$$B$$
$$(\overline{A + B}) + (\overline{C + D})$$
$$\overline{A} \cdot \overline{B} + \overline{C} \cdot \overline{D}$$
$$C$$
$$D \quad \overline{C + D}$$

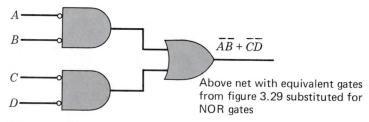

$$A$$
$$B$$
$$\overline{\overline{A}\,\overline{B}} + \overline{\overline{C}\,\overline{D}}$$
$$C$$
$$D$$

Above net with equivalent gates from figure 3.29 substituted for NOR gates

FIGURE 3.35
NOR-to-OR gate network and equivalent network.

TABLE 3.26

A	B	C	Output	Product terms
0	0	0	1	$\overline{A}\,\overline{B}\,\overline{C}$
0	0	1	0	$\overline{A}\,\overline{B}C$
0	1	0	1	$\overline{A}B\overline{C}$
0	1	1	0	$\overline{A}BC$
1	0	0	0	$A\overline{B}\,\overline{C}$
1	0	1	1	$A\overline{B}C$
1	1	0	1	$AB\overline{C}$
1	1	1	1	ABC

have as inputs $\overline{A}$ and $\overline{B}$, from the product term AB; the second NOR gate will have as inputs $\overline{B}$ and $\overline{C}$, from the product term BC; and the third NOR gate will have as inputs A and C, from the product term $\overline{A}\,\overline{C}$. Figure 3.36 shows this design.

3.18 WIRED OR AND WIRED AND GATES*

In certain integrated-circuit technologies, it is possible to form OR and AND gates by means of a simple connection. Figure 3.37(a) shows a NAND-to-AND gate combination in which the AND gate is formed by simply connecting the NAND gate outputs. The wired AND gate in Fig. 3.37(a) requires no additional circuitry beyond that required for the NAND gates. This is shown by the dotted lines used for the NAND symbol.

Only certain NAND gates can have their outputs connected in this way and still form an AND gate. The designer of the NAND gates arranges for this feature, and the manufacturer will indicate on the specification sheet when this can be done.

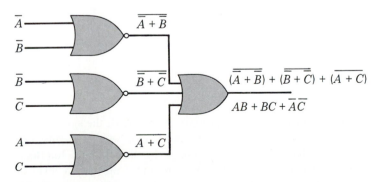

FIGURE 3.36
Design for NOR-to-OR gate network.

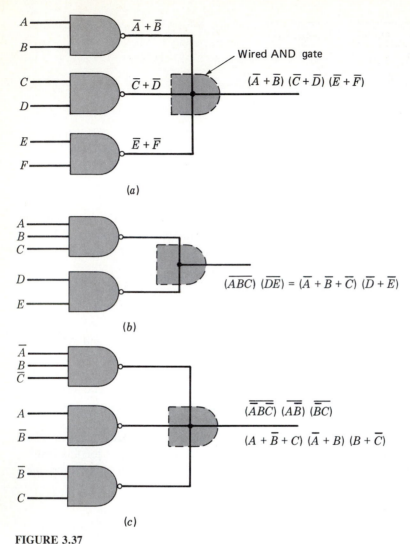

FIGURE 3.37
NAND to wired AND networks. (*a*) NAND-to-AND with wired AND gate. (*b*) NAND-to-AND with wired AND for Fig. 3.33(*a*). (*c*) NAND to wired AND for Fig. 3.34.

For example, when transistor-transistor logic (TTL) circuits are used, the specification sheets sometimes refer to the gates as having "open collectors," which means they can be formed into NAND-to-AND nets by simply connecting their outputs. In effect, the circuits are designed so that when the gates are connected, the output level of all gates will be the lowest level any gate would output if the gates were operated singly.

Figure 3.37(*b*) and (*c*) shows examples of NAND-to-wired-AND nets that correspond in function to those in Figs. 3.33 and 3.34. Again, we emphasize that not all NAND gates can be wire-ANDed by using a simple connection. When this is possible, however, the savings in circuitry and speed improvement make the configuration desirable.

An important observation should be made here: If inputs are wire-ANDed by using a simple connection, a single variable cannot be tied to the AND connection. A single-input NAND gate (inverter) must be used. Refer to Fig. 3.38, which shows a design where a single variable *B* occurs in the minimal expression.

To explain this problem, if in Fig. 3.38 *A* and *C* are each 1 and *B* is 0, then the NAND gate output should be 0 and the value of $\overline{B}$ 1. What would the value at

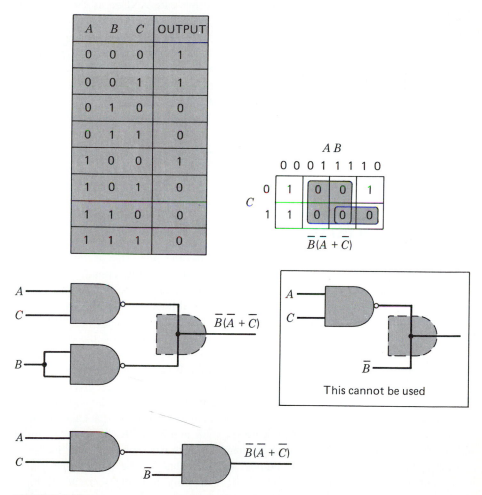

FIGURE 3.38
NAND-to-AND gate design with a single variable.

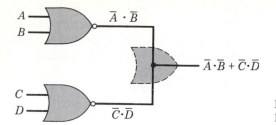

FIGURE 3.39
NOR-to-wired-OR gate network.

the wired AND junction be? Will the NAND gate output pull $\overline{B}$ down, or will the 1 on $\overline{B}$ force the level up? The situation is to use an AND gate, not a wired AND, or to use a NAND gate with the ability to have its output wire-ANDed as shown in Fig. 3.38.

Some NOR gates will form an OR gate at their output when they are connected. Figure 3.39 shows a NOR-to-wired-OR net with output function $\overline{(A + B)} + \overline{(C + D)} = \overline{A} \cdot \overline{B} + \overline{C} \cdot \overline{D}$. This expression shows that the NOR-to-OR gate network functions as an AND-to-OR gate network with each variable complemented. Again, the dotted symbol indicates that the gate is wired OR.

The above result shows that we can design for NOR-to-wired-OR networks just as for NOR-to-OR networks.

Again, note that only certain NOR gates can be connected at their outputs to form wired ORs. Some ECL circuits make this possible, and the manufacturer will note this on the specification sheets.

3.19   PLAs AND PALs*

Once a design has been made for a gate network, the next step is to implement the design using integrated circuits. Figure 3.40(a) shows an IC container, and Fig. 3.40(b) shows the gate layout in that container. This is called the *pin out* for the IC package. The package in Fig. 3.40(b) is one of several hundred different gate layouts from which a designer can choose. Using this particular IC package, the NAND-to-NAND gate network for $A\overline{B} + BC$ can be realized by connecting the pins of the package as shown in Fig. 3.40(c). These connections are often made as conducting metallic strips on printed-circuit boards on which the IC containers are mounted.

The container shown has only 14 pins, whereas some chips have over 100 pins. Chips of this size (and chips of 16 pins) are widely used, however, as will be seen.

In a given design, as the number of gates increases, more IC packages such as that in Fig. 3.40 are required. To decrease the total number of IC packages required and to simplify their interconnection, IC manufacturers have evolved manufacturing processes that greatly increase the number of gates that can be placed in a single IC container. The IC package in Fig. 3.40, with only four gates, is an example of small-scale integration. Large chips can have several hundred thousand gates in a package. This large-scale integration leads to several basic design problems, however.

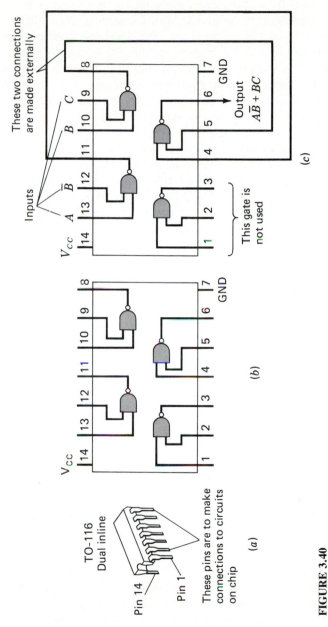

FIGURE 3.40
Integrated-circuit container and pin-out. (*a*) Integrated-circuit container. (*b*) Pin-out showing gate layout in container in (*a*).
(*c*) NAND-to-NAND gate set realizing $A\bar{B} + BC$.

107

For example, the inputs and outputs for the gates in Fig. 3.40 are all available, and the gates can be interconnected in any desired manner, but if more gates are placed in a container, the number of pins must be increased. This increases the cost of the container substantially and decreases the ability of the designer to select the right combination of gates for the network. Also, connections must still be made outside the IC container. If the same connections were made inside the container (on the IC chip), they would cost less and be more reliable. Also, circuits would be faster and use less power. This leads to the idea of a chip with a specific gate layout in which the gates are interconnected on the chip. Such an IC chip made for a particular design is called a *custom* chip.[13] Unfortunately, generating a complete design for a new, individual custom IC chip can be very expensive (costs can be from several thousand to several hundred thousand dollars). This means that start-up costs for a design that requires a number of custom chips can be very high. Once custom chips are made, however, for large runs, the cost per manufactured chip is low.

The high start-up costs for custom chips have caused designers to use IC packages with only a few gates, as in Fig. 3.40, and form the networks by interconnecting the gates outside the IC packages (using a printed-circuit board, as previously noted), particularly when small numbers of the design are to be made. However, although this approach is practical and economical for small production runs, it does not utilize the level of integration possible for present ICs.[14]

To aid designers in reducing the number of chips required, IC manufacturers make *programmable logic device* (PLD) chips in IC containers with many gates. The gates can be interconnected by the designer under certain constraints. Two examples of these are *programmable logic arrays* (PLAs) and *programmable array logic* devices (PALs).[15] Figure 3.41 shows a layout for a small PLA. This particular array has three AND gates and two OR gates. (In actual practice, an array would have several hundred to several thousand gates.) Note that the connections from inputs A, B, and C to the AND gates are not complete and that the AND gate outputs are not connected to the OR gates. These connections are made as desired by the designer.

Figure 3.42 shows a design that uses the PLA in Fig. 3.41 to realize the two boolean algebra expressions $AB\overline{C} + \overline{A}\,\overline{B}$ (for output 1) and $\overline{A}\,\overline{B} + AC$ (for output 2).

PLAs are manufactured in several different ways. In one method, the manufacturer places a fused connection at every intersection point in the PLA between the inputs and the AND gates and between the AND and OR gates. Thus, every possible connection is made when the PLA is manufactured, and then the undesired connec-

---

[13] A custom IC chip is one made from scratch for a particular purpose. A particular gate configuration can be manufactured into a chip by developing the masks used to produce the chip design.

[14] The level of integration is the complexity in terms of gates per chip. *Small-scale integration* (SSI) is roughly 1 to 20 gates per chip, *medium-scale integration* (MSI) is 20 to 100 gates per chip, *large-scale integration* (LSI) is 100 to 1000 gates per chip, and *very large-scale integration* (VLSI) is more than 1000 gates.

[15] PAL is a registered trademark of Monolithic Memories.

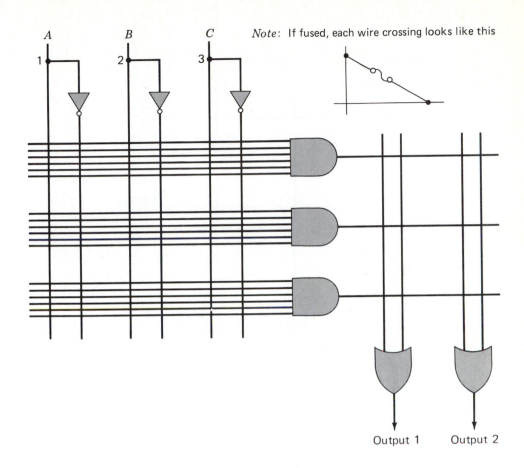

FIGURE 3.41
Layout for three-input two-output PLA.

tions are removed by blowing the fuses.[16] This type of PLA is often called a *field programmable logic array* (FPLA).

There is also a version of FPLAs called EFPLAs (erasable FPLAs), where connections are made by the user but can be changed. In one version of EFPLAs, the IC chip is housed in a windowed ceramic package. When the lid to the window is opened, UV light erases existing connections, allowing new ones to be made.

In another manufacturing technique, the desired connections are made during manufacture. The manufacturer originally makes the IC array layout so that stipu-

---

[16] The fuses are blown by selecting a fuse using logic levels at the inputs and then applying a relatively high voltage to a pin on the IC container. Electronic instruments can be purchased that blow selected fuses on a PLA. This is called *programming* the PLA. As mentioned, some chips are electrically reprogrammable; they can be programmed and reprogrammed using only electrical inputs. (These are not fused but have solid state mechanisms. Chapter 4 gives more details.)

110

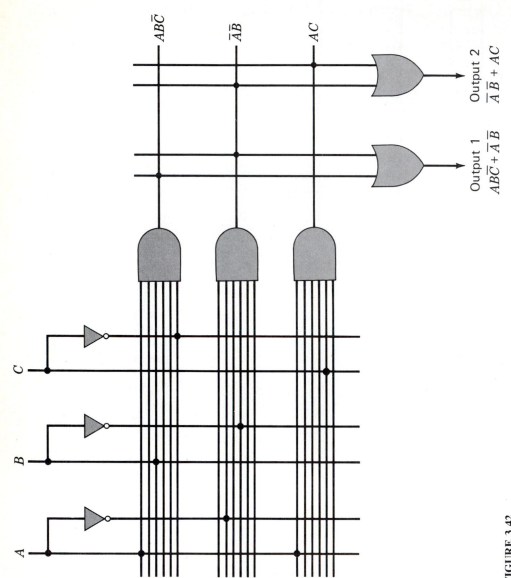

FIGURE 3.42
Connection design for three-input two-output PLA.

lated connections can be made, and the logic designer tells the manufacturer which connections to make for a particular design. Then the manufacturer creates a *mask*, which generates the desired connections when layers of metallization are added to the chip during manufacture. Setting up this mask costs far less (several hundred dollars, perhaps), than designing an entire new chip with the precise logic array desired by the logic designer, and production runs of these chips are inexpensive.

Note that the AND gate that generates $\overline{A}\,\overline{B}$ in Fig. 3.42 has its output connected to both OR gates. This is sometimes a useful and desirable feature for PLAs, enabling a single AND gate to be used for two outputs.

Most larger PLAs contain several hundred gates, 15 to 25 inputs, and 5 to 15 outputs. This offers the logic designer great flexibility. The low cost per unit of these IC gate networks has led to widespread use of PLAs.

To design these large arrays, a simplifying symbology has proved useful. Figure 3.43 shows this for the array in Fig. 3.42. The crosses drawn on the function indicate ANDs, and the squares indicate ORs. The figure also shows that the AND can be realized by a single semiconductor junction (called a *diode*), and the OR can be realized by a single junction pointed the other way. In practice, the manufacturer lays out the chip with junctions at every intersection of the lines, and only the desired diode connections are made.[17] This is simply a redrawing of Fig. 3.42 using

---

[17] For FPLAs the diodes are fused so they can be blown by an instrument called a *programmer*. This sets the FPLA as desired. Programmers are made with standard chip connectors (sockets) utilizing standard inputs. These are called JEDEC programmers. More on this subject will be presented in Chapter 4.

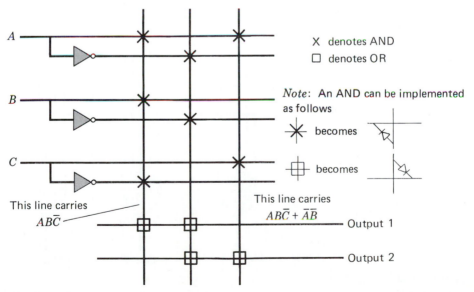

FIGURE 3.43
A frequently used way to draw PLA designs.

a different symbology. This symbology is very useful when there are many inputs and gates.

Figure 3.44 shows the layout for a PAL. PALs are very similar to PLAs except that the OR gates are fixed and permanently connected to a set of AND gate output lines. As a result, AND gates cannot be shared, but the fixed OR gate connections lead to an ease of manufacture that has proved popular. Figure 3.45 shows a PAL design using the AND symbology (crosses) at intersections, as in Fig. 3.43.

The current nomenclature calls the version of Fig. 3.44, in which the AND element connections are fused, a PAL and calls the version in which the manufacturer makes the connections *hard array logic*, or HAL.

Example of Design Using a PLA

Since PLAs and PALs are widely used because of their economy and speed of operation, we examine the design of a small network employing a widely used table listing.

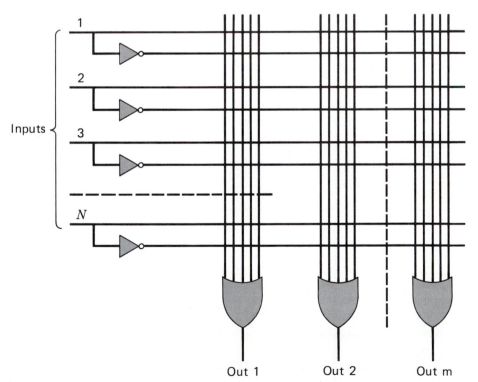

FIGURE 3.44
Layout for PAL.

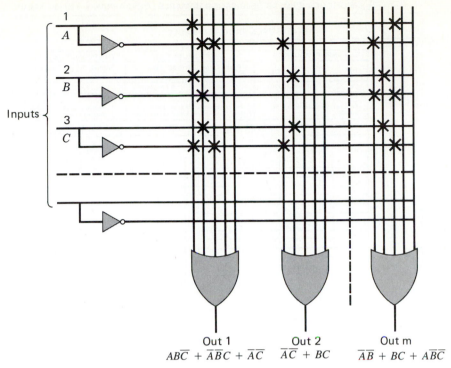

Inputs

Out 1
$$A B \overline{C} + \overline{A} \overline{B} C + \overline{A} \overline{C}$$

Out 2
$$\overline{A} C + B C$$

Out m
$$\overline{A} \overline{B} + B C + A \overline{B} \overline{C}$$

FIGURE 3.45
PAL design for three functions.

Figure 3.46 shows a program table for a small PLA manufactured by Signetics. This PLA has 16 input variables and 8 outputs from OR gates. Also, 48 AND gates can be formed on the chip. This PLA is packaged in a 28-pin IC container, and the pin-out is shown in Fig. 3.47.

The table in Fig. 3.46 can be filled out to describe a particular gate network and then mailed to an IC manufacturer, who will produce chips with a gate network corresponding to the table. Although a Signetics table is used here, the table is typical of those used by other manufacturers who provide the same service.

The table is filled out as follows: First, the logic input variables are identified in the "input variable" column using numbers 0 to 15 in the table. We fill out the table for Fig. 3.42 as a (small-scale) example. We identify A with input 2, B with input 1, and C with input 0 on the program table. We now wish to form the product terms $A B \overline{C}$, $\overline{A} \overline{B}$, and $A C$. The rule is that if an input is not complemented (inverted), an H is written in the table; if the input is to be complemented, an L is written; and if the input is not used, a — is written. To form $A B \overline{C}$, then, we form a row in the table containing dashes everywhere except in input variable columns 2, 1, and 0; in these we write H, H, and L. This is shown in Fig. 3.48.

SIGNETICS BIPOLAR FIELD-PROGRAMMABLE LOGIC ARRAY • 82S100, 82S101

16X48X8 FPLA PROGRAM TABLE

PROGRAM TABLE ENTRIES

INPUT VARIABLE			OUTPUT FUNCTION		OUTPUT ACTIVE LEVEL	
Im	Īm	Don't Care	Prod. Term Present in Fp	Prod. Term Not Present in Fp	Active High	Active Low
H	L	— (dash)	A	• (period)	H	L

NOTE

Enter ı—ı for unused inputs of used P-terms

NOTES

1 Entries independent of output polarity
2 Enter A for unused outputs of used P-terms

NOTES

1 Polarity programmed once only
2 Enter ıHı for all unused outputs

THIS PORTION TO BE COMPLETED BY SIGNETICS

CF (XXXX)
CUSTOMER SYMBOLIZED PART #
DATE RECEIVED
COMMENTS

	PRODUCT TERM¹ INPUT VARIABLE¹																	ACTIVE LEVEL¹ OUTPUT FUNCTION¹							
NO	15	14	13	12	11	10	9	8	7	6	5	4	3	2	1	0		7	6	5	4	3	2	1	0
0																									
1																									
2																									
3																									
4																									
5																									
6																									
7																									
8																									
9																									
10																									
11																									
12																									
13																									
14																									
15																									
16																									
17																									
18																									
19																									
20																									
21																									
22																									
23																									
24																									
25																									
26																									
27																									
28																									
29																									
30																									
31																									
32																									
33																									
34																									
35																									
36																									
37																									
38																									
39																									
40																									
41																									
42																									
43																									
44																									
45																									
46																									
47																									

CUSTOMER NAME
PURCHASE ORDER #
SIGNETICS DEVICE #
TOTAL NUMBER OF PARTS
PROGRAM TABLE #
REV_____ DATE

(1) Input and Output fields of unused P-terms can be left blank. Unused inputs and outputs are FPLA terminals left floating

vi   **signetics**

FIGURE 3.46
Program table for a PLA. (*Courtesy Signetics Corp.*)

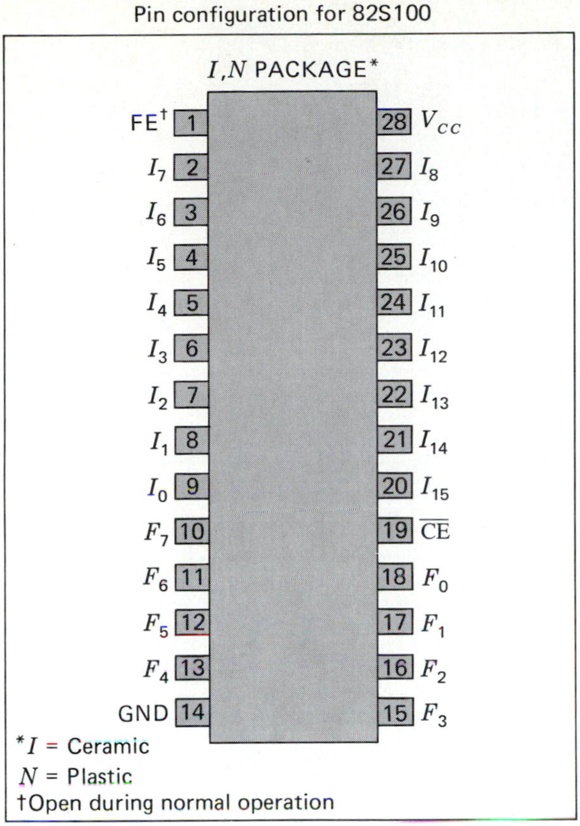

Pin configuration for 82S100

I,*N* PACKAGE*

FE†	1	28	V_{cc}
I_7	2	27	I_8
I_6	3	26	I_9
I_5	4	25	I_{10}
I_4	5	24	I_{11}
I_3	6	23	I_{12}
I_2	7	22	I_{13}
I_1	8	21	I_{14}
I_0	9	20	I_{15}
F_7	10	19	$\overline{CE}$
F_6	11	18	F_0
F_5	12	17	F_1
F_4	13	16	F_2
GND	14	15	F_3

*I = Ceramic
N = Plastic
†Open during normal operation

FIGURE 3.47
Pin-out for PLA. (*Signetics Corp.*)

The OR gate inputs are written as follows: If the AND term in a particular row is to be used in an OR output, an A (for active) is written in the row; if not, a • is written. In Fig. 3.48, the "output function" column 0 in the table is associated with output 1 in Fig. 3.42, and column 1 is associated with output 2 in Fig. 3.42.

A final example is shown in Fig. 3.49. In this case, there are three output lines, 0, 1, and 2. *A* is associated with input variable 3 on the table, *B* with 2, *C* with 1, and *D* with 0. The functions formed are

$$\text{Output } 0 = A + BC + \overline{A}\,\overline{C}D$$

$$\text{Output } 1 = AB + BC + A\overline{B}\,\overline{C}D$$

$$\text{Output } 2 = \overline{B}\,\overline{C} + \overline{A}\,\overline{C}D + A\overline{B}\,\overline{C}D + AC$$

Clearly, PLAs provide a convenient way to fabricate IC chips with gate networks. Field-programmable arrays with a given design can be made by blowing selected fuses, and then the computer design can be tested by using these trial chips. Later, for production runs, the chips made by a manufacturer from the table can be used.

16X48X8 FPLA PROGRAM TABLE

PROGRAM TABLE ENTRIES

INPUT VARIABLE			OUTPUT FUNCTION		OUTPUT ACTIVE LEVEL	
Im	$\overline{Im}$	Don't Care	Prod Term Present in Fp	Prod Term Not Present in Fp	Active High	Active Low
H	L	— (dash)	A	• (period)	H	L
NOTE Enter (—) for unused inputs of used P-terms			NOTES 1 Entries independent of output polarity 2 Enter (A) for unused outputs of used P-terms		NOTES 1 Polarity programmed once only 2 Enter (H) for all unused outputs	

PRODUCT TERM

NO	INPUT VARIABLE																OUTPUT FUNCTION							
	15	14	13	12	11	10	9	8	7	6	5	4	3	2	1	0	7	6	5	4	3	2	1	0
0	—	—	—	—	—	—	—	—	—	—	—	—	—	H	H	L							H	L
1	—	—	—	—	—	—	—	—	—	—	—	—	—	L	L	—						H	L	
2	—	—	—	—	—	—	—	—	—	—	—	—	—	H	—	H						H		H
3																								
4																								
5																								
6																								
7																								
8																								
9																								
10																								

Forms $AB\overline{C}$ (row 0) $A\ B\ C$
Forms $\overline{A}\overline{B}$ (row 1)
Forms AC (row 2)

Realizes $A\overline{B}C + AC$
Realizes $AB\overline{C} + \overline{A}\overline{B}$

ACTIVE LEVEL

OUTPUT FUNCTION							
7	6	5	4	3	2	1	0
•	•	•	•	•	•	•	A
•	•	•	•	•	•	A	A
•	•	•	•	•	•	A	•

FIGURE 3.48
Program table for the PLA design in Fig. 3.42.

16X48X8 FPLA PROGRAM TABLE

PROGRAM TABLE ENTRIES						
INPUT VARIABLE			OUTPUT FUNCTION		OUTPUT ACTIVE LEVEL	
Im	Im̄	Don't Care	Prod Term Present in Fp	Prod Term Not Present in Fp	Active High	Active Low
H	L	— (dash)	A	• (period)	H	L

Enter (—) for unused inputs of used P-terms

NOTES
1 Entries independent of output polarity
2 Enter (A) for unused outputs of used

NOTES
1 Polarity programmed once only
2 Enter (H) for all unused outputs

PRODUCT TERM — INPUT VARIABLE

NO	15	14	13	12	11	10	9	8	7	6	5	4	3	2	1	0
0	—	—	—	—	—	—	—	—	—	—	—	—	H	—	—	—
1	—	—	—	—	—	—	—	—	—	—	—	—	—	H	H	—
2	—	—	—	—	—	—	—	—	—	—	—	—	L	—	L	H
3	—	—	—	—	—	—	—	—	—	—	—	—	H	H	—	—
4	—	—	—	—	—	—	—	—	—	—	—	—	H	L	L	H
5	—	—	—	—	—	—	—	—	—	—	—	—	—	L	L	—
6	—	—	—	—	—	—	—	—	—	—	—	—	H	—	H	—
7																
8																
9																
10																
11																
12																
13																

ACTIVE LEVEL — OUTPUT FUNCTION

7	6	5	4	3	2	1	0
•	•	•	•	•	•	•	A
•	•	•	•	•	•	A	A
•	•	•	•	•	A	•	A
•	•	•	•	•	A	A	•
•	•	•	•	•	A	A	•
•	•	•	•	•	A	•	•
•	•	•	•	•	A	•	•

Output 0 = $A + BC + \overline{A}CD$

Output 1 = $BC + AB + A\overline{B}CD$

Output 2 = $\overline{A}CD + A\overline{B}CD + \overline{B}C + AC$

Note: Input variable 3 = A
2 = B
1 = C
0 = D

FIGURE 3.49
Program table for three AND-to-OR gate networks.

QUESTIONS

3.1. Prepare a truth table for the following boolean expressions:

(a) $XYZ + \overline{X}\,\overline{Y}\,\overline{Z}$

(b) $ABC + A\overline{B}\,\overline{C} + \overline{A}\,\overline{B}\,\overline{C}$

(c) $A(B\overline{C} + \overline{B}C)$

(d) $(A + B)(A + C)(\overline{A} + \overline{B})$

3.2. Prepare a table of combinations for the following boolean algebra expressions:

(a) $\overline{X}\,\overline{Y} + \overline{X}Y$

(b) $XY\overline{Z} + \overline{X}\,\overline{Y}Z$

(c) $\overline{X}Y\overline{Z} + \overline{X}\,\overline{Y}$

(d) $\overline{X}\,\overline{Y}\,\overline{Z} + X\overline{Y}\,\overline{Z} + \overline{X}YZ$

(e) $\overline{X}\,\overline{Y} + \overline{Y}\,\overline{Z}$

(f) $\overline{AB}(\overline{A}\,\overline{B}\,\overline{C} + \overline{B}C)$

3.3. Prepare a truth table for the following boolean expressions:

(a) $A\overline{B} + \overline{A}B$

(b) $A\overline{B} + B\overline{C}$

(c) $A\overline{C} + AC$

(d) $A\overline{B}C + AB\overline{C} + \overline{A}BC$

(e) $A(A\overline{B}C + A\overline{B}\,\overline{C} + AB\overline{C})$

3.4. Prepare a table of combinations for the following boolean algebra expressions:

(a) $X(\overline{Y} + \overline{Z}) + X\overline{Y}$

(b) $X\overline{Y}(Z + Y\overline{Z}) + \overline{Z}$

(c) $[X(Y + \overline{Y}) + \overline{X}(\overline{Y} + Y)]\cdot\overline{Z}$

(d) $AB(\overline{AB} + \overline{A}\,\overline{B})$

(e) $A[(\overline{B} + C) + \overline{C}]$

(f) $\overline{A}\,\overline{B}\,\overline{C}(AB\overline{C} + \overline{A}BC)$

3.5. Prepare a table of combinations for the following boolean algebra expressions:

    (a) $XY + \overline{X}\,\overline{Y}Z$ (b) $ABC + \overline{A}\,\overline{B} + \overline{A}B$ (c) $ABC + \overline{A}\,\overline{C}$

3.6. Prepare a table of combinations for the following boolean algebra expressions:

    (a) $A\overline{B}\,\overline{C} + \overline{A}B$ (b) $\overline{A}\,\overline{B}\,\overline{C} + AC + AB$ (c) $XZ + X\overline{Y} + \overline{X}\,\overline{Z}$

3.7. Simplify the following expressions, and draw a block diagram of the circuit for each simplified expression, using AND and OR gates. (Assume the inputs are from flip-flops.)

(a) $\overline{A}\overline{B}\,\overline{C} + \overline{A}\overline{B}\,C + \overline{A}B\overline{C} + \overline{A}BC$

(b) $\overline{A}BC + \overline{A}B\overline{C} + A\overline{B}C + AB\overline{C} + \overline{A}\overline{B}\,\overline{C} + \overline{A}B\overline{C} + \overline{A}\overline{B}\,\overline{C}$

(c) $A(A + B + C)(\overline{A} + B + C)(A + \overline{B} - C)(A + B + \overline{C})$

(d) $(A + B + C)(A + \overline{B} + \overline{C})(A + B + \overline{C})(A + \overline{B} + C)$

3.8. Simplify the expressions in Question 3.4 and draw block diagrams of gating networks for your simplified expressions using AND gates, OR gates, and inverters.

3.9. Simplify the following expressions:

(a) $ABC(AB\overline{C} + A\overline{B}C + \overline{A}BC)$

(b) $AB + A\overline{B} + \overline{A}C + \overline{A}\,\overline{C}$

(c) $XY + XY\overline{Z} + XY\overline{Z} + XZY$

(d) $XY(\overline{X}Y\overline{Z} + X\overline{Y}\,\overline{Z} + \overline{X}\,\overline{Y}\,Z)$

3.10. Simplify the expressions in Question 3.6 and draw block diagrams of gating networks for your simplified expressions, using AND gates, OR gates, and inverters.

3.11. Form the complements of the following expressions. For instance, the complement of $(XY + XZ)$ is equal to $\overline{(XY + XZ)} = (\overline{X} + \overline{Y})(\overline{X} + \overline{Z}) = \overline{X} + \overline{Y}\,\overline{Z}$.

(a) $(A + BC + AB)$

(b) $(A + B)(B + C)(A + C)$

(c) $AB + \overline{B}C + C\overline{D}$

(d) $AB(\overline{C}D + \overline{B}C)$

(e) $A(B + C)(\overline{C} + \overline{D})$

3.12. Complement the following expressions (as in Question 3.11):

    (a) $\overline{X}\,\overline{Y} + X\overline{Y}$ (b) $X\overline{Y}Z + \overline{X}Y$ (c) $\overline{X}(Y + \overline{Z})$

    (d) $X(Y\overline{Z} + \overline{Y}Z)$ (e) $XY(\overline{Y}Z + X\overline{Z})$ (f) $XY + \overline{X}\,\overline{Y}(Y\overline{Z} + \overline{X}\,\overline{Y})$

3.13. Prove the two basic De Morgan theorems, using the proof by perfect induction.

3.14. Prove the following rules using the proof by perfect induction:

    (a) $X\overline{Y} + XY = X$ (b) $X + \overline{X}Y = X + Y$

3.15. Convert the following expressions to sum-of-products form:

(a) $(A + B)(\overline{B} + C)(\overline{A} + C)$

(b) $(\overline{A} + C)(\overline{A} + \overline{B} + \overline{C})(A + \overline{B})$

(c) $(A + C)(A\overline{B} + AC)(\overline{A}\,\overline{C} + \overline{B})$

3.16. Convert the following expressions to sum-of-products form:

(a) $(\overline{A} + \overline{B})(\overline{C} + B)$

(b) $\overline{AB}(\overline{BC} + \overline{BC})$

(c) $(A + B\overline{C})(\overline{A}B + \overline{A}B)$

(d) $AB(A\overline{B}\,\overline{C} + \overline{A}C)$

(e) $(\overline{A} + B)[A\overline{C}(B + C)]$

(f) $(\overline{A} + C)(AB + \overline{A}\,\overline{B} + AC)$

3.17. Which rule is the dual of rule 12 in Table 3.10?

3.18. Give the dual of the rule $X + \overline{X}Y = X + Y$.

3.19. Multiply the following sum terms, forming a sum-of-products expression in each case. Simplify while multiplying when possible.

(a) $(A + C)(B + D)$

(b) $(A + C + D)(B + D + C)$

(c) $(A + C + DC)(B + BC + D)$

(d) $(A\overline{B} + \overline{A}B + A\overline{C})(\overline{A}\,\overline{B} + A\overline{B} + A\overline{C})$

3.20. Convert the following expressions to product-of-sums form:

(a) $A + \overline{A}B + \overline{A}\,\overline{C}$

(b) $BC + \overline{A}B$

(c) $A\overline{B}(\overline{B} + \overline{C})$

(d) $\overline{A}B(\overline{B}\,\overline{C} + \overline{B}\,\overline{C})$

(e) $(A + \overline{B} + C)(AB + \overline{A}C)$

(f) $(\overline{A} + \overline{B})A\overline{B}C$

3.21. Write the boolean expression (in sum-of-products form) for a logic circuit that will have a 1 output when $X = 0$, $Y = 0$, $Z = 1$ and $X = 1$, $Y = 1$, $Z = 0$; and a 0 output for all other input states. Draw the block diagram for this circuit, assuming that the inputs are from flip-flops.

3.22. Convert the following to product-of-sums form:

(a) $AB + \overline{A}(B + \overline{C})(D + \overline{B})$

(b) $(B + C)[(\overline{B} + \overline{C})(A + \overline{C})(B + C)]$

3.23. Convert the following to product-of-sums form:

(a) $AB\overline{C} + A\overline{B}C + \overline{A}BC$ (b) $ABC + \overline{BC}(A + CD)(B + C)$

3.24. Prove the following theorem, using the rules in Table 3.10:

$$(X + Y)(X + \overline{Y}) = X$$

3.25. Write the boolean expression (in sum-of-products form) for a logic network that will have a 1 output when $X = 1$, $Y = 0$, $Z = 0$; $X = 1$, $Y = 1$, $Z = 0$; and $X = 1$, $Y = 1$, $Z = 1$. The circuit will have a 0 output for all other sets of input values. Simplify the expression derived and draw a block diagram for the simplified expression.

3.26. Derive the boolean algebra expression for a gating network that will have an output of 0 only when $X = 1$, $Y = 1$, $Z = 1$; $X = 0$, $Y = 0$, $Z = 0$; $X = 1$, $Y = 0$, $Z = 0$. The outputs are to be 1 for all other cases.

3.27. Prove rule 18 in Table 3.10 using the proof by perfect induction.

3.28. Develop sum-of-products and product-of-sums expressions for F_1, F_2, and F_3 in Table 3.27.

3.29. Develop both the sum-of-products and the product-of-sums expressions that describe the function of Table 3.28. Then simplify both expressions. Draw a block diagram for logical circuitry that corresponds to the simplified expressions, using only NAND gates for the sum-of-products expression and NOR gates for the product-of-sums expression.

3.30. Draw block diagrams for F_1, F_2, and F_3 in Question 3.28, using only NAND gates.

TABLE 3.27

Inputs			Outputs		
X	Y	Z	F_1	F_2	F_3
0	0	0	0	0	1
0	0	1	0	1	1
0	1	0	1	1	1
0	1	1	1	1	0
1	0	0	1	0	0
1	0	1	0	1	0
1	1	0	1	1	1
1	1	1	1	0	1

TABLE 3.28

Inputs			Output,
X	Y	Z	A
0	0	0	0
0	0	1	1
0	1	0	1
0	1	1	0
1	0	0	0
1	0	1	1
1	1	0	1
1	1	1	0

3.31. Write the boolean algebra expressions for Tables 3.29 to 3.31, showing expressions in sum-of-products form. Then simplify the expressions and draw a block diagram of the circuit corresponding to each expression.

3.32. Draw block diagrams for F_1, F_2, and F_3 in Question 3.28, using only NOR gates.

3.33. Draw block diagrams for F_1, F_2, and F_3 in Question 3.28, using OR-to-NAND networks.

3.34. Draw block diagrams for F_1, F_2, and F_3 in Question 3.28, using AND-to-NOR gate networks.

3.35. Draw Karnaugh maps for the expressions in Question 3.2.

3.36. Draw Karnaugh maps for the expressions in Question 3.3.

3.37. For a four-variable map in W, X, Y, and Z, draw the subcubes for:
   (a) $WX\overline{Y}$ (b) WX (c) $XY\overline{Z}$
   (d) Y

3.38. For a four-variable map in W, X, Y, and Z, draw the subcubes for:
   (a) $\overline{WX\,YZ}$ (b) $W\overline{Z}$ (c) $\overline{WZ}$
   (d) $\overline{Y}$

3.39. Draw maps of the expressions in Question 3.40; then draw the subcubes for the shortened terms you found.

3.40. Apply the rule $AY + A\overline{Y} = A$, where possible, to the following expressions:
   (a) $X\overline{Y} + \overline{X}\,Y$
   (b) $\overline{A}\,\overline{B}\,\overline{C} + A\overline{B}\,\overline{C}$
   (c) $A\overline{B}C + ABC$

TABLE 3.29

Inputs			Output,
A	B	C	Z
0	0	0	0
0	0	1	1
0	1	0	1
0	1	1	0
1	0	0	1
1	0	1	1
1	1	0	0
1	1	1	0

TABLE 3.30

Inputs			Output,
A	B	C	Z
0	0	0	1
0	0	1	0
0	1	0	0
0	1	1	1
1	0	0	1
1	0	1	0
1	1	0	0
1	1	1	1

TABLE 3.31

Inputs			Output,
X	Y	Z	P
0	0	0	1
0	0	1	1
0	1	0	1
0	1	1	1
1	0	0	1
1	0	1	0
1	1	0	0
1	1	1	0

(d) $ABC + A\overline{B}\,\overline{C} + A\overline{B}C + AB\overline{C}$

(e) $ABC + \overline{A}\,\overline{B}\,\overline{C} + A\overline{B}C$

(f) $ABC + \overline{A}BC + \overline{A}\,\overline{B}\,\overline{C}$

Note: There is a technique for writing minterms that is widely used. It consists of writing the letter m (to represent *minterm*) along with the value of the binary number given by the row of the table and combinations in which the minterm lies. For instance, in the variables X, Y, Z we have the unfinished table of combinations given in Table 3.32.

For this table $m_0 = \overline{X}\,\overline{Y}\,\overline{Z}$, $m_1 = \overline{X}\,\overline{Y}Z$, $m_2 = \overline{X}Y\overline{Z}$, and so on to $m_7 = XYZ$. Now we can substitute m_s for actual terms and shorten the writing of expressions. For instance, $m_1 + m_2 + m_4$ means $\overline{X}\,\overline{Y}Z + \overline{X}Y\overline{Z} + X\overline{Y}\,\overline{Z}$. Similarly $m_0 + m_3 + m_5 + m_7$ means $\overline{X}\,\overline{Y}\,\overline{Z} + \overline{X}YZ + X\overline{Y}Z + XYZ$.

This can be extended to four or more variables. An expression in W, X, Y, Z can be written as $m_0 + m_{13} + m_{15} = \overline{W}\,\overline{X}\,\overline{Y}\,\overline{Z} + WX\overline{Y}Z + WXYZ$. Or $m_2 + m_5 + m_9 = \overline{W}\,\overline{X}Y\overline{Z} + \overline{W}X\overline{Y}Z + W\overline{X}\,\overline{Y}Z$. As can be seen, to change a minterm to an m_i, simply make uncomplemented variables 1s and complemented variables 0s. Thus $\overline{W}XY\overline{Z}$ would be 0110, or 6 decimal; $\overline{W}X\overline{Y}\,\overline{Z}$ would be 0010, or 2 decimal. These two terms would then be written m_6 and m_2. (Notice that we must know how many variables a minterm is in.)

3.41. Draw the Karnaugh maps in X, Y, Z for:

(a) $m_o + m_1 + m_5 + m_7$ (b) $m_1 + m_3 + m_5 + m_4$ (c) $m_1 + m_2 + m_3 + m_5$

(d) $m_0 + m_5 + m_7$

3.42. Draw the subcubes for a three-variable map in X, Y, Z for:

(a) $m_1 + m_3 + m_5 + m_0$ (b) $m_4 + m_7$ (c) $m_0 + m_3$

3.43. Find the maximal subcubes for the maps drawn for Question 3.42.

3.44. Find minimal expressions for the maps drawn in Question 3.42.

3.45. Using maps, simplify the following expressions in four variables, W, X, Y, and Z:

(a) $m_2 + m_3 + m_5 + m_6 + m_7 + m_9 + m_{11} + m_{13}$

(b) $m_0 + m_2 + m_4 + m_8 + m_9 + m_{10} + m_{11} + m_{12} + m_{13}$

3.46. Using maps, simplify the following expressions in four variables W, X, Y, and Z:

(a) $m_1 + m_3 + m_5 + m_7 + m_{12} + m_{13} + m_8 + m_9$

(b) $m_0 + m_5 + m_7 + m_8 + m_{11} + m_{13} + m_{15}$

3.47. Using maps, derive minimal product-of-sums expressions for the functions given in Question 3.46.

3.48. Using maps, derive minimal product-of-sums expressions for the functions given in Question 3.42.

TABLE 3.32

Input					Designation
X	Y	Z	Output	Product terms	(m_i)
0	0	0		$\overline{X}\,\overline{Y}\,\overline{Z}$	m_0
0	0	1		$\overline{X}\,\overline{Y}Z$	m_1
0	1	0		$\overline{X}Y\overline{Z}$	m_2
0	1	1		$\overline{X}YZ$	m_3
1	0	0		$X\overline{Y}\,\overline{Z}$	m_4
1	0	1		$X\overline{Y}Z$	m_5
1	1	0		$XY\overline{Z}$	m_6
1	1	1		XYZ	m_7

3.49. Using maps, simplify the following expressions, using sum-of-products form:

don't-cares

(a) $\overline{A}\,\overline{B}\,\overline{C} + A\overline{B}\,\overline{C} + \overbrace{ABC + \overline{A}B\overline{C} + \overline{A}BC}$

don't-cares

(b) $ABC + A\overline{B}\,\overline{C} + \overbrace{A\overline{B}\,\overline{C} + \overline{A}\overline{B}C}$

don't-cares

(c) $ABCD + \overline{A}\,\overline{B}\,CD + \overline{A}BCD + \overbrace{\overline{A}\overline{B}CD + \overline{A}\,\overline{B}CD + ABC\overline{D}}$

3.50. Using maps, derive minimal product-of-sums expressions for the functions given in Question 3.49.

3.51. Using maps, simplify the following expressions, using sum-of-products form:

don't-cares

(a) $ABC + \overline{A}\,BC + \overbrace{\overline{A}B\overline{C} + A\overline{B}C + AB\overline{C}}$

don't-cares

(b) $ABCD + \overline{A}\,\overline{B}CD + \overbrace{A\overline{B}CD + A\overline{B}CD + \overline{A}\,\overline{B}\,\overline{C}\,\overline{D}}$

don't-cares

(c) $\overline{A}\overline{B}C\overline{D} + A\overline{B}CD + \overbrace{\overline{A}B\overline{C}D + \overline{A}B\,\overline{C}\,\overline{D}}$

3.52. (a) Design an AND-to-OR gate combinational network for the boolean algebra expression

$$ABCD + AB\overline{C}\,\overline{D} + \overline{A}\,\overline{B}CD + \overline{A}B\overline{C}D + ABC\overline{D} + \overline{A}BCD$$

Use as few gates as you can.

(b) Design a NOR gate combinational network for the boolean algebra function in part (a), again using as few gates as you can.

3.53. The following is a NAND-to-NAND gate network. Draw a block diagram for a NOR-to-NOR gate network that realizes the same function, using as few gates as possible.

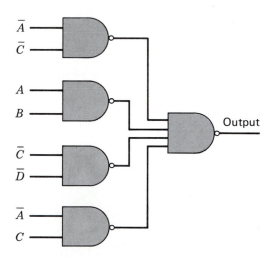

3.54. (a) Derive a boolean algebra expression for the output Y of the network shown.

(b) Convert the expression for Y derived in (a) to product-of-sums form.

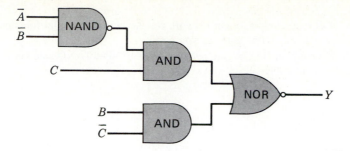

3.55. (a) Design an OR-to-AND gate combinational network for the boolean algebra expression

$$ABCD + \overline{A}B\overline{C}\,\overline{D} + \overline{A}B\overline{C}D + \overline{A}BC\overline{D} + (\overline{A}\,\overline{B}\,\overline{C}\,\overline{D} + \overline{A}\,\overline{B}CD)$$

The two terms in parentheses are don't-cares.

(b) Using only NAND gates, design a combinational network for the boolean algebra function given in part (a).

3.56. (a) Design an OR-to-AND gate combinational network for the boolean algebra expression

$$\overline{A}BCD + \overline{A}BC\overline{D} + \overline{A}B\overline{C}D + (\overline{A}BC\,\overline{D} + \overline{A}\,\overline{B}CD)$$

The two terms in parentheses are don't-cares.

(b) Using only NOR gates, design a combinational network for the boolean algebra function given in part (a).

3.57. The following NAND-to-AND gate network is to be redesigned using a NOR-to-OR gate configuration. Make the change, using as few gates as possible.

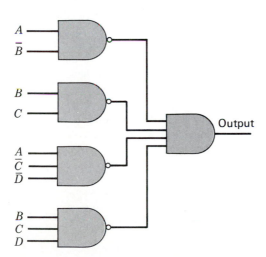

3.58. (a) Design an AND-to-OR gate combinational network for the boolean algebra expression

$$ABCD + AB\overline{C}D + \overline{A}\,\overline{B}C\overline{D} + AB\overline{C}\,\overline{D} + ABC\overline{D} + \overline{A}BC\,\overline{D}$$

Use as few gates as you can.

(b) Design a NOR gate combinational network for the boolean algebra function in part (a), again using as few gates as you can.

3.59. Convert the following NOR-to-OR gate network to a NAND-to-AND gate network. Use as few gates as possible.

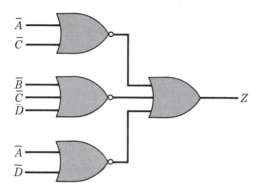

3.60. (a) Design an AND-to-OR gate combinational network for the boolean algebra expression

$$\overline{A}\overline{B}CD + AB\overline{C}D + \overline{A}\,\overline{B}CD + AB\overline{C}\,\overline{D} + A\overline{B}\,\overline{C}\,\overline{D} + \overline{A}BCD$$

Use as few gates as you can.

(b) Design a NOR-to-NOR gate combinational network for the boolean algebra function in part (a), again using as few gates as you can.

3.61. A combinational network has three control inputs C_1, C_2, and C_3; three data inputs A_1, A_2, and A_3; and a single output Z. ($\overline{A}_1$, $\overline{A}_2$, $\overline{A}_3$, $\overline{C}_1$, $\overline{C}_2$, and $\overline{C}_3$ are also available as inputs.) Each input is a binary-value signal. Only one of the control inputs can be a 1 at any given time, and all three can be 0s simultaneously. When C_1 is a 1, the value of Z is to be the value of A_1; when C_2 is a 1, the value of Z is to be the value of A_2; and when C_3 is a 1, the value of the output is to be the value of A_3. If C_1, C_2, and C_3 are 0s, the output Z is to have value 0. Design this network, using only NOR gates. Use a two-level network with as few gates as possible.

3.62. The following NAND-to-AND gate network is to be redesigned to use a NOR-to-OR gate configuration. Make the change, using as few gates as possible.

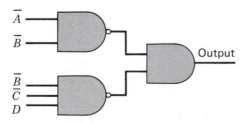

3.63. Convert the following NOR-to-NOR gate network to a NAND-to-AND gate network. Use as few gates as possible.

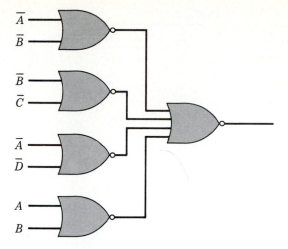

3.64. Will the minimal expression for the function in Table 3.33 require fewer NAND gates or NOR gates? (d means don't-care.) Assume complements are available. How many gates of each kind are required? Give your minimal expressions.

3.65. The following NAND-to-AND gate network must be converted to a NOR-to-OR gate network. Make the conversion, using as few gates as possible in your final design.

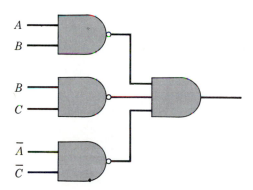

3.66. Will the minimal expression for the function in Table 3.34 require fewer NAND gates or NOR gates? (d means don't-care.) Assume complements are available. How many gates of each kind are required? Give your minimal expressions.

3.67. Simplify:

(*a*)
$$(\overline{W} + \overline{X} + Y + Z)(\overline{W} + X + \overline{Y} + Z)(\overline{W} + X + Y + Z) \cdot$$
$$\overbrace{(W + X + \overline{Y} + Z)(W + \overline{X} + Y + Z)(\overline{W} + \overline{X} + Y + \overline{Z})}^{\text{don't cares}} \cdot$$
$$(W + X + Y + Z)$$

(*b*)
$$\overline{A}\,\overline{B}\,\overline{C}\,\overline{D} + \overline{A}B\overline{C}D + ABC\overline{D} + \overbrace{\overline{A}\,\overline{B}\,\overline{C}D + \overline{A}BCD + ABCD + \overline{A}BC\overline{D}}^{\text{don't cares}} + A\overline{B}C\overline{D}$$

TABLE 3.33

X_1	X_2	X_3	X_4	Output
0	0	0	0	0
0	0	0	1	1
0	0	1	0	1
0	0	1	1	0
0	1	0	0	0
0	1	0	1	d
0	1	1	0	1
0	1	1	1	d
1	0	0	0	d
1	0	0	1	1
1	0	1	0	0
1	0	1	1	0
1	1	0	0	d
1	1	0	1	0
1	1	1	0	d
1	1	1	1	0

TABLE 3.34

X_1	X_2	X_3	X_4	Output
0	0	0	0	0
0	0	0	1	1
0	0	1	0	1
0	0	1	1	0
0	1	0	0	0
0	1	0	1	0
0	1	1	0	1
0	1	1	1	d
1	0	0	0	d
1	0	0	1	1
1	0	1	0	1
1	0	1	1	0
1	1	0	0	d
1	1	0	1	0
1	1	1	0	1
1	1	1	1	0

(c) For parts (a) and (b), design block diagrams for the logical circuitry of the simplified expressions, using either NAND gates only or NOR gates only. Assume that complements of the inputs are available. [The same type of gates do not have to be used for both (a) and (b).]

3.68. Write a boolean algebra expression in sum-of-products form for a gating network with three inputs, A, B, and C (and their complements $\overline{A}$, $\overline{B}$, and $\overline{C}$), that is to have a 1 output only when two or three of the inputs have a 1 value. Implement this function using a NAND-to-wired-AND gate network.

3.69. Draw a block diagram for a NOR-to-OR gate network with three inputs, A, B, and C (and their complements), that has a 1 output only when two or three of the inputs have a 1 value.

3.70. Will the minimal expression for the function in Table 3.35 require fewer NAND

TABLE 3.35

X_1	X_2	X_3	X_4	Output
0	0	0	0	0
0	0	0	1	1
0	0	1	0	1
0	0	1	1	0
0	1	0	0	d
0	1	0	1	0
0	1	1	0	1
0	1	1	1	d
1	0	0	0	d
1	0	0	1	1
1	0	1	0	1
1	0	1	1	d
1	1	0	0	d
1	1	0	1	0
1	1	1	0	1
1	1	1	1	0

gates or NOR gates? (d means don't-care.) Assume that complements are available. How many gates of each kind are required? Give your minimal expressions.

3.71. The following is a NAND-to-NAND gate network. Draw a block diagram for a NOR-to-NOR gate network that realizes the same function, using as few gates as possible.

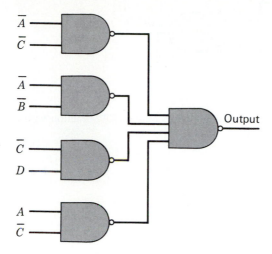

3.72. Convert the following NOR-to-OR gate network to a NAND-to-NAND gate network. Use as few gates as possible.

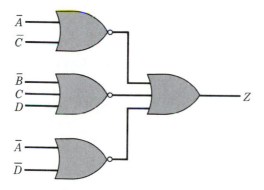

3.73. (*a*) Design an AND-to-OR gate combinational network for the boolean algebra function

$$F = \overline{W}\,\overline{X}\,\overline{Y}\,\overline{Z} + W\overline{X}\,\overline{Y}Z + W\overline{X}\,\overline{Y}\,\overline{Z} + W\overline{X}YZ + \overline{W}X\overline{Y}\,\overline{Z}$$

Use as few gates as you can.

(*b*) Design a NOR gate combinational network for the boolean algebra function in part (*a*), again using as few gates as you can.

3.74. This chapter has explained a number of two-level networks that can be used to implement all possible functions of a given number of variables. There are also two-level networks that can implement only a few of the many functions possible. For instance, an AND-to-AND gate network accomplishes only the AND function, as shown below:

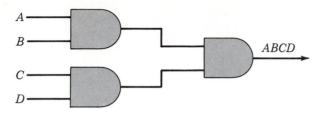

Similarly, a NAND-to-OR network implements only an OR function with complemented inputs, as shown below:

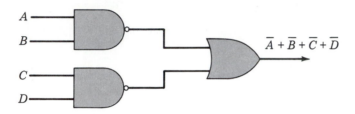

In all, 8 of the possible 16 two-level network arrangements that can be made with NOR, NAND, OR, and AND gates will realize all functions; the other 8 are degenerate and yield only a few of the functions. Identify the degenerate forms and the forms that will yield all functions.

3.75. This chapter did not treat the two-level AND-to-NOR form. Derive a rule for designing AND-to-NOR gate networks, and show how it works for a problem of your choice.

3.76. This chapter did not treat OR-to-NAND gate networks, although all boolean functions can be realized using that configuration. Derive a sample network, using your rule.

3.77. Show how the following NOR-to-NAND gate network can be replaced by a single gate.

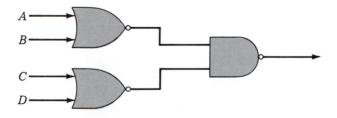

3.78. Convert the following NAND-to-NAND gate network to a (two-level) NOR-to-OR gate network.

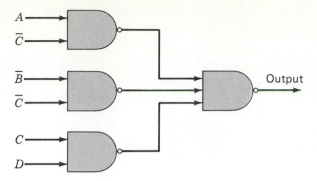

3.79. Using as few gates as possible, design a NAND-to-AND gate network that realizes the following boolean algebra expression:

$$\overline{AB}\overline{C}D + AB\overline{C}\,\overline{D} + A\overline{B}C\overline{D} + ABC\overline{D} + A\overline{B}\,\overline{C}\,\overline{D}$$

3.80. Convert the following NAND-to-NAND gate network to a (two-level) NOR-to-OR gate network.

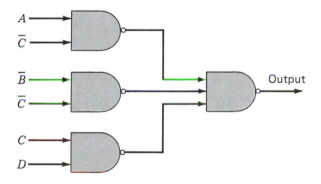

3.81. Convert the following NAND-to-NAND gate network to a NOR-to-NOR gate network.

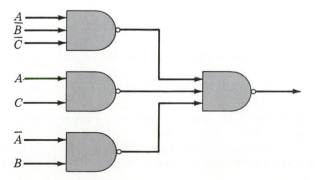

3.82. Convert the following NOR-to-OR gate network to a NAND-to-AND gate network. Use as few gates as possible.

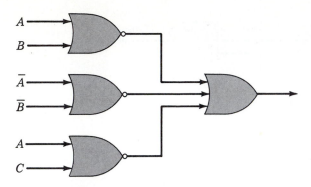

3.83. Convert the following NAND-to-AND gate network to a NOR-to-OR gate network. Use as few gates as possible.

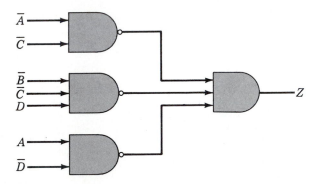

3.84. Using a PLA table like the one in Fig. 3.46, design a three-input, six-output gate network that squares each input. (Inputs and outputs are unsigned binary integers.)

3.85. Using a PLA table like the one in Fig. 3.46, design a network that forms the 9s complement of a BCD number in 2,4,2,1 form.

3.86. Using the PAL in Fig. 3.44, design a three-input gate network that finds the 2s complement of a positive input number.

3.87. Using the PLA symbology in Fig. 3.43, design a logic network that converts a BCD number in 2,4,2,1 form to 8,4,2,1 form.

3.88. Using a PLA table as in Fig. 3.46, design a four-input, five-output circuit that adds 3 to a BCD number in 8,4,2,1 form.

3.89. Using the PLA in Fig. 3.41, show how to form the two outputs $X = \overline{A}\,\overline{B}C + A\overline{B}\,\overline{C}$ and $Y = \overline{A}\,\overline{B}C + AB$.

3.90. Using the symbology in Fig. 3.43, form a design for a PLA with two outputs $X = AB\overline{C} + A\overline{B}$ and $Y = AB\overline{C} + A\overline{B}C + \overline{A}B$.

3.91. A light is controlled by three switches. The light is turned on when a majority of the switches are on. Design a combinational circuit for controlling the operation of the light.

3.92. A *majority circuit* is a combinational circuit with an odd number of inputs such that the output is 1 only if a majority of the inputs are 1s. Design a five-input majority circuit.

3.93. Use the Quine-McCluskey method to obtain the minimal sum for the following functions:

(*a*) $F = \Sigma$ (3, 6, 7, 8, 10)
(*b*) $F = \Sigma$ (2, 4, 6, 7, 8, 10, 11, 15)
(*c*) $F = \Sigma$ (0, 2, 3, 5, 8, 11)
(*d*) $F = \Sigma$ (1, 7, 11, 12, 13, 15)
(*e*) $F = \Sigma$ (6, 7, 8, 9, 10, 11, 14, 15)
(*f*) $F = \Sigma$ (0, 1, 3, 5, 6, 7, 8, 9, 10, 14)
(*g*) $F = \Sigma$ (6, 8, 14, 18, 23, 25, 27, 29, 41, 45, 57, 61)

3.94. Derive an expression for determining if one 4-bit positive binary number is greater in magnitude than another, and design a circuit using SSI gates.

3.95. Two 4-bit numbers A and B are in signed-magnitude form. Develop expressions to determine if $A < B$, $A = B$, or $A > B$.

3.96. Describe the principal characteristics and applications of the PLA and the PAL.

CHAPTER
4

LOGIC
DESIGN

Chapter 3 described gates and the analysis of gating networks using boolean algebra. The basic devices used in the operational or calculating sections of digital computers consist of gates and *flip-flops*. It is remarkable that even the largest of computers is constructed primarily of these devices. This chapter first describes flip-flops and their characteristics. From an intuitive viewpoint, flip-flops provide memory, and gates provide operations on, or functions of, the values stored in these memory devices.

Following the introduction of flip-flops, a discussion of the use of flip-flops and gates to perform several of the most useful functions in computers is presented. The particular functions described include counting in binary and binary-coded decimal, transferring values, and shifting or scaling values stored in flip-flops.

Several other names have been used as alternatives to *flip-flop*. These include *binary* and *toggle*, but *flip-flop* is the most frequently used. Also, there are several other types or memory devices in computers, and these are covered in Chap. 6. However, for actual operations, flip-flops remain dominant, because of their high speed, the ease with which they can be set or read, and the natural way in which gates and flip-flops can be interconnected.

This chapter also contains a section on clocks in digital computers. Computers do not run by taking steps at random times, but proceed from step to step at intervals precisely controlled by a clock. Some knowledge of the uses of clocks in computers is indispensable, and the subject is introduced here.

4.1 FLIP-FLOPS

The basic circuit for storing information in a digital machine is called a *flip-flop*. There are several fundamental types of flip-flops and may circuit designs. However, two characteristics are shared by all flip-flops:

1. The flip-flop is a bistable device, that is, a circuit with only two stable states, which we designate as the 0 state and the 1 state.

   The flip-flop circuit can remember, or store, a bit of information because of its bistable characteristic. The flip-flop responds to inputs. If an input causes it to go to its 1 state, it will remain there and "remember" a 1 until some signal causes it to go to the 0 state. Similarly, once placed in the 0 state, the flip-flop will remain there until it is converted to the 1 state. This simple characteristic, the ability of the flip-flop to retain its state, is the basis for information storage in the operating or calculating sections of a digital computer.

2. The flip-flop has two signals, one of which is the complement of the other.

Figure 4.1 shows the block diagram for a particular type of flip-flop, the *RS flip-flop*. There are two inputs, designated S and R, and two outputs, marked with X and $\overline{X}$. To describe and analyze flip-flop operation, certain conventions are used in the computer industry:

1. Each flip-flop is given a "name." Convenient names are letters, such as X, Y, A, or B; or letter-number combinations, such as A_1 or B_2, or because of difficulty in subscripting on typewriters or printers, A1 or B2. The flip-flop in Fig. 4.1 is called X. It has two outputs, the X output and the $\overline{X}$ output.

   The X and the $\overline{X}$ output lines are always complements; that is, if the X output line has a 1 signal, the $\overline{X}$ output line has a 0 signal; and if the X output line has a 0 signal, output line $\overline{X}$ has a 1 signal.

2. The state of the flip-flop is taken to be the state of the X output. Thus, if the output line X has a 1 signal on it, we say that flip-flop X is in the 1 state. Similarly, if the X line contains a 0 signal, we say that flip-flop X is in the 0 state.

These conventions are very important and convenient. Note that when flip-flop X is in the 1 state, the output line $\overline{X}$ has a 0 on it; and when flip-flop X is in the 0 state, the output line $\overline{X}$ has a 1 on it.

There are two input lines to the *RS* flip-flop. These are used to control the state of the flip-flop. The rules governing the inputs are as follows:

1. As long as both input lines S and R carry 0 signals, the flip-flop remains in the same state; that is, it does not change state.

2. A 1 signal on the S line (the SET line) and a 0 signal on the R line cause the flip-flop to "set" to the 1 state.

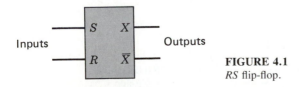

Inputs   Outputs

FIGURE 4.1
RS flip-flop.

3. A 1 signal on the R line (the RESET line) and a 0 signal on the S line cause the flip-flop to "reset" to the 0 state.

4. Placing a 1 on the S line and a 1 on the R line at the same time is forbidden. If this occurs, the flip-flop can go to either state. (This is, in effect, an ambiguous input in that it is telling the flip-flop to both set and reset at the same time.)

An example of a possible sequence of input signals and the resulting state of the flip-flop is as follows:

S	R	X	X is the state of the flip-flop after inputs S and R are applied.
1	0	1	
0	0	1	Flip-flop remains in same state.
0	0	1	
0	1	0	Flip-flop is reset.
0	0	0	
0	0	0	
0	1	0	Flip-flop is told to reset but is already reset.
0	0	0	
1	0	1	Flip-flop is set.
0	0	1	

Although these conventions may seem formidable at first, they can be summarized by simply noting that a 1 on the S line causes the flip-flop to set (that is, assume the 1 state) and a 1 on the R line causes the flip-flop to reset (that is, assume the 0 state). The flip-flop does nothing in the absence of 1 inputs and would be hopelessly confused by 1s on both S and R inputs.

It is very convenient to draw graphs of the inputs and outputs from computer circuits to show how they act as inputs vary. We assume the convention that a 1 signal is a positive signal and a 0 is a ground signal, or 0-V, signal. This is conventional in most present-day circuits and is called *positive logic*. Figure 4.2 shows several signals as they progress in time, with the current binary values of each signal written above. The X and $\overline{X}$ output line signals from the flip-flop corresponding to the S and R signal sequences are also shown. We have arbitrarily chosen $+2$ V for the 1 state of the signals and 0 V for the 0 state because these are very frequently used levels.

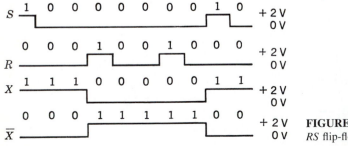

FIGURE 4.2
RS flip-flop waveforms.

Notice that the flip-flop changes only when the input levels command it to, and that it changes at once. (Actually, there would be a slight delay from the instant when the flip-flop is told to change states and the time when it changes, since no physical device can respond instantly; however, the flip-flop's delay in responding is quite small.)

Transfer Circuit

The RS flip-flop, although simple in operation, is adequate for all purposes and is a basic flip-flop circuit. Let us examine the operation of this flip-flop in a configuration called a *transfer circuit*. Figure 4.3 shows two sets of flip-flops named X_1, X_2, and X_3 and Y_1, Y_2, and Y_3. The function of this configuration is to transfer the states, or *contents*, of Y_1 into X_1, Y_2 into X_2, and Y_3 into X_3 upon the TRANSFER command, which consists of a 1 on the TRANSFER line.

Assume that Y_1, Y_2, and Y_3 have been set to some states that we want to remember, or store , in X_1, X_2, and X_3, while the Y flip-flops are used for further calculations. Placing a 1 on the TRANSFER line will cause this desired transfer of information. To understand the transfer of the state of Y_1 into X_1, note that if Y_1 is in the 0 state, the Y_1 output line connected to the AND gate will be a 0 and the AND gate will place a 0 on the S input line of X_1. At the same time the $\overline{Y}_1$ output from Y_1 will be a 1, causing, in the presence of a 1 on the TRANSFER line, a 1 on the R input of X_1. Similar reasoning will show that a 1 in Y_1 will cause a 1 to be placed in X_1 in the presence of a 1 on the TRANSFER line. As long as the TRANSFER line is a 0, both inputs to the X flip-flops will be 0s, and the flip-flop will remain in the last state it assumed.

This simple operation, the transfer operation, is quite important. Related sets of flip-flops in a computer are called *registers*: the three flip-flops Y_1, Y_2, and Y_3 would be called, simply, *register Y*, and the three flip-flops, X_1, X_2, and X_3 would be called *register X*. A 1 on the TRANSFER line would transfer the contents of register Y into register X.

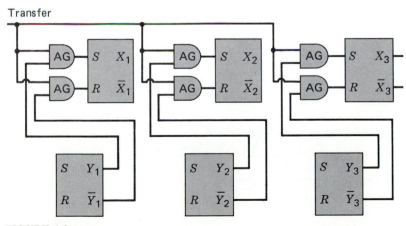

FIGURE 4.3
Transfer circuit.

4.2   CLOCKS

A very important fact about digital computers is that they are clocked. This means that there is a "master clock" somewhere sending out signals that are carefully regulated. These signals initiate the operations performed.

There are excellent reasons why computers are designed this way. The alternative way, with operations triggering other operations as they occur, is called *asynchronous operation* (the clocked way is called *synchronous operation*) and leads to considerable difficulty in design and maintenance. As a result, genuinely asynchronous operation is rarely used.

The clock is the mover of the computer in that it carefully measures time and sends out regularly spaced signals that cause things to happen. We can examine the operation of the flip-flops and gates before and after the clock initiates an action. Initiating signals are often called *clock pulses*.[1]

Figure 4.4 shows a typical clock waveform called a *square wave*. The figure shows two important portions of a square wave: the *leading* or *rising edge*, also called the *positive-going edge*; and the *falling* or *negative-going edge*. This distinction is particularly important since most flip-flops now in use respond to either (but not both) a falling edge or a rising edge. In effect, a system that responds to rising edges of the clock "rests" between such edges and changes state only when such positive-going edges occur. (The reason for the rest periods is to give the circuits time to assume their new states and to give all transients time to die down. The frequency at which such edges occur is generally determined by the speed with which the circuits can go to their new states, the delay times for the gates that must process the new signals, etc.)

Since clock signals are used to initiate flip-flop actions, a clock input is included on most flip-flops. This input is marked with a small triangle, as shown in Fig. 4.5(*a*). A clocked flip-flop can respond to either the positive-going edge of the clock signal

---

[1] The term *clock pulse* has a historical origin. The early computers used short electric pulses to initiate operations: these were naturally called *clock pulses*. Few circuits still use these narrow pulses. The majority of circuits now respond to the edges of square waves, as in Fig. 4.4.

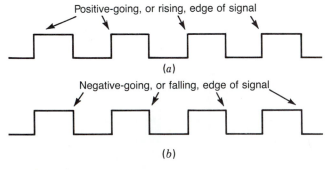

FIGURE 4.4
Clock waveforms.

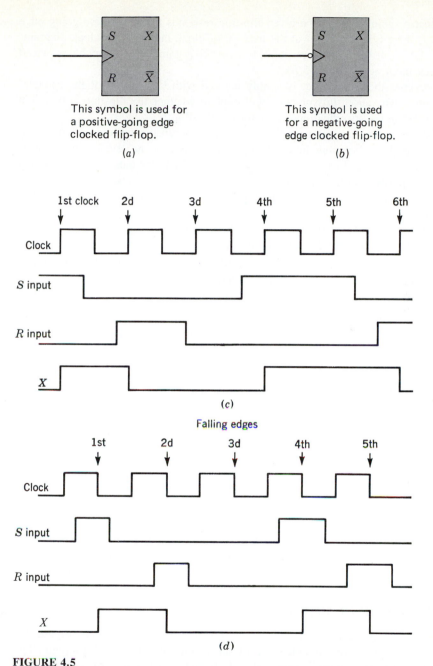

This symbol is used for a positive-going edge clocked flip-flop.

(a)

This symbol is used for a negative-going edge clocked flip-flop.

(b)

1st clock   2d   3d   4th   5th   6th

Clock

S input

R input

$\overline{X}$

(c)

Falling edges

1st   2d   3d   4th   5th

Clock

S input

R input

X

(d)

FIGURE 4.5
Clocked flip-flops and waveforms. (*a*) Positive-edge-triggered flip-flop. (*b*) Negative-edge-triggered flip-flop. (*c*) Waveforms for positive-edge-triggered flip-flop in (*a*). (*d*) Waveforms for flip-flop in (*b*).

or the negative-going edge.[2] If a given flip-flop responds to the positive-going edge of a signal, there is no "bubble" at the triangle or clock input on the block diagram, as in Fig. 4.5(a). If the flip-flop responds to a negative-going edge, a bubble is placed at the clock input, as in Fig. 4.5(b).

Sometimes the clock input is simply marked with CL instead of the triangle. Manufacturers who adopt this practice will explain whether the flip-flop is or is not edge-triggered in the specifications sheet for the flip-flop.

It is important to understand this convention because most clocked flip-flops actually respond to a *change* in clock input level, not to the level itself. This is shown in Fig. 4.5(c) and (d). The flip-flop in Fig. 4.5(a) responds to positive-going clock edges (positive shifts); a typical set of signals for the *clocked RS flip-flop* in Fig. 4.5(a) is shown in Fig. 4.5(c). The flip-flop is operated according to these rules:

1. If the S and R inputs are 0s when the clock edge (pulse) occurs, the flip-flop does not change states but remains in its present state.
2. If the S input is a 1 and the R input is a 0 when the clock pulse (positive-going edge) occurs, the flip-flop goes to the 1 state.
3. If the S input is a 0 and the R input is a 1 when the clock pulse occurs, the flip-flop is cleared to the 0 state.
4. Both the S and R inputs should not be 1s when the clock signal's positive-going edge occurs.

Of course, nothing happens to the flip-flop's state between occurrences of the initiating positive-going clock signal. Figure 4.5(c) shows this with a square-wave clock signal. The flip-flop is set to a 1 by the first positive-going edge and to a 0 at the occurrence of the second clock signal. No change occurs at the third positive-going clock edge. The flip-flop is set to 1 again on the fourth edge and remains a 1 until the sixth clock edge occurs. Notice that the S and R inputs can have any value between the clock edges without affecting the operation of the flip-flop. (They can even both be 1s without effect, except when the positive-going edge occurs.)

Figure 4.5(d) shows typical waveforms for the flip-flop in Fig. 4.5(b). This flip-flop is *negative-edge-triggered* because it responds to shifts in the clock level that are negative-going. The rules of operation are as before: 0s on S and R lead to no change; a 1 on S sets the flip-flop; and a 1 on R clears the flip-flop. The flip-flop responds to the S and R inputs only at the precise time the clock input goes negative.

4.3   FLIP-FLOP DESIGNS

Flip-flops can be made from gates; in fact, this is a common practice. Figure 4.6 shows two NOR gates cross-coupled to form an *RS* flip-flop. The cross-coupled NOR gates in Fig. 4.6(a) have two inputs, S and R, and two outputs, Q, and $\overline{Q}$. This configuration realizes the *RS* flip-flop in Fig. 4.6(b).

---

[2] A flip-flop that responds to a rising or falling clock signal (as opposed to responding to a dc level) is called an *edge-triggered* or *master-slave* flip-flop for reasons that will be explained.

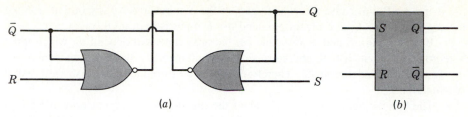

FIGURE 4.6
RS flip-flop formed by cross-coupling NOR gates. (*a*) Cross-coupled NOR gates. (*b*) *RS* flip-flop corresponding to (*a*).

The operation of the NOR gates is as follows: Consider both S and R to be 0s. If Q is a 1, the the rightmost NOR gate has a 1 input and a 0 input, so its output will be a 0. This places a 0 on the $\overline{Q}$ output and two 0s at the inputs to the leftmost NOR gate, which will have a 1 output, and the configuration will be stable. Similar reasoning will show that the configuration will be stable with a 1 on $\overline{Q}$ and a 0 on Q.

The S and R inputs work as follows: If a 1 is placed on the R input and a 0 on the S input, this will force the leftmost NOR gate to a 0 output, which will cause the rightmost NOR gate to have two 0s as inputs and a 1 output. The flip-flop has now been cleared, with a 0 on the Q and a 1 on the $\overline{Q}$ output. Similar reasoning will show that a 1 on the S input and a 0 on the R input will force the NOR gate flip-flop to the 1 state with Q a 1 and $\overline{Q}$ a 0.

Gated Flip-Flop

Just as two NOR gates can be used to form an *RS* flip-flop, Fig. 4.7 shows that two NAND gates can be used to form an *RS* flip-flop (however, the inputs are complemented). In this case, the inputs operate as follows: When both $\overline{S}$ and $\overline{R}$ are 1s, the flip-flop will remain in its present state, that is, it will not change states. If, however, the $\overline{R}$ input goes to a 0, the NAND gate connected to $\overline{R}$ will have a 1 output regardless of the other feedback input to the NAND gate. This will force the flip-flop to the 0 state (provided the $\overline{S}$ input is kept high, or a 1). Similar reasoning shows that making

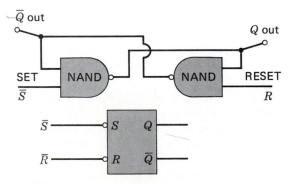

S	R	NEXT STATE
0	0	NOT USED
0	1	1
1	0	0
1	1	NO CHANGE

FIGURE 4.7
Two NAND gates used to form an *RS* flip-flop.

the $\overline{S}$ input a 0 will cause the NAND gate at the $\overline{S}$ input to have a 1 output, forcing the flip-flop to the 1 state (again provided the $\overline{R}$ input is kept high, or 1).

If both inputs $\overline{R}$ and $\overline{S}$ are made 0s, the next state will depend on which input is returned to 1 first. If both are returned to 1 simultaneously, the resulting state of the flip-flop will be indeterminate. Therefore, this is a "forbidden" or "restricted" input combination.

The block diagram in Fig. 4.7 shows the flip-flop to be a conventional *RS* flip-flop, except that the two inputs are inverted. This is shown by the two bubbles at the $\overline{R}$ and $\overline{S}$ inputs. The circuit is activated by 0s, and inputs are normally at 1.

A limited form of clocked flip-flop called a *latch* can be formed by using four NAND gates, as shown in Fig. 4.8(*a*). The circuit has an *R* and an *S* input and also a clock input, CL. This latch flip-flop is activated by a positive level on the clock input, and not by a positive transition. Thus, the flip-flop "takes" its input levels during positive portions of clock signals, not changes in clock levels. Let us see how the circuit works. (Fig. 4.8(*b*) shows a sample waveform.) If the clock signal is at the 0 level, both NAND gates *A* and *B* will have 1 outputs, so the NAND gate inputs to *C* and *D* will be a 1 and, as before, the flip-flop will remain in its present state, with either *C* or *D* on. (Both cannot be on because of the cross-coupling.)

If the clock signal goes to the 1 level and both inputs *R* and *S* are at the 0 level, the NAND gate outputs of *A* and *B* will still be 1s, and the flip-flop will remain in the same state.

If the *R* input is a 1 and the *S* input a 0, when the clock input goes positive (a 1), the NAND gate connected to *R* will have a 0 output and the NAND gate connected to *S* a 1 output, forcing the flip-flop consisting of *C* and *D* to the 0 state.

Similarly, a 1 at the *S* input and a 0 at the *R* input during a positive clock signal will cause gate *A* to have a 0 output and gate *B* a 1 output, forcing the flip-flop to the 1 state.

If both *S* and *R* are 1s and a clock pulse (0 level to 1 level and back to 0) occurs, the next state of the circuit is indeterminate.

A major problem with this circuit is that the *R* and *S* input should remain unchanged during the time the clock is a 1. This considerably limits the use of the circuit, leading to more complicated circuits that can offer the designer more flexibility. The primary value of the circuit is its simplicity.

The block diagram for a latch is the same as for an edge-triggered flip-flop, except for the small triangle at the clock input for edge-triggered flip-flops as opposed to the use of CL for the latch.

Often designers identify latches on block diagrams so that users will realize that the state taken by the flip-flop is determined by the *R* and *S* inputs during the positive clock level, and not at the edge of the clock signal.

Manufacturers often put a number of latches in a single IC package. In this case, a special kind of flip-flop, called the *D* flip-flop, is often used. A *D*-type latch flip-flop is shown in Fig. 4.8(*c*). The advantage of this is the single *D* input. The *D* flip-flop takes the value at its *D* input whenever the clock pulse input is high. It will effectively "track" input levels as long as the clock input is high, as shown in Fig. 4.8(*d*). If the clock input is lowered, the state will be the last state the flip-flop had when the clock input was high. If the clock input returns to 0 just before or during a transition in the input to the *D* latch, the final state the flip-flop takes will depend

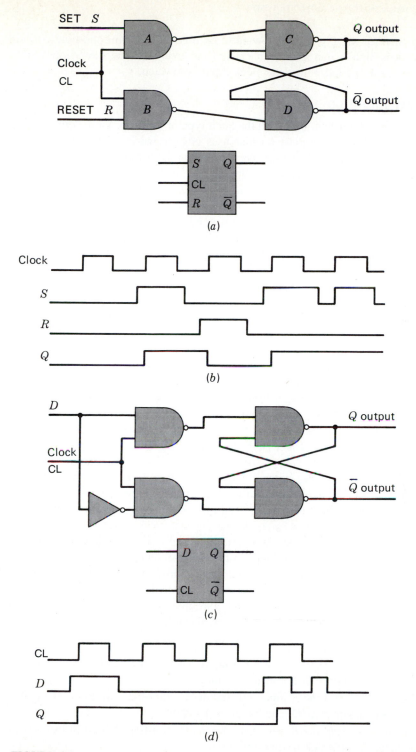

FIGURE 4.8
Latches. (*a*) *RS* latch. (*b*) *RS* flip-flop waveforms. (*c*) *D* latch. (*d*) Waveforms for *D* latch.

on the delay time for the flip-flop. Allowing input transitions during the time period when the clock is high is dangerous, unless there is assurance that the D input will not change for a safe period before the clock input is lowered.

Master-Slave Flip-Flop

To eliminate the problems that arise with the latch type of flip-flop, more complicated flip-flop designs are used. the most popular uses edge-triggering from the clock to initiate changes in the flip-flop's output and is based on the use of two single or latch flip-flops to form a single edge-triggered flip-flop.

The basic flip-flop design is shown in Fig. 4.9. Figure 4.9(*a*) shows that an edge-triggered RS flip-flop consists of two flip-flops plus some gating. The two flip-flops are called the *master* and the *slave*. An expanded logic diagram for Fig. 4.9(*a*) is shown in Fig. 4.9(*b*), in which the master flip-flop is composed of the leftmost NAND gates and the slave flip-flop of the rightmost NAND gates.

The expanded diagram in Fig. 4.9(*b*) can be used to explain the flip-flop's operation. The flip-flop's output changes on the negative-going edge of the clock pulse. The basic timing is also shown in Fig. 4.9(*b*). First, on the positive-going edge and during the positive section of the clock pulse, the master flip-flop is loaded by the two leftmost NAND gates. Then, during the negative-going edge of the clock signal, the two rightmost NAND gates load the contents of the master flip-flop into the slave flip-flop just after the two-input NAND gates are disabled. This means that the master flip-flop will not change in value while the clock is low (0); thus, the slave remains attached to a stable flip-flop, with a value taken during the positive section of the clock pulse.

A more detailed account of the action of the flip-flop is as follows: If the clock signal is low, the two-input NAND gates both have 1 outputs; so the master flip-flop does not change states, since it is a NAND gate flip-flop and can be set or cleared only by 0 inputs.

At the same time, as long as the clock signal is low (a 0), the inverter causes the inputs to the E and F NAND gates to force the value of the master flip-flop into the slave flip-flop. The situation is stable. The master cannot change, and the output flip-flop is "slaved" to the master.

When the clock starts positive, however, the E and F NAND gates are disabled, and NAND gates A and B to the master flip-flop are then enabled.

When the input clock signal is a 1, the master flip-flop will accept information from the S and R inputs; the slave flip-flop is now isolated from the master and will not change states regardless of changes in the master.

The master flip-flop operates according to the following rules when the clock level is a 1:

1. If both S and R are at 0 levels, the two input NAND gates will have 1 outputs, and the master flip-flop will not change values.
2. If the S input is a 1 and the R input a 0, the master flip-flop will go to its 1 state, with the upper master NAND gate having a 1 output.
3. If the S input is a 0 and the R input a 1, the master flip-flop will go to its 0 state, with the upper NAND gate having a 0 output.
4. If both R and S are 1s, the final state is indeterminate.

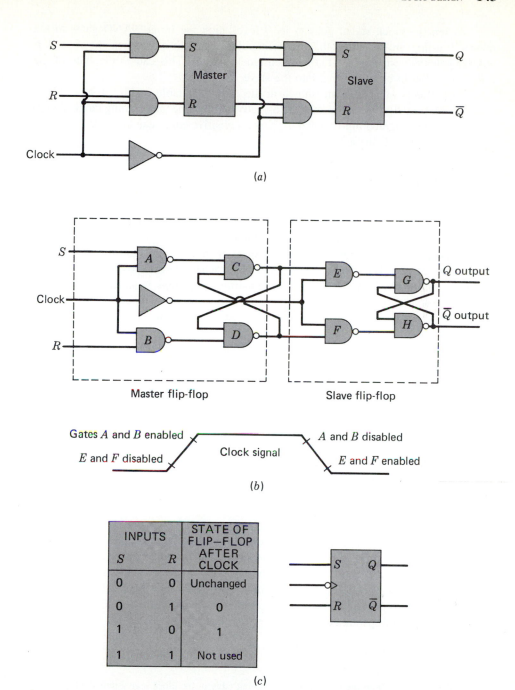

FIGURE 4.9
(*a*) *RS* clocked edge-triggered flip-flop. (*b*) Gate arrangement for master-slave flip-flop. (*c*) Master-slave flip-flop state table and symbol.

When the clock signal goes to its 0 level, first the input NAND gates to the master flip-flop are disabled; that is, each output goes to a 1. Then the E and F NAND gates are enabled (by the inverted clock signal). This causes the state of the master flip-flop to be transferred into the slave flip-flop.

The effects of all this are shown in the next-state table in Fig. 4.9(c), which indicates that the flip-flop is an RS flip-flop activated by a negative-going clock signal.

An edge-triggered flip-flop that triggers on positive edges can be made by adding an inverter at the CL input.

4.4   SHIFT REGISTER

Figure 4.10 shows a *shift register*. This circuit accepts information from some input source and then shifts this information along the chain of flip-flops, moving it one flip-flop each time a positive-going clock signal occurs.

Figure 4.10 also shows a typical sequence of input signals and flip-flop signals in the shift register. The input value is taken by X_1 when the first positive-going clock signal arrives.[3] Anything in this and the remaining flip-flops is shifted right at this time. (We have assumed that all the flip-flops are initially in their 0 states.) In the figure, the input waveform is at 1 when the first clock occurs, so X_1 goes to the 1 state.

When the second positive-going clock signal arrives, the input is at 0: so X_1 goes to the 0 state, and the 1 from X_1 is shifted into X_2. When the third clock edge appears, the input is a 1; so X_1 takes a 1, the 0 previously in X_1 is shifted into X_2, and the 1 from X_2 goes into X_3. This process continues. The values in X_3 are simply dropped off the end of the register.

Notice that each flip-flop takes the value in the flip-flop on its left when the shift register is stepped. The reasoning is as follows: If, for instance, X_1 is in the 1 state, then its X output line is a 1 and, thus, the S input to X_2 will be a 1 also, the $\overline{X}$ output of X_1 will be a 0, and so the R input of X_2 will be a 0. This causes X_2 to take its 1 state when the clock pulse occurs. A 0 in X_1 will cause X_2 to go 0 when the clock pulse occurs.

There is one problem that could occur if certain design precautions were not taken with the flip-flops. If the flip-flop outputs changed too fast, or if latches were used, a state could ripple, or race, down the chain. This is called the *race problem*. It is handled by designing flip-flops so that they take the value at their inputs just as the clock's positive-going edge occurs, and not slightly after the clock's rise time. This leads to the complexity in flip-flop design, which has been discussed. Edge-triggered (master-slave) flip-flops are necessary for proper operation.

---

[3] There is some delay from the time the positive-going edge of the clock signal tells the flip-flop to "go" until the flip-flop's outputs are able to change values. The clock signal itself will also require a small amount of time to rise, for physical reasons. For present systems, the rise time on the clock signals, that is, the time to 90 percent of total rise, ranges from about 1×10^{-9} to about 50×10^{-9} s. The delay from the clock signal change until a flip-flop's output changes 90 percent, which is called the *delay time*, ranges from 10.5×10^{-9} to 50×10^{-9} s for most circuits.

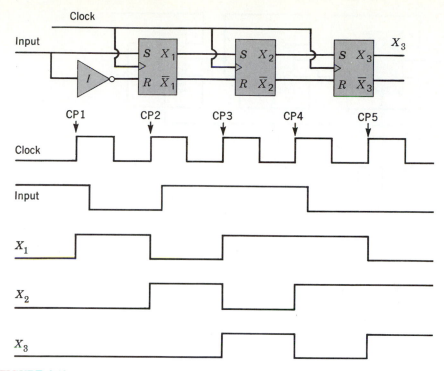

FIGURE 4.10
Shift register with waveforms.

4.5 BINARY COUNTER

Inasmuch as the binary counter is one of the most useful logical circuits, there are many kinds. The fundamental purpose of the binary counter is to record the number of occurrences of some input. This is a basic function, and it is used over and over.

The first type of binary counter to be explained is shown in Fig. 4.11. This counter records the number of occurrences of a positive-going edge (or pulse) at the input.

It is desirable to start this counter with 0s in all three flip-flops so an extra line is added to each flip-flop: a DC RESET line. This line is normally at the 0 level; when it goes positive, or to 1, it places a 0 in the flip-flop. This action does not depend on the clock. When a DC RESET line is at the 1 level, the flip-flop goes to 0 regardless of any other input and in the absence or presence of a clock pulse. It is quite common for a flip-flop to have a DC RESET line. Notice that this input "overrides" all other inputs when it is a 1, forcing the flip-flop to the 0 state. A 0 on this line, however, does not affect flip-flop operation in any way.

Before counting begins, then, a 1 is placed temporarily on the DC RESET line, clearing the three flip-flops to 0. The RESET line is then returned to 0.

When the first positive edge of the clock occurs, flip-flop X_1 goes to its 1 state. This is because when flip-flop X_1 is in the 0 state, the $\overline{X}_1$ output is high, placing a

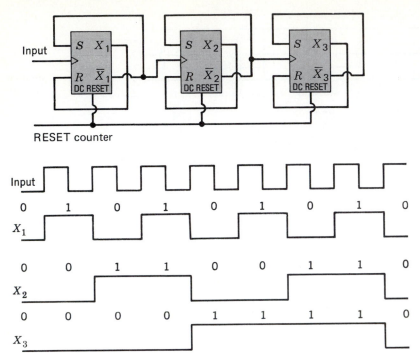

RESET counter

FIGURE 4.11
Binary counter.

1 on the S input (refer to Fig. 4.11), and the X_1 output is low, placing a 0 on the R input; therefore, a 1 goes into flip-flop X_1.

Flip-flops X_2 and X_3 are not affected by this change, for although the $\overline{X}_1$ output is connected to the clock input of X_2, the signal has gone from 1 to 0. This is a negative shift, which does nothing to X_2.

The counter now has $X_3 = 0$, $X_2 = 0$, and $X_1 = 1$, or binary 001. Thus, the first input clock edge has stepped the counter from 000 to 001.[4]

The occurrence of the second positive-going clock edge causes flip-flop X_1 to go from the 1 state to the 0 state. The reasoning is as follows: When X_1 is a 1, the X_1 output is a 1 and is connected to the R input; the $\overline{X}_1$ output is a 0 and is connected to the S input. This tells the flip-flop to reset to 0 at the second clock pulse.

This is important: When a flip-flop is cross-coupled, that is, when its uncomplemented output is connected to its R input and its complements output to its S

---

[4] Note that the binary numbers are written in the opposite direction from the block diagram layout, which has the least significant bit on the left. This makes for a neater block diagram and is frequently used. The standards, in fact, ask for left-to-right signal flow.

input, the occurrence of a clock edge will always cause it to *complement*, or change values.

The change of value from 1 to 0 of flip-flop X_1 causes X_2 to change from a 0 to a 1. This is because the $\overline{X}_1$ output is connected to the CL input of X_2 and has gone from 0 to 1, a positive shift; and since X_2 is cross-coupled, it will complement (change values) and go from 0 to 1. This does no affect X_3, whose CL input has gone from 1 to 0, a negative shift.

The counter has now progressed to $X_1 = 0, X_2 = 1$, and $X_3 = 0$, so the sequence of states has been 000, 001, 010.

Further reasoning of this type will show that the progression of states by the counter is as follows:

X_3	X_2	X_1
0	0	0
0	0	1
0	1	0
0	1	1
1	0	0
1	0	1
1	1	0
1	1	1
0	0	0
0	0	1
0	1	0

This is a list of binary numbers from 0 to 7, which repeats over and over. After five input pulses, the counter contains 101, or binary 5; after seven pulses, the counter contains 111, or binary 7. The maximum number of pulses this counter can handle without ambiguity is seven. After eight pulses, the counter contains 0; after nine pulses, 1; and so on. In the trade this is called a *modulo 8*, or *three-stage*, counter.

The counter can be extended by another flip-flop, X_4, which is also cross-coupled and has its CL input connected to the output of flip-flop $\overline{X}_3$. This forms a *four-stage*, or *modulo 16*, counter, which can handle up to 15 counts. A fifth flip-flop would form a counter which would count to 31, a sixth to 63, and so.

We now consider a *gated-clocked binary counter*. This is an exceedingly popular counter in modern computers, and it demonstrates the fact that most operations are *enabled* by logic levels and activated by clock signals. The preceding counter is called a *ripple counter* because changes "ripple" down the flip-flop chain.

In Fig. 4.12 the ENABLE input to the first flip-flop in the chain, X_1, goes to two AND gates, which also have the outputs of the flip-flop as inputs. If the ENABLE signal is a 0, the two AND gates will have 0 outputs, and X_1 will remain in the same state regardless of how many clock pulses occur.

When the ENABLE signal is a 1, however, the outputs from flip-flop X_1 cause that flip-flop to change values whenever a clock pulse occurs. Thus, the counter

ENABLE

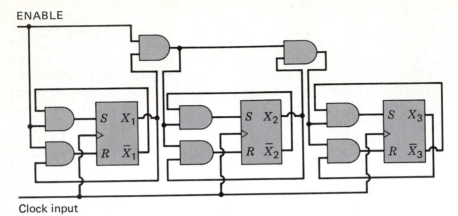

Clock input

FIGURE 4.12
Gated-clocked binary counter.

records the number of clock pulses that occur while the ENABLE is on. Flip-flop X_2 will change only when X_1 is a 1, the ENABLE signal is a 1, and a positive-going clock signal occurs. Similarly, X_3 will change states only when X_1 and X_2 are 1s, the ENABLE is a 1, and a clock positive edge occurs.

The two AND gates combined with an RS flip-flop in Fig 4.12 are so useful that most popular lines of flip-flops contain in a single integrated-circuit container the flip-flop and its two AND gates, as shown in Fig. 4.13(a).

Figure 4.13(b) shows another very popular and useful flip-flop, which consists of the RS flip-flop and its two AND gates, but with the cross-coupling of the AND gates made permanent. In this form the two lines taken outside are called J and K, and the flip-flop is called a JK flip-flop. Analysis of this flip-flop indicates that the J and K inputs act just as RS inputs for two 0 inputs—the flip-flop never changes states. With a 0 on J and a 1 on K, the flip-flop goes to the 0 state when a clock positive edge appears; with a 1 on J and a 0 on K, the flip-flop goes to 1 when a clock positive edge appears. The significant fact is that when both J and K are 1s, the flip-flop always changes states when a clock positive edge appears.

The flip-flops in Fig. 4.13(a) and (b) both have DC RESET and DC SET inputs. The bubbles at the input on the block diagram indicate that these are activated by 0 inputs and are normally held at a 1 level. When, for instance, a 0 is placed on the DC SET input, the flip-flop goes to a 1 level regardless of the clock or other inputs. DC SET and DC RESET should not be 0s at the same time; this is forbidden and leads to an undetermined next state.

It is a general rule that bubbles, or small circles, at the DC SET and DC RESET inputs mean that these inputs are activated by 0 levels. The absence of bubbles means that the inputs are activated by 1 levels and are normally at 0.

There is one other type of edge-triggered flip-flop now in general use, the D flip-flop. This flip-flop simply takes the value at its input when a clock pulse appears and remains in the same state until the next clock pulse appears. As shown in Fig. 4.13(c),

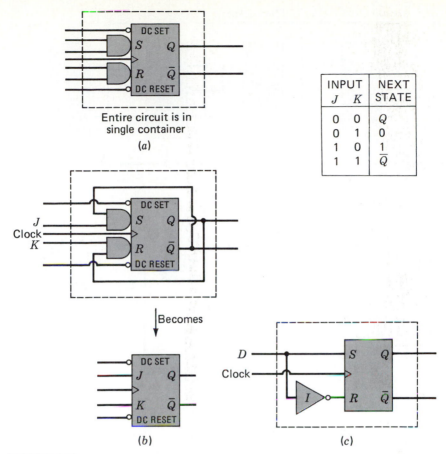

INPUT		NEXT
J	K	STATE
0	0	Q
0	1	0
1	0	1
1	1	$\overline{Q}$

FIGURE 4.13

JK and *D* flip-flops. (*a*) *RS* flip-flop with AND gates. (*b*) How a *Jk* flip-flop is made from an *RS* flip-flop. (*c*) *D* flip-flop.

the *D* flip-flop can be made from an *RS* flip-flop and an inverter. The operation is essentially the same as that of the *D* latch previously explained, except the *D* flip-flop operates on a clock edge and the latch is activated by a clock level.

The *D* flip-flop is very useful because, when clocked, it takes the state on its input and holds it until clocked again. Only a single input line is needed for a transfer, whereas the *RS* or *JK* flip-flops require two input lines.

Examples of the use of *JK* flip-flops are shown in Fig. 4.14(*a*) and (*b*). Figure 4.14(*a*) shows the simplicity of a gated binary counter made with *JK* flip-flops. Figure 4.14(*b*) shows a block diagram for a *binary up-down counter*. When the UP ENABLE line is high, or a 1, the counter will count up, that is, 0, 1, 2, 3, 4, ... When the DOWN ENABLE line is a 1, the counter will count down, that is, 6, 5, 4, ... In general, the counter will increase its value by 1 if the UP ENABLE line is a 1 and

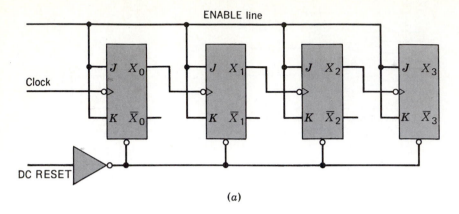

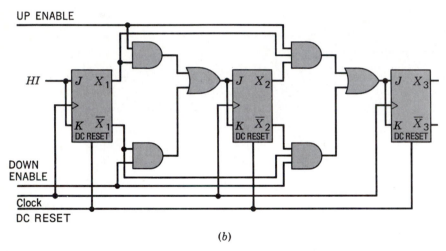

FIGURE 4.14
Binary counters made with *JK* flip-flops. (*a*) Gated ripple counter. (*b*) Up-down counter.

a clock pulse arrives, and it will decrease its value by a 1 if the DOWN ENABLE input is a 1 and the clock pulse occurs.

A DC RESET line is provided, which is used to reset the counter to 0. This is activated by a 1.

4.6 BCD COUNTERS

The binary counters considered so far count to the limit before resetting to all 0s. Often it is desirable to have counters count in binary-coded decimal (BCD). Figure 4.15(*a*) shows a typical BCD counter. Examination of this counter shows that it counts normally until it reaches 1001; that is, the sequence until that time is as follows:

Carry out

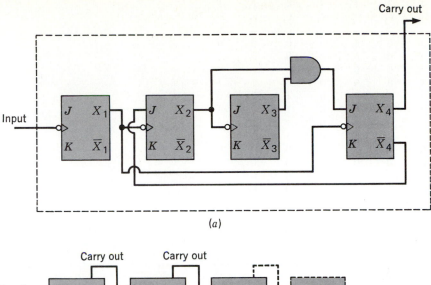

(a)

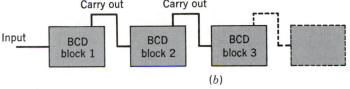

(b)

FIGURE 4.15
BCD counters. (*a*) Decade, or BCD, counter. (*Note*: Unconnected inputs are 1s.) (*b*) Cascading BCD counter blocks.

X_4	X_3	X_2	X_1
0	0	0	0
0	0	0	1
0	0	1	0
0	0	1	1
0	1	0	0
0	1	0	1
0	1	1	0
0	1	1	1
1	0	0	0
1	0	0	1

When the next negative-going edge at the input occurs, however, the BCD counter returns to all 0s. At the same time (that is, during the interval when the counter goes from 9 to 0), a negative-going signal edge occurs at the CARRY output. This CARRY output can be connected to the input of another BCD counter, which will then be stepped by 1 when the first BCD stage goes from 9 to 0. This is shown in Fig. 4.15(*b*), where several four-flip-flop BCD stages are combined to make a large counter.

If we consider just two of the "BCD boxes," we find the sequence to be as follows:

8 Y_4	4 Y_3	2 Y_2	1 Y_1	8 X_4	4 X_3	2 X_2	1 Y_1	Value of bits
0	0	0	0	0	0	0	0	
0	0	0	0	0	0	0	1	
0	0	0	0	0	0	1	0	
0	0	0	0	0	0	1	1	
0	0	0	0	0	1	0	0	
0	0	0	0	0	1	0	1	
0	0	0	0	0	1	1	0	
0	0	0	0	0	1	1	1	
0	0	0	0	1	0	0	0	
0	0	0	0	1	0	0	1	
0	0	0	1	0	0	0	0	
0	0	0	1	0	0	0	1	
.	.	.	.	.	.	.	.	
0	0	0	1	1	0	0	1	
0	0	1	0	0	0	0	0	
0	0	1	0	0	0	0	1	
.	.	.	.	.	.	.	.	

Here we have counted to 21. This would continue until the counter reached 99, when the Y stage would put out a signal that could be used to gate another stage, forming a counter that could count to 999. This repetition of various "boxes," or "modules," for a BCD counter is facilitated by manufacturers placing an entire four-stage BCD counter in a single integrated-circuit container.

One point should again be noted about the block diagram in Fig. 4.15(*a*). The flip-flops are activated by negative-going shifts in input levels. This is indicated by the small circles at the inputs. As a result, a flip-flop such as X_3 is activated when X_2 goes from a 1 to a 0, that is, when the output makes a negative transition.

Also note that unconnected inputs, such as the K inputs of all the flip-flops and the J inputs of X_1 and X_3, are at 1 levels. This is due to the circuit construction.

4.7 INTEGRATED CIRCUITS

The flip-flops and gates used in modern computing machines—which range from calculators and microcomputers to the large, high-speed computers—are constructed and packaged using what is called *integrated-circuit technology*. When integrated circuits are used, gates or flip-flops are packaged in integrated-circuit (IC) containers. The IC containers provide input and output pins or connections, which are interconnected by plated strips on circuit boards, wires, or other means to form complete computing devices.

Two typical IC containers are shown in Fig. 4.16(a). One is called a *dual inline package* (in the trade it is called a "coffin" or a DIP); this particular package has 14 pins for external connections. For years 14-pin and 16-pin packages were standard in the industry, and plastic and ceramic DIPs of this sort were the largest-selling IC packages.

As IC technology has improved, however, there has been a tendency to increase the number of pins per package. Packages with up to 40 pins are popular, and packages with up to 200 pins can now be found in some IC manufacturers' products.

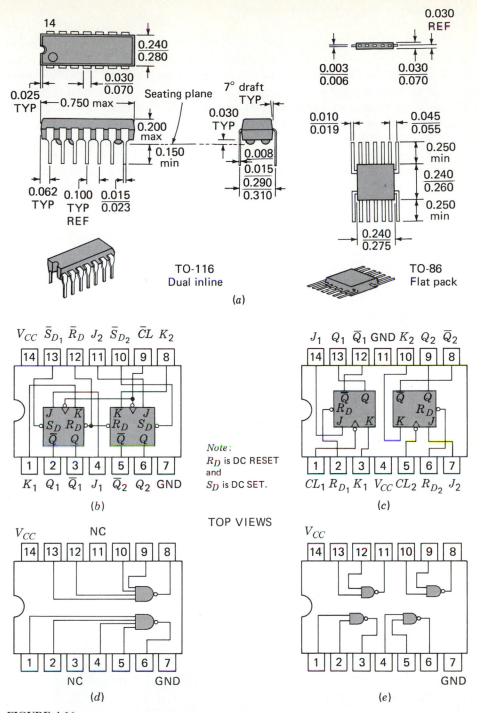

FIGURE 4.16
IC containers and flip-flop and gate circuits. (*a*) Dual inline and flat-pack IC containers. (*b*) Dual *JK* flip-flop with common clock and resets and separate sets. (*c*) Dual *JK* flip-flop with separate resets and clocks. (*d*) Dual four-input NAND gates. (*e*) Quadruplex two-input NAND gates.

153

Figure 4.16(*b*) through (*e*) shows how several gates and flip-flops are packaged in a single container. The inputs and outputs are numbered, and each number refers to an external pin on the IC container. A ground connection and a positive power voltage are both required for each container, so that only 12 pins remain to be used for the actual inputs and outputs to gates and flip-flops. (For these circuits, the V_{CC} pin is connected to a 5.5-V power supply and GND to 0 V or system ground.)

The particular circuits in Fig. 4.16 are made in *transistor-transistor logic* (TTL) circuits and (CMOS). These circuits have a 3.5-V level for a 1 and 0.2-V level for a 0 (see Chapter 12 for details). The particular configurations shown are manufactured by just about every major IC manufacturer, and packages from one manufacturer can be fairly easily substituted for another manufacturer's packages (provided the speed requirements or loading capabilities are not violated). There are many other packages with, for instance, three 3-input NAND gates, two *RS* flip-flops, exclusive OR gates, etc.

To illustrate the use of IC packages in logic design, we now examine an implementation of Fig. 4.17 using the packages shown in Fig. 4.16. The logic circuit in Fig. 4.17 is called a *shift register with feedback,*[5] for it consists of four flip-flops connected in a shift-register configuration and "feedback" from these four flip-flops to the first flip-flop's inputs. This particular counter is started by setting a 1 in X_1 and 0s in X_2, X_3, and X_4. The sequence of states taken is then

---

[5] This particular type of shift register with feedback is so widely used that complete books have been written about it. It is sometimes called a *linear shift register,* a *random sequence generation,* or a *linear recurring sequence generator.* With similar feedback connections, a register can be made with as many flip-flops as desired, thus forming counters with sequences of $2^N - 1$ for any reasonable N (where N is the number of flip-flops).

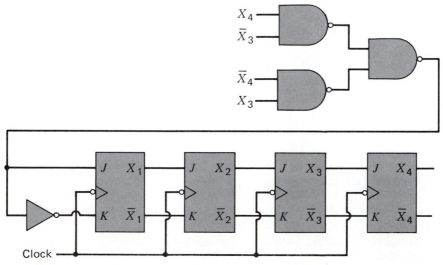

FIGURE 4.17
Shift register with feedback.

1	0	0	0	
0	1	0	0	
0	0	1	0	
1	0	0	1	
1	1	0	0	
0	1	1	0	
1	0	1	1	Basic sequence, which repeats
0	1	0	1	
1	0	1	0	
1	1	0	1	
1	1	1	0	
1	1	1	1	
0	1	1	1	
0	0	1	1	
0	0	0	1	
1	0	0	0	
0	1	0	0	

Notice that this sequence contains 15 of the 16 possible 4-bit numbers that might be represented by this circuit. (Only the all-0 combination is excluded.) This is a sequence that has many uses in radar systems, sonar systems, coding encryption boxes, and other instruments.

The sequence of states assumed by a logic circuit is often specified in a *counter table*. The counter table for the above sequence is

X_1	X_2	X_3	X_4
1	0	0	0
0	1	0	0
0	0	1	0
1	0	0	1
1	1	0	0
0	1	1	0
1	0	1	1
0	1	0	1
1	0	1	0
1	1	0	1
1	1	1	0
1	1	1	1
0	1	1	1
0	0	1	1
0	0	0	1

In the counter table, the flip-flops' names are first listed, followed by the starting states. Then the successive states taken are listed in order, and the final line contains the state preceding the starting state.

There is a straightforward technique for designing a logic circuit to realize a counter table; this technique is developed in a later section. For now, we return to the implementation of the counter in Fig. 4.17.

To implement this counter, we require four flip-flops and a gate circuit to yield $\overline{X_3}X_4 + X_3\overline{X_4}$. As shown, this can be made with a NAND-to-NAND gate network with three 2-input NAND gates. An inverter is also required. (A NAND gate can be used for this by connecting both inputs.)

One problem remains: We need to start the counter with X_1 in state 1 and the other three flip-flops in state 0. Since DC RESET inputs are connected on the flip-flops [see Fig. 4.16(b)], it is necessary to use a trick for flip-flop X_1. This simply involves renaming the J and K inputs and the two outputs so that J becomes K, K becomes J, and the two output names are reversed. The DC RESET input then becomes a DC SET input for the new (renamed) flip-flop. Figure 4.18 shows the circuit as finally designed. Notice how X_1 differs in connections from X_2 and X_3.

The logic circuit in Fig. 4.18 could be implemented by using a printed-circuit board to make the connections between IC containers. Or the connections could be made with individual wires by using any of a number of interconnection boards manufactured by various companies. Placing a 0 (ground) on the DC RESET input sets the flop-flops to the desired starting conditions: the circuit will then step through the desired states.

There are several major lines of integrated circuits now being produced in substantial quantities. Table 4.1 lists several basic lines and gives some of the characteristics of each line. The IC lines listed in the table (except for CMOS) are called *bipolar logic* because they utilize conventional transistors in the IC packages; the CMOS lines use what are called *field-effect transistors* (FETs) and are fabricated using metal-oxide semiconductor (MOS) technology. The bipolar logic lines are widely used for configurations on circuit boards that realize high-speed logic. Generally there

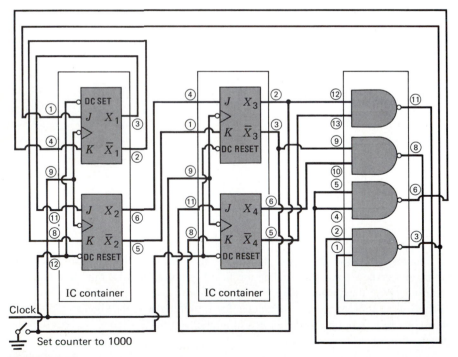

FIGURE 4.18
Design of shift register in Fig. 4.17 using TTL. Circled numbers are pin numbers on IC containers.

TABLE 4.1
IC lines

74XXX	The original TTL family
74LXXX	Lower-power version of standard TTL
74LSXXX	Low-power Schottky TTL; widely used
74SXXX	Early Schottky (TTL)
74ALSXXX	Advanced low-power Schottky
74ASXXX	Advanced Schottky
74CXXX	CMOS equivalents to TTL lines
74HCXXX	High-speed CMOS (about like LS TTL)
74HCTXXX	High-speed CMOS with TTL input compatibility
74ACXXX	Advanced CMOS
74ACTXXX	Advanced CMOS with TTL-compatible inputs
ECL	Includes MECL and others; high-speed, high-power, low packing density; MSI only; fastest lines
GaAs	Gallium Arsenide: High Speed, good packing density, expensive

Note: XXX represents three digits. For a given set of three digits each line has the same pin-out. For example, a 74166 8-flip-flop parallel-load shift register has the same pin-out as the 74S166, 74HC166, and 74ALS166, and each package contains the same logic.

are not as many gates and flip-flops in a package using bipolar logic, but these lines are fast and can be interconnected more readily than the MOS lines. The reason is that the bipolar logic lines use more power (primarily more current) for each gate or flip-flop and can, as a result, produce more current and thus drive long cables, long wires, and, in general, additional circuits.

Associated with each gate and flip-flop in a line of integrated circuits are data concerning the gate's or flip-flop's ability to drive other circuits and be driven by other circuits. Typically the manufacturer gives data concerning the delays through the circuit; rise and fall times for output waveforms: the circuit's ability to drive other electrical loads, circuits, and long wires or cables. The manufacturer also generally provides information on how many other inputs to similar gates a given gate can drive (refer to Chapter 12). In its simplest form, every input to every gate and flip-flop is the same, and the manufacturer simply indicates how many inputs can be connected to a given output. Each input is called a *standard load,* and an output is said to be able to drive, for instance, eight standard loads. For some circuit lines, different gates and flip-flop inputs present different loads. Thus, an input to a particular kind of gate might have a number such as 2 or 3 associated with it, and an output may have a drive number such as 12. The designer must see that the sum of the input loads does not exceed the output drive number.

Figure 4.19 shows a binary counter in MSI packaged in a single IC container with 16 pins. The counter has several features:

1. The counter counts up (from 0000 to 1111) if $U/\overline{D}$ is a 1 and down (from 1111 to 0000) if $U/\overline{D}$ is a 0.

2. The four flip-flops can be "loaded" from the four DATA inputs by making the LOAD line a 1 when a clock pulse occurs (the LOAD line is normally a 0, so making it a 1 causes each of DATA input values to be taken by the corresponding flip-flops.).

3. The counter can be gated on or off by the two ENABLE lines.

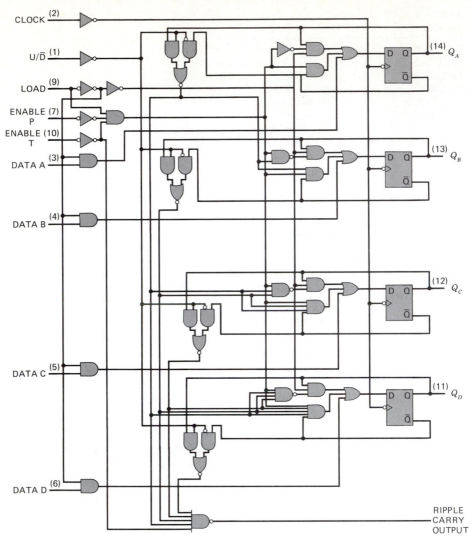

FIGURE 4.19
Binary counter in IC container.

4.8   MEDIUM-, LARGE-, AND VERY LARGE-SCALE INTEGRATION

Most circuits are now fabricated using the general technology of integrated circuitry. The transistors, diodes, resistors, and any other components are fabricated together, using solid state physics techniques, in a single container. In the most common technology, called *monolithic integrated circuitry,* a single semiconductor wafer is processed by photomasking, etching, diffusions, and other steps, thus producing a complete array of diodes, transistors, and resistors already interconnected to form one or more logic gates or flip-flops.

When more than a few flip-flops or gates are packaged in a single container, the process is called *medium-scale integration* (MSI). This name still refers to integrated circuits, but even more circuits are housed in a single container. There are no fixed rules; however, generally, if more than 10 but less than 100 gates or flip-flops are housed in a single package, the manufacturer will refer to it as MSI.

When more than 100 gates or flip-flops are manufactured in a single small container, the process is called *large-scale integration* (LSI). Some notion of the complexity of arrays of this sort is provided in later chapters, where memories and arithmetic-logic units consisting of over one million gates in a single package are studied.

Finally, there is *very large-scale integration* (VLSI), in which 50,000 to several million gates and flip-flops are packaged in a single package. The memories and microprocessors presented in later chapters will illustrate this.

Figure 4.20 shows several integrated circuit packages and how they mount on circuit boards. As the number of gates in a package is increased, more external connections (leads) are required for inputs and outputs.

The dual inline package remains a standard. Connections are made to a circuit board by inserting the leads into holes drilled in the metal conductors on the board and then soldering the contact points. Connectors or sockets are also used, into which the ICs are inserted.

There is also a technology called *surface mounting*, in which IC containers are mounted on pads on the board surface rather than having their leads pushed through holes. This technology and the allied chip carrier packages are popular in large manufacturing operations. Higher density is possible on circuit boards, but placement machines for mounting the chip carrier ICs are expensive.

Despite the various levels of integration, the circuits are surprisingly similar in principle, except that VLSI tends to use a technology based on MOS, whereas MSI, LSI, and "conventional" integrated circuits use "conventional" *npn* and sometimes *pnp* transistors fabricated on silicon chips. There are good reasons for this. MOS circuits require very small chip areas and use very little power, which is quite important given

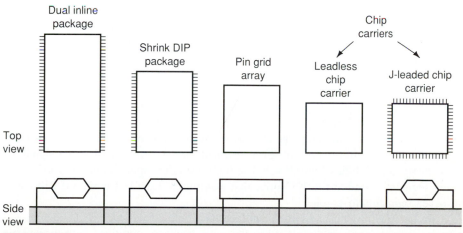

FIGURE 4.20
Integrated circuit packages.

the volume/complexity factor. However, conventional bipolar circuits are faster and more readily interconnected. As a result, MOS technology is used more often for larger arrays treated as complete single units rather than on a circuit-by-circuit basis. MOS is more likely to be used in large memories and microprocessors, for example.

Figure 4.21(a) shows a typical MSI package containing a complete BCD counter. This counter steps from 0 to 9 and then resets to 0 when X_1 (which is pin 5) is connected to clock 2 (which is pin 6). The counter is stepped each time an input clock waveform connected to clock 1 (pin 8) goes negative (i.e., on negative edges). The counter can be reset to the all 0s by connecting a 0 to the RESET line (pin 13). Data from four input wires connected to Y_1, Y_2, Y_3, and Y_4 will be loaded into flip-flops X_1, X_2, X_3, and X_4, respectively, if the LOAD input is pulled down to a 0 (it is normally a 1).

An example of a gate network in an MSI package is shown in Fig. 4.21(b), which shows a *seven-segment decoder*. When decimal numbers are to be read from a digital calculator, instrument, microcomputer, or similar electronic device, display devices using light-emitting diodes (LEDs) or liquid crystals are often used. Each digit of the display is formed from seven segments, each consisting of one light-emitting diode or crystal that can be turned on or off. A typical arrangement is shown in Fig. 4.21(c), which assigns the letters a through g to the segments. To represent the digit 5, for example, segments a, f, g, c, and d are turned on. A set of digits as formed by these segments is shown in Fig. 4.21(d).

The seven-segment decoder in part (b) can be connected to the outputs of the four flip-flops in the BCD counter in part (a) by connecting the X_1, X_2, X_3, and X_4 outputs from part (a) to the X_1, X_2, X_3, and X_4 inputs of (b). If the seven outputs a through f of Fig. 4.21(b) are then connected to the decimal digital display device, a counter with a decimal digit display, as found in the familiar calculator will be formed.

The BCD counter in Fig. 4.21(a) can be extended to several digits by connecting the X_4 output from one digit to the CLOCK 1 input of the next-higher-order digit in the counter.

The seven-segment decoder in Fig. 4.21(b) has the ability to blank leading zeros in a multidigit display, which is commonly done on calculators. Consider a multistage BCD counter connected to several seven-segment decoders, with one decoder per BCD counter stage. If the ripple blanking output (RBO) of each seven-segment decoder is connected to the ripple blanking input (RBI) of the decoder of the next-higher-order digit in the counter, and if the RBI of the most significant digit's decoder is connected to a 0 input, then a blanking circuit will be formed. Then, for instance, in a four-stage counter the number 0014 will have the leading two 0s turned off, or *blanked;* the number 0005 will be displayed as simply 5, with the 0 displays not activated. In effect, the circuit tests for a 0 value at its input. If the value is 0 and all the digits to its left are 0s, the circuit turns off all seven segments and generates a blanking signal for the next rightmost digit's light driver. The light test (LT) input can be used to test all seven segments simultaneously. Notice that making the light test input a 0 will cause all seven segments to go on.

In the MSI products of some manufacturers, both a four-stage BCD counter and a seven-segment decoder are placed in the same package, complete with a blanking input and output for each digit. This gives some feeling for MSI packages.

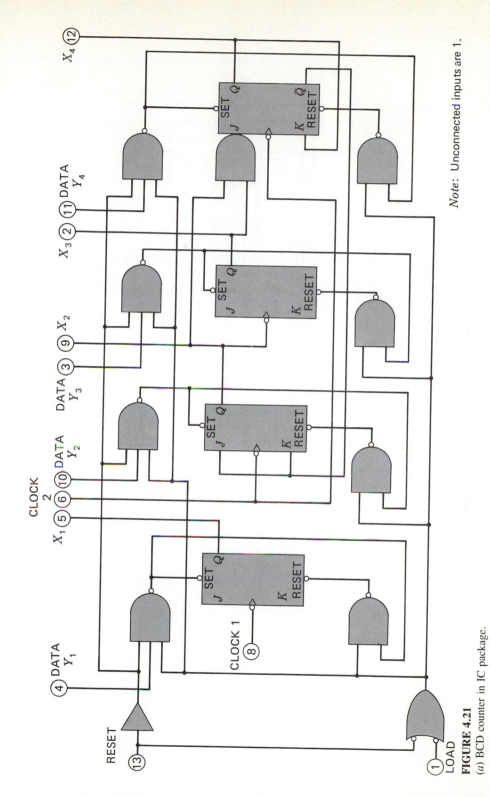

Note: Unconnected inputs are 1.

FIGURE 4.21

(*a*) BCD counter in IC package.

161

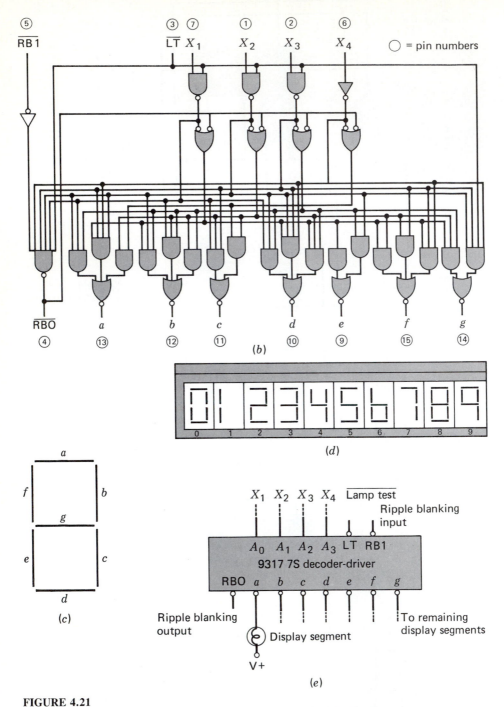

FIGURE 4.21

(b) Logic diagram for seven-segment decoder. (c) Designation for the seven segments. (d) Numbers formed by seven segments. (e) General arrangement for connecting seven-segment decoder.

4.9   COUNTER DESIGN*

The design of a counter to sequence through a given set of states is straightforward. First, a counter table is made up listing the states to be taken. Assume that we wish a counter using three flip-flops to sequence as follows:

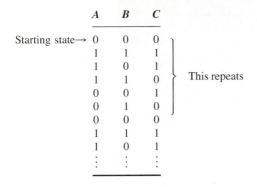

	A	B	C	
Starting state→	0	0	0	
	1	1	1	
	1	0	1	
	1	1	0	This repeats
	0	0	1	
	0	1	0	
	0	0	0	
	1	1	1	
	1	0	1	
	⋮	⋮	⋮	

This table shows that if the counter is in the state $A = 0$, $B = 0$, $C = 0$ and a clock pulse (edge) is applied, the counter is to step to $A = 1$, $B = 1$, $C = 1$. As another example, if $A = 0$, $B = 1$, and $C = 0$ and a clock pulse occurs, the counter is to step to $A = 0$, $B = 0$, $C = 0$. As can be seen, the counter cycles: after taking the state 010, it returns to 000 and then goes to 111, as before. If clock pulses continue, the counter will cycle through the six different states indefinitely.

We use RS flip-flops for our first design. So we give the R input to A the name A^R, the S input to A the name A^S, the R input to B the name B^R, and so on through C^S.

The problem is now to derive boolean algebra expressions for each of the six inputs to the flip-flops. To do this, we place the state table in a *counter design table*, listing the three flip-flops and their states and also listing the six inputs to the flip-flops. This is shown in Fig. 4.22(*a*).

The values for A^R, A^S, B^R, B^S, C^R, C^S are then filled in according to the following rule.

DESIGN RULE

For a specific row in the table and a specific flip-flop:

1. If the flip-flop's state is a 0 in the row and a 0 in the next row, place a 0 in the S input column and a d in the R input column for the flip-flop input.
2. If the flip-flop's state is a 1 in the row and a 1 in the next row, place a 0 in the R input column and a d in the S input column.
3. If the flip-flop's state is a 0 in the row and a 1 in the next row, place a 1 in the S column and a 0 in the R column.
4. If the flip-flop's state is a 1 in the row and a 0 in the next row, place a 1 in the R column and a 0 in the S column.

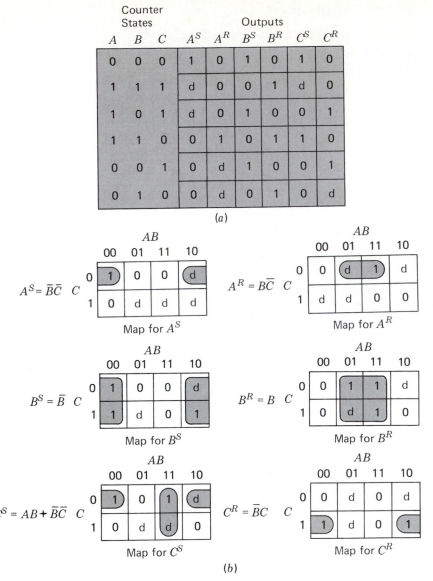

Counter States			Outputs					
A	B	C	A^S	A^R	B^S	B^R	C^S	C^R
0	0	0	1	0	1	0	1	0
1	1	1	d	0	0	1	d	0
1	0	1	d	0	1	0	0	1
1	1	0	0	1	0	1	1	0
0	0	1	0	d	1	0	0	1
0	1	0	0	d	0	1	0	d

(a)

$A^S = \bar{B}\bar{C}\ C$ — Map for A^S

$A^R = B\bar{C}\ C$ — Map for A^R

$B^S = \bar{B}\ C$ — Map for B^S

$B^R = B\ C$ — Map for B^R

$C^S = AB + \bar{B}\bar{C}\ C$ — Map for C^S

$C^R = \bar{B}C\ C$ — Map for C^R

(b)

FIGURE 4.22
Designing a counter using *RS* flip-flops.

As an example, consider flip-flop A in Fig. 4.22(*a*). The flip-flop has the value 0 in the first row and changes to a 1 in the second row. We therefore place a 1 in the column for the A^S in row 1 and a 0 in the column for A^R in row 1. In row 2, A has value 1, and it remains in 1 in row 3. So we fill in a d in column A^S and a 0 in column A^R.

The reasoning behind these rules is as follows: Suppose flip-flop A is in the 0 state and should stay in the 0 state when the next clock pulse is applied. The S input must then be 0, and the R input can be a 1 *or* a 0. Thus, we must have 0 for A^S and can use a d (for don't-care) at the A^R input.

If A is a 0 and should change to a 1, however, and S input to A must be a 1 and the R input a 0 when the next clock pulse is applied. Therefore, a 1 is placed in A^S and 0 in A^R. It is instructive to examine several entries in the counter table in Fig. 4.22(*a*) to see how this rule applies.

Our goal is to generate the flip-flop inputs (A^R, A^S, etc.) for a given row so that when the counter is in the state specified by that row, each input will take the value listed. Then the next clock pulse should cause the counter to step to the state indicated in the next row in the counter table.

A boolean algebra expression is formed from this table for A^R, A^S, B^R, B^S, C^R, and C^S, the inputs to the flip-flops, and then each expression is minimized. This is shown in Fig. 4.22(*b*), which shows the maps for the flip-flops' inputs. Notice that any unused counter states can be included as d's in the map. The minimal expressions are shown beside each map.

The final step is to draw the block diagram for the counter using the minimal expressions. The final design for this counter is shown in Fig. 4.23.

Now suppose that we desire to design the same counter using JK flip-flops. The procedure is basically the same, except that the rules for filling in the counter design table using JK flip-flops differ. The inputs will now be A^J, A^K, B^J, B^K, C^J, and C^K. The rules for JK flip-flops are as follows:

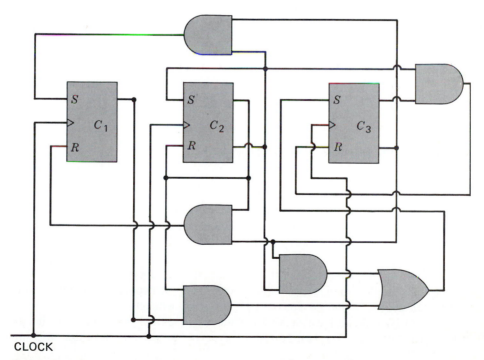

CLOCK

FIGURE 4.23
Counter with RS flip-flops.

DESIGN RULE

For a given flip-flop in a selected row, the J and K inputs to the flip-flop are as follows:

1. If the flip-flop is a 0 in the row and remains a 0 in the next row, place a 0 in the J input column and a d in the K input column.
2. If the flip-flop is a 1 in the row and remains a 1 in the next row, place a 0 in the K input column and a d in the J input column.
3. If the flip-flop is a 0 in the row and changes to a 1 in the next row, place a 1 in the J input column and a d in the K input column.
4. If the flip-flop is a 1 in the row and changes to a 0 in the next row, place a d in the J input column and a 1 in the K input column.

The reasoning behind these rules is as follows: Suppose a given flip-flop (say, A) is in the 0 state and should stay in the same state when the next clock pulse occurs. Input A^K must be a 0 at that time, but A^J can be either a 0 or a 1, so A^J is essentially a d (or don't-care) input. If A must go from a 0 to a 1, the A^K input must be a 1, but the A^J input can be either a 0 or a 1 (since the flip-flop will change states if both inputs are 1s). Notice that there are more d's in the table for JK flip-flops than for RS flip-flops because of the ability of the flip-flops to change states when both inputs are 1s.

The maps for each input to the flip-flops A^J, A^K, B^J, B^K, C^J, and C^K are drawn as before, the expression for each flip-flop's input is minimized, and the block diagram for the counter is then drawn, as shown in Fig. 4.24. Notice that fewer gates are used for the counter in Fig. 4.24 than for that in Fig. 4.23 because of the additional d's in the maps. This will generally, although not always, be the case. (Sometimes the RS and JK designs will be the same; JK flip-flops, however, cannot require more gates for a given counter sequence.)

4.10   STATE DIAGRAMS AND STATE TABLES

A set of interconnected gates with inputs and outputs is called a *combinational network*. The outputs from a combinational network at a given time are completely determined by the inputs at that time. As a result, the function of a combinational network can be described by using a table of combinations that simply lists the input-output values.

When flip-flops are combined with gates, a more complicated situation arises because the flip-flops progress through various states—depending on inputs—and the output can depend on the previous as well as the immediately preceding inputs.

To analyze and design a circuit using both flip-flops and gates, several techniques have been developed. The best known involves the use of *state diagrams* and *state tables*.

A simple design problem requiring flip-flops as well as gates is a *binary sequence detector*. The sequence detector looks for some specified sequence of inputs

A	B	C	A^J	A^K	B^J	B^K	C^J	C^K
0	0	0	1	d	1	d	1	d
1	1	1	d	0	d	1	d	0
1	0	1	d	0	1	d	d	1
1	1	0	d	1	d	1	1	d
0	0	1	0	d	1	d	d	1
0	.1	0	0	d	d	1	0	d

$A^J = \bar{B}\bar{C}$

$$\begin{array}{c|cccc} & \multicolumn{4}{c}{AB} \\ & 00 & 01 & 11 & 10 \\ \hline 0 & 1 & 0 & d & d \\ 1 & 0 & d & d & d \end{array}$$

$A^K = \bar{C}$

$$\begin{array}{c|cccc} & \multicolumn{4}{c}{AB} \\ & 00 & 01 & 11 & 10 \\ \hline 0 & d & d & 1 & d \\ 1 & d & d & 0 & 0 \end{array}$$

$B^J = 1$

$$\begin{array}{c|cccc} & \multicolumn{4}{c}{AB} \\ & 00 & 01 & 11 & 10 \\ \hline 0 & 1 & d & d & d \\ 1 & 1 & d & d & 1 \end{array}$$

$B^K = 1$

$$\begin{array}{c|cccc} & \multicolumn{4}{c}{AB} \\ & 00 & 01 & 11 & 10 \\ \hline 0 & d & 1 & 1 & d \\ 1 & d & d & 1 & d \end{array}$$

$C^J = A + \bar{B}$

$$\begin{array}{c|cccc} & \multicolumn{4}{c}{AB} \\ & 00 & 01 & 11 & 10 \\ \hline 0 & 1 & 0 & 1 & d \\ 1 & d & d & d & d \end{array}$$

$C^K = \bar{B}$

$$\begin{array}{c|cccc} & \multicolumn{4}{c}{AB} \\ & 00 & 01 & 11 & 10 \\ \hline 0 & d & d & d & d \\ 1 & 1 & d & 0 & 1 \end{array}$$

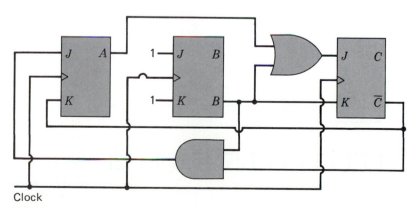

Clock

FIGURE 4.24
Design for a *JK* flip-flop counter.

on a single input line and outputs a 1 when this sequence is found.[6] An example of a specified sequence is three consecutive 1s. In this case, if the sequence detector is presented with the inputs 1001011101, it will output a 0 at all times except immediately following the third 1, when it will output a 1; this is shown in Fig. 4.25. The sequence detector is like a lock that unlocks (outputs a 1) only when the combination (in this case, three consecutive 1s) appears. Sequence detectors can be designed to detect any specified sequence, such as 11011, 1110101, or any other.

Figure 4.26(a) shows a state diagram describing a binary sequence detector that detects three consecutive 1s. A state diagram is formed from what mathematicians call a *directed graph*. State diagrams have *nodes,* which are the circles in Fig. 4.26(a), and *links,* which are the arrows. There are four nodes in Fig. 4.26(a) and eight links.

The nodes in a state diagram correspond to flip-flop states in the final design, so they are also called *states* and given names. For Fig. 4.26(a), the states are named A, B, C, and D. To the right of each state name is a comma, followed by the output value for that state. This corresponds to the output from the detector in Fig. 4.25. For this diagram, if the present state is A, the output is 0; if the state is D, the output is 1; and so forth. Each link of the graph is labeled with the input value $X = 1$ or $X = 0$. These links show how transitions are made from state to state. The X inputs in Fig. 4.26(a) correspond to the X inputs in Fig. 4.25.

The interpretation of the state diagram in Fig. 4.26(a) is as follows. The machine is started in state A, at which time the output is a 0. If the input X is 0 when the first clock pulse arrives, the detector stays in state A and continues to output a 0. This is shown by the loop connected to A and labeled $X = 0$.

If the detector is in state A and a 1 is input (when the clock pulse arrives), the system goes to state B and continues to output a 0.

With the detector in state B, if a 0 is input, the detector goes back to state A and continues to output a 0. If a 1 is input with the detector in state B, the detector goes to state C and continues to output a 0.

---

[6] The sequence of 1s and 0s on the input line occurs in time, and each 1 and 0 is generally clocked into the flip-flops.

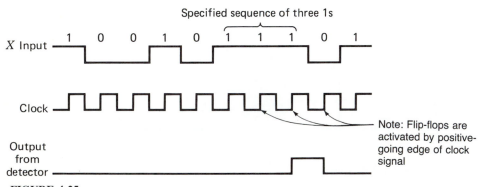

FIGURE 4.25
Input and output waveforms for binary sequence detector.

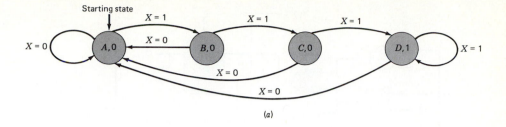

(a)

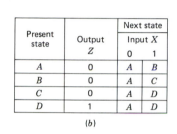

Present state	Output Z	Next state Input X	
		0	1
A	0	A	B
B	0	A	C
C	0	A	D
D	1	A	D

(b)

Z → Output

(c)

Present state $Q_1 Q_2$	Output Z	Next state Input X	
		0	1
00	0	00	01
01	0	00	10
10	0	00	11
11	1	00	11

(d)

$Q_1 \; Q_2$
00 01 11 10

X	0	0	0	0	0
1	0	1	1	1

$D_1 = Q_1 X + Q_2 X$

$Q_1 \; Q_2$
00 01 11 10

X	0	0	0	0	0
1	1	0	1	1

$D_2 = Q_1 X + \bar{Q}_2 X$

Q_1
0 1

Q_2	0	0	0
1	0	1

$Z = Q_1 Q_2$

(e)

FIGURE 4.26
(a) State diagram. (b) State table. (c) Circuit for (a) and (b). (d) State table with assigned values to state flip-flops. (e) Maps for design.

This analysis of the detector's operation can be continued. The important thing is that if the detector is in state C and an input of 1 is given, the detector goes to state D and outputs a 1. If more 1s are input with the machine in state D, it remains in that state and continues to output a 1. If a 0 is input, the detector returns to A.

As can be seen, the detector outputs a 0 until three successive 1s are input, at which time it outputs a 1; this 1 output is continued until a 0 is input.

Figure 4.26(b) is a *state table* representing the same sequence detector as the state diagram in Fig. 4.26(a). There are three major columns in the table; *present state, output,* and *next state.* The interpretation of this table is as follows. If the

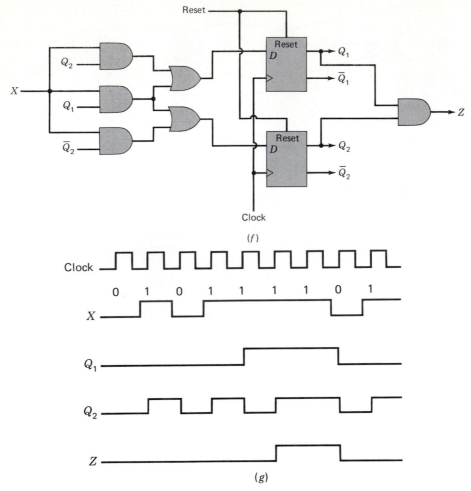

FIGURE 4.26
(*f*) Gates and flip-flops for sequence detector. (*g*) Waveforms for design.

detector is in present state A and a 0 is input, the next state will be A and a 0 will be output. If the system is in state A and a 1 is input, the detector will go to state B and output a 0 while in that state.

If the detector is in state A and two successive 1s are input, the resulting state will be C. If another 1 is input, the detector will go to the D state and a 1 will be output. Inputs of 1 will keep the system in D and the outputs will continue to be 1s until a 0 is input; then the next state will be A and a 0 will be output. The state diagram in Fig. 4.26(*a*) and the state table in Fig. 4.26(*b*) should be compared to see how they describe the same operations.

We now make a design using flip-flops and gates to realize the state diagram and table using integrated circuits. Two flip-flops will be required for the four states A, B, C, and D in the state diagram and table. Figure 4.26(*c*) shows the overall layout, with two flip-flops, a set of gates, an input X, and an output Z. What remains is to design the gate network in Fig. 4.26(c). First, however, it is necessary to assign values to the flip-flops for each of states A, B, C, and D.

A natural assignment of flip-flop values is to let $Q_1 = 0$, $Q_2 = 0$ represent state A; $Q_1 = 0$, $Q_2 = 1$ represent B; $Q_1 = 1$, $Q_2 = 0$ represent C; and $Q_1 = 1$, $Q_2 = 1$ represent D. Replacing A, B, C, and D in Fig. 4.26(b) with this assignment of values leads to the table in Fig. 4.26(d), which is otherwise the same as Fig. 4.26(b).

It is now possible to design the actual gate structure. There are three inputs to the gating network: Q_1 and Q_2, which are the flip-flop outputs, and the X input. There are also three outputs from the gate network; the D inputs to Q_1 and Q_2 and the Z output. Since there are three outputs, three maps are required. The maps for D_1 and D_2 (the inputs to Q_1 and Q_2) will have three inputs: Q_1, Q_2, and X. However, the map for the output has only two inputs, Q_1 and Q_2, since the output Z is determined by the present state of the system and not the current input.

The maps for the system are shown in Fig. 4.26(e), and the complete design is shown in Fig. 4.26(f). A RESET line has been added, which can be used to start the machine. The operation of this design should be checked by noting the resulting states of the flip-flops for several sequences of X inputs. Figure 4.26(g) shows a set of waveforms.

The design in Fig. 4.26(f) is an example of a state machine.[7] The same procedure, involving state diagrams and state tables, can be used to design many things, including interfaces and sections of a computer. In general, a state machine is simply a collection of interconnected flip-flops and gates with a set of inputs and outputs. This is a very general concept, and in following section we treat it in more detail.

4.11 DESIGN OF A SEQUENTIAL MAGNITUDE COMPARATOR

The preceding section described the design of a state machine with a single input and output. The same technique can be used to design a state machine with several inputs and outputs.

Consider the design of a *sequential comparator* whose function is to determine which of two binary numbers A and B, having the same number of bits, is larger. The most significant bits of the numbers are input to the comparator, followed by the second most significant bits, then the next most significant bits, and so on until the least significant bits are presented. (The numbers A and B could be stored in two shift registers.) There are to be two outputs, Z_1 and Z_2. If $A > B$, Z_1 is to be a 1; if $A < B$, Z_2 is to be a 1; and if $A = B$, both Z_1 and Z_2 are to be 0s. Figure 4.27 shows a block diagram of the comparator and a set of waveforms for inputs and outputs.

The design of this comparator is begun by developing a state diagram. The most significant bits of A and B are to be presented first. If the most significant bit of A is 1 and that of B is 0, then $A > B$. Therefore, we can draw a starting node K and a

---

[7] State machines are often called *finite-state machines* in computer science literature, but computer designs and IC manufacturers generally use the shorter form.

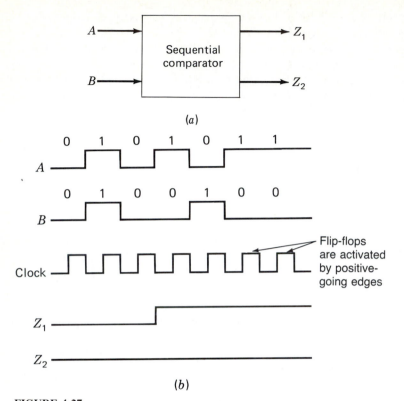

(a)

(b)

FIGURE 4.27
Sequential comparator and waveforms. (*a*) Block diagram. (*b*) Waveforms for two 7-bit binary numbers, A = 0101011 and B = 0100100.

link to a state L with the input value 10 (for A = 1, B = 0); see Fig. 4.28(*a*). The output for the starting state will be Z_1 = 0, Z_2 = 0, or simply 00; the output for state L will be Z_1 = 1 and Z_2 = 0. If the most significant bit of A is 0 and that of B is 1, then $A < B$. Therefore, a third state, M, is added with a link going to it from state K.

If the machine is in state L, no sequence of inputs can change the fact that $A > B$. So a loop with 00, 01, 10, 11 is added to L, indicating that it will stay in that state regardless of the inputs. Similarly, if the comparator is in state M, then $A < B$, and no sequence of inputs can change this relation. Thus, 00, 01, 10, and 11 are placed on a loop leading from M.

If the most significant bits of A and B are the same, the numbers can be equal or either A or B can be larger. So for inputs A = 0 and B = 0, or A = 1 and B = 1, the comparator has next state K and outputs Z_1Z_2 = 00. It can be seen that this process will continue for the next most significant bits used and all those that follow, so the state diagram is complete. As an example, if $A_2A_1A_0$ = 101, or decimal 5, and if $B_2B_1B_0$ = 110, or decimal 6, the state diagram will output 01 after the second bits arrive.

A state table can be made for the state diagram in Fig. 4.28(*a*). This table is shown in Fig. 4.28(*b*).

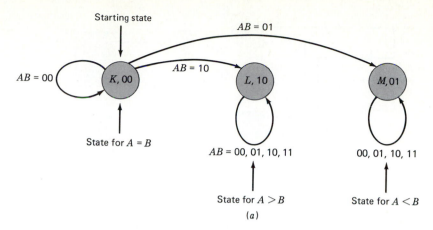

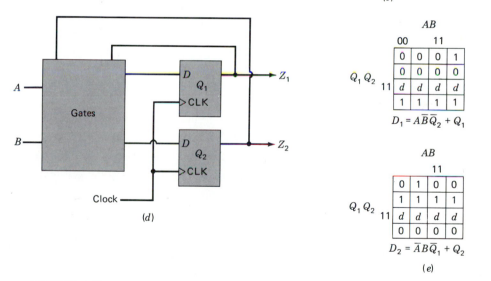

FIGURE 4.28

Design for sequential comparator. (*a*) State diagram. (*b*) State table for (*a*). (*c*) State table for sequential comparator with flip-flop values assigned. (*d*) Block diagram of layout for comparator. (*e*) Maps for sequential comparator.

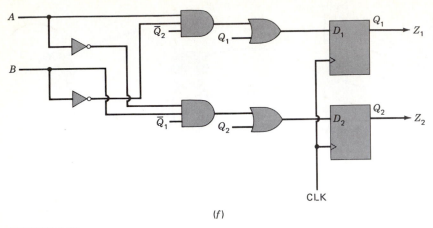

FIGURE 4.28
(*f*) Gate and flip-flop design for sequential comparator.

To design a logic network to realize the state table and state diagram, it is necessary to use flip-flops. Since there are three states, two flip-flops, Q_1 and Q_2 will be used. A natural assignment of states to Q_1 and Q_2 is to let them have the same state as the outputs Z_1 and Z_2. Thus, no gates are required to produce Z_1 and Z_2 since the Q_1 and Q_2 outputs can be used for this purpose.

The resulting state table is shown in Fig. 4.28(*c*). The overall block diagram for the design is shown in Fig. 4.28(*d*). Only the gating network for the two *D* inputs to Q_1 and Q_2 needs to be designed since Z_1 and Z_2 are simply outputs from Q_1 and Q_2. The maps for these two inputs are shown in Fig. 4.28(*e*), and the final design is seen in Fig. 4.28(*f*).

4.12   COMMENTS—MEALY MACHINES

What we have called state machines are also called *sequential machines, sequential systems, sequential circuits,* and *finite-state machines.* Many issues in the theory of computing are concerned with what finite-state machines can compute. A finite-state machine that can read a tape and write on it is called a *Turing machine.* For a Turing machine in which the tape is potentially infinite in length, there have been many interesting results concerning what the machine can compute, some of which are due to Turing, a brilliant early-20th-century mathematician. The references discuss these results.

There are several variations on the state diagrams and design procedures that have been described. When the outputs are determined only by the state of the flip-flops, as in the two previous designs, the machine is called a *Moore machine,* in honor of Edward Moore. When the outputs are determined by the input value as well as the internal state, the machine is called a *Mealy machine.* Figure 4.29 shows a Mealy machine state diagram, state table, block diagram, and some output waveforms. The machine depicted is a sequential detector that looks for three 1s (as in Fig. 4.25). Note that the output values are on the links, not the nodes, in Fig. 4.29(*a*).

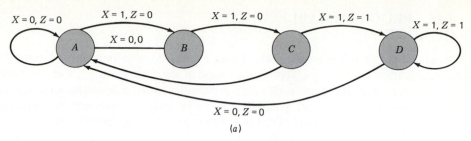

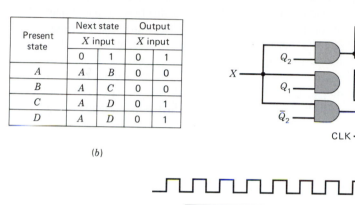

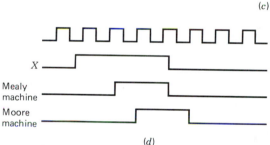

(a)

Present state	Next state		Output	
	X input		X input	
	0	1	0	1
A	A	B	0	0
B	A	C	0	0
C	A	D	0	1
D	A	D	0	1

(b)

(c)

(d)

FIGURE 4.29.
Mealy machine design. (a) State diagram. (b) State table. (c) Design for Mealy version of sequence detector. (d) Waveforms for Mealy and Moore machine designs.

Occasionally it is possible to reduce the number of states in a first design. For completely specified tables, a technique for doing this was discovered by Edward Moore. If not all next states and outputs are specified, the problem is much harder, but Steve Unger solved this problem.[8] The state table of Fig. 4.29, for example, is reducible.

The assignment of values to the flip-flops in the final design can influence the number of gates used, but no one knows how to make the best assignment, short of trying every one possible. This is called the *assignment problem*.

---

[8] Edward Moore did his work at Bell Laboratories, and George Mealy did his at IBM. Both have changed jobs but are still around, as is Steve Unger, who is at Columbia. Detailed descriptions of their work can be found in Birkhoff and Bartee, or in Ed McCluskey's book on switching theory.

4.13 PROGRAMMABLE ARRAYS OF LOGIC*

Integrated-circuit manufacturers have found natural ways to implement layouts for state machines on IC chips. The regular shape of the state machine, with its gating array preceding the flip-flops, makes for a rectangular, ordered design for an integrated circuit. As a result, chips are available that can be used to implement state machine designs in a single IC package. The basic idea is to present the designer with a layout that is sufficiently flexible that most actual designs can be fabricated on this layout.

Figure 4.30 shows the basic block diagram for a state machine. What is needed is a set of flip-flops and a set of gates so that this general structure can be used for many different designs. Figure 4.31 shows a programmable array of logic cells that can be used as a state machine by forming AND gates at the junctions of the vertical lines and connecting the horizontal lines to the OR gates. The particular array shown has three inputs, three flip-flops, and outputs from the flip-flops. The AND-to-OR gate networks are formed as for the PAL in Fig. 3.44; in fact, this particular array is called a PAL.

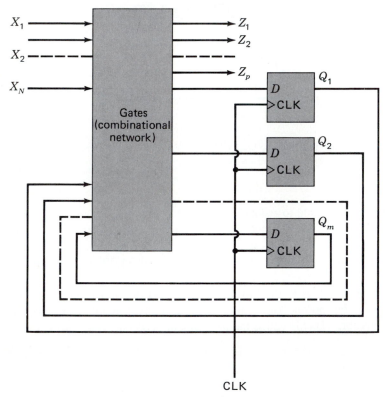

FIGURE 4.30
Block diagram of a state machine.

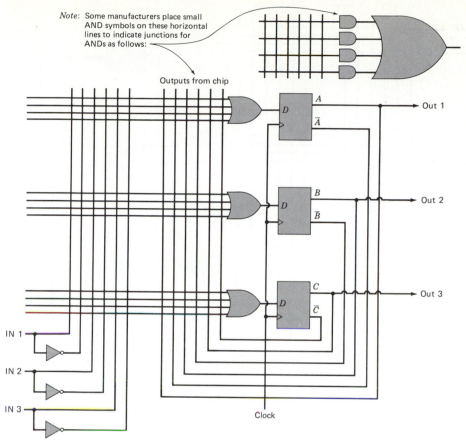

FIGURE 4.31
Programmable array of logic cells.

Figure 4.32 shows the design using the PAL in Fig. 4.31 for the sequence detector in Fig. 4.26. Since there are three flip-flops and three inputs in Fig. 4.32, only part of the logic shown in the figure is used. The idea, however, is that by working from a framework such as Fig. 4.32, most designs can be realized. In this way, the chip can be manufactured in sufficient volumes so that the cost per chip will be less than the cost of assembling a given design from several IC packages with fewer gates and flip-flops per package.

The IC packages on the market at present have up to several thousand gates and flip-flops per package. Sometimes there are several arrays in a single package, enabling the user to form several machines in a single IC container. Figure 4.33 shows a PAL layout for a state machine from a particular manufacturer.

The gating connection required for a particular design using the layout in Fig. 4.33 can be implemented in two ways: (1) The manufacturer works from a submitted design, in which case a particular mask or pattern is made for the design and is

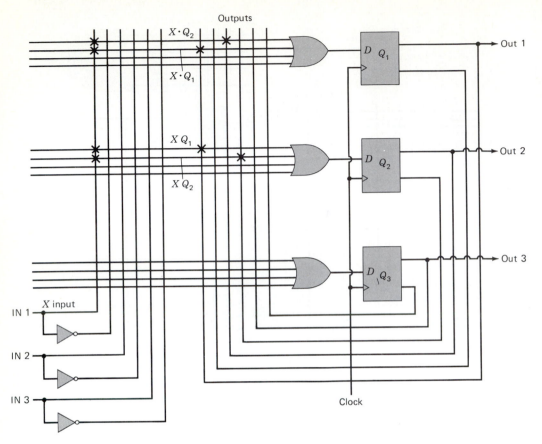

FIGURE 4.32
Design for state machine in Fig. 4.25 using PAL.

used for each chip manufactured. (2) The chip can be user-programmable, in which undesired connections are destroyed by the user (using high currents) blowing fuses.[9]

Arrays of logic cells such as that shown in Fig. 4.33 are becoming increasingly popular and frequently used in commercial and laboratory equipment. Such *semicustom fabrication processes* are very popular in IC manufacture because of the very high cost of designing and manufacturing completely original, or custom, chips.

The PLAs and PALs that have been described are typical of parts produced by a large industry that manufactures programmable logic devices (PLDs). A PLD is a digital integrated circuit that can be altered to provide different logical functions. As a result, a PLD can be used in many applications. PLDs are one of the fastest growing segments of the IC industry.

---

[9] This is called *programming* the chip. Instruments are made that allow the introduction of a particular design into a chip by blowing selected fuses.

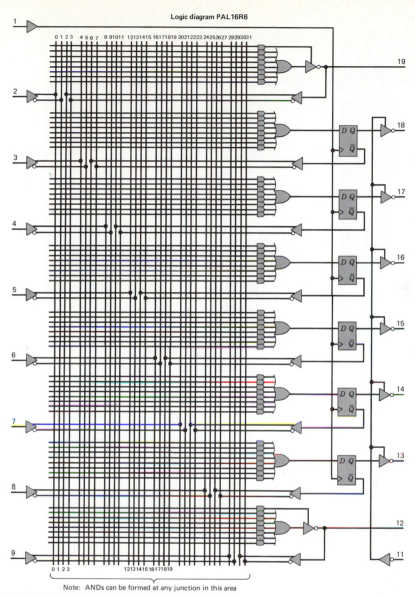

FIGURE 4.33
PAL with six flip-flops. (*Monolithic Memories.*)

PAL16R6

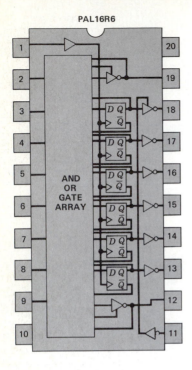

Conventional Symbology

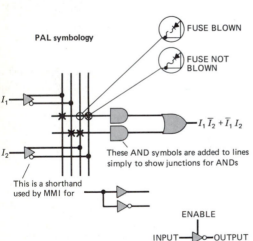

PAL symbology

FUSE BLOWN

FUSE NOT BLOWN

I_1

$I_1 \bar{I}_2 + \bar{I}_1 I_2$

These AND symbols are added to lines simply to show junctions for ANDs

I_2

This is a shorthand used by MMI for

ENABLE

INPUT — OUTPUT

In general a ▷ symbol represents an amplifier which passes a larger signal at the same level but with increased current drive.

I_1

I_2

$I_1 \bar{I}_2 + \bar{I}_1 I_2$

LOGIC STATE

$\overbrace{H\ L\ L\ H}$

INPUT HIGH

PRODUCT WITH ALL FUSES BLOWN REMAINS HIGH ALWAYS

H

INPUT LOW

PRODUCT WITH ALL FUSES INTACT REMAINS LOW ALWAYS

SHORTHAND NOTATION FOR ALL FUSES INTACT

This is the symbol for a three-state driver. If the ENABLE line is high the OUTPUT will be the complement of the INPUT. If ENABLE is low the OUTPUT will be at a high impedance and can be driven to any value by another three-state driver. These are used on buses (see Chap. 8)

FIGURE 4.33

(*continued*)

The primary approaches to IC chip design are:

1. *Mask-programmable ICs*. Mask-programmable ICs are arrays of gates that are prefabricated with the silicon dies complete except for the final two or three metallization layers. The final metallization layers are made to provide the required interconnect wiring for the gates, thereby defining the logic functions to be implemented by the array. *Gate array* designs, which provide tens of thousands of gates, involve high nonrecurring engineering charges, which include mask tooling charges and, generally, charges for the use of a computer-aided design (CAD) system, for production of the metallization layers. Although the cost varies depending on several factors, typical gate array nonrecurring engineering charges are in the $10,000–$50,000 range.

2. *Standard-cell devices*. Standard-cell devices utilize a set of standard cells fixed in place on the chip that can be interconnected. The cells consist of several gates and one or more flip-flops permanently connected in a useful logic configuration. A computer program generates the appropriate masks for producing the standard-cell devices from engineering specifications. Nonrecoverable engineering charges for standard-cell designs are less than for gate array designs.

3. *Custom devices*. Custom chip design refers to complete chip design and involves the largest nonrecoverable engineering charges. As a result, custom design is used only for large productions runs and includes, for example, microprocessor design.

4. *PLDs*. PLDs are of many types, among which are the following:
   a. *Field-programmable logic arrays* (FPLAs). (FPLAs) consist of a programmable AND array followed by a programmable OR array. These are typically fused. The PLAs fall in this category.
   b. *Field-programmable logic sequencers* (FPLS). FPLSs consist of FPLAs plus flip-flop registers.
   c. *Field-programmable gate arrays* (FPGAs). The FPGA contains programmable AND arrays with programmable-polarity inputs and outputs. Since an AND gate can become a NAND gate (by inverting the output), a NOR gate (by inverting all inputs), or an OR gate (by inverting all inputs and the output), each AND gate in an FPGA can be used to realize any of these other gates.
   d. *Programmable array logic* (PAL, ZPAL, HAL, ZHAL, NML). The programmable array logic (PAL) family is the most-used PLD family currently. The patented architecture consists of a programmable AND array followed by a fixed OR array.
   e. *Generic array logic* (GAL). Generic array logic (GAL) consists of electrically erasable PLDs, also called E^2PLDs. These devices present the designer with programmable architecture through the use of programmable cells.

There are several other types of PLDs, and manufacturers continually add new configurations and features (reprogrammability, for example). The use of these devices is now considerable and constitutes a major item in the computer industry.

4.14 COMPUTER-AIDED DESIGN OF COMPUTER LOGIC

As the amount of logic required to implement a design becomes very large, problems in making the design and in making the physical layouts for circuit boards and ICs increase greatly. To alleviate this, a number of programs have been developed to aid the designer. These programs run on workstations and PCs and make heavy use of graphics to display chip layouts, circuit board layouts, and other major design features. The programs are not a substitute for knowlege of logic design but are intended as design aids—hence the name *computer-aided design* (CAD). CAD programs generally present the design on a computer display and add written information concerning the details of the design.

Many of the CAD programs that are available are related to specific manufacturers' products. There are, for instance, programs to aid in minimization and layout for manufacturer chips including PLAs, PALs, and state machines. There are also programs that lay out custom designs, and some of these do actual circuit design and layout, offering such features as checking for IC mask problems arising from long parallel conductor paths or high electrical capacity on mask lines. Programs are also available that provide the layouts for standard IC cells—flip-flop arrays and two-level logic arrays, for example. The designer then arranges these cells as he or she pleases on the display and draws in interconnections to complete the desired design. The masks used in IC manufacture are then produced from the program runs or by photographing the display.

There are also programs to aid in verifying that a given design is going to work as desired. The verification tools include programs for layout rule checking, in which masks are examined to see if the chip geometries are correct for the technology used. These programs verify that long lines are spaced further apart than short lines, for example, so that interline capacitance problems do not arise. For custom designs using standard cells, the programs check that cells are properly placed and that adjacent cells satisfy the constraints for the circuits.

There are also programs that simulate the operation of the design, producing lists or outputs for selected or for automatically generated inputs. Some of these programs even provide waveform analysis, estimating signal delays and signal degradation caused by interconnections. Logic verification programs make sure that two-level designs correspond to the original boolean or logic table description.

The most advanced CAD programs aid in the systhesis of state machines or computer sections described by register transfer language (to be described). These are still directed toward specific technologies, such as a particular manufacturer's PLAs or PALs, and include algorithms for placement of cells or circuit elements and for interconnections.

Computer-aided design is a rapidly expanding field fueled by the ability of manufacturers to place more and more gates and flip-flops on a chip, thereby increasing the potential for a design but also increasing the design problems. CAD programs are necessary aids in very large designs but require designers expert in the use of the logic principles contained in this book. Such programs are no substitute for knowledge of the subject and can lead to catastrophe if misused. Nevertheless, CAD programs can be most welcome for designers of large logic arrays.

QUESTIONS

4.1. Draw a set of waveforms for S and R and X and $\overline{X}$ (as in Fig. 4.2) so that the flip-flop in Fig. 4.1 will have the signals 0011010 on the output line.

4.2. If the AND gate connected to the R input of X_1 in Fig. 4.3 fails so that its output is always 1, we would expect, after a few transfers, that X_1 will always be in what state? Why?

4.3. If the $\overline{X}$ output of a flip-flop is connected to an inverter, the inverter's output will always be the same as the X output of the flip-flop. True or false? Why?

4.4. Draw a set of waveforms for S and R (as in Fig. 4.2) so that the flip-flop in Fig. 4.1 will have the output signals 101110001 on the X output line.

4.5. Draw a set of waveforms as in Fig. 4.5(d) for the flip-flop in Fig. 4.5(b) so that the flip-flop will have the output signals 0010110 on its Y output line.

4.6. Draw an input waveform as in Fig. 4.10 so that X_3 will have the output signal 010011010 if X_1, X_2, and X_3 are all started in the 0 state.

4.7. In Fig. 4.10, if flip-flop X_2 "sticks" (that is, fails) in its 0 state, will X_3 have a 1 output after: (a) Clock pulse 1? (b) Clock pulse 2? (c) Clock pulse 3 and for each clock pulse thereafter?

4.8. Draw a set of waveforms as in Fig. 4.5(c) for the flip-flop in Fig. 4.5(a) so that the flip-flop will have the output signals 10111001 on its X output line.

4.9. The binary counter in Fig. 4.11 uses flip-flops that act on positive transitions. Draw a block diagram of a binary counter with bubbles on the clock inputs (that is, with flip-flops that act on *negative*-going clock inputs).

4.10. Redraw Fig. 4.11 with a bubble on each clock input to X_1, X_2, and X_3 [that is, make the same drawing, but use the flip-flop in Fig. 4.5(b) instead of that in Fig. 4.5(a)]. Redraw the waveforms in Fig. 4.11 for this circuit.

4.11. If the X_3 line (the output of X_3) is connected to the input line in Fig. 4.10, a *ring counter* is formed. If this circuit is started with $X_1 = 0$, $X_2 = 1$, and $X_3 = 1$, draw the waveform at X_1, X_2, and X_3 for six clock pulses.

4.12. Does the counter in Question 4.10 count up or down?

4.13. Make a single change to Fig. 4.11 by connecting the X_2 output instead of the $\overline{X}_2$ output to the clock input of X_3. Redraw the waveforms for this changed configuration.

4.14. After answering Question 4.13, use the flip-flop in Fig. 4.5(a) to design a counter that counts as follows:

X_3	X_2	X_1
0	0	0
0	1	1
0	1	0
1	0	1
1	0	0
1	1	1
1	1	0
0	0	1
0	0	0
0	1	1
0	1	0
1	0	1
.	.	.

4.15. After answering Question 4.13, use the flip-flop in Fig. 4.5(*a*) to design a counter that counts as follows:

X_3	X_2	X_1
0	0	0
1	1	1
1	1	0
1	0	1
1	0	0
0	1	1
0	1	0
0	0	1
0	0	0
1	1	1

This counter counts *down*. The counter of Fig. 4.11 counts *up*.

4.16. For Fig. 4.14(*b*), draw UP ENABLE, DOWN ENABLE, and clock waveforms so that the counter starts at 000 and counts as follows:

X_3	X_2	X_1
0	0	0
0	0	1
0	1	0
0	1	1
1	0	0
0	1	1
0	1	0
0	1	1

4.17. In Fig. 4.14(*a*), when the ENABLE line is a 1, the counter counts at the occurrence of a negative-going clock edge. Draw the output waveforms for flip-flops X_0, X_1, and X_2 for the following waveforms. Start the flip-flops at 0.

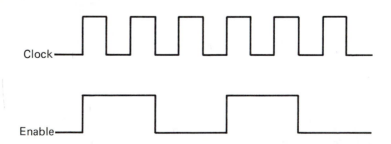

4.18. Suppose the AND gate in Fig. 4.15(*a*) fails such that its output is always a 0. Write the sequence or show the waveform through which this counter will go in response to clock signals.

4.19. Draw a clock waveform and the waveforms for the output of the AND gate connected to the S input of X_1, the R input of X_2, and 1 outputs of X_1, X_2, and X_3 for Fig. 4.12.

4.20. For Fig. 4.15(*b*), the carry-out from block 1 to block 2 goes from 1 to 0 every _____clock pulses. The carry-out from block 3 to block 4 goes from 1 to 0 every _____clock pulses.

4.21. Suppose that the AND gate's output in Fig. 4.15(*a*) is connected to the K input of X_4 instead of the J input. How will the computer count.

4.22. Using the circuits in Fig. 4.16, design a gated-clocked binary counter.

4.23. (*a*) If we replace block 2 in Fig. 4.15(*b*) with the four-stage ripple counter in Fig. 4.14(*a*), using the 1 output of X_3 in that counter as the carry-out line, the carry-out line from block 2 will go from 1 to 0 after how many clock pulses?

(*b*) For the configuration in (*a*), after how many clock pulses will the carry-out from block 2 go from 0 to 1?

4.24. Using the circuits in Fig. 4.16, design a gating network with inputs A, B, and C that will have output 1 when $\overline{A}BC$ or $AB\overline{C}$ are 1s.

4.25. Design a BCD counter using the flip-flops in Fig. 4.16.

4.26. Using the circuits in Fig. 4.16, design a gated binary counter.

4.27. Using the circuits in Fig. 4.16, design a gate network with inputs A, B, and C and output $A\overline{B} + \overline{A}C$.

4.28. Does a four-input NAND gate (as shown in Fig. 4.16), with the third input held at 1, act as a three-input gate would if only two inputs were used? Explain your answer.

4.29. Design the counter in Fig. 4.12 using the blocks in Fig. 4.16.

4.30. Redesign the following circuit, using only RS flip-flops and NOR gates.

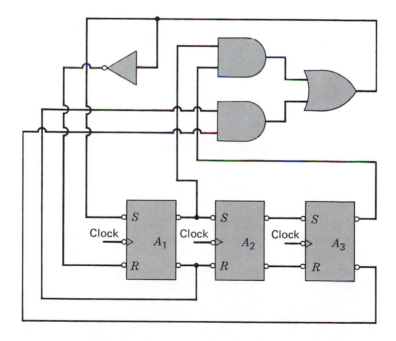

4.31. Give the states of the flip-flops in the following circuit after each of the first five clock signals (pulses) are applied. The circuit is started in the state $A_1 = 0$, $A_2 = 0$, $A_3 = 1$.

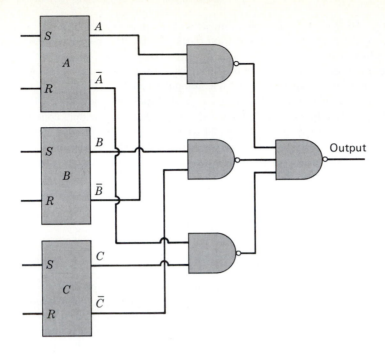

4.32. The following circuit is started in the state $C_1 = 1$ and $C_2 = 0$. The circuit divides the number of positive-going input edges (positive pulses) by what number? (That is, after every _____ input pulses, the output will return to 0.) Justify your answer.

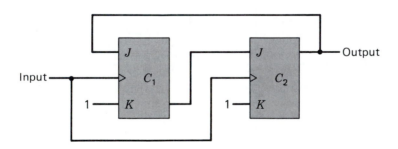

4.33. The gate block in the following circuit is an "equal to" combinational network realizing the boolean function $\overline{X_3}\overline{X_2} + X_3X_2$. If this set of three flip-flops is started in the state $X_1 = 1$, $X_2 = 0$, and $X_3 = 0$, what will the sequence of internal states be? As a start, the first three states are as follows:

X_1	X_2	X_3	
1	0	0	
1	1	0	After first clock pulse
0	1	1	After second clock pulse

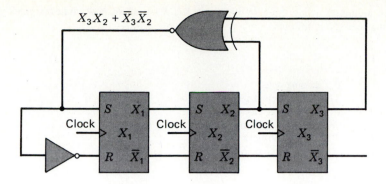

$$X_3X_2 + \overline{X}_3\overline{X}_2$$

4.34. In Fig. 4.9, why are E and F enabled at a lower level than A and B?

4.35. In Fig. 4.9, write 0s and 1s for all gate inputs and outputs when the clock input is 1, R is a 1, S is a 1, and the flip-flop is in the 1 state.

4.36. Using your result from Question 4.35, explain how the flip-flop in Fig. 4.9 operates when R and S are 0s and a negative edge appears.

4.37. In Fig. 4.9, if the feedback connection from the C NAND gate output to the input of the D NAND gate is broken (i.e., open), in what state will we probably find the flip-flop?

4.38. Design a counter, using only JK flip-flops, AND gates, and OR gates, that counts in the following sequence:

0	0	0
0	1	0
0	1	1
1	0	0
0	0	0
0	1	0
0	1	1
1	0	0
0	0	0

This repeats

4.39. The following sequence is to be output by a counter consisting of three RS flip-flops. Use AND and OR gates in your design.

A_1	A_2	A_3	
0	0	0	Starting state
0	1	0	
0	1	1	
0	0	1	
1	0	0	
1	1	0	
0	0	0	

Sequence repeats after this segment

4.40. Design a counter, using three JK flip-flops X_1, X_2, and X_3 and whatever gates you like, that counts as follows:

X_1	X_2	X_3	
0	0	0	Starting state
0	1	1	After first clock pulse
0	1	0	After second clock pulse
1	1	1	After third clock pulse
1	0	1	After fourth clock pulse
0	0	0	After fifth clock pulse
0	1	1	
0	1	0	

4.41. The following sequence is to be output by a counter consisting of three JK flip-flops. Use AND and OR gates in your design.

	A_1	A_2	A_3	
	0	0	0	Starting state
	0	1	1	
	0	1	0	
Sequence repeats after this segment	0	0	1	
	1	0	1	
	1	1	0	
	0	0	0	

4.42. If the S and R inputs for Fig. 4.7 are both 0s and S is made a 1 followed by R, what will be the resulting state of the flip-flop?

4.43. The NAND gate flip-flop in Fig. 4.7 will have what outputs on the 0 and 1 lines if both SET and RESET are made 0s?

4.44. Design a counter, using three JK flip-flops X_1, X_2, and X_3 and whatever gates you like, that counts as follows:

X_1	X_2	X_3	
0	0	1	Starting state
0	1	1	After first clock pulse
0	1	0	After second clock pulse
1	1	1	After third clock pulse
1	0	1	After fourth clock pulse
0	0	1	After fifth clock pulse
0	1	1	
0	1	0	

4.45. The rules for designing counters using JK and RS flip-flops have been given. Derive the rules for designing a counter using D flip-flops.

4.46. Design a counter using D flip-flops that counts in the same manner as the example given for JK and RS flip-flops.

4.47. Design a binary sequence detector that recognizes four consecutive 1s. Display the state diagram, state table, and final design.

4.48. Using the PAL in Fig. 4.31, design a state machine that realizes this state diagram:

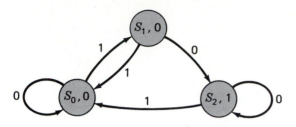

4.49. Design a state machine to realize this state diagram:

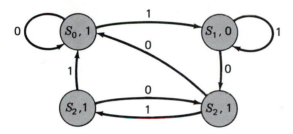

4.50. Design a two-input magnitude comparator, but use the Mealy configuration instead of the Moore configuration shown in Fig. 4.29.

4.51. What are SSI, MSI, LSI, and VLSI? Give an application in which each is useful.

4.52. Design a divide-by-25 circuit. The output should be true (i.e., a 1) only 1 of every 25 clock periods. This is called *a frequency divider.*

4.53. Design a sequential circuit that multiplies a binary number N by 3. N is entered serially, can be of any length, and is entered with its least significant bit first. The output 3N comes serially from the circuit's single output line. Show a state table and draw a logic circuit that uses only *JK* flip-flops and NOR gates.

CHAPTER
5

THE ARITHMETIC-LOGIC UNIT

The arithmetic-logic unit (ALU) performs arithmetic and logical operations on input data. This section of the machine can be relatively small, consisting of as little as part of a microprocessor chip. On the other hand, for large "number crunchers," it can consist of a considerable array of high-speed logic components. Despite the variations in size and complexity, arithmetic and logical operations are always performed using the same principles.

Although many functions can be performed by ALUs, the basic arithmetic operations—addition, subtraction, multiplication, and division—continue to be "bread-and-butter" operations. Even the literature reinforces the fundamental nature of these operations, for when a new machine is described, the times required for addition and multiplication are always included as significant features. Accordingly, this chapter first describes the means by which a computer adds, subtracts, multiplies, and divides. Other basic operations, such as shifting, logical multiplication, and logical addition, are then described.

Remember that the control unit directs the operation of the ALU. What the ALU does is add, subtract, shift, and so on, when it is provided with the correct sequence of input signals. It is up to the control element to provide these signals, and it is the function of the memory units to provide the arithmetic element with the information that is to be used. These sections of the computer are discussed in Chaps. 6 and 9.

5.1 CONSTRUCTION OF THE ALU

The information handled in a computer is generally divided into "words," each consisting of a fixed number of bits.[1] For instance, the words handled by a microcomputer may be 32 bits in length, in which case the ALU would have to be capable of performing arithmetic operations on 32-bit words. The operands used are supplied to the ALU, and the control element directs the operations. If addition is to be performed, the addend and augend will be supplied to the ALU, which must add the numbers and then, at least temporarily, store the results (sum).

To introduce several concepts, let us consider the construction of a typical computer ALU. The storage devices consist of a set of registers, each of which consists of one or more flip-flops. For convenience, the various registers of the ALU are generally given names, such as the X register, B register, or MQ register. The flip-flops are then given the same names, so that the X register would contain flip-flops X_1, X_2, X_3, and so on.[2]

Most computers (especially microprocessors) have one or more registers called *accumulators* or *general registers*, which are the principal registers for arithmetic and logical operations. These registers store the results of all arithmetic or logical operations, and gating circuitry is attached to the registers so that the necessary operations can be performed.

The accumulator (or general register) is the basic register of an arithmetic operation. If the machine is instructed to *load* an accumulator, the control element will put the operand selected into the accumulator register. If the computer is instructed to *add*, the number stored in the accumulator will represent the augend. Then the addend will be located, and the computer's circuitry will add this number (the addend) to the number previously stored in the accumulator (the augend), storing the sum in the accumulator. Notice that the original augend will no longer be stored in the accumulator after the addition. In this chapter we deal only with the processes of adding, subtracting, and similar operations, and not with the process of locating the numbers to be added.

5.2 INTEGER REPRESENTATION

The numbers used in digital machines must be represented using storage devices such as flip-flops. The most direct number representation system for binary storage devices is an integer representation system. Figure 5.1(a) shows a register of four flip-flops. X_3, X_2, X_1, and X_0, used to store numbers. Simply writing the values or states of the flip-flops gives the number in integer form. Thus $X_3 = 1$, $X_2 = 1$, $X_1 = 0$, $X_0 = 0$ gives 1100, or decimal 12; and $X_3 = 0$, $X_2 = 1$, $X_1 = 0$, $X_0 = 1$ gives 0101, or decimal 5.

It is generally necessary to represent both positive and negative numbers, so an additional bit is required, called the *sign bit*. This is generally placed to the left of the magnitude bits. In Fig. 5.1(b) X_4 is the sign bit, and X_3, X_2, X_1, and X_0 give the

---

[1] A few computers also provide the ability to handle variable-length operands.
[2] Often the numbering is $X1$, $X2$, $X3$, ...

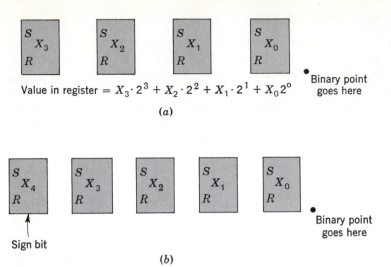

Value in register $= X_3 \cdot 2^3 + X_2 \cdot 2^2 + X_1 \cdot 2^1 + X_0 2^0$

• Binary point goes here

(a)

• Binary point goes here

Sign bit

(b)

FIGURE 5.1
Representation systems. (a) Integer representation. (b) Sign-plus-magnitude system.

magnitude. A 0 in X_4 means that the number is positive, and a 1 in X_4 means that the number is negative (this is the usual convention).[3] Therefore, $X_4 = 0$, $X_3 = 1$, $X_2 = 1$, $X_1 = 0$, and $X_0 = 1$ gives positive 1101, or +13 decimal; and $X_4 = 1$, $X_3 = 1$, $X_2 = 1$, $X_1 = 0$, and $X_0 = 1$ gives negative 1101, or −13 decimal.

This system is called the *signed-integer binary system* or *signed-magnitude binary integer system*. If a register contains eight flip-flops, a signed binary number in the system will have 7 magnitude, or integer, bits and a single sign bit. Thus, 00001111 would be +15, and 10001111 would be −15.

The magnitudes of numbers that can be stored using each of the two representation systems in Fig. 5.1 are as follows:

1. For binary integer representation, an *n*-flip-flop register can store numbers from (decimal) 0 to $2^n - 1$. A 6-bit register can therefore store numbers from 000000 to 111111, where 111111 is 63, which is $2^6 - 1$ or 64 − 1.
2. The signed binary integer representation system has a range of $-(2^{n-1} - 1)$ to $+(2^{n-1} - 1)$ for a binary register. For instance, a seven-flip-flop register can store numbers from −111111 to +111111, which is −63 to +63.

The following sections describe how to perform various arithmetic and logical operations on registers.

---

[3] Some companies number registers with the sign bit A_0, the most significant bit A_1, and so on to the least significant bit, A_n, in a register with $n + 1$ bits. IBM does this for some of its computers, for example.

TABLE 5.1

Input	Sum bits
$0 + 0$	0
$0 + 1$	1
$1 + 0$	1
$1 + 1$	0 with a carry of 1

5.3 BINARY HALF-ADDER

A basic module used in arithmetic elements is the *half-adder*. The function of the half-adder is to add two binary digits, producing a sum and a carry according to the binary addition rules shown in Table 5.1. Figure 5.2 shows a design for a half-adder. There are two inputs, designated X and Y in Fig. 5.2, and two outputs, designated S and C.

The half-adder performs the binary addition operation for two binary inputs as specified in Table 5.1. This is arithmetic addition, not logical or boolean algebra addition. If either of the inputs is a 1, but not both, the output on the S line will be a 1. If both inputs are 1s, the output on the C (for *carry*) line will be a 1. For all other states, there will be a 0 output on the C line. These relationships may be written in boolean form as follows:

$$S = X\overline{Y} + \overline{X}Y$$

$$C = XY$$

A *quarter-adder* consists of the two inputs to the half-adder and the S output only. The logical expression for this circuit is therefore $S = X\overline{Y} + \overline{X}Y$. This is the *exclusive OR* relationship for boolean algebra.

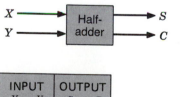

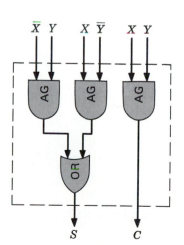

FIGURE 5.2
Half-adder.

5.4 FULL ADDER

When more than two binary digits are to be added, several half-adders will not be adequate, since the half-adder has no input to handle carries from other digits. For example, consider the addition of the following two binary numbers:

$$
\begin{array}{r}
1011 \\
+\ 1110 \\
\hline
11001 = \text{Sum}
\end{array}
\qquad
\begin{array}{r}
1011 \\
+\ 1110 \\
\hline
0101 = \text{Partial sum} \\
1\ 1\quad = \text{Carry bits} \\
\hline
11001 = \text{Complete sum}
\end{array}
$$

As shown, the carries generated in each column must be handled in the addition process. Therefore, adder circuitry capable of adding the contents of two registers must include provision for handling carries as well as addend and augend bits. So there must be three inputs to each stage of a multidigit adder—except the stage for the least significant bits—one for each input from the numbers being added and one for any carry that might be generated or propagated by the previous stage.

The block diagram symbol for a *full binary adder*, which will handle these carries, is illustrated in Fig. 5.3, as is the complete table of input-output relationships for the full adder. There are three inputs to the full adder: the X and Y inputs, for the respective digits of the registers to be added, and the C_i input, which is for any carry generated by the previous stage. The two outputs are S, which is the output value for that stage of the addition, and C_o, which generates the carry to be added into the next stage.[4] The boolean expressions for the input-output relationships for each of the

---

[4] C_i is for *carry-in* and C_o for *carry-out*.

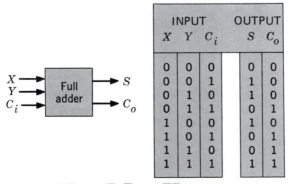

INPUT			OUTPUT	
X	Y	C_i	S	C_o
0	0	0	0	0
0	0	1	1	0
0	1	0	1	0
0	1	1	0	1
1	0	0	1	0
1	0	1	0	1
1	1	0	0	1
1	1	1	1	1

$$S = \overline{X}\,\overline{Y}C_i + \overline{X}Y\overline{C}_i + X\overline{Y}\,\overline{C}_i + XYC_i$$
$$C_o = \overline{X}YC_i + X\overline{Y}C_i + XY\overline{C}_i + XYC_i$$

or

$$C_o = XC_i + XY + YC_i$$

FIGURE 5.3
Full adder.

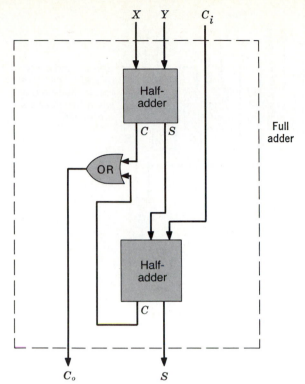

FIGURE 5.4
Half-adder and full adder relations.

two outputs are also presented in Fig. 5.3, as is the expression for the C_o output in simplified form.

A full adder may be constructed of two half-adders, as illustrated in Fig. 5.4. Constructing a full adder from two half-adders may not be the most economical technique, however; generally, full adders are designed directly from the input-output relations illustrated in Fig. 5.3

5.5 A PARALLEL BINARY ADDER

A 4-bit parallel binary adder is illustrated in Fig. 5.5. The purpose of this adder is to add two 4-bit binary integers. The addend inputs are named X_0 through X_3, and the augend bits are represented by Y_0 through Y_3.[5] The adder shown does not possess the ability to handle sign bits for the binary words to be added; it only adds the magnitudes of the numbers stored. The additional circuitry needed to handle sign bits

---

[5] These inputs would normally be from flip-flop registers X and Y, and the adder would add the number in X to the number in Y, giving the sum, S_0 through S_3.

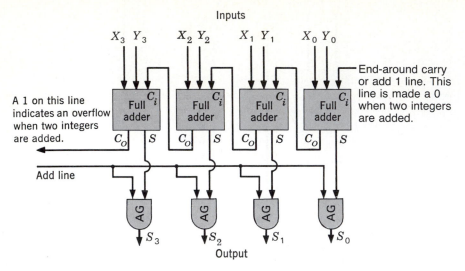

FIGURE 5.5
Parallel adder.

depends on whether negative numbers are represented in true magnitude or using the 1s or 2s complement systems. This will be described later.

Consider the addition of the following two 4-bit binary numbers:

$$0111 \quad \text{where } X_3 = 0, \ X_2 = 1, \ X_1 = 1, \ \text{and } X_0 = 1$$
$$0011 \quad \text{where } Y_3 = 0, \ Y_2 = 0, \ Y_1 = 1, \ \text{and } Y_0 = 1$$
$$\text{Sum} = 1010$$

The sum should be $S_3 = 1$, $S_2 = 0$, $S_1 = 1$, and $S_0 = 0$.

The operation of the adder may be checked as follows. Since X_0 and Y_0 are the least significant digits, they cannot receive a carry from a previous stage. In the problem above, X_0 and Y_0 are both 1s, their sum is therefore 0, and a carry is generated and added into the full adder for bits X_1 and Y_1. Bits X_1 and Y_1 are also both 1s, as is the carry input to this stage. Therefore, the sum output line S_1 carries a 1, and the carry line to the next stage also carries a 1. Since X_2 is a 1, Y_2 is a 0, and the carry input is 1, the sum output line S_2 will carry a 0, and the carry to the next stage will be a 1. Both inputs X_3 and Y_3 are equal to 0, and the carry input line to this adder stage is equal to 1. Therefore, the sum output line S_3 will represent a 1, and the carry output line, designated as "overflow" in Fig. 5.5, will have a 0.

The same basic configuration illustrated in Fig. 5.5 may be extended to any number of bits. A 7-bit adder may be constructed by using 7 full adders, and a 20-bit adder may be made by using 20 full adders.

Note that the overflow line could be used to enable the 4-bit adder in Fig. 5.5 to have a 5-bit output. This is not generally done, however, because the addend and augend both come from storage, so their length is the length of the basic computer word, and a longer word cannot be readily stored by the machine. It was explained earlier that a machine with a word length of n bits (consisting of a sign bit and $n - 1$

bits to designate the magnitude) could express binary numbers from $-2^{n-1} + 1$ to $2^{n-1} - 1$. A number within these limits is called *representable*. Since the simple 4-bit adder in Fig. 5.5 has no sign bit, it can represent only binary integers from 0 to 15. If 1100 and 1100 are added, there will be a 1 output on the overflow line because the sum of these two numbers is 11000. This number is 24 decimal, which cannot be represented in this system. Such a number is referred to as *nonrepresentable* for this particular, very small register. When two integers are added such that their sum is nonrepresentable (that is, contains too many bits), we say the sum *overflows*; a 1 on the carry line for the full adder connected to the most significant digits indicates this.

The AND gates connected to the S output lines from the four adders are used to gate the sum into the correct register.

5.6 ADDITION AND SUBTRACTION IN A PARALLEL ARITHMETIC ELEMENT

We now examine the design of a gating network that will either add or subtract two numbers. The network is to have an ADD input line and a SUBTRACT input line as well as the lines that carry the representations of the numbers to be used. When the ADD line is a 1, the sum of the numbers is to be on the output lines; and when the SUBTRACT line is a 1, the difference is to be on the output lines. If both ADD and SUBTRACT are 0s, the output is to be 0.

First we note that if the computer is capable of adding both positive and negative numbers, subtraction may be performed by complementing the subtrahend and then adding. For instance, $8 - 4$ yields the same result at $8 + (-4)$, and $6 - (-2)$ yields the same result as $6 + 2$. Subtraction may thus be performed by an arithmetic element capable of adding. For instance, in the 1s complement system, four cases may arise:

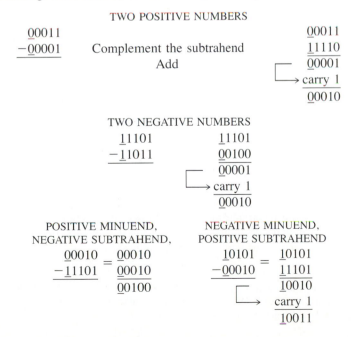

TWO POSITIVE NUMBERS

$\underline{00011}$
$-\underline{00001}$ Complement the subtrahend
                    Add

$\underline{00011}$
$\underline{11110}$
$\underline{00001}$
$\rightarrow$ carry 1
$\underline{00010}$

TWO NEGATIVE NUMBERS

$\underline{11101}$ $\underline{11101}$
$-\underline{11011}$ $\underline{00100}$
                  $\underline{00001}$
          $\rightarrow$ carry 1
                  $\underline{00010}$

POSITIVE MINUEND,   NEGATIVE MINUEND,
NEGATIVE SUBTRAHEND,   POSITIVE SUBTRAHEND
$\underline{00010}$ $=$ $\underline{00010}$ $\underline{10101}$ $=$ $\underline{10101}$
$-\underline{11101}$ $\underline{00010}$ $-\underline{00010}$ $\underline{11101}$
          $\underline{00100}$ $\underline{10010}$
                              $\rightarrow$ carry 1
                                     $\underline{10011}$

The same basic rules apply to subtraction in the 2s complement system, except that any carry generated in the sign-bit adders is simply dropped. In this case the 2s complement of the subtrahend is formed, and the complemented number is added to the minuend with no end-around carry.

We now examine the implementation of a combined adder and subtracter network. The primary problem is to form the complement of the number to be subtracted. This complementation of the subtrahend may be performed in several ways. For the 1s complement system, if the storage register is composed of flip-flops, the 1s complement can be formed by simply connecting the complement of each input to the adder. The 1 that must be added to the least significant position to form a 2s complement may be added by connecting a 1 at the carry input of the adder for the least significant bits.

A complete logical circuit capable of adding or subtracting two signed 2s complement numbers is shown in Fig. 5.6. One number is represented by X_4, X_3, X_2, X_1, and X_0, and the other number by Y_4, Y_3, Y_2, Y_1, and Y_0. There are two control signals, ADD and SUBTRACT. If neither control signal is a 1 (that is, both are 0s), the outputs from the five full adders (S_4, S_3, S_2, S_1, and S_0) will all be 0s. If the ADD control line is made a 1, the sum of the number X and the number Y will appear as S_4, S_3, S_2, S_1, and S_0. If the SUBTRACT line is made a 1, the difference between X and Y (that is, $X - Y$) will appear on S_4, S_3, S_2, S_1, and S_0.

Notice that the AND-to-OR gate network connected to each Y input selects either Y or $\overline{Y}$, so that, for instance, an ADD causes Y_1 to enter the appropriate full adder, and a SUBTRACT causes $\overline{Y}_1$ to enter the full adder.

To either add or subtract, each X input is connected to the appropriate full adder. When a subtraction is called for, the complement of each Y flip-flop is gated into the full adder, and a 1 is added by connecting the SUBTRACT signal to the C_i input of the full adder for the lowest-order bits, X_0 and Y_0. Since the SUBTRACT line will be a 0 when we add, a 0 carry will be on this line when addition is performed. The simplicity of the operation of Fig. 5.6 makes 2s complement addition and subtraction the most commonly used system.[6] It will be instructive to try adding and subtracting several numbers in 2s complement form, using pencil and paper and this logic circuit.

The configuration in Fig. 5.6 provides a simple, direct means for either adding or subtracting positive or negative numbers. Quite often the S_4, S_3, . . . , S_0 lines are gated back into the X flip-flops, so that the sum or difference of the numbers X and Y replaces the original value of X.

An important consideration is overflow, which occurs when the performance of an operation results in a quantity beyond the capacity of the register (or storage register) that is to receive the result. Since the registers in Fig. 5.6 have a sign bit plus 4 magnitude bits, they can store from $+15$ to -16 in 2s complement form. Therefore, if the result of an addition or a subtraction were greater than $+15$ or less than -16, an overflow occurs. Suppose we add $+8$ to $+12$; the result should be $+20$,

---

[6] A 1s complement parallel adder-subtracter can be made by connecting the CARRY-OUT line for the X_0, Y_0 adder to the CARRY-IN line for the X_4, Y_4 adder (and disconnecting the SUBTRACT line to this full adder, of course).

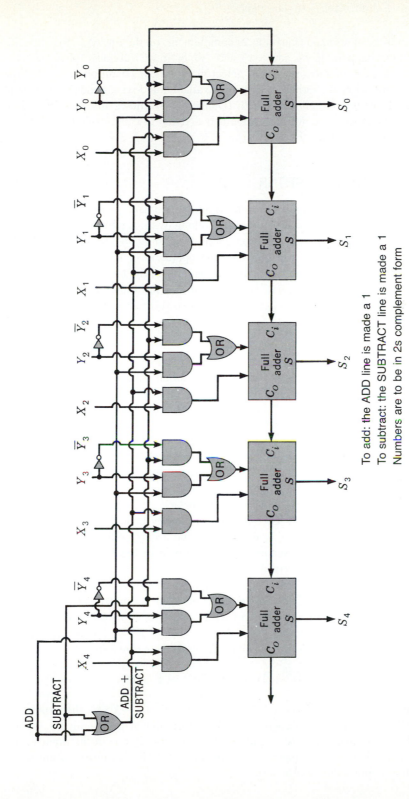

FIGURE 5.6
Parallel addition and subtraction.

To add: the ADD line is made a 1
To subtract: the SUBTRACT line is made a 1
Numbers are to be in 2s complement form

but this cannot be represented (fairly) in 2s complement, on the lines $S_4, S_3, \ldots, S_0$. The same thing happens if we add -13 and -7 or if we subtract -8 from $+12$. In each case, logical circuitry is used to detect the overflow condition and signal the computer control element. Various options are available, and what is done can depend on the type of instruction being executed. (Deliberate overflows are sometimes used in double-precision routines. Multiplication and division use the results as they are.) We defer this topic to Chap. 9.

5.7   FULL ADDER DESIGNS

The full adder is a basic component of an arithmetic element. Figure 5.3 illustrated the block diagram symbol for the full adder, along with a table of combinations for the input-output values and the expressions describing the SUM and CARRY lines. Succeeding figures and text described the operation of the full adder. Notice that a parallel ALU requires one full adder for each bit in the basic word.

There are, of course, many gate configurations for full binary adders. Examples of an IBM adder and an MSI package containing two full adders follow.

Full Binary Adder

Figure 5.7 illustrates the full binary adder configuration used in several IBM computers. There are three inputs to the circuit. The X input is from one of the storage devices in the accumulator. The Y input is from the corresponding storage device in the register to be added to the accumulator register. The third input is the carry (C) input from the adder for the next least significant bit. The two outputs are SUM and CARRY. The SUM output will contain the sum value for this particular digit of the output. The CARRY output will be connected to the C input of the next most significant bit's adder (refer to Fig. 5.5).

The outputs from the three AND gates connected directly to the X, Y, and C inputs are logically added by the OR gate circuit directly beneath. If either the XY, XC, or YC input lines contains a 1, there should be a carry output. The output of this circuit, written in logical equation form, is shown in the figure. This may be compared with the expression derived in Fig. 5.3.

The derivation of the SUM output is not so straightforward. The CARRY output expression $XY + XC + YC$ is first inverted (complemented), yielding $\overline{(XY + XC + YC)}$. The logical product of X, Y, and C is formed by an AND gate and logically added to this, forming $\overline{(XY + XC + YC)} + XYC$. The logical sum of X, Y, and C is then multiplied by this value, forming the expression

$$[\overline{(XY + XC + YC)} + XYC](X + Y + C)$$

When simplified, this expression is $\overline{X}\,\overline{Y}C + \overline{X}Y\overline{C} + X\overline{Y}\,\overline{C} + XYC$, the expression derived in Fig. 5.3. Tracing through the logical operation of the circuit for various values will indicate that the SUM output will be 1 when only one of the input values is equal to 1 or when all three input values are equal to 1. For all other combinations of inputs, the output value will be a 0.

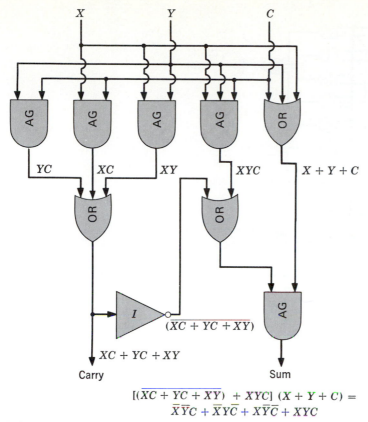

FIGURE 5.7
Full adder used in IBM machines.

Two Cascaded Full Adders

Figure 5.8 shows two full adders in one IC container.[7] The maximum delay from an input change to an output change for an S output is on the order of 2 nanoseconds (ns).[8] The maximum delay from any input to the $C2$ output is about 1.5 ns.

The amount of delay associated with each carry is an important figure in evaluating a full adder for a parallel system, because the time required to add two numbers is determined by the maximum time it takes for a carry to propagate through the adders. For instance, if we add 01111 to 10001 in the 2s complement system, the carry generated by the 1s in the least significant digit of each number must propagate through four carry stages and a sum stage before the sum can be safely gated into the accumulator. A study of the addition of these two numbers using the configuration in Fig. 5.5 will make this clear. This is called the *carry-ripple problem*.

---

[7] The circled numbers are pin numbers for the container.
[8] 1 ns $= 10^{-9}$ s.

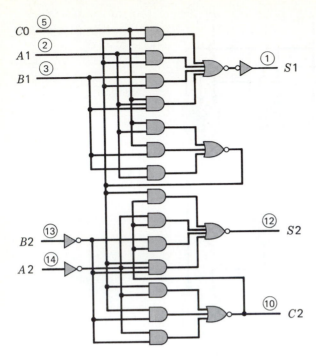

FIGURE 5.8
Two full adders.

A number of techniques are used in high-speed machines to alleviate this problem. The most common remedy is a bridging, or carry-look-ahead, circuit, which calculates the carry-out of a number of stages simultaneously and then delivers this carry to the succeeding stages. (This is covered in a later section.)

5.8 BINARY-CODED-DECIMAL ADDER

Arithmetic units that perform operations on numbers stored in BCD form must have the ability to add 4-bit representations of decimal digits. To do this, a BCD adder is used. A block diagram symbol for an adder is shown in Fig. 5.9. The adder has

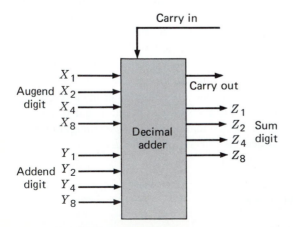

FIGURE 5.9
Serial-parallel addition.

an augend digit input consisting of four lines, an addend digit input of four lines, a carry-in and a carry-out, and a sum digit with four output lines. The augend digit, addend digit, and sum digit are each represented in 8,4,2,1 BCD form.

The purpose of the BCD adder in Fig. 5.9 is to add the augend and addend digits and the carry-in and produce a sum digit and carry-out. This adder could be designed using the techniques described in Chap. 3 and the rules for decimal addition. It is also possible to make a BCD adder by using full adders and AND or OR gates. An adder made in this way is shown in Fig. 5.10.

There are eight inputs to the BCD adder: four X_i, or augend, inputs; and four Y_i, or addend, digits. Each input will represent a 0 or a 1 during a given addition. If 3 (0011) is to be added to 2 (0010), then $X_8 = 0$, $X_4 = 0$, $X_2 = 1$, and $X_1 = 1$; $Y_8 = 0$, $Y_4 = 0$, $Y_2 = 1$, and $Y_1 = 0$.

The basic adder in Fig. 5.10 consists of the four binary adders at the top of the figure; this configuration performs base-16 addition when the intent is to perform

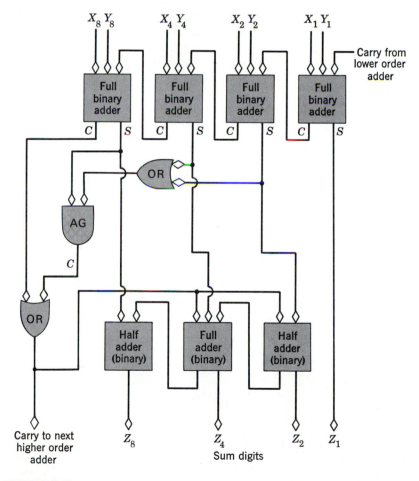

FIGURE 5.10
BCD adder.

base-10 addition. Thus, some provision must be made to (1) generate carries and (2) correct sums greater than 9. For instance, if 3_{10} (0011) is added to 8_{10} (1000), the result should be 1_{10} (0001) with a carry generated.

The actual circuitry used to determine when a carry is to be transmitted to the next most significant digits consists of the full binary adder, to which sum (S) outputs from the adders for the 8,4,2 inputs are connected, and the OR gate to which the carry (C) from the 8-position bits is connected. Examination of the addition process indicates that a carry should be generated when the 8 AND 4, the 8 AND 2, or the 8 AND 4 AND 2 sum outputs from the base-16 adder represent 1s, or when the CARRY output from the 8-position adder contains a 1. (This occurs when 8s or 9s are added.) Whenever the sum of two digits exceeds 9, the CARRY TO NEXT HIGHER ORDER ADDER line will contain a 1 for the adder in Fig. 5.10.

A further difficulty arises when a carry is generated. If 7_{10} (0111) is added to 6_{10} (0110), a carry will be generated, but the output from the base-16 adder will be 1101. The value 1101 does not represent any decimal digit in the 8,4,2,1 system and must be corrected. The method used to correct this is to add 6_{10} (0110) to the sum from the base-16 adders whenever a carry is generated. This addition is performed by adding 1s to the 4- and 2- position output lines from the base-16 adder when a carry is generated. The two half-adders and the full adder at the bottom of Fig. 5.10 perform this function. Essentially, then, the adder performs base-16 addition and corrects the sum, if it is greater than 9, by adding 6. Examples of this are shown below.

$$8 + 7 = 15 \qquad 1000 + 0111 = $$

	(8)	(4)	(2)	(1)	
	1	1	1	1	
+	0	1	1	0	
1	0	1	0	1	= 5

with a carry generated

$$9 + 5 = 14$$

	(8)	(4)	(2)	(1)	
	1	0	0	1	
	0	1	0	1	
	1	1	1	0	
+	0	1	1	0	
1	0	1	0	0	= 4

with a carry generated

Figure 5.11 shows a complete BCD adder in an IC package.[9] The inputs are digits A and digits B, and the outputs are S. A carry-in and a carry-out are included. The circuit line used is CMOS.

---

[9] The IC packages in Figs. 5.11, 5.13, 5.14, and 5.15 are typical BCD MSI packages. The notation $A1$, $A2$, $A3$, $A4$ (instead of X_1, X_2, X_4, X_8) is often used for the 4 bits of a BCD digit, and the weights 1, 2, 4, 8 are understood. Thus, a BCD digit in $B1$, $B2$, $B3$, $B4$ would have weight 1 on $B1$, weight 2 on $B2$, weight 4 on $B3$, and weight 8 on $B4$.

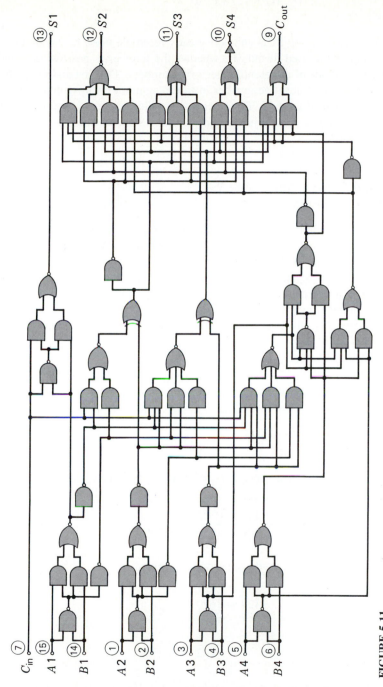

FIGURE 5.11
Complete BCD adder in an IC package.

205

5.9   POSITIVE AND NEGATIVE BCD NUMBERS

The techniques for handling BCD numbers greatly resemble those for handling binary numbers. A sign bit is used to indicate whether the number is positive or negative. There are three methods of representing negative numbers. The first and most obvious method is to represent a negative number in true magnitude form with a sign bit, so that -645 is represented as $\underline{1}645$. The other two possibilities are to represent negative numbers in 9s or a 10s complement form, which resembles the binary 1s and 2s complement forms.

Addition and Subtraction Using 9s and 10s Complements

A negative decimal number can be represented in 9s complement form, a situation roughly the same as using the 1s complement to represent a negative binary number. In adding or subtracting BCD numbers, four cases may arise: two positive numbers may be added; a positive and negative number may be added, yielding a positive result; a positive and negative number may be added, yielding a negative result; and two negative numbers may be added. Since there is no problem when two positive numbers are added, we illustrate the last three situations.

NEGATIVE AND POSITIVE NUMBER—POSITIVE SUM

$$
\begin{array}{rl}
+692 = & \underline{0}692 \\
-342 = & \underline{1}657 \\
\hline
+350 & \underline{0}349 \\
& \underline{1} \\
& \underline{0}350
\end{array}
$$

POSITIVE AND NEGATIVE NUMBER—NEGATIVE SUM

$$
\begin{array}{rl}
-631 = & \underline{1}368 \\
+342 = & \underline{0}342 \\
\hline
-289 & \underline{1}710 = -289
\end{array}
$$

TWO NEGATIVE NUMBERS

$$
\begin{array}{rl}
-248 = & \underline{1}751 \\
-329 = & \underline{1}670 \\
\hline
-577 & \underline{1}421 \\
& \underline{1} \\
& \underline{1}422 = -577
\end{array}
$$

The rules for handling negative numbers in the 10s complement system correspond to those for the binary 2s complement system in that no carry must be wrapped around. Therefore, a parallel BCD adder may be constructed using only the full BCD adder as the basic component; all combinations of positive and negative numbers may be handled thus.

There is an additional complexity in BCD addition, however, because the 9s complement of a BCD digit cannot be formed by simply complementing each bit in the representation. A gating block called a *complementer* must be used.

A block diagram of a logical circuit that will form the 9s complement of a code group representing a decimal number in 8, 4, 2, 1 BCD form is shown in Fig. 5.12. There are four inputs to the circuit, X_1, X_2, X_4, and X_8; X_1 has weight 1, X_2 has weight 2, X_4 has weight 4, and X_8 has weight 8. If the inputs represent a decimal digit of the number to be complemented, the outputs will represent the 9s complement of the input digit. For instance, if the input is 0010 (decimal 2), the output will be 0111 (decimal 7), the 9s complement of the input.

Figure 5.13 shows a complete 9s complementer in an IC package. When the COMP input is a 1, the outputs $F1$–$F4$ represent the complement of the digit on $A1$–$A4$; but if COMP is a 0, the $A1$–$A4$ inputs are simply placed on $F1$–$F4$ without change.

By connecting the IC packages in Figs. 5.11 and 5.13, a BCD adder-subtracter can be formed, as shown in Fig. 5.14. This figure shows a two-digit adder-subtracter IC package. To add the digits on the inputs, the ADD/SUBTRACT input is made a 1; to subtract, this signal is made a 0. (Making the ZERO input a 1 will cause the value of B to pass through unchanged.)

BCD numbers may be represented in parallel form, as we have shown, but a mode of operation called *series-parallel* is often used. If a decimal number is written in binary-coded form, the resulting number consists of a set of code groups, each of which represents a single decimal digit. For instance, decimal 463 in a BCD 8, 4, 2, 1 code is 0100 0110 0011. It is convenient to handle each code group representing a

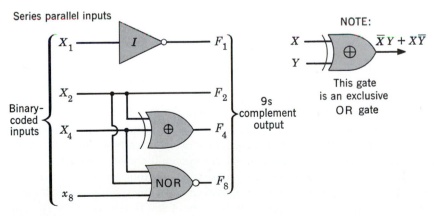

FIGURE 5.12
Logic circuit for forming 9s complement of 8,4,2,1 BCD digits.

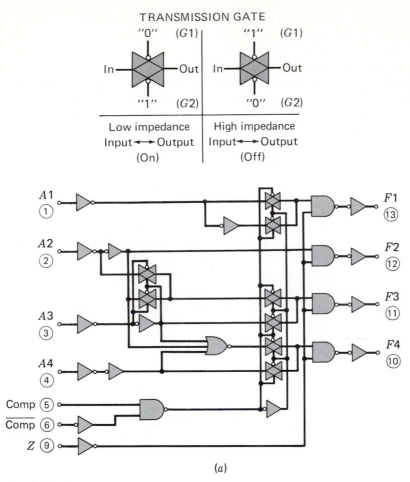

FIGURE 5.13
9s complementer. (*a*) Logic diagram.

decimal digit as a unit, that is, in parallel. At the same time, since the word lengths for decimal computation are apt to be rather long, it is desirable to economize in terms of the amount of equipment used.

The *series-parallel* system provides a compromise in that each code group is handled in parallel, but the decimal digits are handled sequentially. This requires four lines for each 8, 4, 2, 1 BCD character, each input of which carries a different weight. The block diagram for an adder operating in this system is shown in Fig. 5.15. There are two sets of inputs to the adder; one consists of the four input lines that carry the coded digit for the addend, and the other four input lines carry a coded augend digit. The sets of inputs arrive sequentially from the *A* and *B* registers, each of which consists of four shift registers. The least significant addend and augend BCD digits arrive first, followed by the more significant decimal digits.

DECIMAL EQUIVALENT INPUT	INPUTS				DECIMAL EQUIVALENT OUTPUT	OUTPUTS			
	$A4$	$A3$	$A2$	$A1$		$F1$	$F2$	$F3$	$F4$
0	0	0	0	0	9	1	0	0	1
1	0	0	0	1	8	1	0	0	0
2	0	0	1	0	7	0	1	1	1
3	0	0	1	1	6	0	1	1	0
4	0	1	0	0	5	0	1	0	1
5	0	1	0	1	4	0	1	0	0
6	0	1	1	0	3	0	0	1	1
7	0	1	1	1	2	0	0	1	0
8	1	0	0	0	1	0	0	0	1
9	1	0	0	1	0	0	0	0	0
10	1	0	1	0	7	0	1	1	1
11	1	0	1	1	6	0	1	1	0
12	1	1	0	0	5	0	1	0	1
13	1	1	1	1	4	0	1	0	0
14	1	1	1	0	3	0	0	1	1
15	1	1	1	1	2	0	0	1	0

Illegal BCD input codes (rows 10–15)

(b)

FIGURE 5.13
9s complementer. (b) Table of combinations.

Using the 8,4,2,1 code, let 324 represent the augend and 238 the addend. The ADD signal will be a 0. First the adder will receive 0100 on the augend lines, and at the same time it will receive 1000 on the addend lines. After the first clock pulse, these inputs will be replaced by 0010 on the augend lines and 0011 on the addend lines. Before the first clock signal, the sum lines should contain 0010; and before the second, 0110. A carry will be generated during the addition of the first two digits; this will be delayed and added in using the D flip-flop. The process will continue until each of the three digits has been added. To subtract B from A, we have only to make the ADD/SUBTRACT input a 1 and then apply the clocks.

5.10   SHIFT OPERATION

A *shift operation* moves the digits stored in a register to new positions in the register. There are two distinct shift operations: shift left and shift right. A shift-

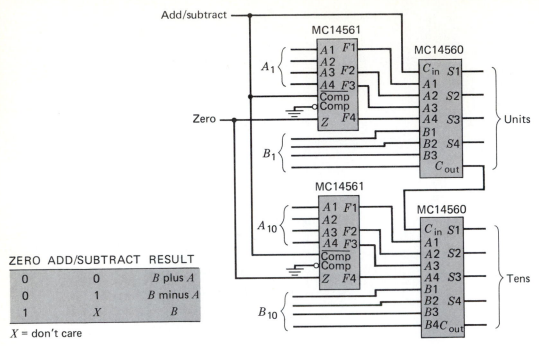

ZERO	ADD/SUBTRACT	RESULT
0	0	B plus A
0	1	B minus A
1	X	B

X = don't care

FIGURE 5.14
Parallel add/subtract circuit (10s complement).

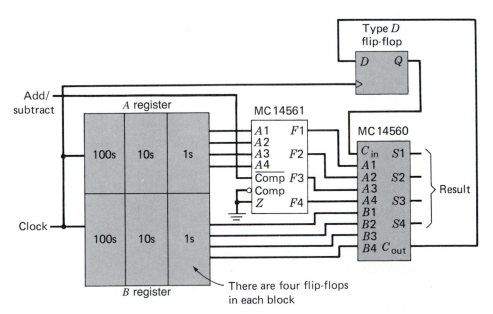

FIGURE 5.15
Series-parallel BCD adder/subtracter using shift register.

left operation moves each bit of information stored in a register to the left by some specified number of digits. Consider the six binary digits 000110, which we assume to be stored in a parallel binary register. If the contents of the register are shifted left 1, the shift register will then contain 001100. If a right shift of 1 is performed on the word 000110, the shift register as a result will contain 000011. The shifting process in a decimal register is similar: if the register contains $\underline{0}01234$, after a right shift of 1 the register will contain $\underline{0}00123$; after a left shift of 1 the register will contain $\underline{0}12340$. The shift operation is used in the MULTIPLY and the DIVIDE instructions of most machines and is provided as an instruction that may be used by programmers. For instance, a machine may have instructions SHR and SHL, where the letters represent in mnemonic form SHIFT RIGHT and SHIFT LEFT instructions, respectively.

A block diagram of logic circuitry for a single stage (flip-flop) in a register that can be shifted either left or right is shown in Fig. 5.16. As can be seen, the bit to the left is shifted into X_m when SHIFT RIGHT is a 1, and the bit to the right is shifted into X_m when SHIFT LEFT is a 1.

Figure 5.17 shows an MIS package containing four flip-flops and gating circuitry so that the register can be shifted right or left and so that the four flip-flops can be parallel-loaded from four input lines W, X, Y, and Z. The circuits are TTL circuits and are clocked in parallel. By combining modules such as this one, a register of a chosen length can be formed that can be shifted left or right or parallel-loaded.

5.11 BASIC OPERATIONS

The arithmetic-logic unit of a digital computer consists of a number of registers in which information can be stored and a set of logic circuits that make it possible to

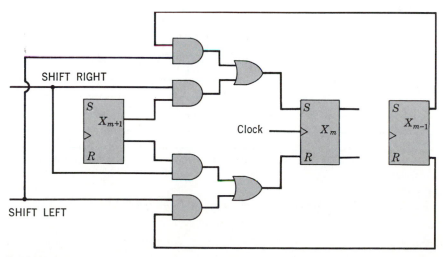

FIGURE 5.16
Shift-left and shift-right stages of register.

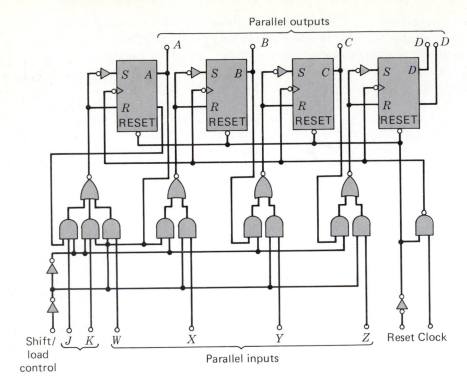

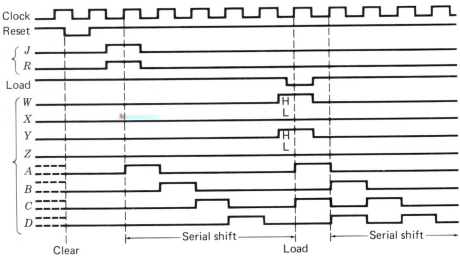

FIGURE 5.17
Shift register (model SN74195) with parallel-load ability. (*Texas Instruments.*)

perform certain operations on the information stored in the registers and between registers.

As we have seen, the data stored in a given flip-flop register may be operated on in the following ways:

1. The register may be reset to all 0s.

2. The contents of a register may be converted to either 1s or 2s complement form, for binary, or to 9s or 10s complement form, for decimal.

3. The contents of a register may be shifted right or left.

4. The contents of a register can be incremented or decremented.

Several operations between registers have been described. These include:

1. Transferring the contents of one register to another register

2. Adding to or subtracting from the contents of one register the contents of another register

Most of the arithmetic operations performed by an ALU consist of these two types, or sequenced sets of these two types, of operations. Complicated instructions, such as multiplication and division, can require a large number of these operations, but these instructions may be performed using only sequences of the simple operations already described.

One other important point needs to be made. Certain operations that occur within instructions are *conditional:* that is, a given operation may or may not take place, depending on the value of certain bits of the numbers stored. For instance, it may be desirable to multiply using only positive numbers. In this case, the sign bits of the two numbers to be multiplied will be examined by control circuitry, and if either is a 1, the corresponding number will be complemented before the multiplication begins. This operation, complementing the register, is a conditional one.

Many different sequences of operations can yield the same result. For instance, two numbers could be multiplied by simply adding the multiplicand to itself the number of times indicated by the multiplier. If this were done with pencil and paper, 369 × 12 would be performed by adding 369 to itself 12 times. This would be a laborious process compared with the easier algorithm we have developed for multiplying, but we would get the same result. The same principle applies to computer multiplication. Two numbers could be multiplied by transferring one of the numbers into a counter that counted down each time an addition was performed, and then adding the other number to itself until the counter reached zero. This technique has been used, but much faster techniques are also used and will be explained.

Many algorithms have been used to multiply and divide numbers in digital computers. Division is an especially complicated process and in decimal computers, in particular, many different techniques are used. The particular technique used by a computer is generally based on the cost of the computer and the premium placed on speed. In almost all operations, speed is expensive, and a faster division process generally means a more expensive computer.

To explain the operations of binary multiplication and division, we use a block diagram of a generalized binary computer. Figure 5.18 illustrates, in block diagram form, the registers of an ALU. The computer has three basic registers: an accumulator, a Y register, and a B register. The operations that can be performed have been described:

1. The accumulator can be cleared.

2. The contents of the accumulator can be shifted right or left. Further, the accumulator and the B register may be formed into one long shift register. If we then shift this register right two digits, the two least significant digits of the accumulator will be shifted into the first two places of the B register. Several left shifts will shift the most significant digits of the B register into the accumulator. Since there are 5 bits in the basic computer word, there are five binary storage devices in each register. A right shift of five places will transfer the contents of the accumulator into the B register, and a left shift of five places will shift the contents of the B register into the accumulator.

3. The contents of the Y register can be either added to or subtracted from the accumulator. The sum or difference is stored in the accumulator register.

4. Words from memory may be read into the Y register. To read a word into the accumulator, it is necessary to clear the accumulator, to read the word from memory into the Y register, and to add the Y register to the accumulator.

An arithmetic element that can perform these operations on its registers can be sequenced to perform all arithmetic operations. It is, in fact, possible to construct a machine using fewer operations than these, but most general-purpose computers have an arithmetic element with at least these capabilities.

Binary Multiplication

The process of multiplying binary numbers may be best examined by writing out the multiplication operation:

$$
\begin{array}{r}
1001 \quad = \text{Multiplicand} \\
1101 \quad = \text{Multiplier} \\
\hline
1001 \\
0000 \\
1001 \\
1001 \\
\hline
1110101 \quad = \text{Product}
\end{array}
$$

Partial products

The important thing to note in this process is that there are only two rules for multiplying a binary *number* by a binary *digit:* (1) If the multiplier digit is a 1, the

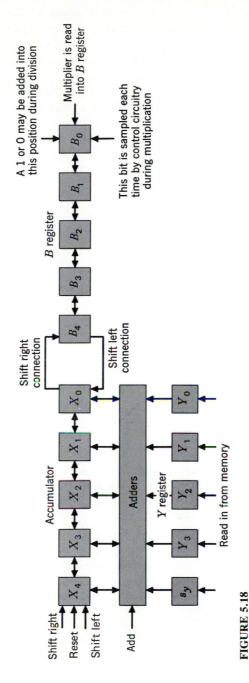

FIGURE 5.18

Generalized parallel arithmetic element.

215

multiplicand is simply copied to form the partial product. (2) If the multiplier digit is a 0, the partial product is 0. The above example illustrates these rules. Each time a partial product is formed, it is shifted one place to the left of the previous partial product. Even if the partial product is a 0, the next partial product is shifted one place to the left. This process is continued until all the multiplier digits have been used, and then the partial products are summed.

The three operations that the computer must be able to perform to multiply in this manner are, therefore, (1) to sense whether a multiplier bit is either a 1 or a 0, (2) to shift partial products, and (3) to add the partial products.

It is not necessary to wait until all the partial products have been formed before summing them; they may be summed two at a time. For instance, starting with the first two partial products in the above example, we have

$$\begin{array}{r} 1001 \\ \underline{0000} \\ 01001 \end{array}$$

The next partial product may be added to this sum, displacing it an extra position to the left:

$$\begin{array}{r} 01001 \\ \underline{1001} \\ 101101 \end{array}$$

And finally,

$$\begin{array}{r} 101101 \\ \underline{1001} \\ 1110101 \end{array}$$

A multiplier can be constructed in just this fashion. By sampling each bit of the multiplier in turn, adding the multiplicand into some register, and then shifting the multiplicand left each time a new multiplier bit is sampled, a product can be formed as the sum of the partial products. The process of multiplying in most binary machines is performed in a manner very similar to this.

To examine the typical technique for multiplying, the generalized arithmetic elements in Fig. 5.18 are used. Let the multiplier be stored in the B register and the multiplicand in the Y register. The accumulator initially contains all 0s as shown:

Accumulator B register

| 0———0 | | Multiplier |

Y register

| Multiplicand |

Let us assume that both multiplier and multiplicand are positive. If either is negative, it must be converted to positive form before the multiplication begins. The sign bits will therefore be 0s.

The desired result format is shown, with the product being the combined accumulator and *B* register:

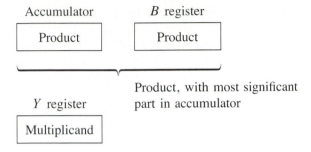

A multiplication requires *n* *basic steps*, where *n* is the number of bits in the magnitude of the numbers to be multiplied, and a final right shift to position the product. Each basic step is initiated by the control circuitry examining the rightmost bit in the *B* register. The basic step is as follows.

BASIC STEP

If the rightmost bit in the *B* register is a 0, the combined accumulator and *B* register are shifted right one place. If the rightmost bit in the *B* register is a 1, the number in the *Y* register is added to the contents of the accumulator, and then the combined accumulator and *B* register are shifted right one place.

After each basic step, the new rightmost bit of the *B* register is examined and the next of the *n* steps is initiated.

Let us consider the same multiplication used in the previous example, that is, 1101 × 1001, where 1101 is the multiplier. In the beginning, the accumulator contains 00000, the *B* register 01101, and the *Y* register 01001 (the leftmost 0s are sign bits). Four basic steps and a final shift are required.

1. Since the rightmost bit of the *B* register is a 1 (the least significant bit of the multiplier), during the first step the contents of the *Y* register are added to the accumulator, and the combined accumulator and *B* register are shifted to the right. The second least significant bit of the multiplier now occupies the rightmost bit of the *B* register and controls the next operation. The *Y* register still contains the multiplicand 01001, the contents of the accumulator are 00100, and the contents of the *B* register are 10110.

2. The rightmost bit of the B register is a 0, and since it controls the next operation, the accumulator and B register are shifted right, giving 00010 in the accumulator and 01011 in the B register.

3. A 1 is now in the rightmost bit of the B register. Therefore, the Y register is added to the accumulator again, and the combined accumulator and B register are shifted right, giving 00101 in the accumulator and 10101 in the B register.

4. The least significant bit of the B register is another 1, so the Y register is added to the accumulator and the accumulator and B register are shifted right. After the shift right, the combined accumulator and B register contain 0011101010. A final right shift gives 0001110101, the correct product of our integer number system. The most significant digits are stored in the accumulator, and the least significant digits in the B register.

Accumulator	B register	
00000	01101	At beginning
00100	10110	After step 1
00010	01011	After step 2
00101	10101	After step 3
00111	01010	After step 4
00011	10101	After shift right

Now the reason for combining the accumulator and B register can be seen. The product of two 5-bit signed numbers can contain up to nine significant digits (including the sign bit), so two 5-bit registers, not one, are required to hold the product. The final product is treated like a 10-bit number extending through the two registers with the leftmost bits (most significant bits) in the left register, the rightmost bits (least significant bits) in the right register, and the least significant binary digit in the rightmost bit. Thus, our result in the two registers is 0001110101, which is +117 in decimal.

The control circuitry is designed to examine the multiplier bits, then either shift or add and shift the correct number of times, and stop. In this case, the length of the multiplier, or Y register, is 4 bits plus a sign bit; so four such steps are performed. The general practice is to examine each bit of the computer word, except the sign bit, in turn. For instance, if the basic computer word is 32 bits (that is, 31 bits in which the magnitude of a number is stored plus a sign bit), each time a multiplication is performed, the computer will examine 31 bits, each in turn, performing the add-and-shift or just the shift operation 31 times. This makes the multiplication operation longer than such operations as addition or subtraction. Some parallel computers double their normal rate of operation during multiplication: if the computer performs such operations as addition, complementation, and transferring at a rate of 10 MHz/s for ordinary instructions, the rate will be increased to 20 MHz for the add-and-shift combinations performed during multiplying. Some computers are able to shift right while adding; that is, the sum of the accumulator and Y register appears shifted one place to the right each time, so the shift-right operation after each addition may be omitted.

The sign bits of the multiplier and multiplicand may be handled in a number of ways. For instance, the sign of the product can be determined by means of control circuitry before the multiplication procedure is initiated. This sign bit is stored during the multiplication process, after which it is placed into the sign bit of the accumulator, and then the accumulator is complemented, if necessary. Therefore, the sign bits of the multiplier and multiplicand are examined first. If they are both 0s, the sign of the product should be 0; if both are 1s, the sign of the product should be 0; and if either but not both are a 1, the sign of the product should be 1. This information, retained in a flip-flop while the multiplication is taking place, may be transferred into the sign bit afterward. If the computer handles numbers in the 1s or 2s complement system, both multiplier and multiplicand may be handled as positive magnitudes. If the sign of either number is negative, the number is complemented to a positive magnitude before the multiplication begins. Sometimes the multiplication is performed on complemented numbers using more complicated algorithms. These are described in the questions and bibliography.

Decimal Multiplication

Decimal multiplication is a more involved process than binary multiplication. Whereas the product of a binary digit and a binary number is either the number or 0, the product of a decimal digit and decimal number involves the use of a multiplication table plus carrying and adding. For instance,

$$7 \times 24 = 7 \times 4 + 7 \times 20 = 28 + 140 = 168$$

Even the multiplying of two decimal digits may involve two output digits; for instance, 7×8 equals 56. In the following discussion we call the two digits that result when a decimal digit is multiplied by a decimal digit the *left-hand* and the *right-hand* digits. Thus, for 3×6 we have 1 for the left-hand digit and 8 for the right-hand digit. For 2×3 we have 0 for the left-hand digit and 6 for the right-hand digit.

Except for just adding the multiplicand to itself the number of times indicated by the multiplier, a straightforward but time-consuming process, the simplest method for decimal multiplication involves loading the rightmost digit of the multiplier into a counter that counts downward and then adding the multiplicand to itself and simultaneously indexing the counter until the counter reaches 0. The partial product thus formed may be shifted right one decimal digit, the next multiplier digit loaded into the counter, and the process repeated until all the multiplier digits have been used. This is a relatively slow technique, however.

The process may be speeded up by forming products using the multiplicand and the rightmost digit of the multiplier, as in the previous scheme, but by actually forming the left-hand and right-hand partial products obtained and then summing them. For instance, 6×7164 would yield 2664 for the right-hand product digits and 4032 for the left-hand product digits. The sum would be

$$2664$$
$$+4032$$
$$\overline{42984}$$

Computer decimal multiplication is, in general, a complicated process if speed is desired, and there are almost as many techniques for multiplying BCD numbers as there are types of machines.[10] IC packages are produced that contain a gate network having two BCD characters as inputs to produce the two-digit output required. The questions and bibliography explore this in more detail.

Division*

The operation of division is the most difficult and time-consuming for ALUs of most general-purpose computers. Although division may appear no more difficult than multiplication, several problems in connection with the division process introduce lengthy additional steps.

Division using pencil and paper is a trial-and-error process. For instance, if we are to divide 77 into 4610, we first notice that 77 will not go into 46; so we attempt to divide 77 into 461. We may guess that it will go six times; however,

$$
\begin{array}{r}
6 \\
77\overline{)\,4610} \\
462 \\
\hline
-1
\end{array}
$$

We have guessed too high and must reduce the first digit of the quotient, which we will develop, to 5.

The same problem confronts the computer when it attempts to divide in this manner. It must "try" a subtraction at each step of the process and then see whether the remainder is negative. Consider the division of 1111 by 11:

$$
\begin{array}{r}
101 \\
11\overline{)\,1111} \\
11 \\
\hline
0011 \\
11 \\
\hline
00
\end{array}
$$

It is easy to determine visually at any step of the process whether the quotient is to be a 1 or a 0, but the computer cannot determine this without making a trial subtraction each time. After a trial quotient has been tried and the divisor subtracted, if the result is negative, either the current dividend must be "restored" or some other technique for dividing used.

---

[10] Several systems use table look-up techniques for forming products, where the product of each pair of digits is stored in the memory.

There are several points to note concerning binary fixed-point integer division. The division is generally performed with two signed binary integers of the same, fixed length. The result, or quotient, is stored as a number, with as many digits as the divisor or dividend, and the remainder is also stored as a number of the same length.[11]

Using the registers in Fig. 5.18, we will show how to divide a number stored in the accumulator by a number in the Y register. The quotient is stored in the B register and the remainder in the accumulator. This is the most common division format.

Assume that the B and Y registers in Fig. 5.18 are 5 bits in length (4 bits plus a sign bit), and the accumulator is also 5 bits in length. Before we start the procedure, the dividend is read into the accumulator and the divisor into the Y register. After the division, the quotient is stored in the B register, and the remainder is in the accumulator. Both divisor and dividend are to be positive.

For example, say the accumulator (dividend) originally contains 11 (decimal) and the Y register (divisor) contains 4. The desired result is the quotient 2 in the B register and the remainder 3 in the accumulator.

Accumulator	B register
01011	00000

At beginning
of division

Y register

00100

Accumulator	B register
00011	00010

After division

Y register

00100

There are two general division techniques for binary machines: the *restoring* and the *nonrestoring* techniques. Our first example illustrates the restoring technique.

Just as in multiplication, the restoring technique for division requires that a *basic step* be performed repeatedly (in this case, as many times as there are significant bits in the subtrahend).

---

[11] If we divide one integer into another, both the quotient and the remainder will be integers. The rule is as follows: If a is the dividend, y the divisor, b the quotient, and r the remainder, then $a = y \times b + r$.

BASIC STEP

A "trial division" is made by subtracting the Y register from the accumulator. After the subtraction, one of the following steps is executed.

1. If the result is negative, the divisor will not "go" into the dividend; so a 0 is placed in the rightmost bit of the B register, and the dividend (accumulator) is restored by adding the divisor to the result of the subtraction. The combined B register and accumulator are then shifted left.
2. If the result of a subtraction is positive or zero, there is no need to restore the partial dividend in the accumulator, for the trial division has succeeded. The accumulator and B register are both shifted left, and then a 1 is placed in the rightmost bit of the B register.

The computer determines whether the result of a trial division is positive or negative by examining the sign bit of the accumulator after each subtraction.

First it is necessary to understand how to initiate the division and how to start and stop performance of the basic steps. Unfortunately, these are complicated procedures, just as determining the position of the decimal point and how to start and stop the division is complicated for ordinary division.

1. As described above, if the divisor is larger than the dividend, the quotient should be 0, and the remainder is the value of the dividend. (For instance, if we attempt to divide 7 by 17, the quotient is 0, and the remainder is 7.) To test this, the dividend in Y can be subtracted from the accumulator. If the result is negative, all that remains is to restore the accumulator by adding the Y register to the accumulator. The B register now has value 0, which is right for the quotient, and the accumulator has the original value, which is the remainder.
2. After the preceeding test is made, it is necessary to align the leftmost 1 bit in the divisor with the leftmost 1 bit in the dividend by shifting the divisor left and recording the number of shifts required to make this alignment. If the number of shifts is M, then the basic step must be performed $M + 1$ times. [12]
3. The basic step is now performed the necessary $M + 1$ times.
4. Finally, to adjust the remainder, the accumulator must be shifted right $M + 1$ times after the last basic step is performed. Examples are shown in Tables 5.2 and 5.3. Step 1, testing for a zero quotient, is not shown in the two examples.

---

[12] This can be accomplished by making Y a shift register and providing a counter to count the shifts until the first 1 bit of Y is aligned with the 1 bit of the accumulator. Both the accumulator and Y could be shifted left until there is a 1 bit in their first position, but the remainder will have to be adjusted by moving it right in the accumulator.

TABLE 5.2

B register	Accumulator	*Y* register	Remarks
00000	00110	00011	We divide 6 by 3.
00000	00110	00110	*Y* register is shifted left once to align 1s in accumulator and *Y* register. The basic step must be performed two times.
00000	00000	00110	*Y* register is subtracted from accumulator. The result is 0.
00001	00000	00110	*B* register and accumulator are shifted left, and a 1 is placed in the rightmost bit of *B* register.
00001	11010	00110	*Y* register is subtracted from accumulator.
00010	00000	00110	*Y* register is added to accumulator, and *B* register and accumulator are shifted left 1. A 0 is placed in *B* register's last bit.
00010	00000	00110	Accumulator must now be shifted right two times, but it is 0, so no change results. The quotient in *B* register is 2, and the remainder in accumulator is 0.

TABLE 5.3

B register	Accumulator	*Y* register	Remarks
00000	01101	00011	We divide 13 by 3.
00000	01101	00110	Shift *Y* register left.
00000	01101	01100	Shift *Y* register left again. Leftmost 1 bits in accumulator and *Y* register are now aligned. Basic step will be performed three times.
00000	00001	01100	*Y* register is subtracted from accumulator. Result is positive.
00001	00010	01100	*B* register and accumulator are shifted left, and 1 is placed in *B* register.
00001	10110	01100	*Y* register is subtracted from accumulator. Result is negative.
00010	00100	01100	*Y* register is added to accumulator. *B* register and accumulator are shifted left, and a 0 is placed in *B* register.
00010	11000	01100	*Y* register is subtracted from accumulator. Result is negative.
00100	01000	01100	*Y* register is added to accumulator. Accumulator and *B* register are shifted left. A 0 is placed in *B* register's least significant bit.
00100	00001	01100	Accumulator is shifted right three times. The quotient is 4, and the remainder is 1.

Figure 5.19 shows a flowchart of the algorithm. A detailed flowchart divides the steps such as "shift the accumulator right $M + 1$ times" into single shifts performed in a loop that is controlled by a counter. For reasonably complicated algorithms, such as this one, it is often convenient to draw a flowchart of the algorithm before attempting to implement the control circuitry.

During division, the sign bits are handled in much the same way as during multiplication. The first step is to convert both the divisor and the dividend to positive magnitudes. The value of the sign bit for the quotient must be stored while the division is taking place. The rule is that if the signs of the dividend and divisor are both either 0s or 1s, the quotient will be positive. If either but not both of their signs is a 1, the quotient will be negative. The relationship of the sign bit of the quotient to the sign bit of the divisor and dividend is, therefore, the quarter-adder, or exclusive OR, relationship, that is, $S = X\overline{Y} + \overline{X}Y$. The value for the correct sign of the quotient may be read into a flip-flop while the division is taking place; this value is then placed in the sign bit of the register containing the quotient after the division of magnitudes has been completed.

There are several techniques for nonrestoring division. One widely used algorithm employs a procedure in which the divisor is alternately subtracted and added. Another uses a technique in which the divisor is compared to the dividend at each trial division. This material is covered in detail in the bibliography.

5.12 LOGICAL OPERATIONS

In addition to the arithmetic operations, many logical operations are performed by ALUs. Three logical operations are described here: logical multiplication, logical addition, and *sum modulo 2* addition (the exclusive OR operation). Each of these operations takes place between registers, where the operation specified is performed on each of the corresponding digits in the two registers. The result is stored in one of the registers.

Logical multiplication is often referred to as an *extract masking*, or *AND operation*. The rules for logical multiplication are $0 \cdot 0 = 0$, $0 \cdot 1 = 0$, $1 \cdot 0 = 0$, and $1 \cdot 1 = 1$. Suppose the contents of the accumulator register are logically multiplied by another register. Let each register consist of 5 bits. If the accumulator contains 01101 and the other register contains 00111, the contents of the accumulator after the operation will be 00101.

The logical addition operation and the sum modulo 2 operation are also provided in most computers. The rules for these operations are as follows:

LOGICAL ADDITION	MODULO 2 ADDITION
$0+0=0$	$0 \oplus 0 = 0$
$0+1=1$	$0 \oplus 1 = 1$
$1+0=1$	$1 \oplus 0 = 1$
$1+1=1$	$1 \oplus 1 = 0$

Figure 5.20 shows how a single accumulator flip-flop and B flip-flop can be gated so that all three of these logical operations can be performed. The circuit in Fig. 5.20 would be repeated for each stage of the accumulator register.

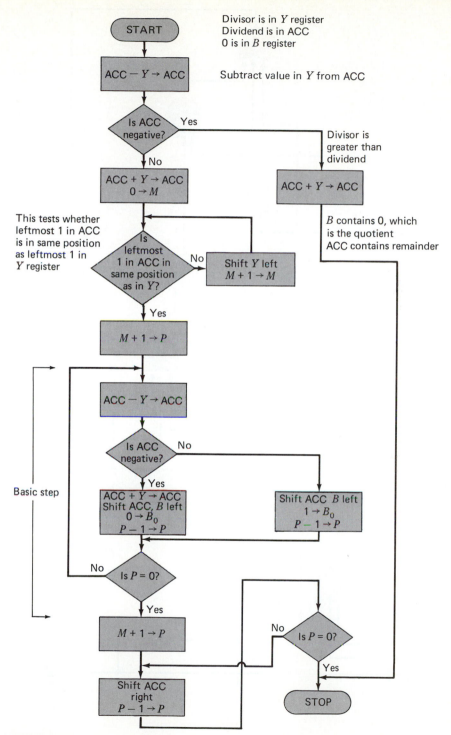

FIGURE 5.19
Flowchart of division algorithm.

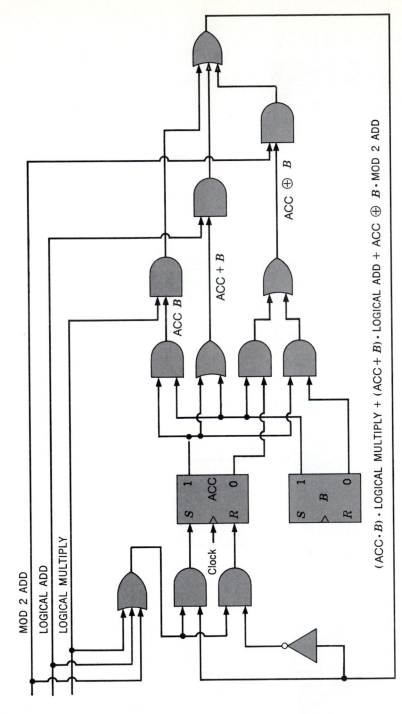

FIGURE 5.20
Circuit for gating logic operations into accumulator flip-flop.

226

There are three control signals: LOGICAL MULTIPLY, LOGICAL ADD, and MOD 2 ADD. If one of these is a 1, then when a clock pulse arrives, the respective operation is performed, and the result placed in the ACC (accumulator) flip-flop. If none of the control signals is a 1, nothing happens, and ACC remains as it is.

The actual values desired are formed by three sets of gates: that is, ACC·B, ACC + B, and ACC $\oplus$ B are all formed first. Each is then ANDed with the appropriate control signal. Finally, the three control signals are ORed, and this signal is used to gate the appropriate value into the ACC flip-flop when one of the control signals is a 1.

Figure 5.20 shows how a choice of several different function values can be gated into a single flip-flop using control signals. We could include an ADD signal and a SHIFT RIGHT and a SHIFT LEFT by simply adding more gates.

Figure 5.21 shows an example of the logic circuitry used to form sections of an ALU. All the gates are contained in a single chip (package) with 24 pins. There is a 7-ns maximum delay through the package. This chip, the 74S181, is called a *4-bit arithmetic-logic unit* and can add, subtract, AND, OR, and perform other operations on two 4-bit register sections. Two chips could be used for the logic in an 8-bit accumulator, four chips would form a 16-bit accumulator, and so forth.

The function performed by this chip is controlled by the mode input, M, and four function select inputs, S_0, S_1, S_2, and S_3. When M is low (a 0), the 74S181 performs such arithmetic operations as ADD or SUBTRACT. When M is high (a 1), the ALU does logic operations on the A and B inputs "a bit at a time." (Notice in Fig. 5.21 that the carry-generating gates are disabled by $M = 1$.) For instance, if M is a 0, S_1 and S_2 are also 0s, and S_0 and S_3 are 1s, then the 74S181 performs arithmetic addition. If M is a 1, S_0 and S_3 are 1s, and S_1 and S_2 are 0s, the 74S181 chip exclusive-ORs (mod 2 adds) A and B (it forms $A_0 \oplus B_0$, $A_1 \oplus B_1$, $A_2 \oplus B_2$, and $A_3 \oplus B_3$).

The table in Fig. 5.21 further describes the operation of this chip. Questions at the end of the chapter develop some operational characteristics of this 4-bit ALU section.

5.13   MULTIPLEXERS

The function of a *multiplexer* is to select from several inputs a single input. Control lines are used to make this selection.

Figure 5.22 shows an eight-input multiplexer on a single IC chip. The eight inputs are labeled I_0, I_1, ... , I_7. There are three control wires, S_2, S_1, and S_0. These three control lines can take eight different values (from 000 to 111), and for each value a different input is selected. The value of the input selected appears on Z. An examination of this multiplexer shows that if $S_2 S_1 S_0$ are all 0s, input I_0 is selected. If $S_2 S_1 S_0$ are 001, I_1 is selected; if $S_2 S_1 S_0$ are 010, I_2 is selected; and so on.

For example, if $S_2 S_1 S_0 = 010$, the output Z will be 0 if I_2 is a 0 and a 1 if I_2 is a 1. The input values on I_0, I_1, I_3, I_4, I_5, I_6 and I_7 will not affect the output value on Z. The E input enables the multiplexer.

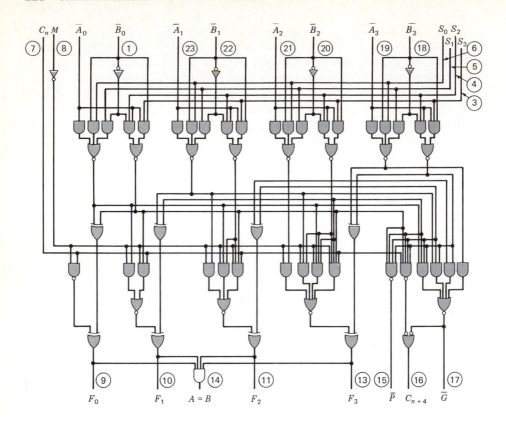

MODE SELECT INPUTS				ACTIVE LOW INPUTS & OUTPUTS	
				LOGIC	ARITHMETIC
S_3	S_2	S_1	S_0	$(M = H)$	$(M = L)$ $(C_n = L)$
L	L	L	L	$\bar{A}$	$A - 1$
L	L	L	L	$\overline{AB}$	$AB - 1$
L	L	H	L	$\bar{A} + B$	$A\bar{B} - 1$
L	L	H	H	Logical 1	-1
L	H	L	L	$\overline{A + B}$	$A \mp (A + \bar{B})$
L	H	L	H	$\bar{B}$	$AB \mp (A + \bar{B})$
L	H	H	L	$A \oplus B$	$A - B - 1$
L	H	H	H	$A + \bar{B}$	$A + \bar{B}$
H	L	L	L	$A\bar{B}$	$A \mp (A + B)$
H	L	L	H	$A \oplus B$	$A \mp B$
H	L	H	L	B	$AB \mp (A + B)$
H	L	H	H	$A + B$	$A + B$
H	H	L	L	Logical 0	$A \mp A$
H	H	L	H	$A\bar{B}$	$AB \mp A$
H	H	H	L	AB	$AB \mp A$
H	H	H	H	A	A

*L = 0; H = 1.

Note:

x ———⟩ z
y ———

is the symbol for a mod 2 adder (exclusive OR gate)
$z = x \oplus y$

$\mp$ is the sign for arithmetic addition

FIGURE 5.21
A 4-bit arithmetic logic unit.

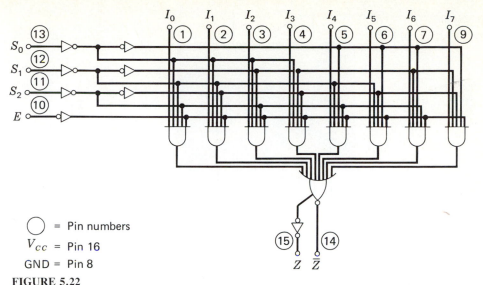

FIGURE 5.22
Eight-input multiplexer in a single IC container.

Multiplexers are useful in many ways. Suppose we are to select as inputs to a gate network a single register from four flip-flop registers, with two flip-flops in each register. Figure 5.23 shows a dual four-input multiplexer that will accomplish this. The two multiplexers each have four inputs, and the inputs selected are in the same respective positions. There are two control inputs, S_1 and S_0. If S_1 and S_0 are both 0s, then A_0 and B_0 are selected and placed on the A and B outputs; if S_1 is a 0 and S_0 is a 1, then the values of A_1 and B_1 are placed on the A and B outputs; and so on.

The $ENABLE$ input is used to enable or disable both multiplexers. A 0 on $\overline{ENABLE}$ enables the outputs, and a 1 on $\overline{ENABLE}$ forces both outputs to 0.

Figure 5.24 shows four flip-flop registers, W, X, Y, and Z, each with two flip-flops. The control lines S_0 and S_1 select from each of the four sets of inputs a single two-flip-flop register, whose outputs are then placed on the output lines. This shows how multiplexers can be used to select a single register from a set of registers. If each register contained more than two flip-flops, another dual four-input multiplexer would be needed for each additional two flip-flops.

Multiplexers are useful in many ways, and Figs. 5.22 and 5.23 should be examined carefully.

5.14   HIGH-SPEED ARITHMETIC*

Speeding up Addition

Since additions and subtractions are often performed in computers, it is desirable to perform them quickly. In this section we describe how the time required may be shortened. This also will speed up multiplication and division, which in most cases involve a number of additions or subtractions.

230

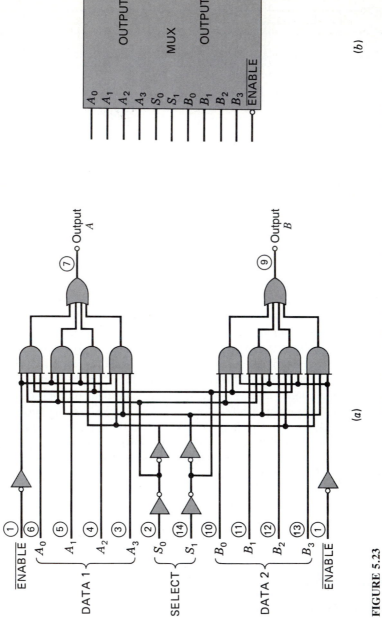

(a)

(b)

FIGURE 5.23
Two multiplexers in a single IC container (SN54153 and SN74153). (a) Block diagram showing gates. (b) Block diagram symbol.

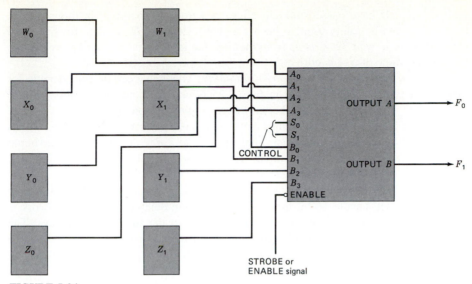

FIGURE 5.24
Using a dual four-input multiplexer IC to select from four flip-flop registers.

Figure 5.25 shows a set of full adders as they might be interconnected to form a 16-bit full adder for two registers of 16 flip-flops each (i.e., for two 16-bit numbers). Note that a carry arising in the rightmost adder (if X_0 and Y_0 are both 1s) will propagate all the way through the leftmost adder (for X_{15} and Y_{15}) if there is a 1 input at each adder in the chain.

Each gate in a network delays a signal by some time period. Thus, if a set of new inputs is placed on the inputs to the adder configuration, it is necessary to wait

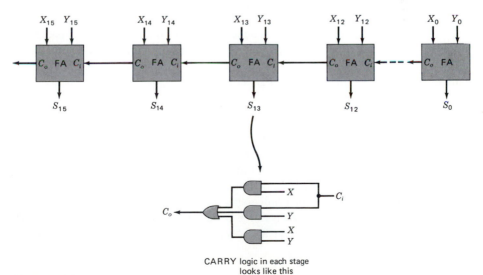

FIGURE 5.25
Chain of full adders.

until the signals have passed through all gates before the outputs, in this case S_{15} through S_0, can be safely used. If each gate has a delay of D ns, then for Fig. 5.25 it is necessary to wait $32 \times D$ ns from the time the inputs are changed before we can be sure the value of S_{15} is correct.

This is called the *carry propagation delay*. This delay can be considerable for long registers if the configuration in Fig. 5.25 is used without modification. Fortunately, there are several ways to shorten the carry propagation delay.

Figure 5.26 shows an IC chip layout containing gates to add two 4-bit inputs plus a carry to the group. Note here that the C_0, or carry output, has a maximum delay path of three gates for any input. That is, the maximum delay path from any input to the output C_o is a three-gate delay.

Figure 5.27 shows how four of these IC containers can be interconnected to form an adder that will handle 16-bit inputs. The maximum delay through this network is shorter than that for the layout in Fig. 5.25 because of the shorter carry delays. The maximum path length for the C_i input to the leftmost four-adder package is nine gates, or $9 \times D$ ns if a gate delay is D ns. The delay through the final package—to S_{15}, for example—is four gate delays, however, because a carry input to C_i must pass through an AND gate, a NOR gate, and exclusive OR gates to reach S_{15}; and exclusive OR gates require two delays. (Exclusive OR gates are often made from a two-level network of conventional gates.)

The reduction of carry propagation delay using the adder in Fig. 5.26 is due to the development of the C_o output directly from the eight inputs A_1, B_1, $\ldots$, A_4, B_4, and C_i. For example, if we wish to put a 3-bit adder in a single container, with inputs A_1, B_1, A_2, B_2, A_3, B_3, and C_i, then the C_o output can be written as follows:[13]

$$C_o = C_i(A_3 + B_3)(A_2 + B_2)(A_1 + B_1)$$
$$+ A_3B_3(A_2 + B_2)(A_1 + B_1) + A_2B_2(A_1 + B_1) + A_1B_1$$

This expression results in a three-level network, and thus three-gate delays, but the expression can be "multiplied out," and a two-level net will result.

The amount of delay reduction in adders depends on the complexity (and therefore cost) of the gating network used. As an example, the network of Fig. 5.21 has a reasonably fast carry, but this chip also develops a P and G output that can be used with another chip to further speed up adder operation.

Parallel Multipliers

The multiplication technique described earlier is called the *add-and-shift algorithm*. This technique is used in most smaller computers because it is implemented directly. Also, it is often used in programs for multiplication because many smaller computers (microcomputers, in particular) have no multiplication instruction.

Larger computers and signal-processing computers have a need for high-speed multiplication. To achieve this, arrays of gates are used that multiply several binary digits at the same time. These arrays are of various sizes and range from moderately

---

[13] This is the expression for a *carry look-ahead* or *carry bridging* net. Placing carry look-aheads every few adders will speed up adder operations.

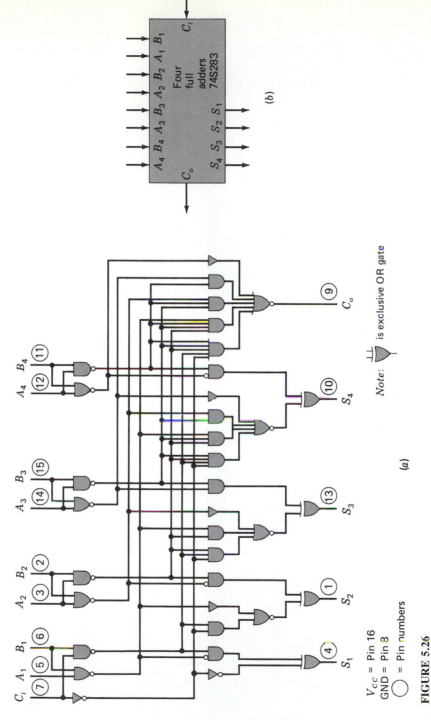

FIGURE 5.26

Full adders with carry bridge. (*a*) A 74S283 chip with four full adders. (*b*) Block diagram for (*a*).

V_{CC} = Pin 16
GND = Pin 8
◯ = Pin numbers

Note: is exclusive OR gate

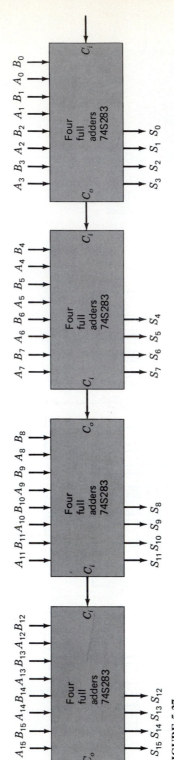

FIGURE 5.27
A 16-bit adder made from IC chips.

inexpensive to quite expensive. Their use is based on economic considerations and the requirements for the system.

We will now illustrate how two binary numbers can be multiplied in a gating network. Suppose a_1a_0 and b_1b_0 are two binary 2-bit numbers, for example, $a_1a_0 = 10$, which is 2 in decimal, $b_1b_0 = 11$, which is 3 in decimal. If these numbers are multiplied using our familiar technique, this array is formed:

$$
\begin{array}{cccc}
 & & b_1 & b_0 \\
 & \times & a_1 & a_0 \\
\hline
 & a_0b_1 & a_0b_0 & \\
a_1b_1 & a_1b_0 & & \\
\hline
p_3 \quad p_2 & p_1 & p_0 &
\end{array}
$$

where

$$
\begin{aligned}
p_0 &= a_0b_0 \\
p_1 &= a_0b_1 \oplus a_1b_0 \\
p_2 &= a_1b_1 \oplus a_0b_1a_1b_0 \\
p_3 &= a_1b_1a_0b_0
\end{aligned}
$$

Here

$$
\begin{array}{ll}
0 \oplus 0 = 0 & \quad 1 \oplus 0 = 1 \\
0 \oplus 1 = 1 & \quad 1 \oplus 1 = 0
\end{array}
$$

Figure 5.28 shows the boolean algebra expression for the product bits, p_3, p_2, p_1, and p_0, realized in gate network form. If a_1a_0 and b_1b_0 are input to the network, $p_3p_2p_1p_0$ will give the product in binary integer form. The net in Fig. 5.28 is called a *parallel multiplier*.

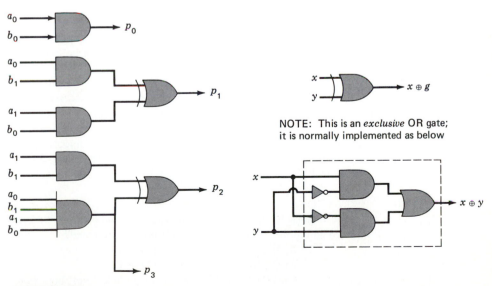

FIGURE 5.28
A two-digit parallel binary multiplier.

This technique for deriving boolean algebra expressions for the product bits can be used for multiplications involving more digits. Unfortunately, for 8-bit or 16-bit multipliers and multiplicands, the expressions become very large and costly to implement. However, this technique works well for small numbers.

To make parallel multipliers for larger numbers of inputs and outputs, an array of full adders is commonly used. Consider the multiplication of two 3-bit numbers shown in Fig. 5.29(a). The partial products are shown, with the product bits $p_5 p_4 p_3 p_2 p_1 p_0$ immediately below. In Fig. 5.29(b) a set of nine AND gates is used to produce all the $a_i b_j$ terms in Fig. 5.29(a). In Fig. 5.29(c) an arrangement of full adders is shown that have as inputs the outputs from the AND gates in Fig. 5.29(b) and that will implement the multiplication shown in Fig. 5.29(a). It is instructive to see how the multiplication is performed by the full adders. The operation of this circuit should be carefully examined.

The maximum length of the carry path for Fig. 5.29(c) is along the top row to the p_5 output. If the full adders have two-gate delays for each carry, then Fig. 5.29(c) has as a worst case an eight-gate delay, and another delay arises from the AND gates in Fig. 5.29(b). As the number of bits in the numbers being multiplied increases, so does the size of the array of full adders, and so does the delay through the array. There are several ways to rearrange the adders slightly and to add more gates to reduce this delay; these are covered by selections in the bibliography.

Parallel multiplier arrays are packaged in IC containers by several manufacturers. The largest array in a single IC container multiplies two 16-bit numbers; the delay through this package is about 25 ns. Eight-bit parallel multipliers are common. Several of these multipliers can be grouped along with some full adders to form multipliers for even larger numbers. Parallel multipliers also can be used to shorten multiplication time by using an add-and-shift algorithm and multiplying several bits at each step.

QUESTIONS

5.1. Draw a block diagram of circuitry for two registers, X and Y, of three flip-flops each, so that Y can be transferred into X, or the 1s complement of Y can be transferred into X.

5.2. Two parallel binary registers, designated register X and register Y, each consist of three flip-flops. Draw a block diagram of the registers and the necessary logic circuitry so that (a) register X can be cleared, or 1s complemented, and (b) the 1s complement of the contents of register Y can be transferred into register X.

5.3. If a binary computer handles numbers in the sign-plus-magnitude integer system and numbers are 5 bits (sign plus 4 bits) each, how would the following decimal numbers be represented? (For example, $+5 = \underline{0}0101$.)

(a) $+6$ (b) $+10$ (c) -12
(d) -16

5.4. If a binary computer represents numbers in a sign-plus-magnitude form with 5 bits per number, how would the following decimal numbers be represented?

(a) $+8$ (b) $+11$ (c) -7
(d) -4 (e) -15 (f) -12

5.5. If a binary machine handles negative numbers in true magnitude form, how would -4 be stored in a register with a sign bit and 4 bits representing magnitude? If

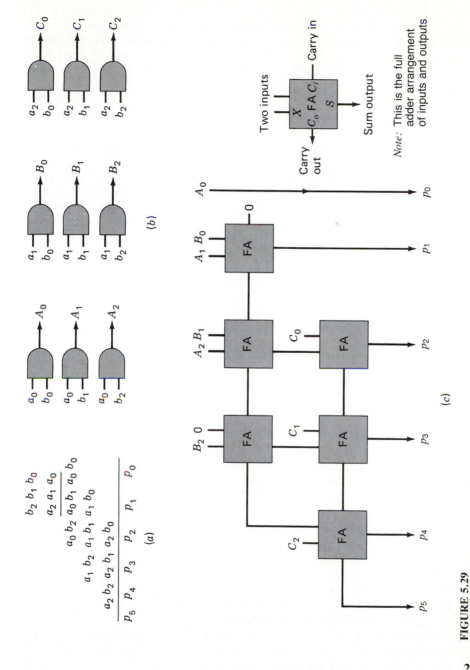

FIGURE 5.29

A parallel multiplier. (*a*) Multiplication of 3-bit numbers. (*b*) Forming product terms. (*c*) Parallel multiplier made of full adders.

237

the same machine stored numbers in the 1s complement system, how would -4 be stored?

5.6. If a register contains five flip-flops, as in Fig. 5.1(b), with $X_0 = 1$, $X_2 = 1$, $X_3 = 0$, $X_4 = 0$, $X_5 = 1$, give the decimal value of the number in the register if the 1s complement number system is used. What is the value if 2s complement is used?

5.7. The inputs to the full adder in Fig. 5.3 are as follows: $X = 1$, $Y = 1$, and $C_i = 1$. What will the output on the S and C_o lines represent?

5.8. If we use the $\oplus$ symbol to mean exclusive OR, defined as $X \oplus Y = \overline{X}Y + X\overline{Y}$, then the output S from a full adder can be written as $S = X \oplus Y \oplus C_i$. Show why this is the case.

5.9. If we load the binary number $\underline{1}0011$ into the flip-flops in Fig. 5.1(b), that is, if $X_4 = 1$, $X_3 = 0$, $X_2 = 0$, $X_1 = 1$, and $X_0 = 1$, what will the value of the register be in the 1s complement number system? Give the answer in decimal. What will the value of this number be if the 2s complement number system is used?

5.10. If register X contains $\underline{0}0111$ and register Y contains $\underline{1}1011$, what do the two numbers represent in decimal if 1s complement is used? If 2s complement is used? Add the two numbers in 1s complement, then in 2s complement, and give the results in decimal.

5.11. Register X contains $\underline{0}1100$, and register Y contains $\underline{0}1101$ (where the underscored 0s designate that the number stored is positive). If the two registers are added, what will the result be?

5.12. If 1s complement is used, for which of the following expressions will an overflow or end-around carry be generated? Why? Assume 5-bit registers, including a sign bit.
(a) $+5 + (-7)$ (b) $+5 + (-4)$ (c) $+12 + (-13)$
(d) $+12 + 3$

5.13. Add a stage to the load-and-shift register in Fig. 5.17. Copy only D in your drawing, omitting A, B, and C.

5.14. A binary register consists of five binary storage devices; one stores the sign bit, and the other four store the magnitude bits. If the number stored is $\underline{0}0110$ and this number is then shifted right one binary place, what will be the result? Assume a 0 goes into the sign bit.

5.15. Design a half-adder, using only NOR gates.

5.16. A binary half-subtracter has two inputs, x and y, and two outputs, which are the difference value $x - y$ and a BORROW output that is 1 if the value of $x - y$ is negative ($x - y$ is then given the value 1). Draw a block diagram for a half-subtracter, using NAND gates, assuming x, $\overline{x}$, y, and $\overline{y}$ are all available as inputs.

5.17. Design a half-adder, using only NAND gates.

5.18. If a BORROW input is added to the half-subtracter in Question 5.16, a full subtracter is formed. Design a full subtracter using only NAND gates.

5.19. Design a half-subtracter, using only NOR gates.

5.20. Design a full subtracter, using only NOR gates.

5.21. Design a full adder, using only NAND gates.

5.22. Explain how the 2s complement of the subtrahend is formed during subtraction, using the configuration in Fig. 5.6. How is the 1 added in to form this complement?

5.23. Can an overflow occur during multiplication in a binary machine with numbers stored in fixed-point sign-plus-magnitude form? Assume a double-length product.

5.24. Show how the configuration in Fig. 5.6 adds and subtracts by adding and subtracting $+11$ and $+3$ in binary, showing what each output will be.

5.25. Draw a multiplexer using only NAND gates that selects from four inputs, I_0 to I_3, using two select inputs, S_0 and S_1.

5.26. Using the configuration in Fig. 5.6, add and subtract $+6$ and -4, showing what each output will be and checking the correctness of the sum and difference.

5.27. Design a multiplexer for four inputs, using a two-level NOR gate combinational network. The inputs are to be X_0, X_1, X_2, and X_3. The output is to be called W. The X_0, X_1, X_2, and X_3 lines are selected by S_0 and S_1. If S_0 and S_1 are each 0, then W should equal X_0. If S_1 and S_0 equal 01, then W should equal X_1. If S_0 and S_1 are 10, then W should equal X_2. If S_0 and S_1 are 11, then W should equal X_3.

5.28. Add a control line NAND and circuitry to Fig. 5.20 so that the NAND of ACC and B can be transferred into ACC.

5.29. If a register containing $\underline{0}110011$ is logically added to a register containing $\underline{0}101010$, what will the result be? What will be the result if the registers are logically multiplied? If the registers are exclusive ORed?

5.30. Find a sequence of logical operations that will cause ACC to have value 0 regardless of how ACC and B start in Fig. 5.20.

5.31. Referring to Fig. 5.20, show that a logical multiplication followed by a logical addition will transfer the contents of B to ACC.

5.32. Add a control line NOR and circuitry to Fig. 5.20 so that the NOR of ACC and B can be transferred into ACC.

5.33. Demonstrate by means of a table of combinations that two half-adders plus an OR gate do make a full adder, as shown in Fig. 5.4.

5.34. Add gates and a flip-flop X_{m+2} so that we can shift left and right into X_{m+1} in Fig. 5.16.

5.35. Design a gate network with inputs A, B, C, X, and Y so that if the control input signal C is made a 1, the value $\overline{XY}$ will appear on the output line. If A is a 1, then $X + Y$ appears on the output; if B is a 1, then $X \cdot Y$ appears on the output; if A, B, and C are 0s, then the output is to be a 0; and only one of A, B, or C can be a 1 at a given time. Use only NAND gates in the design.

5.36. Design a parallel multiplier gate network with two inputs, A_1A_0 and $B_2B_1B_0$, where A_1A_0 are two binary digits forming a binary number (with decimal values 0 to 3) and $B_2B_1B_0$ is a 3-bit binary number (with values 0 to 7). Use only AND gates and OR gates, and see that no signal passes through more than four levels of gates. (Assume input complements are available.)

5.37. In what case will subtracting a negative number from 0 cause an overflow in the 2s complement system?

5.38. Write the boolean algebra expressions for the four least significant bits in a parallel multiplier that multiplies two 4-bit binary numbers.

5.39. Design a gating network for a module in an ALU that will add two 2-bit binary inputs, A_j, A_{j-1} and B_j, B_{j-1}, and an input carry-in, C_{j-1}. The network is to generate the two sum digits and a carry-out C_{j+2}. Use only AND or OR gates and inverters, but assume that both complemented and uncomplemented inputs are available. The output carry, C_{j+2}, should have a delay of no more than three gates (that is, a change in an input must pass through no more than three gates in any path to an output).

5.40. Most microprocessors address memory in 8-bit bytes. This means there can be a single alphanumeric decimal digit or two BCD digits at each address. Discuss instructions to convert alphanumeric characters to BCD format.

5.41. A reduced instruction set computer (RISC) contains many general registers, and all arithmetic is done between these registers (i.e., there are no arithmetic operations between memory and registers). Discuss the effect of this on speed of operation.

5.42. Develop a flowchart for floating-point addition, using the IEEE standard for 32-bit numbers, similar to that for division shown in the chapter.

5.43. The Booth algorithm for multiplication uses a setup like the one in Sec. 5.11 except that an extra flip-flop is added to the right of the B register. Bits from B_o shift into this flip-flop, which is started at 0. The two rightmost bits in the multiplicand are examined during each step instead of only the rightmost bit. If B_o and the extra flip-flop are 11 or 00, the registers are simply shifted; if they are 10, the multiplicand is subtracted from the partial product, which is then shifted; and if they are 01, the multiplicand is added to the partial product, which is then shifted. This algorithm multiplies signed 2s complement numbers, positive or negative, and delivers the signed product. Work through this algorithm by multiplying 4×-7 and -6×-5 in 5-bit formats.

5.44. Ignoring the handling of sign bits, does the Booth algorithm speed up multiplication? (Consider that an addition or subtraction takes longer than a shift, but be careful in your answer.)

5.45. Design an arithmetic element like the one in Fig. 5.18, and show how it works for the Booth algorithm.

5.46. The boolean algebra expressions on the output lines from the gates in Fig. 5.8 are not filled in. Develop the boolean algebra expressions for the $S1$, $S2$, and $C2$ outputs from the network.

5.47. When the 2s complement number system is used and addition is performed, let us designate the carry-out of the full adder connected into the full adder for the sign digits as C_3 (refer to Fig. 5.6). The rule for overflow is that two numbers added cause an overflow either if both numbers are positive and C_3 is a 1, or if both numbers are negative and C_3 is not a 1. Therefore, by examining the sign digits of the two numbers and the carry-out of the full adder that adds the two most significant digits of the magnitudes, we can form a logic network whose output will be a 1 when an overflow condition arises and a 0 if the addition is legitimate. Let X_4 store the sign digit of the addend, let Y_4 store the sign digit of the augend, and let C_3, again, be the carry-out of the full adder connected to the X_3 and Y_3 flip-flops. Show that the logic equation for an overflow condition is $X_4 Y_4 \overline{C_3} + \overline{X_4} \overline{Y_4} C_3 =$ Overflow.

5.48. Which of the following number systems has two 0s?
(*a*) Sign plus magnitude (*b*) 1s complement   (*c*) 2s complement

5.49. Modify Fig. 5.16 so that the complement of X can be shifted into X_m, that is, so that SHIFT LEFT causes $\overline{X}_{m-1}$ to go into X_m.

5.50. Show that when we add 7 to 9 in the BCD system using the series-parallel BCD adder in Fig. 5.10, the answer will be correct. Do this by tracing the outputs of the circuit, filling in the binary value for each X and Y shown in the figure, and showing the values of Z_8, Z_4, Z_2 and Z_1.

5.51. Show how the BCD adder in Fig. 5.11 adds +6 to +5, by calculating each output from the gates and then the final outputs.

5.52. Explain the operation of Fig. 5.15 by explaining how 234 can be added to or subtracted from 523 in this configuration.

5.53. Check how the gates in Fig. 5.12 form a 9s complement by trying 5 and 3 in BCD at the inputs.

5.54. Explain how to load the input values on W, X, Y, and Z into the flip-flops in Fig. 5.17.

5.55. What is the function of the D flip-flop in Fig. 5.15?

5.56. Explain how to cause the flip-flops in Fig. 5.17 to shift right three times. Suppose we (1) make the RESET input a 0 then a 1, (2) hold J and K at 1 and shift at 1, and (3) apply three clock pulses to the CLOCK line. Draw the output waveforms for A, B, C, and D for this sequence of inputs.

5.57. What is the result if we multiply 01101 by 00011 in our generalized machine in Fig. 5.18? Give the values in each X and B flip-flop.

5.58. What is the binary number that represents -3 in the 2s complement system if we represent the number by using a sign digit plus four magnitude digits?

5.59. Using the 8,4,2,1 BCD system with a single digit for the sign digit, write the following numbers, using a sign-plus-magnitude number system:
(a) $+0014$ (b) $+0291$ (c) -2346
(d) -0364

5.60. Using the 8,4,2,1 code, give the same numbers as in Question 5.59, but use 9s complement for the negative numbers.

5.61. Using the 8,4,2,1 BCD system, write in binary form the following decimal numbers. Use a single digit for the sign digit, and express the numbers as magnitude plus sign.
(a) $+0043$ (b) -0222 (c) $+1234$
(d) -1297

5.62. Write the binary forms of the numbers in Question 5.61 using 8,4,2,1, but use 10s complements for negative numbers.

5.63. Express each of the numbers in Question 5.61 using the 9s complement and the 8,4,2,1 BCD system. For example, $-1024 = 11000\ 1001\ 0111\ 0101$.

5.64. If we add two 20-digit binary numbers using the full adders shown in Fig. 5.8, and if 3 ns is required for a signal to pass through a gate, what is the maximum time it will require a CARRY signal to propagate from the lowest-order bits to the highest-order bits, assuming a parallel full adder as in Fig. 5.6?

5.65. Write the decimal numbers in Question 5.61 using the 10s complement number system and, again, the 8,4,2,1 BCD system. For example, $-1420 = 11000\ 0101\ 1000\ 0000$.

5.66. If we multiply 6×11 in the registers in Fig. 5.18, show the placement of binary digits at the start and end of the multiplication.

5.67. Explain how you would add gates and inputs to Fig. 5.17 so that the flip-flop register could be shifted left as well as right.

5.68. Draw a flowchart (as in Fig. 5.19) for the binary multiplication procedure described.

5.69. Show how 7×9 and 5×5 would be multiplied in the registers in Fig. 5.18.

5.70. Explain how to divide 14 by 4 by using the registers in Fig. 5.18 and showing how the quotient and the remainder are placed after the division.

5.71. If we divide 23 by 6 in the registers in Fig. 5.18, show the beginning positioning of the numbers (in binary) and the result at the end. (Show where the quotient and the remainder are placed.)

5.72. Using the algorithm shown in Fig. 5.19, show how to divide 11 by 4.

5.73. Go through the division of 14 by 3, using the technique shown in the text.

5.74. Explain the function of the multiplexer.

5.75. Modify the algorithm for division that was given to handle positive and negative integers in 2s complement form.

5.76. Design a *serial adder* using D flip-flops and NOR gates. The design is to have two inputs that accept the two binary numbers to be added, least significant bits first, and two output lines that give the sum bits and carry bit. Give a description of your design in state table form.

5.77. The principle of *carry-save addition* can be applied when a number of summands need to be added to generate a sum. The simplest example is in adding three numbers, W, X, and Y. With carry-save addition, the three operands are added using n full adders to generate two numbers, S (sum bits) and C (carry bits), which are then added in a ripple-carry adder to generate the desired sum. Apply this idea to the multiplication of two n-bit positive numbers. Start by considering the problem as one of adding n summands, appropriately shifted, as in the paper-and-pencil method. This principle is used in many high-performance computers.

5.78. Why should the sign of the remainder after a division be the same as the sign of the dividend?

5.79. A binary computer with a basic 16-bit data word uses an integer 2s complement system. The arithmetic element contains an accumulator and MQ register, each containing 16 flip-flops (or bits). When a multiplication is performed, the 16-bit word taken from the memory is multiplied by the 16-bit word in the accumulator, and the product is stored in the combined ACC-MQ with the least significant bit in the rightmost bit of the MQ. The sign bit of the MQ is set the same as the sign of the ACC; it is not used to store a magnitude bit. In what bit of the ACC does the most significant bit of a product appear for numbers of maximum magnitude?

5.80. For the 74S181 chip in Fig. 5.21, write the boolean algebra expression for $\overline{F}_0$ in terms of A_0, B_0, and C_n if M, S_3, S_1, and S_0 are 1s and S_2 is a 0.

5.81. For the 74S181 chip in Fig. 5.21, how would you set M, S_0, S_1, S_2, and S_3 to subtract B from A?

5.82. For the 74S181 chip in Fig. 5.21, if we set $M = 1$, $S_3 = S_1 = S_0 = 1$, and $S_2 = 0$, the chip will add A to B. Write the boolean algebra expression for F_1 in terms of the A, B, C_{n+4} inputs.

5.83. How would you set the M, S_0, S_1, S_2, and S_3 inputs to the 74S181 chip in Fig. 5.21 to form the AND of A and B?

5.84. How would you set the M, S_0, S_1, S_2, and S_3 inputs to perform an OR operation on the A and B inputs for the chip in Fig. 5.21?

5.85. Explain how the carry output C_n is formed for the chip in Fig. 5.21.

5.86. The statement was made that the maximum delay through the 74S181 chip in Fig. 5.21 is 7 ns. This means, for instance, that if all the inputs are held in the same state except for $\overline{A}_0$, then from the time $\overline{A}_0$ is changed, the maximum time for C_{n+4} to change will be 7 ns. Find the maximum number of gates through which this delay must propagate. Then determine typical single-gate delays.

5.87. The inputs to the 74S181 chip in Fig. 5.21 are each complemented, as are the outputs. Suppose we connect the A and B inputs to the uncomplemented outputs of the A and B flip-flops, changing the diagram by removing the bars over the A and B inputs and the F outputs. Now if M is a 1, the functions yielded by each S_0, S_1, S_2, and S_3 state (input combination) will differ from those shown in Fig. 5.21. For instance, $M = S_3 = S_2 = S_1 = 1$ and $S_0 = 0$ will cause the circuit to form $A + B$. Give three more different output functions and their S_0, S_1, S_2, and S_3 values.

5.88. Using the setup of Question 5.87, give three more functions.

5.89. The following is the block diagram for a 74S182 chip in the TTL series. This works with four 74S181 chips, shown in Fig. 5.21. The $\overline{G}_0$, $\overline{P}_0$, $\overline{G}_1$, $\overline{P}_1$, ... inputs here are connected to the $\overline{G}$ and $\overline{P}$ outputs for the four 74S181 chips to be used. The 74S182 chip forms a carry-look-ahead generator for all four chips, forming high-speed carries for inputs to these chips. A complete 16-bit addition can be performed in 22 ns. Explain how this works.

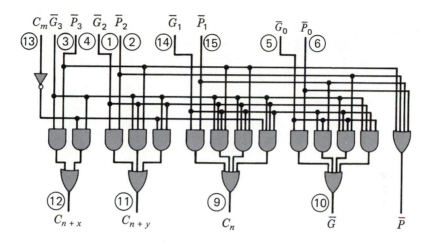

5.90. For the carry generator in Question 5.89 and four 74S181 chips as in Fig. 5.21, find the longest carry propagation path and determine how many gates are in it.

5.91. Develop the boolean algebra expression for the carry output in Fig. 5.29.

5.92. Convert the boolean algebra expression for the carry-out in a 3-bit adder to two-level AND-to-OR gate form.

CHAPTER
6

THE MEMORY ELEMENT

The memory of a computer is not actually concentrated in one place: storage devices are scattered throughout the machine. For instance, the *operation registers* are flip-flop registers used in the arithmetic and control sections of the computer. Arithmetic operations, including additions, multiplications, shifts, etc., are all performed in these registers of the machine. The actual processing of information is performed in and directed by these registers.

Moving outward, the next category of storage device encountered is called the *high-speed memory, inner memory, main memory,* or the *random access memory* (RAM). This section of the computer's memory consists of a set of storage registers, each of which is identified with an address that enables the control section either to write into or read from a particular register.

It is desirable that the operating speed of this section of the computer's memory be as high as possible, for most of the transfers of data to and from the information processing section of the machine will be via the main memory. For this reason, storage devices with very fast access times are generally chosen for the main memory: unfortunately, the presently available devices that are fast enough to perform this function satisfactorily do not possess the storage capacity that is sometimes required. As a result, additional memory, called the *auxiliary memory* or *secondary memory*, is added to most computers. This section of the computer's memory is characterized by low cost per digit stored, but it generally has an operating speed far slower than that of either the operation registers or the main memory. This section of the memory is sometimes designated the *backup memory*, for its function is to handle quantities of data in excess of those that may be stored in the inner memory.

Each division of memory has certain characteristics. For instance, the premium on speed is very high for the operation registers. These registers generally must perform operations at many times the speed of the main memory. The main memory also requires high operating speeds, but because it is desirable to store larger quantities of data (perhaps 10^6 to 10^9 bits) in this section, a compromise between cost and speed generally must be made. Often the same sort of compromise must be made in the case of the auxiliary memory. In a large machine, the auxiliary memory may have to store from 10^9 to 10^{15} bits making it generally too expensive to use devices such as those employed in the main memory.

An important point in the consideration of operating speed is that before a word can be read, it must be located. The time required to locate and read a word from memory is called the *access time*. The procedures for locating information may be divided into two classes: random access and sequential access. A *random-access* storage device is one in which any location may be selected at random, access to the information stored is direct, and an approximately equal access time is required for each location. A flip-flop register is an example of a random-access storage device, as are the IC memories that will be described. A *sequential-access* device is one in which the arrival at the location desired may be preceded by sequencing through other locations, so that access time varies according to location.[1] For instance, if we try to read a word stored on a reel of magnetic tape, and the piece of tape on which the word is stored is near the center of the reel, it is necessary to sequence through all the intervening tape before the word can be read.

This chapter will concentrate on the most frequently used devices for storing digital information: IC memories, which are high-speed and moderate-cost; magnetic disk and optical memories, which are used for auxiliary storage; and magnetic-tape memories, which are also used almost exclusively as an auxiliary, or backup, storage but are capable of storing large quantities of information at low cost. Following the sections on disk and magnetic-tape devices, the techniques used to record digital information on a magnetic surface are described.

6.1 RANDOM-ACCESS MEMORIES

The main memory of a computer is organized in a way that is particularly desirable. Figure 6.1 shows that a high-speed main memory is organized into words of fixed length. As the figure indicates, a given memory is divided into N words, where N generally is some power of 2, and each word is assigned an *address*, or location, in the memory. Each word has the same number of bits, called the *word length*. If we read, for instance, the word at address 72, we receive a word from the memory with the given word length.

The addresses, or location numbers, in the memory run consecutively, starting with address 0 and running up to the largest address. At address 0 we find one word, at address 1 a second word, at address 2 a third word, and so on up to the final word at the largest address.

---

[1] Sequential-access devices are further separated into *direct-access storage devices* (DASD) and *serial-access devices*. Direct-access storage devices have addresses, but the access time to reach the data at a given address may vary. For instance, the time to locate data on a movable-head disk depends on the head position and disk position when the address is given. Serial-access devices are truly serial in their access properties; magnetic tape is the classic example.

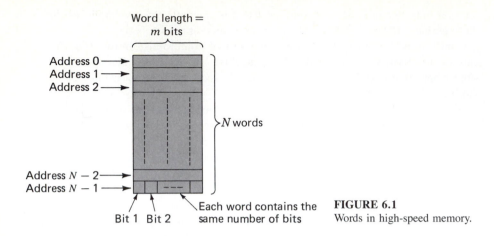

Bit 1   Bit 2   Each word contains the same number of bits

FIGURE 6.1
Words in high-speed memory.

Generally, the computer can read a word from or write a word into each location in the memory. For a memory with an 8-bit word, if we write 01001011 into memory address 17 and later read from this same address, we shall read the word 01001011. If we again read from this address at a later time (and have not written another word in), the word 01001011 will be read again. Such a memory is *nondestructive read*, which means that reading does not destroy or change a stored word.

It is important to understand the difference between the contents of a memory address and the address itself. A memory is like a large cabinet containing as many drawers as there are addresses in memory. In each drawer is a word, and the address of each word is written on the outside of the drawer. If we write or store a word at address 17, it is like placing the word in the drawer labeled 17. Later, reading from address 17 is like looking in that drawer to check its contents. We do not remove the word at an address when we read. We change the contents at an address only when we store or write a new word.

From an exterior viewpoint, a high-speed main memory is very much like a "black box" with a number of locations or addresses into which data can be stored or from which data can be read. A memory with 4096 locations, each with a different address and each storing 8 bits, is called a *4096-word 8 bit-memory*, or in the vernacular of the computer trade, a *4K 8-bit memory*. Since memories generally come with a number of words equal to 2^n for some n, if a memory has $2^{14} = 16,384$ words, computer literature and jargon would refer to it as a 16K memory,[2] because it is always understood that the full 2^n words actually occur in the memory. Thus, a 2^{15}-word 8-bit memory is called a 32K 8-bit memory.

Memories can be read from (that is, data can be taken out) or written into (data can be entered into the memory). Memories that can be both read from and written

---

[2] The symbol K is generally used to represent 1000 in engineering. In this case 1024 would be more precise.

into are called *read-write memories*. Some memories have programs or data that are permanently stored and are called *read-only memories*.

A block diagram of a read-write memory is shown in Fig. 6.2. The computer places the address of the location into which the data are to be read into the *memory address register*. This register consists of n binary devices (generally flip-flops), where 2^n is the number of words that can be stored in the memory. The data to be written into the memory are placed in the *memory buffer register*, which has as many binary storage devices as there are bits in each memory word. The memory is told to write by means of a 1 signal on the WRITE line. Then the memory will store the contents of the memory buffer register in the location specified by the memory address register.

Words are read by placing the address of the location to be read from into the memory address register. Then a 1 signal is placed on the READ line, and the contents of that location are placed by the memory in the memory buffer register.

As can be seen, the computer communicates with the memory by means of the memory address register, the memory buffer register, and the READ and WRITE inputs. Memories generally come in separate modules or packages. It is possible to buy a memory module of a specified size from a number of different manufacturers. For instance, a 4-megabit 8-bit word memory module might be purchased on a circuit board ready for use. Similarly, if a computer is purchased with a certain amount of main memory, more memory can usually be added later by purchasing additional modules and "plugging them in."

If it is possible to read from or write into any location "at once," that is, if there is no more delay in reading from one address than another, the memory is called a random-access memory. Computers almost invariably use random-access read-write memories for their high-speed main memory and use backup or slower-speed memories to hold auxiliary data.

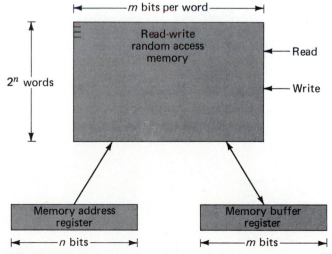

FIGURE 6.2
Read-write random-access memory.

6.2 LINEAR-SELECT MEMORY ORGANIZATION

In any memory there must be a basic memory cell. Figure 6.3 shows a basic memory cell consisting of an *RS* flip-flop with associated control circuitry. A memory that uses flip-flops for its memory cells is called a *static random access memory* (SRAM). To use a flip-flop memory cell requires a technique for selecting those cells addressed by the memory, as well as a method to control whether the selected cells are written into or read from.

Figure 6.4 shows the basic memory organization for a *linear-select* SRAM. This is a four-address memory with 3 bits per word. The memory address register (MAR) selects the memory cells (flip-flops) to be read from or written into through a *decoder*, which selects three flip-flops for each address in the memory address register.

Figure 6.5(*a*) shows the decoder in expanded form. It has an input from each flip-flop (bit) to be decoded. For 2 input bits, as in Fig. 6.5(*a*), there will be four output lines, one for each state (value) the input register can take. For instance, if the MAR contains a 0 in both flip-flops, then the upper line of the decoder will be a 1 and the remaining three lines a 0. Similarly, if both memory cells contain 1s, the lowest output line will be a 1 and the remaining three lines a 0. For each possible input state there will be a single output line with a 1, and the remaining lines will always be 0s.

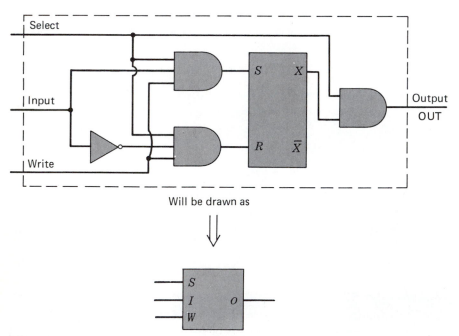

Will be drawn as

FIGURE 6.3
Basic memory cell.

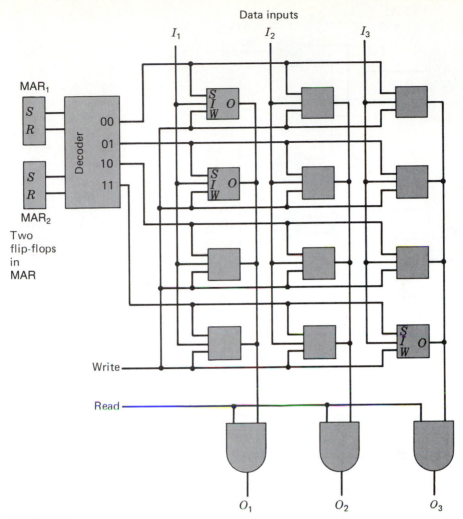

FIGURE 6.4
Linear-select SRAM.

Figure 6.5(*b*) shows a decoder for three inputs. The decoder has eight output lines. In general, for *n* input bits a decoder will have 2^n output lines. This decoder operates in the same manner as that in Fig. 6.5(*a*). For each input state, the decoder will select a particular output line, placing a 1 on the selected line and 0s on the remaining lines.

Returning to Fig. 6.4, we now see that corresponding to each value that can be placed in the MAR, a particular output line from the decoder will be selected and carry a 1 value. The remaining output lines from the decoder will contain 0s, that is, the AND gates at the inputs and outputs of the flip-flops for these rows will not be selected. (Refer also to Fig. 6.3.)

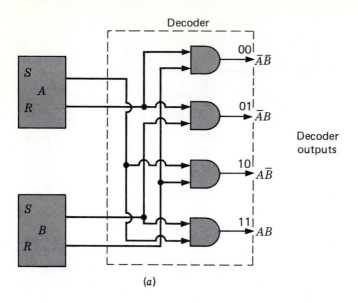

(a)

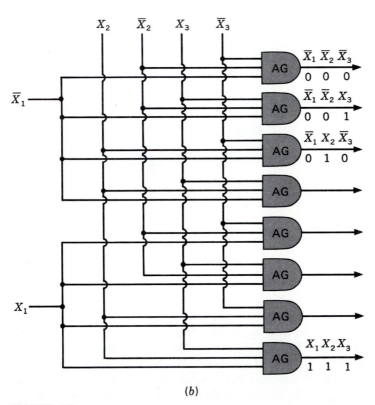

(b)

FIGURE 6.5
Decoders. (a) Four-output decoder. (b) Parallel decoder.

The memory in Fig. 6.4 is organized as follows. There are four words, each represented by a row of three memory cells. At a given time the MAR selects a word in memory. If the READ line is a 1, the contents of the three cells in the selected word are read out on the O_1, O_2, and O_3 lines. If the WRITE line is a 1, the values on I_1, I_2, and I_3 are read into the memory.

The AND gates connected to the OUT lines of the memory cells (see Fig. 6.3) must have the property that when a number of output lines are connected, and any one is high, the overall output goes to the highest level (if any OUT is a 1, the line goes to 1; otherwise, it is a 0). This is called a *wired-OR*. In Fig. 6.4, all four memory cells in the first column are wire-ORed; if any output line is a 1, the entire line will be a 1. Memory cells in IC memories are constructed in this manner.

If the READ line is a 1 in Fig. 6.4, the output values for the flip-flops in the selected row will all be gated onto the output line for each bit in the memory. For example, if the second row in the memory contains 110 in the three memory cells, and if the MAR contains 01, the second output line from the decoder (marked 01) will be a 1, and the input gates and output gates to these three memory cells will be selected. When the READ line is made a 1, the outputs from the three memory cells in the second row will be sent to the AND gates at the bottom of the figure, which will transmit the value 110 as an output from the memory.

If the WRITE line is a 1 and the MAR again contains 01, the input values on I_1, I_2, and I_3 will be read into the flip-flops in the second row.

As may be seen, this is a complete memory, fully capable of reading and writing. The memory will store data for an indefinite period and will operate as quickly as the gates and flip-flops permit. There is only one problem with the memory— its complexity. The basic memory cell (the flip-flop with its associated circuitry) is complicated, and for large memories the decoder will be large.

6.3   DECODERS

The part of the system that selects the cells to be read from and written into is the decoder. This particular circuit is also called a *many-to-one-decoder* or a *decoder matrix*. For each of the possible 2^n binary numbers that can be taken by the n input cells, the matrix will select a unique output line out of the total of 2^n lines.

Figure 6.5(*b*) shows a decoder that is completely parallel in construction and is designed to decode three flip-flops. There are $2^3 = 8$ output lines; for each of the eight states the three inputs (flip-flops) may take, a unique output line will be selected. This type of decoder is often constructed by using transistors (or diodes) in the AND gates. The rule is that the number of transistors (or diodes) used in each AND gate is equal to the number of inputs to each AND gate. For Fig. 6.5(*b*) this is equal to the number of flip-flops to be decoded. Further, the number of AND gates is equal to the number of output lines, which is equal to 2^n (n is the number of input flip-flops to be decoded). So the total number of transistors is equal to $n \times 2^n$. For the binary decoding matrix in Fig. 6.5(*b*), 24 transistors are required to construct the network. As may be seen, the number of transistors required increases sharply with the number of inputs to the network. For instance, decoding an eight-flip-flop register would require $8 \times 2^8 = 2048$ transistors if the decoder were constructed in this manner.

As a result, several other types of structures are sometimes used in building decoder networks. One such structure, called a *tree-type* decoding network, is shown in Fig. 6.6. This tree network decodes four flip-flops and so has $2^4 = 16$ output lines, a unique one of which is selected for each state of the flip-flops. An examination will show that 56 transistors are required to build this particular network, whereas $2^4 \times 4 = 64$ transistors would be required for this network using the parallel decoder type.

Still another type of decoder network is shown in Fig. 6.7. It is called a *balanced multiplicative decoder network*. Notice that this network requires only 48 transistors.

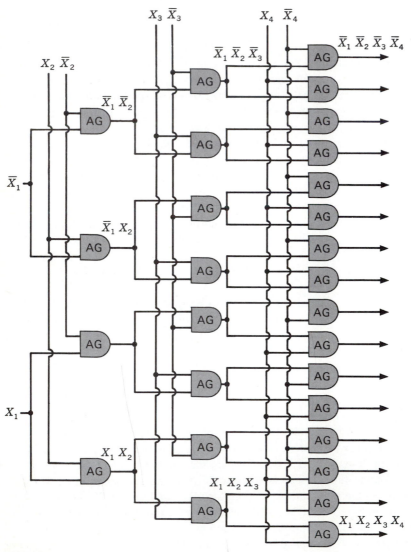

FIGURE 6.6
Tree decoder.

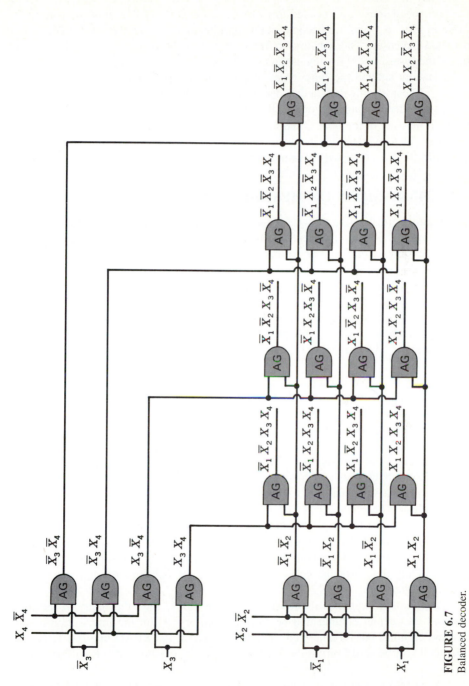

FIGURE 6.7
Balanced decoder.

It can be shown that the type of decoder network illustrated in Fig. 6.7 requires the minimum number of transistors for a complete decoder network. The difference in the number of transistors needed to construct a network such as this compared with those in Figs. 6.5 and 6.6 becomes more significant as the number of flip-flops to be decoded increases. The network shown in Fig. 6.5, however, has the advantage of being the fastest and most regular in construction of the three types.

Having studied the three types of decoding matrices now used in digital machines, we can simply draw a decoder network as a box with n inputs and 2^n outputs, with the understanding that one of the three types of circuits shown in Figs. 6.5 to 6.7 will be used in the box. Often only the uncomplemented inputs are connected to decoders, and inverters are included in the decoder package. Then a three-input (or three-flip-flop) decoder will have only three input lines and eight outputs.

6.4   DIMENSIONS OF MEMORY ACCESS

The memory organization in Fig. 6.4 has a basic linear-select (one-dimensional) selection system. This is the simplest organization. However, the decoder in the selection system becomes quite large as the memory size increases.

As an example, consider a parallel decoder for a 4096-word memory. There will be 12 inputs per AND gate, and 4096 AND gates are required. If a transistor is required at each AND gate's input, then $12 \times 4096 = 49,152$ transistors will be required. For a 64K memory there would be 16×2^{16} transistors (or diodes) and for a megabit memory 20×2^{20}, or over 20 million, transistors would be needed. This requirement of a large number of components is the primary objection to this memory organization.

Let us now consider a *two-dimensional selection system*. First we need to add another SELECT input to our basic memory cell; this is shown in Fig. 6.8. Now both SELECT 1 and SELECT 2 must be 1s for a flip-flop to be selected.

Figure 6.9 shows a two-dimensional memory selection system using this cell. Two decoders are required for this memory, which has 16 words of only 1 bit per word (for clarity of explanation). The MAR has 4 bits and, thus, 16 states. Two of the MAR inputs go to one decoder and two to the other.

To illustrate the memory's operation, if the MAR contains 0111, the value 01 goes to the left decoder and 11 goes to the right decoder. This will select the second row (line) from the left decoder and the rightmost column from the top decoder. The result is that only the cell (flip-flop) at the intersection of the second row and the rightmost column will have both its SELECT lines (and, as a result, its AND gates) enabled. Only this particular cell will be selected, and only this flip-flop can be read from or written into.

As another example, if the MAR contains 1001, then the lines for the third row and the second column will be 1s. The memory cell at the intersection of this row and column, but no other cell, will be enabled. If the READ line is a 1, the enabled cell will be read from; if the WRITE line is a 1, the enabled cell will be written into.

Now let us examine the number of components used. If a 16-word 1-bit memory were designed using the linear-select, or one-dimensional, system, a decoder with

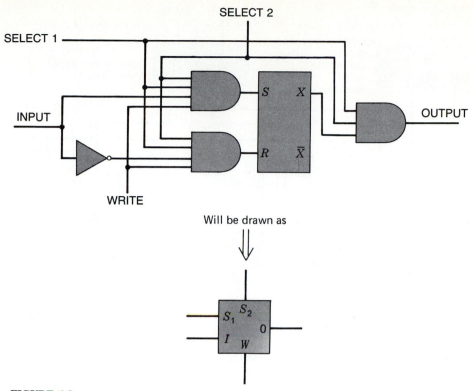

FIGURE 6.8
Two-dimensional memory cell.

16×4 inputs and, therefore, 64 transistors would be required. For the two-dimensional system, 2 two-input, four-output decoders are needed, each requiring 8 transistors; so 16 transistors are required for both decoders.

For a 4096-word 1-bit-per-word memory, the numbers are more striking. A 4096-word linear-select (one-dimensional) memory requires a 12-bit MAR. This decoder therefore requires $4096 \times 12 = 49,152$ transistors. The two-dimensional selection system would have two decoders, each with six inputs. Each would require $2^6 \times 6 = 384$ diodes or transistors, that is, a total of 768 transistors for the decoders. These remarkable savings can be extended for even larger memories. For example, whereas a 1-megabit memory requires about 20 million diodes or transistors with linear-select, only $2(2^{10} \times 10)$, or about 20,000, are required for a two-dimensional system.

Figure 6.10 shows a small, very high-speed IC memory with 256 bits on a single chip. As can be seen, this is a two-dimensional memory. For a memory with more bits per word, we simply use one chip per bit.

In a two-dimensional memory simplification in decoder complexity is paid for with cell complexity. In some cases this extra cell complexity is inexpensive, but it can be a problem, so a variation of this scheme is used. The most common variation

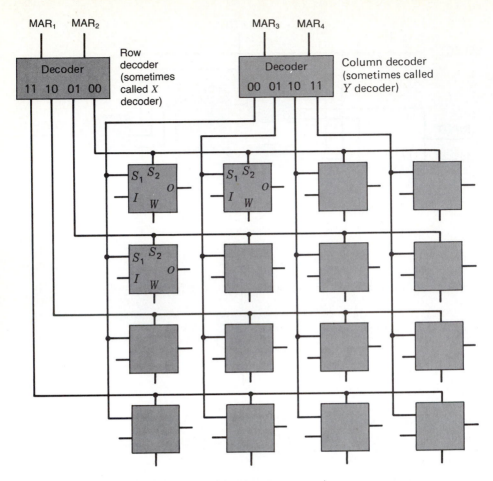

WRITE— (All *W* inputs on cells are connected to this input)

INPUT— (All *I* inputs on cells are connected to this input line)

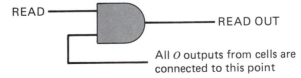

All *O* outputs from cells are connected to this point

FIGURE 6.9
Two-dimensional IC memory organization.

on the basic two-dimensional selection system is illustrated in Fig. 6.11. This memory uses two decoders, as in the previous scheme; however, the memory cells are basic memory cells of the type shown in Fig. 6.3.

The selection scheme uses gating on the READ and WRITE inputs to achieve the desired two-dimensionality. Let us consider a WRITE operation. First assume that the MAR contains 0010. This will cause the 00 output from the upper decoder to be a 1, selecting the top row of memory cells. In the lower decoder the 10 output

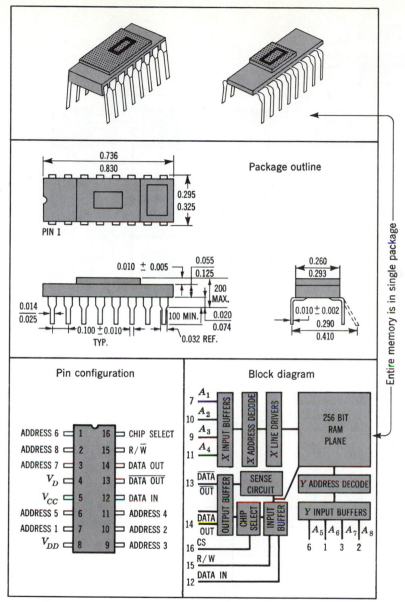

FIGURE 6.10
Single-chip 256-bit memory.

will become a 1, and this, in conjunction with the AND gate near the bottom of the diagram, turns on the W inputs in the third column. As a result, for the memory cell in the top row and third column, the S input and the W input will be 1s. For no other memory cell will both S and W be 1s, so no other memory cell will have its RS flip-flop set to the input value. (Notice that all I inputs on the memory cells are connected to the input value D_1.)

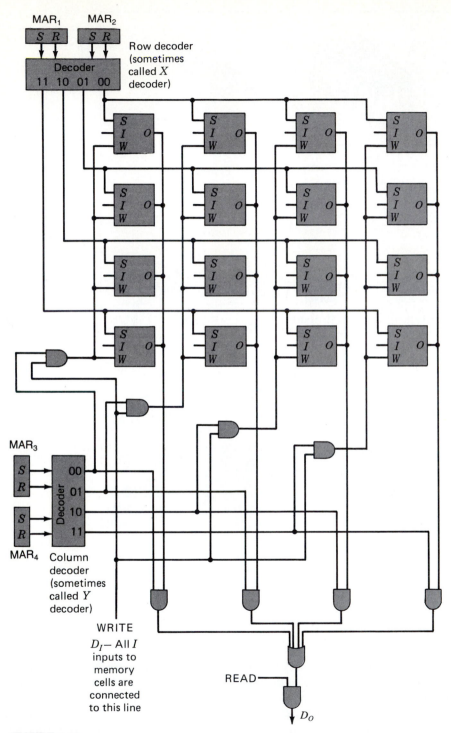

FIGURE 6.11
IC memory chip layout.

Consideration of other values for the MAR will indicate that for each value a unique memory cell will be selected for the WRITE operation. Therefore, for each MAR state only one memory cell will be written into.

The READ operation is similar. If the MAR contains 0111, then the upper decoder's 01 line will be a 1, turning on the S inputs in the second row of memory cells. As a result, only these four cells in the entire array are capable of producing a 1 on the output lines. (Again, the memory cells are wire-ORed by having their outputs connected, this time in groups of four.)

The lower decoder will have input 11, so its lowest output line will carry a 1. This 1 turns on the rightmost AND gate in the lowest row, which enables the output from the rightmost column of memory cells. Only the second cell down has its output enabled, however, so the output from the rightmost AND gate will show the value in the cell. This value then goes through the OR gate and the AND gate at the bottom of the diagram, the AND gate having been turned on by the READ signal.

Examination will show that each input value from the MAR will select a unique memory cell to be read from, and that will be the same cell as would have been written into if the operation were a WRITE.

6.5 CONNECTING MEMORY CHIPS TO A COMPUTER BUS

The present trend is to connect the computer central processing unit (CPU)[3] to the memory by means of a *bus*. The bus is simply a set of wires that are shared by all the memory elements to be used.

All microprocessors use buses to interface memory. In this case, the memory elements will be IC chips, which are in IC containers like those described in Chap. 4 and shown in Fig. 6.10.

The bus used to connect the memory generally consists of (1) a set of *address lines* to carry the address of the word in memory to be used (these are effectively an output from a MAR on the microprocessor chip); (2) a set of *data wires* to input data from the memory and output data to the memory; and (3) a set of *control wires* to control the READ and WRITE operations.

Figure 6.12 shows a bus for a microcomputer. To simplify drawings and clarify explanations, we use a memory bus with only three address lines, three output data lines, two control signals, and three input data lines. Thus, the memory to be used is an 8-word 3-bit-per-word memory.

The two control signals work as follows. When the read-write ($R/\overline{W}$) line is a 1, the memory is to be read from; when the $R/\overline{W}$ line is a 0, the memory is to be written into.[4] The MEMORY ENABLE signal (ME) is a 1 when the memory is either to be read from or to be written into; otherwise, it is a 0.

---

[3] A CPU includes the arithmetic and control sections of a computer.

[4] This is quite similar to the READ and WRITE signals used in prior memory description. An AND gate connected to ME and $R/\overline{W}$ will generate a READ signal, and an inverted $R/\overline{W}$ ANDed with ME will give a WRITE signal.

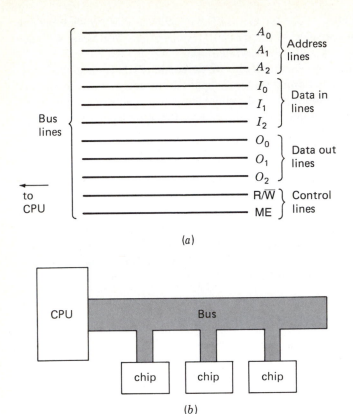

(a)

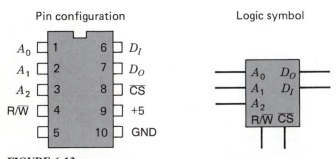

(b)

FIGURE 6.12
Bus for computer system. (a) Bus lines. (b) Bus, CPU, and memory organization.

The IC memory package is shown in Fig. 6.13. Each IC package has three address inputs (A_0, A_1, and A_2), an R/$\overline{W}$ input, an output bit (D_O), an input bit (D_I), and a CHIP SELECT (CS). Each package contains an 8-word 1-bit memory.

The IC memory chip works as follows. The address lines, A_0, A_1, and A_2, must be set to the address to be read from or written into (refer to Fig. 6.13). If the operation is a READ, the R/$\overline{W}$ line is set to a 1 and the $\overline{CS}$ line is brought

Pin configuration   Logic symbol

A_0	1	6	D_I
A_1	2	7	D_O
A_2	3	8	$\overline{CS}$
R/$\overline{W}$	4	9	+5
	5	10	GND

FIGURE 6.13
IC package and block diagram symbol for RAM chip. (a) Pin configuration. (b) Logic symbol.

to 0 (the $\overline{CS}$ line is normally a 1). The data bit may then be read on line D_O. Certain timing constraints must be met, however, and these will be supplied by the IC manufacturer. Figure 6.14 shows several of these. The value T_R is the minimum cycle time a READ operation requires. During this period the address lines must be stable. The value T_A is the access time, which is the minimum time from when the address lines are stable until data can be read from the memory. The value T_{CO} is the minimum time from when the $\overline{CS}$ line is made a 0 until data can be read.

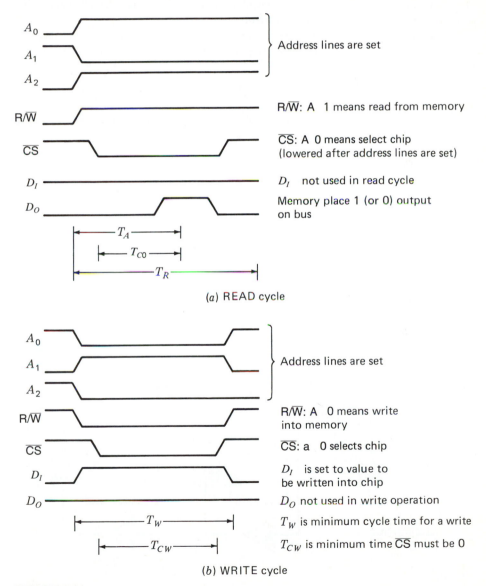

FIGURE 6.14
Timing for bus IC memory. (*a*) READ cycle. (*b*) WRITE cycle.

The bus timing must accommodate these times. It is important that the bus not operate too fast for the chip and that the bus wait for at least the time T_A after setting its address lines before reading, and wait at least T_{C0} after lowering the $\overline{CS}$ line before reading. Also, the address line must be held stable for at least the period T_R.

For a WRITE operation, the address to be written into is set up on the address lines, the R/$\overline{W}$ line is made a 0, $\overline{CS}$ is brought down, and the data to be read are placed on the D_I line.

The time interval T_W is the minimum time for a WRITE cycle. Different types of memories have different timing constraints that the bus must accommodate. We assume that our bus meets these constraints.[5]

To form an 8-word 3-bit memory from these IC packages (chips), the interconnection scheme in Fig. 6.15 is used. Here the address line to each chip is connected

---

[5] On the other hand, if a specific microprocessor is used, the memory must be fast enough to accommodate the bus.

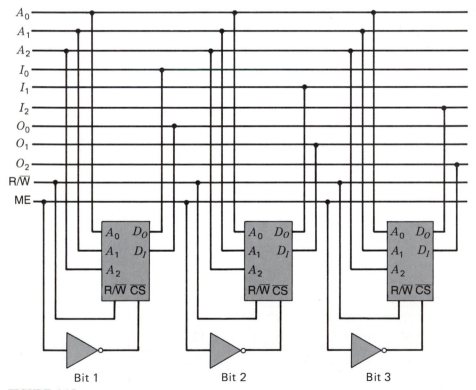

Bit 1   Bit 2   Bit 3

FIGURE 6.15
Interfacing chips to a bus.

to a corresponding address output on the microcomputer bus. The CHIP SELECT input ($\overline{\text{CS}}$) of each chip is connected to the MEMORY ENABLE output (ME) from the microprocessor via an inverter, and the R/$\overline{\text{W}}$ bus line is connected to the R/$\overline{\text{W}}$ input on each chip.

If the microprocessor CPU wishes to read from the memory, it simply places the address to be read from on the address lines, puts a 1 on the R/$\overline{\text{W}}$ line, and raises the ME line. Then each chip places the selected bit onto its output line, and the CPU can read these values on its I_0, I_1, and I_2 lines. (Notice that a chip's output is a bus input.)

Similarly, to write a word into the memory, the CPU places the address to be written into on the address lines, places the bits to be written on the O_0, O_1, O_2 lines, lowers R/$\overline{\text{W}}$, and then raises ME.

In practice, for microprocessors, memory words now generally contain 8 bits each. There are generally 24–32 address lines, so 2^{24}–2^{32} words can be used in the memory. However, memory chips tend to have 16–22 memory address lines. Fortunately, there is a simple way to expand memories, and this is shown for our small system in Fig. 6.16.

In this example the chips again have three address lines, but the microprocessor bus has five lines. To enable connection, a two-input decoder is connected to the two most significant bits of the address section of the bus; the three least significant bits are connected to the chip address buses as before.

The decoder outputs are each gated with the ME control signal by a NAND gate; when ME is raised, a single CHIP SELECT line is lowered (the outputs from the NAND gates are normally high). The decoder therefore picks the chip that is enabled, and the address lines on the enabled chip select the memory cell to be written into or read from.

The technique shown in Fig. 6.16 is widely used in computers. Memory chips almost invariably have fewer address inputs than buses, so this expansion is necessary for memory usage. Notice that only 1 bit of the memory word is completely drawn in Fig. 6.16 (One chip from the second bit is also shown.) An entire 32-word 3-bit memory would require 12 chips of the type shown here. Most buses combine the input and output data lines into a single set of lines.

As may be seen, a microcomputer or minicomputer (or any computer) can be purchased with a minimal memory, and then the memory can be expanded by adding more chips, up to the size that the bus address lines can accommodate.

6.6 STATIC RANDOM-ACCESS MEMORIES

Static random-access memories (SRAMs) are memories that use flip-flop storage for the bits in the memory. So far we have used only static random-access memories in our descriptions. There are also random-access memories that use dynamic storage devices, and these will be discussed in later sections.

Figure 6.17 shows the pin-out for a 256K static memory; Fig. 6.18 gives timing details of the memory. Memories of this type have good access times, ranging from

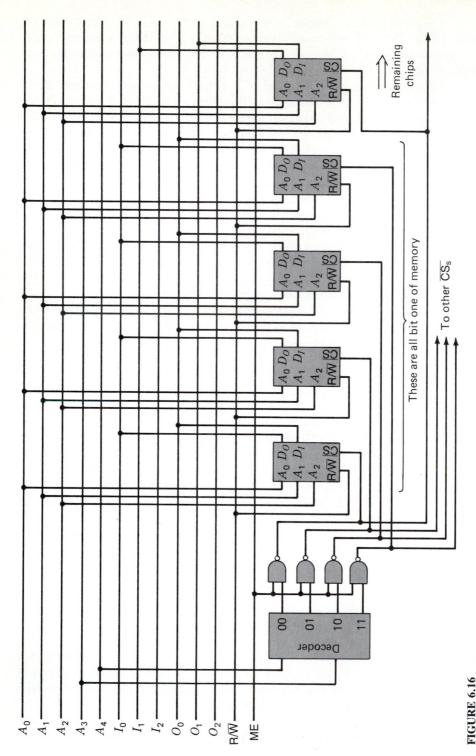

FIGURE 6.16
Layout for adding memory to a bus.

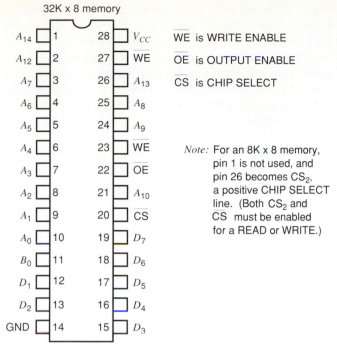

FIGURE 6.17
Pin-out for 32K-8 bit SRAM chip.

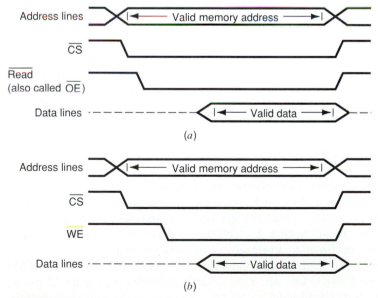

FIGURE 6.18
SRAM memory timing. (*a*) Memory READ timing. (*b*) Memory RAM timing.

a few to tens of nanoseconds. There has been some attempt to develop "standard" static 26-pin and 28-pin RAM packages (Fig. 6.17 is an example) with 8 bits at each memory location. These packages have 2K to 32K words of 8 bits each. Larger static RAMs (1 megabit and 4 megabit) use different pin-outs (1 or 4 output bits).

The overall organization for static memories follows the principles that have been presented here. The timing signals used in interfaces are fairly standard and are shown in Fig. 6.18. Notice there is a separate READ signal called OUTPUT ENABLE ($\overline{\text{OE}}$) and a WRITE signal called WRITE ENABLE ($\overline{\text{WE}}$) to select whether a READ or a WRITE is to be performed.

The $\overline{\text{CS}}$ signal enables the memory, selecting the chip for operation. In a READ from the chip, when $\overline{\text{CS}}$ is brought low, the chip reads the address on the address lines. Then $\overline{\text{OE}}$ is lowered, indicating a READ. The chip then places the data on the output lines, and when $\overline{\text{OE}}$ goes positive these data will be read.

For a WRITE operation, the timing is similar. The address is placed on the address lines, and $\overline{\text{CS}}$ is brought low. Then $\overline{\text{WE}}$ is made a 0, and the data to be written into the chip must be placed on the data lines before $\overline{\text{WE}}$ is returned to its normal 1 state (the chip inputs from the data lines on the transition from 0 to 1).

6.7   DYNAMIC RANDOM-ACCESS MEMORIES

The memories discussed so far have all used flip-flops for the basic memory cells in an array and are called SRAMs (static RAMs). There is another class of random-access memory called *dynamic random-access memories* (DRAMs). These memories have individual cells composed of one or more transistors plus a capacitor. The cell's state is determined by placing or not placing a positive charge on the capacitor. If the capacitor has no charge, the cell represents a 0; with a positive charge, the cell represents a 1. The advantage of this kind of memory is that the individual cells are simpler than flip-flops, requiring less area on the chip and lower power consumption. The disadvantages are that DRAMs are slower, and the charge slowly leaks from the capacitor. As a result, the contents of each cell must be rewritten into each cell periodically. This is called *refreshing* the memory. Despite the difficulties of refreshing dynamic memories and their relatively slow speed (50–500 ns access times are representative whereas some SRAMs can access in less than 10 ns), the memory costs are sufficiently lower than those for static memories to make dynamic memories the most widely used in present-day systems.

Dynamic random-access memories are organized in the same manner as flip-flop memories. The organization of Fig. 6.11 is the most common; however, some circuit "tricks" enable the combining of each column input line and output line into a pair of lines called *bit lines*. Two-dimensional selection with decoders is standard. Dynamic memory chips now contain up to 4 megabits of memory per chip.

Figure 6.19(*a*) shows the standard pin layout for 64K and 256K dynamic RAM (A_8 is not used for a 64K). One and four-megabit memories require an 18-pin IC package. There are not enough address lines into this chip, so the addresses are time-multiplexed (that is, put on the bus in two sections, one right after the other). This is

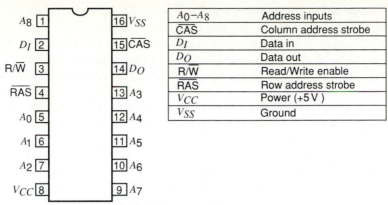

A_0-A_8	Address inputs
$\overline{CAS}$	Column address strobe
D_I	Data in
D_O	Data out
R/$\overline{W}$	Read/Write enable
$\overline{RAS}$	Row address strobe
V_{CC}	Power (+5 V)
V_{SS}	Ground

Note: 64K memory does not use A_8; 256K memory does.

(a)

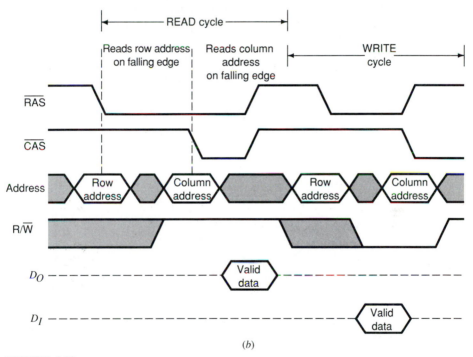

(b)

FIGURE 6.19
Dynamic memory chips. (a) Pin-out for dynamic memory chip. (b) Dynamic RAM timing.

shown in Fig. 6.19(*b*). First the row address[6] is placed on A_0–A_7 and $\overline{RAS}$ is lowered; then the column address is placed on A_0–A_7 and $\overline{CAS}$ is lowered. To use RAMs of this kind, extra circuitry for multiplexing address lines and generating the REFRESH signals must be used.[7] Nevertheless, because of their high packing density and low cost, the extra complexity of these specialized circuits is compensated for, and these memories are widely used.

The primary advantage of dynamic memories lies in the simplicity of the individual cells. There is a secondary advantage in that power need not be applied to the cells when they are not being read from or written into, so power is conserved. This makes for higher packing densities per chip. The obvious disadvantage lies in the need to refresh these cells every few milliseconds since charge continually leaks from the capacitors. External circuitry to control the refresh rewrite is sometimes required, or the memories may include special circuits to refresh when commanded. As a result, extra refresh memory cycles are required, but these occupy only a small percentage of the overall operating time.

Figure 6.20 shows memory sizes for single dynamic and static RAM chips, as a function of time. To give some feeling for the complexity of SRAMs versus DRAMs,

---

[6] The row address is the first half of the field 16-bit address, and the column address is the second half.

[7] IC manufacturers make special chips for this purpose. For these particular memories, refreshing is done a column at a time, so only the rows must be sequenced through. To refresh a row, the row address is placed on the address lines and $\overline{RAS}$ is lowered. Each row must be refreshed in a 2-ms period.

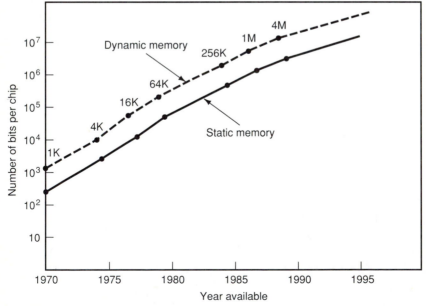

FIGURE 6.20
Single-chip static and dynamic memory capacity.

Fig. 6.21 shows schematics for typical cells. The SRAM cell generally uses four or six transistors; memories with four transistors per cell are called *4T memories*, and those with six transistors are *6T memories*. In each case the two transistors Q_1 and Q_2 form flip-flops; resistors are tied to the positive voltage, V_{cc}, for 4T cells, and transistors Q_3 and Q_4 are used in 6T cells. The data lines are used for column selection as well as to write data into the cells and read from them. The DRAM memory cells each require a single transistor and a capacitor. The sense amplifier reads from cells,

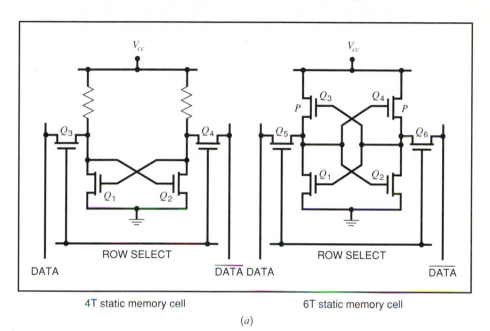

4T static memory cell   6T static memory cell

(*a*)

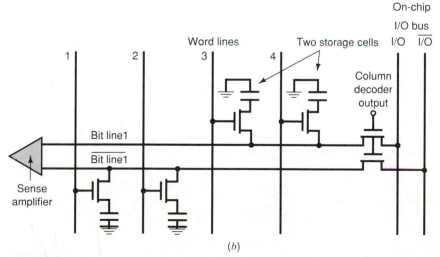

(*b*)

FIGURE 6.21

Memory cell schematics. (*a*) SRAM storage cells. (*b*) DRAM storage cell.

sensing whether a capacitor is charged or not (i.e., whether a cell is a 0 or 1), by reading differences on the bit lines. Bit lines also write into the cells, and the word lines select cells [see Fig. 6.21(*b*)]. Because of the simplicity of the DRAM cells, DRAM memories have about four times more bits per chip than SRAMs.

Figure 6.22 shows another example of the timing for the inputs to standard DRAM chips. DRAMs read the row address before the column address. $\overline{RAS}$ is the *row address strobe*, which causes the chip to read the row address. The column address is then placed on the address lines, and $\overline{CAS}$ is lowered, causing the chip to read the column address; if the R/$\overline{W}$ line is a 1, the chip then places its output on the data line(s). (For a WRITE, the chip accepts data.)

Some DRAMs have modes of operation that allow successive READs to be made faster. A typical one is the *paging mode* shown in Fig. 6.22(*b*). After the row address is read, the $\overline{RAS}$ line is held low, and successive lowerings of the $\overline{CAS}$ line

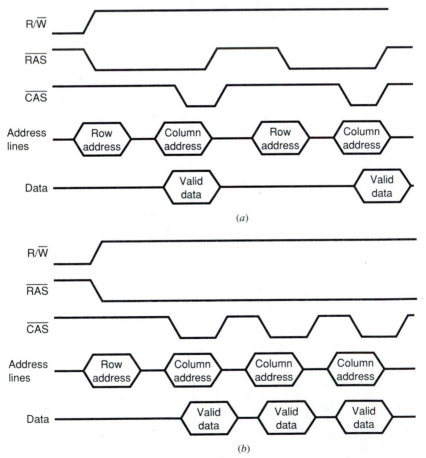

FIGURE 6.22
DRAM timing signals. (*a*) DRAM in normal operation. (*b*) DRAM in paging mode.

cause the memory to produce data without the need to reload the row address. When addresses follow one another in memory, this feature can be used by letting the most significant memory address bits be the row address lines and the least significant the column lines. When paged systems (to be explained) are used, this is most useful.

6.8   READ-ONLY MEMORIES

A type of storage device called a *read-only memory* (ROM) is also widely used. ROMs have the unique characteristic that they can be read from, but not written into. Thus, the information is introduced into the memory in such a manner that the information is semipermanent or permanent. Sometimes the information stored in a ROM is entered at the time of construction, and sometimes devices are used in which the information can be changed. In this section we study several types of ROMs that are characteristic of this particular class of memory devices.

A ROM is a device with several input and output lines such that for each input value there is a unique output value. Thus, a ROM physically realizes a truth table or table of combinations. A typical table is shown in Table 6.1. This list of input-output values is actually a list of binary-to-Gray code values. (The Gray code is discussed in the next chapter.) It is important to see that the list can be looked at in two ways: (1) as a table for a gating network with four inputs and four outputs and (2) as a list of addresses from 0 to 15, given by the X values, along with the contents of each address, given by the values of Z. Thus, we might construct a gating network as in Fig. 6.23, which would give the correct Z output for each X input. (The boxes marked $\oplus$ are mod 2 adders.)

TABLE 6.1
Binary-to-Gray code values

Input				Output			
X_1	X_2	X_3	X_4	Z_1	Z_2	Z_3	Z_4
0	0	0	0	0	0	0	0
0	0	0	1	0	0	0	1
0	0	1	0	0	0	1	1
0	0	1	1	0	0	1	0
0	1	0	0	0	1	1	0
0	1	0	1	0	1	1	1
0	1	1	0	0	1	0	1
0	1	1	1	0	1	0	0
1	0	0	0	1	1	0	0
1	0	0	1	1	1	0	1
1	0	1	0	1	1	1	1
1	0	1	1	1	1	1	0
1	1	0	0	1	0	1	0
1	1	0	1	1	0	1	1
1	1	1	0	1	0	0	1
1	1	1	1	1	0	0	0

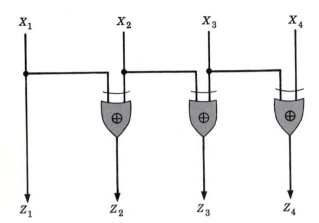

FIGURE 6.23
Combinational network for binary-to-Gray code.

Table 6.1 could also be realized by a 16-word 4-bit-per-word IC memory into which we have read 0000 at address 0, 0001 at address 1, 0011 in the next address, and so on to 1000 at the last address. Were we never to write into this memory afterward, it would be a ROM memory and would serve the same purpose as the gating network in Fig. 6.23.

Figure 6.24(a) shows a scheme for implementing Table 6.1 by using a decoder network with four inputs, X_1, X_2, X_3, and X_4, and four OR gates. With a given input combination (or address), a single output line from the decoder will be high. Let us assume that the input value is $X_1 = 0$, $X_2 = 1$, $X_3 = 1$, $X_4 = 1$. This corresponds to 0111 on the decoder output in Fig. 6.24(a). OR gates are connected to this line for outputs that are 1s; no OR gates are placed where 0s are to appear. Thus, for the input 0111 we have a single OR gate connected to output line Z_2, since the desired output is 0100. Similarly, for the input 0110 we connect OR gates to Z_2 and Z_4 since the output is to be 0101.

This scheme realizes the ROM with OR gates. Arrays of this sort can be inexpensively fabricated in small containers at low prices. Figure 6.24(b) shows how the configuration of Fig. 6.24(a) might be implemented using diodes to form the OR gates. The diodes OR the inputs to which they are connected. The manufacturer of a conventional ROM will have an IC layout in which diodes can be placed between every input and output line. Only the specified diodes would be actually used, with the remainder omitted during manufacture. Transistors are often used for the diodes as in Fig. 6.24(b), and the manufacturing processes are of various types. Both one- and two-dimensional selection is used in ROMs.

When a ROM is constructed so that the user can electrically (or using other techniques) write in the contents of the memory, the memory is called a *programmable*

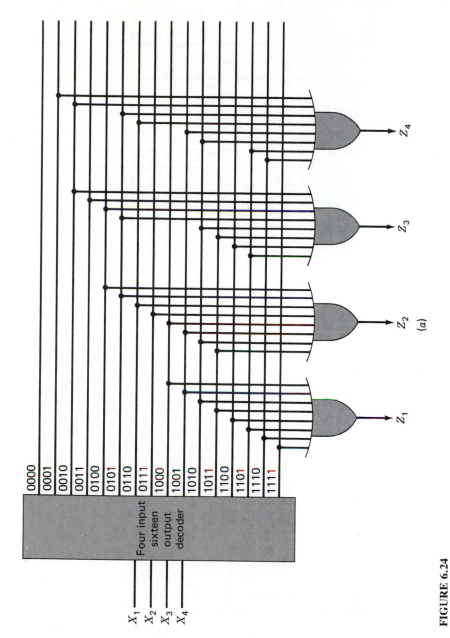

FIGURE 6.24
Read-only memory. (*a*) Read-only memory layout.

273

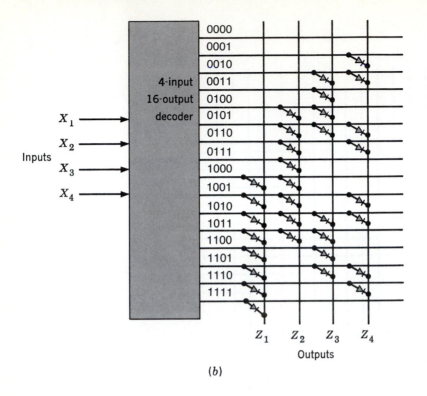

(b)

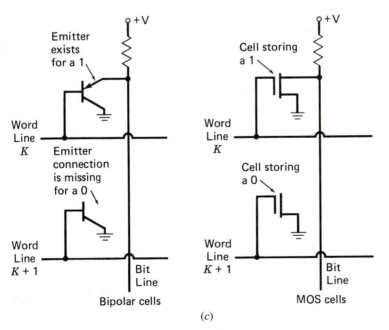

(c)

FIGURE 6.24
(b) Diode ROM. (c) ROM cells using MOS and bipolar transistor.

ROM, or *PROM*.[8] Often a scheme is used in which a memory chip is delivered with 1s in every position; 0s are then introduced by placing an address on the input lines and raising each output line that is to be a 0 to a specified voltage, thus destroying a connection to the selected cell. (Sometimes the memories contain all 0s, and 1s are written in by the user.) Devices are also manufactured that program PROMs manually and also by reading diskettes, magnetic tapes, punched cards, or other media, placing their contents into the PROM.

Custom ROM manufacturers provide forms or diskette formats where a user can fill in 1s and 0s; the manufacturer then will produce a custom-made mask and chips to realize the memory contents specified by the user.

Figure 6.25 shows a block diagram of a 64K-bit memory organized as a 4096-word 8-bit-per-word memory. The user places the address on the 13 input lines, A_0 to A_{12}, and then raises CS_1 and CS_2 ($\overline{CE}$ must be low). This will enable the output, and the desired word will appear on lines O_0 to O_7. This is a custom-made memory in which the desired contents are supplied to the manufacturer by the user on a form. Then the manufacturer makes a mask to create the desired bit patterns on an IC chip and manufactures ROMs with this pattern.

A ROM manufactured so that the memory's contents can be set as desired by the user, and later erased so that new values can be written in, is said to be *erasable and reprogrammable* and is often called an *EPROM*. For example, some memory chips are made with a transparent lid. Exposing the semiconductor chip (through the lid) to ultraviolet light[9] will erase the pattern on the chip, and a new pattern can be written in electrically. This can be repeated as often as desired.

EPROMs normally have 8-bit words and are widely used to store programs in microprocessor systems. EPROMs are programmed by an instrument called a PROM *programmer* before being inserted into a circuit board. EPROMs range up to more than a megabit in size and require several minutes for the contents to be entered. There is a 28-pin "semistandard" pin-out in fairly widespread usage. A ROM chip that can be written into and changed electrically is called an *electrically alterable erasable programmable ROM*.

6.9 MAGNETIC DISK MEMORIES

The magnetic disk memory provides large storage capabilities and moderate operating speeds. A number of different types of magnetic disk memories are now on the market. Although they differ in specific details, all are based on the same principles of operation.

Magnetic disk memories store information on one or more circular platters, or disks, which are continually spinning. These rotating disks are coated with a magnetic

---

[8] These memories are also called *field-programmable ROMs*.

[9] Standard ultraviolet lamps can be used to erase the memory. About a 20- to 30-min exposure is required.

PIN CONFIGURATION

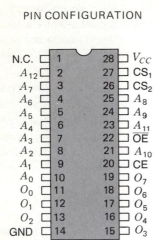

BLOCK DIAGRAM

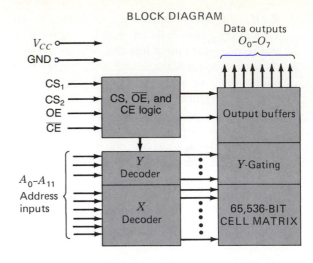

PIN NAMES

A_0–A_{12}	Addresses
$\overline{OE}$	Output enable
$\overline{CE}$	Chip enable
CS	Chip select
N.C.	No connection

(a)

FIGURE 6.25
A 64K ROM. (a) Pin-out and block diagram.

material and stacked with space between them. Single disks are also used. Information is recorded on the surface of the rotating disks by magnetic heads such as that in Fig. 6.26. These heads are mounted on *access arms*. Information is recorded in bands rather than on a spiral. Each band of information on a given disk is called a *track*, and tracks are divided into *sectors*. On one side of a typical disk there will be several thousand data tracks. Bits are recorded along a track at a density of 20,000–100,000 bits/in. In some systems the outer tracks contain more bits than the inner tracks, because the circumference of an outer track is greater; but many disks have the same number of bits around each track. The rotational speed of the disks varies, of course, with the manufacturer, but typical speeds are on the order of 3600 rpm.

Since each disk contains a number of tracks of information, and there may be several disks in a given memory, several techniques have evolved for placing a magnetic read-write head in the correct position on a selected track. Since the same head is generally used for reading and for writing, the problem becomes one of placing this head accurately and quickly on the selected track.

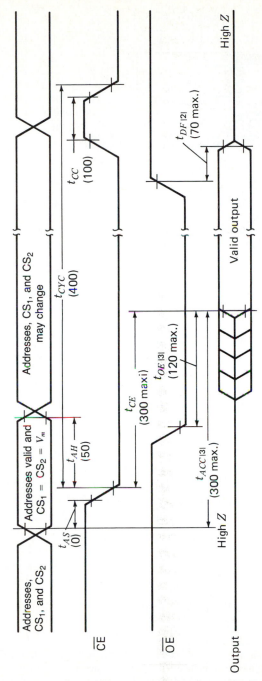

Notes

1. All times shown in parentheses are minimum times and are nanoseconds unless otherwise specified.

2. t_{DF} is specified from $\overline{OE}$ or $\overline{CE}$, whichever occurs first.

3. t_{ACC} may be delayed up to 180 ns after the falling edge of $\overline{CE}$ without impact on t_{ACC}.

(b)

FIGURE 6.25

(b) Timing diagram. (*Intel Corporation.*)

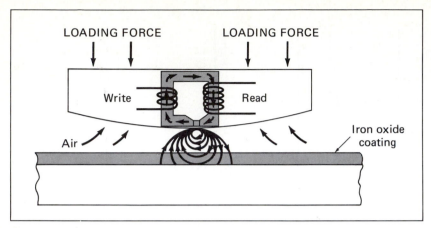

FIGURE 6.26
Flying head in a disk memory. The loading force is applied by the access arm pressing down, using a springlike mechanism. The flying height is determined by the amount of loading force. Passing a film of magnetic material by a head while passing current through the write winding will magnetize the surface of the material, forming simple magnets. Passing this same area by a head at a later time will induce currents in the read winding in the read writing.

There are two basic tapes of disk head placement systems. In the first type, the heads are fixed in position on each track. These are called *fixed-head systems*, and there are now very few of these. In the second kind of system, one or more pairs of read-write heads exist for each pair of adjacent disk surfaces (because information is generally written on both the top and the bottom of each disk). These heads are mounted on arms that can be moved in and out. These are called *movable-head systems*.[10] The positioning of the heads by means of the mechanical movement of arms is a difficult and tricky business, particularly since the tracks are recorded thousandths of an inch apart on the disk.

The total time it takes to begin reading selected data or to begin writing on a selected track in a particular place is called the *access time*. The time it takes to position a head on the selected track is called the *seek time*, and it is generally several milliseconds. The other delay in locating selected data is the *latency*, or *rotational delay*, which is the time required for the desired data to reach the magnetic head once the head is positioned. Thus, the total access time for a disk is the seek time plus the latency. For a rotational speed of 2400 rpm, for example, latency is a maximum of 25 ms and an average of 12.5 ms.

---

[10] A few systems have been made with only one pair of read-write heads for the entire memory. In these systems, the two recording heads are positioned on an arm that first is moved between the correct pair of disks and then selects the correct surface (again, because information is written on both the top and the bottom of each disk). The read-write head is finally placed upon the selected track.

The rate at which bits can be transferred once the reading (or writing) begins must also be considered. The *transfer rate* of a disk is the number of bits per second that can be transferred (this is sometimes called the *burst transfer rate*). Twenty to 30 million bits per second is a good transfer rate. The importance of transfer rate depends on how the disk drive is used. For small transfers it is not significant, but for large block transfers it becomes more important than seek time.

Although track spacing is limited by *crosstalk* between adjacent tracks and mechanical tolerances, spacing of 2 mils between adjacent tracks is common. Further, track widths of approximately 0.3 mil are consistent with head-positioning accuracies of 0.25 mil.

The read-write heads used on magnetic disk memories are almost invariably of the *flying head* type. A simplified diagram of a flying head is shown in Fig. 6.26. When a disk rotates at a high speed, a thin but resilient boundary layer of air rotates with the disk. The head is shaped so that it rides on this layer of rotating air, which causes the disk to maintain separation from the head, thus preventing wear on the disk surface. In effect, the layer of air rotating with the disk acts like a spring with a stiffness exceeding several thousand pounds per inch, thus forcing the head away from the surface of the disk. To force the head into correct proximity with the disk, a number of mechanisms have been used, but current memories use a spring-loading system based on a flexible arm on which the read-write head is mounted. These floating heads are normally about 10 microinches (μ in.) from the disk surface.

Some disk memories have changeable disk packs (or modules[11]). Each disk pack contains a set of disks that rotate together. These disk packs are inexpensive enough that a user can store records or programs on them and keep them in files. The cost per bit is much higher than for tape, however, so disk packs are used mostly in applications requiring high operating speeds.

In the mid-1970s, modules were the most-used devices. At that time, however, an IBM unit with fixed disks, the 3350, brought in a new disk technology with greater recording density, more tracks per data surface, and a faster transfer rate. This disk technology is referred to as *Winchester* technology and features a low head loading force (10 versus 300 grams on earlier devices) and a low-mass head. Also, since disks in this technology are generally not changeable, alignment and other tracking problems are reduced. Further, the disks are lubricated so that the lightweight heads can "crash" without damage, and they are stored with power off against the disk.

The technology was quickly picked up by manufacturers of smaller drives, and Winchester drives are now made by many companies. Winchester systems are the most popular for microcomputer systems as well as for large systems. The Winchester disk drives manufactured by most concerns use 14-, 8-, $5\frac{1}{4}$-, or $3\frac{1}{2}$-in. disks. Capacities range from 5 megabytes (Mbytes), for $3\frac{1}{2}$- in. drives, to several thousand Mbytes, for very large drives. These disk memories are often referred to as hard disks. Both hard disk and soft disk (or *floppy disk*) memories are often called *direct access storage devices*, or DASDs.

---

[11] A *module* is a disk pack with the read-write heads and positioning arms all packaged together with the disks. These modules are costly but enable a higher-performance system.

6.10   FLEXIBLE-DISK STORAGE SYSTEMS—THE FLOPPY DISK

The floppy disk uses a flexible plastic base in place of the more conventional rigid, metal-based disk. Floppy disks are changeable, and each disk comes in an envelope, as shown in Fig. 6.27. The disks are mounted on the disk drive with the envelope in place, and information is written and read through an aperture in the envelope. The envelope gives handling protection; in addition, it has a special liner that provides a wiping action to remove wear products and dirt, which would be abrasive to the media and head if left on the surface.

In most floppy-disk drives, the read-write head assembly is in actual physical contact with the recording material. (For increased life, head contact is maintained

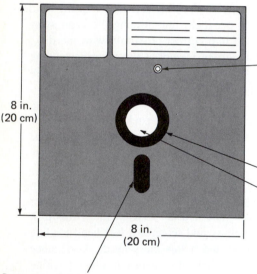

8 in.
(20 cm)

8 in.
(20 cm)

Index hole
The outer circle shows a hole in the jacket; the inner circle shows the index hole in the disk. When these two holes are aligned as the disk revolves during data processing operations, a beam of light shining on one side of the diskette is sensed from the other side and used for timing functions.

Drive access opening in jacket

Drive spindle hole in disk
After the diskette has been placed in the machine and the disk drive spindle has been inserted into the drive spindle hole in the disk, the drive mechanism clamps onto a portion of the disk exposed by the drive access opening in the jacket.

Pressure pad slot
(A similar opening on the other side of the diskette is called the head slot.)
The head slot exposes the recording surface of the disk as the disk turns in its jacket in the machine. The data recording and sensing unit of the disk drive, which is called a *read-write head* and is similar to the record/play-back head in a tape recorder, moves to specified positions along the length of the slot. Moving to a specified position is called *accessing a track*. (Data are recorded only on the side of the diskette that contains the head slot.)

FIGURE 6.27
Floppy disks with envelopes. (*a*) 8-in. floppy.

only during reading or writing.) Track life for a diskette is generally on the order of 3 to 5 million contact revolutions.

There are three standard sizes for floppy disks, as shown in Fig. 6.27. Most disks now use the $5\frac{1}{4}$- or $3\frac{1}{2}$-in. format. To increase disk capacity, manufacturers now supply double-density and two-sided double-density drives.

6.11 MAGNETIC TAPE

Although magnetic tape is not a desirable medium for the main high-speed storage (or even the primary backup storage) of a computer because of its long access time,

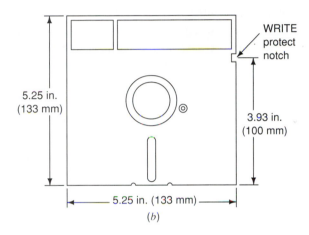

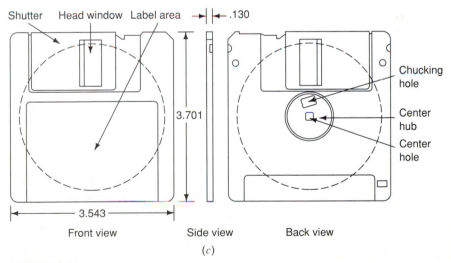

FIGURE 6.27
(*b*) $5\frac{1}{4}$-in. Minifloppy. (*c*) Microfloppy.

modern mass-production techniques have made the cost of tape very low, enabling vast quantities of information to be stored inexpensively. Furthermore, since it is possible to erase and rewrite information on tape, the same tape may be used again and again. Another advantage of magnetic tape is that the information stored does not "fade away," and data or programs stored one month may be used again the next.

Another advantage of using magnetic tape for storing large quantities of data stems from the fact that the reels of tape on a tape mechanism may be changed. In this way the same tape-handling mechanism and its associated circuitry may be used with many different reels of tape, each reel containing different data.

There are four basic parts of a digital magnetic-tape system:

1. *Magnetic tape:* Generally a flexible plastic tape with a thin coating of some ferromagnetic material along the surface.

2. *Tape transport:* A mechanism designed to move the tape past the recording heads at the command of the computer. Included are the heads themselves and the storage facilities for the tape being used, such as the reels on which the tape is wound.

3. *Reading and writing system:* The part of the system that includes the reading and writing amplifiers and the *translators*, which convert the signals from the tape to digital signals that may be used in the central computing system.

4. *Switching and buffering equipment:* The section consisting of the equipment necessary to select the correct tape mechanism, if there are several; to store information from the tape and also information to be read onto the tape (i.e., to provide buffering); and to provide such tasks as manually directed rewinding of the tape.

The tape transports used in most digital systems have two unique characteristics: the ability to start and stop very quickly and high tape speed. The ability to start and stop the tape very quickly is important for two reasons. First, since the writing or reading process cannot begin until the tape is moving at a sufficient speed, a delay is introduced until the tape gains speed, thus slowing down operation. Second, information is generally recorded on magnetic tape in *blocks*, or *records*. Therefore, the tape between blocks of information that passes under the heads during the stopping and starting processes is wasted. This is called the *interblock* or *interrecord gap*. Fast starting and stopping conserves tape.[12]

Figure 6.28(*a*) shows a typical tape system. To accelerate and decelerate the tape very quickly, an effort is made to isolate the tape reels, which have a high inertia, from the mechanism that moves the tape past the recording heads. Both *mechanical* and *vacuum column* systems are used to accomplish this. When systems of this

---

[12] There is a type of tape drive called a *streaming tape drive* that does not start or stop quickly but has a high tape speed. This is described in a later section.

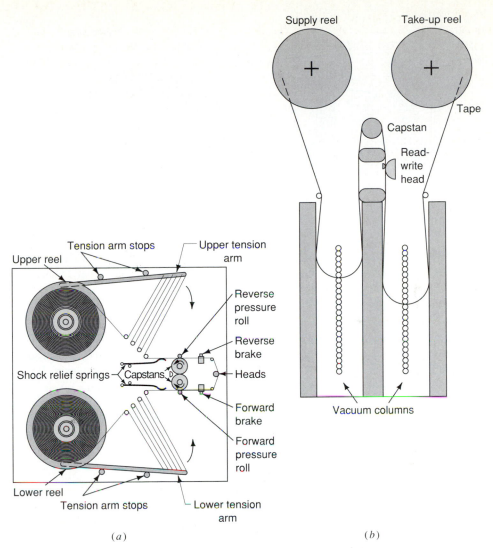

FIGURE 6.28
Magnetic tape drives. (*a*) Mechanical system. (*b*) Vacuum column system.

sort are used, the start and stop times can be less than 3 ms. These are, respectively, the times required to accelerate a tape to a speed suitable for reading or writing and the time required to fully stop a moving tape. The speed at which the tapes are moved past the heads varies greatly, with most tape transports having speeds in the range of 12.5 to 250 in./s.

Some systems have changeable cartridges with a reel of tape in each cartridge. The manufacturers of these systems feel that this protects the tape and facilitates changing the reels. These are discussed in a following section.

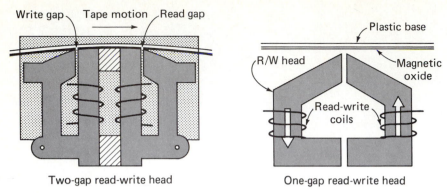

FIGURE 6.29
One- and two-gap tape heads.

Most tape systems have two-gap read-write heads. The two gaps (refer to Fig. 6.29) are useful because, during writing, the read gap is positioned after the write gap and is used to check what has been written by reading and comparing.

Tapes vary from $\frac{1}{4}$ to 3 in. in width; however, most tape is $\frac{1}{2}$-in. wide, 1.5-mil-thick (or less) Mylar. A $10\frac{1}{2}$-in. reel typically has 2400 or 3600 ft of tape. Generally about nine channels or tracks are used for each $\frac{1}{2}$ in. of width. The surface of the tape is usually in contact with the read-write heads. Output signals from the read heads are generally in the 0.1- to 0.5-V range. The recording density varies; however, 200, 556, 800, 1600, 6250, and even 12,500 bits/in. per channel are standard.

Data are recorded on magnetic tape by using some coding system. Generally one character is stored per row (refer to Fig. 6.30) along the tape. The tape in Fig. 6.30 has seven tracks or channels; one of these is a parity bit, which is added to

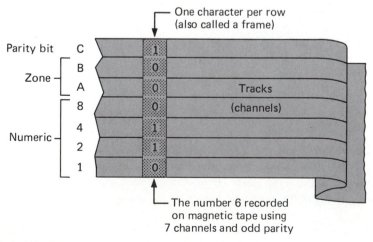

FIGURE 6.30
Basic layout of magnetic tape.

make the number of 1s in every row odd (we study this in the next chapter, 8 or 9 tracks is more common than 7). Data are recorded on magnetic tape in blocks, with gaps between the blocks and usually with unique start and stop characters to signal the beginning and the end of a block.

A small piece of metallic reflective material is sometimes fastened to the tape at the beginning and end of the reel, and photoelectric cells are used to sense these markers to prevent overrunning of the tape [refer to Fig. 6.31(a)].

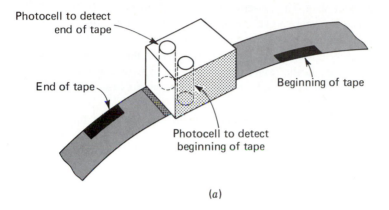

(a)

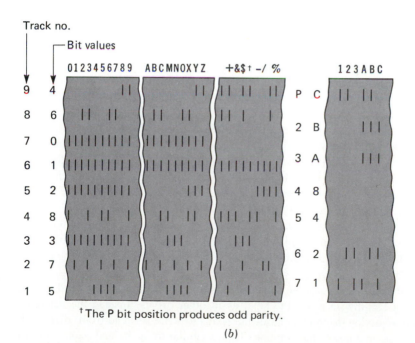

†The P bit position produces odd parity.

(b)

FIGURE 6.31
Magnetic-tape coding. (a) Beginning- and end-of-tape markings. (b) Nine-track (EBCDIC) and seven track tape data format.

The codes used to record on tape vary; a commonly used code is shown in Fig. 6.31(b). Recording densities are 200, 556, 800, 1600, 6250, or 12,500 bits (or rows) per inch, which means 200 to 12,500 characters (or bytes) per inch, since a character is recorded in each row.

6.12   TAPE CASSETTES AND CARTRIDGES

At first glance, the tape cassette used in the familiar home recorder appears an attractive means for recording digital data. The cassettes are small, changeable, and inexpensive; moreover, they are used in some "home" computers. Unfortunately, the tape-moving mechanism in the conventional home cassette system is not of sufficient quality for larger business and scientific computer usage. However, a number of high-quality digital cassettes with prices in the dollar region ($2 to $15, in general) have been developed. These are small — on the order of the familiar audio cassette — and have a similar appearance.

There are also larger tape cartridges that contain long strips of magnetic tape and resemble large cassettes. These cartridges provide a more convenient way to package tape and greatly simplify the mounting of tape reels (which can be a problem with conventional systems where the tape must be manually positioned on the mechanism). The sealed tape cartridges also provide protection against dirt and contamination.

Because most Winchester drives have fixed disks, there is often a need to back up — that is, to write and store elsewhere — the contents of a Winchester disk. This can be done with floppy disks, but they are expensive per bit and somewhat slow. Therefore, a small, inexpensive type of drive, the *streaming tape drive*, now competes in the market for the Winchester backup function.

Most streaming tape drives use $\frac{1}{4}$-in. tape in a cartridge. An important design characteristic is that the tape is moved past the read-write heads by driving the reels, not by using a capstan, as in most tape systems. This leads to fast tape movement, but starts and stops are slow, so interrecord gaps are long. As a result, a streaming tape drive can be used to transfer (or read) large quantities of data once the tape is in motion. Tape speeds of 90 in./s are common, and tape lengths are about 450 ft per cartridge. Transfer rates can be as high as 100 Kbytes/s, and a single tape can store up to 67 Mbytes per cartridge. Densities of 6400 bits/in. along a track are common, and four or five tracks are generally used.

There are also digital audio tape (DAT) storage systems, which use audio-type cassettes. These cassettes have high storage capacity, perhaps 1.2 gigabytes of data in a single cassette the size of a credit card. This is because of the high packing density (over 60,000 bits per inch).

The read-write heads are not in a fixed position on the tape, each head writing a track running lengthwise along the tape, as in other drives. Instead the heads are mounted on a revolving drum that causes the heads to write (or read from) diagonally recorded tracks at an angle to tape motion. This is similar to the helical scan recording used in VHS videotape.

Because of the access time, this tape is used primarily for recording large amounts of data and is a reasonable choice for archiving.

6.13   MAGNETIC BUBBLE AND CCD MEMORIES

The secondary, or backup, memory devices that have been most successful so far are all electromechanical devices (drums, disks, tape, etc.), which store bits as magnetic fields on a surface and rely on mechanical motion to locate the data. However, two devices for secondary storage with no moving parts have started to appear in some commercial applications. These are *magnetic bubble* and *CCD* memories.

Magnetic bubble memories compete primarily with floppy disks, small disks, cartridges, and small tape devices. Bubble memories are more reliable (having no moving parts), consume less power, are smaller, and cost less per unit. However, disks have higher transfer rates, and the cost per bit is lower except for very small systems.

Bubble memories trace their history to research at the Bell Laboratories, which showed that bits can be stored as "bubbles" in a thin magnetic film formed on a crystalline substrate. A bubble device operates as a set of shift registers. The storage mechanism consists of cylindrically shaped magnetic domains called *bubbles*. These bubbles are formed in a thin-film layer of single-crystal synthetic ferrite (or garnet) when a magnetic field is applied perpendicular to the film's surface. A separate rotating field moves the bubbles through the film in shift register fashion. The presence of a bubble is a 1; no bubble is a 0. The bubbles move along a path determined by patterns of soft magnetic material deposited on the magnetic epitaxial film.

To the user, the physics of the bubble memory's operation are less important than its operating characteristics. The memories appear as long shift registers that can be shifted under external control. Storage is permanent, since if shifting is stopped, the bits in the memory will remain indefinitely. To better utilize the shift register characteristics and to reduce access time, the registers are generally made of only modest lengths, perhaps 50 to 100 bits. A memory package is liable to contain from a few hundred kilobits to several megabits. The shift rate is relatively slow, perhaps 400 MHz, so access times are on the order of a few milliseconds. (Reading and writing are performed only at the ends of the shift register.)

Bubble memories require relatively complex interface circuitry, but IC manufacturers have produced reasonable IC packages for this purpose.

Charge-coupled devices (CCDs) are constructed using IC technology. The bits are stored on capacitors as charges similar to the dynamic IC memories, except that the storage is arranged in a shift register configuration, with the charge "packets" shifted from cell to cell under clock control. Since the storage mechanism is a charge on a capacitor, if shifting stops for very long (a few milliseconds), the charges will leak from the capacitors and the memory's contents will be lost.

CCD memories generally have from 500 kilobits to several megabits of storage. The shift registers are read from and written into from the ends, so access time is dependent on shift register lengths. The shift rate is generally 200 to 500 kHz, so for reasonable-length shift registers access times are in milliseconds.

Since CCD memories use IC technology, they require less interface circuitry than bubble memories. The strategy involved in determining how long the shift registers should be for both bubbles and CCDs is based on a cost/performance analysis. A greater number of shorter loops results in faster access times but more interface circuits and more complicated system usage strategies. Long loops give economy but long access times.

Both bubble and CCD technologies are in the early stages, but they are already considered to be competitive with the smaller, more conventional disk memories.

6.14 OPTICAL STORAGE DEVICES

Most optical storage devices record data on a thin film by burning microscopic holes (pits) in the film with a laser. A laser-reader device reads the data by sensing the presence or absence of holes. Optical storage devices are used to record and retrieve video, audio, and image data as well as text and computer data. The extremely high-density recording capability of optical devices enables one 5-in. optical disk to store more than 5 gigabytes of data. Twelve-in. disks can store well over twice this amount.

Most optical disks are read-only and are used for long-term "archival" storage. Stored optical data are relatively unaffected by magnetic fields, so optical disks can be mailed and taken through x-ray machines and airport scanning devices.

There are three basic types of optical disks: compact disk read-only memory (CD-ROM), write-once read-many (WORM), and erasable units and media.

CD-ROM uses the same techniques as audio disks and is most efficiently used for prerecorded optical storage. It can be used to distribute a database that doesn't have to be frequently updated, for example.

CD-ROM is often used for archival purposes. A standard CD-ROM system stores 600 Mbytes of data on a 4.7-in. disk and drive (half-height $5\frac{1}{4}$-in. drives are also available).

WORM storage devices provide one-time writing but unlimited reading of data. Data cannot be overwritten or erased but can be updated by writing new information into a file at another location on the disk. The new file is then linked to the original file through software. The WORM memory format is available in $5\frac{1}{4}$-, 8-, 12-, and 14-in. disks.

WORM optical disks are used to handle data that must be occasionally updated and changed. WORM's long life expectancy eliminates periodic updates (magnetic tape is generally rewritten about every five years).

Erasable optical storage media is an emerging area where improvements are continually being made. Erasable optical media are used in applications where stored data require frequent changes.

There are several techniques used for changeable read/write video systems. One uses *magneto-optic* technology, which differs from the kind of optical storage in which holes are physically burned into a film substrate, making the data nonerasable. These read-only optical drives read 1s and 0s according to the reflectivity of the burned holes to an incident laser beam. With magneto-optic technology (see Fig. 6.32) the write laser heats material in the presence of a magnetic bias field. The heated bit positions take on the magnetic polarization of the field and retain it after they cool. To erase bits, the bias field is reversed, and all bits are heated by the laser.

To read data, the drive takes advantage of *Kerr rotation*, in which the polarization of the read laser is rotated by the magnetic field. The polarization of the light

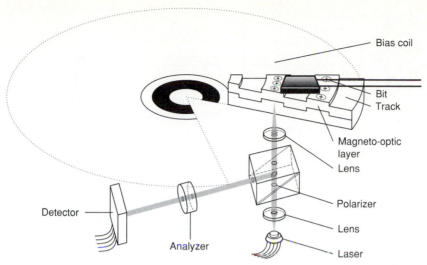

FIGURE 6.32
Changeable read/write video memory system.

striking the written bit positions will be opposite that striking the rest of the media. Overwriting data on magneto-optic media is slower than for magnetic media, since one revolution is required to erase a bit and a second is required to write back to that location. Large storage capacities are the main attraction of magneto-optic drive technology.

6.15 COMPUTER WORD STRUCTURES

The data and instruction words in computers tend to be organized systematically. The simplest organization is to have the basic instruction words and data words be of the same length and to have the memory word be this length also. This was the case for most early computers and is still the case for some large computers. Figure 6.33 shows this organization.

In the past 15 years there has been a considerable change in the way memories are addressed and computer words are organized. Most memories now are *byte-addressable*, which means that a single 8-bit byte in the memory is addressed by a complete memory address.[13] This is shown in Fig. 6.34, where for m = 32, for ex-

---

[13] The actual physical memory may have a word length different from a byte. The physical memory might have 64 bits lying at each address, and additional gates would be required to select a byte or several bytes from the memory word read each time. This has the advantage that full words and double words can be accessed much faster, and even successive bytes can be obtained quickly if called for. Generally, large computers have large numbers of bits in the physical memory word because it helps them to operate faster.

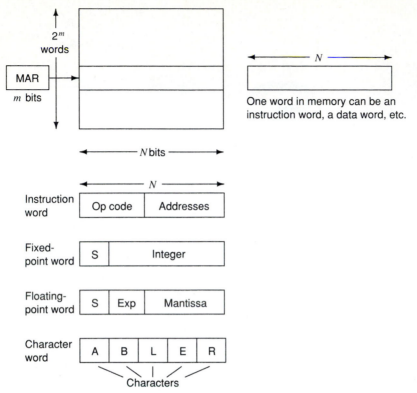

FIGURE 6.33
Conventional memory word structure.

ample, an address of 32 bits accesses a memory of as many as 2^{32} bytes and, therefore, 8×2^{32} bits. Normally the byte at a given location will not constitute a complete computer word, however. In microprocessors there is a tendency to let 16-bit entities be called *words*, so a word would consist of 2 bytes. To address a word, only the numerically lowest address for the 2 bytes used must be given; it is understood that the following memory address will contain the remainder of the word.

When this scheme is used, it is possible for the central processing unit (CPU) to call for bytes, or *half-words*, consisting of a single byte each. *Double words* are then 4-byte words. (In the Intel 80386 and 80486, double words are called *dwords*.)

This nomenclature is not consistent, however. In the IBM 370 series, words are 32 bits, half-words 16 bits, bytes are 8 bits, nibbles are 4 bits, and double words are 64 bits.

6.16 STORAGE HIERARCHIES

Storage in a computer is organized in a hierarchy, with the fastest, most expensive memory devices closest to the CPU. A typical configuration appears in Fig. 6.35,

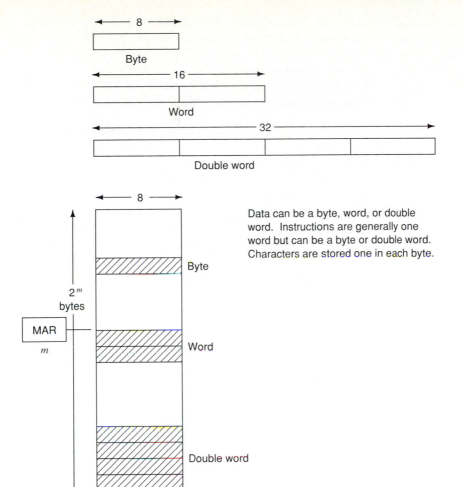

Data can be a byte, word, or double word. Instructions are generally one word but can be a byte or double word. Characters are stored one in each byte.

FIGURE 6.34
Byte-organized word structure.

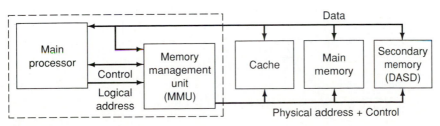

FIGURE 6.35
MMU and memory devices.

which shows a CPU with cache, main memory, and "secondary" DASD devices (these are generally hard Winchester disks). (Cache memories will be explained. They are SRAMs and are much faster than the main memory.) Tape or optical disk devices can be used to add a larger and slower *archival* storage. A memory management unit (MMU) is used to obtain data and instructions from the memories; this unit generally works in cooperation with the operating system. MMUs can be very simple or quite complex.

The MMU permits division of the memory into cache, backup or secondary memory, main memory, and bytes. Computers organize the MMU in various ways. Large computers (VAXs, for example) have large MMUs. A microprocessor may or may not have an MMU on the basic chip (it can be on a separate chip).

Figure 6.36 shows the same hierarchy represented differently. The slower memories are depicted below the faster memories. When the processor asks for data at a particular address, if it is in the cache, the access is fastest; if main memory must be accessed, it will take longer; and if a DASD must be used, the processor must wait still longer.

When a designer chooses a memory organization, the idea is to assemble and operate the memory devices so that the speed of computer operation is close to that of the fastest memory device (the main memory, or cache if one exists) and so that the average cost per bit approaches the cost of the least expensive device (generally the DASD).

To achieve speed of operation with a collection of many memory devices, the *principle of localized reference* is used. The idea is that at a particular point in the processing of data, the instructions run by a program and the data used in a program generally are located in relatively small areas of the memory. The areas used move through the overall memory as the program progresses, but for a reasonable time interval, by placing the currently used sections of memory in the fastest memory devices, most instructions and operands will be taken from the fast devices. The

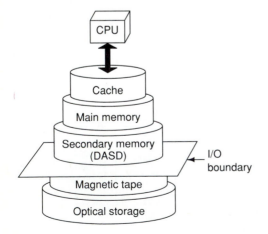

FIGURE 6.36
Hierarchy of memory devices.

average access time will thus be close to the speed of the fastest devices. As an example, if a program contains a loop of 50 instructions, these instructions can be placed in the fastest memory device, and the operating speed for instruction accesses will be that of this device. The general strategy is that the overall program and data are placed on the slowest devices and moved into the faster devices when used.

The memory devices should be operated in a way that takes advantage of their basic characteristics. For example, DASDs are slow in locating data but can transfer large amounts quickly once the data are located (i.e., the transfer rate is high). This means when data from a DASD are called for, many words should be transferred into the main memory. The main memory will then also contain nearby words, which ensures that succeeding words in a program will already be in the main memory. The set of words in the main memory at a given time is called the *working set*. The idea in memory management is to have the words about to be used by the program reside in main memory after the DASD is read from. Similarly, an attempt is made to keep the most-used words in the cache memory so as many words as possible can be taken from it when the program is run.

As can be seen, reading a program or subprogram and the section of data it uses from a DASD is one way to efficiently transfer words to and from the DASD. The actual techniques are somewhat more general and are used blindly by the operating system and MMU.

After a section of program and data have been transferred into main memory, inevitably the program (CPU) will ask for a word not in main memory but still in a DASD; the word called for and other words in the same region will then be read into main memory from the DASD. This leads to another problem. At some point the main memory will be filled, and to make room, words must be read from the main memory back into the DASD(s). The *least recently used* algorithm is generally utilized to determine what is to be moved from main memory. This algorithm is also sometimes used by the cache and is fundamental to memory management. The *least recently used* algorithm consists of keeping track of when each block of data is used and reading out the block that has not been used for the longest period of time.

Using this algorithm, data are moved up and down through the storage hierarchy of Fig. 6.36 based on reference activity. All this is controlled by the operating system and the other memory management hardware. The design strategy is intended to cause maximum throughput for the CPU.

In the following sections the most common memory management techniques, virtual memory and cache memory, will be explained.

6.17   VIRTUAL MEMORY

Many applications require large programs that, along with all subprograms, cannot be placed entirely in the main memory. Also, it is convenient for programmers to write programs with the assumption that memory space is practically unlimited. In addition, large programs may need to be transported from computer to computer, and the memories of these computers may vary in size. Some may have less main memory than the overall program size.

To address these problems, computer designers use memory management techniques offering a feature called *virtual memory*, enabling programmers to write programs as if the memory is very large. This large imaginary memory is called *virtual memory*, and the computer's actual main (IC) memory is called *real memory* or *physical memory*.

The computer and its operating system cause the program to be run in the main memory by first placing the program in DASD and then transferring part of it into the main memory. The program is run until something not in main memory is called for. The section required is then moved from DASD into main memory.

Eventually, a section of program will be called for, and main memory will be filled. A section of program must then be moved back into the DASD before the required section can be moved into main memory. The computer continues exchanging program and data sections between DASDs and main memory as necessary.

The same mechanisms that provide a large virtual memory to a single user can be used to facilitate *multiprogramming systems* or *multitasking systems*, where several programs are alternately run using the same memory. The idea is that a program is operated until it calls for a slow device (such as a printer or tape drive). Another program is then run until the device called for by the first program is ready, and then the first program is run again. The main memory can thus be shared by several programs, sections of which are moved back and forth between a DASD and main memory. When programs are operated so that each uses a certain maximum amount of time before another program is operated, the programs are said to *time-share* the computer; the computer is then being operated in a *time-shared multiprogramming* or *time-shared multitasking* mode.

It will facilitate discussion to first concentrate on the virtual-memory mode of operation ignoring multiprogramming considerations. There are two approaches to virtual memory organization.

1. *Linear virtual memory.* In the linear approach the programmer is provided with a very large imaginary memory in which to write programs, place data, and so on. The memory starts with address 0, and address numbers increase up to some large value (such as 2^{32}). However, the actual (physical) main memory in the computer may have only 2^{20} locations. In such a case, the addresses used for virtual memory are called *virtual addresses* or *logical addresses*, and those in "real" main memory are called *real addresses* (refer to Fig. 6.37). The program(s) are stored on a DASD with virtual addresses (32 bits for a 2^{32} location virtual memory).

   The operating system loads part or all of a program into real memory, assigning locations for this section, and the memory-mapping unit then maps virtual addresses to physical addresses. Sections of program and data are interchanged between DASD and main memory at the direction of the operating system. In Fig. 6.37, all of the program sections are loaded into main memory, but only some of the sections might be loaded if the program and data were large.

2. *Segmented virtual memory.* In the segmented approach the program and data are divided into modules by the programmer. Each module has an address space be-

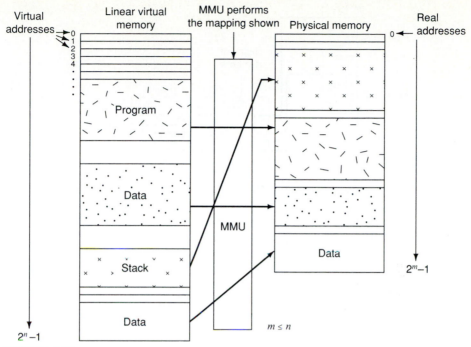

FIGURE 6.37
Linear virtual memory.

ginning at 0 and is linear. Figure 6.38(*a*) shows an example where the program is broken into five modules: two modules for the main program, two data modules, and a stack module. (A stack module is a particular memory organization that will be described later.) Each module is given a *segment number*, and an address consists of the segment number and the address within that segment, which is called the *displacement* or *offset*. An operating system can place a segment anywhere in memory by determining a beginning physical address for the segment, which is sometimes called the *base address* or *segment pointer*. This physical address is then added by the memory management unit to each logical address (displacement) in the segment to form the final physical address, as shown in Fig. 6.38(*b*). This method of determining addresses makes programs *relocatable* in that a given module containing a program can be placed anywhere in the memory and run. Data modules can also be placed anywhere. Since the operating system knows the approximate physical size and can allocate physical storage based on the size, modules can be read into and out of main memory according to demand.

Virtual memory implementation is based on two techniques: *paging* and *segmentation*. Paging is generally used to implement linear virtual memories, and segmentation mapping is used for segmented virtual memories. These can also be combined, as will be shown.

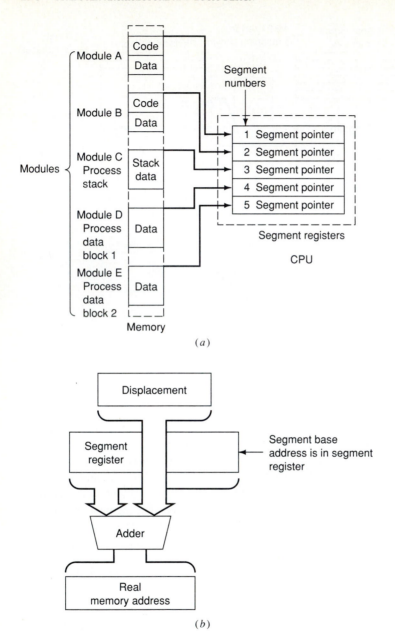

FIGURE 6.38
(a) Segmented virtual memory. (b) Address calculation for segmented virtual memory.

Paged Virtual Memory

When paged virtual memory is used, the overall program generally resides on DASD (any large storage medium can be used). The address space used by the programmer, the virtual memory, is divided into *virtual pages*, all of equal size. (The programmer need not be aware of this division or of any other feature of virtual memory. The program is simply written as if the main memory space is the size of the virtual memory.)

The program is operated by reading the page containing the beginning of the program into the main memory. The computer begins to operate the program, and if addresses are called for that are not in the main memory, the pages containing these addresses are read from disk (DASD) into the main memory. This is called *demand paging*. When an instruction or operand address not currently in the main memory is called for during program operation, this is called a *page fault*. A page fault causes the page containing the address called for by the program to be read from DASD into main memory.[14] Eventually, of course, a page will be called for and there will be no more room in main memory. Generally the strategy is used where the page in memory which was least recently used is removed and replaced by the new page.

Obviously, some strategy must be developed for translating the virtual addresses to the physical addresses. The architecture of the computer is designed to facilitate this translation using the memory management unit.

It is general practice to divide the main memory into *page frames*, which are the same size as the pages in the virtual memory. Figure 6.39 shows a layout for address translation where the virtual memory has 32-bit addresses (so the programmer can use up to 2^{32} addresses) and the computer has 32-bit addresses, but the physical memory has only 2^{21} addresses. The virtual page size for virtual memory and the page frame size for physical memory is 2^{12} addresses, so there are 2^9 pages in the physical memory. Figure 6.40 shows that a virtual address consists of a 20-bit *virtual page number* (there are 2^{20} pages in the virtual memory) and a 12-bit displacement; a main memory address consists of a 9-bit *physical page number* and a 12-bit displacement. (The words *offset* and *displacement* are used interchangeably by different manufacturers and mean the same thing.)

The job to be done by the memory management unit is thus to map or translate virtual page numbers to real page numbers and then add on the displacements. To accomplish this, a *page table* is used, which is part of the memory management unit. When a page is read from disk to main memory, a page frame number is assigned the page in physical memory, and the virtual page number and physical page number are placed together in the page table. Each time an instruction or operand address is

---

[14] When an instruction word's address is called for and the instruction word is not in main memory, the MMU causes the generation of an interrupt; the computer then jumps to a page fault interrupt program. This program decides what memory addresses to transfer from DASD to main memory, what page(s) to replace, and so on. If an instruction has begun to operate and calls for an operand not in main memory, the computer must also "back up" the instruction's operation before jumping to the page fault service program so that the instruction can be restored once the operand is available. It is also possible to "freeze" the instruction's operation when the operand is called for and to restart it when the operand has been obtained. Interrupts and more details are discussed in Chapter 10.

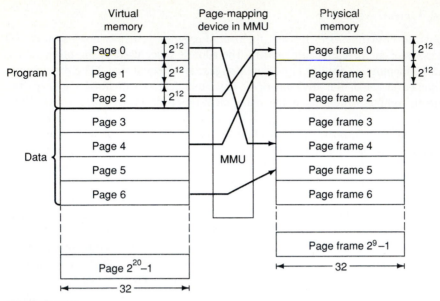

FIGURE 6.39
Paged virtual memory.

asked for by the CPU, the virtual page number is looked up in the page table, and the corresponding real page number is added to the displacement to form the final physical address. Figure 6.40 shows this, and it is a good idea to mentally try a few addresses to see how this works. This process is called *address translation*, and it requires that each virtual address be translated to a physical address before it can be used. The computer operating system manages the page table and the transfer of pages from and to the DASDs.

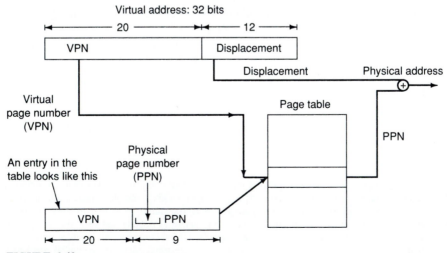

FIGURE 6.40
Address calculation using the page table.

There is a type of memory called an *associative memory* or a *content-addressable memory* that can be used to implement the page table and speed up operation. It is also useful in other applications.

Figure 6.41 shows an associative memory with eight locations. The memory is not addressed in the normal way. Memory is in two sections, one that selects and one that stores data. The selection section stores "addresses" that are examined in parallel by gates to see if the value in the input register is in the selection section (ANDed with the mask register). If it is, there will be a 1 output to the cell of the selection register at the corresponding location; if not, that cell will contain a 0. It is important to note that the output is determined by gates only; the memory is not searched sequentially. Many gates are required.

Typical values are shown in the selection section to provide an example. Note these values are read in, and other values could be used. For these values, if the input is 01101 and the mask 11111, there will be a 1 in the top cell of the selection register. If the mask is 11100 and the input is 10101, then the second and sixth cells from the top of the selection register will be 1s. If the mask is 01111 and the input 10110, only the second cell from the top will contain a 1. The word in the data memory at the location with a 1 output in the selection register can be read on demand in these memories. This memory can also be written into (loaded).

Associative memories can be constructed with as many bits per word as desired and as many words as desired. It is, of course, necessary to be able to read values into

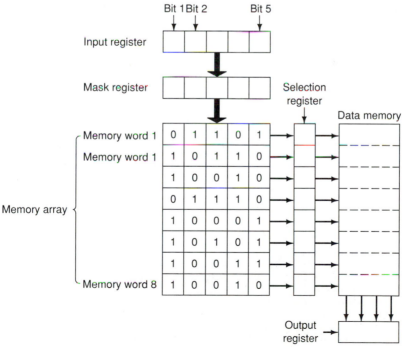

FIGURE 6.41
Associative or content-addressable memory.

the selection section, the data memory, and the input and mask registers. Associative memories are expensive to manufacture, and many gates (and flip-flops) are required for even small memories. They are primarily used where high speed is required.

An associative memory with the selection section containing the virtual page numbers and the data memory containing the physical page numbers can be used to make a high-speed page table. A page table of this type is very fast, but it is also very expensive if it must address the entire physical memory. To alleviate cost, a compromise is often used where only part of the overall page table is placed in the high-speed associative memory page table,[15] which is then called a *translation look-aside buffer* (TLB) (see Fig. 6.42). The most recently used page numbers are

---

[15] The look-aside buffer can also be placed in a cache memory (to be described).

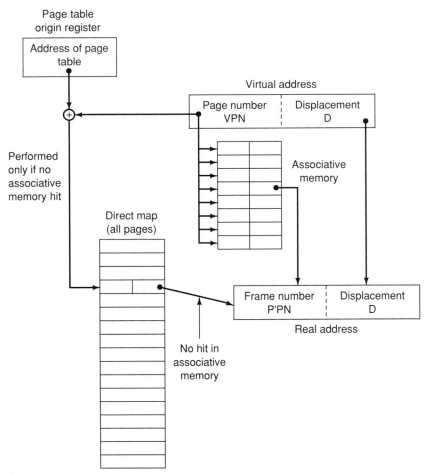

FIGURE 6.42
Address translation mechanism using an associative memory to form a look-aside buffer.

placed in the look-aside buffer, and the entire table is placed in main memory. Most memory accesses will use the look-aside buffer, and only a few will require a trip to main memory for the physical page number. This results in fast overall operating speed with reasonable implementation cost, and this method is frequently used.

Implementing Segmented Virtual Memory

With segmented addressing, a program is not viewed as a single sequence of instructions and data, but as several modules of code, data, stack, and so on. The virtual address space is thereby broken into several linear address spaces as defined by the programmer. Each of these modules of program and data is called a *segment* and is given a separate segment number (or name), which is also called a *segment selector*. A physical address is computed as a combination of the segment selector number, which is a pointer to a block in memory, and the segment displacement (refer to Fig. 6.43). Each segment is treated as a linear address space by the programmer, starting with address 0 and continuing upward.

Advocates of this type of memory feel that segmented addressing schemes reflect the user's view of memory as a collection of segments of variable sizes, which is how the programmer writes the program, decomposing it into a main program, subroutines, data structures, and other elements. Figure 6.44 shows how several virtual segments in two programs operating in a multitasking mode can be mapped to sections of main memory. Each segment is mapped to a section of main memory that is selected by the operating system and whose base location is loaded into the segment-mapping device.

A good way to provide segmentation (which has been used in several computers, including the Intel 8086, 8088, 80386, and 80486) is to use a set of *segment registers*. Each of these registers is associated with a particular usage in programming. As an example, consider a microprocessor with three segment registers: a program register, P; a data register, D; and a stack register, S (stacks will be explained). The program-

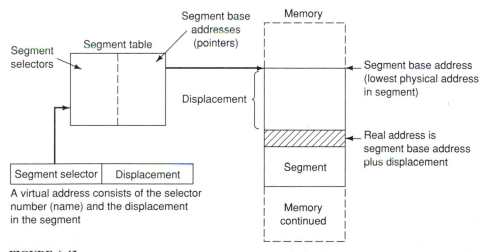

FIGURE 6.43
Segment table operation.

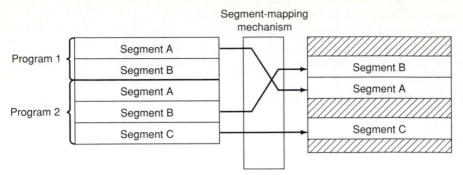

FIGURE 6.44
Mapping two programs in segmented memory.

mer then writes his program instructions in a program virtual memory, P*; places all data in a data virtual memory, D*; and uses the stack, S*, as desired. The segmented virtual memory program then consists of the three program modules P*, S*, and D*. The operating system assigns memory locations for each of the three sections, as shown in Fig. 6.45, and loads the P, S, and D registers with the starting addresses or *segment base addresses*. Each virtual address displacement is then added to the correct starting address by the memory mapping device. (The MMU must be told whether an address is an instruction, data, or stack address; a segment selector number gives this information.)

Example

The Intel 80386 and 80486 microcomputers use both segmentation and paging. The segmentation is controlled by six segment registers, as shown in Fig. 6.46. The pro-

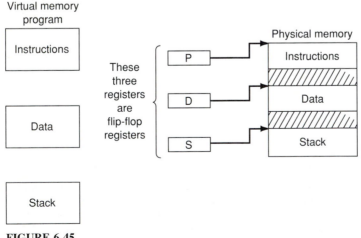

FIGURE 6.45
Segment registers.

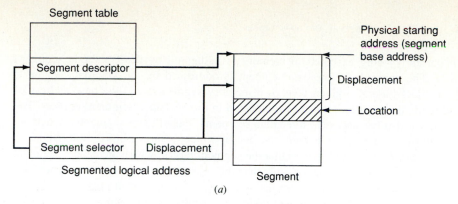

Segment table

Segment descriptor

Physical starting address (segment base address)

Displacement

Location

Segment selector | Displacement

Segmented logical address

Segment

(a)

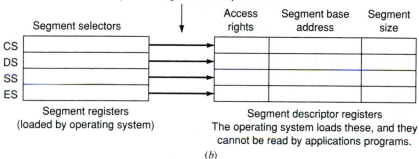

Segment selectors in table point to segment descriptors in segment descriptor table

Segment selectors

Access rights | Segment base address | Segment size

CS
DS
SS
ES

Segment registers
(loaded by operating system)

Segment descriptor registers
The operating system loads these, and they
cannot be read by applications programs.

(b)

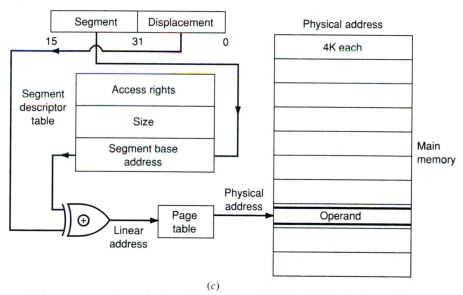

Segment | Displacement

15 · 31 · 0

Physical address

4K each

Segment descriptor table

Access rights

Size

Segment base address

Linear address

Page table

Physical address

Main memory

Operand

(c)

FIGURE 6.46

80386/80486 virtual memory. (*a*) Address translation mechanism. The segment selector points to the segment descriptor in the segment map table. The physical memory address is formed as a sum of the memory address of the segment, stored in the segment descriptor, and the displacement in the logical address. (*b*) Segment registers with the corresponding segment descriptors. Segment descriptors are invisible to applications programs and are loaded by the CPU. The information they contain includes access rights, the segment base address in the physical memory, and the segment size. (*c*) Segmented addressing scheme with paging.

gram currently being executed in memory is addressed by the CS (code segment) register. The currently active data segment is addressed by the DS (data segment) register. Stacks are also given their own memory segments, and the base address of the currently active stack segment is contained in the SS (stack segment) register. The programmer also has access to three data segments, called extra segments, which are addressed by ES, FS, and GS registers, one of which is shown in Fig 6.46(*b*).

Figure 6.46(*b*) and (*c*) shows that the segment tables, which are called "segment descriptor tables" by Intel, contain more than the segment base address. Segment tables also contain the *size*, so that an erroneous address (one generated outside the bound formed by adding the size to the base address) will be detected, and an *access rights* section, which tells whether the segment can be written into (changed) or is read-only, who can read or write (access privileges), and other conditions.

The 80386/80486 combines segmentation with paging as shown in Fig. 6.46(*c*).

6.18   CACHE MEMORY

There is a basic problem caused by the relatively low speeds of large main memories. The processor section of a computer is constructed of flip-flops and gates, which are very fast, whereas the main memory uses less expensive, higher-packing-density IC devices, which are much slower in operation. If the processor obtains all of its instructions and operands from the main memory, the speed at which instructions are executed will be limited by the speed of main memory and its cycle time rather than by the speed of the processor section.

There are several ways to address this problem. One straightforward method to reduce the average time required for many accesses to main memory is called *interleaving*. The access time for large RAMs, particularly large DRAMs, is only a part of the total time needed for a memory cycle. After a DRAM has been read, for example, a *precharge* time (a wait time) is required before the memory can be accessed again. This and other factors slow overall operation of a memory composed of a set of chips operating as a single memory module.

The basic concept behind interleaving is to break the main memory into independent modules, each consisting of several chips. Each module can then be addressed and operated independently. By providing buffering flip-flops in the interface, the modules can be addressed as soon as addresses are available, and each memory module can respond and recover while other modules are being addressed and sequenced through their cycles. This speeds up overall operation speed beyond what can be expected from a single chip and its cycle time. Interleaving requires additional interface buffering and timing circuitry and sufficient logic to ensure that the separate modules are correctly operated.

Interleaving, however, does not speed up memory operation by a factor equal to the number of the modules. One reason for this is that several consecutive requests for data from the same module will require the full chip cycle time. To distribute requests among the modules so that successive requests go to different modules, the least significant bits in memory addresses are generally used to select modules. This causes requests for successive addresses to go to different modules (successive instructions generally come from successive addresses, for example).

When interleaving is used, memories are divided into two to eight modules. Using more than eight modules will generally not provide further significant benefit.

Another frequently used technique for reducing average memory access time involves adding a small memory, called a *cache memory*, to the processor. This cache memory is constructed of very high-speed devices (flip-flops and gates) and is used to hold the most-used data and instructions. References to the main memory are made only when something is not in the cache.

The basic procedure is to load a section of program into the cache from the main memory as the program begins to operate (the cache starts out empty). It is important to note that since the cache is much smaller than the main memory, address information as well as the contents of addresses must be stored in the cache.

A reference from the processor to the memory is said to be a *hit* if it is to something in the cache and a *miss* if it necessitates going to main memory. The *miss ratio* is the probability that a reference to memory is a miss. If the miss ratio were 0, the computer would operate at the speed of the cache; if it were 1, the computer would operate at the speed of the main memory. Since the cache is much faster than the main memory, the lower the miss ratio the better. Clearly, a large cache will lower the miss ratio, but cache memory is expensive. As is the case with all engineering, a tradeoff must be made between cache cost and the gain in operating speed.

Generally, cache memories are 5 to 40 times faster and 50 to 1000 times smaller than the main memory. Considering only READ operations from the memory, a formula for the average memory cycle time is

$$T_{average} = h \times T_{cache} + m \times T_{main}$$

where $T_{average}$ is the average memory cycle time, h is the hit ratio, m is the miss ratio, and T_{cache} and T_{main} are the cycle times for the cache and main memory, respectively. If a cache were 20 times faster than the main memory, and the miss ratio were 0.02, the computer would obtain operands from the memory with an average cycle time of about 1.38 times the cache cycle time; if the miss ratio were 0.05, the average memory cycle time would be 1.95 times the cache memory cycle time. The importance of lowering the cache miss ratio is readily seen.

The first strategy we will describe is called the *direct mapped cache* organization and is used in many microprocessors (with one variation). We will then describe other strategies.

Cache Organization

A basic problem with any cache design is determining if the word at the address requested by the processor is in the cache memory and, if so, where. Since the cache is smaller than main memory, the number of addresses (address space) is smaller, and some way must be found to put data in the cache and mark it using main memory addresses. The most straightforward method is called *direct mapped cache memory*.

Figure 6.47 shows a block diagram for a direct mapped cache memory. The memory is basically a high-speed RAM. The computer main memory is divided into

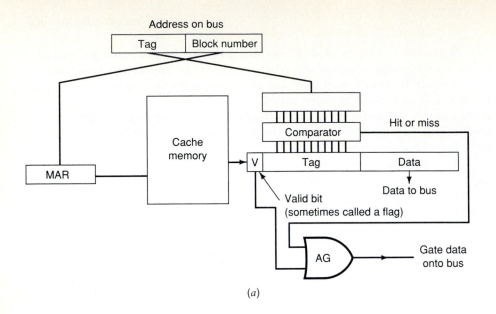

(a)

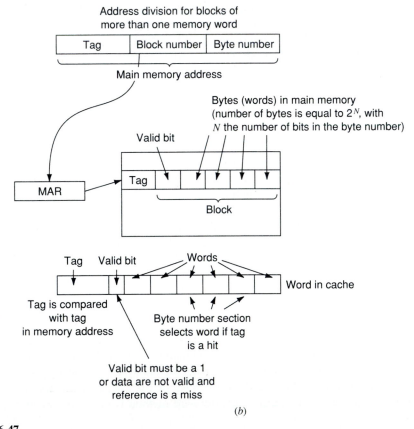

(b)

FIGURE 6.47
Direct mapped cache. (a) Direct mapped cache memory with one word per block. (b) Direct mapped cache memory with several words per block.

a number of *blocks*, each containing 2^N main memory words, where N is an integer. If N is 3, each block contains eight words; the words at memory addresses 0 to 7 are in block 0, the words at memory locations 8 to 15 are in block 1, the words at memory addresses 16 to 23 are in block 2, and so on. The cache stores a block at each location plus a tag and a valid bit, which will be explained.

To make the initial explanation more straightforward, we will use selected word lengths for cache and main memory. Also, there will be only one main memory word in each block. The more general case will be described after this specific case has been made clear.

The main memory is assumed to have words of 32 bits each. Memory addresses are assumed to be 24 bits, and the cache has 2^9 locations (addresses). The tag sections will then have $24 - 9$ bits (15) each. When a word is called for from the memory, the 24-bit address is broken into two sections. The nine least significant bits are placed in the address register for the cache; these bits are called the *block number*, as shown in Fig. 6.47(*b*). The 15 most significant bits represent the *tag* and are stored in a flip-flop register. To determine if the word in the address called for is in the cache, the cache control reads the word in cache at the address given by the block number and then determines if the tag in this cache word is the same as the tag in the main memory address. If this is the case, the reference is a hit, and the word can be delivered from the cache to the processor. If the tag at the address specified by the 9 bits is not the same, the word called for must be obtained from main memory. In this event, the direct mapped strategy calls for writing the word currently in the cache at the proper address in main memory, placing the new word (block) that was called for in the cache along with the tag section of its address, and making the valid bit a 0.

This approach is called *direct mapping* because the nine least significant bits directly address the cache memory to obtain the tag and corresponding word. The use of the least significant bits to address the cache memory allows consecutive addresses to be distributed through the cache. (Try a few addresses to see how this works.)

There are several techniques used to write words from cache into main memory (store instructions). In a *write-through* cache memory, when a processor instruction writes a word into memory (generally from the CPU), the word is written into both the cache and main memory at the same time (a valid bit is not required). In a *copy-back* cache memory, updates are made only to the cache, and a valid bit is set. Then, when a memory word must be replaced in the cache and written into the main memory, the valid bit is examined to see if the transfer is actually necessary. This requires more logic and costs more but can speed up operation. It is sometimes called *flagged copy-back*.[16]

In effect, the valid bit is used to determine if the word in the cache is the same as the word in memory. When a word is read from memory into the cache, the valid

---

[16] There is also an *always copy-back* strategy (with no flags), which always copies into memory for replacements.

bit is set to 0. If the word is changed, the valid bit is set to 1. When a miss occurs, it is not actually necessary to read the word that is replaced in the cache back into the main memory if it has not been changed, and this speeds up operation.

When there is more than one main memory word per block, the direct mapped technique is a little more involved. If the memory is byte-addressable, the reason for having more than one memory word per block can be readily seen: the tags will be longer than the memory words in the cache, and the overhead will be considerable. Also, if *computer* words consist of several bytes, it is faster to read more bytes (and, therefore, complete computer words) from the cache.

Figure 6.47(*b*) shows a direct mapped cache with several memory words (bytes) in each block. Let us assume there are eight words in a block. The three least significant bits in each memory address give the position of a byte in a block. The overall addressing technique for the direct mapped cache then involves dividing each address into three sections: (1) the block number, which gives the address in the cache; (2) the tag section, which identifies a particular block; and (3) the byte number, which selects a particular byte in the block.

All that must be added to Fig. 6.47(*a*) to implement the multiword block is a selection network to choose the correct byte (or bytes) from a block for a hit. These bits from the three-part address must be stored in flip-flops.

The primary problem with direct mapping occurs when a program continually calls two or more instructions or data addresses that map to the same address in the cache. The most common way to alleviate this problem is to have more than one block and tag at each location in the cache memory. The contents at a given location in the cache is then called a *set*. For example, if two blocks and their tags lie at each location in cache, then when an address is called for by the processor, the tags for the two blocks must each be examined to see if there is a hit. This is called a *block set associative* technique, or *set associative* technique, and the *degree of associativity* refers to the number of blocks at each location in cache. Two or four blocks are often contained in each set.

Figure 6.48 shows how one version of a set associative organization operates. The scheme tends to alleviate the problem of pairs of words that are frequently called for by the program going into the same cache location and causing continual replacement of this cache location; however, the additional gates needed to examine each of the tags is expensive, and the extra cost could be used for more locations in cache. Also, there must be an algorithm to determine which memory word to replace when there is a miss (generally the *least recently used* algorithm is used). Choosing between the set associative and the direct mapped cache is an example of an engineering tradeoff decision.

Finally, an *associative cache* can be constructed using an associative memory. In this case, the associative memory holds a complete address and data or instruction word at each location. Each address is looked for in the cache and if found results in a hit. This method is very fast but also expensive. The *least recently used* algorithm is generally used for replacement, and the words are ordered according to this usage, which increases the complexity. As a result, the direct mapped and set associative organizations are more often used.

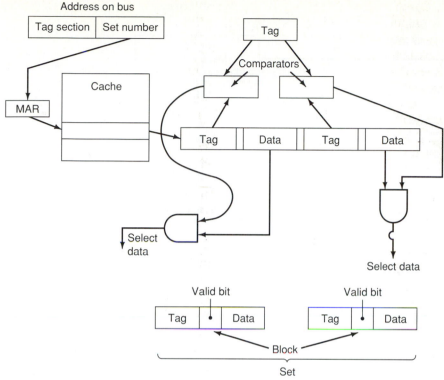

FIGURE 6.48
Set associative cache memory.

Figure 6.49 shows how virtual memory combines with cache memory. The steps taken to determine a memory location are shown in flowchart form. It is remarkable that this complexity leads to fast memory access, but this is because of the parallelism in the process and the high speed of the gates and flip-flops used.

In microprocessors there are often two caches, one for instruction words and one for data words. Large computers tend to have large single caches. The speed advantage using even small caches is so impressive that caches are used very frequently.

6.19 DIGITAL RECORDING TECHNIQUES

Although the process of recording a 0 or a 1 on a surface may appear straightforward, considerable research has gone into both the development of the recorded patterns used to represent 0s and 1s and the means for determining the value recorded. There are two necessities here: (1) The packing density should be made as great as is possible; that is, each cell or bit should occupy as little space as possible, thus economizing on the amount of tape or disk used to store a given amount of information. (2) The reading and writing procedure should be made as reliable as possible. These two interests

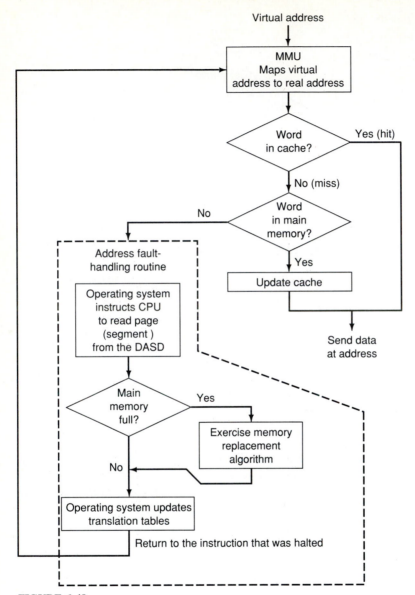

FIGURE 6.49
The flowchart for virtual memory system with cache memory.

conflict because as the recorded bits are packed more closely together, the distortion of the playback signal is increased.

In writing information on a magnetic surface, the digital information is supplied to the recording circuitry, which codes this information into a pattern that is recorded by the write head. There are three techniques used to write information on a magnetic medium: the *return-to-zero* (RZ) technique, the *return-to-bias* (RB) technique, and the *nonreturn-to-zero* (NRZ) technique.

Return-To-Zero and Return-to-Bias Recording Techniques

Figure 6.50(*a*) illustrates the return-to-zero recording technique. No current goes through the winding of the write head except when a 1 or a 0 is to be recorded. If a 1 is to be recorded, a pulse of positive polarity is applied to the winding; if a 0 is to be written, a negative pulse is applied to the winding. In either case, the current through the winding is returned to zero after the pulse and remains there until the next bit is recorded. The second set of waveforms on this drawing illustrates the remnant flux pattern on the magnetic surface after the write head has passed. There is some distortion in this pattern because of the fringing of flux around the head.

If this pattern of magnetization is passed under a read head, some of the magnetic flux will be coupled into the core of the head. The flux takes the lower reluctance path through the core material of the head instead of bridging the gap in the head (see Fig. 6.26). When the amount of flux through the core material changes, a voltage is induced in the coil wound around the core. Thus, a change in the amplitude of the recorded magnetic field results in a voltage being induced in the coil on the read head. The waveforms in Fig. 6.50(*a*) and (*b*) illustrate typical output signals on the read-head windings for each technique. Note that the waveform at the read head is not a reproduction of the input current during the write process, nor of the pattern actually magnetized on the material.

The problem is, therefore, to distinguish a 1 from a 0 output at the sense winding. Several techniques have been used. One involves first amplifying the output waveform from the read winding in a linear amplifier. Then the output of this amplifier is strobed to determine whether a 1 or 0 was written. If the output from the read amplifier is connected to an AND gate and the strobe pulse is connected as an input to the same AND gate, the output will be a positive pulse when the recorded signal represents a 1.

A fundamental characteristic of RZ recording should be noted: For a 1, the output signal during the first half of each bit time will be positive with regard to the second half; for a 0, the first half of the output signal during each bit time will be negative with regard to the second half of the signal. This fact is sometimes exploited in translating the signal.

In the RZ system of Fig. 6.50(*a*), the magnetic field returns to zero flux when a 1 or a 0 pulse is not present. This makes it impossible to write over information that has previously been written unless the position of each cell is very accurately located. If a 0 pulse is written directly over a previously recorded 1, the flux generated will reverse the polarity of the recorded field only if the write head is in exactly the right position when the 0 is recorded. Thus, the timing of the writing of information is very critical for this system, and it is rarely used.

The second method for recording information shown in Fig. 6.50 is the *return-to-bias* system. In this case, the current through the winding keeps the head saturated in the negative direction unless a 1 is to be written. When a 1 is written, a pulse of current in the opposite direction is applied to the winding at the center of the bit time. Also as illustrated in the figure, there will be an output at the sense winding only when a 1 is written. This output may be amplified and strobed just as in the previous method. The timing here is not so critical when information is being written

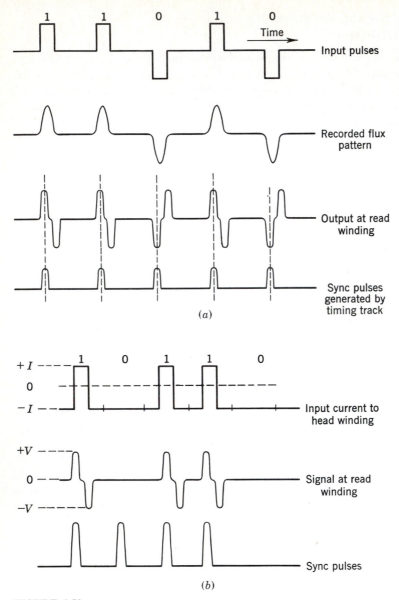

FIGURE 6.50
Recording techniques. (*a*) Return-to-zero recording. (*b*) Return-to-bias technique.

over, because the negative flux from the head will magnetize the surface in the correct direction, regardless of what was previously recorded. The current through the winding in this case, and in all those that follow, is assumed to be sufficient to saturate the material on which the signals are being recorded. A primary problem here concerns sequences of 0s. For magnetic tape, either a clock track must be used or the code must be such that at least one 1 occurs in each line of the tape. This is because only 1s generate magnetic flux changes and, therefore, output signals at the read head.

Nonreturn-to-Zero Recording Techniques

Figure 6.51 illustrates three recording techniques, each of which is classified as a nonreturn-to-zero system. In the first, the current through the winding is negative through the entire bit time when a 0 is recorded, and it is positive through the entire bit time when a 1 is recorded. So the current through the winding will remain constant when a sequence of 0s or 1s is being written and will change only when a 0 followed by a 1 or when a 1 followed by a 0 is written. Thus, a signal will be induced in the sense winding only when the information recorded changes from a 1 to a 0 or vice versa.

The second technique illustrated is sometimes referred to as a *modified nonreturn-to-zero* or *nonreturn-to-zero* mark (NRZI) technique. In this system the polarity of the current through the write winding is reversed each time a 1 is recorded and remains constant when a 0 is recorded. If a series of 1s is recorded, the polarity

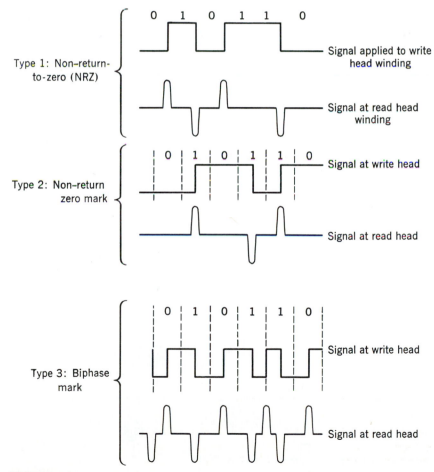

FIGURE 6.51
Three types of nonreturn-to-zero recording.

of the recorded flux will change for each 1. If a series of 0s is recorded, no changes will occur. Notice that the polarity has no meaning in this system; only changes in polarity matter. Therefore, a signal will be read back only when a 1 has been recorded. This system is often used for tape recording when, in order to generate a clock or strobe, a 1 must be recorded somewhere in each cell along the tape width. That is, if 10 tracks are recorded along the tape, then one of these must be a timing track that records a sequence of 1s, each of which defines a different set of cells to be read; or the information must be coded so that a 1 occurs in each set of 10 cells read. Alphanumeric coded information, to be described later, is often recorded on tape, and the code may be arranged so that a 1 occurs in each code group.

The third nonreturn-to-zero technique in Fig. 6.51 is called a *phase encoded, biphase-mark, Harvard, Manchester,* or *split-frequency* system. In this case a 0 is recorded as a half-bit-time negative pulse followed by a half-bit-time positive pulse, and a 1 is recorded as a half-bit-time positive pulse followed by a half-bit-time negative pulse. This technique is often used in high-speed systems.

The reading of information that has been recorded consists of two steps. First the output from the read head is amplified, and then the amplified signals are translated by logic circuitry. Figure 6.52 shows a translation technique for the first nonreturn-to-

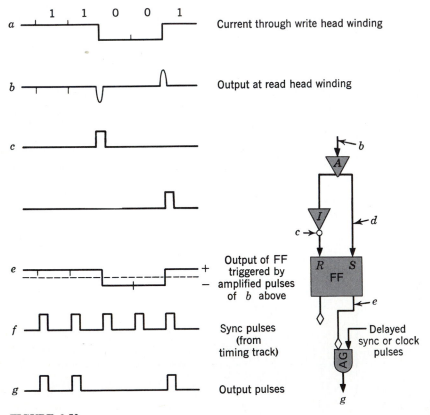

FIGURE 6.52
Nonreturn-to-zero recording.

zero system illustrated in Fig. 6.51. The output signals may be either from the output flip-flop or from serial pulses. The sync pulses occur each time a cell passes under the read heads in the system.

The flip-flop in Fig. 6.52 responds to positive pulses only. Positive pulse signals at the recording head will therefore set the flip-flop to 1. The inverter at the c input will cause negative pulses to be made positive. These positive pulses then will clear the flip-flop. The output of the flip-flop may be used directly by the computer; or pulse outputs can be generated by connecting an AND gate to the 1 output, delaying the sync pulses, and connecting them to the AND gate. Also, a serial representation of the number stored along the surface may be formed.

QUESTIONS

6.1. Determine the AND gate decoder count for an IC memory with 4096 words of 1 bit each, using the selection schemes in Figs. 6.4 and 6.9.

6.2. Determine the number of AND gates and OR gates used in a two-dimensional and a one-dimensional IC memory. The memory is to have 1 bit per word and 512 words. (Show how you got your numbers.)

6.3. The interface circuitry for dynamic memories is more complicated than for static memories. However, the cost per bit of actual memory is less for dynamic memories. As a result, for small memories static devices are less expensive, and for larger memories dynamic devices are less expensive. If the interface for a static memory costs $1.00 compared to $5.00 for a dynamic memory, and if static memory costs $0.00002 per bit and dynamic memory costs $0.00001 per bit, determine how many bits must be in a memory to make dynamic memory less expensive.

6.4. Consider decoder matrices that are rectangular but not square. For instance, to encode a 256-bit memory, we might use a "square" 16×16 matrix in two-dimensional form or an 8×32 two-dimensional rectangular array. Show that keeping the array "as square as possible" will reduce the number of AND gates in the decoders.

6.5. As the size of the memory goes up, the advantage of using a two-dimensional selection scheme increases with regard to the number of AND gates used for the decoders. The two-dimensional memory, however, requires more complicated memory cells. For a 64K-bit memory with a single output bit, compare the number of AND gates in the decoder for linear and for two-dimensional memories, and also the number of gates in the linear memory cells versus the two-dimensional memory cells. Try to draw some conclusion regarding which is more economical.

6.6. Does the two-dimensional selection system slow down operation in any way compared to the linear selection scheme?

6.7. A 2^{20}-word memory is to be assembled with SRAM chips having 4096 bits each. Explain how a memory bus can be connected so that the full 2^{20}-word memory can be implemented.

6.8. There is a scheme whereby as the power declines, the contents of the IC memory are read into a secondary (disk or tape) memory. When the power is returned, the data are reentered into the IC memory. It is important that the power not decline too much before the transfer of information can be made. As a result, it is generally necessary to have some sort of backup power (battery) to carry the memory through until the contents of the IC memory can be read out. Calculate how long this would take for a 256K memory with a cycle time of 250 ns.

6.9. Question 6.8 concerned dumping an IC memory on a disk in case of power failure. It is also necessary to find a spare area on the disk and to transfer the contents of the memory onto the disk. For one of the disk memories described in this chapter, discuss this problem for the preceding 256K 250-ns IC memory.

6.10. Several microcomputers come with a basic 1 megaword 8-bit memory. How many flip-flops are in (*a*) the memory address register and (*b*) the memory buffer register?

6.11. Draw the waveforms for recording the binary sequence 101, showing the signal applied to the write-head winding and the signal at the read-head winding for the type 1, type 2, and type 3 nonreturn-to-zero recording techniques.

6.12. A block diagram of a memory chip is shown in Fig. 6.10. R/$\overline{\text{W}}$ tells whether to read or write (a 0 on this line is READ, a 1 is WRITE). The CHIP SELECT disables the memory for a 1 input and enables the memory with a 0 output. Discuss the construction of a 1K-word 8-bit memory using these packages. How many packages are required? Each flip-flop in the address register (external) would have its 1 output connected to how many chips? Each DATA OUT line would go to how many MBR flip-flops?

6.13. Draw the schematic for a many-to-one decoder matrix with inputs from four flip-flops and 32 output lines. Use the same basic configuration as is illustrated in Fig. 6.6.

6.14. The package in Fig. 6.10 is representative of several IC manufacturers' products. Show how the CHIP SELECT can be used to add words to a memory.

6.15. What are the primary advantages of SRAM memory over DRAM memory?

6.16. Explain the operation of the DRAM memory cell shown in Fig. 6.21.

6.17. Explain the difference between SRAM and DRAM memory cells.

6.18. Contrast the parallel tree and balanced decoder networks for a 32-output decoder. Figure the number of diodes used for each and the delay incurred because of the number of gates a signal must pass through for each, assuming diode AND gates are used.

6.19. Given eight 8-bit registers, *A*, *B*, *C*, ... , *H*, show how a transfer circuit can be made by using multiplexers so that the contents of any register can be selected by a 3-bit register *S* and transferred to an 8-bit register *X*.

6.20. In larger machines, when the ac power drops below a certain level, the contents of the control unit and arithmetic-logic unit are dumped on tape or disks so that the computer can be restarted with no loss of data. If IC memories are used, their contents must be dumped also. Explain why.

6.21. Explain the operation of the memory cell in Fig. 6.3.

6.22. Explain the operation of the memory cell in Fig. 6.8.

6.23. When linear selection is used for IC memories, individual cells tend to be simpler than for two-dimensional cell select systems, but the decoders tend to be more complicated. Explain why.

6.24. Why are both floppy disks and hard disks used in microcomputers?

6.25. The memory in Fig. 6.11 has linear-select memory cells. This simplifies individual memory cell complexity. Explain why this is cost-effective for a large memory of this type.

6.26. Dynamic memories that require external refreshing introduce extra complexity into computer operation. Why?

6.27. Explain the advantages and disadvantages of dynamic IC memories.

6.28. In designing a 256-word 8-bit memory, pin i is connected to pin i for each container of the chip shown in Fig. 6.10. This applies to all address inputs and to CHIP SELECT bits and R/$\overline{\text{W}}$, but not to DATA OUT or DATA IN. Why?

6.29. Make up a formula to calculate how many bits per second can be read from a disk memory that has a rate of r revolutions per second and has b bits per track. What will the average latency time be?

6.30. Show how to expand the 256-word 1-bit memory in Fig. 6.10 to a 2048-word 1-bit memory by using the CHIP SELECT and a three-input, eight-output decoder.

6.31. Assuming that a disk with 1500 bits/in. has a speed of 2400 rpm and that we read from eight tracks simultaneously, how many bits per second can be read from one of these disks?

6.32. Explain seek time and latency for disk memories.

6.33. A magnetic-tape system has seven tracks for each $\frac{1}{2}$-in. width of tape. The packing density per track is 1280 bits/in., and the tape is moved at a speed of 75 in./s. If the tape width is $\frac{1}{2}$ in., how many bits may be read per second?

6.34. Fixed-head disk memories reduce total access time by avoiding either seek time or latency. Which is avoided and why?

6.35. Tape cassettes and tape cartridges have advantages and disadvantages compared to conventional tape systems. Cite several of each.

6.36. What devices would you choose for the following kinds of computers and why?
(*a*) Microcomputers   (*b*) Minicomputers   (*c*) Large computer systems

6.37. Draw a diode ROM that adds 3 to each of the first six BCD numbers.

6.38. An IC memory could be made three-dimensional by breaking the MAR into three pieces and having three decoders. The memory cell would be more complex, however. Design a 4096-word memory of this type, comparing it with the two-dimensional memory.

6.39. Design four locations in a ROM by adding gates to the following diagram. The signal C_1 is to be a 1 in locations 01111 and 11110 and a 0 otherwise; the signal

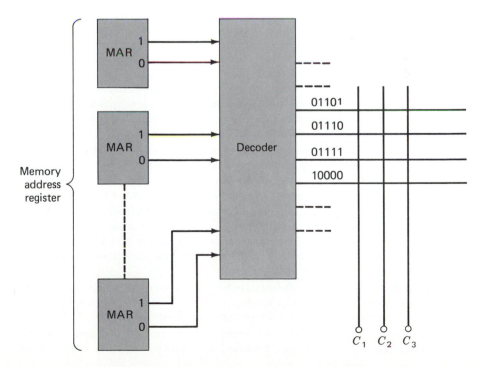

C_2 is to be a 1 in locations 01111 and 10000 and a 0 otherwise; the signal C_3 is to be a 1 in 01101, 11110, and 01111 and a 0 otherwise. A given decoder output line is high when selected.

6.40. Following are some data on a disk pack:

Number of cylinders: 203	Seek time S to move N cylinders:
Tracks per cylinder: 2	For $N = 0$ to 8, $S = 6 + 2N$
Bytes per track: 6144	For $N = 9$ to 24, $S = 16 + 3N/4$
Disk rotation time: 40 ms	For $N > 24$, $S = 26 + N/3$

Discuss the total search time for finding a specific piece of data, considering the heads to be positioned in the center cylinder when the search order is given. (A cylinder is the set of all tracks that can be read from or written on for a given position of the head-positioning mechanism.)

6.41. Compare conventional disk memory with floppy disk memory with regard to operating characteristics and costs.

6.42. Memory systems, disk packs, tape drives, cassettes, and floppy disks all have different characteristics. However, in general the units with lower entry prices (that is, lower unit prices) have higher bit prices. Explain this and give examples.

6.43. *Hard sectoring* refers to a disk system in which sectors are determined by some mechanical technique. For instance, sectors on some floppy disks are determined by punching a number of holes around the disk, and a sector begins where a hole occurs in the disk. *Soft sectoring* refers to a technique in which headers are written at the beginning of sectors, and the reading circuitry locates sectors and information without the use of mechanical devices. What are the advantages and disadvantages of these systems?

6.44. The very high-speed high-bit-packing-density tape drives use an encoding technique in which bits are encoded in groups. For instance, in one commonly used technique, 4 input bits are encoded into 5 bits. Since the 16 possible combinations of 4 bits that can occur in the data are mapped onto only 16 of the 32 possible combinations of 5 bits, these sixteen 5-bit patterns should be carefully selected so that the recording characteristics are optimal. When the 5 bits are read back, they are changed back to the original input data. This plus the use of powerful error-correcting codes allows a packing density of 6250 bits/in. (and sometimes more). Give some advantages and disadvantages of a complicated encoding and decoding scheme such as this one with regard to tape drive mechanisms and user characteristics.

6.45. Formulate a memory system for a microprocessor that has 64K of ROM, 512K of RAM, and an initial backup memory of 10 Mbytes with a possibility of expanding to 50 Mbytes. Choose the memory devices you think would be reasonable, and justify your choice both economically and from a performance viewpoint.

6.46. Bubble and CCD memories are generally considered to be competitive with floppy disk and small disk packs and are useful in replacing these devices, since disks require mechanical motion for reading and writing and are thus less reliable than straight integrated circuitry or nonmoving media. In what applications might bubble or CCD memories be particularly useful?

6.47. A dynamic memory must be given a refresh cycle 128 times each 2 ms. Each refresh operation requires 150 ns, and a memory cycle is 250 ns. What percentage of the memory's total operating time must be given to memory refreshes?

6.48. If a memory is made up of dynamic memory chips, then the time lost to refreshing can be reduced by breaking the memory into sections, or banks, and when one bank is addressed, refreshing another bank. Sketch how this might be arranged by a memory controller chip.

6.49. Describe the characteristics of RAM, ROM, PROM, and EPROM.

6.50. How do static and dynamic RAMs differ? What advantages do dynamic RAMs offer? What disadvantages?

6.51. When the contacts of a mechanical switch close, they generally "bounce," causing several openings and closings of the contacts before the closure is stable. Why can a mechanical switch output often not be directly used in a digital design? Draw a "switch-debouncing" gate circuit.

6.52. Why are synchronous data transfers on a bus so fast?

6.53. A *stack* is a data structure often implemented in hardware. A stack looks like a stack of plates in a cafeteria; only the top element (plate) is accessible. Removal of the top element exposes the next element, which then becomes the top. Addition of an element to the stack causes the former top element to become next to the top; the added element becomes the top. This is called a *push*, and removing an element is called a *pop*. These are the only allowed stack operations. A stack is sometimes called a *LIFO* (last in, first out) memory and can be implemented using a RAM or an array of flip-flop registers. Using RAM, design a stack that performs push and pop operations.

6.54. The access time of a cache memory is 10 ns, and for main memory it is 100 ns. Eighty-five percent of the memory requests are for READ and 15 percent are for WRITE. The hit ratio for READ accesses is 0.9. A write-through procedure is used. What is the average access time of the system, and what is the hit ratio, taking into consideration write cycles?

6.55. Explain the need for auxiliary memory devices.

6.56. How are auxiliary memory devices different from main memory and from other peripheral devices such as DASD?

6.57. Explain the need for a memory hierarchy.

6.58. Draw the logic diagram of all cells of one word in an associative memory. Include the READ and WRITE logic.

6.59. Draw the logic diagram of all cells along one vertical column in the selection section in an associative memory.

6.60. Describe how multiple matched words might be read from an associative memory.

6.61. A set-associative cache has a block size of 8 words and a set size of 2. The cache will hold 4K words from main memory. The main memory size is 256K by 32. Draw a block diagram of the cache and include details of the cache word construction.

6.62. A *cache sweep* (an operation that clears the cache) is performed in some virtual memory systems when a process finishes and a new process takes its place. Discuss the effect of this strategy on tag bits and cache design.

6.63. A system has a 4K-byte cache. If set-associative mapping is used in the cache, and there are four blocks per set, draw a diagram showing the organization of the cache.

6.64. Discuss the advantages and disadvantages of each of the following:

(a) An *instruction cache*, which stores only program code, not data.
(b) Separate data and instruction caches.

6.65. A four-blocks-per set, set-associative cache can be designed with standard SRAMs. Design a cache of this type.

6.66. Explain the concept of virtual memory and why it is useful.

6.67. A two-dimensional RAM has N storage cells organized as X rows and Y columns. The number of address drivers needed is $X + Y$.

   (a) If $N = M^2$, where M is an integer, show that the number of address drivers is minimal if X equals Y.

   (b) If N has no integer square root, derive an algorithm to determine values of X and Y that minimize the number of address drivers.

6.68. A 256K RAM is to be designed from the 32K by 8 SRAMs in Fig. 6.17. Assume that decoder ICs are available as well as standard logic gates. Try to minimize the total number of ICs used.

6.69. Repeat Question 6.68, but assume the SRAMs are 8K each.

6.70. A disk storage device has the following specifications: Number of tracks per surface, 800; disk rotation speed, 2400 rpm; track storage capacity, 100K bits. Estimate the average latency and the data transfer rate.

6.71. A magnetic-tape drive uses 4800-ft reels of standard nine-track tape. The tape is moved past the recording head at a rate of 2500 in./s. Give the transfer rates for recording with 1K, 2K, and 4K bits per track inch.

6.72. Discuss these memory technologies, relating cost per bit, access time, and data transfer rate: dynamic IC RAMs, static IC RAMs, CD ROMs, magnetic-bubble memories, and magnetic-disk memories.

6.73. A computer with a two-level virtual memory system has a main memory with access time 100 ns and cache memory with access time of 10 ns. Design a paged memory system with a low average access time and discuss the hardware and software costs.

6.74. In the memory hierarchy below, the hit ratio is the fraction of memory access requests that result in a hit. A page swap requires 400 μs plus the access time for secondary memory.

Type	Capacity, in words	Cost per word ($/bit)	Access time (s)	Hit ratio
Cache	8K	10^{-1}	10^{-8}	.9000
Main	2^{16}	10^{-2}	10^{-6}	.998
Secondary	2^{34}	10^{-4}	10^{-2}	1

   (a) Calculate the average time needed for the processor to read one word from the memory system.

   (b) Calculate the effects of reducing: (1) access times for the cache, (2) access time for the secondary memory, (3) improving the hit ratio for the main memory by enlarging it.

   (c) What is the average cost per word in this memory?

6.75. For the memories in the preceding question, show the effect on cost per bit and average access time if the cache is removed.

6.76. Repeat the preceding two questions for the following memory system.

Memory	Capacity, in words	Cost($/word)	Access time (s)	Hit ratio
Cache	2^{12}	10^{-1}	10^{-8}	.99
Main	2^{24}	10^{-3}	10^{-5}	.9998
Secondary	2^{35}	10^{-5}	10^{-3}	.9999
Archival	2^{40}	10^{-6}	10	1

6.77. A variation of the *least recently used* (LRU) replacement algorithm has been used in paged virtual memory systems. For this algorithm, every page in the page table has a reference bit associated with it. Whenever a word is accessed, its reference bit is set to 1. If the access request causes a page fault, then the reference bit is reset to 0 for all pages brought into main memory. When a page is to be selected for replacement, the algorithm scans all the reference bits in a predetermined order, and the first page encountered with a reference bit of 0 is the one replaced. If all reference bits are 1, then the page with the lowest physical address is replaced. Discuss this algorithm. Is it expensive to implement?

6.78. One replacement policy is the *least frequently used* (LFU) in which the block to be replaced is the one that has had the fewest references made to it during the preceding time interval. Compare this with LRU with regard to cost of implementation and effectiveness.

6.79. What are the main functions performed by a memory management unit?

6.80. What are the advantages of an on-chip MMU versus an off-chip MMU for a microprocessor-based PC?

6.81. A cache-based memory system uses FIFO for cache replacement, and it is found that the cache hit ratio is low. The following proposals are made: increase the cache word size, increase the cache size, increase the main memory size. Which would be best? Justify your answer.

6.82. A tape drive has the following characteristics: bit density, 3000 bits/in.; tape speed, 200 in./s; time to reverse direction of motion, 225 ms; minimum delay at an inter-record gap, 3 ms, average record length, 2000 characters. Estimate the improvement in access time resulting from the ability to read records in both the forward and reverse directions. Assume that the distance between two records accessed in sequence is an average of four records.

6.83. When memory interleaving is used, what properties must the memory bus and CPU have for the gains in speed to be realized?

6.84. Give reasons why the page size in a paged virtual memory system should be neither very small nor very large.

6.85. Consider a set of user programs that share the main memory in a virtual memory system, and suggest a strategy for allotting the set of physical main memory pages among the users.

6.86. A digital computer has a memory unit of 128 Kbytes and a cache memory of 4K words. The cache uses direct mapping with a block size of four words. Draw a diagram of a word in cache showing how many bits are in the tag, index, block, and word fields. Include a valid bit.

CHAPTER
7

INPUT/OUTPUT DEVICES

In addition to keys on a keyboard, the input devices to a personal computer include light pens, mice, and analog-to-digital converters. A great variety of output devices are available. The most familiar is certainly the CRT video terminal, which resembles a television display. Business applications generally require that results be printed in tabular form or perhaps on a series of checks, as in a payroll accounting operation. Scientific results are more likely to consist of numeric data, which must be clearly printed with little chance of error (such accuracy is also of prime importance for computers used to produce payroll checks), or graphs showing the results of the calculations. For any of these applications, one type of output device may be more desirable than another. However, a great many applications require that the output from a computer be printed on a piece of paper, and this requires a printer. Printers range from electromechanical typewriters, which print one letter or digit at a time, to high-speed devices capable of printing 100 or more characters at a time.

In this chapter, input devices are discussed first, followed by output devices. Then digital-to-analog (D/A) and analog-to-digital (A/D) converters are described.

7.1 TERMINALS, PERSONAL COMPUTERS, AND WORKSTATIONS

A commonly used I/O device is the *terminal* or *video display terminal* (VDT), which consists of a keyboard, a video screen, and some interface electronics. A terminal with only interface electronics and no ability to compute is called a *dumb* terminal. A terminal including a computer that can interact with the user is called a *smart* terminal.

Dumb terminals are often used in large business (or government) operations. In such applications, a central computer with a large memory interacts with the terminals. An airline reservation system is a good example. The central computer contains all flight information and passenger lists. The reservation clerk with a terminal simply gets flight information and schedules from the computer and enters customer data, including name, credit card information, and flight selected. Banks are also major users of terminals. A central computer keeps all the bank records, and bank employees (tellers, for example) interact with this computer to obtain and pass on information on bank clients.

Terminals can communicate with computers either through direct connection (if they are physically close) or by telephone lines or other long-distance media.

Smart terminals include personal computers and computer workstations which generally are personal computers with powerful graphics capabilities.

7.2   INPUT MEDIA

Keyboards

The most familiar data entry device is the keyboard. Small keyboards with only a few keys (similar to touch-tone telephone keyboards) are sometimes used in industrial applications. These small assemblies of keys are called *keypads*.

When an operator depresses a key, electric signals must be generated to enable the computer (or other device) to determine which key was depressed. This is called *encoding*. The encoding process is dependent on the mechanism used to make the keyboard.

The most direct method for encoding uses keyboard switches, which are similar to the push-button switches used in many electric devices. Figure 7.1 shows such a switch. When the plunger is depressed, the contacts of the switch in the housing are closed, and the two terminals at the output are effectively connected. When the plunger is up (key is not depressed), the switch in the housing is open, and the terminals are not electrically connected.

To encode a keyboard by means of electromechanical switches, OR gates can be used. Figure 7.2 shows the layout for encoding three keys to produce the ASCII characters and functions illustrated in Chapter 2. An odd-parity-check bit has been added at the right end to make an 8-bit character. Each of the horizontal wires on the drawing is normally at a 0 logic level.[1] When a key is depressed, however, the switch in its housing is closed, and this connects the wire to a logic level of 1. Thus, if the A key is depressed, the value 10000011 will appear on the output lines, because a diode connects the horizontal wire attached to the A switch to the leftmost and two rightmost OR gates. This is the ASCII code for A with a parity bit on the right end.

---

[1] The logic level of a 0 can be obtained by grounding the right end of each horizontal wire in Fig. 7.2 through a resistor. Connecting a voltage of, for example, +3V at the point where the "1 level" is shown completes the circuit.

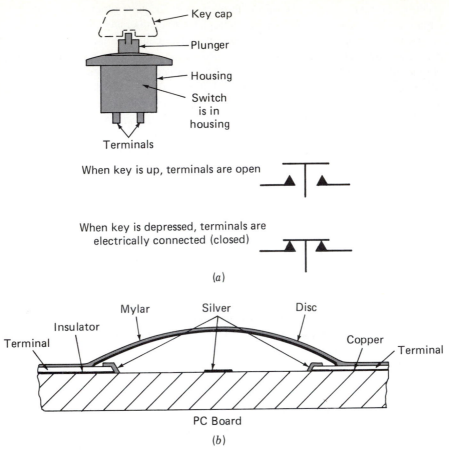

FIGURE 7.1
(*a*) Keyboard switch. (*b*) Keypad switch.

It is a good idea to load the values on the output lines into a flip-flop register before the computer reads the outputs. This has the advantage of storing the values until the computer can read them, particularly if the keyboard operator releases the key before the computer can respond. Figure 7.3 shows a scheme in which a flip-flop is used on each output, and a strobe is used to load the flip-flops by means of a delayed, inverted pulse signal generated whenever any one of the output lines from the encoder goes high. The delay is introduced to compensate for signal *skewing,* a condition where signals arrive at the output lines at different times because of differing delays through the wires of the system. The delay must be adequate to accommodate the largest signal delay that may occur. Also, the length of the strobe pulse should be short compared to the shortest time a key might be depressed. (A delay of 1 ms and a pulse of 1 ms are reasonable.)

Here we are assuming that the switch contacts do not bounce, as is the case with some switches. If the contacts do bounce, the output signals must be "smoothed," and various circuits to accomplish this are available.

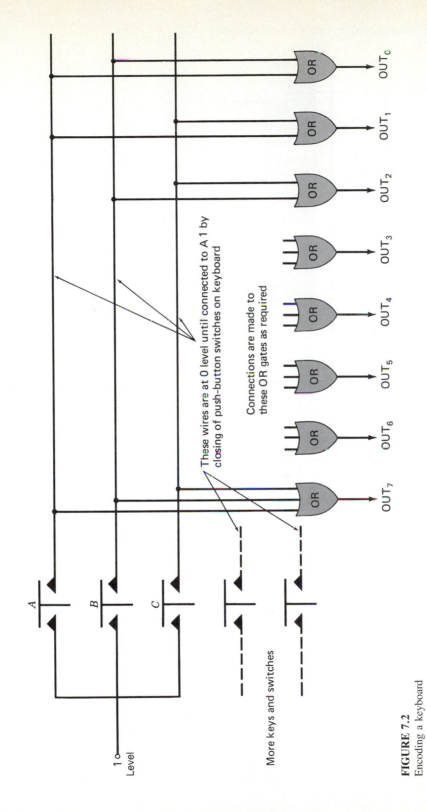

These wires are at 0 level until connected to A 1 by closing of push-button switches on keyboard

Connections are made to these OR gates as required

OUT_0 OUT_1 OUT_2 OUT_3 OUT_4 OUT_5 OUT_6 OUT_7

A

B

C

1

Level

More keys and switches

FIGURE 7.2
Encoding a keyboard

325

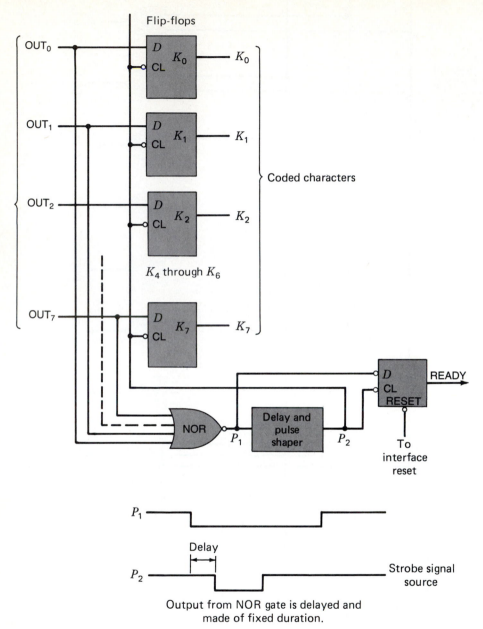

FIGURE 7.3
Keyboard buffer for interface.

In Fig. 7.3 the strobe signal is also used to load a flip-flop, called READY, which will be used in an interface design in the next chapter. Notice that the encoding scheme shown here requires that there be a 1 in the code for each character (so that the strobe pulse will be generated).

The keyboard market is very large, and many kinds of keyboards are now being made as manufacturers compete to see who can produce a lower-cost, more reliable, more durable keyboard. The basic division of keyboards is (1) the electromechanical keyboard, which includes the switch type just explained, and (2) the solid state keyboard.

There are several basic mechanisms for solid state keyboards. Capacitor types have mechanisms to vary the capacitance when a key is depressed. These are low-cost keys, often used in keypads and other inexpensive keyboards. *Hall-effect* keyboards are more expensive, but have long lifetimes and good key feel, as do ferrite-core and photo-optic keyboards. Each of the basic mechanisms has different problems with regard to encoding the keyprinters' output into a form usable by a computer. (The bibliography includes discussions of encoding techniques.)

The encoding technique is often based on a two-dimensional array of keys and wires instead of the "linear" array shown in Fig. 7.2, for reasons of economy. (This is discussed in the questions at the end of the chapter.) IC packages for encoding are made by several manufacturers and can include such features as *smoothing* or *debouncing* for contacts and *key rollover* protection, which protects against two keys being depressed at the same time. (This can happen when an adjacent key is inadvertently depressed or when the next character is struck before a key is released.)

Punched Tape

Punched tape was one of the first popular media for storing the programs and data to be read into a digital machine. When the first large computers were designed, telegraph systems had been using perforated tapes for some time, and devices for punching and reading paper tapes were fairly well developed. The widths of the tapes used have varied from $\frac{1}{2}$ to 3 in.

Figure 7.4 illustrates a section of punched tape. Information is punched into the tape a line at a time. Multiple channels are used (just as for magnetic tape, a channel runs lengthwise along the tape), and a single character of code is punched as a pattern of bits in each lateral line.

The preparation of paper input tapes is sometimes referred as *keyboarding*. When a key on the tape-punch keyboard is depressed, the binary-coded symbol for the character is punched into the tape, and the tape advances to the next line. In most cases, the mechanism used to punch the tape also prints on a separate piece of paper, in the same manner as a typewriter, the character that was punched. There is then a typewritten copy of the program, which may be checked for errors, in addition to the paper tape punched with the coded symbols. This printed copy of the program is referred to as the *hard copy*. Many tape punches are able to read a perforated tape and type printed copy from this tape.

Figure 7.4 shows a code that has been used in many paper tape systems. Eight channels run lengthwise along the tape; a hole in one of these channels represents a 1, and the absence of a hole is a 0. The 8,4,2,1 channels are used to represent the digits

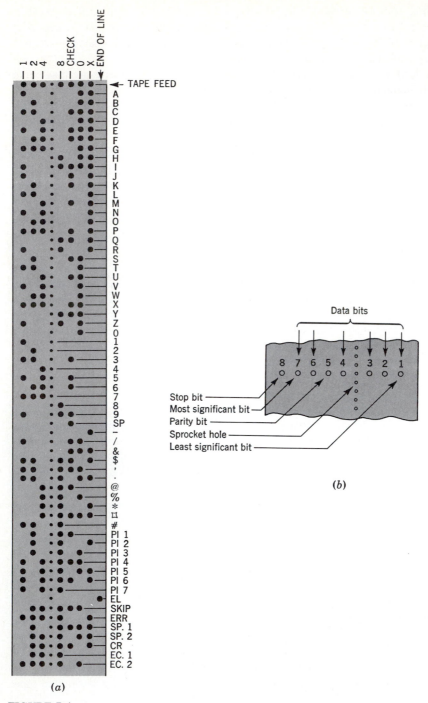

(a)

Data bits

Stop bit
Most significant bit
Parity bit
Sprocket hole
Least significant bit

(b)

FIGURE 7.4
(a) Punched tape with eight-channel code. (b) Format for eight-channel tape.

0 to 9. Thus 0s, or no holes, in positions EL (end of line), X, and 0 indicate that the encoded character is a digit whose value is given by the sum of the 8,4,2,1 positions in which there are holes. The check position is used for an *odd-parity check*. Its value is determined so that the number of 1s, or holes, for each character is odd. The 0 and X positions are used in conjunction with the 8,4,2,1 positions to encode alphabetic and special characters.

Punched Cards

Another input medium that has been widely used is the punched card. There are a number of sizes of punched cards, but the most frequently used card is a 12-row 80-column card $3\frac{1}{4}$ in. wide and $7\frac{3}{4}$ in. long (see Fig. 7.5). The thickness of the cards varies, although at one time most cards were 0.0067 in. thick.

Just as with tape, there are numerous ways in which punched cards may be coded. The most frequently used code is the *Hollerith code*. an alphanumeric code in which a single character is punched in each column of the card. The basic code is illustrated in Fig 7.5.

The card punch usually makes a hard copy of the program as it is punched into the cards. Generally, the card punch also prints the characters punched into a card on the face of the card itself. In this way, a card may be identified without the need to examine the punches. Each character is usually printed at the top of the card directly above the column in which it is punched.

7.3 CHARACTER RECOGNITION

Techniques for data entry extend in many directions. The reading of handwritten or typewritten characters from conventional paper represents an ideal input system for many applications. The systems primarily in use are as follows:

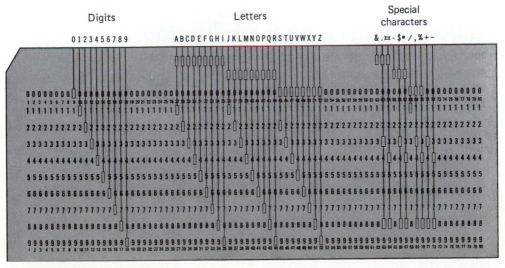

FIGURE 7.5
Punched card with Hollerith code.

1. *Magnetic ink character reading (MICR).* The recording of characters using an ink with special magnetic properties and using characters having special forms was originally used most extensively by banks. The American Banking Association settled on a type font, from which several characters are shown in Fig. 7.6. A *magnetic character reader* "reads" these characters by examining their shapes, using a 7×10 matrix; it determines, from the response of the segments of the matrix to the magnetic ink, which character has passed under the reader's head. This information is then transmitted to the system. Identification of the character is greatly facilitated by the careful design of the characters and the use of the magnetic ink.

2. *Optical character reading (OCR).* In optical character reading, a special type font (or fonts) is used to print on conventional paper with conventional ink. The printed characters are examined through the use of a strong light, a lens system that differentiates light (not inked) areas from inked areas, and a logical system that determines which of the possible characters is being examined. The systems now in use depend heavily on the fact that only a limited number of characters in a particular font are used, but such systems are still quite useful. The standard type font agreed on by the ANSI optical character committee is shown in Fig. 7.7.

Of course, the ideal system would be able to adapt to many different type fonts. Some systems, particularly one developed by the post office, can even read handwritten characters. The limited success of these systems is due to the many

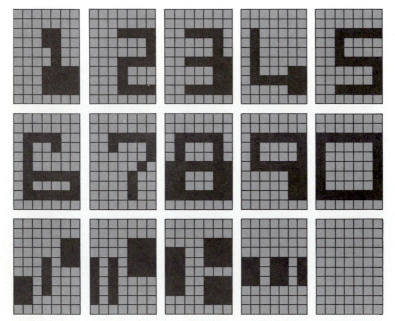

FIGURE 7.6
A magnetic reader character set.

FIGURE 7.7
Type font for optical character recognition.

shapes a given character can take. Consider the ways you can write an *a* and the similarity between a handwritten *a* and an *o* or a *b* and an *f*. These problems are increased by the optical reader's difficulty with the porosity of the paper, ink smearing at the edges of lines, and other factors. Because of the advantages of such systems, much work continues in this area, and much more is needed.

7.4 OUTPUT EQUIPMENT

The most popular form of output from a computer is undoubtedly the printed word, and printers and CRTs are the most-used output devices. There are many other output devices, however, such as loudspeakers and other audio devices used to generate music and voices. Banks commonly use computer-driven audio to give account balances and other information to tellers.

Lights are sometimes used to indicate the states of the storage devices of the principal registers of the machine (the accumulator, selected in/out registers, etc.). Such lights are generally used as troubleshooting aids, often to check the operation of the machine.

Cathode-Ray Tube Devices

Cathode-ray tubes (CRTs) are the most familiar output devices. The CRT is a very fast and inexpensive output device, but it does not deliver permanent copy.

The cathode-ray tubes used in computer displays are the same as those used in television sets; in fact, entire television sets are sometimes used. For these systems, the points are displayed by positioning and turning on an electron beam in the tube, just as in a television set or oscilloscope.

Figure 7.8 shows the arrangement of parts in a conventional raster-scan CRT. The electron gun consists of a heater and a cathode that causes a large number of electrons to be excited. These electrons are attracted to the control electrode, which causes electrons to flow or not flow according to its potential. (This can be used to turn the beam on or off.) The focusing electrode focuses the electrons into a narrow beam, and the deflection yoke controls the beam's direction as it passes through the electromagnetic field generated by voltages applied to sections of the yoke.

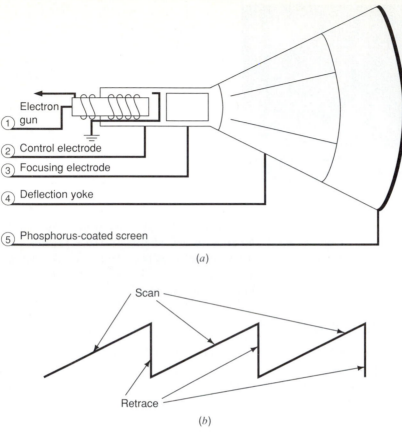

FIGURE 7.8
(*a*) Raster-scan CRT components. (*b*) Signal from a scan generator.

In the conventional raster-scan CRT, the deflection yoke is connected to a scan generator, which places a periodic sawtooth voltage on the horizontal yoke section. This causes the beam to scan across the phosphorous-coated screen, thus drawing a line across the screen. The intensity of light on the screen is determined by the amplitude of the voltage on the control electrode. The beam is gated off while the direction of focus returns to the left side of the screen. The next trace is made slightly lower across the tube's face, and the position of the beam continues downward until the bottom of the screen is reached. The vertical pattern is also a sawtooth but with a much slower rate than for the horizontal sawtooth.

A complete scan of the face is made 60 times per second[2] in the United States and 50 times per second in Europe (for conventional TV) due to the AC power frequencies used.

---

[2] The scanning for TVs requires two vertical scans for a single picture, one slightly below the other.

There are two basic types of CRT displays: *alphanumeric* and *graphic*. Alphanumeric displays are used for alphanumeric characters but not to make drawings or graphs. (They can be tricked by clever programming, however, to provide limited graphics capabilities). Banks and airlines are major users of alphanumeric displays. Graphic displays can be used to draw pictures, maps, and the charts, and they can also display alphanumeric information.

Alphanumeric displays communicate with a computer using only character codes. That is, the computer sends 8-bit or 7-bit character codes to the display, which then forms the characters selected on the face of the CRT in the order sent. Included are character codes for positioning (such as *carriage return*, which moves the position at which the next character will be written to the far left of the screen; *line feed*, which moves the beam position down one line; and others that can be found in the alphanumeric code tables).

Alphanumeric displays generally contain a buffer "refresh" memory, which stores the characters sent to the display. The computer must only send a character once; the character will then be written into the CRT "refresh" memory, which is continually read and whose output is used to refresh or rewrite the characters on the face of the CRT 50 or 60 times per second. (The number of times each character position is rewritten is called the *refresh rate*. For flicker-free displays 50 or 60 rewrites per second are required.)

The CRT electronics also use a read-only memory (or gate networks) to retain the patterns for the characters in alphanumeric form. An alphanumeric code simply selects a pattern from the memory, and it is then written on the screen. (The end-of-chapter questions explore this in more detail.)

Graphics displays are capable of drawing lines and shading areas. Some include the ability to make displays in color. The graphics electronics can be relatively simple, as for some personal computers, or can contain powerful *graphics engines*, which are computers with large memories and special electronics. The latter can produce complicated displays based on instructions from the user's computer. The language used to send instructions to the graphics engine varies from system to system, but attempts have been made to form standard languages to facilitate moving programs from system to system. The graphics engine, in effect, contains subprograms that can be called by the user's main computer and that perform both simple operations (draw a box, draw a circle, fill in the box, etc., which are capabilities provided in PC systems) and complicated procedures (rotate a figure in space, form a window on the screen and draw into it, etc., which are functions provided in workstations).

Techniques for data transmission to CRT electronics are complicated but efficient. If only alphanumeric data are to be displayed, the ASCII code is used for the transmission of each character. The display electronics then convert each 8-bit ASCII character to the sequence of points required to display the character. Typical displays have about 25 lines of 40 to 80 characters per line, as shown in Fig. 7.9(a).

If only alphanumeric characters are displayed, a memory of about 16K bits (for 25 lines of 80 characters) is required to store the display information. When a graphics display is used, the display memory must be on the order of 128K bits to several megabytes (for color).

The individual points in a graphics display are called *pixels* [refer to Fig. 7.9(b) and (c)]. The numbers of pixels goes from a low of 320 per line on the scope face and

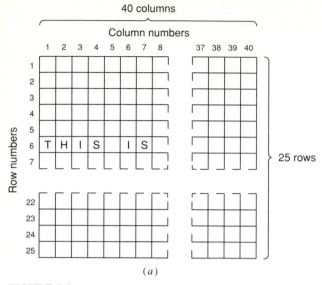

FIGURE 7.9
(a) Screen layout for alphanumeric mode.

200 lines to about 2000 pixels per line and 2000 lines. Two or eight bits are required for each pixel in a color mode of operation. The memory size required to store a display can be calculated from numbers such as these. From these calculations the additional memory and complexity required for graphics displays versus alphanumeric displays becomes clear. The graphics display is generated by a *bit map,* which is a memory containing the pattern to be displayed on the screen.

Most systems use the standard television red-green-blue (RGB) color system to create colors. Separate bits call out each color and, if a high-quality display is required, the amount of each color. The number of bits required in the resulting bit map can be reduced by using "modes," where only a limited "palette" of color possibilities is available at a given time, and the program chooses which palette is in current operation. This makes a large number of colors and gray scales (amplitudes) possible with a reasonable-size bit map but increases system complexity.

Use of the RGB color system in displays requires the generation of amplitudes for each color to be used in each pixel. A scope face of 1000 lines by 1000 pixels per line contains one million pixels. If 8 bits are used to store the amplitude of each RGB color at each pixel, then 24 bits per pixel and a total of 24 million bits in the bit map would result. Some image processing systems use displays of this quality, which results in 16 million possible colors per pixel (this is called the *pallete*).

To reduce the size of the bit map and its memory, tables are sometimes used to define colors. If the system uses 8 bits for each color, a table in a high-speed flip-flop RAM can be used with 256 entries, each with 24 bits (8 for each color). The bit map then would have 8 bits at each pixel; the 8 bits would go into the MAR for the table memory and would select a 24-bit entry. Each of the 8-bit color amplitudes in the entry would then go into a D/A converter, which would output the amplitudes of the three colors to be displayed for the pixel. This scheme makes only 256 colors

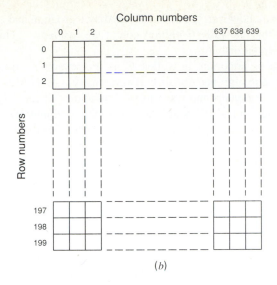

(b)

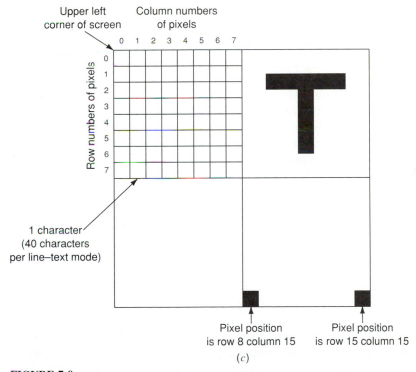

(c)

FIGURE 7.9

(b) Screen layout of pixels in high-resolution mode. (c) Comparison of text mode character size and pixel size.

available for each pixel; however, the table is loaded by a program and can be changed during operation so that the full 16 million colors are available. (This technique is used in many commercial displays.)

Graphics ability is important in workstations. For example, mechanical design applications often require high-performance 3D graphics engines. Although electronic design tasks such as schematics and wave form simulation call for only 2D graphics, electronic enclosure design and PC-board thermal analysis require 3D graphics. Often there is also a graphics requirement for windowing. When 3D displays must be manipulated by the graphics engine, the size of the buffer memory must accomodate 3D figures and the calculation abilities and programs to rotate, expand, and contract these figures. Graphics engines for 3D displays are very large and powerful (and relatively expensive).

Flat Panel Displays

In addition to CRTs, many flat panel displays are now available. These consist of a number of rectangular areas (elements) on a "flat panel." Each element can be turned on or off, causing it to emit light when on. Displays with many elements (thousands) are produced, and these compete with CRTs. The pixels in CRTs correspond to the elements (or cells) in flat panel displays. There are two basic types of flat panel display: those that emit light and those that reflect light. The most popular are: (1) liquid crystal displays (LCDs), (2) electroluminescent (EL) displays, (3) plasma displays, and (4) light-emitting diode (LED) displays. All are capable of color. For each of these display types, individual areas of the panel are selectively turned on or off as separate elements. This means that display elements can be shaped. For small arrays element selection is linear, and for large arrays the selection is generally two-dimensional.

LCD displays have a layer of liquid between two electrically conducting plates. A reflector behind the plates reflects light, which passes or is blocked by the LCD's light-polarizing and -diffusing properties. LCD technology can be divided into two categories: nonactive multiplexed matrix and active matrix. In nonactive multiplexed matrix technology, pixel positions (each of which is a small LCD) are energized by voltages applied via intersecting row and column drivers. Active matrix technology uses a thin-film transistor located at each pixel position. These transistors are addressed by rows and columns, and once a pixel is turned on, it stays on until it is switched off. Active matrix displays require the deposition of thousands of thin-film transistors on a glass substrate.

Electroluminescent panels have two electrically conducting plates with a layer of phosphor in between. Electric potential at intersection points of row and column conductors make the phosphor glow. Plasma displays also use row and column conductors, and small amounts of gas at intersections glow when a sufficient potential is applied.

LEDs are semiconductor devices (diodes) that conduct current in only one direction and glow when current passes through the diodes. They are often used as simple on/off indicators (as panel lights, for example). They are similar to the familiar incandescent light bulb, but because of their low voltage requirement and durability, they are extensively used. LEDs are often packaged in clear epoxy and are widely used in numeric (seven-segment) and alphanumeric displays (which generally have

16 segments). They can be driven by TTL and some MOS devices. When LEDs are pulsed (as in multiplexed operation), they need to be turned on over 1000 times a second to be efficient; however, at 50 to 60 cycles they will not flicker.

Printers

There is a great demand for permanent records of computer results. The primary device for recording results is the computer printer, which we take to include *X/Y* or *flatbed plotters*, which draw lines on paper under computer control.

Most printers are alphanumeric printers and receive streams of 8-bit bytes from the computer, each byte representing a single alphanumeric character. Most such printers receive characters in the 8-bit ASCII code in serial form, but high-speed printers exist that accept bits in parallel at a high rate. Printers can print in black and white or color; we will cover these in turn.

The information delivered to a printer operated *online* will be in the form of electronic signals directly from the computer. If the printer is operated *offline*, the reading and decoding of data stored on magnetic tape is a part of the printing operation. Since the electronic circuitry of a computer is able to operate at speeds much higher than those of printing devices, it is desirable that a printer operated online be capable of printing at a very high speed. Even if the printer is operated offline, speed is highly desirable, since the volume of material to be printed may be quite large.

An example of a fast printer, in which the raised characters are distributed around a print wheel that revolves constantly, is shown in Fig. 7.10. In this case the print

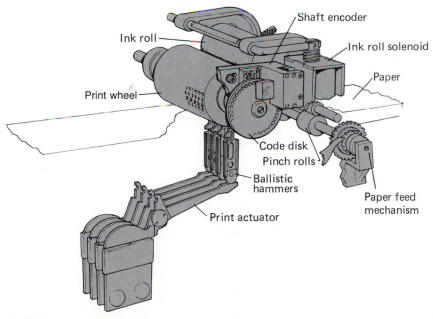

FIGURE 7.10
Line-at-a-time drum printer

wheel does not contain moving parts but consists of a motor-driven drum with a number of bands equal to the number of characters printed per line. A set of all the characters that are used is distributed around each band. As the print wheel revolves, when the selected character is in position, the ballistic hammer strikes the ribbon against the paper and, thus, against the raised character on the print wheel located behind the paper. A printer of this type requires a decoder and a memory for each character position along the line, as well as a character-timing encoder for each position, which determines when the selected character is in position. Printers of this type can print up to 1250 lines per minute with 160 characters per line.

The print wheel is continually inked by an ink roll; no ribbon is used. In the system shown, a code disk and shaft encoder are used to tell which character is currently in a position to be printed. (Shaft encoders are discussed in a later section.) The paper is moved horizontally after each line is printed.

Figure 7.11 shows a printer in which the paper is moved vertically in front of a chain of raised type characters. This chain is continually moving horizontally so that each of the 48 different characters passes by each of the printer's 100 positions in each line. (Other numbers of characters per line are available.) When a character passes the position where it is to be printed, the armature hammer magnet is energized, causing it to strike a hammer and force the paper against the type at that position. An inked ribbon is placed between paper and type so that the inked character is impressed on the paper.

Inexpensive, lower-speed *character-at-a-time* printers are used for minicomputers and microcomputers. Consider the print wheel or drum type of printer shown in Fig. 7.10. The drum can be reduced to a small cylinder with only one set of

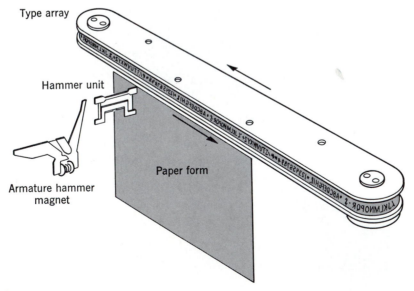

FIGURE 7.11
High-speed chain type line printer.

characters. This single rotating cylinder can be moved across the paper along with a single hammer, making an inexpensive character-at-a-time printer [see Fig. 7.12(*c*)]. Sometimes the characters are distributed around a "daisy wheel," as shown in Fig. 7.12(*b*). A hammer then drives the selected character against the paper when it is in position.

The use of pins driven against the paper to print characters also provides low-cost printing. Sometimes the pins are arranged in a complete dot matrix, but generally only

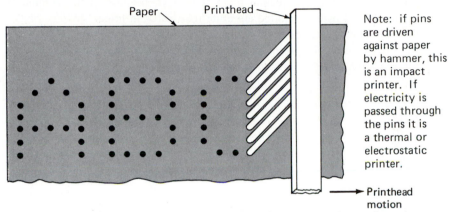

Matrix printhead moves across page. The correct pins are forced against the paper in the proper sequence to form characters as shown. A 5 X 7 matrix is illustrated here; 7 X 9 is also used.

(*a*)

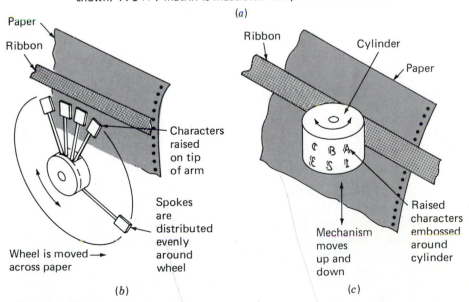

(*b*) (*c*)

FIGURE 7.12
Impact printer mechanisms. (*a*) Matrix print head. (*b*) Daisy wheel printer. (*c*) Cylinder printer.

a single column of seven or eight pins is provided, and this is moved across the paper, requiring five or six positions per character [see Fig. 7.12(*a*)]. Character generator logic determines the sequence for the striking of the pins as the print head is moved across the paper. Although some machines can print several thousand dots per inch, the market centers on printers that produce 300 dots per inch at 6 to 20 pages per minute.

Microprocessors are used to control the timing and other functions required in printers. Character buffering also can be provided by microprocessors.

Many inexpensive printers use thermal or electrostatic papers (see below). The paper generally costs more than regular paper. However, because of the volume of production, the special papers required are quite reasonable in price.

The natural speed limitations of electromechanical devices and cost considerations have led to the development of printers called *nonimpact printers*. These printers fall primarily in the following categories:

1. *Electromagnetic printers.* By using magnetic recording techniques, a magnetic image of what is to be printed is written on the drum surface. This surface is then passed through magnetic powder, which adheres to the charged areas, and the powder is pressed onto the paper. Speeds of up to 250 characters per second are obtained in such systems.

2. *Electrostatic printers.* With electrostatic printers, the paper is coated with a nonconducting dielectric material that holds charges when voltages are applied with writing "nibs" (heads). These heads impress dots on the paper as it passes, as shown in Fig. 7.12(*a*). Then the paper passes through a toner that contains material with colored particles carrying a charge opposite to that introduced by the nibs; as a result, particles adhere to the magnetized areas, forming printed characters.

3. *Thermal printers.* An electric pulse can be converted to heat on selected sections of a printing head or on wires or nibs. When this heat is applied to heat-sensitive paper, a character is printed, as shown in Fig. 7.12(*a*).

4. *Ink-jet printers.* Some printers direct a high-velocity stream of ink toward the paper. This stream is deflected, generally by passing it through an electrostatic field such as that used to deflect beams in oscilloscopes. In some systems the ink stream is broken into droplets by an ultrasonic transducer.

5. *Laser printers.* In laser printer technology, a *print engine* consisting of a laser diode (see Fig. 7.13) emits light onto a rotating mirror. This light is focused by a lens onto an organic photoconductive drum (or belt), which is negatively charged by a corona wire (a high-voltage electrode). Then the drum (or belt) passes under the laser beam, which erases all areas that do not contain a character or image. The drum or belt rotates to a developing area, where a positively charged toner fills the charged areas that haven't been erased. Next, the image and paper come together, and the corona wire applies a negative charge to the back of the paper, causing the toner to be transferred from the drum to the paper. The paper that carries the

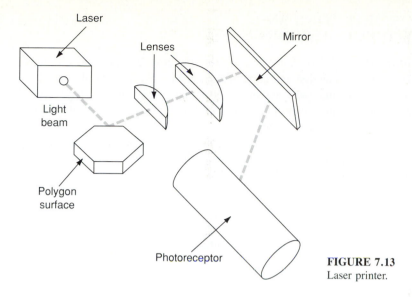

FIGURE 7.13
Laser printer.

image then proceeds through a fixing process that uses heated high-pressure rollers to affix the image to the paper.

Color Printers

There are several ways to produce printed color output from a computer. Pen plotters, which consist of electromagnetically controlled pens, provide good line quality. Color impact dot-matrix printers, with 18 to 24 pin heads and four-color ribbons, are also sometimes used. In addition, cameras can be used to photograph a color image on a CRT directly.

Electrostatic and electrophotographic (laser) printers similar to office photocopiers are sometimes used. In electrostatic printing, a voltage is applied to an array of writing nibs embedded in a stationary writing head. The nibs create minute electrostatic charges on the paper passing over the writing head. The paper is exposed to liquid toners that contain suspended particles, which are attracted to the dots to produce text or images. For color printing, the paper must make four passes over the writing head, one pass for each color toner.

There is also color ink-jet printing. In one version of *drop-on-demand* ink-jet technology, a piezoelectric crystal is used such that when a voltage is applied to the crystal, it physically changes dimension, squeezing a drop of colored ink out of a minute orifice. This drop is then directed to the paper's surface, to form a small dot on the paper. Small (less than 0.005 in.) ink drops are applied with an accuracy of several ten-thousandths of an inch. A print head can have up to 30 independently aimed ink jets.

Color printer technology is in its early stages, but color printers are now being marketed at prices low enough to generate substantial sales and continued development.

7.5 ERROR-DETECTING AND ERROR-CORRECTING CODES

The process of transferring information to and from the computer is especially liable to error. To facilitate the detection and correction of errors, two classes of codes have been invented: error-detecting codes and error-correcting codes. The first type of code enables the equipment to detect errors in the coded groups of bits, and the second type of code corrects the errors automatically.

Both error-detecting and error-correcting codes require that redundant information be sent along with the actual information being processed. The most commonly used type of error-detecting code is the *parity-check code*.

Parity Checking

The parity check is based on the use of an additional bit, known as a *parity bit* or *parity-check bit,* in each code group. The parity bit associated with each code group in an *odd-parity-bit* checking system has a value such that the total number of 1s in each code group plus the parity bit is always odd. (An *even-parity-bit* checking code has a parity bit such that the sum of the 1s in the code group plus the parity bit is always an even number.)

The example shown in Table 7.1, which uses 8,4,2,1 code, has an odd parity bit, which makes the sum of the 1s in each code group an odd number. If a single error occurs in transmitting a code group—for instance, if 0011, 1 is erroneously changed to 0010, 1—the fact that there is an even number of 1s in the code group plus the parity bit will indicate that an error has occurred. (For an even-parity-bit checking code, each parity bit would be the complement of the parity bit shown.)

The technique of parity checking is the most popular method of detecting errors in stored code groups, especially for storage devices such as magnetic tape, paper tape, and even disk systems.

If the parity-bit system is used, an additional bit must be sent with each code group. As another example, if the 7-bit ASCII is used to send characters, each char-

TABLE 7.1

Decimal	BCD	Odd parity bit
0	0000	1
1	0001	0
2	0010	0
3	0011	1
4	0100	0
5	0101	1
6	0110	1
7	0111	0
8	1000	0
9	1001	1

acter will require an 8-bit code consisting of 7-bits for the ASCII character and the parity-check bit.

This type of checking will detect all odd numbers of errors. Suppose an even-parity check is used, and the code group to be sent is 0010; the parity bit in this case will be a 1. If the code group is erroneously read as 0110, the number of 1s in the code group plus the parity bit will be odd, and the error will be detected. If, however, a double error is made and 0010 is changed to 0111, the error will not be detected since the number of 1s will again be even. Thus, a parity-bit check will detect only odd numbers of errors. (This rule will also apply when the parity bit is in error. For instance, consider an odd-parity-bit checking system where 0010 is to be sent and the parity bit is 0. If the parity bit is changed to 1, the number of 1s in the code group plus the parity bit will be even, and the error will be detected.)

There are many types of error-correcting codes, and some very clever and so-phisticated coding schemes are used in both communications and computer systems. For instance, magnetic tape is a memory device that is especially prone to errors. Most errors are due to either imperfections in the tape or foreign matter getting in between the read head and the tape, causing the tape to be physically pushed away from the read head and the recorded signal to be incorrectly interpreted. Such errors are said to be caused by *dropout* and tend to lie in a single track. Several clever codes have been used to detect and correct such errors.

7.6 BUSES FOR PERSONAL COMPUTERS AND WORKSTATIONS

Figure 7.14 shows a general layout for a personal computer or workstation. Printed-circuit (PC) boards contain the CPU, which consists of the arithmetic-logic unit (ALU), the control section[3], and the high-speed (IC) memory. The high-speed memory is connected to the bus, and the control section controls the high-speed memory by using signals it places on the bus. The bus in Fig. 7.14 consists of a set of wires running under the PC boards. PC board connectors are mounted to these wires, and the boards are plugged into these connectors, thus making connection to the logic on the boards. The connectors, bus wires, and their support are called the *backplane*, and this is called a *passive backplane* system. Another system uses a *motherboard* consisting of a PC board on which connectors are mounted. *Baby boards* are plugged into these connectors, and the bus runs along the connectors as in the passive backplane system. The CPU and main memory are generally on the motherboard.

To connect input/output devices to the CPU section boards, *interface boards* are connected to the bus. The boards contain the logic gates and flip-flops to read from and write onto the bus and to control and interface the input/output devices. In a typical system, using a keyboard, a keyboard interface board is attached to the bus

---

[3] The ALU and control section are often on the single chip which is called a *microprocessor chip*.

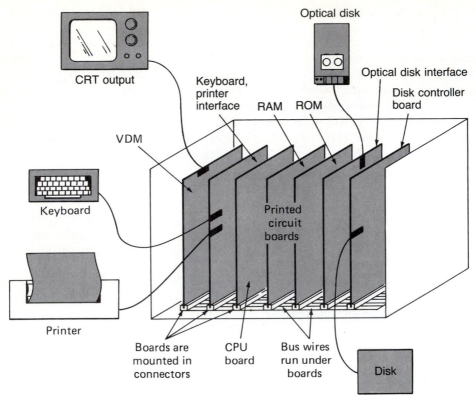

FIGURE 7.14
Microcomputer interface layout for input/output devices.

by a connector, and a cable runs from this board to the keyboard. Similar boards are used to interface a tape unit, a disk drive, and other I/O devices.

Note that communication between input/output devices and the CPU utilizes the interface boards and the bus. In small systems, the CPU memory and one or more interface chips may be placed on a single board with the bus. Cables then connect this board to the input/output devices.

7.7 SERIAL TRANSMISSION OF CHARACTER CODES

When characters must be sent over a single wire (line), the transmission is said to be *serial*. *Parallel* transmission of character involves the use of several lines (8-bit characters would require eight wires in the most straightforward form of parallel operation).

Serial transmission techniques are of two classes: *asynchronous* and *synchronous*. Asynchronous transmissions refers to a technique where characters can occur at any time, and in synchronous transmission characters are clocked into specific time intervals (generally the bits in each character are clocked onto the line).

Figure 7.15 shows how standard-character serial asynchronous transmission operates. The line on which characters are transmitted is normally in the high state,[4] but when a character is sent, a *start bit* at a low level is generated. This start bit is followed by the proper 8-bit ASCII character, and then two *stop bits* at the high level are inserted before another character can be started (that is, before another start bit can be generated). The start bit, each stop bit, and the bits in the ASCII character are all of the same duration and since 11 such time periods, or *bit times,* are required, a single character requires 11 bit times.

There are several standard rates for character transmissions, including 110, 300, 600, 1200, 4800, and 9600 bits/s. In each case, the same character construction using start and stop bits is used, so character rates of $\frac{11}{110}$, $\frac{11}{300}$, $\frac{11}{600}$, $\frac{11}{1200}$, $\frac{11}{4800}$, and $\frac{11}{9600}$ s are attainable. Often, only one stop bit is used, which speeds up character transmission.

The character transmission system described here is called *asynchronous transmission,* for the character and start bits can occur at any time. *Synchronous transmis-*

---

[4] Communications people call this a *mark* value and the other level a *space.*

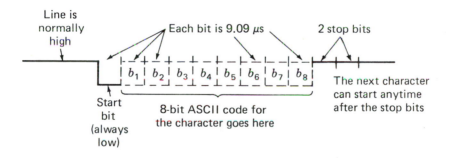

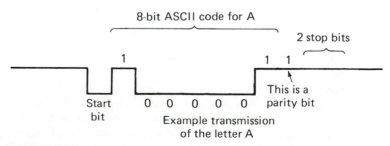

FIGURE 7.15
Sending a character using the standard code.

sion systems have the bits clocked into fixed time periods, and characters are placed in fixed positions in the bit stream. These systems require that both bit timing and character timing be established between the transmitting device and receiver, and they are thus more complicated. Character transmission can be at higher rates, however. (Since start and stop bits are not required, the character beginnings and ends are established by the system.) As a result, high-speed data communication is generally in synchronous form.

The output levels and interface requirements for the coded characters are explained in the end-of-chapter questions.

When terminals or personal computers are operated at some distance from a computer, the telephone system is often used to provide the necessary communications link. In such cases, special devices are needed to translate logic levels produced into signals acceptable for telephone-line transmission.

When output signals in logic-level form are converted to electric signals suitable for telephone transmission by electronic circuitry, the converting device is called a *modem*. A modem can convert logic levels to electric signals for the telephone system and can convert received signals from the telephone line back to logic levels. This means, of course, that the connections are made electrically (generally into a telephone jack) and directly to the telephone line; a handset is not used. It also means that the electric signals must comply with telephone system regulations. The design of modems that will (1) send bits through telephone lines at high speeds, (2) make few errors in transmission, and (3) comply with telephone company regulations is a highly developed and interesting scientific area.

Modems generally use different frequencies for a 1 and a 0. As an example, one Bell modem sends data through telephone lines at either 110 or 300 bits/s. The modem at one end of a telephone line uses 1070 Hz (for 1s) and 1270 Hz (for 0s) to send, and the modem at the other end uses 2025 Hz (for 1s) and 2225 Hz (for 0s). The reason for the two sets of frequencies is that transmission can be in either direction, and while one modem is transmitting a character, the other will still be sending its high (mark) frequency. (That is, a single telephone line handles communications in both directions. Both ends can talk at the same time. You can, for instance, interrupt someone who is talking.)

7.8 INPUT/OUTPUT DEVICES FOR SYSTEMS WITH ANALOG COMPONENTS

Not all inputs to digital machines consist of alphanumeric data. Computers used in data collection systems or in real-time control systems often must measure the physical position of some device or must process electric signals that are analog in nature. Consider a real-time control system in which a computer is used to point a telescope. If, by some system of gears, the position of the telescope along an axis is relayed to the position of a shaft, the position of this shaft may have to be read into the computer. This will involve translation of the shaft position into a binary-coded number that can be read by the computer.

Changing a physical displacement or an analog electric signal to a digital representation is called *analog-to-digital (A/D) conversion*. Two major types of A/D converters are (1) those that convert mechanical displacements to a digital representation and (2) those that convert an electric analog signal to digital-coded signals.

Suppose an analog device has as its output a voltage that is to be used by a digital machine. Let us assume that the voltage varies within the limits of 0 and 63 V dc. We can then represent the voltage values with a set of 6-bit numbers ranging from 000000 to 111111. For each integer value the input voltage may assume, we assign a corresponding value of the 6-bit number. If the input voltage is 20 V, the corresponding digital value will be 010100, and if the input voltage is 5 V, the corresponding number will be 000101. If, however, the input signal is 20.249 V dc, the 6-bit binary number will only approximate the input value. The number of bits in the binary number representing the analog signal is the *precision* of the coder, and the amount of error between the digital output values and the input analog values is a measure of the *accuracy* of the coder.

Not only are the inputs to a computer sometimes in analog form, but it is often necessary for the outputs of a computer to be expressed in analog form. This involves *digital-to-analog* conversion, and a device that performs this is called a *D/A converter*. When digital computers are used in control systems, it is generally necessary to convert the digital outputs from the machine to analog-type signals, which are then used to control the physical system.

Digital-to-Analog Converters

The most-used digital-to-analog converters (DACs) convert a binary unsigned number to either an electric voltage or an electric current. DACs that convert from binary inputs to a voltage are discussed first.

A block diagram for a DAC is shown in Fig. 7.16(a). There are three input lines, X_0, X_1, and X_2, each of which will carry a binary 0 or 1. The number of binary inputs is called the *resolution* of the DAC.[5] The output from this DAC ranges from 0 to 7 V. A list of input-output relations for this DAC is shown in Fig. 7.16(b). For each input value there is a corresponding analog output voltage, which in this case is equal to the value of the input as a binary integer. Examination of this input/output relation will show that the output value can be calculated by giving the input value X_0 a *weight* of 1 V, X_1 a *weight* of 2 V, and X_2 a *weight* of 4 V. Then the output value is equal to the sum of the weights for which the X_1 are equal to 1. This is a general principle for DACs: each input has a *weight*, and the output voltage is the sum of the weights for which the binary inputs are 1s. In this DAC, X_2 is the *most significant bit* (MSB) and X_0 the *least significiacant bit* (LSB).

If a three-flip-flop counter with positive-edge triggering were connected to the DAC's three inputs, with X_0 connected to the counter's LSB, and the counter were clocked, the input/output relation would be as in Fig. 7.16(c). The analog waveform shown here is called a *staircase*.

---

[5] Chapter 12 shows circuits for IC realization of DACs.

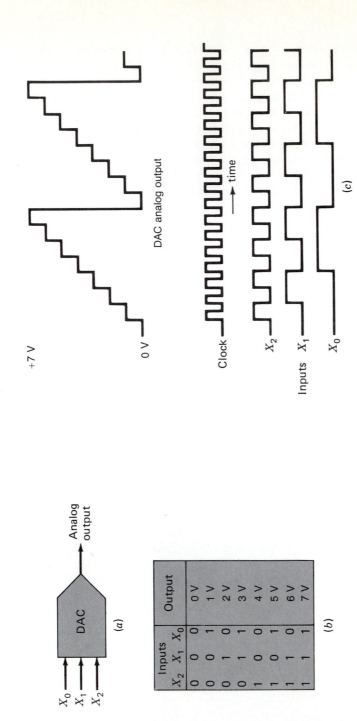

FIGURE 7.16
DAC operation (a) Block diagram. (b) List of input/output values. (c) Staircase DAC output.

The minimum and maximum values the analog output of a DAC can take vary for different DACs. Some manufacturers DACs have only a single built-in minimum and maximum, whereas others allow users to introduce reference signals that control the minimum and maximum output voltages. In most cases the minimum output voltage for a DAC will be 0 V.

If the maximum output voltage of a DAC is V volts,[6] and if the resolution is R bits, then the weight of the least significant bit will be $V/(2^R - 1)$. [For our 3-bit resolution, 7-V maximum output, this gives $7/(2^3 - 1) = 7/7 = 1$ V.] The weight of the second least significant bit will be $2V/(2^R - 1)$, the next least significant bit will have weight $4V/(2^R - 1)$, and so on up to the most significant bit, with weight $(2^{R-1})V/(2^R - 1)$. [For our example this is $(2^{3-1})7/(2^3 - 1) = 4$.]

As a further example, if a DAC had a maximum output voltage of 10 V and a resolution of 8 bits, the least significant bit would have weight:

$$\frac{10}{2^8 - 1} = \frac{10}{255} \approx 0.0392157$$

This means that if an 8-bit counter is connected to the DAC's input, the staircase at the output will have steps of $\frac{10}{255}$ V from 0 to $+10$ V, and there will be 256 steps (counting the 0 step).

Since DACs are made of physical devices, they are imperfect and will have analog outputs that will not exactly equal the output for a "perfect" DAC. To give the user some idea of the size of the DAC's errors, the manufacturer generally specifies the accuracy of the converter. The *absolute accuracy* is defined as the maximum difference between the actual DAC's outputs and a perfect DAC's outputs, divided by the maximum analog output value.

For example, if the maximum output for a 6-bit DAC is $+10$ V, then the "perfect" output for a binary input 000011 is $3 \times 10/(2^6 - 1) \approx 0.4761905$. If the actual output is 0.465, then an error of 0.0111905 exists; and if this is the maximum error for all possible inputs, the absolute accuracy will be $0.0111905/10 = 0.111905$ percent.

Some manufacturers simply specify the absolute value in general terms such as "less than $\frac{1}{2}$ LSB," meaning that the maximum error between perfect and actual values will never exceed half the weight of the least significant bit.

If the maximum error in a DAC is less than the weight of the least significant bit, the output is *monotonic*, which means the output voltage will always increase when the input value to the converter increases. For DACs with many bits of resolution, the manufacturer may only specify that the DAC is monotonic instead of giving an accuracy figure.

Some DACs can be set to have analog outputs that do not range from 0 to a positive voltage, but rather are in an interval from V_1 to V_2. (For instance, V_1 might be -5 V, and V_2 might be $+10$ V.) The principles are the same except that the voltage V

---

[6] In all these examples the DAC is assumed to have outputs ranging from 0 to V volts. DACs with nonzero minimum values are dealt with later.

in the formulas for the weights is obtained by subtracting V_1 from V_2, and weights are added to V_1 to obtain output values. (This would give $V = 15$ for the -5- to $+10$-V example, and the weight of the LSB for a 4-bit DAC with lower voltage -5 V and maximum voltage $+10$ V would be 1 V. The outputs would then be $-5, -4, -3, \ldots,$ 9, 10.)

When a DAC has the ability to be set to some interval, the manufacturer will generally specify two input lines to which the user can connect two input voltages to control the DAC's upper and lower output limits.

Analog-to-Digital Converters

When an analog voltage must be converted to a digital number, an analog-to-digital converter (ADC) is used. Figure 7.17(a) shows the block diagram symbol for a small ADC with a single analog input and 3 bits output. The CONVERT input is normally a 0 and is changed to a 1 signal when a conversion is to occur. The ADC responds to the transition on CONVERT by measuring the input voltage on the analog input and then outputting a binary number that represents the input voltage in digital form.

Converting an analog input signal, such as a voltage, to a digital number is called *quantizing* the input. Since the input can take infinitely many different values and the digital representations can take only a finite number of values, each digital number at the output actually covers a range of input values.

Figure 7.17(b) shows the input signal and digital output numbers for a 2-bit ADC. The input voltage range is to be from 0 to 3 V, and the digital numbers at the outputs that range from 00 to 11. The output number 00 indicates the input voltage is in the interval from 0 to 0.5 V, the output number 01 indicates an input voltage value from 0.5 to 1.5 V, the number 10 indicates an input from 1.5 to 2.5 V, and the number 11 indicates an input greater than 2.5 V.

This is the most commonly used system for ADCs. In this case, the input voltage interval for the output number 01 has its center at 1 V, the interval for 10 has its center at 2 V, and so on. This means that when the ADC reads out a 10, for example, the input is 2 V plus or minus 0.5 V.

Figure 7.17(c) shows the intervals for a 3-bit converter with a normal input voltage range from 0 to 7 V. In this example, the output 011 indicates the input voltage is 3 V $\pm$ 0.5 V.

The final graph in Fig. 7.17(d) shows an analog input along the horizontal axis and digital values along the vertical axis. This graph is included in many manufacturers' manuals and specification sheets and again shows that the 0 interval is half the size of the other intervals (except that the final interval extends on).

Many converters include an *overrange* feature to handle inputs outside the normal interval. This generally consists of an output line indicating that the input is "out of range" when it is 1.[7]

---

[7] The overrange feature reduces the size of the first and highest output intervals to half the size of the other intervals.

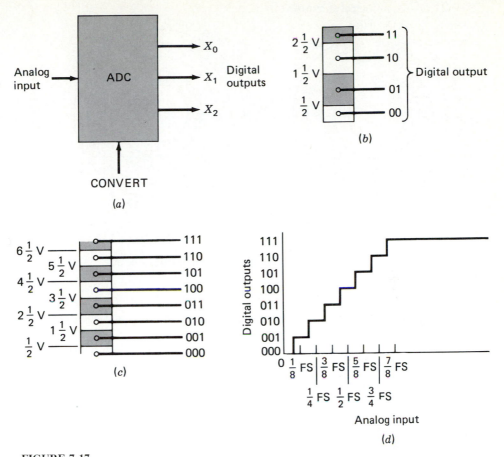

FIGURE 7.17
ADC operation and conversion intervals (*a*) Block diagram. (*b*) Two-output converter intervals. (*c*) Three-output converter intervals (*d*) Graph of intervals.

ANALOG-TO-DIGITAL CONVERTERS—SHAFT ENCODERS. The type of analog-to-digital converter most commonly used to directly convert a physical position to a digital value is the *shaft encoder*. The shaft encoder is connected to a rotating shaft and reads out the angular position of the shaft in digital form.

In the A/D converter in Fig. 7.18(*a*), a coded-segment disk that can rotate is coupled to a shaft. A set of brushes is attached so that a single brush is positioned in the center of each concentric band of the disk. Each band is constructed of several segments made of either conducting material (the darkened areas) or some insulating material (the unshaded areas). A positive voltage is connected to the conducting sections. If a given brush makes contact with a segment of conducting material, a 1 signal will result; if the brush is over the insulating material, the output from the brush will be a 0. The four output lines of the coder shown represent a 4-bit binary number. There are 16 distinct intervals around the coder

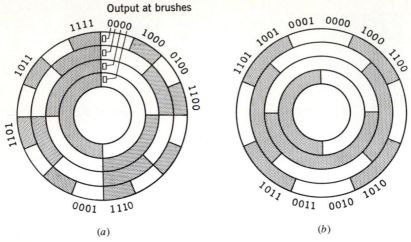

FIGURE 7.18
Shaft-position encoder disks. (*a*) Binary-coded disk. (*b*) Unit-distance-code disk.

disk, each corresponding to a different shaft-position interval, and each causes the coder to have a different binary output.

Photoelectric coders use a coder disk with bands divided into transparent segments (the shaded areas) and opaque segments (the unshaded areas). A light source is put on one side of the disk and a set of photoelectric cells on the other side, arranged so that one cell is behind each band of the coder disk. If a transparent segment is between the light source and a light-sensitive cell, a 1 output will result; if an opaque area is in front of the photoelectric cell, there will be a 0 output. By increasing the number of bands around the disk, more precision may be added to the coder. The photoelectric type of coder has greater resolution than the brush type, and even greater resolution may be obtained by using gears and several disks. The state of the art is about 18 bits or 2^{18} positions per shaft revolution, but most commercial codes have 14 bits or fewer.

There is one basic difficulty with the brush type of coder: If the disk is in a position where the output number is changing from 011 to 100, or in any position where several bits are changing value, the output signal may become ambiguous. Since the brushes are of finite width, they will overlap the change in segments; and no matter how carefully it is made, the coder will have erroneous outputs in several positions. If this occurs when 011 is changing to 100, several errors are possible; the value may be read as 111 or 000, either of which is a value with considerable error. To circumvent this difficulty, a number of schemes have been devised, generally involving two sets of brushes with one set displaced slightly from the other. By logically choosing from the outputs available, the ambiguity may be eliminated at a slight cost in accuracy.

Another scheme for avoiding ambiguity involves the use of the *Gray* or *unit-distance code* to form the coder disk [see Fig. 7.18(*b*)]. In this code, 3 bits retain their value in successive coded binary numbers. By using a Gray-coded disk, a 6 may be read for a 7 or a 4 for a 5, but larger errors will not be made. Table 7.2 shows a listing of a 4-bit Gray code.

If the inputs are from a coder using Gray code, the code groups must be converted to conventional binary or BCD before use.

There are straightforward ways to convert from Gray to binary or from binary to Gray code. The conversion from binary to Gray code is as follows:

1. The leftmost digit of the binary number is also the leftmost digit of the Gray code.
2. The mod 2 sum ($0 \oplus 0 = 1 \oplus 1 = 0$ and $1 \oplus 0 = 0 \oplus 1 = 1$) of the two leftmost digits in the binary number will give the second leftmost digit in the Gray code.
3. The mod 2 sum of the second and third digits of the binary number give the third leftmost digit of the Gray code. This process continues until the mod 2 sum of the two rightmost digits of the binary number give the rightmost Gray code digit.

Here is an example of the conversion of 0111 binary to Gray code:

0	leftmost digit
$0 \oplus 1 = 1$	2d leftmost digit
$1 \oplus 1 = 0$	next digit
$1 \oplus 1 = 0$	rightmost digit

So Gray code for 0111 binary is 0100.

TABLE 7.2

Decimal	Gray code $a_3 a_2 a_1 a_0$
0	0000
1	0001
2	0011
3	0010
4	0110
5	0111
6	0101
7	0100
8	1100
9	1101
10	1111
11	1110
12	1010
13	1011
14	1001
15	1000

Here is an example of the conversion from 1010 binary to Gray code:

$$1 \qquad \text{leftmost digit}$$
$$1 \oplus 0 = 1 \qquad \text{2d leftmost digit}$$
$$0 \oplus 1 = 1 \qquad \text{next digit}$$
$$1 \oplus 0 = 1 \qquad \text{rightmost digit}$$

Thus, Gray code for 1010 binary is 1111.

Here is a five-digit example of converting 10111 to Gray code:

$$1 \qquad \text{leftmost digit}$$
$$1 \oplus 0 = 1 \qquad \text{next digit}$$
$$0 \oplus 1 = 1 \qquad \text{next digit}$$
$$1 \oplus 1 = 0 \qquad \text{next digit}$$
$$1 \oplus 1 = 0 \qquad \text{rightmost digit}$$

So 10111 binary is 11100 in Gray code.

FLASH CONVERTERS. The fastest ADCs are called *simultaneous* or *flash converters*. Figure 7.19(*a*) shows a flash converter with two digital output lines, X_0 and X_1. This converter realizes the converter input/output relations for Fig. 7.17(*b*).

The converter uses an analog circuit called a *comparator*. The block diagram symbol for a comparator is a triangle on its side. When the voltage at the upper (+) input to a comparator is positive relative to the lower (−) input, the comparator outputs a digital 1; when the upper input is negative relative to the lower input, the comparator outputs a digital 0.[8] As an example, the lowest comparator in Fig. 7.19 has a lower (−) input of 0.5 V. If the input is at 0.5 V, the comparator will have a 0 output; if it is at 0.75 V, the comparator will have a 1 output.

The operation of this flash converter is as follows: (1) If the analog input is 0–0.5 V, the three points A, B, and C will all be 0s, and the X_0 and X_1 outputs will also be 0s. (2) If the input is 0.5–1.5 V, then points A and B will be 0s, point C will be a 1, the X_0 output will be a 1, and the X_1 output will be a 0. (3) If the input is between 1.5 and 2.5 V, points B and C will be 1s and A a 0, giving $X_0 = 1$ and $X_1 = 1$. (4) If the input is greater than 2.5 V, then A, B, and C will be 1s and the output will be $X_0 = 1$ and $X_1 = 1$.

This example of a small flash converter shows the basic parts: the reference voltages, the comparators, and a gate network to convert the outputs from the comparators to the proper binary number.

---

[8] The output of a comparator is unspecified when both inputs are equal (it can be a 0 or a 1).

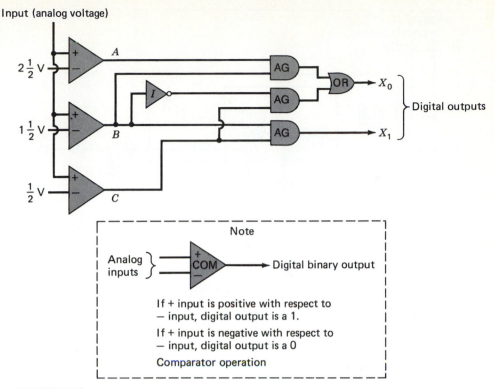

Input (analog voltage)

FIGURE 7.19
A 2-bit flash converter.

Figure 7.20(a) shows a block diagram of a 6-bit flash converter packaged in a single IC container. This ADC operates at a rate of up to 100 million conversions per second. The resistor chain at the left provides the correct reference voltages for the inputs to the comparators. The CONV and $\overline{\text{CONV}}$ inputs, which control conversions, operate as follows: When CONV is made a 1, the outputs from the 63 comparators go into the 63 latches (flip-flops) to their right. The C on each of the latches is the clock input, which works on a positive 1 level. When $\overline{\text{CONV}}$ goes to 1, this transfers the outputs from these latches to the latches to their right. The ROM contains the conversion codes for the inputs from the latches, converting these inputs to the correct binary number. This ROM replaces the gate network shown in the preceding figure and provides an example of how ROMs and gate networks are sometimes interchangeable. When CONV is next made a 1, the outputs from the ROM are transferred into the latches to its right. These latches now contain the correct conversion number. Finally, when $\overline{\text{CONV}}$ is made a 1, the output latches take the six output values for the ADC. (The triangles to the right of these latches are simply amplifiers or buffers providing drive for chip output; they do not shift 0 and 1 output levels from the latches.) The interval through which the ADC converters are set is established by connecting the

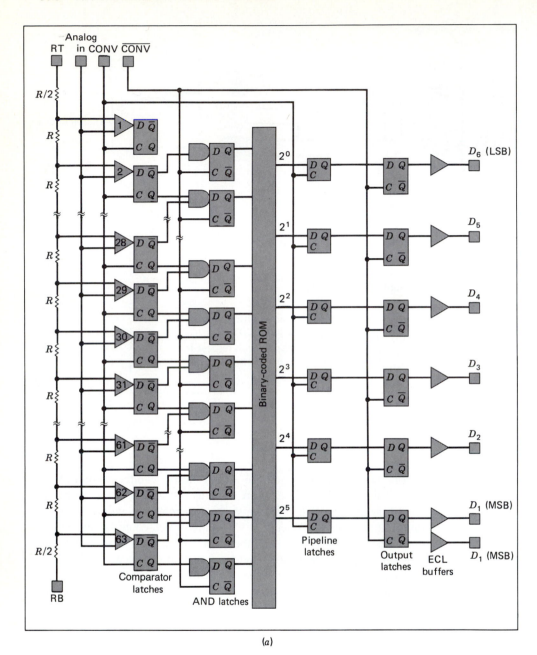

(a)

FIGURE 7.20
A high-speed flash A/D converter. (a) Block diagram of 6-bit 100-MHx flash converter. (*Courtesy TRW, LSI Products Division.*)

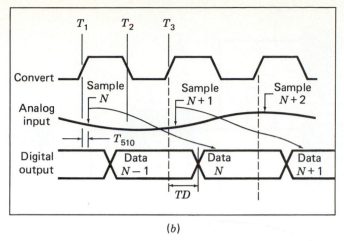

(b)

FIGURE 7.20
(b) Waveforms for flash converter in (a). (*Courtesy TRW, LSI Products Division.*)

desired upper and lower voltages to the RT and RB inputs to the ADC's container. Figure 7.20(b) shows the waveforms for conversion.

Flash converters come in many sizes and speeds. The fastest single-chip converters now perform 8-bit conversions at a rate of 100 million conversions per second; smaller, slower, and less expensive devices are also readily available.

The principal problem with flash converters is the large number of comparators required. For an n-bit converter, $2^n - 1$ comparators are needed, and this involves considerable circuitry if n is very large.

COUNTER AND SUCCESSIVE-APPROXIMATION CONVERTERS. Quite often ADCs are made from the DAC and some flip-flops and other logic. These ADCs are generally slower than the flash ADCs but are less expensive and ordinarily have more output bits (resolution) and, thus, greater accuracy. (Flash converters can be combined to give more bits, but more logic and one or more DACs are required.)

The most conceptually straightforward nonflash ADC uses a binary counter, a DAC, and a comparator and is called a *counter* ADC. The block diagram for a counter ADC is shown in Fig. 7.21(a). This uses a 3-bit counter, a 3-bit input DAC, and a comparator.

A conversion by this ADC is initiated by lowering the $\overline{\text{CONVERT}}$ line and then raising it (this line is normally a 1, so making it a 0 tells the ADC to convert). The actual conversion begins when the $\overline{\text{CONVERT}}$ line is returned to the 1 state which "frees" the counter that has been reset. The CLOCK input is supplied with clock signals continuously, and the three-flip-flop counter then begins to count. Also, while $\overline{\text{CONVERT}}$ is down, the ("bottom conversion complete") flip-flop is set to 0 ($\overline{\text{CONVERT}}$ must be a 0 long enough for this flip-flop to be set).

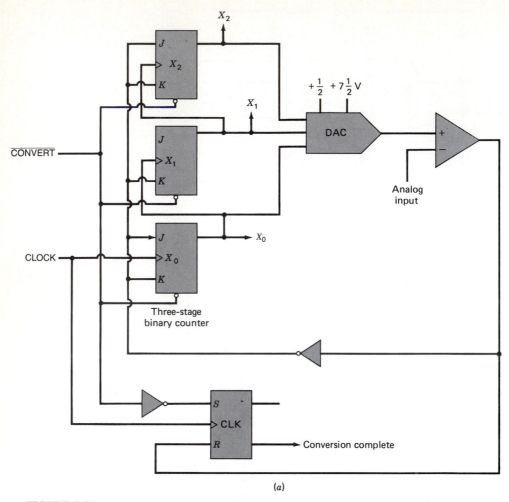

FIGURE 7.21
Counter ADC. (*a*) Block diagram.

As the counter counts, the output from the DAC increases in voltage,[9] as shown in Fig. 7.21(*b*). Until the output from the DAC exceeds the analog input voltage, the comparator output will be a 0 and the *JK* inputs to the counter will be 1s (notice the inverter), and the counter will count. When the DAC's output exceeds the analog input, the counter will be stopped, and the signal on the bottom output line in Fig. 7.21(*a*) will go to 1, indicating the conversion is complete.

[9] Note the DAC is biased +0.5 V positive; that is, a 0 input to the DAC gives a +0.5 V output. The DAC then increases its output voltage in 1-V steps as the counter is incremented.

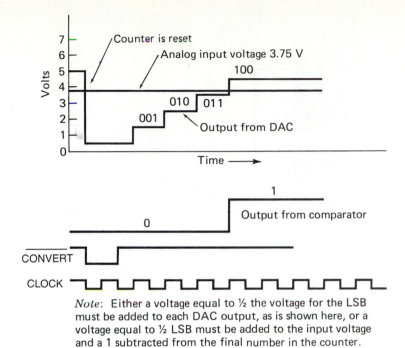

Note: Either a voltage equal to ½ the voltage for the LSB must be added to each DAC output, as is shown here, or a voltage equal to ½ LSB must be added to the input voltage and a 1 subtracted from the final number in the counter.

(*b*)

FIGURE 7.21
Counter ADC. (*b*) Waveforms.

As can be seen, the counter ADC is less expensive but slower than the flash converter. Another type of ADC, called a *tracking* ADC, simply follows the analog input up and down continuously, giving a continuous output of its value. This is formed by connecting the flip-flops in an up/down counter and then connecting the comparator's output to the DOWN input and the inverted comparator's output to the UP input. In this way the counter-DAC combination will continually track the analog input signal.

The most-used ADC of this type is the *successive-approximation* ADC. Figure 7.22(*a*) shows an ADC similar to the counter ADC but with control logic where the counter logic was. This ADC works as follows. First, all flip-flops are set to 0. Then the most significant bit (MSB) is set to 1. The output of the comparator is examined by the control logic: if it is a 1, the MSB flip-flop (the flip-flop connected to the MSB of the DAC) is turned off; if it is a 0, the flip-flop is left on. Next the second most significant bit's flip-flop is turned on. Again, if the comparator's output is a 1, the flip-flop is turned off; if the comparator's output is a 0, then the flip-flop is left on. This continues for each flip-flop up to and including the LSB flip-flop. The final number in the flip-flop will represent the input voltage. Figure 7.22(*b*) shows the waveform for a 3-bit successive-approximation ADC.

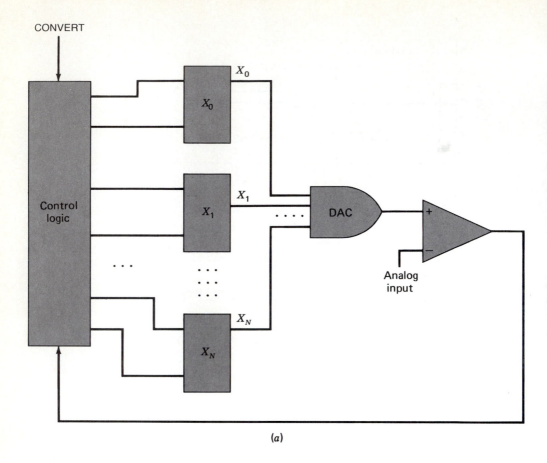

(a)

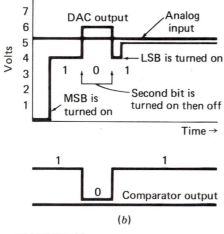

(b)

Note: Either a voltage equal to ½ LSB must be added to the analog input voltage or the output from the DAC must biased down ½ LSB

FIGURE 7.22
Successive-approximation ADC.

The important thing to notice is that a counter ADC with n binary outputs can take up to $2^n - 1$ clock signals to convert an input and will take $(2^n - 1)/2$ steps on the average. The successive-approximation ADC requires only n clock signals or steps to make each conversion. For a 12-bit ADC then, the successive-approximation ADC would require 12 steps, whereas the counter ADC would require 4095/2 steps, on average, and could require up to 4095.

ADCs are packaged in IC containers, or on PC boards when several IC chips are used. The block diagram and input/output signal lines for a 12-bit ADC using the successive-approximation technique with a 3-μs conversion time are shown in Fig. 7.23(a) and (c). Waveforms for this device are seen in Fig. 7.23(b). Lowering $\overline{\text{WR}}$ to 0 initiates a conversion. At this time the $\overline{\text{ACK}}$ line goes high (a 1), and it goes back to 0 when the conversion is complete. Data are read from the chip in two steps.[10] (To conserve on in/out connections, the data output lines are time-multiplexed.) When $\overline{\text{RD}}$ is low, the ADC outputs appear on D_0 to D_7. If $C/\overline{D}$ is low when $\overline{\text{RD}}$ is low, the 8 least significant bits are output on D_0 to D_7. If $C/\overline{D}$ is high, the 4 most significant bits appear on D_0 to D_3. $\overline{\text{CS}}$ is a CHIP SELECT input (as in memories) that enables the ADC when low (a 0); holding this line high disables the chip (this permits easy connection to microcomputer buses). GND_A is analog ground, and GND_D is digital ground. The outputs and inputs are TTL levels—approximately 0 V = 0 and 3.5 V = 1.

Computer Data Acquisition Systems

Computer data acquisition and computer control systems are important areas in computer technology. Computers have long been used to make measurements in laboratories and to monitor and control manufacturing processes. Machine tools are often controlled by computers, as are plastic-forming machines and other industrial devices. Now the advent of microprocessors is moving the level of control down to consumer items such as automobiles, stoves, and home temperature control. For example, for some time the automobile industry has used computers to test motors and perform other manufacturing operations. Now cars themselves have computer controls. Some Ford models use a microcomputer-based logic control system with inputs from six sensors. A vane airflow meter in the air induction system outputs a voltage proportional to the amount of air drawn into the engine. The temperature of this air is measured by a second sensor, while still another gives engine temperature. The amount of free oxygen in the exhaust gas is also measured, as is the crankshaft position. By using data from these sensors as input, the ignition spark timing is set, and the amount of fuel discharged through the injector nozzles is controlled, as is the exhaust-gas recirculation system. Other manufacturers use computers to control transmissions, shock absorber pressure, fuel pumps, and other key components.

All such applications rely on the measuring of analog inputs by computer, which involves extensive use of ADCs. In these and in laboratory data systems, blood

---

[10] These outputs utilize three-state drivers, which are explained in Chap. 8.

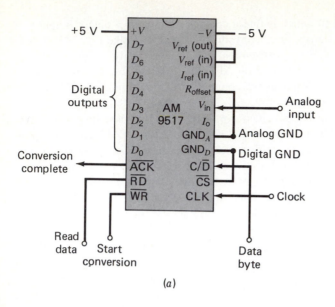

(a)

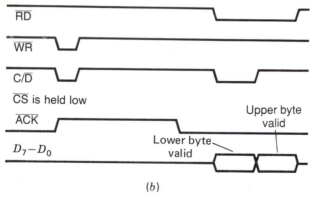

(b)

FIGURE 7.23
A successive-approximation A/D converter. (a) Pin-out for the AM 9517 showing input-output signals. (b) Waveforms for (a) and (c) showing how C/$\overline{D}$ controls multiplexing for digital output. (*Courtesy Advanced Micro Devices Inc.*)

processing laboratories, computer patient monitoring, and many other such systems, different sensors must be monitored by the computer continuously. This general area is called *data acquisition* and is rapidly expanding.

Figure 7.24(a) shows a section of a waveform to be monitored by a computer. This waveform is to be sampled periodically and the values at sample points input to the computer. The sampling process is not perfect, however. If counter or successive-approximation ADCs are used, the conversion times are liable to be long; and if the signal is changing during the conversion process, the output from the ADC can represent almost any point in the sampling interval. Figure 7.24(b) shows an expanded

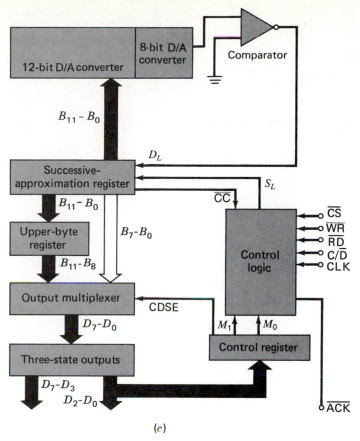

(c)

FIGURE 7.23
(c) Block diagram of successive-approximation ADC in (a). (*Courtesy Advanced Micro Devices Inc.*)

section of the waveform; clearly, the output from the ADC could be from any point on this curve.

The indeterminacy in output value caused by the change of input during the sample interval may or may not be important. However, if the analog signal changes rapidly, so that a significant change can occur during the sample interval, then mathematical analyses of the digital inputs or attempts to reconstruct the original input signal from the sample values can be severely degraded.

To alleviate this problem, a device called a *sample-and-hold amplifier* is often used. Figure 7.24(c) shows a functional representation of this device (it is an electronic circuit on a chip), and Fig. 7.24(d) shows the block diagram symbol. The sample-and-hold amplifier works as follows: When a positive pulse is placed on the SAMPLE input, the current value at the input is placed on the output and remains there until the SAMPLE input again is given a positive pulse. The functional representation shows a relay whose contracts are closed by the positive edge on the SAMPLE input and reopened by the negative edge of the positive pulse. (In actual practice, a high-speed

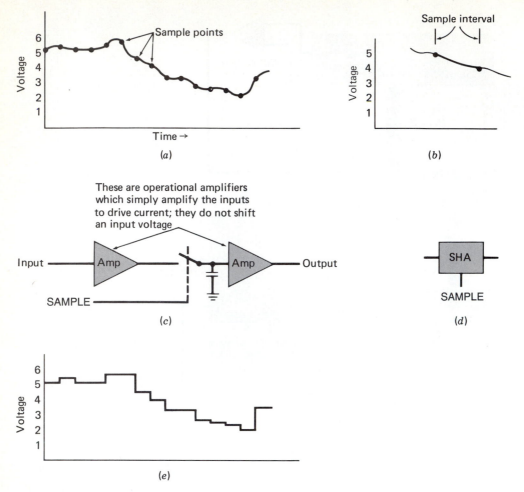

FIGURE 7.24

Sampling of an analog signal. (*a*) Waveform to be sampled. (*b*) Typical sample interval. (*c*) Functional representation. (*d*) Block diagram symbol for sample-and-hold amplifier. (*e*) Output of sample-and-hold amplifier based on waveform in (*a*).

semiconductor switch is used — not a relay). When the contacts of the relay are closed, the leftmost amplified charges the capacitor to the input value. When the contacts are opened, the capacitor stores this value until the contacts are again closed.

Figure 7.24(*e*) shows the output from a sample-and-hold amplifier based on the input waveform in (*a*) and the same sample points. If an ADC is connected to the sample-and-hold output and told to convert, the analog output from the sample-and-hold amplifier will be constant in the interval between the sample points, and the ADC will have a constant input to convert. The output of the ADC will thus represent the value of the analog input at the time the sample-and-hold amplifier was told to sample.

There are important considerations concerning the operation of a sample-and-hold amplifier:

1. The *aperture time* is the time that elapses between the command to hold and the actual opening of the hold switch. (This can be as low as 1 ns for some switches.)

2. The *settling time* is the time required for the output to reach the input value when the switch is closed. If the switch is closed by the positive edge of a pulse, as in our example, and opened by the negative edge, then the time between positive and negative edges (pulse width) must be long enough for the output value to change from the prior to the new value. [This will involve charging the capacitor in Fig. 7.24(c).] The manufacturer's specification will give the settling time. Reasonable figures might be a 10-ns aperture delay, 0.25-ns aperture jitter (variation in delay), a 100-ns settling time.

3. *Droop* is the amount or rate of drift in the output between samples. A typical figure would be $100 \mu V/\mu s$, which means that a maximum change of $100 \mu V$ might occur during $1 \mu s$.

Another important device in data acquisition systems is the *analog multiplexer,* or AMUX. This is shown in Fig. 7.25(a) and (b). An AMUX has several analog inputs [four are shown in Fig. 7.25], enough digital *select inputs* to select one of the analog inputs, and a single analog output. The function of the AMUX is to select one of several possible analog inputs by using the digital select inputs and to output only this particular input. Figure 7.25(a) shows this in the functional diagram by a rotary switch, where the position of the wiper arm on the switch selects and connects one of the four inputs to the output. In practice, AMUXs are made of semiconductors and are often packaged in a single IC container. The inputs and outputs are generally connected to amplifiers, and the switch is a semiconductor switch. As can be seen, each select value will cause a particular input to be output. In Fig. 7.25(a), $S_0 S_1 = 00$ would cause A_0 to be output. $S_0 S_1 = 01$ would output A_1, and so on.

Figure 7.26 shows a typical data acquisition system. There are four analog signals, A_0, A_1, A_2, and A_3. Each is connected to the AMUX; the computer selects

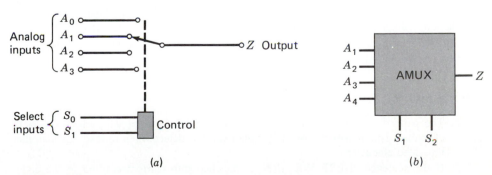

FIGURE 7.25
Analog multiplexer. (*a*) Functional diagram of four-input analog multiplexer. (*b*) Block diagram.

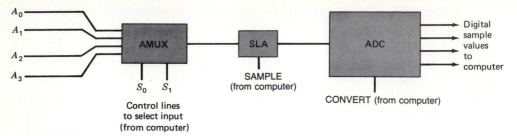

FIGURE 7.26
Data acquisition system.

from these inputs the one it wants to be sampled and places its number on S_0S_1. Then the selected analog signal is connected to the sample-and-hold amplifier. When the correct time for a sample occurs, the computer raises and lowers the SAMPLE input, causing the selected input voltage to be held at its current value. Next the CONVERT signal to the ADC is raised, causing the ADC to measure and output the value of the selected analog signal. The computer can now read the output signal from the ADC and proceed to the sampling of another signal.

With this data acquisition system, the analog inputs can be sampled at varying rates in case some signals change more rapidly than others or are more critical than the others. Also, the exact time at which the sample was taken will be known by the computer since it issues the SAMPLE signal (generally this signal is combined with some precise timing source).

AMUXs are produced with more than four analog inputs to handle large systems. Sometimes several sample-and-hold amplifiers are used, and these are connected to the analog inputs rather than the AMUX's output. This makes it possible to sample two or more inputs at the same time and then read them by addressing one and then the other, using the AMUX.

Sometimes the analog signals have voltage amplitudes outside the normal range of the ADC. The sample-and-hold amplifiers (and sometimes the AMUX) often use amplifiers that can be set to accommodate these inputs, increasing or decreasing signal values and even inverting (converting from negative to positive) input values. There are also circuits for *offsetting,* or *translating,* input signals; this consists of adding a selected voltage to them, thereby changing their range. This area is called *signal conditioning* and generally involves the use of operational amplifiers. Some material on this can be found in the following questions.

QUESTIONS

7.1. The paper tape code shown in Fig. 7.4 uses at least one punch or hole for each character. This makes it possible for the reader to detect when to read. Explain the tape feed character.

7.2. If the sentence "HERE WE ARE" is punched into cards according to the code shown in Fig. 7.5 using normal procedures, how many holes will be punched into the cards? If a mistake is made during keyboarding, will it be easier to correct if cards or tape is used? Explain why.

7.3. List the binary code groups for each decimal digit in the 2,4,2,1 BCD code in Chap. 2, and assign a parity bit for an even-parity-bit checking system to each code group.

7.4. The *tape feed* character (see Fig. 7.4) can be used to take out any character in the code shown except one. Which character and why? (*Hint:* Remember the parity checks.)

7.5. Discuss any problems you can foresee in attempting to read characters optically and that would not occur for magnetic characters. Do these problems help to explain why banks adopted magnetic readers before optical readers?

7.6. More powerful parity-check systems can be formed by adding columns at the end indicating the number of 1s in each original column written as a binary number. For instance, if we wish to encode

$$
\begin{array}{l}
1011 \\
1101 \\
1100 \\
1110
\end{array}
$$

we add

$$
\left.\begin{array}{l}
0 \\
0 \\
1 \\
0
\end{array}\right\} \text{ parity checks}
$$

$$
\left.\begin{array}{l}
01001 \\
01110 \\
10000
\end{array}\right\} \text{ number of 1s in each column}
$$

$$
\begin{array}{l}
\text{indicates two 1s} \\
\text{indicates four 1s}
\end{array}
$$

Adding this to the original data forms this encoded block of data:

$$
\begin{array}{l}
10110 \\
11010 \\
11001 \\
11100 \\
\left.\begin{array}{l}
01001 \\
01110 \\
10000
\end{array}\right\} \text{ check digits}
\end{array}
$$

Now if one or more errors occur in the same column, they can be corrected by simply noting that the number of 1s in the column does not agree with the total recorded at the end, and that there are parity checks in the rows of the block of data containing errors. By simply changing these errors, we convert the message back to its original form.

Following are two blocks of data that include errors. Correct the errors in these blocks of data, and write the alphanumeric code for each set of seven digits in a row to the right of the rows. (The code is that of Fig. 2.4.)

(a) 10100100
10010010
10001101
10010001
10101000
Check digits { 10000010
00111111 } Check digits
10000000

(b) 10000011
10011101
10100011
10010010
00101011
00010111 } Check digits
10000010

7.7. Using the error-detecting and error-correcting scheme in the following question, and using a single odd-parity-check row at the bottom, a message has been sent. It arrives as follows. Determine if errors have occurred, and correct any that you find.

10100100
10000010
10001101
10010001
10101000
01111111

7.8. Each of the following rows of digits consists of a code group in ASCII. A single parity check has been added as the rightmost bit in each row, and a single row of parity checks has been added at the end, as explained in the preceding question. In addition, errors have been added so that the data are not correct at present. Correct these groups of data, and then convert each seven-digit code to the alphanumeric character it represents. (The parity checks are odd-parity-checks.)

(a) 10101000
10010001
10000011
10101000
01001111
10100111
01100000
10000100
10110010
10001111
10010001
10101000
11000101   parity-check row

(b) 10001001
10011110
10011101
01001111
10101000
01001000
10100111
10101000
10011110
10100001
01011011
10111001   parity-check row

7.9. How many bands must a coder disk similar to that shown in Fig. 7.18 have for an A/D converter with a precision of 10 binary digits? List the successive code groups for a 5-bit unit-distance Gray code that counts from 0 to 31_{10}.

7.10. Put errors into the message in Question 7.8 that the coding will neither correct nor detect.

7.11. A 3,3,2,1 code for encoding the 10 decimal digits into 4 binary digits can be made so that no more than two positions change each time a single digit is increased by 1. Write this code down.

7.12. Characters are generally read from punched paper tape a line at a time. When the code in Fig. 7.4(a) is used, the computer will be supplied with information bits each time a line is read. If the computer is a serial computer, the bits will arrive in parallel and must be changed to serial form. By loading a seven-place shift register in parallel and then shifting the register at the machine's pulse-repetition frequency, the bits representing the character can be converted to serial form. Draw a block diagram of a seven-flip-flop shift register, along with the input lines necessary to load the register. (Assume that there are seven input lines—one to each flip-flop—from the tape reader and that a given input line will contain a pulse if a hole is in the respective position of the tape.)

7.13. If the ASCII code in Fig. 2.4 is transmitted serially in binary, draw the waveform for the character 6, assuming a 1 is +4 V and a 0 is a −4 V.

7.14. Which of the sets of errors in Question 7.7 would have been detected if the error-catching system in Question 7.6 had been used? Which of the sets of errors in Question 7.6 could have been corrected by the error-detecting and error-correcting-scheme in Question 7.7, and which would only have been detected?

7.15. Is it possible to invent a 7-bit code that includes an odd-parity-check bit and that contains 70 characters? Give a reason for your answer.

7.16. The code in Question 7.6 is generally not able to correct double errors in a row or errors in the checking numbers at the end, but it will almost always detect either of these. Explain this statement.

7.17. Show how a keyboard would read out the character *B* in standard serial. Draw the output waveform.

7.18. What is ASCII for *line feed?* Show the serial waveform.

7.19. What is EBCDIC for *E?* What would the serial waveform be?

7.20. Notice that the characters in the magnetic reader character set of Fig. 7.6 are "blocked," not curved. Why might this be a good idea?

7.21. Notice the difference in a 0, a Q, and an O in the character sets shown in 7.7. Find other letters that have similar printed shapes and have been altered to make them more machine-readable.

7.22. Consider a computer connected by a cable or telephone lines to a terminal. When a character is typed in the terminal keyboard, it is said to be "echoed" if it is printed by the computer and not by the local terminal electronics. Why might this be a good idea, and what might be the problem be?

7.23. Why are start bits and at least one stop bit necessary for the serial code transmission explained for terminals?

7.24. Explain the difference between synchronous and asynchronous transmission of digital data.

7.25. Explain how the Bell modem described would send the ASCII character *G* on a line in a chosen direction. How would it send in the other direction? Use the teletypewriter scheme to encode, using start and stop bits.

7.26. Design an A/D converter that uses the successive-approximation technique.

7.27. Show how long it would take an A/D converter using the successive-approximation technique to convert 7 bits. Assume that it takes 10 ms for the D/A converter–resistor network to stabilize its output. Explain by showing how conversions are made for three specific input voltages.

7.28. Again assuming that it takes 10 ms for a D/A converter network to stabilize, show how a 6-bit converter uses the successive-approximation technique for three voltages +9, +1, and +7 V, assuming a 0- to 10-V range for inputs (0 and +10 V as voltage levels for the converter outputs).

7.29. Show how the converter in Fig. 7.21 converts the three voltages in the preceding question, and compare the conversion times.

7.30. Using the information in the preceding three questions, can you compare the average time for conversion for a counter ADC with that of a successive-approximation converter? Assume 6 bits.

7.31. Show how a flash converter works for a 3-bit system. Draw the gates from the comparator outputs to the binary numbers.

7.32. Explain how the successive-approximation converter converts -0.5, $+3.2$, and $+5.4$ V.

7.33. Discuss *resolution* and *quantizing error*. Can the quantizing error be less than the resolution? Why or why not?

7.34. Discuss A/D converters, bringing out the important characteristics that must be considered in choosing a converter. What is the primary advantage of a flash ADC, and what is its primary disadvantage? Can a flash converter convert an analog input directly to digital form, using a Gray code instead of binary? Justify your answer.

7.35. Draw a table of combinations for a gate network that converts a 3-bit Gray code to a 3-bit conventional binary number.

7.36. A straightforward technique for encoding a keyboard is shown in this chapter. Several other methods are sometimes used, and these are primarily intended to either reduce the number of semiconductors in the decoder mechanism or simplify the wiring.

One technique involves a two-dimensional array similar to the selection systems used in memories. The following figure shows a two-dimensional array. The horizontal wires are connected to the vertical wires by switches, which are activated by keys on the keyboard. Thus, depressing a key closes a switch connecting a single X wire to a single Y wire. Each key that is depressed produces a unique X wire–Y wire combination. Determining which key has been closed, however, is nontrivial. A common technique is to raise one of the X (horizontal) wires and then scan (i.e.,

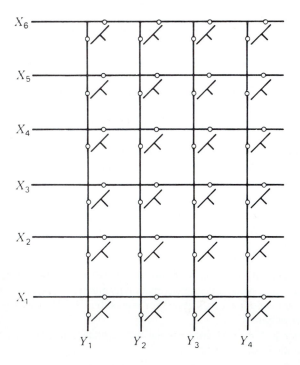

sample) each of the Y wires. If one of the wires is high and the other wires are low, then the correct intersection of X and Y wires can be determined. Sometimes a microprocessor is programmed to generate the X wire sequence and sample the Y wires, but special *keyboard encoding chips* are also made for this process. The X wires are normally low, and the microprocessor or scanner raises a single X wire and examines each Y wire to see if it is high. If it is, a key has been depressed, and since the microprocessor is aware of which X wire and which Y wire have been raised, it can identify the key. By encoding each X wire with a unique 3-bit code and each Y wire with a unique 2-bit code, a unique 5-bit combination results. For larger keyboards the ASCII code can be used by proper choice of the X and Y values. Draw a simple encoder that encodes only eight of the ASCII characters shown in Fig. 2.4, assigning values to the X and Y access wires.

7.37. What is the weight of the least significant bit in a DAC with with a resolution of 6 bits and an output voltage in the range of 0 to $+10$ V?

7.38. What is the weight of the most significant bit for a DAC with 5 bits of resolution and an output voltage range of 0 to $+5$ V?

7.39. If a 6-bit DAC has a 0- to $+5$-V output range, what is expected output for an input of 010101?

7.40. A 7-bit DAC has an output range of 0 to $+10$ V. The manufacturer specifies that the DAC has a monotonic output with perfect values of 0 and $+10$ V. In terms of voltage, what is the maximum error that can occur?

7.41. What is the Gray code for 10111 binary? For a Gray code of 11011, what is the corresponding binary code?

7.42. Derive a rule for converting from Gray code to binary.

7.43. Draw the waveform from the DAC and input voltage for a 4-bit counter converting the input voltage of $+2.75$ V. The conversion range for the ADC is 0 to $+5$ V.

7.44. Draw the DAC output waveform for a 5-bit successive-approximation ADC converting the input voltage of -3.33 V. The ADC has an input voltage range of 0 to $+7$ V.

7.45. Design a 4-bit successive-approximation ADC, showing gates, flip-flops, and other elements.

7.46. Design a 4-bit tracking ADC using an up-down counter as in Chap 4. The input voltage range should be 0 to $+15$ V.

7.47. Lay out the block diagram for a data acquisition system that samples the output from four ADCs connected to temperature-measuring devices and an ADC connected to an accelerometer in a jet sled. Use sample-and-hold amplifiers, multiplexers, and an ADC. Have a computer control the sampling.

CHAPTER
8

BUSES AND INTERFACES

To interconnect memories, I/O devices, and other sections of a computer, a bus is often used. Several examples of buses were given in Chap. 6; buses are covered in greater depth in this chapter. When a given I/O device or memory module is connected to a bus, an *interface* is required. This interface consists of the logic necessary for the I/O device or memory module to communicate successfully with the bus. Since each device must be interfaced, there are as many interfaces in a system as there are devices. In general, whenever one part of a digital system is connected to another, the logic effecting the interconnection is called the interface. In this chapter, buses will be discussed in some detail, interfaces will be developed for a keyboard and printer, and a program to drive these interfaces will be shown.

8.1 INTERCONNECTING SYSTEM COMPONENTS

The components of a computer system, that is, the memories, input/output devices, and other elements, must be interconnected. The way these components are put together and how they communicate with each other profoundly affect the system's performance characteristics.

The arithmetic-logic unit and control unit are generally placed together and called the central processing unit (CPU). The CPU is then "in charge" of the system's operation, directing the operation of the other parts of the system.

In earlier computers the CPU was connected directly to each input/output device and memory unit by a separate cable for each connection.[1] This is shown in Fig. 8.1.

---

[1] A cable is a set of electric conductors (wires). Connections are made to a cable only at each of the two ends, whereas a bus has connections made along the conductors.

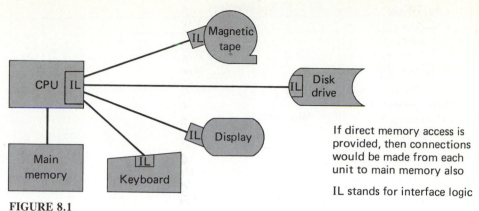

FIGURE 8.1
Individual connections between computer system units.

Using this setup, if a word is to be read from a disk drive, the CPU must accept the information; if it is to be stored in memory, the CPU must store it. The CPU is therefore central and involved directly in each transaction. This system has the disadvantage of many different cables and considerable interface logic (at each end of each cable).

To make interconnection of the system components less expensive and to standardize the interface logic used, a very popular technique is to interconnect all components using a single *bus*. This bus consists of a number of wires or connections, and in the bus are provisions for addressing the components and transferring data from or to each component.

Figure 8.2 shows a typical organization. Notice that the same wires are used to transfer data from the CPU to the high-speed main memory and from the CPU to a tape-punch or other input/output device.

In the simplest systems, the CPU is the director of all traffic on the bus. If a transfer of data must be made from, for instance, a disk pack to the main memory, then the CPU, under program control, will read each piece of data into its general registers and store each piece of data in the memory.

8.2 INTERRUPTS AND DIRECT MEMORY ACCESS

There is a problem involving the computer's ability to determine when a *peripheral device*[2] has performed a given operation. Suppose we wish to find some data on a magnetic tape but are unwilling to suspend operations while the tape is searched, desiring to perform other calculations while waiting. If the computer must continually look to see whether the tape drive now has the data available, time is lost and programming complexity is increased. To alleviate this, the computer bus is generally

---

[2] *Peripheral devices* are the input/output devices, disk packs, tape drives, and other devices not including the main (IC) memory.

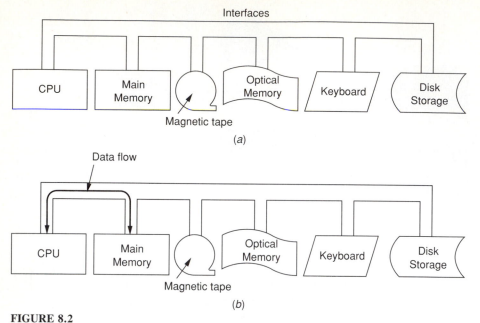

Interfaces

FIGURE 8.2
Buses. (*a*) CPU, memory, and other devices are connected by a single bus. (*b*) In normal use, CPU controls transfer of data.

provided with control lines[3] called *interrupt lines,* and a peripheral device can raise one of these lines when ready for attention.

The computer must be provided with some kind of interrupt facility so that it can "service" the interrupt without losing its place in the program being executed. This problem becomes serious in systems where a number of peripheral devices must be serviced frequently, and computers are designed to service these interrupts as efficiently as possible.

Even if there is a good interrupt facility, the CPU is still involved in every data transfer, and this can be very time-consuming. It is possible to add a *direct memory access* (DMA) feature to most systems, where a disk pack or other device transfers data directly into high-speed main memory using the bus and bypassing the CPU (see Fig. 8.3). This is called *cycle stealing.* The CPU is simply held in its present state for one or more clock cycles while data are transferred from the disk pack directly into the main memory. The CPU does not "see" each transfer when it occurs; it simply continues executing its program, which is slowed down a little because of the cycle stealing, but not nearly as much as if the CPU had to make each transfer itself. The CPU must, of course, originate these DMA transfers by telling where in the disk memory the data are to be read from and into which locations in the main memory the data are to be written. (Transfers generally can be made in either direction when

---

[3] The lines are normally at 0; to raise a line means to place a I on it. In microcomputers and minicomputers there may be only one line. (The word *lines* is often used for the electric conductors (wires) on a bus.)

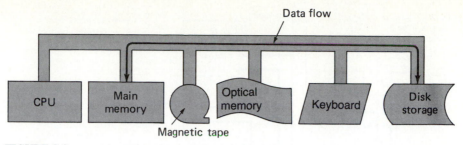

FIGURE 8.3
DMA mode.

the DMA feature is added to a system—for example, from tape to main memory or from main memory to tape.)

8.3 LARGE AND SMALL COMPUTER PERIPHERAL ORGANIZATION

Large computer systems have problems quite different from those of small systems, so different interconnection configurations are used. Since large systems contain many components, they are quite expensive, and it is important to utilize the CPU and other components to the maximum. The cost of more expensive interconnection configurations is thus warranted.

As a small system example, Fig. 8.4 shows the bus and interfaces for the Macintosh portable. This bus is shown with address A_{1-23} and data D_{0-15} sections but is physically in a single piece. Notice the flexibility of the organization. The extensive bus usage is typical of small systems. Large systems use more complex organizations. To keep large-processor configurations working at maximum speed, the systems are operated in *multiprogramming mode*. This means that several programs are kept in memory at the same time, and a given program is executed until it demands an input/output device or perhaps a disk drive. Since these devices are slow compared to the CPU, the device is started in its function, and the CPU begins executing a different program until this program asks for input/output. When this happens, the CPU begins executing a third program, and this process continues.

When a program completes execution, another program is read in. As can be seen, the CPU must keep track of where it is in each program and must control all the data transfers between system components; but it would be hopelessly held up if it had to participate in each transfer.

One way to configure a large system of this sort is shown in Fig. 8.5(*a*), which illustrates an IBM configuration. It shows a single CPU and two input/output processors, one of which IBM calls a *multiplexer channel* and the other a *selector channel*.[4] Some systems have more input/output processors, and others even have more than one CPU, in which case the system is called a *multiprocessor*.

---

[4] A multiplexer channel has logic particularly suited to relatively slow devices with random characteristics. Selector channels are for fast bursts of data generated by disk packs and tape drives, for instance.

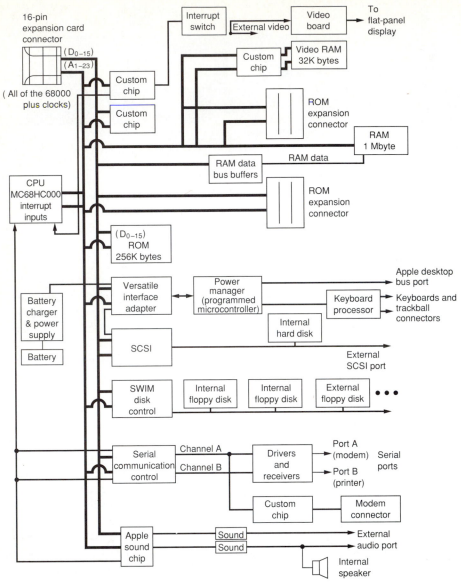

FIGURE 8.4
Macintosh portable computer organization.

The system operates as follows: All transfers to and from peripherals devices (such as card readers, printers, and tape drives) are initiated by the CPU telling an input/output processor what is to be done. The actual transfers are then made by the special-purpose processors, which work independently of the CPU. To initiate a data transfer, the CPU tells the input/output processor where in memory to put (or find) the data, which IO device to use, and (if necessary) where in that device the data

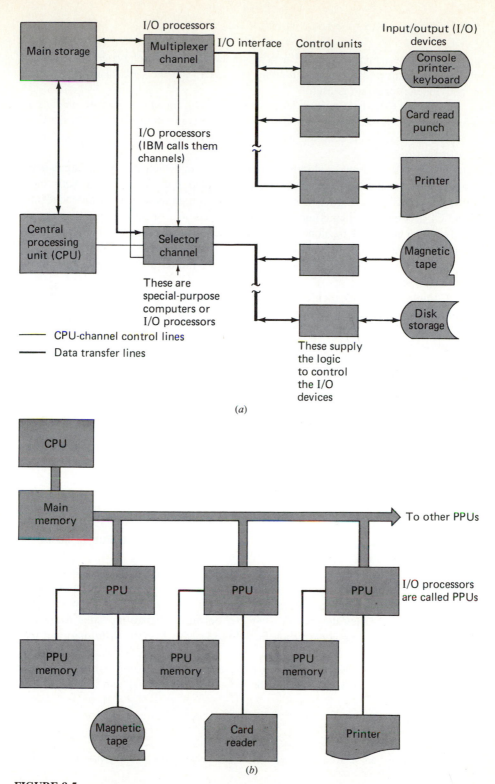

FIGURE 8.5
(a) Organization of IBM computer series. (b) Parallel computer organization.

are located. The actual transfer of data is guided by a *channel program* written in advance and executed by the input/output processor, and the CPU also sees that the correct channel program is used.

Once the CPU has initiated an input-output data transfer, it can go about executing other programs. When the input/output processor completes its work, the CPU is notified so that it can continue where it left off in the program that called for the input-output transfer.

Figure 8.5(*b*) shows a different organization, in which the input/output operations are all handled by small "computers" called *peripheral processing units* (PPUs). The PPUs have their own memories and programs and work independently of the CPU. The CPU plants messages to the PPUs in a specified area in memory, specifying what should be done. The PPUs then search this memory, looking for orders; when they find one, they execute the necessary operations and plant a message notifying the CPU that its orders have been fulfilled and the necessary operations performed.

Complex structures such as these are practical because a number of peripheral or input/output devices can be operating simultaneously at relatively low speed while the CPU races from job to job. The overall throughput for the computer system can be increased because of the parallel operation of all parts of the system.

The idea of using several CPUs to execute programs in parallel is an attractive one. As just mentioned, such systems are called multiprocessor systems. They have high throughput and make good usage of both large memories and several input/output devices. Figure 8.6 shows a particular configuration using 8086 and 8088 microprocessors, and Fig. 8.7 depicts the basic structure of a multiprocessor system.

8.4 INTERFACING — BUSES

As has been stated, a widely used technique to interface modules efficiently at low cost employs a single bus to interconnect all the units. Some systems have more than one bus to speed up operations. When bus traffic becomes too heavy for a single bus to carry it, operation speed is said to be *bus-limited*, and additional buses can alleviate this condition.

Figure 8.8 shows several lines or conductors that form the bus pass through and connect to a number of units or modules. In general, each module can read from or write onto the bus. The bus interface is usually standardized since the same bus connects all units. Often the modules together on the bus share the same data lines, in which case it is necessary for each module to be able to both write onto and read from a given line.

For sharing of lines on a bus,[5] a logic circuit called a *three-state* or *tristate driver* is used. The block diagram for the three-state driver is shown in Fig. 8.9(*a*).

---

[5] Three-state drivers are used in many applications other than buses, but the sharing of a line is always the reason for their use.

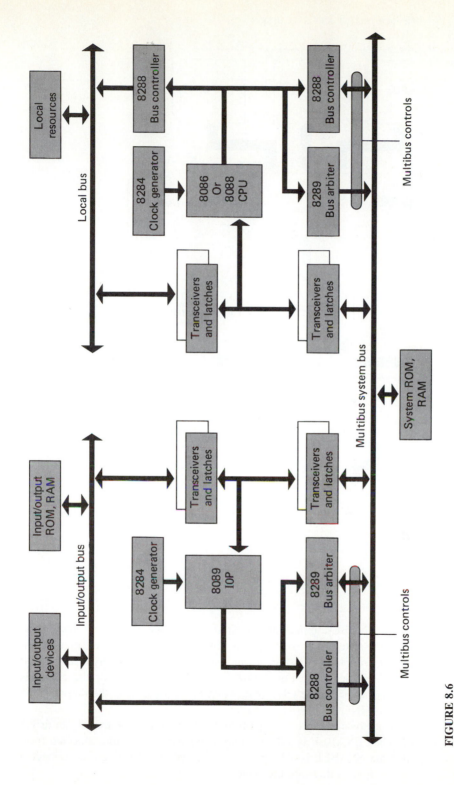

FIGURE 8.6

Multiprocessor configuration using 8086 and 8088 microprocessors.

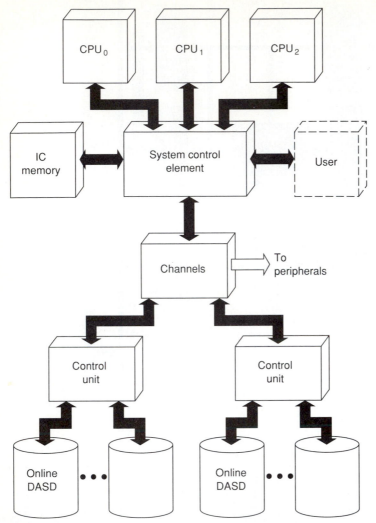

FIGURE 8.7
Typical multiprocessor system organization.

There are IN and ENABLE inputs and a single OUT line. A table showing the operation of the three-state driver is also given. The three-state driver has three output states: a 0 output, a 1 output, and a state in which the circuit is effectively disconnected from the output. As indicated in Fig. 8.9(a), when ENABLE is a 0, the circuit is effectively disconnected from the OUT line; when ENABLE is a 1, the output is the same as the input on IN.

Figure 8.9(c) shows a way of interpreting the operation of the three-state driver in Fig. 8.9(a). When ENABLE is a 0, the relay is open and IN is disconnected from the output; when the ENABLE is a 1, the relay is closed and the output is connected to the input, so the logic values are the same.

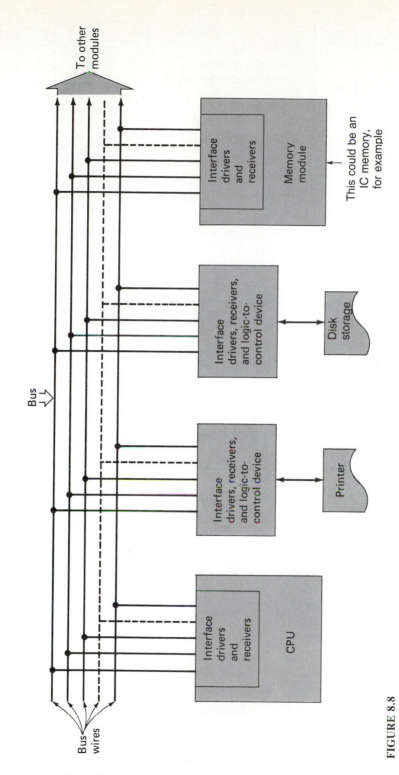

FIGURE 8.8
Computer organization of single-bus system.

IN	ENABLE	OUT
0	0	—
1	0	—
0	1	0
1	1	1

— indicates driver is electrically disconnected

IN	ENABLE	OUT
0	0	—
1	0	—
0	1	1
1	1	0

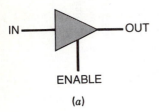

(a)

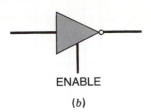

(b)

IN	ENABLE	OUT
0	0	Relay open
1	0	Relay open
0	1	0
1	1	1

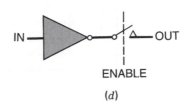

(d)

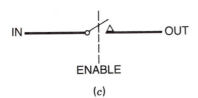

(c)

IN	DISABLE	OUT
0	0	1
1	0	0
0	1	—
1	1	—

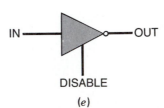

(e)

FIGURE 8.9

Three-state driver operation. (a) Three-state driver. (b) Three-state driver with inverted output. (c) Functional representation of (a). (d) Functional representation of (b). (e) Three-state driver with DISABLE input.

The important thing to understand is that if several three-state drivers have their outputs connected to the same line, and if only one of the drivers has as its ENABLE input a 1, then that particular driver will control the state of the line. When three-state drivers are used for interfaces, only one interface on a line (conductor) must have its ENABLE input a 1 at a given time, and this interface will control the state of the line.

Inverters or other logic gates can have their inputs connected to a line controlled by several three-state drivers. Generally, manufacturers arrange to have the three-state driver capable of driving a line of considerable length and with several gate inputs connected to it, which is often the case for a bus line.

Figure 8.9(*b*) shows a three-state driver that inverts its input. As the table shows, when ENABLE is a 0, the driver is effectively disconnected from the output; when ENABLE is a 1, the OUT value is the complement of the IN value. Figure 8.9(*d*) is a functional representation of (*b*) showing that the driver operates much like an inverter and a relay connected.

Sometimes manufacturers make three-state drivers with a DISABLE input instead of an ENABLE input [see Fig. 8.9(*e*)]. In this case the driver is disconnected when DISABLE is a 1, and the output—which is inverted in this case—is the complement of the input when DISABLE is a 0.

Three-state drivers are widely used in the interfaces for buses. They enable control of bus lines to pass from interface to interface as is appropriate.

Figure 8.10 shows a tristate octal *D*-type latch IC package with eight latches equipped with tristate drivers. Each latch reads the input at *D* when the clock input is high. The outputs from the latches are forced on the outputs from the chip when ENABLE is a 1. When ENABLE is a 0, the outputs represent "high impedances" (and another chip can drive the lines as they are connected to a desired state).

Figure 8.11 shows an octal tristate buffer with positive-edge-triggered flip-flops in which the outputs are forced to the flip flop states only when the ENABLE input is high (a 1).

Since several units share the same bus lines, the interface procedures for bused modules must be carefully worked out to ensure that, for instance, two modules do not attempt to write data on the bus at the same time, and to identify the module for which the data are intended.

Bus Formats and Operation

There are a number of different types of buses and several different standards for buses. All buses can be divided into three major sections, however: the *address,* *data,* and *control* sections. This is shown in Fig. 8.12, along with two common ways to represent multiple lines on the bus. Figure 8.12(*a*) shows the three sections, using a wide, ribbonlike representation for the multiple lines (wires). Figure 8.12(*b*) shows the convention of a single printed line with a slash to indicate that there are actually a number of lines (wires). There are 16 address lines, 8 data lines, and 4 control lines. Both representations are frequently used.

Most buses now use tristate drivers to write data on the data lines. In the most straightforward systems, the address lines are completely controlled by the *bus master,*

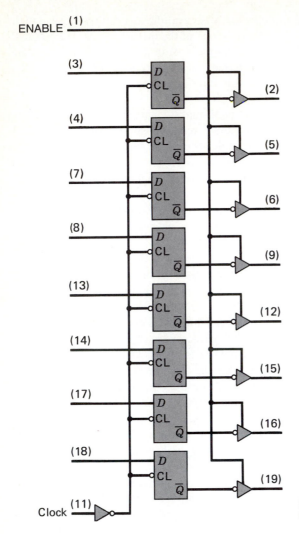

FIGURE 8.10
Octal latches with tristate drivers.

which is generally a microprocessor CPU. If there is a single bus master, the remaining devices connected to the bus are called *slaves*. Each slave has an address number, and the bus master uses the address lines to control which slave is to use the bus. In some systems, however, devices other than the CPU can take control of the bus. In this case, a controlling device is called the bus master only when it has control, and at that time the responding devices are called slaves. For buses in which control is shared among several devices, the address lines also are driven by tristate drivers.

Some of the control lines may be permanently controlled by the CPU, and others may be used by several devices and will thus require tristate drivers (or wired-OR or wired-AND drivers).

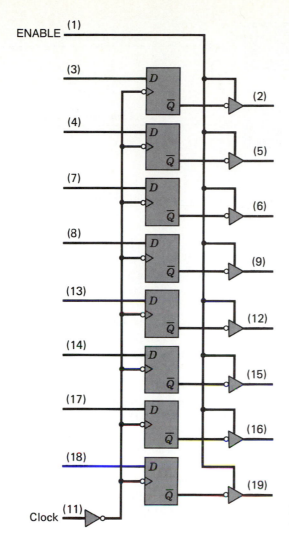

FIGURE 8.11
Octal flip-flops with tristate drivers.

Note that any device can read from a line driven by a tristate driver, and conventional inverter or gate inputs can be connected to these lines. (The only restriction is that the gates connected to the lines not load the lines unduly.)

Synchronous Versus Asynchronous Bus Operation

Buses transfer information over data wires by using either a *synchronous* or *asynchronous* technique. Different manufacturers and bus designers have different philosophies about which is better, with the result that there are several standards.

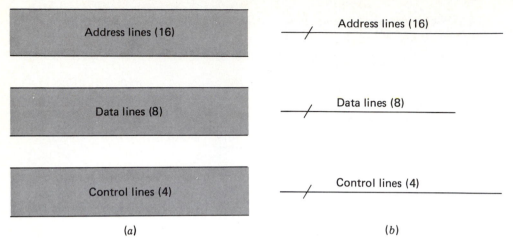

FIGURE 8.12

Address, data, and control sections of a bus. (*a*) The three sections of a bus. (*b*) Alternative representation for (*a*).

For synchronous transfers, the bus works as follows. Let us assume a CPU wishes to read from and write to peripheral devices. Each device is given a separate number, and a device is selected by the CPU's placing that number on the address lines.[6]

Figure 8.13 shows the timing of synchronous data transfers involving a set of address wires, data wires, and $\overline{\text{READ}}$ and $\overline{\text{WRITE}}$ control lines. All transfers are controlled by the CPU. Note that the meaning of READ and WRITE is always relative to the master or CPU on buses. Therefore, a READ means the CPU (master) reads data from the bus, and a WRITE means the CPU (master) writes data on the bus.

Figure 8.13 shows that to read, the CPU places the number of the device to be read from on the address lines. Then the CPU lowers the $\overline{\text{READ}}$ line,[7] and the selected device must place data on the data lines, which means enabling its tristate drivers connected to the bus data wires. When the $\overline{\text{READ}}$ line goes back to a 1, the device must disable its tristate drivers.

When the CPU desires to write data to a device, the device's number is placed on the address line, and then the data are placed on the data lines. The CPU lowers the $\overline{\text{WRITE}}$ line to 0, and the device must read the data at that time. The data must have been read by the time the $\overline{\text{WRITE}}$ line goes back to a 1.[8] The interface designer must know how long $\overline{\text{WRITE}}$ will be a 0 so that the data can be read safely during that time.

---

[6] A disk drive might be given the number 1, a keyboard the number 3, and so on.

[7] It is common practice to use a 0 signal to activate devices on a bus. This is indicated by the bar over the name of the line ($\overline{\text{READ}}$). If a device is activated by a 1 signal, no bar is used.

[8] Sometimes the interface reads on the positive-going edge. This is a decision to be made by the interface designer: Does the interface generate its own timing or use the edges for timing?

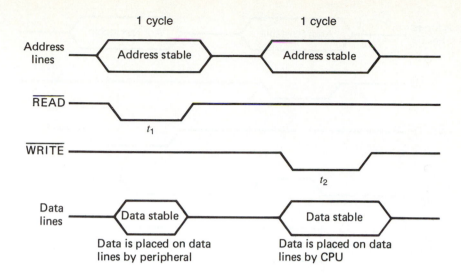

1 cycle   1 cycle

Address
lines — Address stable — Address stable —

$\overline{\text{READ}}$

t_1

$\overline{\text{WRITE}}$

t_2

Data
lines — Data stable — Data stable —

Data is placed on data   Data is placed on data
lines by peripheral   lines by CPU

Note: t_1 and t_2 are fixed in duration.

FIGURE 8.13
Timing signals for synchronous transfers.

Note here that the device being written to or read from must respond during the fixed time period permanently established by the CPU. If a READ is performed, the device must place data on the data lines at once and keep them there while the READ line is active. Similarly, for a WRITE the device must have already read the data by the time that the $\overline{\text{WRITE}}$ line goes high (or must read it when it goes high for edge-triggered flip-flops.)

Synchronous transfers are generally thought to be the fastest way to transfer data and are often used for memory data transfers and sometimes for transferring data to other types of devices. The problem is that all devices must be able to respond at the same speed unless the CPU has READ and WRITE signals of different durations for different devices.[9] To alleviate this problem (that is, to accommodate devices with differing response times), the asynchronous transfer technique is often used.

When the asynchronous bus transfer technique is used, another control line is required, called DATA VALID OR RECEIVED (see Fig. 8.14). This line is controlled by the devices and not by the CPU, however. If there is more than one device on the bus, a tristate driver will be required for each device using this line.[10]

The sequence of timing steps performed in Fig. 8.14 is as follows. To read from the bus, the CPU sets the number of the device on the address lines and then lowers the $\overline{\text{READ}}$ line. The selected device then places data on the data lines and a 1 on the DATA VALID OR RECEIVED line. This tells the CPU that the data are on the lines

---

[9] This would be a complicated strategy. Another bad alternative is for all devices to operate at the speed of the slowest device.

[10] A driver which wire-ORs its output could also be used.

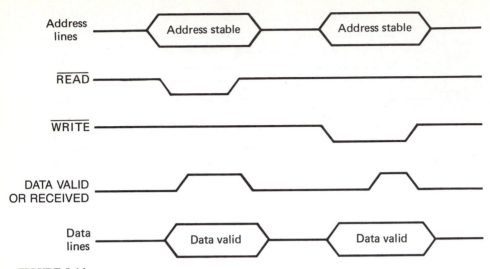

FIGURE 8.14
Timing signals for asynchronous transfers.

and can be read. The CPU cannot read from the data lines until the DATA VALID OR RECEIVED line is a 1. If the device is slow in preparing its data, the CPU must wait until the data are on the data lines and the DATA VALID OR RECEIVED line is raised. Next the CPU reads the data and raises the $\overline{\text{READ}}$ line to a 1. This means the selected device must keep its data on the data line until $\overline{\text{READ}}$ goes to a 1. The selected device then turns off its tristate drivers to the data lines and lowers the DATA VALID OR RECEIVED line.

A WRITE operation is performed similarly. First the CPU places the number of the selected device on the address lines and the data on the data lines. Then the CPU lowers the $\overline{\text{WRITE}}$ line. The selected device now reads the data and raises the DATA VALID OR RECEIVED line. The CPU must keep its data and address lines stable until it receives this signal, so the device can be "slow to read" and still get the data. After the CPU receives the DATA VALID OR RECEIVED high signal, it removes the address and data from the bus and then raises the $\overline{\text{WRITE}}$ line; this allows the selected device to lower the DATA VALID OR RECEIVED line.

The asynchronous procedure involves what is called a *handshake*. The effect is that the CPU tells what device is selected if it is reading or writing and then waits for the selected device to respond (with a handshake) before continuing. This means fast and slow devices can be accomodated on the same bus. This is the reason for the wide use of asynchronous buses.

For both synchronous and asynchronous buses, there are several variations on Figs. 8.13 and 8.14. Instead of separate $\overline{\text{READ}}$ and $\overline{\text{WRITE}}$ lines, a single R/$\overline{W}$ line may be used (1 for READ, 0 for WRITE), and a separate ADDRESS VALID line may be used to indicate when the address is on the address lines. Sometimes there are separate DATA VALID and DATA RECEIVED lines. The principles of synchronous and asynchronous data transfers remain, and the combining or splitting of control lines can be figured out easily if the general principles are understood.

One other strategy is used in some systems. These systems are essentially synchronous but have another control line, generally called a WAIT line, which is controlled by the devices being written to or read from. If a device is too slow to respond to the normal system synchronous timing, it simply activates the WAIT line, and this forces the bus master (a microprocessor, for example) to hold up its timing cycle until WAIT is returned to normal (i.e., turned off). A system of this type is called *semisynchronous*. (As is often the case with control signals, the control line is commonly $\overline{\text{WAIT}}$, which is normally high and pulled low when activated.)

8.5 I/O ADDRESSING TECHNIQUES

There are two general techniques commonly used to identify input/output (I/O) devices on the bus. The first keeps the I/O device addresses (or numbers) separate from memory addresses; this is often called *isolated I/O*. The second, called *memory-mapped I/O*, mixes memory addresses with I/O device numbers.

In the isolated I/O technique, I/O devices are each given a separate number on the bus. For instance, a printer would be assigned device number 3, a keyboard number 4, a disk drive number 5, and so on. A number is placed in binary on the address section of the bus when an I/O device is to be read from or written to by the CPU. The I/O devices may have a separate I/O address bus, as shown in Fig. 8.15(*a*), or the I/O devices may share the address section of the bus with memory, as in Fig. 8.15(*b*). In either case, the I/O device number is placed on the bus by the CPU, and the control lines tell the I/O device whether to place data on the lines or to read data. If the I/O devices share bus lines with the main (IC) memory, the control signals must tell whether an address on the bus is for I/O devices or for memory.

The 8080, 8086, 80286, 80386, 80486 microprocessor series provides an example of an I/O system that has device numbers on the address lines shared with memory, as in Fig. 8.15(*b*). Figure 8.16 shows the sections of the 8080 bus, which we will use as an initial example. To read from a memory device, the 8080 places the memory address to be read from on A_0 to A_{15} and then lowers $\overline{\text{MEMR}}$; next the memory places the contents at this address on data wires DB_0 to DB_7. To write into memory, the 8080 places the address to be written into on A_0 to A_{15}, places the data to be written on DB_0 to DB_7, and lowers $\overline{\text{MEMW}}$; the data are then written at the selected location.

The 8080 uses only eight of the address lines A_0 to A_{15} to select I/O devices; these lines are A_0 to A_7. As a result, only 256 I/O devices can be used. Suppose a keyboard is device number 3_{10}. Then, to read from the keyboard, the CPU places 00000011 on A_7 to A_0 and then lowers $\overline{\text{I/O R}}$; next the keyboard places an 8-bit character (data) on DB_0 to DB_7.[11]

As another example, if a printer is device number 5 and the CPU wishes to print a character, the CPU places 00000101 on A_7 to A_0, places the character on DB_0 to DB_7, and then lowers $\overline{\text{I/O W}}$. This bus is synchronous, so the devices must read

---

[11] The most significant bit is A_7; the least significant bit is A_0. For numbers on DB_7 to DB_0, the sign bit goes on DB_7, and the least significant bit is DB_0.

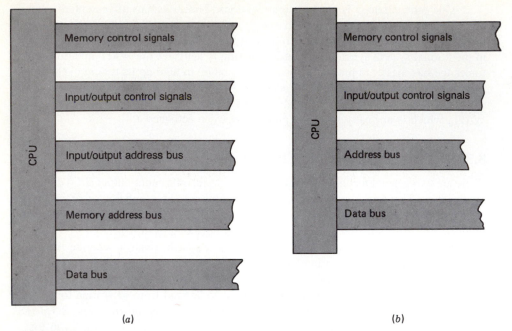

(a)   (b)

FIGURE 8.15
Bus structure for input/output and memory. (a) Separate memory and input/output address lines.
(b) Shared memory and input/output address bus.

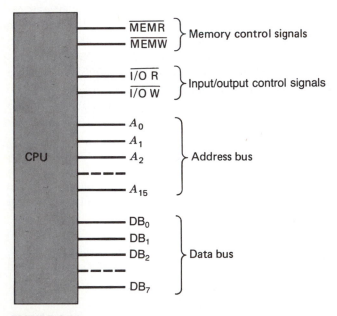

FIGURE 8.16
8080 series memory and input/output bus sections.

or write data at the specified time since the $\overline{\text{I/O W}}$ and $\overline{\text{I/O R}}$ lines are lowered only for a time determined by the clock rate of the 8080.

The 8080 is only the original member of a line of microprocessors produced by Intel. Other processors have numbers such as 8085, 8086, 80286,80386, and 80486. Each model has particular features. The bus interfaces for different microprocessors are compatible; however, the speed of transfer is determined by the clock rate of the particular chip, which varies from device line to device line. (A memory or I/O device that responds in 10 ns could interface any of the current devices.)

This is a good example of the consistency of interfacing principles for buses from upwards-compatible systems. The 80386 has 32-bit data, so the data would be placed on lines DB_0 to DB_{31}. It also has 30 address lines, so A_0–A_{15} would become A_0–A_{29}; there are also BYTE ENABLE pins to select from the 4 bytes in the data lines (DB_0–DB_{31}). Address lines A_0–A_7 provide the same 256 I/O addresses (called 8-bit ports) as for the 8080, and the DB_0–DB_7 lines work the same for byte IN/OUT instructions. The changes are primarily in the ability of the 80386 to transfer 8, 16, or 32 bits at a time on the DB_0–DB_{31} lines and to address 2^{32} bytes of memory directly, as opposed to 2^{16} for the 8080.

8.6   MEMORY-MAPPED I/O

The second general technique for addressing I/O devices is called *memory-mapped I/O*. When this is used, the I/O devices are assigned addresses in memory. These locations must not conflict with addresses given to memory devices such as ROM and RAM chips. The I/O devices are read from and written into by using the same control lines as for the IC memory chips.

The memory-mapped I/O technique requires making a map of memory showing which locations are devoted to IC memory and which to I/O devices. Figure 8.17 shows a memory map for a bus with 16 address bits and 8 data bits. The computer has a 4K-word read-only memory, a 4K-word random-access memory, a printer, and a keyboard. The ROM is connected to addresses 0 to 4095 and the RAM to addresses 4096 to 8191; the keyboard is given locations 9472 and 9473, and the printer is given locations 9671 and 9672. (The keyboard and printer are each given two locations because each requires a status register; we discuss this later.)

The programmer for this system must know where the RAM, ROM, keyboard, and printer are located. To print a character, the particular address allocated to the printer must be used; to read a character from the keyboard, the address given to the keyboard must be employed.

Memory-mapped computers have no I/O instructions in their list of instructions. To read a character from a keyboard, the keyboard address is simply used; any instruction that reads from memory can read from that address. Data from a keyboard would be added to or ANDed with the current contents of an accumulator by using a single instruction, for example; or a character from the keyboard could be simply transferred into an accumulator. The PDP-11 series and the 6800 and 68000 microprocessors are examples of memory-mapped computers.

In systems having separate I/O control lines and device numbers, the CPU will have specific I/O instructions. For example, the 8080–80386 series has IN and

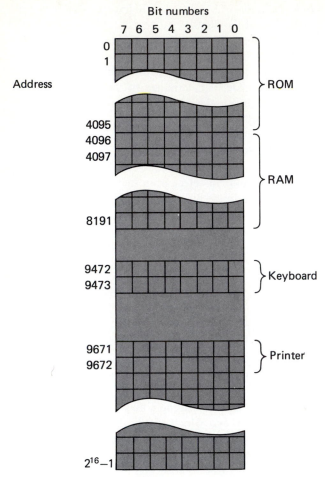

FIGURE 8.17
Map of memory layout for memory-mapped I/O.

OUT instructions, and these specifically cause transfers to and from I/O devices. The programmer must then know the I/O device numbers.

Advocates of isolated I/O point out that interfaces may be simpler and that programmers' use of I/O instructions seems more natural. Advocates of memory-mapped I/O claim that the CPU is simpler, as is the bus, and that the instructions in the CPU for data manipulation can be used for I/O data, simplifying programs.

MEMORY-MAPPED I/O IN 68000 SERIES MICROPROCESSORS. The 68000 is a memory-mapped asynchronous microcomputer. A section of the 68000 bus is shown in Fig. 8.18(*a*). This is a bus with 24 address lines and 16 data lines. There are a number of control signals, five of which are shown. The 68000 is part of a series that begins with the 6800 and progresses through many versions, including the 68040, which has

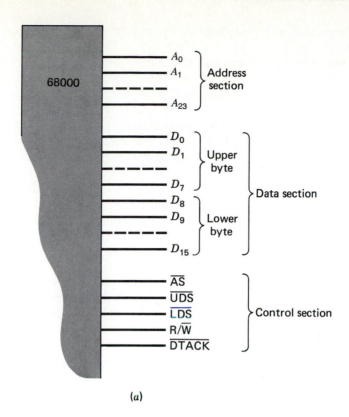

(a)

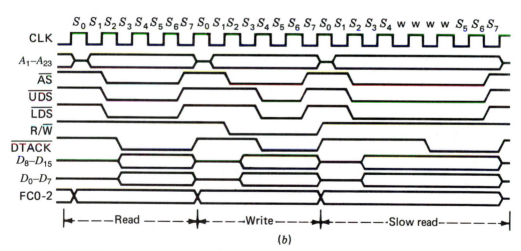

(b)

FIGURE 8.18
68000 bus signal. (a) Bus layout. (b) Read-write timing.

32 address lines and 32 data lines. The principles are the same and interfaces are upwards-compatible.

The 68000 has a 16-bit word, which is the normal unit for data transfer. However, each word is divided into two 8-bit bytes, called the *upper byte* and *lower byte*. Memory and I/O READS and WRITES can transfer either a complete 16-bit word or an upper or lower byte. To indicate an I/O device or memory, whether 1 or 2 bytes are to be transferred, two control signals, $\overline{UDS}$ (upper data strobe) and $\overline{LDS}$ (lower data strobe) are used. If $\overline{LDS}$ is low, data are placed on lines D_0 to D_7; if $\overline{UDS}$ is low, data lines D_8 to D_{15} are used. If both are low, an entire 16-bit word is transferred.

Figure 8.18(*b*) shows the timing for a READ and a WRITE. Since the 68000 is memory-mapped, I/O devices use addresses in memory, and data transfers to and from I/O devices use the same timing signals as memory transfers.

Let us assume the 68000 wants to read a 16-bit word from a disk drive interface that uses location $000FF6_{16}$. The timing would be as follows [refer to Fig. 8.18(*b*)]:

1. The 68000 places the address 000FF6 on the address lines, lowers $\overline{AS}$, $\overline{UDS}$, and $\overline{LDS}$ and makes R/$\overline{W}$ a 1. A 0 on $\overline{AS}$ tells the devices on the bus that the address is valid, both $\overline{UDS}$ and $\overline{LDS}$ low indicates all 16 data lines are to be used, and a 1 on R/$\overline{W}$ indicates a READ operation.
2. The disk drive interface places 16 bits of data on D_0 to D_{15} and then lowers $\overline{DTACK}$ (for data acknowledge), which indicates the data are on lines D_0 to D_{15}.
3. The 68000 reads the data from D_0 to D_{15}.
4. The 68000 raises $\overline{AS}$ to indicate that the disk interface can release the data because they have been read.
5. The disk interface turns off its tristate drivers to lines D_0 to D_{15} and raises $\overline{DTACK}$.

A WRITE is performed similarly. Assume a tape drive interface accepts data on address $00076F4_{16}$. When data are written into the tape drive interface, the following occurs:

1. The 68000 places 00076F4 on address lines A_1 to A_{23}, places the data to be transferred on D_0 to D_{15}, and then lowers $\overline{AS}$, $\overline{UDS}$, $\overline{LDS}$, and R/$\overline{W}$. This indicates that the address is valid, all lines D_0 to D_{15} are to be used, and the operation is a WRITE.
2. The tape drive interface reads the data from D_0 to D_{15}.
3. After it has the data, the tape drive interface lowers $\overline{DTACK}$ to indicate that the data transfer is complete.
4. The 68000 releases its address from the address bus and the data from the data bus and then raises $\overline{AS}$, R/$\overline{W}$, $\overline{UDS}$, and $\overline{LDS}$.

Note that these transfers are asynchronous because the I/O device or memory must signal the acceptance of data or the placing of data on D_0 to D_{15} by using $\overline{DTACK}$. The 68000 will not proceed until $\overline{DTACK}$ is lowered. This is shown in Fig 8.18(*b*) by the "slow read" indicated where $\overline{DTACK}$ is not lowered quickly, resulting in a longer read time.

8.7   INTERRUPTS IN INPUT/OUTPUT SYSTEMS

In most systems, it is necessary for the computer to determine when a peripheral has data and is ready to be read. (For example, when a keyboard key is depressed, the keyboard has data and is ready to be read.) There are two distinct ways to determine the states of peripherals:

1. By polling or examining each peripheral in turn, using program instructions to test each device.

2. Using an *interrupt system*. In this case the peripherals are provided with one or more interrupt lines on the bus. When a peripheral requires servicing, it raises the interrupt line. The computer then stops executing the current program and jumps to an interrupt routine (a section of program that services the interrupt, reading from or writing into the peripheral.) The computer then jumps back to execute the instruction following the one it was executing before the interrupt was serviced.

Polling peripherals requires each peripheral to be be tested by the CPU at regular intervals to see if it has data. This is time consuming and can only be used for a few peripherals. In many cases, there will be too many devices for this scheme to be successful. Or there may be a great amount of computation to be performed, so that continually taking time out to examine the status of input/output devices cannot be tolerated. For these reasons, interrupt systems are commonly used.

The operation of such a system can best be shown by an example. Suppose that we have a computer system with a keyboard, a printer, and an input from an ADC measuring temperature in a physics experiment. A great deal of computation is required to process each temperature reading from the ADC. The operator of the keyboard examines the results of the computations, which are output on the printer, and occasionally the operator comments using the keyboard. These comments are to be printed by the printer along with the temperature and the results of the calculation. In this case the keyboard inputs are made infrequently, the printer is kept quite busy, and we assume that the ADC inputs are read at fairly frequent intervals.

The interrupt system works as follows. The computer normally is processing the inputs from the ADC. Each time a key on the keyboard is depressed, however, an interrupt signal is generated by the keyboard, the program in operation is interrupted, the keyboard is serviced, and the program that was interrupted is thus returned to. In addition, a short list of characters to be printed may be stored in the computer, and the program adds to this list as it gathers results. Whenever the printer can print, it generates an interrupt, current program operation is interrupted long enough to service the printer by giving it another character (or line) to print, and the original program operation then continues at the point at which it had been interrupted. The ADC will also generate interrupts, which must be serviced by reading the output, and the readings are processed as soon as time is available.

To effect this procedure, there are some features an interrupt system should have. For instance, it may be necessary to turn off the interrupt feature of the printer, because when there is nothing to print, the printer would simply generate many time-consuming interrupts. (It can always print when there is nothing to print.) It might be necessary to turn off the entire interrupt system for a short time, since during servicing of the keyboard, an interrupt from the printer might cause an interrupt of an interrupt.

To understand the interrupt feature more closely, note that the following things must be done each time an interrupt is generated:

1. The state of the program[12] in operation when the interrupt is executed and the location of the next instruction in memory must be saved. Then the program can be reentered when the interrupt servicing program is finished.
2. The device that generated the interrupts must be identified.
3. The CPU must jump to the program that will service the interrupt.
4. When the interrupt has been serviced, the state of the program that was interrupted must be restored.
5. The original program's operation must be reinitiated at the point at which it was interrupted.

Discussion of how the interrupted program is handled and how returns are made to this program is deferred to Chap. 10 since more information is first required about program execution. The mechanism for interrupt generation and identifying the device to be serviced can be dealt with here, however.

An interrupt is initiated by a device placing a 1 on an interrupt wire in the bus. This notifies the CPU that a device wishes to be serviced. The CPU then completes the instruction it is executing and transfers control to a section of program designed to service the interrupt.

In some microprocessors, the various devices can then be polled by examining *status registers,* each in turn, until the interrupting device is located. This device is then serviced. These status registers can be assigned memory locations (for memory-mapped I/O systems) or device numbers (for isolated I/O systems). The status registers have a bit position that is set to 1 when the associated peripheral is ready.

In the 8080, 80286, 80386, 80486, and the 68000 series microcomputers, as well as in the PDP-11 microcomputer and VAX series, the place in memory that holds the address of the service program for the particular device that generated the interrupt is read into the CPU by the interrupt device. This is called a *vectored interrupt.* In effect, the interrupting device tells the CPU "who did it" and does not wait to be asked. The approach used for vectored interrupts is to have the processor jump to the address in memory given by the interrupt vector placed on the bus data lines. (The peripherals are assigned addresses in memory that correspond to their numbers.) At this address is an instruction word that causes a jump to the service routine for the peripheral. This jump instruction is in effect the first instruction in the service routine.

In all systems the final instruction(s) in the service routine restores the status of the CPU when it was interrupted and causes a jump to the next instruction to be executed.

---

[12] "The state of the program" basically refers to the contents of the registers in the CPU.

There can be a problem when several devices generate a 1 signal on the interrupt wire at the same time. If the devices are polled, the polling order determines who gets serviced first; a device not serviced will continue to interrupt until it is serviced. For the vectored interrupt, however, if two devices attempted to write their identifiers into the CPU at the same time, they might overwrite each other, so a scheme must be devised to inform the CPU which device to service. This is accomplished by chip(s)[13] external to the CPU, which set a priority for the devices and cause only the highest-priority device requesting an interrupt to place its number on the bus.

As microcomputer system become larger and more peripheral devices are used, the interface design problem increases. To use the microprocessor CPU chip to its utmost ability, it is necessary to use an interrupt system for peripheral devices so that the CPU is not burdened with polling and servicing peripherals continuously. To remove the load of servicing peripherals from the CPU, several microprocessor manufacturers produce separate chips that are I/O processors and work closely with the CPU in handling peripheral servicing. Other important chips now produced to facilitate peripheral handling convert serial input signals (such as the serial ASCII signals) to parallel and place the parallel form on the bus, as well as converting from parallel to serial (to drive some printers and modems). Chips are also produced to aid in interrupt processing, including chips to select the highest-priority peripheral demanding service.

Figure 8.19 shows a block design of a system based on the 8086 microprocessor chip. (This system is similar to IBM's personal computer (PC) system, which uses the 8088.[14]) Examination of this layout reveal how chips are assembled to interface devices in larger systems.

Figure 8.19 shows the parts of the 8086 microprocessor:

1. An 8234 clock generator produces the clock signal for the 8086 and is involved in resets.

2. The 8081 I/O processor (IOP) handles interrupts for the 8086. (The 8086 can be interfaced without this chip; it simply takes some I/O processing load from the 8086.)

3. The 8288 bus controller buffers control signals and handles the time multiplexing of the control signals (the 8086 uses the same lines for address lines and control lines, producing control signals to tell which is being output at a given time).

4. The 8282 latches hold the address information and provide tristate drivers for the bus. This is necessary for two reasons. First, the 8086 outputs are not capable of driving many other circuits. Second, the 8086 time-multiplexes its address signals, and the latches are used to hold the address while control signals are output on the same lines.

5. The 8286 transceivers provide tristate drivers and considerable drive capability for the data bus and receivers to read from the data bus.

---

[13] The IC packages used range from gate arrays that examine and allocate priority to programmable interface controllers that contain ROMs with programs for the specific interfaces to be implemented.
[14] The 8086 handles data 16 bits at a time whereas the 8088 has 8-bit data paths, so a 16-bit data bus would be used for the 8086.

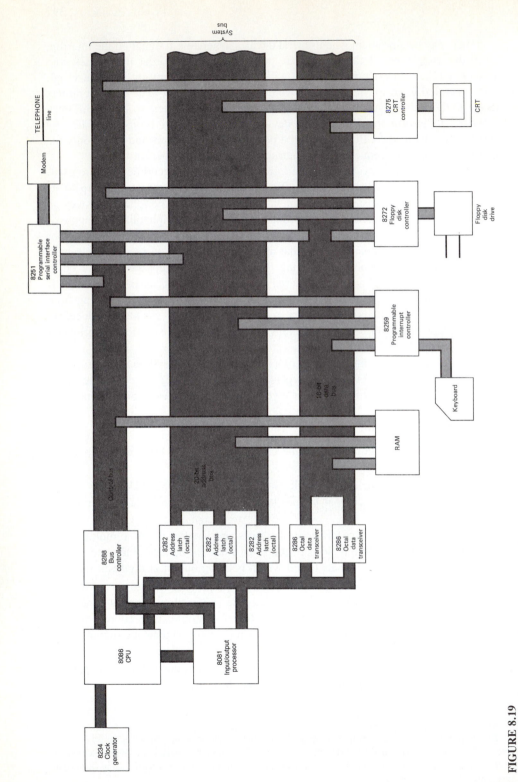

FIGURE 8.19
8086/8088 microcomputer system showing bus layout.

398

6. The 8259 is a programmable interrupt handler that examines demands for service from the peripherals, determines the highest-priority demand, and then interrupts the 8086, outputting a "vector" telling which peripheral requires service.

7. The 8259 programmable parallel interface controller handles keyboard interrupts. The term *programmable* means that the input/output configuration and data-handling functions of the chip are set up by means of data transfers from the 8086 under program control.

8. The 8251 programmable serial interface controller is used to handle serial data and to provide control signals for modems. This chip is programmable, and a register in the 8251 that is loaded from a program over the data lines by the 8086 is used to control such parameters as:

   (*a*) the number of stop bits in a character transmission,
   (*b*) the speed of transmission and reception (controlled by a clock and a divide action, and
   (*c*) whether parity is odd or even.

9. The floppy disk and CRT controllers are special interface chips made to service particular devices.

8.8   STANDARD BUSES

There have been many attempts to standardize on buses, particularly by such organizations as the IEEE and the National Bureau of Standards. Most buses that have become standards were developed by computer and electronic concerns and were used and adopted by several manufacturers before the standards organization developed an official document.

Note that these bus standards do not simply specify pin connections and line operation procedures, but also connectors and printed-circuit board sizes. Thus, a system built around one of these buses can add printed-circuit boards containing more memory, interfacing for I/O devices, and other features, as long as the board and bus operation for the board meet the standard specifications. So when the organization of Fig. 7.14 is used, the connectors, boards, and interfaces are all as prescribed by the standard.

Standard buses take several forms. The original IBM PC bus is designed around the 8088 chip and the PC AT bus (also called the *industry standard bus*) is an extension of the PC bus designed around the 80286 chip. Some buses are designed to be chip-independent so that any chip can be used. Such buses are generally complex but are widely used.

Bus standards have arisen for different reasons. The IBM PC bus was designed so that "standard" boards could be designed by IBM and other manufacturers and plugged into the PC to provide additional features such as I/O interfaces, and memory expansion. The STD bus was designed by Pro-Log and Mostek as a general-purpose bus and has been used with a number of different chips. The STD bus standard is also an IEEE standard (P-96).

Figure 8.20(*a*) shows the signals for the PC bus. (The 8088 signals can easily be located in this bus). There are 62 signals, and a 62-pin connector is used. The data bus section is 8 bits, and the address section is 20 bits. The PC AT bus [see

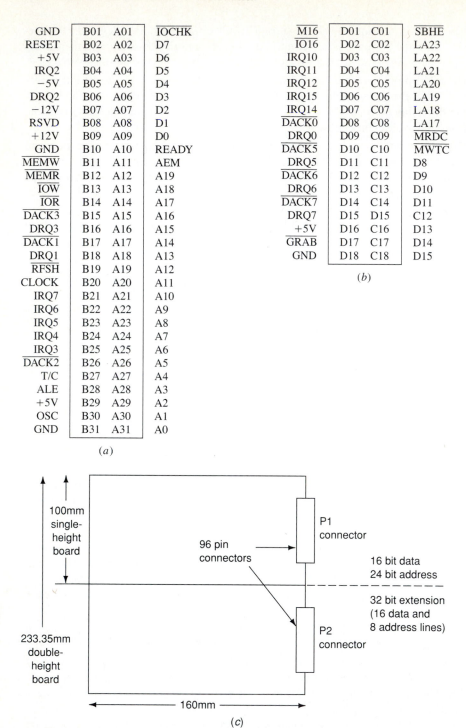

GND	B01	A01	IOCHK
RESET	B02	A02	D7
+5V	B03	A03	D6
IRQ2	B04	A04	D5
−5V	B05	A05	D4
DRQ2	B06	A06	D3
−12V	B07	A07	D2
RSVD	B08	A08	D1
+12V	B09	A09	D0
GND	B10	A10	READY
MEMW	B11	A11	AEM
MEMR	B12	A12	A19
IOW	B13	A13	A18
IOR	B14	A14	A17
DACK3	B15	A15	A16
DRQ3	B16	A16	A15
DACK1	B17	A17	A14
DRQ1	B18	A18	A13
RFSH	B19	A19	A12
CLOCK	B20	A20	A11
IRQ7	B21	A21	A10
IRQ6	B22	A22	A9
IRQ5	B23	A23	A8
IRQ4	B24	A24	A7
IRQ3	B25	A25	A6
DACK2	B26	A26	A5
T/C	B27	A27	A4
ALE	B28	A28	A3
+5V	B29	A29	A2
OSC	B30	A30	A1
GND	B31	A31	A0

(a)

M16	D01	C01	SBHE
IO16	D02	C02	LA23
IRQ10	D03	C03	LA22
IRQ11	D04	C04	LA21
IRQ12	D05	C05	LA20
IRQ15	D06	C06	LA19
IRQ14	D07	C07	LA18
DACK0	D08	C08	LA17
DRQ0	D09	C09	MRDC
DACK5	D10	C10	MWTC
DRQ5	D11	C11	D8
DACK6	D12	C12	D9
DRQ6	D13	C13	D10
DACK7	D14	C14	D11
DRQ7	D15	D15	C12
+5V	D16	C16	D13
GRAB	D17	C17	D14
GND	D18	C18	D15

(b)

100mm single-height board

96 pin connectors

P1 connector

16 bit data
24 bit address

32 bit extension
(16 data and
8 address lines)

P2 connector

233.35mm double-height board

160mm

(c)

FIGURE 8.20
Bus examples. (a) PC bus. (b) PC at bus extension to PC bus. (c) VME board showing boards can be of two sizes.

	VME bus	Multibus II	Futurebus	STD Bus	IBM PC/AT
Data Paths (primary bits)	non-multiplexed 16	multiplexed 32	multiplexed 32	non-multiplexed 8	non-multiplexed PC = 8
(secondary bits)	32,24,16,8	32,24,16,8	32,24,16,8	–	AT = 16
Primary addr. range	2^{24}	2^{32}	2^{32}	2^{16} (or 2^{32} max)	PC = 2^{20}, AT = 2^{24}
Standard number	IEEE P1014	IEEE P1296	IEEE P896.1	IEEE P961	
Board dims. (mm)	233.4 × 160	233.4 × 220	366.7 × 280	4.5 × 6.5 in.	PC = 4.2 × 13.2 in. AT = 4.8 × 13.2 in.
Board area (cm²)	373	514	1027	25 in²	PC = 51 in² AT = 106 in²
Connectors (pins)	96 + 96	96	96	56	PC = 62 pin AT = 36 pin
Bus drivers	TTL	TTL	special (BTL)	TTL	TTL
Power supply	+5V, ±12V	+5V	+5V	+5V	+5V
Bus control	Async	Semisync	Async	Semisync	Semisync

FIGURE 8.20
(d) Table of bus characteristics.

Fig. 8.20(*b*)] is an extension of this and calls for a separate 36-pin connector, in addition to the connector in 8.20(*a*), so that the total number of connections is 62 + 36 = 98. Figure 8.20(*c*) shows a board and connectors for the VME bus, which uses the same scheme and two connectors.

The PC AT bus allows use of only the original 8-bit PC data line section used by the original PC board, which is roughly half the size of the PC AT board. This means that the original PC boards for printers, disk interfaces, and other peripherals can still be used (only 8 bits can be transferred each time on this section). A full PC AT transfer is 16 bits, and 24-bit addresses can also be used, versus only 20 address lines for the original PC boards.

The VME board arrangement also uses two sections, and half-size boards that interface only one connector can be used. These connectors, are pin in-socket connectors, which require connectors with pins on the circuit boards; the PC AT uses card edge connectors, which are simply rectangular printed areas on the edge of printed-circuit boards. Fig. 8.20(*d*) shows the characteristics of several bus standards.

Each bus standard has several features that distinguish it from the others. Among these are the number of address wires, which determines the address space for the bus unless the addresses can be multiplexed. The number of data wires is also very important because it determines the speed at which transfers on the bus can be made. Whether the bus is asynchronous or synchronous is also important, as is the presence of such features as DMA, number of interrupt levels and how interrupts are handled, and so forth. Another important factor is whether there is a "bus master" controlling the bus, or whether the bus is a *multimaster* bus, where different "masters" can take control.

A number of buses are important historically as indicated by the number of these buses in existence. These include the IBM PC and PC AT buses, the DEC buses, the VME bus, Multibus I and II, NUBUS, the IBM Microchannel, the Macintosh II Nubus, Futurebus, and the IEEE EISA bus.

The number of pins on the connectors of buses has steadily grown due to the demand for longer addresses and wider data paths. An example is the progression from the PC bus, which as 8-bit data paths and 20-bit addresses with 62 pins, to the PC AT bus, with 16 data lines, 24 address lines and 98 pins. The Microchannel, the bus associated with the IBM PS/2, has a basic 90-pin segment for 8-bit systems, a 22-pin 16-bit extension, and a 62-pin 32-bit extension.

In the transfer of data from a transmitting module, or *talker*, to a receiving module, or *listener*, certain basic problems arise in the operation of any bus.[15] These problems are solved by a handshaking procedure whereby talker and listener interact using the control lines. It is convenient to describe this procedure with a flowchart, as shown in Fig. 8.21. This diagram shows that three control lines, called DAV, NRFD,

---

[15] These problems concern how the listener knows when data are on the bus and how the talker knows when the listener has received the data. The bus described here is an asynchronous bus. Microprocessors and minicomputers often use synchronous buses, where one wire in the bus contains a clock and the clock signal is used to time data transfers. In these systems, the talker must place the data on the data wires, and the listener must be ready to receive data when the clock edge arrives. A synchronous system is faster and simpler but less flexible.

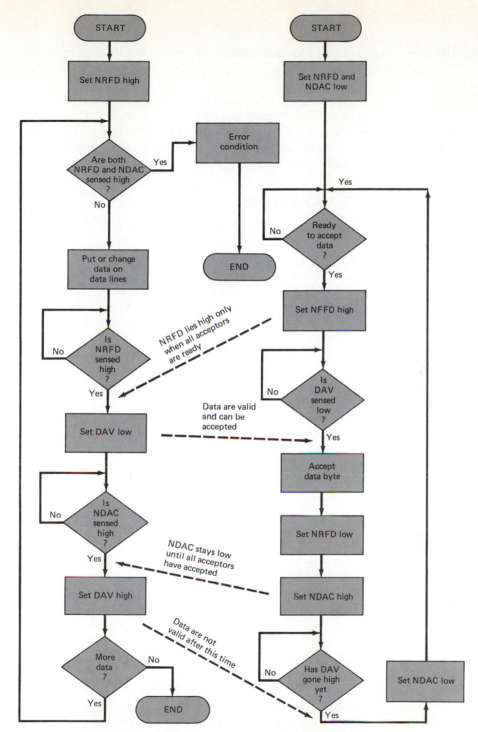

The DAV line is controlled by the talker, NRFD and NDAC by the listeners.

FIGURE 8.21
Flowchart for handshaking on a bus. (*Hewlett-Packard Co.*)

and NDAC, are used to control each data transfer. The talkers and listeners each raise and lower the control signals, as shown by the flow chart, and the talker places data on the data bus at the appropriate time.

The necessary control circuitry to implement this handshaking and the other required functions must be provided by each module's interface circuitry. It is possible to design a line of input/output equipment and to interface each device to the same bus by using the interface specification. IC manufacturers often furnish single chips made to provide the necessary logic for an interface.

8.9 INTERFACING A KEYBOARD

In this section we describe the interfacing of a keyboard with a bus. The interface developed will be a straightforward, typical design.

There are two basic bus designs, one for Intel chips and one for Motorola chips. The Intel 8080, 8085, 8086, 8088, 80286, 80386, 80486, and related series all use the Intel interface, as do the Z-80, Z-8000 family. Chips in the 6800, 6802, 6809, 68000, 68020, 68030, 68040 family use the Motorola-type interface. It is very easy to convert from one to the other with no delay problems. The Intel-type interface will be discussed first, and the Motorola interface will follow.

Figure 8.22 shows the bus signals. Typical 1-byte I/O transfer will be made from a keyboard and to a printer. The interface will be to a chip. The bus has three basic classes of input/output lines: address lines A_{15} to A_0, data lines D_7 to D_0, and control lines such as $\overline{WR}$, DBIN, and $\overline{I/O\ R}$.

The address signals are used both to address the IC memory and to select which input device is to be written to or read from. The data lines are bidirectional; that is, data are written into the chip by using D_7 to D_0. These same lines are also used to output data to memories and input/output devices. Bidirectional lines are widely used in buses for computers, the main advantage being fewer connections to and from chips and fewer pins on chips. If data wires D_7 to D_0 were not bidirectional, a set of both eight input wires and eight output wires would be required instead of the eight bidirectional wires.[16]

Using bidirectional data lines means that the various system components such as memories and keyboards must be carefully controlled and timed in their operations so that only one device writes on a wire at a time and so that system components know exactly when to examine wires with signals on them.

Each input and output device that interfaces the system is given a unique *device number*. The numbers given devices can have up to 8 bits. Thus, 256 different devices can be handled directly.

The microprocessor system selects and input-output device as follows:

1. The number of the selected device is placed on address lines A_7 to A_0.
2. If the device is to be read from by the bus, $\overline{I/O\ R}$ (which is normally 1) is made a 0. While $\overline{I/O\ R}$ is a 0, the selected device to be read from places its data on D_7

---

[16] Three-state drivers are normally used to drive these lines.

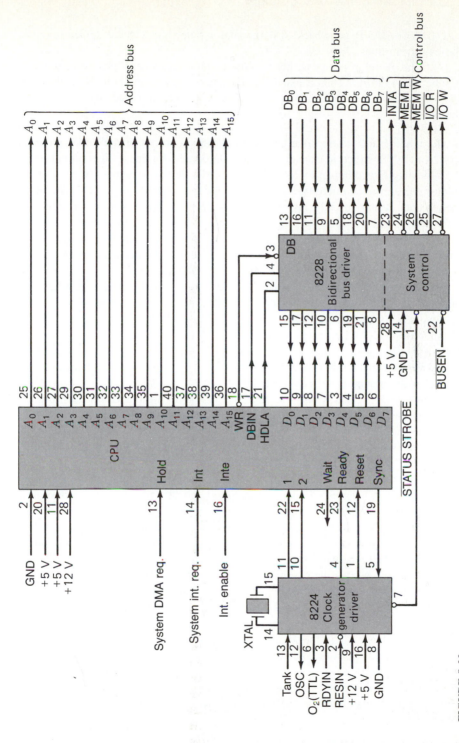

FIGURE 8.22
Microprocessor bus signals.

to D_0. When $\overline{\text{I/O R}}$ goes back to its normal 1 state, the selected device removes the data from lines D_7 to D_0.[17]

If the micro processor wishes to output data to a device, it places the device's number on A_7 to A_0. Then it places the data to be output on D_7 to D_0 and makes $\overline{\text{I/O W}}$, which is normally 1, a 0. The selected device then reads these data from the bus.

The reading and writing operations for the microprocessor are under program control. An OUT instruction executed by the microprocessor causes the outputting of data to a device. Executing an IN instruction causes a device to be read from. The accumulator register in the microprocessor system receives data during an IN instruction and sends data during an OUT instruction. If an IN instruction is executed, the data from the selected device are read onto D_7 to D_0 and from there into the accumulator. If an OUT instruction is executed, the data are read from the microprocessor system's accumulator onto D_7 to D_0, and the selected device accepts the data on D_7 to D_0. (This is the same accumulator used for arithmetic operations.)

An interface design for the keyboard of Fig. 7.1–7.3 is shown in Fig. 8.23. The keyboard is device number 1, or binary 00000001. Therefore, the lines A_7 to A_0 are 0's and A_0 is a 1 when the keyboard is selected. The NAND gate in Fig. 8.23 shows these inputs to be NANDed along with $\overline{\text{I/O R}}$. When $\overline{\text{I/O R}}$ is a 0, the 8080 bus is saying, "Place the selected device's data on D_7 to D_0." In this design, if A_7 to A_0 contain 00000001 and $\overline{\text{I/OR}}$ is a 0, then the output of the NAND gate becomes a 0. This enables the tristate drivers connected to K_7 to K_0, the keyboard output from the flip-flops in Fig. 7.3. As a result, the values of K_7 to K_0 are placed on bus lines D_7 to D_0 where the 8080 bus can read them (into its accumulator).

Notice that the output of the NAND gate is normally a 1, which disables the tristate drivers so that they have high impedance and write nothing on bus lines D_7 to D_0.

A major question now arises: At any given time the operator of the keyboard may or may not have depressed a *key*, so that the keyboard may or may not have new information. If the keyboard is simply read, the microprocessor cannot tell whether the character supplied is new or old. (The same key could be pressed twice in succession.) To compensate for this, a system is used in which a *keyboard status word* is read by the bus and will tell whether a new character is ready to be read from the keyboard. The scheme shown here is the one most used for this kind of interface.

Figure 8.24 shows the *status word generator* interface for the keyboard. We have given this keyboard status word generator the device number 2. The keyboard status word is used as follows. If a new character is available from the keyboard, the status word will have a 1 in the D_7 position. If there is no new keyboard character, a 0 will be in the D_7 position. The remaining bits, D_0 to D_6, of the keyboard status word will always be 0s.

The interface operates as follows. The program in the microprocessor reads the status word (an IN instruction is executed). The accumulator now contains the status

---

[17] This $\overline{\text{I/O R}}$ line corresponds to the $\overline{\text{READ}}$ line in Fig. 8.13; the $\overline{\text{I/O W}}$ line corresponds to the $\overline{\text{WRITE}}$ line in that figure.

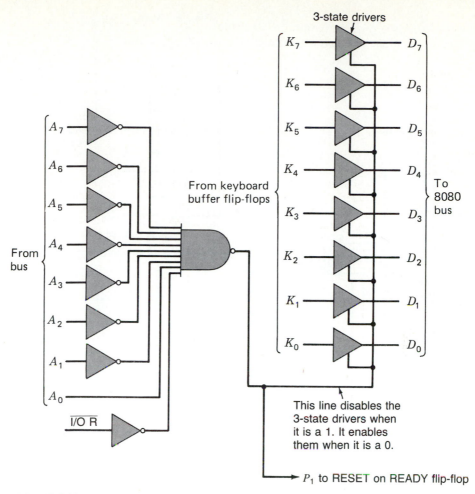

FIGURE 8.23
Interfacing a keyboard to a microprocessor.

word, and the program sees whether it has a 1, in which case the keyboard should be read. If the status word is all 0s, the program goes on to other programs or devices. If it has nothing else to do, it simply continues to read the status word until a 1 is found.

The operation of the keyboard status word interface is shown in Fig. 8.24. When a key is depressed, the READY flip-flop is set to a 1, as shown in Fig. 7.3. Therefore, when I/O R is made a 0, indicating a device READ, and the device number on A_7 to A_0 is 00000010, the NAND gate output in Fig. 8.24 goes to a 0, enabling the tristate devices. As a result, a 10000000 is placed on D_7 to D_0, indicating that the keyboard is ready to be read.

When the keyboard is read, the READY flip-flop is cleared (reset) by the signal generated in Fig. 8.23. Therefore, if keyboard status words are read in the interval

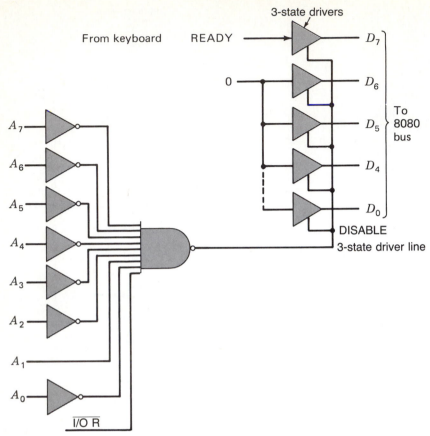

FIGURE 8.24
Keyboard status word generator.

between when the keyboard is read and when a key is depressed, the output on D_7 to D_0 will be all 0s.

The described use of a status register in the interface circuitry to give the status of an input/output device to the CPU is the most widely used technique for interfacing of this sort. In more complicated input/output devices, such as disk memories, there are more bits in the status word that have a meaning, and these bits are set and reset by the processor and disk controller as operations are sequenced.

Motorola uses somewhat different bus control signals. First, since an I/O device is interfaced in the same manner as memory chips and simply has addresses in memory for the data inputs and for status registers, the addresses are longer and run 2 or more bytes. Thus, the A_i lines will go from A_0 to A_{20}, for example.

In the Motorola 68000 series, 16 bits can be transferred as well as 8 bits, so there are 16 D_i lines. Two control signals, $\overline{UDS}$ and $\overline{LDS}$, tell whether the high byte or both bytes ($\overline{UDS}$ and $\overline{LDS}$ both low) are to be transferred [refer to Fig. 8.18 (b)]. When Intel interfaces are extended to handle 16 bits, a control line called $\overline{BHE}$ is added, which causes a full 16-bit transfer when low. If the $\overline{BHE}$ is high, the least significant A_i bit (A_0) tells whether the least significant or the most significant byte is to be transferred.

Program Control of Keyboard Interface

The interface design for the keyboard is intended to be under program control. Thus, a section of the program in the microprocessor will examine the keyboard status register to see if the keyboard has data; if it does, data are read from the keyboard.

Table 8.1 shows a section of program for a microprocessor that reads from a keyboard. The microprocessor has an 8-bit byte at each address in memory. Each op (operation) code, which tells what the instruction is to do, is a single byte in memory. An IN instruction with op code 11011011 (binary) tells the microprocessor to read from an input/output device. The number of the device (device code) immediately follows the IN instruction's op code in the next byte.

In Table 8.1 the presentation of the program listing is arranged as follows. The program in assembly language is to the right. The program as actually stored is in the two left columns, which lists addresses in memory followed by the contents of each address in hexadecimal. The *label* column lists names for locations in the memory, enabling programs to use names in memory instead of actual numeric addresses.

This program starts at location 030 in memory. At this location is the value DB, the op code for the IN instruction. Comments (shown to the right) are always preceded by a slash so the assembler will ignore them. The location 030 in memory is given the label KEYSTAT.

In location 031 is the device number 2; therefore, the microprocessor will read location 030, find the IN instruction op code, and read location 031, finding in it the device number 2. The microprocessor will then place the value 2 on the address lines and issue an input/output device READ sequence on the bus.

This will result in the status register interface placing 00000000 on the data lines if there is no character to be read from the keyboard, and placing 10000000 if there is a character. This value will be read by the microprocessor into its accumulator, completing the instruction.

The next instruction is an ANI instruction with op code E6. The ANI instruction performs a bit-by-bit AND of the byte following the instruction, in this case 10000000

TABLE 8.1

Location in memory	Contents	Label	Op code	Operand	Comments
					Assembly language
030	DB	KEYSTAT	IN	2	/READ STATUS WORD
031	02				/INTO ACCUMULATOR
032	E6		ANI	80H	/AND ACCUMULATOR BITS
033	80				
034	CA		JZ	KEYSTAT	/JUMP BACK IF ZERO
035	30				
036	00				
037	DB		IN	1	/READ KEYBOARD
038	01				

(binary), with the accumulator. If the keyboard is ready to be read, this will result in a 1 in the leftmost position; if not, a 0 results.

The ANI instruction also sets a flip-flop called Z (for zero) to a 1 if the results of the AND contain a 1 and a 0 if not. Therefore, if a character is ready to be read, Z will contain a 1; if not, it will contain a 0.

JZ is the op code for a "jump-on-zero" instruction. If the Z flip-flop is a 0, the microprocessor will take its next instruction word from the address given in the bytes following the JZ; if Z is a 1, the instruction following these 2 bytes will be executed. As a result, if a character is ready to be read, the microprocessor will read the IN instruction 037 next; if no character is ready, the microprocessor will jump back to location 030. Notice that the programmer has used the label KEYSTAT instead of giving the numeric value in the address part of the instruction, but the actual address appears in the *contents* column. (The assembler determined the location.) Also, note that a complete address requires 2 bytes (2^{16} words can be used in memory). The lower-order (least significant) bits come first in an instruction word, followed by the higher-order bits.

When the keyboard is to be read, the instruction word beginning at location 037 will be executed. This is an IN instruction, but the device number is 1, so the keyboard itself will be read from.

When the instruction is executed, the microprocessor will place the device number 1 on its address lines and then generate a device READ sequence of control signals. As a result, the keyboard interface will place the character in the keyboard buffer register on the data lines, and this character will be read into the accumulator, ending the READ process.

8.10 INTERFACING A PRINTER

The preceding sections have detailed the reading of data from a keyboard into a microprocessor (CPU). We now examine the outputting of characters from a microprocessor to a printer.

We assume that the printer uses an ASCII character in 8-bit parallel form to cause the printing of a single character. In our interfacing, first the printer is selected. To do this, since different output devices may be connected to the microprocessor, the printer is given a unique device number; we will assume that the number is 3 (decimal). When the printer is selected, this number will appear on the microprocessor address lines A_7 to A_0 in binary.

Figure 8.25 shows an interface design. A NAND gate and six inverters are connected so that the NAND gate will have a 0 output only when the number 3 appease on A_7 to A_0 and $\overline{\text{I/O W}}$ is a 0. This NAND gate's output is used as a GO signal, which ultimately causes the printer to print the character on data lines D_7 to D_0. The $\overline{\text{I/O W}}$ signal is pulled negative (to a 0) when the character to be printed is available on D_0 to D_7 and the device address (3 in this case) is on lines A_7 to A_0.

A flip-flop called CHARACTER READY is used to signal the printer that a character is ready to be printed. The printer must read this flip-flop and then print the character.

The program instruction that causes this character transfer is called an OUT instruction. The OUT instruction occupies two 8-bit bytes in memory, with a second

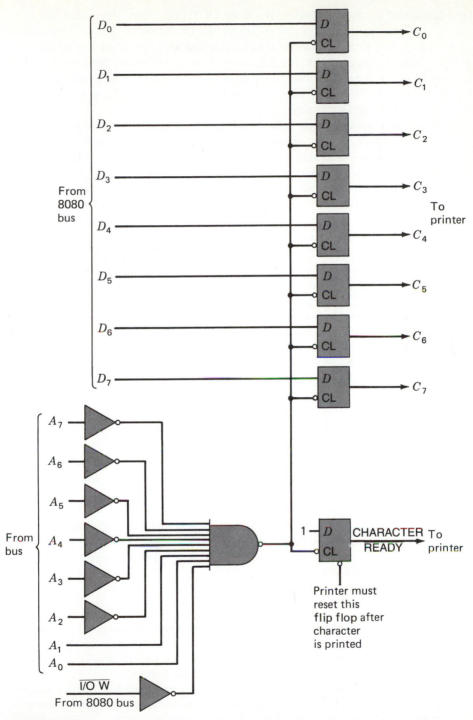

FIGURE 8.25
Interfacing a printer.

byte containing the device number. When the OUT instruction is executed, the contents of the accumulator are placed on D_0 to D_7. Execution of the OUT instruction causes the printer to print a character corresponding to whatever code was stored in the accumulator. This implies that the computer program in the 8080 memory has previously stored the ASCII code for the character to be printed in the accumulator. (A LOAD ACCUMULATOR instruction will effect this. For now we restrict our discussion to the interface strategy.)

There is a basic problem with this scheme. A printer is a very slow electromechanical device, and the microprocessor, because of its high speed, is capable of flooding the printer with more characters than it can possibly print. An attempt to print only after a pause following each character will be difficult to implement because the printer may require different time intervals to respond to different characters.

There are two basic solutions to this problem. One is to have the microprocessor examine the printer at regular intervals to see when a new character can be printed. If the printer is ready to accept a character, it "raises a flag" (turns on a flip-flop), which the microcomputer reads. If the flag is a 1, the microcomputer outputs the character to be printed; if the flag is a 0, the microcomputer goes back to what it was doing and examines the printer again at a later time. (The computer may simply continue to examine the flag until it goes high.) The other solution is to have the printer signal the computer with an interrupt line when it is able to print. The computer then services this interrupt by feeding the printer a character.

In regard to the first technique, all that is required to respond to a query from the microprocessor is shown in Fig. 8.26. When the printer is able to handle a character, it turns the flag flip-flop on. The flag is then made a bit in a status register of 8 bits.

The program step to read the flag involves transferring an entire 8-bit character placed on the data lines from the status registers into the accumulator. The status register is given device number 4. When an IN instruction with device number 4 is executed by the microprocessor, the number 4 (in binary) comes up on A_7 to A_0, and the $\overline{\text{I/O R}}$ line is brought low. This causes the transfer of the flag and its associated 0s into the microprocessor accumulator. Another instruction examines the accumulator to see whether it is all 0s or contains a 1. If the accumulator sign bit is a 1, the printer is ready for a character; if not, the computer must wait.

This interfacing technique is widely used because of its simplicity of implementation. Using a flag (or several flags) to determine an output device's status, placing the flag(s) in a status register, and then reading the status register using a program are a standard computer interface scheme.

QUESTIONS

8.1. How would you convert a three-state driver with a DISABLE input to one with an ENABLE input?

8.2. Discuss the problems that might be encountered when several devices connected to the same bus can each become the bus master for a time.

8.3. If the high-speed memory for a microcomputer were assembled from a collection of IC memories including 100-, 200-, and 500-ns memories, would a synchronous or an asynchronous data bus be better? Explain your reasoning.

8.4. Cite some advantages and disadvantages of memory-mapped I/O versus specific I/O instructions.

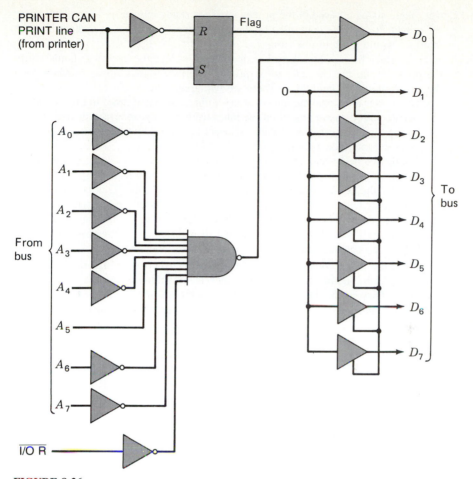

FIGURE 8.26
Printer status generator.

8.5. Explain how a keyboard with an 8-bit output would be interfaced to the 68000 bus.

8.6. Draw waveforms for the 68000 bus for an 8-bit transfer of data to a printer.

8.7. The 8086 configuration shown in this chapter is fairly complex. Discuss the benefits of such a configuration for a personal computer, and contrast it with a microprocessor used as a traffic light controller or an automobile ignition control system.

8.8. Explain the handshake on an asynchronous bus.

8.9. Design an interface for a 256-word 8-bit memory using the chip in Fig. 6.10 for the bus timing in Fig. 8.14.

8.10. Design an interface for a 256-word 8-bit memory using the chip in Fig. 6.10 for the bus timing in Fig. 8.13.

8.11. In the status register scheme used to interface a microprocessor to a keyboard, only 1 bit is used to determine the status of the keyboard. A status register could have several status bits, however, each with a different meaning. Discuss the use of the AND instruction to test various bits in conjunctions with the JUMP instruction for the system shown.

8.12. The single status bit used in the printer interface status register is set on and off by the printer. It could be controlled by the printer and the interface. Explain how the interface would work in this case.

8.13. In an interface for a printer there is a question as to how the interface should notify the printer when the character to be printed is on the signal wires, and how long the signal should be held there. There are two approaches:

(a) The printer must read the information within a stipulated time. In this approach, signals with data are placed on the interface wires (the interface device address having already been placed there) and are held for some fixed time acceptable to all the interface circuitry used.

(b) The device being read into notifies the interface when it has received the characters. In this case another interface wire is used, and a signal is placed on this wire by the device when it has accepted the input data. This is a handshake procedure, where the interface device address is placed on the wires, data are then placed on the wires, and a wire to the device is raised that says, "The data are on the lines." The interface device then raises another wire saying, "The data have been accepted."

IBM used the first technique in its 3081 interfaces, whereas the IEEE (and several other standards organizations and computer manufacturers) use the handshaking technique. Discuss the advantages and disadvantages of each technique.

8.14. With some interfaces it is possible to read into several devices at the same time. In this case the system controller places the data on the wires and then raises the wire showing that the data are there. In responding, the devices accepting data use the *open-collector* circuit shown in Chapter 12 so that if any device has not yet accepted the data, the response wire will be set low. Explain how this circuit works.

8.15. Show how the circuitry in Fig. 8.23 can be modified to interface a keyboard with address 6 (device number 6).

8.16. Show how the program in Table 8.1 would be modified to service a keyboard with device number 8 and status register number 7.

8.17. Write a sequence of instructions that will read a keyboard and then print the characters read on a printer. Give the keyboard device number 5 and the printer device number 7. Number the status registers as you please.

8.18. Design an interface that will accept serial bit strings using ASCII and the serial format in Chapter 7. The interface should buffer this bit string of characters into the microprocessor.

8.19. Design an interface that will take a parallel data byte from a microprocessor bus and convert it to serial for a teletypewriter.

8.20. Explain handshaking on a bus when data are transferred from a sender to a receiver. How can this be used to prevent errors due to signal skew caused by signals on different wires arriving at different times (skewed) because of differences in line length and characteristics and differences in delays through IC line drivers?

8.21. For the standard handshake, draw the signals DAV, NRFD, and NDAC for a data transfer from a talker to a listener. Assume that there are no problems in transferring data, and indicate who is raising and lowering each signal.

8.22. For the handshake technique, indicate how the controller selects a talker and a listener.

8.23. How is signal skew handled on the standard handshake?

8.24. Explain how peripheral devices interrupt a computer with a single-bus organization.

8.25. Explain the meaning of *direct memory access* (DMA) and why it is desirable in some cases.

8.26. Can you think of any problems that might arise in multiprocessor systems?

8.27. If devices and status registers are numbered 1, 2, 4, 8, . . . and only a few are used (less than or equal to the number of address wires), the gate to determine which device is selected in an interface can be simplified (or omitted). Show why.

8.28. Explain how IBM PC boards (or clone boards) can be plugged into a PC AT bus.

8.29. Compare the VME and PC AT approaches to multiple-board sizes.

8.30. Can buses with 32 address lines be used in microcomputers with only 1 Meg of RAM? How?

8.31. How would you suggest smoothing the bounce from the contacts on the keyboard?

8.32. Design an interface for an ASCII serial input.

8.33. The signal that strobes the values into the flip-flops that read from the encoder on the keyboard must be slightly delayed. Explain why.

8.34. The IBM series of computers uses a priority delegation scheme where interrupt devices are interconnected as shown below. When an interrupt service is issued, the leftmost point of the "daisy-chain" wire is raised. If a device wishes to be serviced, it does not forward this 1 to the device on the right. If it does not wish to be serviced, it forwards this 1 to the device on the right. Each device in turn makes this decision, either passing the 1 to the right or passing a 0. (A 0 on the left is always passed right.) Design a logic circuit to effect this. Use an interrupt flip-flop that is turned on by the device utilizing the interface and that has a 1 output if the device wishes service and a 0 output if not.

To input-output controller

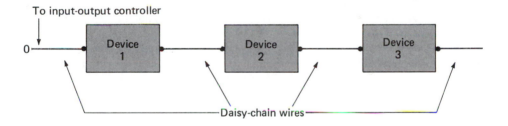

Daisy-chain wires

8.35. The daisy-chain interrupted scheme in Question 8.34 assigns interrupt priorities according to the position in the daisy chain. Explain this statement.

8.36. The passing of a 1 or a 0 along the daisy chain by each device must be carefully controlled with regard to time. Strict standards are given concerning maximum delays for each device. Explain the advantages and disadvantages of the daisy-chain scheme in assigning priorities and determining which device has generated an interrupt.

8.37. Notice that when the daisy-chain scheme explained in Question 8.34 is used a device can place its identity or interrupt vector on the bus without the danger of other devices placing their vectors on at the same time and overwriting at the same time. In some microcomputers combinational logic is used to determine which device is to be serviced first. Explain how this might be done, assuming that each device uses an interrupt flip-flop as in Question 8.34.

8.38. Compare the disadvantages and advantages of using combinational logic versus the daisy-chain technique for interrupt servicing.

8.39. When DMA (direct memory access) is used on a bus, a line to the CPU on the bus is raised by the device wishing to read into memory using the bus. The CPU then stops executing instructions at the first possibility, and raises another line on the bus, indicating that it has stopped execution of instructions. The device wishing access to the bus then uses the bus; when it is done, it lowers the wire that was used to stop the CPU. The CPU then continues to execute instructions. Explain the danger of having several devices able to generate interrupts of this kind at the same time.

8.40. Why does the control in a digital computer wait until the end of an instruction to execute an interrupt request?

8.41. A bus has a data section with 16 lines, and its address section contains 24 lines. What is the maximum memory that can be directly addressed?

8.42. What is the basic advantage of the priority interrupt over a nonpriority system?

8.43. A microcomputer has a bus with a single interrupt line that is to be raised by an external device that wishes to be serviced. The bus is controlled by the microcomputer's CPU chip. Explain the CPU's problem in determining which input/output device(s) generated an interrupt, and discuss two possible solutions.

8.44. What is the difference between a program-controlled transfer and a DMA transfer?

8.45. Assume an interface that handles serial character inputs. How many characters per second can be transmitted over a 1200-bit-per-second line in each of the following modes? (Assume a character code of 8 bits.)
(*a*) Synchronous serial transmission
(*b*) Asynchronous transmission with 2 stop bits
(*c*) Asynchronous transmission with 1 stop bit

8.46. Compare synchronous and asynchronous buses from the viewpoint of interface circuit cost and reliability.

8.47. Analyze the bus arbitration methods of daisy-chaining, polling, and independent interrupts.

8.48. Generally interrupts are not acknowledged until the end of execution of the current machine instruction. Consider suspending operation of the CPU in the middle of execution of an instruction in order to acknowledge an interrupt, and discuss the difficulties that may arise.

8.49. When an interrupt system for several I/O devices is used that places the number associated with the interrupting device on the bus, a priority encoder is required. This device has a single connection from each I/O device as inputs and an output that is a binary number identifying a device. The I/O devices present 0s to the priority encoder except for when an interrupt is requested. They are prioritized so that if two devices generate 1 inputs at the same time, the one with the higher priority has its identifying number output. Design a priority encoder with five inputs, I_1, I_2, ..., I_5, and three outputs, X_1, X_2, X_3 such that if I_3, for example, raises its input to a 1, X_1 will be a 0 and X_2 and X_3 will be 1s. That is, if I_i is a 1, then the X output will have value i, and if two or more inputs have value 1, the input I_i with the lowest i will have its i value output.

8.50. A computer has a vectored interrupt architecture, where an I/O device supplies the starting address of the interrupt service routine when the interrupt is acknowledged. The processor status is saved in memory. Describe the sequence of events from the time the device requests an interrupt until execution of the interrupt service routine is started.

8.51. Design a 16-bit priority encoder using four copies of a 4-bit priority encoder and whatever gates are needed. An n-bit priority encoder has n inputs and m outputs, where Z is greater than or equal to n and the inputs are numbered from 0 to $n - 1$. The value on the m output lines is a binary number equal to the largest number that has a 1 input.

CHAPTER 9

THE CONTROL UNIT

The *control unit* is defined as "the parts that effect the retrieval of instructions in proper sequence, the interpretation of each instruction, and the application of the proper signals to the arithmetic unit and other parts in accordance with this interpretation."[1]

The function of the control circuitry in a general-purpose computer is to interpret the instruction words and then sequence the signals to those sections of the computer that will cause the instructions to be performed. Previous chapters have shown how the application of the correct sequence of control signals to the logic circuitry in the arithmetic element enables the computer to perform arithmetic operations, and how binary words may be stored and later read from various memory devices. For the computer to function, the operation of its sections must be directed. The control circuitry performs that function.

This chapter first presents some introductory material concerning instruction word execution. Two general-purpose computers are used as examples. Then the control circuitry of a small general-purpose computer is described. The basic ideas in the design of control circuitry are presented in these sections, and register transfer concepts are emphasized. The final sections describe microprogrammed computer control concepts.

9.1 CONSTRUCTION OF AN INSTRUCTION WORD

A computer word is an ordered set of characters handled as a group. Basically all words consist of a set of binary digits, and the meaning of the digits depends on

---

[1] From *IEEE Standard Dictionary of Electrical and Electronics Terms*. IEEE Standard 100. Institute of Electrical and Electronics Engineers, Inc.

417

several factors. For instance, the bits 01000100 could represent the decimal number 68 in a pure binary computer, and the decimal number 44 in a BCD computer that uses an 8,4,2,1 code. Thus, the meaning of a set of digits is determined by its usage. Other interpretations are possible, for instruction words are stored just as data words are, and the digits could represent an instruction to the computer. Since memory locations can store either instruction words or data words, the programmers and system operators must see that the instruction words are used to determine the sequence of operations that the computer performs, and that reasonable meanings are assigned to the words.

If we assume that each memory location can contain a single instruction word, then a computer will start with the word stored in a specified address, interpret the contents of this location as an instruction, and then continue taking instruction words from the memory locations in order unless a HALT or BRANCH instruction is encountered. The data to be used in the calculations will be stored in another part of the memory. Since the computer can store either instructions or data at a given memory address, considerable flexibility of operation results.

An instruction word in a digital machine consists of several sections. The number of divisions in the word depends on the type of computer. We describe what are called *single-address instruction words* in this and the following sections, leaving more complicated formats for later. This will allow us to develop a control design that is easily understood. Basically each single-address instruction word contains two sections: the *operation code* (op code), which defines the instruction to be performed (addition, subtraction, etc.); and the *address part*, which contains the location in memory of the number to be added, subtracted, or otherwise used (the operand).

We will first describe the operation of a small single-address computer. The microprocessor to be described is used in the DEC word processors, in one of their personal computers, and in several other items, including disk drive controllers and printer controllers. The instruction word format, instruction repertoire, and general architecture originated in the DEC PDP-8 series, which was DEC's first "big winner" in the minicomputer area and the largest-selling minicomputer for some years. This microprocessor is manufactured in an IC chip by Harris as the 6100. For simplicity we will refer to our design as the 6100.

The 6100 has a basic memory word and instruction word of 12 bits.[2] The instruction word comprises two sections, an op-code part and an address part, as shown in Fig. 9.1(*a*). There are only 3 bits in the op-code part, so only eight basic instruction types are possible. In this section we describe only three of these. The instructions we study are the TAD (2s complement add), the DCA (deposit and clear), and the JMP (jump) instructions.

The TAD instruction [Fig. 9.1(*b*)] has an op code of 001 (in binary). It tells the computer to add the number located in memory at the address given in the address part of the instruction to the number currently in the accumulator and to place the

---

[2] This is a good size for a word processor because a character plus underscore, overbar, and other options in word processors can be stored in the 12 bits at each location.

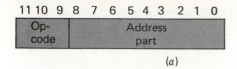

(a)

001000000111   Example: This instruction
word tells computer to
add word at location 7
in memory into
the accumulator

(b)

011   Address   Op-code for DCA
part   instruction is 011

011000001101   Example: This instruction
word tells computer to
deposit the contents of
the accumulator at
the address in memory
given in the address
section, which is 13_{10}

(c)

FIGURE 9.1
6100 instruction words. (a) Instruction word format. (b) TAD instruction format. (c) DCA instruction format.

sum in the accumulator. If the address part of the instruction were 000100110, this would reference the number at address 38 (decimal) in memory. Thus, the computer instruction word that will cause the 12-bit number at address 38 to be added to the number in the accumulator is 001000100110. (Words are generally written in octal in the 6100, and this word would be 1046 in octal.)

The DCA instruction has op code 011. This instruction tells the CPU to deposit or store the present contents of the accumulator at the address given by the address part of the instruction. Thus, the instruction word 011000001101 tells the CPU to store the current contents of the accumulator at location 13 in the memory. The DCA instruction also clears the accumulator to all 0s.

Let us now examine two program steps, a DCA followed by a TAD. Let these two instruction words be at memory locations 41 and 42 (octal). Let DCA refer to location 50 (octal) and TAD to location 51. The arrangement is as follows:

Location in memory (octal)	Memory contents (octal)	Memory contents (binary)
41	3050	011000101000
42	1051	001000101001
⋮	⋮	⋮
50	0222	000010010010
51	0243	000010100011

We now analyze the action of the computer as it executes these two instructions. Suppose that the accumulator contains 0102 (octal) when the instruction at address 41 is executed. The value 0102 will then be deposited (stored) at location 50, overwriting or destroying the value 0222, which was in location 50. The accumulator will be cleared to all 0s.

Next, the instruction at location 42 in memory is executed. This instruction will add the value at location 51, which is 0243 (octal), to the current value in the accumulator.

Therefore, when execution is begun on the instruction word at location 43 (not shown), the accumulator will contain 0243, and the contents of memory location 50 will be 0102.

Another instruction in the 6100's repertoire is the JMP instruction, with op code 101. This instruction causes a jump in memory to the location given in the address part on the instruction word. For example, suppose the value at location 71 (octal) in memory is 101001000011 (binary) or 5103 (octal). When the CPU reads this as the instruction word JMP 0103, it will cause the next instruction to be taken from location 103 in memory, and not from location 72.

Table 9.1 shows the three instructions combined into a five-instruction-word section of program. Assembly language and octal values are both shown in this table.

The operation of these instructions by a CPU would be as follows. When location 41 is read, the DCA instruction stores the current contents of the accumulator, which is

TABLE 9.1
Section of 6100 Program

Address in memory (octal)	Contents (octal)	Assembly language			
		Label	Op code	Address	Comments
0041	3051		DCA	LOC1	/CLEARS ACC
0042	1052		TAD	LOC2	/LOADS 0200
0043	1053		TAD	LOC3	/ADDS 212
0044	3054		DCA	LOC4	/STORES AT 54
0045	5071		JMP	71	/GO TO 71
⋮	⋮		⋮		
0051	0600	LOC1	0600		
0052	0200	LOC2	0200		
0053	0212	LOC3	0212		
0054	0310	LOC4	0310		

then cleared to 0s. The next instruction word is TAD LOC2, which causes the number 0200 at location 52 to be added to the accumulator, giving 0200 in the accumulator.

When the TAD LOC3 instruction is read, it causes the number 0212 at location 53 in memory to be added to the number 0200 in the accumulator, giving 0412 in the accumulator. The CPU then executes the instruction DCA LOC4, causing the value in the accumulator, 0412, to be stored at address 54 in the memory. The CPU then reads the JMP 71 instruction, causing it to fetch the next instruction word from location 71 in the memory (and not from location 46).

After this section of the code has been executed, the sum of the numbers at locations 52 and 53 is stored in location 54, and the CPU jumps to location 71 in memory.

9.2   INSTRUCTION CYCLE AND EXECUTION CYCLE ORGANIZATION OF CONTROL REGISTERS

We now proceed to the design of a small computer similar to, but somewhat larger than, that just described. A digital computer proceeds through the execution of a program with a basic sequence of operation that is based on the necessity of drawing both instructions and operands from the same memory.

The basic sequence of operations for most instructions in a single-address digital computer consists of the alternation of a time period called the *instruction cycle* or *instruction fetch* and a period called the *execution cycle*. During the instruction cycle, an instruction word is obtained from the memory and interpreted, and the memory is given the address of the operand to be used. During the execution cycle, the memory obtains the operand to be used (for instance, the multiplier if the instruction is a multiplication, or the augend if the instruction is an addition), and the operation called for by the instruction word is performed on this operand.

Most computers now being made use an IC memory to store both instruction words and operands or data. The cycle time for the memory is fixed. Once we tell the memory that we wish to read from it or write into it, a certain time will elapse before we can instruct the memory that we are again ready to read or write. If we are reading from the memory, the selected word will be delivered a short time after the memory has been given the address of the word to be read and has been instructed to read.

If the memory is to be written into, the word to be written as well as the address we wish to write to must be given to the memory. A WRITE signal also must be given. As discussed in Chap. 6, the address that we write to or read from in the memory will be put into a *memory address register*, and the word to be written into the memory will be put into the *memory buffer register*. When we read from the memory, the word read is delivered to the memory buffer register.

During each instruction cycle, the instruction word is transferred by the memory into the memory buffer register. To obtain this word, we must tell the memory to read and give it the address to read from. During the instruction cycle, the instruction word that was read into the memory buffer register is interpreted, and the address of the operand to be used is delivered to the memory address register. For many instructions this will be the address part of the instruction word read from the memory during the instruction cycle. During the execution cycle, an operand is obtained from or written into the memory, depending on the instruction word that was interpreted during the previous instruction cycle.

For example, if the instruction being interpreted is an ADD, the location of the augend is given in the address part of the instruction word, and this address must be given to the memory address register. The memory then obtains the desired word and puts it into the memory buffer register. The computer then adds this word to the word already in the accumulator. Afterward the computer gives to the memory the address of the next instruction word to be used and commands the memory to read this word.

Note that the machine alternates between an instruction cycle and an execution cycle. Also note that during an execution cycle we must store somewhere in our control circuitry the op code of the instruction word read from the memory, the address of the operand to be used (which is a part of the instruction word read from the memory), and the address of the next instruction word to be read from the memory.

As a result, several registers are basic to almost every digital computer. These are shown in Fig. 9.2 and are described as follows:

1. *Instruction counter.*[3]   The instruction counter is of the same length as the address section of the instruction word. The counter can be either reset or incremented. A

---

[3] In some computers the instruction counter is called the *program counter.*

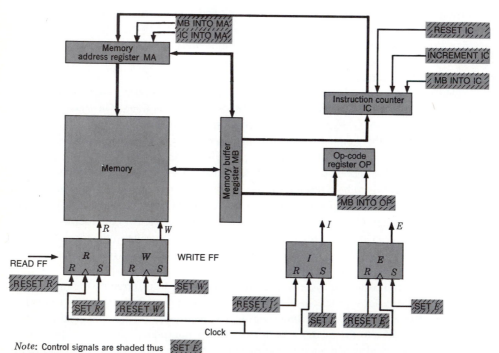

Note: Control signals are shaded thus SET E

FIGURE 9.2
Control registers.

typical logic diagram could consist of the counter shown in Fig. 4.14(*a*), having a RESET line and an INCREMENT or ENABLE line. This counter keeps track of the instructions to be used in the program, so during each instruction time, the counter is normally incremented by 1, which will give the location of the next instruction word to be used. If, however, the instruction is a BRANCH or JUMP, we may wish to place part of the *B* register's contents into this counter: the MB INTO IC line does this. The counter can be reset to 0 when a program is started.[4]

It must also be possible to transfer the contents of this counter into the memory address register, which is used to locate a word in memory. Normally the instruction counter is increased by 1 during the performance of each instruction, and the contents of the counter are transferred into the memory address register at the beginning of each instruction time.

2. *Op-code register.* When an instruction word is read from the memory, the op-code section of this word must be stored to identify the instruction to be performed. If the computer has an op-code length of 5 bits (which we will use in our design), the operation register will be 5 bits in length and will contain the op-code part of the instruction word that is read from the memory. Therefore, we must be able to transfer a section of the memory buffer register into the op-code register during the instruction time period.

3. *Memory address register.* The memory address register contains the location of the word in memory to be read or the location to be written into.

4. R *flip-flop.* When the *R* flip-flop is turned on, it tells the memory to read a word. (The flip-flop can be turned off shortly afterward; it need not be on during the entire memory cycle.)

5. W *flip-flop.* Turning on the *W* flip-flop tells the memory to write the word located in the memory buffer register at the location given by the memory address register.

6. I *flip-flop.* When the *I* flip-flop is on, the computer is in an instruction cycle.

7. E *flip-flop.* The computer is in an execution cycle when the *E* flip-flop is on.

Sequence of Operation of Control Registers

Let us consider further the construction of the control circuitry of a digital computer, again using the block diagram of the control registers, memory, memory address register, and memory buffer register shown in Fig. 9.2.

The control signals necessary to the operation of this small single-address computer are shown on the diagram and are as follows. There is a RESET IC line, which clears the instruction counter to 0. (This is often connected to a push-button that clears the counter when the program is to be started.) There is an MB INTO IC control signal, which causes the contents of the memory buffer register to be transferred into the instruction counter, and an INCREMENT IC control signal, which causes

---

[4] Most computers make it possible to load a selected address into the operation counter and thereby start the machine at that address.

the instruction counter to be incremented by 1. Another control signal is MB INTO OP, which transfers the first five digits of the memory buffer register containing the op code of an instruction word into the five flip-flops in the operation register. The memory address register has two control signals. IC INTO MA causes the contents of the instruction counter to be transferred into the memory address register, and MB INTO MA causes the last 16 digits of the memory buffer register (which constitute the address part of an instruction word) to be transferred into the memory address register.

During each instruction cycle of the computer, we must turn on the READ flip-flop and at the same time (or earlier) transfer the contents of the instruction counter into the memory address register. The memory will now read an instruction word into the memory buffer register, after which time we can enable the MB INTO OP line, transferring the op-code section of the instruction word into the op-code register. The next actions that the computer will take depend on the contents of the op-code register.

9.3   CONTROLLING ARITHMETIC OPERATIONS

Consider the problem of directing the arithmetic element as it performs an instruction. Let us add an accumulator and a B register to the registers shown in Fig. 9.2, forming the block diagram shown in Fig. 9.3. Five more control signals are required to perform such instructions as ADD, SUBTRACT, CLEAR AND ADD, and STORE:

1. *RESET ACC.*   This signal sets all the flip-flops in the accumulator to 0.
2. *ADD.*   This signal causes the B register to be added to the accumulator and the sum transferred into the accumulator.
3. *SUBTRACT.*   This signal causes the B register to be subtracted from the accumulator and the difference placed in the accumulator.
4. *MB INTO BR.*   This signal transfers the memory buffer register into the B register.
5. *AC INTO MB.*   This signal causes the contents of the accumulator to be transferred into the memory buffer register.

Figure 9.4 shows a single accumulator flip-flop and a single B register flip-flop, along with the control signals and gates required for the above operations. The accumulator and B register are basically composed of as many of these blocks as there are bits in the basic computer word. (The carry-in to the least significant bit is connected to the SUBTRACT signal when 2s complement addition is used and to the carry-out of the sign digit when the 1s complement system is used.)

One further thing is needed. We must distribute our signals in an orderly manner. Some sort of a time base, which will indicate where we are in the sequence of operations to be performed, is required. To achieve this, each memory cycle is broken into four equal time periods, T_0–T_3. If we are in the first time period, we need a signal to tell us that it is time T_0; during the second period, we need a signal that will tell us that it is time T_1; and so on.

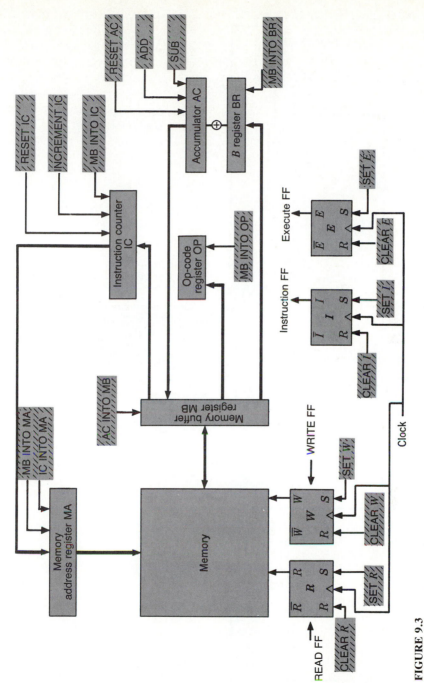

FIGURE 9.3
Control registers and arithmetic registers.

425

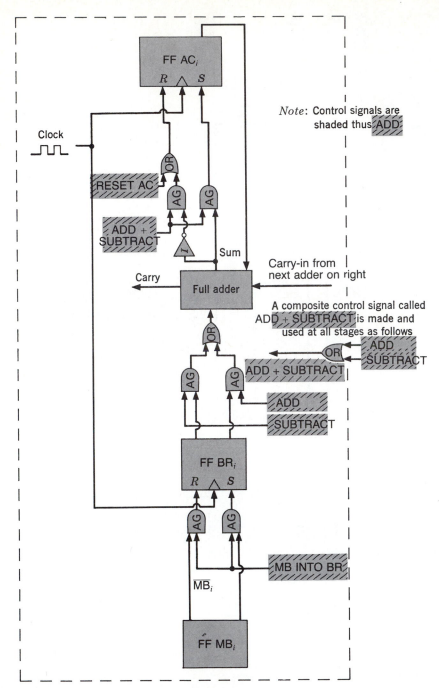

FIGURE 9.4
Accumulator flip-flop and *B* register flip-flop with control signals.

Figure 9.5 shows a way of generating such timing signals. There is a clock signal input, and the clock is assumed to operate such that during a memory cycle we obtain four clock pulses. If it requires 0.1 μs to read into or write from the memory, a clock pulse should be generated every 0.025 μs. Therefore, the clock will run at a rate of 40 MHz.

The circuit has four output lines, designated T_0, T_1, T_2, and T_3. When the computer is in time period T_0, the output line T_0 will carry a 1 signal, and T_1, T_2, and T_3 will be 0s; at time T_1, only line T_1 will have a 1 signal on it; and so on.

Let us now develop a short table specifying the sequence of operations that occur during each of the ADD, SUBTRACT, CLEAR AND ADD, and STORE instructions. Notice that when the instruction cycle flip-flop is on, the operations during times T_0 and T_1 are always the same. In Table 9.2 the control signal to be turned on (or made a 1) is listed to the left, and the effect of the signal is listed to the right. From this table of operations it is possible to design the control section of this small computer. The inputs are the op code stored in the op-code register, the timing-signal distributor, and the I and E flip-flops.

Notice, for instance, that during time T_0 in an instruction cycle, we always turn on the READ flip-flop, telling the memory to read the instruction word located at the address in the memory address register. Then we assume that the memory places this word in the memory buffer register before time T_1, so at time T_1 we transfer the op-code part of the instruction word into the op-code register. These two facts tell us that we should logically AND the output line T_0 from the timing signal distributor with the 1 output of the I flip-flop and then connect the $T_0 \cdot I$ signal to the SET input of the READ flip-flop. Next we should connect a $T_1 \cdot I$ signal to the control line that

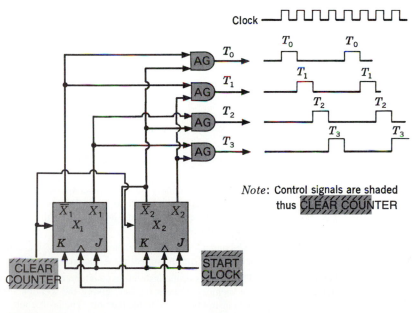

FIGURE 9.5
Timing signal distributor.

TABLE 9.2
Sequencing of control signals

Instruction	List of control signals to be turned on	Comments
ADD		
I and T_0	SET R	Tells memory to read instruction word.
I and T_1	MB INTO OP, RESET R	Transfers op-code part of instruction word into op-code register; turns off READ flip-flop.
I and T_2	INCREMENT IC	Adds 1 to the instruction counter, preparing for the next instruction.
I and T_3	MB INTO MA, RESET I, SET E	Transfers the address part of the instruction word (which is in the memory buffer register) into the memory address register. Puts the computer in the execution cycle.
E and T_0	SET R	Turns on the READ flip-flop telling the memory to read a word.
E and T_1	MB INTO BR, RESET R	Transfers the message of the memory buffer register into the B register. Since the memory buffer register now contains what was read from the memory, the addend is transferred into the B register. Also turns off READ flip-flop.
E and T_2	ADD	The contents of the B register are added to the accumulator, and the sum is placed in the accumulator.
E and T_3	IC INTO MA, SET I, RESET E	The contents of the instruction counter are transferred into the memory address register, giving the location of the next instruction word to the memory. The instruction cycle flip-flop is turned on, and the execution cycle flip-flop is turned off.
CLEAR AND ADD		
I and T_0	SET R	Tells memory to read instruction word.
I and T_1	MB INTO OP, RESET R	Transfers op-code part of instruction word into op-code register; turns READ flip-flop off.
I and T_2	INCREMENT IC	Adds 1 to the instruction counter, preparing for the next instruction.
I and T_3	MBA INTO MA, RESET I, SET E	Transfers the address part of the instruction word (which is in the memory buffer register) into the memory address register.
E and T_0	SET R	Turns on the READ flip-flop, telling memory to read a word.
E and T_1	MB INTO BR, RESET AC, RESET R	Transfers the memory buffer register into the B register and also clears the accumulator, so if the B register is now added to the accumulator, the accumulator will contain the word read from memory.
E and T_2	ADD	The contents of the accumulator are added to the B register, and the sum is placed in the accumulator.
E and T_3	IC INTO MA, SET I, RESET E	The contents of the instruction counter are transferred into the memory address register, giving the location of the next instruction word to the memory. The instruction cycle flip-flop is turned on, and the execution cycle flip-flop is turned off.

TABLE 9.2
Sequencing of control signals (*continued*)

Instruction	List of control signals to be turned on	Comments
SUBTRACT		
I and T_0	SET R	Tells memory to read instruction word.
I and T_1	MB INTO OP, RESET R	Transfers op-code part of instruction word into op-code register; turns off READ flip-flop.
I and T_2	INCREMENT IC	Adds 1 to the instruction counter, preparing for the next instruction.
I and T_3	MB INTO MA, RESET I, SET E	Transfers the address part of the instruction word (which is in the memory buffer register) into the memory address register. Puts the computer in the execution cycle.
E and T_0	SET R	Turns on the READ flip-flop, telling the memory to read a word.
E and T_1	MB INTO BR, RESET R	Transfers the contents of the memory buffer register into the B register. Since the memory buffer register now contains what was read from the memory, the subtrahend is transferred into the B register. Also turns off READ flip-flop.
E and T_2	SUB	The contents of the B register are subtracted from the accumulator, and the difference is placed in the accumulator.
E and T_3	IC INTO MA, SET I, RESET E	The contents of the instruction counter are transferred into the memory address register, giving the location of the next instruction word to the memory. The instruction cycle flip-flop is turned on, and the execution cycle flip-flop is turned off.
STORE		
I and T_0	SET R	Tells memory to read the instruction word.
I and T_1	MB INTO OP, RESET R	Transfer op-code part of instruction word into op-code register; turns off READ flip-flop.
I and T_2	INCREMENT IC	Adds 1 to the instruction counter, preparing for the next instruction.
I and T_3	MB INTO MA, RESET I, SET E	Transfers the address part of the instruction word (which is in the memory buffer register) into the memory address register.
E and T_0	SET W, AC INTO MB	Transfers word to be read into memory from accumulator into the memory buffer register.
E and T_1	RESET W	Turns off WRITE flip-flop.
E and T_2		Contents of memory buffer register are written into memory.
E and T_3	IC INTO MA, SET I, RESET E	The contents of the instruction counter are transferred into the memory address register, giving the location of the next instruction word to the memory. The instruction cyle flip-flop is turned on, and the execution cycle flip-flop is turned off.

transfers the first 5 bits of the memory buffer register into the OP register. This is shown in Fig. 9.6.

What happens next depends on the op-code register. We now connect a decoder with $2^5 = 32$ outputs to that register (assuming that we will use all the combinations by adding more instructions). We then have a set of signal lines, so that line 00000 = ADD will carry a 1 signal when we are adding (since the operation code for ADD is 00000); 00001 = SUB will carry a 1 if and only if we are subtracting; and 00010 = CLA will be a 1 only when we CLEAR AND ADD. We combine these lines, the timing signal distributor lines, and the I and E flip-flop lines to give us all the control signals needed to run the computer. Fig. 9.6 shows the complete control circuitry required. A comparison of this figure with the timing and control signal chart in Table 9.2 will show how the control circuitry works and how signals are manufactured when they are needed.

Additional instructions can be carried out by adding the required gates to the control circuitry. Analyzing the computer in this way, we can readily see how the control circuitry directs the operations performed in the machine, alternating the acquisition of instructions from the memory and the performance of the instructions.

9.4   TYPICAL SEQUENCE OF OPERATIONS

It is instructive to analyze the control circuitry in Fig. 9.6 during an ADD instruction and a STORE instruction. Each instruction is started with the I (instruction cycle) flip-flop on and with the timing signal distributor having an output on line T_0. The top AND gate in the figure will therefore be turned on by I and T_0, thus setting the READ flip-flop to the 1 state and initiating a READ from the memory. At this time, the memory address register is assumed to have the address of the instruction that will be read into the memory buffer register.

By time T_1 the word read from the memory will have been read into the memory buffer register, so that when we have the control state I and T_1, the contents of the memory buffer register, which constitute the op-code section of the instruction, will be transferred into the op-code register, and the computer will be in a position to decode the op code and determine what instruction is to be performed.

At time I and T_2 the instruction counter is incremented by 1, so that the instruction counter now contains the address of the next instruction to be read from the memory. The AND gate connected to the I and T_2 input signals is used to turn on the INCREMENT IC control signal, and its output is designated by the name of the control signal.

Similarly, at time I and T_3 the contents of the memory buffer register are transferred into the memory address register by the MB INTO MA signal, thus transferring the address part of the instruction word into the memory address register. The next word read from or written into the memory will then be at the address designated by the address part of the instruction word just read from the memory.

At the same time, the instruction cycle flip-flop is cleared by the RESET 1 signal, and the execution cycle flip-flop is set on by the SET E signal, thus changing the state of the computer from an instruction cycle to an execution cycle.

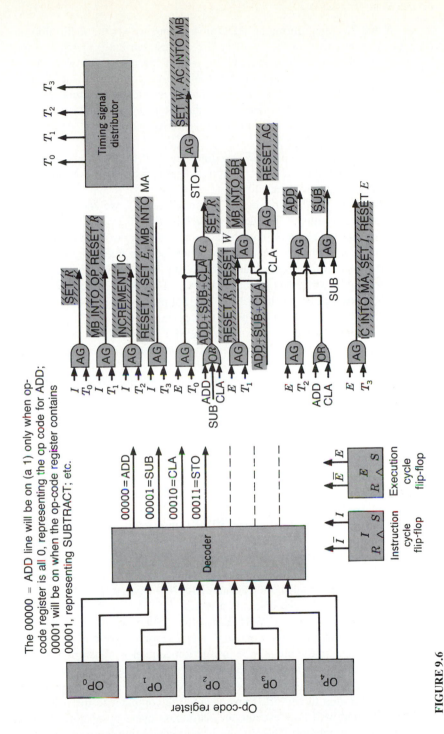

FIGURE 9.6
Control circuitry for four-instruction computer.

431

At time E and T_0, then, during an ADD instruction, we set the R flip-flop on, thus telling the memory to read the word at the address currently in the memory address register. In this case, this is the address part of the instruction word that is being executed. Then, at time E and T_1, we transfer the contents of the memory buffer register into the B register. The memory buffer register at that time contains the word that has been read from the memory, so that we now have the word that has been addressed by the instruction word in the B register for the addition. At the same time we reset the READ flip-flop.

Notice that the RESET R and RESET W lines are used to reset both the READ and the WRITE flip-flops simultaneously. There is no harm in resetting both flip-flops, since only one will be on at any given time.

If the instruction is an ADD instruction at time E and T_2, we add the contents of the B register to the contents of the accumulator. The B register contains the word that has been read from the memory, and the accumulator has not been changed; so their sum will be transferred into the accumulator. Then, at time E and T_3, we transfer the instruction counter into the memory address register (thus giving the address of the next instruction to be performed to the memory), at the same time clearing the EXECUTE flip-flop and setting the instruction cycle flip-flop on, thus changing the computer from an execution cycle to an instruction cycle.

Since the I flip-flop is on and it is time T_0, the SET R control line will go high, telling the memory to read a word. The next instruction word will be read from the memory and can then be interpreted.

Let us now examine the operation of the STORE instruction. When the instruction flip-flop is on and we are in an instruction cycle, the R flip-flop will be set on when time T_0 arrives, telling the memory to read, just as for an addition, subtraction, or clear and add. Since at time I and T_1 the memory buffer register flip-flops contain the op code of the instruction, these will be transferred into the op-code register.

At time I and T_2 we increment the instruction counter so that the address of the next instruction in memory lies in the instruction counter; and at time I and T_3 we reset the instruction flip-flop and turn on the execution cycle flip-flop, thus putting the computer in an execution cycle.

At time E and T_0, if the instruction is a STORE instruction, we set the WRITE flip-flop on, thus initiating a WRITE into the memory. We also transfer the contents of the accumulator into the memory buffer register, so that the word written into the memory will be the current contents of the accumulator register, and so that after the WRITE cycle has been terminated the accumulator will have been written into the memory at the address given by the instruction word.

At time E and T_1 we reset the WRITE flip-flop. Since we have already told the memory to write, nothing need be done at E and T_2, for we are now writing the word into the memory. At time E and T_3 the instruction counter is transferred into the memory address register by the IC INTO MA control signal, thus giving the address of the next instruction to the memory. The instruction cycle flip-flop is turned on, and the execution cycle flip-flop turned off, transforming the computer to the instruction cycle state. The machine will now execute an instruction cycle by reading the next instruction word from the memory, interpreting it, and continuing the program.

This example demonstrates how it is possible to design a computer to execute a given sequence of operations that will cause it to perform each instruction read from the memory. Although only four instructions are demonstrated in this particular example, more instructions can be added in exactly the same manner, simply by writing what must be done when an instruction word is read from the memory, listing the operations that must be performed, and providing gates to generate the control signals necessary to the performance of each instruction. Subsequent sections discuss shifting instructions and branching instructions. All these may be incorporated into the computer design shown by simply adding gates to the control circuitry and providing for the additional gates necessary for the transfers and operations between registers.

Figure 9.7 shows the overall organization of the control section. The control section can be thought of as a state machine with inputs from memory and outputs to memory. The control registers are flip-flops in the state machine, and the clock steps the control section (state machine) through its states. The design problems in this approach concern the many states in an actual design and the difficulty of making changes in a completed design. If automated, this approach might be workable for very small designs (for small controllers, for example).

9.5 BRANCH, SKIP, OR JUMP INSTRUCTIONS

The BRANCH, SKIP, or JUMP instruction varies from the normal instruction in several ways.[5] For single-address machines, only one word, the instruction word, must

---

[5] A survey indicates that some manufacturers call these instructions BRANCH instructions, others call them TRANSFER instructions, and still others call them SKIP or JUMP instructions. All refer to the same thing.

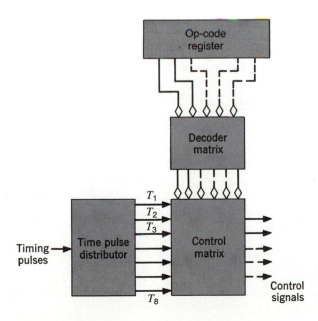

FIGURE 9.7
General configuration of control in state machine configuration.

be located in memory. Also, the contents of the instruction counter may be modified instead of simply increased by 1. There are two types of BRANCH instructions: conditional and unconditional. In response to an *unconditional* BRANCH instruction, the contents of the address portion of the memory buffer register are always transferred into the instruction counter. The next instruction performed will be the instruction at the location indicated by the address section of the instruction word. In a *conditional* branch instruction the branch may or may not occur depending on some condition. For example, in single-address computers the conditional BRANCH ON MINUS instruction will cause the machine to branch only if the number stored in the accumulator register of the arithmetic element is negative. If the number in the accumulator is positive, the contents of the instruction counter will simply be increased by 1, and the next instruction will be taken in the normal order.

As can be seen, during a conditional BRANCH ON MINUS instruction, the sign bit of the accumulator of the arithmetic element must be examined by control circuitry. If the sign bit is a 1, the number stored is negative, and the number in the address part of the instruction word is transferred into the instruction counter. If the sign bit is a 0, a 1 is added to the instruction counter, and the computer proceeds.[6]

To demonstrate how a typical BRANCH ON MINUS (BRM) instruction operates in a single-address computer, we modify the control circuitry shown in Fig. 9.6 to include a BRM instruction. Let us assign the op code 00100 to BRM, so that the line beneath the $00011 = $ STO line from the decoder attached to the op-code register in Fig. 9.6 will be high when a BRM instruction is in the register.

The first two time periods of the instruction cycle are the same for all instructions. First the memory is told to read, and then the instruction word is read from memory into the memory buffer register. The op code is transferred into the op-code register, so that after time T_1 and the beginning of time T_2, the line $00100 = $ BRM will be high and all the other output lines from the decoder will be low. Table 9.3 shows the steps that must be taken to carry out this instruction.

If at time T_2 during the instruction cycle a BRM instruction op code is in the op-code register, one of two things must happen. Either we wish to increment the instruction counter and give this number as the address of the next instruction to be taken from the memory, or we wish to transfer the contents of the address portion of the instruction word into the instruction counter. The choice depends on the sign bit of the accumulator, called AC_N. If the accumulator contains a negative number, it will have a 1 in AC_N; if it contains a positive number, it will have a 0 in flip-flop AC_N. Therefore, for I AND T_2 AND AC_N, we want to increment the instruction counter. For I AND T_2 AND AC_N, we wish to transfer the memory buffer register into the instruction counter. This is shown in the table. During time T_3 of this instruction cycle, we want to transfer the instruction counter into the memory address register. We do not need to put the machine in an execution cycle; rather, we can simply continue to another instruction cycle, taking the word at the address that has been transferred into the memory address register as the next instruction. Therefore, we do not clear

---

[6] Many computers have a set of *status bits* (flip-flops) that are set and reset depending on the results of operations performed. Jumps or transfers are then taken based on these flip-flops.

TABLE 9.3

	List of control signals to be turned on	Comments
BRANCH ON MINUS		
I and T_0	SET R	Tells memory to read instruction word.
I and T_1	MB INTO OP, RESET R	Transfers op-code part of instruction word into op-code register; turns off READ flip-flop.
I and T_2 and $\overline{AC_n}$	INCREMENT IC	If the sign digit of the accumulator (AC_n) is a 0, we want to increment the instruction counter and use its contents as the address of the next instruction.
I and T_2 and AC_n	MB INTO IC	If the sign digit of the accumulator is a 1, the accumulator is negative, and we want to use the address in the next instruction word as the address of the next instruction word.
I and T_3	IC INTO MA	Transfers the the instruction counter into the memory address register. Notice that the E flip-flop is not turned on as we are ready to read another instruction word; execution cycle is not needed.

the instruction cycle flip-flop or put a 1 in the execution cycle flip-flop; we simply transfer the instruction counter into the memory address register.

The control circuitry to implement these operations is shown in Fig. 9.8. The two AND gates in Fig. 9.6, that are connected to the I, T_2 and I, T_3 inputs will be replaced with the two circuits shown in Fig. 9.8. Notice that this logical circuitry, plus the circuitry in Fig. 9.6, is all that is needed to generate the control signals required for the BRM instruction. Also notice that the BRM instruction requires only one access to memory and, thus, only one instruction cycle for its execution.

9.6   SHIFT INSTRUCTIONS

The instructions we have examined so far are always performed within a fixed number of memory cycles. That is, the ADD, SUBTRACT, CLEAR AND ADD, and STORE instructions are performed within two memory cycles, and the TRANSFER and BRANCH instructions require only one memory cycle. Several types of instructions may require more time than two memory cycles. Typical of these are multiplication and division. An instruction such as SHIFT RIGHT or SHIFT LEFT could conceivably be performed in a single memory cycle, since the operand is in the accumulator when the instruction word is obtained. However, if the instruction calls for a large number of shifts, more than one memory cycle may be needed. In this case we could not initiate another memory cycle until we had finished shifting the requisite number of times. Similarly, for multiplication and division we cannot initiate another memory cycle until we finish our multiplication and division process.

To implement such instructions, we turn over control of the computer to a simple control element that is dominated by a counter. This counter will sequence and count the number of steps that must be performed until the instruction is completed, and

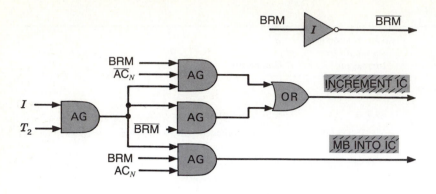

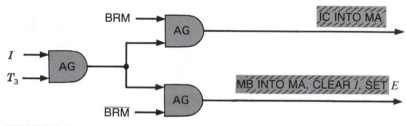

FIGURE 9.8
Modification of control circuitry for BRANCH instruction.

then it will put the computer in an instruction cycle and tell the memory to read the next instruction word. We illustrate with a SHIFT RIGHT instruction.

The SHIFT RIGHT instruction word consists of two parts: an op code and an address part. The OP code 00101 tells the machine to shift the word in the accumulator to the right the number of times given in the address part. If we write 00101 for the op code in an instruction word and then write 8 in binary form in the address part, the computer will be instructed to shift the binary number in the accumulator to the right 8 bits.

Assuming that we have an accumulator with gates so that we can shift the accumulator digits to the right, as explained in Chap. 5, all we need to do is apply eight consecutive SHIFT RIGHT control signals to the accumulator. Since there are only four pulses per memory cycle, we do not want to use the memory until we have completed our shifting. If, for instance, the instruction were SHIFT RIGHT 1, we could finish in one pulse time and start the next instruction cycle immediately afterward. But for an instruction of SHIFT RIGHT 4, 5, or 15 or more times, we would have to complete shifting before we could initiate another instruction cycle and fetch the next instruction word from the memory.

To do this, we first prepare the computer for the shifting operation by incrementing the instruction counter so that the next word obtained will contain the address of the next instruction word. To count the number of shifts that we perform, we add another register, called a *step-counter register*, that counts downward from a given number to 0. We then transfer the address part of the memory buffer register into the step counter so that the step counter contains the number of shifts to be performed. Then each time we shift, we decrement the counter by 1; when the counter reaches 0, we will have performed the requisite number of shifts.

Figure 9.9 shows two stages of a decrementing counter and the gates necessary to transfer the memory buffer register contents into the step counter, designated SC. The two rightmost (least significant) digits of the counter are shown (SC_1 and SC_0), as are the two rightmost digits of the memory buffer register (MB_1 and MB_0).

The actual number of stages in the step counter is determined by the maximum number of shifts the machine must ever make and, since we will also use the same counter for multiplication and division, by the maximum number of steps that will ever be required for multiplying or dividing. For a computer with 21 binary digits in the basic computer word, the counter might well contain five flip-flops. For a computer with a basic computer word of perhaps 35 or 36 binary digits, the step counter might well contain six or even seven flip-flops.

Consider a sequence of operations for a SHIFT instruction. Time I and T_0 and time I and T_1 are as usual. At time I and T_2 we increment the instruction counter and transfer the count into the step counter. At I AND T_3, we set a flip-flop called SR (shift right) on, which tells the computer to start shifting. At the same time we clear the I flip-flop so that the machine is in neither an instruction nor an execution cycle, although it is actually executing an instruction. Thus, we do not initiate subsequent memory cycles, and the machine effectively freezes in the shifting state

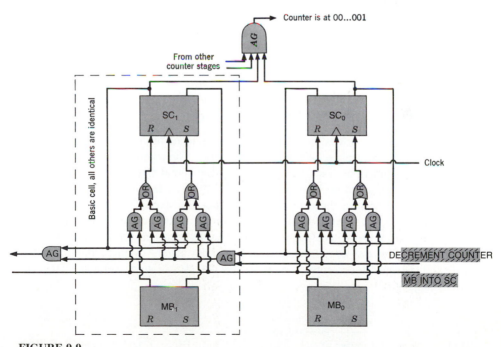

FIGURE 9.9
Two stages of decrementing counter and transfer network.

TABLE 9.4

	Control signal turned on	Comments
SHIFT RIGHT		
I and T_0	SET R	Tells memory to be read.
I and T_1	MB INTO OP, RESET R	Op-code of instruction word is transferred into op-code register. READ flip-flop is turned off.
I and T_2	INCREMENT IC, MB INTO SC	The instruction counter is prepared to obtain the next instruction word. The address part of the instruction word is transferred into the step counter.
I and T_3	RESET I, SET SR	The instruction cycle flip-flop is turned off. The SHIFT RIGHT flip-flop is turned on.

until the step counter has counted to 0, indicating that the requisite number of shifts has been performed. (Actually the step counter counts only to binary 1 rather than to 0 before the order to stop counting is given, for counting when the counter is at 0 would introduce an extra shift.) If we turn off the counter SR flip-flop when the output of the counter is at the 00 ... 001 signal, and if at the same time we turn on the I or instruction cycle, the computer will proceed to the next instruction cycle, fetching the next instruction word from the memory and performing it. Table 9.4 shows this.

When the SR flip-flop is on, it will be necessary to stop the timing signal distributor. Thus, we arrange to disable this circuit using the SR flip-flop's output.

Implementation of this procedure is straightforward. A three-input AND gate with inputs I, T_3, and $00101 =$ SHR (the output from the decoder in Fig. 9.6) can be used to turn on an SR flip-flop, and the STOP output from the step counter can be used to turn it off, also turning on I. The input to the clock can be turned off when SR is on.

9.7   REGISTER TRANSFER LANGUAGE

The preceding design showed how to generate a sequence of control signals to cause instruction words read from a memory to be executed. The control signals were named to indicate their functions. For example, the control signal INCREMENT IC causes the instruction counter to be incremented, RESET W causes flip-flop W to be reset, and MB INTO BR causes the contents of MB to be transferred into the BR register.

To document a design, a notational technique is used to represent the operations on and between registers. The most common way to represent register operations is called *register transfer language*, invented by I. S. Reed.[7] Manufacturers' design efforts and manuals documenting computer designs all use some version of register transfer language.

---

[7] The book *Theory and Design of Digital Machines* by T. C. Bartee, I. L. Lebow, and I. S. Reed (McGraw-Hill, New York), first presented this design technique in detail.

An example of a transfer between registers in register transfer language is

$$B \leftarrow A$$

This says, "Transfer the contents of register A into register B." A control signal to effect this might be conveniently called A INTO B.

Another example of register transfer language is

$$D \leftarrow 0$$

This says, "Set D to a 0." If D is a flip-flop, this simply means to reset D, so an appropriate control signal name would be RESET D.

Here is another example:

$$A \leftarrow A + B$$

This says, "Add the numbers in A and B and place the sum in A." A control signal for this operation might be called ADD or ADD AB.

Such operations on and between registers are sometimes called *microoperations*, particularly if the computer is microprogrammed, as will be discussed.

An interesting statement in register transfer language is

$$A \leftarrow A + 1$$

This says, "Add 1 to A and place the sum in A." A name for the corresponding control signal might be INCREMENT A.

In some cases, register transfers or operations affect only parts of registers. An example was shown earlier, where the first 5 bits in the memory buffer register MBR were transferred into the op-code register. Subscripts are generally used to indicate specific bits, so a particular transfer can be written

$$P_{0-4} \leftarrow B_{0-4}$$

This assumes that the B register flip-flops have been named $B_0, B_1, \ldots , B_N$. The procedure called for is the transfer of B_0, B_1, B_2, B_3, and B_4 into P_0, P_1, P_2, P_3, and P_4, respectively.

A specific bit in a register also can be transferred. Consider

$$B_2 \leftarrow A_3$$

This transfers bit A_3 of register A into B_2 of register B.

Sometimes an operation or transfer is dependent on certain conditions. This is indicated as follows:

$$R = 0 : B \leftarrow A$$

This statement means, "If R has value 0, transfer A into B." Here is another example:

$$R \cdot T_2 : IC \leftarrow IC + 1$$

This statement says, "If R is a 1 and T_2 is a 1, then increment the IC register." The colon is used to indicate a conditional operation.

Following is the CLEAR AND ADD instruction in Table 9.2 rewritten in register transfer language. We will use the CLEAR AND ADD control signal CLA from the decoder in Fig. 9.6.

$$I \cdot T_0 : R \leftarrow 1$$

$$I \cdot T_1 : OP_{0-4} \leftarrow MB_{19-23}$$

$$CLA \cdot I \cdot T_2 : IC \leftarrow IC + 1$$

$$CLA \cdot I \cdot T_3 : MA_{0-18} \leftarrow MB_{0-18}$$

$$I \leftarrow 0, E \leftarrow 1$$

$$CLA \cdot E \cdot T_0 : R \leftarrow 1$$

$$CLA \cdot E \cdot T_1 : BR \leftarrow MB$$

$$AC \leftarrow 0, R \leftarrow 0$$

$$CLA \cdot E \cdot T_2 : A \leftarrow A + B$$

$$CLA \cdot E \cdot T_3 : MA \leftarrow IC$$

$$I \leftarrow 1, E \leftarrow 0$$

This usage assumes 24 bits in the A and MB registers and 19 bits in the memory address register. Thus, MB_{0-18} is the address part of an instruction word and gets transferred into MA_{0-18}.

Notice that the entire circuitry for generating the gates for control signals can be read directly. The final statement,[8] for example, says: "If you AND CLA, E, and T_3, then the output from the AND gate can be used to initiate the transfer MA$\leftarrow$ IC, $I \leftarrow 1$ and $E \leftarrow 0$." This means the output from the AND gate can be connected to (perhaps being ORed with other signals) the control signals IC INTO MA, SET I, and RESET E.

Various register transfer languages have been designed and used by different individuals and companies. One frequent variation is in making transfers move from left to right. In this variation we find

$$A \rightarrow B$$

instead of [9]

$$A \leftarrow B$$

Sometimes equals signs are used. For example,

$$B = A$$

means "Transfer A into B." Occasionally we see

$$B := A$$

This also means transfer A into B in some variations. It is generally not difficult to read a particular register transfer language once the basic principles are understood.

One further usage concerns memory addressing. The notation MEM[120], for example, refers to the word at location 120 in memory. The expression

---

[8] Notice the control signal CLA from the decoder in Fig. 9.6 can be used after time T_1 because the op code is in OP after that time.

[9] Motorola uses $A \rightarrow B$, Intel uses $B \leftarrow A$, and IBM uses both. This presents no problem once the principle is understood (i.e., "go with the arrow").

$$A \leftarrow MEM[135]$$

means "Take the word (beginning) at location 135 in memory and move it into register *A*."

As an additional example, if the variable *able* has value 36, then MEM[*able*] refers to the word at location 36 in memory.

The wide success and usage of register transfer language to describe the internal operations of a computer is primarily due to the facility with which a design can be organized and directly translated from register transfer language into the control gating structure. Register transfer language is also widely used in giving the details of instruction repertoires.

Flowcharts can also be used to describe control circuit operation. Fig. 9.10 shows a flowchart for the instructions described so far. We have used register transfer language in the boxes. The flowchart for a design is very similar to the state diagram for the same design.

9.8   MICROPROGRAMMING

In the preceding sections, the control signals determining the sequence of operations to execute computer instructions were generated using gates. There is another method, called *microprogramming*, that is also used to generate the control signals in an orderly fashion. This method generally involves use of a ROM to effectively store the control signals in a manner that will be described.

When a computer is microprogrammed, the individual operations between and on registers are called *microoperations*. For instance, transferring the program counter's contents into the memory address register is a microoperation. Similarly, incrementing the program counter is a microoperation, as is transferring the accumulator's contents into the memory buffer register.[10] In each case, a microoperation is initiated by raising a single control signal. Sequencing microoperations involves sequencing the appropriate control signals.

Determining the sequence of microoperations to perform some function is called *microprogramming*. The microprogrammer generally writes the list of operations (the *microprogram*) using a special language. Quite often a computer program is used to translate the microprogram into a listing describing the appropriate contents for the ROM used to store the microprogram. The statements are in a microprogramming language, which can be very primitive or very complex.

To explain microprogramming, we use the computer layout and instructions given in the previous sections and redo the design using a ROM to store the control signals. Therefore, the registers and control signals in Fig. 9.3 are used in the design. The basic list of microoperations needed is shown in Table 9.5. Each microoperation is described by using a symbolic notation (in effect, a microprogramming or

---

[10] Microoperations are just the same as register operations. The term *microoperations* is used in this area along with *microprogramming* for historical reasons. Microoperations and register transfers and operations are physically realized using the same control signals and associated gating structures.

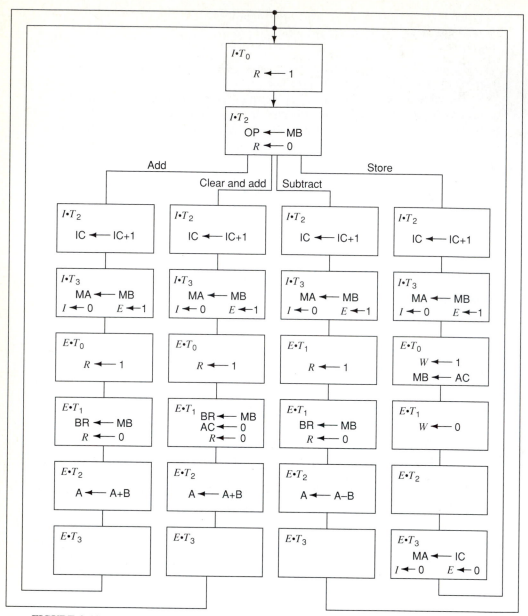

FIGURE 9.10
Control flowchart.

register transfer language); the corresponding control signal causing this operation is also shown.

For instance, the microoperation BR ← MB, which transfers the contents of the memory buffer register (MB) into the B register (BR), is made to occur by raising the control signal MB INTO BR. Notice the considerable similarity between the description in the microprogramming language and the control signal's name. This is a

TABLE 9.5
Microoperations

Microoperation	Control signal name	Bit in read-only control memory
IC ← 0	RESET IC	C_7
IC ← IC + 1	INCREMENT IC	C_8
IC ← MB	MB INTO IC	C_9
0 ← AC	RESET AC	C_{10}
AC ← AC + BR	ADD	C_{11}
AC ← AC − BR	SUBTRACT	C_{12}
W ← 1	SET W	C_{13}
W ← 0	RESET W	C_{14}
R ← 1	SET R	C_{15}
R ← 0	RESET R	C_{16}
AC ← 0	CLEAR AC	C_{17}
MA ← MB_{0-0}	MB INTO MA	C_{18}
MA ← IC	IC INTO MA	C_{19}
MB ← AC	AC INTO MB	C_{20}
OP ← MB_{11-15}	MB INTO OP	C_{21}
BR ← MB	MB INTO BR	C_{22}
IAR ← IAR + 1	INCREMENT IAR	C_{23}
IAR ← C_{0-6}	C INTO IAR	C_{24}
IAR ← OP + IAR	ADD OP TO IAR	C_{25}
IAR ← 0	RESET IAR	C_{26}

convenient practice, although the control signals could be named X_1, A_1, or anything else desired. Use of a 16-bit instruction word is assumed.

Figure 9.11 shows a block diagram for the control system as it will be implemented. There is a ROM with 64 locations and 30 bits per address, and an address register for this memory called IAR (microinstruction address register). Each output bit from the ROM is a control signal that will generate a microoperation; these control signals are named C_0 to C_{26}. Seven of these outputs are special because they are *next addresses* that can be loaded into the IAR and used to sequence the IAR. (This ROM is often called a *control memory*.)

The following operations can be performed on this control unit. A 1 can be added to the IAR (in microprogramming language, IAR ← IAR + 1; the control signal is called INCREMENT IAR), and the output bits from the control memory, labeled C_0 to C_6, can be transferred into the IAR. It is also possible to add the value in OP (see Fig. 9.3) plus 1 to the current contents of the IAR.

The basic scheme is this: The control signals to generate a given computer instruction—say, ADD—are stored in a section of the control memory. The IAR sequences through this section, and at each location the outputs from the control memory constitute the control signals. These ROM outputs thus replace the control signals generated by the gates in Fig. 9.6.

The first problem is that the IAR must be set to the address at the beginning of the section in control memory that contains the bits storing the control signals for the instruction to be executed. To do this, we must examine the op-code register's

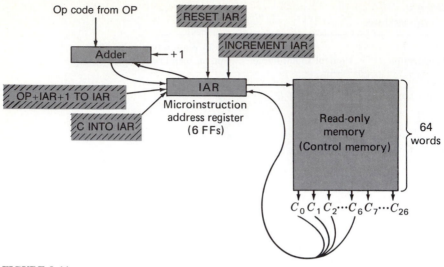

FIGURE 9.11
Block diagram for control system.

contents after we have read the instruction word from memory and then moved the op-code section from the memory buffer register into the op-code register. The complete microprogram for the control memory is shown in Table 9.6. Notice that the first microoperations performed are as follows:

Location in control memory	Microprogram
0	R ← 1 IAR ← IAR +1
1	OP ← MB$_{11-15}$ IAR ← IAR +1
2	IAR ← OP +IAR +1
3	IAR ← C$_{0-6}$
4	IAR ← C$_{0-6}$
5	IAR ← C$_{0-6}$
6	IAR ← C$_{0-6}$

The operation here is as follows. First the memory is told to read. (The prior instruction has loaded the memory address register with the location of the instruction word.) The instruction word is then in the memory buffer register when the next microoperation is performed. This microinstruction loads the op-code register with the first 5 bits in the memory buffer register. Next this value is added to the IAR register plus 1. Now if the instruction is an ADD, with op code 00000, then 1 will be added to the IAR's current contents (which will give 3 decimal). Thus, the next word in the control memory to be accessed will be at location 3, and in location 3 the value for C in the first 7 bits is 20. When C is loaded into the IAR, the next microinstruction word addressed will be that at address 20 in the ROM, which contains the first microinstruction in the ADD section. If the instruction in OP is a SUBTRACT, the op code will be 00001, so the next word in the control memory to be used will be at location 4 decimal. This will cause a transfer to location 25, which contains the microinstructions for the SUBTRACT instruction.

Thus, an ADD instruction will cause a jump to location 20(decimal) in the control memory, and a SUBTRACT will cause a branch to location 25. Each of these locations begins the section of memory containing the microinstructions that will cause the instruction to be executed.

At the end of each microprogram section that causes an instruction to be executed, the IAR is set to 0, which is the starting point for the operations that cause the next instruction to be read and that branch to the section in the control memory causing the instruction to be executed.

Variations in Microprogramming Configurations

Figure 9.12 shows the microprogram of Table 9.6 stored in a memory. The implementation here has the control memory in Fig. 9.11 with its contents, as shown in Fig. 9.12. This basic configuration is used in most modern microprogrammed computers. There are many variations on this idea, however, and there are many microprogramming languages.

The microprogramming configuration shown in Fig. 9.12 has an output bit from the memory for each control signal. This is called *horizontal microprogramming*. For larger computers there may be many control signals and, thus, many bits in the control memory. (In general, the number of control signals varies from about 60 for small computers to about 3000 for the largest machines.) Since this would involve too large a control memory, the control signals are examined, and an attempt is made to reduce the number of outputs from the memory. The resulting configuration is said to use *vertical microprogramming*.

As an example of how the number of outputs might be reduced, consider that, in some cases, when one control signal is raised, another is always raised, so these two signals could be combined into a single signal. In other cases different control signals are never turned on at the same time. If N such signals can be found, then only M control lines, where $2^M \geq N$, will be required, and a decoder can be used to provide the necessary control signals. For instance, the ADD, SUB, RESET AC, and MB INTO BR signals are never turned on at the same time. Thus, two control output lines with a four-output decoder could be used to generate these signals.

A system based on vertical microprogramming is less flexible because fewer options in control signal generation are available when microprograms are enlarged or otherwise changed. As a result, most commercial computers use a configuration somewhere between horizontal and vertical. (Many schemes have been used, and several are described in the questions.)

Microprogramming is widely used in the new computer lines. Since the instruction repertoire for the computer is effectively stored in the ROM, the instructions provided can be changed or added to by changing or adding to the ROM.

TABLE 9.6
Microprogram for four-instruction computer

Location control memory	Microprogram	Comments
0	$R \leftarrow 1$, $IAR \leftarrow IAR + 1$	Tell memory to read, increment IAR
1	$OP \leftarrow MB_{11-15}$, $IAR \leftarrow IAR + 1$	Place op code instruction in OP
2	$IAR \leftarrow OP + IAR + 1$	Add op code to 3; this gives next address in IAR to be used
3	$IAR \leftarrow C_{0-6}$, C_{0-6} has value 20 decimal	Instruction was ADD; go to location 20 in ROM
4	$IAR \leftarrow C_{0-6}$, C_{0-6} has value 25 decimal	Instruction was SUBTRACT; go to location 25 in ROM
5	$IAR \leftarrow C_{0-6}$, C_{0-6} has value 30 decimal	Instruction was CLA; go to location 30 in ROM
6	$IAR \leftarrow C_{0-6}$, C_{0-6} has value 35 decimal	Instruction was STO; go to location 35 in ROM
7 8 9 10 11 12 13 14 15 16 17 18 19	Left blank to add more instructions (*Note:* $IAR \leftarrow IAR + 1$ occurs in every following line except 24, 29, 34, 39	
20	$I \leftarrow 0$, $E \leftarrow 1$, $MA \leftarrow MB_{0-10}$	Begin ADD instruction microoperations; place address of augend in memory address register
21	$R \leftarrow 1$, $IC \leftarrow IC + 1$	Read augend from memory; increment instruction counter
22	$BR \leftarrow MB$, $R \leftarrow 0$	Place augend in B register
23	$AC \leftarrow AC + BR$	Add and place sum in accumulator

Further, microprogramming is useful in simulating one computer on another. Suppose that we have a computer with a basic set of registers and operations between registers, and we have the ability to microprogram this computer. Further, we have a second computer with a certain set of instructions and a set of programs written to run on this second computer. We now wish to make the first computer run these programs and deliver the same results as the second computer would have delivered. This is called *simulation,* and the first computer is said to *simulate* the second computer. To do this, we microprogram the simulator computer so that a given instruction has the same effect as the same instruction in the second

TABLE 9.6
Microprogram for four-instruction computer (*continued*)

Location control memory	Microprogram	Comments
24	MA ← IC, I ← 1, E ← 0, IAR ← 0	Set up for next instruction by placing instruction counter in memory address register and going to location 0 in control memory
25	MA ← MB$_{0-10}$, I ← 0, E ← 0, IAR ← 0	Begin SUBTRACT instruction micro-operations
26	R ← 1, IC ← IC +1	
27	BR ← MB, R ← 0	Place subtrahend in B register
28	AC ← AC −BR	Subtract and place difference in accumulator
29	MA ← IC, I ← 1, E ← 0, IAR ← 0	Place address of next instruction word in memory address register and go to 0 in control memory
30	MA ← MB$_{0-10}$, I ← 0, E ← 1	Begin CLA instruction operations
31	R ← 1	
32	BR ← MB, AC ← 0, R ← 0	Reset accumulator
33	AC ← AC +BR	Add B register to the accumulator
34	MA ← IC, I ← 1, E ← 0, IAR ← 0	End CLA instruction; place address of next instruction in memory address register and go to 0 in control memory
35	I ← 0, E ← 1, MA ← MB$_{0-10}$	Begin STO instruction
36	W ← 1; MB ← AC	Place accumulator's contents in memory buffer register so that it can be stored; tell memory to write
37	W ← 0	
38	IC ← IC +1	Set up for next instruction
39	MA ← IC, I ← 1, E ← 0, IAR ← 0	End of instruction: place address of next instruction in memory address register and go to 0 in control memory

machine.[11] As can be seen, a computer that is microprogrammed can be made to simulate another computer. Clearly, some computers have architectures much better suited for simulation than others.

The microprograms provided by a manufacturer (or anyone else) to be used on a microprogrammed computer are generally called *firmware*. The instructions that a

---

[11] This is often called *emulation*. When microprogramming is used, it is necessary to rename registers and arrange for other changes to really effect this, but the principle is essentially as given here.

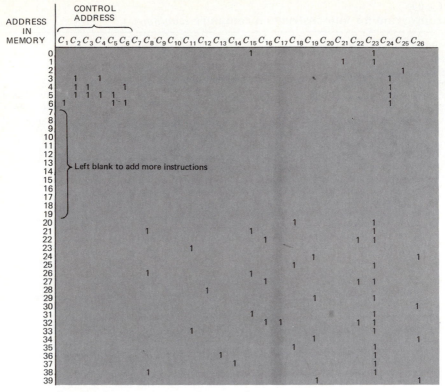

Note: Only 1s are shown; remaining positions are 0s.

FIGURE 9.12
Microprogram in memory. Control address C_0 has 0s in all positions.

microprogrammed computer provides can be very complex and carefully designed to satisfy the programmer's needs. The primary objections to microprogramming are: (1) speed, because the logic gates used in a "conventional" computer will be faster than the ROM in most cases, so the conventional machine may run faster; and (2) the gates can be minimized in number since the instructions are to be fixed. As a result, most large, fast "super" computers tend to use logic gates for control, whereas the medium and smaller computers now tend to be microprogrammed. The fastest small computers, called *RISCs* (to be explained), use gates for their control.

QUESTIONS

9.1. A single-address, one-instruction-per-word computer has a word length of 32 binary digits. The computer can perform 128 different instructions, and it has three index registers. The inner memory is a 4M-word IC memory. Draw a diagram of the computer word, allocating space for each part of the basic instruction word (op-code part, address part, index register part).

9.2. Design a single stage of an accumulator and B register that will add and shift left in one operation (step) or will simply shift left in one step. Use SHIFT LEFT and

ADD AND SHIFT LEFT as control signals, a full adder, AND and OR gates, *RS* flip-flops.

9.3. Construct a timing table and modify the control circuitry in Fig. 9.6, including the modification in Fig. 9.8, so that the machine has an unconditional BRANCH instruction (BRA), as well as a conditional BRANCH instruction (BRM), generating the necessary control signals.

9.4. Discuss how you would expand or perhaps improve the register transfer language in Table 9.5. Do you think that microprogramming in a higher-level language, such as Pascal or one or its variations, would yield an efficient microprogram in the control memory? Discuss this.

9.5. Show how to modify Fig. 9.8 so that the BRM instruction becomes a BRP instruction (meaning that the computer jumps or branches when the ACC is positive instead of negative).

9.6. Show how to generate timing signals (such as T_0, T_1, T_2, and T_3 in Fig. 9.5) by using a shift register with the rightmost stages' outputs connected to the leftmost stages' inputs. This is called a *ring counter*. In what states would you set the flip-flops to start?

9.7. Explain why some instructions require both execution and instruction cycles and others require only instruction cycles. Give examples of both kinds of instructions.

9.8. Why is the instruction counter always placed in the memory address register at time T_3 during the execution part of an instruction in Table 9.2?

9.9. Why can the SET W and AC INTO MB control signals be combined in Fig. 9.6?

9.10. Why can the IC INTO MA, SET I, and CLEAR E control signals be combined in Fig. 9.6?

9.11. Show how to add a pushbutton connected to a RESET AND START wire that will (using DC SETs and DC RESETs on the flip-flops) cause the computer in Fig. 9.6 to start executing a program beginning at location 0 in the memory when it is depressed.

9.12. Add a BRANCH ON ZERO instruction similar to that in Table 9.3 and Fig. 9.8, except that the computer branches when the accumulator value is all 0s.

9.13. Add a SHIFT LEFT instruction to the computer control example, using a technique as shown in Table 9.4 and Figs. 9.8 and 9.9.

9.14. When microprogramming is used with a ROM to generate control signals, how can the instruction repertoire of the computer be changed?

9.15. In Fig. 9.11 the control signals could be loaded into D flip-flops and the flip-flops' outputs used as the actual control signals. Give advantages and disadvantages of this arrangement.

9.16. Explain the difference between a microoperation and the control signal that implements it.

9.17. In writing microprograms it is convenient to have an IF microoperation. For instance, to implement a BRANCH instruction, we might use the IF $(AC_0 = 1)$ THEN IAR $\leftarrow C_{0-6}$ / IAR $\leftarrow$ IAR $+ 1$ microoperation. This says if AC_0 is a 1, place the current value of C_0 to C_6 in IAR, which means that the next microinstruction will be from the address given in C_0 to C_6. If AC_0 is a 0, the next microinstruction will be from the next location in the control store. Write a microprogram for the BRANCH REGISTER MINUS (BRM) instruction, using this microoperation.

9.18. To implement BRANCH or JUMP ON ACCUMULATOR NEGATIVE instructions, another control signal, C_{30}, can be added that, when a 1, causes a test of the sign bit of the accumulator and a jump in the control memory to a section of microoperations that causes the desired change in the computer's sequence of operations. Design this instruction.

9.19. Write a microprogram for a BRP (BRANCH ON POSITIVE) instruction, using the information in Question 9.17.

9.20. Show how to implement the instruction in Question 9.19.

9.21. Write a microprogram for a SHIFT RIGHT instruction, using the IF type of statement just described. (You will also need a counter.)

9.22. Show how to implement the microprogram in Question 9.21.

9.23. Write a microprogram to implement a multiplication instruction.

9.24. Show how to implement the multiplication instruction in Question 9.23.

9.25. Write a microprogram to implement a DIVIDE instruction.

9.26. Show how to implement your DIVIDE instruction from Question 9.25.

9.27. Reduce the number of control signals used in Fig. 9.12.

9.28. Explain what features you might like in a computer, which is to be microprogrammed to simulate several other computers.

9.29. Most computers now use a branch or jump scheme where status bits stored in flip-flops are continually set during arithmetic and logic operations. For instance, status bits Z and N are commonly used to indicate if the result of an operation is "all zero" or "negative." Show how to add such status bits to the arithmetic section of the computer shown in Fig. 9.6.

9.30. Discuss some of the advantages and disadvantages of microprogramming.

9.31. When status bits are used, JUMP instructions are of the form JUMP ON ZERO (jump if the Z flip-flop is a 1) or JUMP NEGATIVE (jump if the N flip-flop is a 1). Design these two instructions, using the Z and N circuitry from Question 9.29.

9.32. Discuss the advantages and disadvantages of *random logic* (gate-generated logic) versus microprogramming for a computer control section. Assume that the computer is a minicomputer.

9.33. Compare the microprogramming and conventional random logic techniques for generating the control signals in a general-purpose digital computer. Assume that the computer is to be sold in a large market where both business and scientific programs are to be run. Give the advantages and disadvantages of both techniques for implementing control logic.

9.34. The control of a small single-address computer normally passes through two major phases in executing an instruction to fetch a single operand from memory (an ADD or SUBTRACT instruction, for example). We call these the *instruction cycle* and the *execution cycle*. In order for control to know which phase or cycle it is in, a conventional random logic control unit uses an E flip-flop and an I flip-flop.
(*a*) Why are two flip-flops used instead of one?
(*b*) Why does a microprogrammed version of the same computer not require E and I flip flops?

9.35. Write a register transfer statement to transfer every other bit (starting with bit X_0) from a register X with 10 flip-flops into a register Y with 5 flip-flops.

9.36. Write the transfers in Table 9.3 in register transfer language. Write the transfers for a SUBTRACT instruction (as in Table 9.2) in register transfer language.

9.37. A frequently used configuration is a combinational "barrel" shifter, which provides for high-speed shifting left or right. Design a barrel shifter for 4-bit numbers. The inputs are:
(*1*) The 4-bit number to be shifted.
(*2*) A 2-bit input that specifies the length of the shift in bits.

(*3*) A direction bit that, if 1, causes a right shift and, if 0, causes a left shift.

(*4*) A bit that gives the value of all bits shifted in at the right or left.

The barrel shifter's output is a number that has been shifted as specified.

9.38. You are to design a new microprocessor with an architecture using single-address instructions and 16-bit words. Due to physical constraints, only 16 distinct op codes are allowed. What 16 instructions would you implement?

9.39. Compare horizontal and vertical microinstruction formats from the viewpoints of speed, cost, and ease of microprogramming.

9.40. Design a five-element stack using flip-flop (MSI) registers.

9.41. Add two signals, FULL and EMPTY, to your stack design, and suggest how these might be used in PUSH and POP operations.

9.42. A *queue* is a structure that is sometimes implemented in hardware. The queue has a front and a rear, like a line for tickets at a theater. A WRITE instruction adds an element to the rear of the queue; a READ instruction removes the element at the front of the queue. The queue is also called a *FIFO* (first in, first out) memory. A queue can have two status indicators, EMPTY and FULL. Show how to implement a queue instruction using the computer's RAM.

9.43. Design a five-word queue with 4 bits in each word using MSI.

9.44. Write a microprogram that can implement the MUL (multiply) instruction.

9.45. What are the advantages and disadvantages of horizontal and vertical microprogramming?

9.46. Write a microprogram for the instruction ASL (arithmetic shift left).

9.47. A BGT (branch if greater than zero) instruction has the value $Z + (N + V) = 0$ as its branch condition, where Z, N, and V are the zero, negative, and overflow condition flags, respectively. Write a microprogram to implement this instruction.

9.48. Write the register transfer statements for the following four instructions: EXCLUSIVE OR, SHIFT LEFT, BRANCH ON OVERFLOW, SUBTRACT MAGNITUDE.

9.49. Write the microprogram for a DIVIDE instruction.

CHAPTER

10

COMPUTER ARCHITECTURE

Computers are available in a wide range of sizes and capabilities. The smallest computers are called microcomputers, and the next largest are minicomputers. These are followed by small, medium-sized, and the large "super" or "maxi" computers. The prices range from a few dollars (for a chip set for a microcomputer) to several million dollars. Speeds are from microseconds per instruction to hundreds of instructions per microsecond.

A microcomputer generally consists of several integrated-circuit (IC) chips, including a central processing unit (CPU) chip (or chips), called a *microprocessor chip* (or chips); several memory chips; and one or more input/output interface chips. These sets of chips can be quite inexpensive (a few dollars in large quantities) or fairly expensive (several hundred dollars for very high-speed chip sets). Hand calculators are often assembled from IC chips including one of the lower-priced microprocessor chips. Personal computers also use microcomputer chip sets.

Microprocessor chips also are widely used in so-called original equipment manufacturer (OEM) devices or systems. Traffic lights, printers, communications controllers, automatically controlled instrument complexes, cash registers, and automatic checkout facilities in grocery and department stores, for example, all make wide use of microprocessors.

Similarly, minicomputers, which generally have prices of tens of thousands of dollars (including memory and input/output devices), are widely used in control systems and OEM systems, as well as in scientific applications and in business data processing for small businesses, schools, laboratories, and other institutions. The minicomputer preceded the microcomputer, and minicomputers continue to be widely used since they provide many users with enough additional capabilities to warrant the extra cost.

452

The small- and medium-scale computer market finds applications in businesses and laboratories of all kinds as well as in hospitals, warehouses, and small banks, for example. The largest computers are found in large corporations such as insurance companies, banks, scientific laboratories, and universities. These "super" computers range from scientific application–oriented "number crunchers" to large complexes of input/output devices and memories used in businesses where emphasis is on maintaining large files of data, producing management reports, billing, automatic ordering, or inventory control.

The characteristics of these different computers vary considerably from category to category and from design to design. Computers for business data processing have different system features than those for scientific work. There is also considerable variation in opinion as to how computers for the same application area should be configured, which leads to differing computer designs. The general subject of how computers should be configured and what features should be included is called *computer architecture*.

The principles of computer architecture extend through almost every aspect of computer organization. Included are the lengths of the instruction words, whether or not the length is variable, and how many addresses in memory are referenced by an instruction word. Other architectural considerations concern the number of bits in each memory word, whether instructions and data words are of the same size as the memory words, whether numbers are handled in 1s or 2s complement form or in BCD, or some combination of these. What are the instructions provided, how are the memories organized, and how are input/output devices interfaced? As can be seen, computer architecture is a large and rich subject that deals with most aspects of computer design and organization.

10.1   INSTRUCTION WORD FORMATS: NUMBER OF ADDRESSES

The number of divisions in the basic instruction word is determined primarily by the number of addresses referred to. The single-address instruction has been covered. Most current computers, however, have two-address instruction words with three sections [see Fig. 10.1(*a*)]; the first section consists of the op code and the second and third sections generally each contain the address of an operand. Different computers use these addresses differently.

In many computers, instead of a single accumulator, there are two or more registers called either *multiple* or *general-purpose* registers, or simply general registers. Figure 10.1(*b*) shows general registers and memory. As indicated in the figure, instruction words with two addresses can operate in one of the following modes:

Memory, memory. Both addresses refer to memory locations. For two memory addresses A and B, the instruction ADD A,B would cause the operation[1]

$$MEM[A] \leftarrow MEM[A] + MEM[B]$$

---

[1] Here, as in Chapter 9, MEM[A] means "The contents of address A in memory."

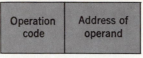

Single-address instruction

Two-address instruction

(a)

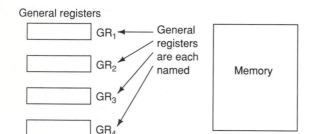

General registers

General
registers
are each
named

Memory

The number of bits in the general
register is generally either 16 or 32
for microprocessors. It can be greater
for large computers.

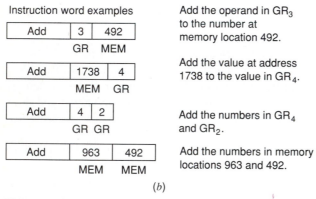

Instruction word examples

Add	3	492
	GR	MEM

Add the operand in GR_3
to the number at
memory location 492.

Add	1738	4
	MEM	GR

Add the value at address
1738 to the value in GR_4.

Add	4	2
	GR	GR

Add the numbers in GR_4
and GR_2.

Add	963	492
	MEM	MEM

Add the numbers in memory
locations 963 and 492.

(b)

FIGURE 10.1
(a) Formats for instructions. (b) General registers and instruction words.

General register, memory. Address A in the instruction word specifies the
general register to be used, and the second address indicates the location in memory.
A LOAD ACCUMULATOR instruction (LOAD A,B) would cause the contents at
location B in memory to be transferred into the general register denoted A. In symbols,
$GR_A \leftarrow MEM[B]$.

Memory, general register. The memory address A gives the location of the operand in memory, and the general register code B is the register involved. An instruction might be a STORE instruction (STO A,B), which would move the contents of the general register into memory:

$$MEM[A] \leftarrow \text{GR}_B$$

General register, general register. Only general registers are involved. An ADD A,B instruction would cause either $\text{GR}_A \leftarrow \text{GR}_A + \text{GR}_B$ or $\text{GR}_B \leftarrow \text{GR}_A + \text{GR}_B$ depending on the computer. (IBM goes left, for example, and Motorola goes to the right.) This and the *general register, memory* format are the primary formats used for RISCs (to be explained).

Stacks

Basically a stack is a set of consecutive locations in a memory into which operands can be placed. The name *stack* is derived from the fact that the memory is organized like a stack of plates in a cafeteria. (Each operand can be thought of as a plate.) The first operand placed on the stack is said to be at the *bottom* of the stack. Placing an operand on the stack is called *pushing*, and removing an operand is called *popping* the operand. The operand most recently placed on the stack is said to be on the *top* of the stack. Only this top operand is immediately available.

If we push operands A, B, and C onto an empty stack and then pop an operand, C will be removed. If we push A, B, and C in order and then pop three operands, first C will be popped, then B, and finally A. (This last-in, first-out principle leads to stacks sometimes being called *LIFO* lists.)

Figure 10.2 shows the operation of a stack. Stacks are generally maintained as a set of words in a memory. Each word therefore has a fixed length (number of bits) and an address. The *stack pointer* is a register that contains the address of the top operand in the stack. The stack pointer is incremented or decremented when an operand is pushed or popped.

Most computers provide stack instructions in their instruction repertoires. These instructions primarily use PUSH and POP operands. A typical instruction is PUSH A, where A is the number of a general register. This would effect the operation $MEM[P] \leftarrow \text{GR}_A$, where P is the address in the stack pointer; the stack pointer would also be incremented. POP A would cause the operation $\text{GR}_A \leftarrow MEM[P]$, and in this case P would be decremented.

A few computers have been made which use stacks instead of general registers for basic operations. If an ADD instruction is given to a computer using a stack architecture, the top two operands in the stack will be removed and added, with the sum placed on the top of the stack. Similarly, a MULTIPLY instruction would cause the top two operands to be multiplied and the product placed on the stack.

Since only the op-code section of an arithmetic instruction need be given to specify an arithmetic operation, these instruction words can be very short. It is still necessary, however, to move operands from memory onto the stack and from the stack back into the memory, and the instruction words for this will be longer since memory addresses must be specified. (These instruction words will be like single-

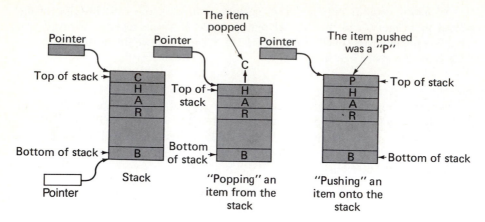

Note: In this case each item in the stack is a single character. The stack items could be numbers, words, records, etc. The pointer contains the address of the "top of the stack." There is also generally a pointer that limits the size of a stack. Sometimes this is a second pointer to the upper location in memory to be used.

FIGURE 10.2
Stack operations.

address instruction words, except that the operands are moved to and from the stack instead of to and from the accumulator.)

The advocates of stacked computer architecture have some convincing arguments, but problems do exist. Stacked computers included the Burroughs 5500 and 1700.

10.2 REPRESENTATION OF INSTRUCTIONS AND DATA

Important features of a computer's architecture are the number of bits in instruction words, the size of memory words, and the way data are represented in the computer. In most early computers and in some present-day computers, the high-speed memory contains the same number of bits at each address (in each location) as the instruction words, and numbers are represented using the same number of bits. This makes for straightforward implementation. Most of the large scientific number-crunching machines use this structure. CDC produced a number of 64-bit/word large computers with this basic structure, as well as some smaller, 24-bit/word computers. CRAY also makes computers of this type as do several Japanese manufacturers.

Business data processing involves much manipulation involving character strings (names, addresses, text, etc.). The desire to create computer architectures that conserve on instruction word length and also permit efficient storage of character strings of arbitrary length has led to a number of computer architectures with (1) only 8 bits at each address in memory, so that a single alphanumeric character can be stored at each address, and (2) instruction words with variable lengths (each word length is some multiple of 8 bits).

As a result, most computers now have memories where addresses are 8-bit bytes. Instruction words are then of variable length, with each being some multiple of 8 bits. Data words are also multiples of 8 bits, with many computers having 8-, 16-, 32-, and even 64-bit data word lengths.

10.3 ADDRESSING TECHNIQUES

To specify a memory address in an instruction word, the most obvious technique is simply to give the address in binary form. This is called *direct addressing*: The instruction words in the examples in Chap. 9 all use direct addressing.

Although direct addressing provides the most straightforward (and fastest) way to give a memory address, several other techniques are also used. Use of one of these techniques is generally motivated by one of the following considerations:

1. *Desire to shorten address section*.
2. *Programmer convenience*.
3. *System operation facilities*.   In many computer systems, the computer will have several different programs in memory at a given time and will alternate the running of these programs. To efficiently load and remove these programs from memory in differing locations, addressing techniques are provided that make the program *relocatable*, meaning that the same program can be run in many different sections of memory. The operating systems in microcomputers use this facility and this subject was introduced in Chapter 6.

The following sections describe the basic addressing techniques now in use: direct addressing, immediate addressing, relative addressing, indirect addressing, and indexed addressing. Numerous examples of these techniques are given for actual computers so that each principle can be clearly understood.

10.4 DIRECT ADDRESSING

Simply giving the complete binary memory address is the most direct way to locate an operand or to jump. As a result, most computers provide for some form of *direct addressing*. The computers used in the following examples will also be used in the sections on more complex addressing strategies.

8080 Series Example

Microprocessors of the 8080 series have single 8-bit accumulators. An 8080's memory is organized into words of 8 bits each (bytes). An op code for this microprocessor occupies 8 bits, or 1 byte, an entire memory location. The address bits are then located in the following memory locations. Since 2^{16} words can be used in a memory, 2 bytes are required for a direct address. As a result, a direct-address instruction requires 3 bytes in memory—one for the op code and two for the address.

In executing an instruction, the 8080 CPU[2] obtains the op code from memory first. It then reads the necessary bytes from memory and assembles a complete instruction word in its registers, which it then proceeds to execute.

A typical direct-access instruction in the 8080 is the LDA (load accumulator) instruction, with op code 00111010 (3A hexadecimal). This op code is followed by 2 bytes giving the address in memory of the 8-bit word to be loaded into the accumulator. The low-order (least significant) bits of the address are given in the first byte of the address and the high-order bits in the second byte.

Assume that the memory contains these values:

Address (hexadecimal)	Contents (hexadecimal)
0245	3A
0246	49
0247	03
$\vdots$	$\vdots$
0349	23

The 3 bytes in locations 245, 246, and 247 contain a single LDA instruction which, when executed, will cause the value 23_{16} to be transferred into the accumulator of the 8080 microprocessor.

Example

The 6800 series of microprocessors, which includes the 6802, 6805, 6809, and 68HC11, has two 8-bit accumulators, which are referred to as accumulator A and accumulator B. The microprocessor has 8 bits per memory word. The op code of an instruction occupies 8 bits, or a complete memory word. The address bits for an instruction word are in the memory location(s) indicated following the op code. The memory can encompass up to 2^{16} locations.

As an example of direct addressing, the op code for ADDA, which causes the contents of the address specified to be added to and then stored in accumulator A, is BB (hexadecimal), or 10111011 (binary). If the microprocessor reads this op code, it knows that the address is given in the following 16 bits. In other words, if a 6800 CPU reads an op code of BB, it then reads the next 2 bytes in memory to obtain the address. The microprocessor reads from this address and performs the required addition. The next op code is then read from the memory location following the two locations containing the address.[3]

---

[2] Each microprocessor in the 8080 series consists of a CPU constructed on a single chip. This chip is called a *microprocessor chip*. It interprets and executes instructions. Memory is on separate chips, as are input/output interface circuits. The 8080 series includes the 8086, 8088, 8085, 8089, etc. Perhaps 808X might represent it. There are differences between each chip but the basic architecture remains.

[3] Notice that the 6800 series places the most significant address bits in the second byte and the least significant bits in the third byte. (The 8080 does the reverse.)

The op code for an ADDB instruction, which causes the number stored in the memory location indicated by the next 16 bits to be added to accumulator B, is FB (hexadecimal). Now examine Fig. 10.3. If the microprocessor reads the two instruction words shown, it will cause addition first into accumulator A and then into accumulator B, and it will take the next instruction word from location 17 in the memory.

In the 6800 microprocessor, instruction words can have addresses with 1 byte or 2 bytes. [Some instructions use only "implied addresses" (i.e., no address bits); HALT is such an instruction.] The microprocessor must therefore read the op code before it can determine how many more locations from the memory need to be read to form the instruction word. In its manuals Motorola calls the 8-bit address instruction words *direct-addressing instructions* and the 16-bit address instruction words *extended direct-addressing instructions*. The 16-bit addresses have been used to illustrate the direct-addressing technique because they are more natural and enable all the memory to be accessed.

Example

The PDP-11 is a DEC minicomputer and microcomputer series incorporating several model sizes. A particular size is designated by the model number; the PDP-11/05 is a small computer, the PDP-11/45 is a medium-sized machine, and the PDP-11/70 is a fairly large system. This series of computers is also typical of what is offered by other manufacturers.

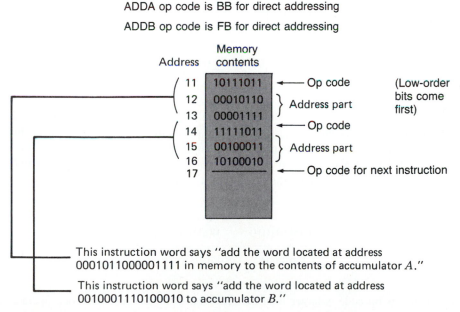

ADDA op code is BB for direct addressing

ADDB op code is FB for direct addressing

Address	Memory contents	
11	10111011	← Op code (Low-order bits come first)
12	00010110	} Address part
13	00001111	
14	11111011	← Op code
15	00100011	} Address part
16	10100010	
17		← Op code for next instruction

This instruction word says "add the word located at address 0001011000001111 in memory to the contents of accumulator A."

This instruction word says "add the word located at address 0010001110100010 to accumulator B."

FIGURE 10.3
6800 series microprocessor instruction execution.

The PDP-11 has eight 16-bit general registers (accumulators). It is common practice to name these general registers R_0 to R_7, and we follow this practice. The PDP-11 memory is organized into 8-bit words, so 1 byte is in each memory location. The PDP-11 has a number of addressing modes and, as a result, a fairly complex instruction word format.

A typical direct-address instruction in the PDP-11 involves adding the numbers in two general registers and storing the sum in one of the registers. The instruction word to do this has three sections: the op code, the source address, and the destination address. (In an ADD, the number in the source register is added to that in the destination register, and the sum is placed in the destination register.)

Since the source and destination are each general registers and there are eight general registers, 3 bits are required to give each address. However, since the PDP-11 has a number of addressing modes, 3 extra bits are included in each of the source and destination addresses to tell which addressing mode is to be used. The instruction word format is as follows:

Op code	Source address	Destination address

```
15   12  11    6  5            0
```

The first (leftmost) 3 bits in the source and destination addresses give the mode: for direct addressing these will be all 0s. The next 3 bits give the register number. The op code for ADD in the PDP-11 is 0110, so the instruction word that will add register 3 to register 5 and store the sum in register 5 is

0110	000011	000101

Another example of direct addressing is the INC (increment) instruction, which simply adds 1 to a selected general register. The instruction word to accomplish this has two sections: an op code and an address section. The address section has 3 bits to indicate the mode and 3 bits to designate the register. The op code for an INC instruction is 0000101010. Thus, the instruction to increment general register 5 is

0000101010	000101

      Op code   Address part

Notice that this op code is larger than the ADD op code, because only one operand is required here. (The first 4 bits are not duplicated in any of these larger op codes; they tell the class of operation.)

80386/80486 Example

In the direct-addressing mode for the Intel 80386/80486, the microprocessor uses the memory location given by the instruction, as shown in this example of assembly language:

MOV   EBX, ABLE

Here EBX is the name of a 32-bit general register, and ABLE is the name of an address in memory. This instruction causes the 32-bit EBX register to be loaded by the memory contents at the address *ABLE*. The 80386 uses segment registers with direct memory addressing (see Chapter 6); the segment register for instructions is called DS. The segment *offset* or *displacement* of the operand is contained in the instruction as a 16-bit offset. This offset is added to the current value of the DS (data segment) register (after shifting DS left 4), and this returns the actual 20-bit physical address.

It should be noted the 80386 microprocessor stores the lowest-order byte of the 4-byte double word at the lowest memory address and the highest-order byte at the highest memory address.

10.5   IMMEDIATE ADDRESSING

A straightforward way to obtain an operand is simply to have it follow the instruction word in memory. Suppose we want to add the number 7 to the accumulator in a single-accumulator computer, and suppose the memory is organized in 8-bit bytes. A direct way to cause this addition would be to have an 8-bit op code indicating an ADD and noting the augend follows "immediately" in memory (the next byte). The computer would then read the op code, get the byte to be added from memory (which would contain 7), add it into the accumulator, and take the next instruction word's op code from the byte following the augend byte. This is essentially how the 8080 and 6800 series computers operate.

In general, immediate addressing simply means that an operand immediately follows the instruction word in memory.

Example

For the 8080 microprocessor, the instruction ADI (add immediate) has op code 11000110 and tells the CPU to take the byte following this op code and add it into the accumulator. Consider the following:

Address	Contents
16_{16}	11000110
17_{16}	00001100
$\vdots$	$\vdots$

When the computer reaches address 16_{16} in memory, it reads the op code, sees that this is an ADI instruction, takes the next byte from the memory (which is 00001100), adds this into the accumulator, and takes the next op code from location 18_{16} in memory.

Example

The 6800 series of microcomputers has two accumulators, so the op code must tell which accumulator to use. The instruction ANDA, with op code 84_{16}, will cause the byte following the op code to be ANDed bit by bit with accumulator A. The instruction ANDB, with op code $C4_{16}$, will cause the byte following the op code to be ANDed bit by bit with accumulator B.

Suppose that accumulator A contains 01100111 and accumulator B 10011101. Then consider these memory contents:

Address	Contents
10_{16}	10000100
11_{16}	11010101
12_{16}	11000100
13_{16}	10100101
14_{16}	
⋮	⋮

A 6800 series microprocessor will read the ANDA at location 10_{16} and AND the next byte with accumulator A, giving 01000101, which will be placed in accumulator A. It will then read the ANDB in location 12_{16}, AND the next byte with B to give 10000101, place this in accumulator B, and read the next op code from location 14_{16}.

Example

The PDP-11 has eight accumulators and so must indicate which accumulator to use in an instruction using immediate addressing. The op code for ADD is 0110, and an instruction word for an immediate ADD looks like this:

0110	010111	000011
Op code	Source	Destination

The source bits say call for an immediate ADD, which means that the augend is in the 2 bytes (since the accumulators have 16 bits) following this word. The destination section here refers to general register 3, so the next 16 bits will be added into general register 3. (Placing 101 in the rightmost bits instead of 011 will cause an addition into general register 5, etc.).

Now assume that general register 4 contains 000061_8, and the memory is as follows (all these numbers are in octal, which is DEC's practice):

Address	Contents
1020–1021	062704
1022–1023	000012
⋮	⋮

Execution of these by the CPU will result in 12_8 being added into general register 4, giving 73_8 in that register.

Notice in the PDP-11 that the ADD instruction op code is the same for immediate and for direct addressing. It is the first 3 bits in the source and destination address sections, not the op code, that specify the addressing mode.

80386/80486 Examples

The 80386/80486 microprocessor assembler determines which addressing mode is being referred to from the syntax of the operation assembly language statement. For example, in the following assembly language instructions,

        MOV   AH,01
        MOV   AL,05

the operand value is contained in the instruction. Here the 4-bit AH register is given value 0001, and the AL register is loaded with 0101 (in binary).

The 80386 microprocessor also provides 8-, 16-, and 32-bit operands. The following instruction moves a 32-bit-wide source operand (a 0 must precede any hexadecimal letter) into the 32-bit EAX register:

        MOV   EAX,0A3C8FFFH

(The H stands for *hexadecimal*.)

In the immediate-addressing mode, all operand values are *sign-extended*, which means that the most significant bit of the operand value is repeated to complete the bit width of the destination operand. The instruction

        MOV   AX,258

takes the 10-bit binary equivalent of decimal 258, 0100000010, and extends it to a 16-bit destination operand width by replicating the sign-bit of 0 into the most significant bit field of the 16-bit AX register, resulting in 0000000100000010.

10.6   RELATIVE ADDRESSING

In general, when relative addressing is used, the address part of the instruction word gives a number to be added to the address following that of the instruction word. Thus, in relative addressing, the address section contains a displacement from the instruction word's location in the memory. Giving only a displacement reduces the number of address bits but makes only part of the memory available. For instance, if the address part contains 8 bits, then only 256 memory locations are available to a given instruction.

Relative addressing is best explained by using examples.

Example

The 6800 microprocessor series can have up to 2^{16} memory words, so 16 bits are required to address the entire memory in a direct-addressing mode. When relative addressing is used, this address is reduced to an 8-bit displacement, shortening the instruction word.

In the 6800 series, a relative-address instruction word contains only the op code and an 8-bit address, so only two locations in memory (bytes) are required. (The op code tells what kind of addressing to use.) The address in the second byte of the instruction is added to the address at which the op code lies, plus 2. The address in the second byte is considered a signed 2s complement number, however, so the address referenced can be at a higher or lower address in memory than the instruction word. In fact, the address can be -125 to $+129$ memory words from the address of the op code.

Figure 10.4 shows this. The op code for a BRA (branch) instruction using relative addressing is 20 (hexadecimal). The microprocessor would read the op code at location 10, see that it is a BRA instruction, get 00000101 from the next memory location, add this 5 (decimal) to 2 plus 10 (where the op code lies), giving 17. The next op code would then come from location 17. In Fig. 10.4 this op code is again BRA, and location 18 contains 11111001, which is -7 decimal. Since $17 + 2 - 7 = 12$, the next op code would come from location 12.

Example

In the PDP-11, the relative-addressing mode can be used for the INC (increment) instruction. The op code for INC in the PDP-11 is 0052_8, and 27_8 in the address part indicates the relative-addressing mode.

Assume that we have the following contents in memory:

Address (octal)	Contents (octal)
1020	005627
1022	000012
1024	
⋮	⋮

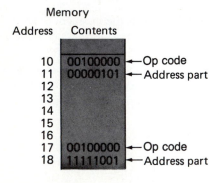

FIGURE 10.4
Relative addressing in 6800 series microprocessor.

The relative-addressing feature operates as follows. The displacement, 12_8 in this example, is added to the address following the instruction word, in this case 1024. This gives 1036, so the number at location 1036 in memory would be incremented.

10.7 INDIRECT ADDRESSING

Another widely used addressing variation is called *indirect addressing*, where the instruction word gives the address not of the operand to be used, but of the address of the operand. For example, if we write ADD 302 and the instruction is a conventional direct-addressing instruction, the number at location 302 will be added to the word currently in the accumulator. If the addition instruction is indirectly addressed, and we write IAD 302 (indirect ADD), then the number stored at address 302 will give the *address* of the operand to be used. As an example, when the instruction word at address 5 in the following memory is performed, it will cause the number 164 to be added to the current contents of the accumulator.

Memory address	Contents
5	IAD 302
⋮	⋮
302	495
⋮	⋮
495	164

Example

In the 8080 microprocessor, there are several registers in the CPU in addition to the accumulator. These are called *scratchpad registers* and may be used in several types of instructions. The scratchpad registers are named *B*, *C*, *D*, *E*, *H*, and *L* and are each 8 bits in length. Sometimes they can be handled in pairs, with a resultant length of 16 bits, thus forming a complete address. Then an indirect-address mode can be used where the number in the register pair points to the address of the operand.

For example, in the 8080 there is a MOV (move) instruction, which moves an 8-bit word from the memory into a designated register. The format for this instruction is as follows:

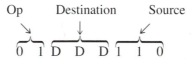

The destination section is 3 bits[4] and simply calls out the register into which the 8-bit word from memory is to be moved. The accumulator has number 111, register *B* has number 000, scratchpad register *C* has number 001, and so on. The location in

---

[4] Each D in the diagram stands for a single destination bit, which can be either a 0 or a 1.

memory from which the word to be moved is taken is always given by the register pair *HL*. Thus if register pair *HL* contains $45A2_{16}$ (*H* contains 45, *L* contains A2), then the memory address used will be $45A2_{16}$.

If the instruction word is 01111110 and register pair *HL* contains 3742_{16}, then the word at location 3742_{16} will be moved up into the accumulator. If the instruction word is 01001110 and the *HL* pair contains 2379_{16}, then the word at location 2379_{16} in memory will be moved into scratchpad register *C*.

80386/80486 Example

In the Intel 80386/80486 indirect-addressing mode, instead of the source operand's address being directly referenced by a memory address, the operand value is obtained from an offset address stored in a specific register. This register is usually denoted SI (source index), DI (destination index), or BX (base register). In the 80386 assembly language, the indirect mode is indicated by enclosing the source operand's designator with square brackets ([]).

The indirect-addressing mode is used mostly to access data in table format.

10.8   INDEXED ADDRESSING

There is a variation on conventional direct memory addressing that facilitates programming, particularly the programming of instruction sequences that are to be repeated many times on sets of data distributed throughout the machine. This technique is called *indexing*.

Indexing was first used in a computer developed at the University of Manchester. A register named the *B box* was added to the control section.[5] The contents of the B box could be added to the contents of the memory address register when desired. The address of the operand in memory would be at the address written by the programmer plus the contents of the B box. The U.S. term for B box is *index register*, and index registers are so useful that some computers provide several.

Use of index registers eases the writing of programs that process data in tables, greatly reducing the number of instructions required in an iterative program. The index registers permit automatic modification of the addresses referred to without altering the instructions stored in memory.

When index registers are included in a computer, a section of the instruction word tells the computer if an index register is to be used and, if so, which one. Thus, the basic instruction word is broken, for a single-address computer, into three parts instead of two. A typical division is shown in Fig. 10.5.

Generally two additional instructions are also used. One loads the index register, and the other modifies the number stored in the specified index register or causes the computer to branch.

If an index register is not to be used, the programmer places 0s in the index-register designation section of the word. If there are three index registers, there will be

---

[5] The idea was so useful that several B boxes were later used.

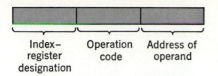

Index–   Operation   Address of
register   code   operand
designation

FIGURE 10.5
Index register instruction word.

two binary digits in the index register section of the word; the index register desired can be selected by placing the correct digits in this section.

To describe the operation of the index registers, we will introduce two instructions. We designate one of these by the mnemonic code SIR (SET INDEX REGISTERS); this instruction will cause the address section of the instruction word to be transferred into the index register designated. For instance, 01 SIR 300 will load the number 300 into index register 01. Since the address section normally contains the address of the computer word, all that is required is that the contents of the address register be transferred into the index register designated.

We designate the second instruction with the mnemonic code BRI (BRANCH ON INDEX). This instruction will cause the contents of the index register designated to be decreased by 1 if the number stored in the index register is positive. At the same time, the computer will branch to the address in the address section of the instruction word, taking its next instruction from that address. If the index register contains a 0, the computer will not branch but will perform the next instruction in normal order.

The index registers may be used with any normal instruction by simply placing the digits indicating the register to be used in the index-register designation section of the computer word. For instance, if index register 01 contains 300 and we write the CAD (CLEAR AND ADD) instruction

01 CAD 200

then the computer will add the contents of index register 01 to the contents of the address section, and the address used will be the total of these. Since index register 01 contains 300 and the address section contains 200, the operand will be taken from address 500 in memory.

An example of the use of an index register is shown in the short program in Table 10.1, which adds all the numbers stored in memory addresses 201 to 300 and stores the sum in address 301.

The program repeats the instructions at addresses 1 to 4 until index register 01 is finally at 0. The computer then does not branch and is halted by the next instruction.

Example

The 6800 microprocessor series has one or two (6800 one, 6809 two) 16-bit index registers. For the ADDA instruction, when indexing is used, the op code is AB_{16} (for the 6809, this uses the X index register). This instruction has only one 8-bit address part, so an entire instruction word requires only 16 bits (two memory locations).

Figure 10.6 shows an example. The instruction word is at locations 68 and 69 in memory and is an indexed ADDA instruction. The 8-bit address part contains 14 (hexadecimal), and the index register in the CPU contains 0102. This results in the number at location 116 in memory being added into accumulator A.

TABLE 10.1

Address in memory	Instruction word			Comments
	Index register designation	Op code	Address section	
0	01	SIR	99	Places the number 99 in index register 01
1	01	CAD	201	Picks up number to be added
2	00	ADD	301	Adds total thus far
3	00	STO	301	Stores the current sum
4	01	BRI	1	Subtracts 1 from index register 01 and then branches to first instruction until index register 01 contains 0, then proceeds to next instruction
5 ⋮	00	HLT	0	
201 to 300				Contain numbers to be added
301				Location at which sum is stored

The 6800 series has instructions to load, increment, or decrement the index register, and these are covered later.

80386/80486 Example

When the 80386/80486 microprocessor is addressed in the indexing mode, the offset address of the operand is calculated by adding the displacement in the instruction word to an index register's contents, and adding this sum to the selected segment register's contents. There are four index registers; SI and DI are 16-bit registers, and ESI and EDI are 32-bit registers. (Actually, SI and DI are the lowest 16 bits of ESI and DSI.) The direct indexed addressing mode is often used to access elements of an array. The

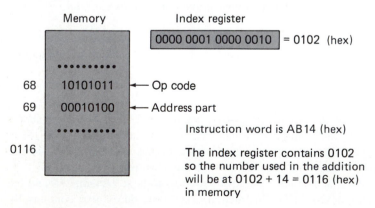

FIGURE 10.6
Index register usage in the 6800 microprocessor series.

displacement value indicates the beginning of the array, and the value stored in the index register selects an element within the array.

Following are two assembly language instructions. The first loads the index register ESI with 4, and the second indexes the value of ARRAY by 4 and moves the value at that address into the 16-bit register AX.

MOV	ESI, 4	(Loads ESI with 4)
MOV	AX, ARRAY, [ESI]	(Moves the contents of memory beginning at ARRAY + 4 into register AX)

In the 80386/80486 only the SI and DI registers can be used as index registers for 16-bit instructions. However, 32-bit operand instructions can use any of the 32-bit general-purpose registers except the ESP register.

10.9   BRANCH and JUMP Instructions

Instructions are normally stored in memory locations in order of execution. When an instruction is fetched from memory, the program counter is incremented until it contains the address of the next instruction in sequence. Execution of a BRANCH or JUMP instruction may change the value in the program counter, causing the flow of instructions to be changed. (In general usage, *BRANCH instruction* and *JUMP instruction* mean the same thing.) The format for a branch or jump instruction is as follows:

BR ADDRESS   JMP ADDRESS

As mentioned earlier, BRANCH or JUMP instructions can be *conditional* or *unconditional*. An unconditional JUMP instruction causes a jump to the address specified by the instruction word without any conditions. The conditional JUMP instruction specifies a condition. When the condition is met, the program counter is loaded with the address in the BRANCH instruction. If the condition is not met, the next instruction is taken in sequence.

Understanding the details of these conditions and how the result is determined requires an explanation of *flags* and *condition codes*, which is given in the next section.

10.10   FLAGS, CONDITION CODES, AND STATUS REGISTERS

Conditional BRANCH or JUMP instructions can be constructed in several ways. In single- (or even double-) accumulator systems the condition to be met generally involves the sign bit of the accumulator. A typical instruction is BRANCH ON NEGATIVE (BRN), which causes a branch to the address given by the address portion of the instruction if the accumulator sign bit is a 1, indicating that the number in the accumulator is negative. A BRANCH ON ZERO (BRZ) instruction will cause a branch if the value of the accumulator is 0. BRANCH or JUMP instructions are in two sections: the op code section and an address. If the branch is taken, the next instruction operated is that at the address in the instruction. If the branch is not taken, the following instruction in sequence is executed.

In general register machines, BRANCH or JUMP instructions operate differently. These computers have several *condition code* or *flag bits* in the CPU, which are set or reset (they are flip-flops) as the CPU performs instructions. Typical flag bits are a *negative* bit (N), a *carry* bit (C), and a *zero* bit (Z). When an arithmetic operation is performed, these bits are set or reset according to the result. For example, consider the following 8-bit ADD instruction:

$$
\begin{array}{r}
00101101 \\
11001001 \\
\hline
11110110 \\
\text{Sign bit}
\end{array}
$$

The result is negative and there is no carry, so N is set to 1, C is reset to 0, and Z is made a 0. For the following ADD operation,

$$
\begin{array}{r}
00000011 \\
11111101 \\
\hline
\text{Carry:} \rightarrow 1 \quad 00000000 \\
\text{Sign bit}
\end{array}
$$

the Z bit will be 1, the C bit a 1, and the N bit a 0.

The condition code or flag values are used to determine if a branch or jump is to be made. Table 10.2 gives a list of several BRANCH instructions. As an example, if a BRANCH IF ZERO instruction is executed, and the Z bit is a 1, the branch or jump to the address in the instruction will be taken; if it is not a 1, the following instruction will be executed.

To show how a specific microprocessor implements condition code bits, we will examine the 68000 series. Figure 10.7 shows the registers available to a programmer in the 68000 series. There are five condition code bits in the *condition code* register: $X, N, Z, V,$ and C; these operate as has been explained. (The X bit, for *extend,* is always the same as the carry bit. This condition code register is a part of a larger register called the status register).

The MC68000 has eight 32-bit data registers, D_0 through D_7. Data registers hold arithmetic values in the form of 1-bit values, 8-bit bytes, 16-bit words, or 32-bit dwords. Byte and word operations on data registers affect only the lower portion of the registers. For example, a byte-sized movement into a data register affects only the least significant 8 bits of the register; the upper 24 bits are not affected.

TABLE 10.2
Conditional BRANCH instructions

Mnemonic	Instruction	Test condition
BZ	BRANCH IF ZERO	$Z = 1$
BC	BRANCH IF CARRY	$C = 1$
BRN	BRANCH IF NEGATIVE	$S = 1$
BV	BRANCH IF OVERFLOW	$V = 1$

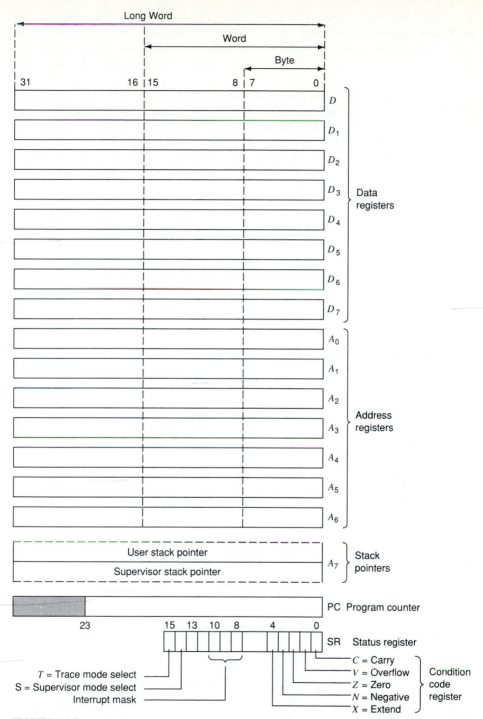

FIGURE 10.7
General registers in 68000 series.

There are eight 32-bit address registers, A_0 through A_7. These are used to hold memory pointers and index values. Operations that move values into an address register affect the entire 32 bits; in a word movement, the CPU "sign-extends" the word to take up the whole 32 bits of the register (i.e., it replicates bit 15 to form bits 16 through 31).

Not all MC68000 series processors have 32-bit memory addresses; the actual number of bits used depends on the size of the address bus. This series is "upward-compatible," however. Table 10.3 summarizes the size of the address buses for each of the processors in this series. When an instruction is executed, the CPU uses only the part of the address register that corresponds to the address bus, ignoring any additional high-order bits.

Seven of the address registers (A_0–A_6) are general-purpose registers. The eighth, A_7, is the user stack pointer. The stack is used to store temporary data and operates in a last in, firsts out (LIFO) mode. (The MC68000 fills a stack from high memory to low memory.) For example, on a subroutine call, the processor decrements the stack pointer, pushes the program counter onto the stack, and then branches to the subroutine. The program counter (PC) keeps track of the address of the next instruction to be executed. The PC is 32 bits long, but the maximum address depends on the size of the address bus.

When executing instructions, the CPU sets and resets the flags in the condition code register (CCR) according to the results of each register operation. The 68000 series has special instructions (to be covered in detail in Chapter 11) that affect only the condition codes. An example is the COMPARE instruction, which simply compares two numbers addressed by a two-address instruction. If the numbers are equal, the Z bit is set to a 0; otherwise it is a 1.

As was mentioned, the condition code register in the 68000 series is part of a larger register called a status register. Most microprocessors now have a status register that includes the condition code flags as well as several other bits that provide other status data for the CPU. Most of the newer computers offer a *supervisor mode* and a *user mode*. (In the 80386/80486 these are called *protected* and *read* modes.) The supervisor mode is intended for operating system usage, and the user mode is for applications programs.

When the computer is in supervisor mode, instructions are available that are not available in the user mode. Also available are registers and certain other privileges

TABLE 10.3
MC68000 series bus sizes

Processor	Bus width	Memory address space
MC68000	24	16 megabytes
MC68008	20	1 megabyte
MC68010	24	16 megabytes
MC68012	31	2 gigabytes
MC68020	32	4 gigabytes
MC68030	32	4 gigabytes
MC68040	32	4 gigabytes

having to do with loading addressing registers (for virtual memory, for example) that are not available for user-mode instruction.

A bit in the status register is generally used to determine if the computer is in user or supervisor mode. It is of interest to note that "hackers" who attempt to access privileged information or to plant "viruses" generally try to maneuver the computer into supervisor mode when their user program is run. This gives them access to supervisor privileges, enabling them to break into the system.

The status register for the MC68000 series consists of the condition codes, which lie in the lower byte and are accessible in the user mode, and the upper byte, which is accessible only in the supervisor mode (the supervisor mode provides access to both bytes). The *supervisor mode select bit* will be a 1 if the processor is in supervisor mode and 0 if the processor is in user mode. The *trace bit* (*T*) when 1 specifies that the processor is operating in trace mode. The *interrupt mask bits* form a binary number that specifies the current operation level for interrupts. External devices attempt interrupts by placing signals on three input lines. The processor compares the bits of the interrupt mask to the values on the interrupt lines, and when the CPU priority is equal to or greater than the interrupt level, the CPU continues execution. If the CPU priority is less than the interrupt level, the CPU suspends execution of the current program, jumps to an interrupt-handler subprogram, and raises its priority level to that indicated by the interrupt lines.

Figure 10.8 shows the *flag register* in the 80386/80486 which is called EFLAGS. The bits shown function as follows:

The *direction flag* (DF) indicates whether string instructions will increase (0) or decrease (1) their pointers.

The *interrupt enable* flag (IF), when a 1, signifies that interrupts are enabled.

The *trap flag* (TF), when a 1, places the processor in a single-step mode.

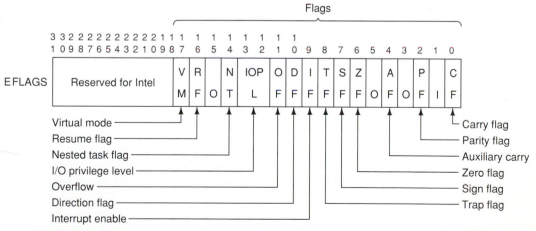

FIGURE 10.8
80386 flag register.

The *sign flag* (SF) indicates whether the result of the last arithmetic (or logical) operation performed resulted in a 1 in the most significant bit.

The *zero flag* (ZF) is a 1 for zero and a 0 for nonzero.

The *auxiliary carry flag* (AF) indicates if the latest arithmetic operation produced a carry from bit 3.

The *parity flag* (PF) indicates whether or not the result of the latest arithmetic or logical operation had even parity (it is a 1 for even parity).

The *carry flag* (CF) is set or reset depending on whether or not the last arithmetic, logical, or shift instruction produced a carry.

10.11 SUBROUTINE (SUBPROGRAM) CALLS

It is good form in writing a computer program to break the program into as many subprograms or subroutines[6] (separable pieces or modules) as possible. These subroutines are then jumped to whenever the function they perform is required.

The problem confronting the designer is that a given subroutine can be jumped to from several different locations in the program. For instance, in microcomputers no square root instruction is provided. If many square roots are called for in a program, the programmer writes a single square root subroutine, and whenever the program must find a square root, a jump is made to this subroutine. After the square root has been formed, the subroutine initiates a jump back to the main program instruction following the jump to the subroutine. The subroutine is said to be *called*, and it is exited by returning to the *calling program*.

The problem is to arrange for a smooth jump to the called subroutine and to make it easy for the subroutine to return to the calling program. To implement this, it is necessary to "plant" the address of the instruction to be returned to in some convenient place for the subroutine. Since the program counter (instruction counter) contains this address when the jump is made, most computers provide a JUMP TO SUBROUTINE instruction that will store the program counter before the jump is made. This instruction is also called a BRANCH TO SUBROUTINE or a CALL SUBROUTINE.

A JUMP TO SUBROUTINE instruction consists of an operation code (generally JMS, BRS, or CALL) followed by the beginning address of the subroutine. The instruction stores the address of the next instruction (the return address) in a temporary location, and control is transferred to the beginning of the subroutine. The last instruction of every subroutine, commonly called RETURN FROM SUBROUTINE (with op code RET) transfers the return address from the temporary location into the program counter. Figure 10.9 shows how subroutine calls and returns are made.

Different temporary locations are used to store the return address in different computers, but the most common way is to store the return address on a memory

---

[6] We use the words *subprogram* and *subroutine* interchangeably and assume they mean the same thing. They are separable modules of code that are called by the main program.

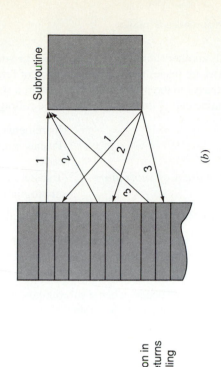

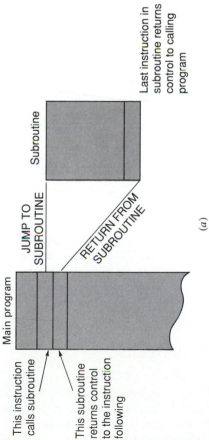

FIGURE 10.9

(a) Calling a subroutine. (b) The same subroutine may be called several times.

475

stack. If a subroutine calls another subroutine, each successive address is placed on the stack, so that when returns are made, the correct sequence of return addresses will be generated (the return is always to the program that last called a subroutine). When this scheme is used, a subroutine call is implemented with the following microoperations:

SP ←   SP + 1   (Increments stack pointer)
MEM[SP] ← PC   (Pushes content of PC onto the stack)
PC ←   *starting address of subroutine*   (Transfers control to the subprogram)

The RETURN TO SUBROUTINE instruction performs these operations:

PC ← MEM[SP]   (Causes jump to PC address stored on stack by JUMP TO SUBROUTINE instruction)
SP ← SP − 1   (Decrements stack pointer)

A *recursive subroutine call* occurs when a subroutine calls itself. Placing return addresses on a stack makes recursive calls possible.

10.12   INTERRUPTS

An *interrupt* refers to the temporary transfer of control from a currently running program to an interrupt service routine as a result of an externally or internally generated request. Control returns to the program that was interrupted after the service routine has been executed. (An interrupt procedure resembles a subroutine call.)

As just mentioned, interrupts can be *externally* generated (by I/O devices, for example) or *internally* generated (by the CPU itself). (An example of the latter occurs when a DIVIDE instruction attempts to divide a number by 0.) Internally generated interrupts are sometimes called *traps*. An example of a service subprogram is a power outage routine, which stores the contents of main memory and the current state of the CPU when a power failure is detected. The computer generally has a reserve power source that will last long enough to store the necessary information. When power returns, the program is restored and begins to operate where it left off when the power outage occurred.

The primary complexity in interrupts concerns the restoration of program operation. After an interrupt occurs, the CPU must be returned to its state as of the time the interrupt occurred. The state of the CPU includes the current contents of the program counter, the contents of all processor registers, and the contents of all status registers. These must be stored before the interrupt is serviced and restored by the interrupt service routine (or user) before operation of the program can be resumed.

10.13   PIPELINED COMPUTERS

Certain techniques can greatly improve CPU speed of operation. The best-known and most-used of these is *pipelining*. Pipelining is the addition of parallel elements to the computer's arithmetic and control element so that several instructions can be worked on in parallel, increasing the throughput of the computer.

The basic idea in pipelining is to begin carrying out new instructions before execution of an old one is completed. To see how this is possible, we examine the execution of a typical instruction involving several clearly defined steps. These steps are shown in the register transfer charts for addition, subtraction, and other operations in Chap. 9, where each step consists of one or more register operations. The steps are also outlined in the microprogram lists, which show the microinstructions that must be executed to perform an instruction.

A possible list of steps to be carried out for an instruction is:

1. *Fetch the instruction.* Read the instruction word from memory.
2. *Decode the instruction.* Identify the instruction based on the op code, and determine what control signals are required and when.
3. *Generate operand addresses.* Determine the addresses of operands to be used.
4. *Fetch operands.* Access the operands to be used.
5. *Execute instruction.* Perform the desired operation (addition, subtraction, etc.).

When pipelining is used, the number of steps in the basic process is less important than fitting the steps into the same framework so that they can be performed in parallel.

Using the preceding steps as a framework, Fig. 10.10(*a*) shows the pipelined execution of a five-step process where a new instruction is read and its execution begins with each new clock period.[7] In this way an instruction's execution is completed each clock period, so throughput is at the rate of one instruction per clock period (cycle). The figure also shows how the five basic operations are performed in parallel during each clock period.

Figure 10.10(*b*) shows the block diagram of a pipeline for the operations outlined. A new instruction word is read into the *fetch instruction* section each clock period. This instruction word is passed to the *decode instruction* section during the next clock period while a new instruction word is read into the *fetch instruction* section. Each instruction is taken in sequence from memory. The blocks shown are implemented separately using gates and flip-flops, and results are passed from block to block over connections. Control signals are generated so that each instruction is properly executed as it passes through the pipeline. All details of the instruction (decoded op code, operand values, etc.) must be passed along each stage of the pipeline. This means that there are many lines between blocks of the pipeline.

Several problems are readily apparent. Instructions such as multiplication and division, which require more than the normal number of instruction steps, must be accommodated and this is done by adding special sections for these operations. Control must then see that subsequent instructions are delayed until these operations are completed. Floating-point instructions also fall into this category. Thus, the pipelines of many larger machines can be quite large as designers add logic to accommodate the more involved instructions. This extra complexity is also one of the reasons for the success of RISCs.

Two other problems are even more severe. One is the occurrence of BRANCH instructions, which can cause the order of instructions taken from memory to vary

---

[7] A clock *period* or *cycle* is the time between a clock pulse and the next clock pulse.

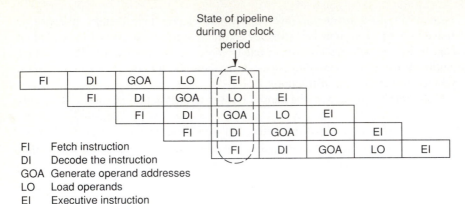

State of pipeline
during one clock
period

FI	DI	GOA	LO	EI				
	FI	DI	GOA	LO	EI			
		FI	DI	GOA	LO	EI		
			FI	DI	GOA	LO	EI	
				FI	DI	GOA	LO	EI

FI   Fetch instruction
DI   Decode the instruction
GOA Generate operand addresses
LO   Load operands
EI   Executive instruction

(a)

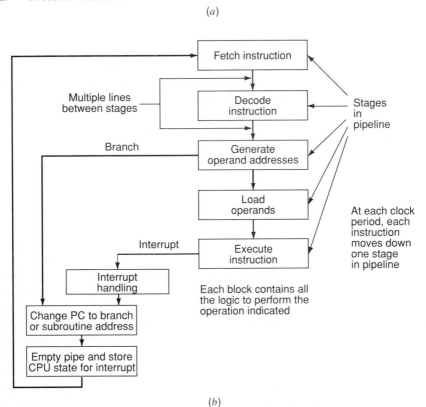

Fetch instruction

Multiple lines
between stages

Decode
instruction

Stages
in
pipeline

Branch

Generate
operand addresses

Load
operands

At each clock
period, each
instruction
moves down
one stage
in pipeline

Interrupt

Execute
instruction

Interrupt
handling

Each block contains all
the logic to perform the
operation indicated

Change PC to branch
or subroutine address

Empty pipe and store
CPU state for interrupt

(b)

FIGURE 10.10
Pipeline operations. (a) CPU pipeline flow. (b) Five-stage CPU pipeline.

from the "normal sequence". The second arises from the fact that an instruction may modify the operand to be used by a following instruction.

BRANCH instructions can be accommodated in several ways. In very large machines, pipelines that allow for both paths through a branch have been constructed. This calls for doubling the size of certain sections of the pipeline; however, consecutive branches must still be accounted for. Another approach is simply to delay the reading of new instructions until the BRANCH instruction is executed. This can slow the pipeline down (in some programs, BRANCH instructions occur as much as 30% of the time). Some systems have compilers that spot a BRANCH instruction and insert instructions that either delay the reading of new instructions or perform other useful tasks while waiting for the BRANCH instructions to finish.

The problem of operand modification can be dealt with by spotting such possibilities with logic and then moving new values in as required, or by simply delaying execution of following instructions until the new values have been formed. Each alternative requires additional logic and complicates pipeline design but constitutes part of the overall design procedure. As can be seen, speed entails extra costs due to complexity of pipeline construction and design, but the additional throughput has made pipelines a component of almost every new machine, including most microprocessors.

10.14 RISC AND CISC ARCHITECTURES

Computer architectures can be divided into two basic types: the *reduced instruction set computer* (RISC) and the *complex instruction set computer* (CISC). The earliest computers had only a few simple instructions because the early vacuum tube and semiconductor technology was too expensive and bulky and generated too much heat to allow complicated instruction repertoires. As semiconductor technology improved, computer designers began adding more instructions to computers, and these instructions became more complex. They were intended to aid operating systems and compiler programmers, and single instructions were made available to implement complete program subroutines. (For example, a single instruction to convert several numbers input in BCD to binary replaced a sequence of instructions, and complicated single instructions to manipulate files were added.) The VAX and IBM 370 are good illustrations of these instruction sets and CISC architecture. The result was that the number of different instructions that were implemented in computers became large, although many of the more complex instructions were rarely used in actual programs.

The basic idea behind CISCs is that when a single instruction does the work of several instructions, fewer instruction words need be read from memory and this reduces trips to memory, saving memory and speeding up operation. There are some negative side effects from large instruction repertoires, however. Each instruction added requires additional electronics (particularly when a pipeline is used). This causes the processor chip(s) to be larger and therefore slower for microprocessors, and much more numerous for larger machines, which also slows down operation. For microprocessors, when chip area is increased, the signal paths become longer and more delay is encountered. Also, more gates increases gate output loading and more current is required to charge inputs. The extra electronics also generates heat, which eventually can require adding still more semiconductor chips, with the result of further slowing instruction operation.

Consideration of these complications led to a new class of designs called RISCs, which use only a small set of carefully chosen instructions, each of which is kept as simple as possible. In this way the processor can be implemented with a small chip area and can execute these few instructions rapidly. More instructions would have to be used in a program, but it was felt the overall operating time for a program would diminish.

Studies and simulations indicated that the RISC architectures would indeed run many programs faster than CISCs (there is still controversy on this), and RISC chips and chip sets became standard items in the semiconductor marketplace.

There are several noteworthy characteristics of RISC instruction repertoires:

1. The instruction set is simple, and instruction words are similar in construction.
2. There are few addressing modes.
3. There is a memory hierarchy that includes cache memory. An attempt is made to execute an instruction word each clock cycle.
4. The processor is pipelined.
5. Control is in gates and flip-flops, and the control is not microprogrammed.
6. The registers in which operands are stored tend to be numerous, and arithmetic instructions are register-to-register (i.e., they do not involve trips to memory). When main memory must be used, LOAD and STORE instructions that load CPU registers from memory or store from CPU registers to memory are used.

The compilers that translate RISC programs often perform operations that optimize the machine code generated and sometimes even add instructions to prevent problems or slowdowns that might occur due to the limited instruction repertoire and pipeline construction. RISCs generally have a queue of instruction words in a "prefetch" buffer ready to be executed.

10.15   SECURITY AND PROTECTION

There is now great concern for security in computer systems. Commercial concerns and government users are very interested in protecting their data and systems from intrusion. The small user also requires protection, whether it is from "wiping out" something on a floppy disk or from "viruses" imported from a program or over communication lines. The architecture of some computers is arranged to make possible more secure operation, and these architectural features generally work in conjunction with the operating system.

There are four areas of major concern in computer security:

Operating system protection
User protection
Security of information
Memory protection

Operating system protection features in the architecture are intended to prevent application programs from modifying the operating system. *User protection* features protect users against each other. *Information security* architectural features allow programs limited access to information, according to established requirements. *Memory protection* mechanisms are designed to detect an addressing error (deliberate or otherwise) before it can cause damage. If an address error is detected, an address fault is generated and a fault-handling routine is activated to analyze the address error. For example, each of the segment registers in the 80386 has an associated *bound* register containing the value of the highest address in memory for that segment. The operating system loads this register when it loads the segment register. Then, if a program attempts to access an address outside its allocated segment, an interrupt is initiated, and a service routine is activated to resolve the problem.

As previously discussed, many processors have two operating modes: *supervisor mode* and *user mode*. In the supervisor mode, the operating system functions are placed at the supervisor level, while application programs execute at the user level, thus protecting the operating system from the application programs. The supervisor level typically enables access to all the processor resources, as well as to all external resources, such as memory and I/O. This allows the operating system to control both processor and external functions. In addition, some processors provide separate address spaces for each running program process, thereby protecting one program from another.

A basic principle in security is to allow a program to access only what it needs. Security of stored information can be provided by assigning each program access rights, such as:

1. *Read-only access rights.* When this is available, a program can obtain information only from the pages or segments for which it is cleared.
2. *Ability to write.* With this feature, a program can modify only certain pages or segments. It may be able to read other pages or segments but cannot write in them. This feature can be used to prevent programs from modifying the operating system or other systems programs.
3. *Execute access.* When a computer has this feature, each segment or page is marked so that the computer can either run it or not run it as a program. Sometimes programmers attempt to smuggle a program in as data and then run it. This feature prevents such a ruse.

Processors such as the IBM 370 series and the 80386 and 68040 store access rights in page or segment descriptor tables. Before the processor accesses a page or a segment, the computer first checks its access rights; if they are verified, it may access the selected page or segment. The diagram in Fig. 10.11 shows how this is done.

Several computers implement a *ring* security system, in which each program and its data are assigned a *security level* and can only access data and subprograms at or above the level assigned. Figure 10.12 shows how the rings are conceptualized. In a given implementation, the status register carries the security level, in binary form, in several bits of the program currently operating. Each segment or page then has a security level associated with it, which is stored in the descriptor tables. When a program instruction attempts to access data or to branch somewhere, the computer security system checks to see if its security level is appropriate for access. If not, an interrupt is generated and a service routine called to determine what is to be done.

As an example, the 80386 has four security levels, 0 to 3, and the status register (see Chaps. 6 and 11) contains the level of the current program.[8] Each segment carries

---

[8] The kernel is a small trusted part of an operating system which controls program and data operations for all other programs.

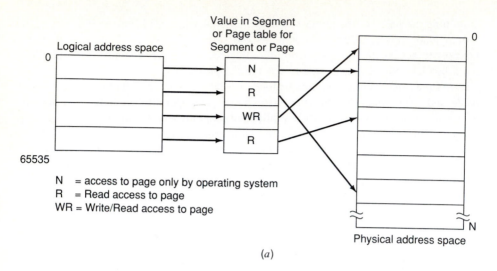

N = access to page only by operating system
R = Read access to page
WR = Write/Read access to page

(a)

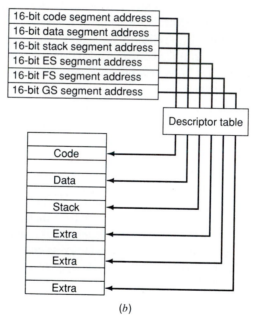

(b)

FIGURE 10.11
Page and segment descriptors. (a) Access rights are stored in page or segment descriptor tables. Each page or segment has access rights that indicate how the page (or segment) can be used. (b) Protected-mode segment addressing.

a descriptor that includes a level code, which is compared against the status register security level before each access is granted.

The emphasis on security features in architecture is increasing, and more examples will appear in Chap. 11. Small controllers in dedicated systems (for refrigerators, irons, manufacturing systems, automobile controls, etc.) do not make use of

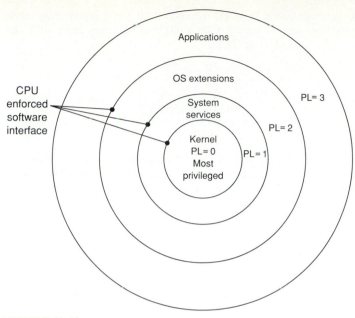

CPU
enforced
software
interface

FIGURE 10.12
Rings in a security system.

these features, but they are used by operating systems in multiuser and multitasking applications.

The segmentation virtual memory system provides a natural security system, since a segment is an entity and can carry a security level and access privilege bits. In the segmentation system, each segment length is defined by the programmer, and protecting segments by using access rights is easy to implement.

QUESTIONS

10.1. Describe some advantages and disadvantages of multiple-accumulator systems (general-purpose registers) versus single-accumulator computer architecture. Include such factors as effects on instruction word length and convenience in programming.

10.2. Discuss the advantages and disadvantages of the following addressing strategies in a microcomputer:

(*a*) Paging (*b*) Indirect addressing (*c*) Index registers

10.3. Discuss the desirability of the following architectural features for a microcomputer to be used as a traffic light controller:

(*a*) Paging of memory
(*b*) Floating-point arithmetic
(*c*) Indirect addressing

10.4. Using the index instructions given in Sec. 10.8, write a program that adds 40 numbers located in the memory, starting at address 200, and stores the sum in register 300.

10.5. A two-address computer has a large IC memory, with a 0.1-μs memory cycle time, and a small high-speed memory, with a 0.025-μs memory cycle time. An addition instruction word looks like this:

ADD	1st address	2d address

The first address refers to the small high-speed memory and the second address to the large memory. The sum is placed in the high-speed memory at the first address. How long will it take to perform an addition instruction? Why?

10.6. Modify the program in Sec. 10.8 so that the numbers located at memory addresses 353 through 546 are added and stored at address 600.

10.7. If we use three binary digits in the instruction word to indicate which index register is used, or if one is to be used at all, how many index registers can be used in the machine?

10.8. The use of paging enables the relocation of programs in the memory without extensive modification of the addresses in the program. Explain why.

10.9. Modify the program in Sec. 10.8 so that the numbers located at addresses 300 through 305 are multiplied and the product stored at address 310.

10.10. Explain how paging and indirect addressing can be useful in relocating subprograms when a program is rewritten. What are some disadvantages of paging and indirect addressing?

10.11. Define the following:
(*a*) Microcomputer   (*b*) Microprogramming   (*c*) Microprocessor
(*d*) Multiprocessor

10.12. Explain each of the following:
(*a*) Program counter   (*b*) Flag register   (*c*) Stack pointer

10.13. A program structure that is related to a stack is a *queue*, which replaces the stack's LIFO access mechanism by first in, first out (FIFO). How can a region of main memory be managed as a queue using registers? What are the instructions needed to write a word into the queue or to read a word?

10.14. Microprocessors such as the Intel 80386 allow the programmer to specify one of four different memory organizations: segmented and paged, unsegmented and unpaged, segmented and unpaged, and unsegmented and paged. Suggest applications where each of these four might be a good choice.

10.15. What are the advantages of having two classes of software processes: supervisor processes and user processes?

10.16. A 16-bit computer has a general register R_1. Determine the values of status bits C, S and V after each of the following instructions. The initial value of R_1 is decimal 65000.
(a) Add immediate operand 5600 to R_1.
(b) Subtract immediate operand 79000 to R_1.

10.17. Two numbers, A and B, are compared by subtracting B from A. C is considered a borrow bit after a COMPARE instruction, so $C = 1$ if $A < B$. Z is set to 1 if $A - B = 0$. Show how the relative magnitudes of A and B can be determined from inspection of C and Z.

10.18. Give three examples of external interrupts and three examples of internal interrupts.

10.19. Some disks have a *disk cache*, which is a high-speed semiconductor memory that buffers disk accesses. Assume the disk controller can control entire page swaps, and give a reasonable design for a disk cache.

10.20. Show that the transfer statement

$$A \leftarrow A + A$$

causes a SHIFT LEFT operation and explain exceptions.

10.21. A main memory with a capacity of 4 megabytes is used in a general-purpose computer that has an instruction word divided into four parts: an indirect-mode bit, code, two bits that specify a general register, and an address part. If only direct addressing is used,

    (*a*) What is the maximum number of different instructions that can be used in the computer if an instruction word uses 32 bits?

    (*b*) Draw an instruction word format indicating the number of bits and the function of each part.

    (*c*) How many processor registers are there in the computer, and how many bits are in each?

    (*d*) How many bits are there in MBR, MAR and PC?

10.22. What is the difference between an immediate, a direct, and an indirect address instruction word? How many references to memory are needed for each type of instruction, assuming two-address instructions with one address referring to memory.

10.23. Designate the address stored in the program counter of a computer P and the address part A; the operand the programmer requires is stored in the memory word at address M. An index register contains I. How should these addresses relate if the addressing mode of an instruction is:

    (*a*) Direct?   (*b*) Indirect?   (*c*) Relative?

    (*d*) Indexed?

10.24. A relative-mode BRANCH instruction is stored in memory at an address of decimal 934. A branch is to be made to address (decimal) 635. What should the value of the relative address field be, in binary, assuming a 16-bit address?

10.25. How many memory fetches does the computer make when it fetches and executes an indirect address-mode instruction if the instruction requires an operand? How many if it is a BRANCH type?

10.26. Register R_6 in the PDP-11 processor is a stack pointer register used with a memory stack. Show how the autodecrement mode with R_6 can be used for a PUSH stack operation and the autoincrement mode for a POP operation.

10.27. Register R_7 in the PDP-11 is the program counter. When R_7 is specified in the register field, the addressing modes are changed into different modes. Explain this statement, and show how some of the modes operate.

10.28. To design a computer with a paged virtual-memory system, what features are needed to permit a multiple-word instruction to start at the end of one page and end in the beginning of the next page?

CHAPTER
11

SELECTED ARCHITECTURES

Steady progress has been made in the architecture for computers. Early computers had very limited instruction repertoires. Later computers increased both the number and the quality of instructions that the computer could execute, in addition to providing many other facilities, such as virtual memory and protection mechanisms.

An important factor in computer architecture concerns the applications for which the computer is intended. Large computers that are business-oriented have architectural features to support multiuser, multitasking applications along with the security features necessary to protect users from each other (and themselves). Cray and other "super" computers are designed for high-speed scientific applications and are magnificent executors of FORTRAN programs, providing vector operations at a dazzling rate.

At the other end of the spectrum are the controller chip microprocessors, the RISC chips for graphics engines, and microprocessor chips for the PC market.

The intended usage is very important. A controller chip for a washing machine, home temperature control system, or electric iron need not have extensive protection features or even floating-point operations. A microprocessor chip for a powerful workstation, on the other hand, should have virtual memory, cache, a pipeline, and other advanced features.

Architectures designed to be used with operating systems include the following features:

1. An efficient system for handling both internal and external interrupts.
2. Virtual memory support, including demand paging interrupts and memory protection features.
3. Both user and supervisor modes to isolate the operating system from application programs.
4. Controllable user program access to system resources.

486

Other possible features include some kind of synchronization technique to permit multiprocessor operations.

Because of cost and speed considerations, designers cannot include every desirable feature. Interaction between operating system programmers, compiler programmers and hardware designers during architecture development is important in minimizing the final costs.

This chapter covers several architectures ranging from 8-bit microprocessors to the more powerful 32-bit systems. It is important to remember that the 8-bit and the 16 bit micros are still in widespread usage, and many designs using them are at this moment in progress. The probability that the average reader of this text will utilize one of these systems in a design is probably as high as the probability that the reader will use the latest super chip. (The small 8085, 8086, 6800, 6802, and 6809 chips are inexpensive, consume little power, are easy to interconnect and interface, and are reliable.)

On the other hand, the latest and fastest RISC or CISC cannot be ignored, since for many applications and for PCs, workstations, and business and scientific processing, all its available power will be used. As a result, these are also included in the discussion.

11.1 MICROPROCESSOR CHIP DEVELOPMENT

To provide an overview of microprocessor chip development, Fig. 11.1 shows the "family tree" for a number of microprocessor chips. (There are other chips, of course.) The tree starts with 8-bit microprocessors (replacing the early 4-bit designs, which were often used in calculators).

The first successful 8-bit microprocessors were the 8080, Z80, and 6800, made by Intel, Zilog, and Motorola, respectively. These were original entries in a competition that includes the chips shown. The last 8-bit chip made by Motorola was the 6809.

The 68000 is a 16–32-bit chip (16-bit external data paths and 32-bit internal operations). The 68008 is an 8-bit, somewhat reduced version of the 68000, and the 68010, 68012, 68020, 68030, and 68040 are steady progressions toward full 32-bit operation, with many features (to be discussed) added along the way. The 80186, 80286, 80386, 80486 are the Intel microprocessors that correspond in time to the Motorola versions and have comparable capabilities.

Some feeling for the complexity involved can be gained from Table 11.1, which gives some bus details.

11.2 INTEL SERIES DEVELOPMENT

The Intel 8080, 8085, 8086, 80286, 80386, 80486 series, shown in Fig. 11.1, is a good example of a microprocessor series used in many controllers and PCs. Before examining specific chips, we will present an overview of the Intel series of microprocessors.

The 8080 was an 8-bit machine and was Intel's first big success in 8-bit microprocessors. It had a single accumulator and six secondary registers. These six registers could be used in 8-bit arithmetic operations or combined as pairs to hold 16-bit mem-

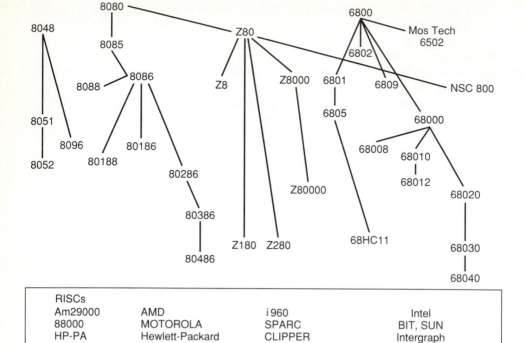

RISCs			
Am29000	AMD	i960	Intel
88000	MOTOROLA	SPARC	BIT, SUN
HP-PA	Hewlett-Packard	CLIPPER	Intergraph
i860	Intel	MIPS	MIPS Computer Systems

FIGURE 11.1
Microprocessor development.

ory addresses, allowing the 8080 to access 2^{16}, or 64 KB (kilobytes) of memory. The 8080 led to chips like the 8085, which do not require an external controller chip and have their own clock generators (which require an external quartz crystal).

In 1977, Intel introduced a 16-bit architecture, the 8086, whose instruction set was compatible with the 8080. (A translator program could convert 8080 assembler programs into 8086 assembler programs.) This upward compatibility has continued, and each new Intel microprocessor is able to run software written for earlier models.

The 8086 introduced memory segmentation. Each 8086 segment is a memory block that begins at an address determined by the appropriate segment register. Each memory segment is 64 KB—equal to one 8080 address space. The 8086 has four segments registers that can point anywhere in a 1 MB (megabyte) address space.

Other 8086-type processors are the 8088, 80186, and 80188. IBM used the 8088 in their PC and the PC/XT, leading this chip's wide usage. Intel also developed the 8087 coprocessor, which connects directly to the 8086 and its successors. This chip gave the 8086 series a floating-point instruction set using the IEEE standard.

The 80286 was announced in 1982. The 80286 has two operating modes: real mode and protected mode. Real mode emulates the 8086, and protected mode supports the 8086 instruction set but places a different interpretation on the contents of

TABLE 11.1
Microprocessor bus information

	6809	6502	8085	Z80	8086	80186	80286	80386/80486	68008	68000/68010	68020/68030/68040
Data bus size	8	8	8	8	16	16	16	32	8	16	32
Address bus size	16	16	16	16	20	20	24	32	20	23	32
Multiplexed	No	No	Yes	No	Yes	Yes	No	No	No	No	No
Control signals	E, $\overline{R/W}$	$\Phi2$, R/W	$\overline{RD}$, $\overline{WR}$, IO/$\overline{M}$	$\overline{RD}$, $\overline{WR}$, $\overline{MREQ}$, $\overline{IORQ}$	$\overline{RD}$, $\overline{WR}$, M/$\overline{IO}$, $\overline{BHE}$	$\overline{RD}$, $\overline{WR}$, M/$\overline{IO}$, $\overline{BHE}$	$\overline{RD}$, $\overline{WR}$, M/$\overline{IO}$, $\overline{BHE}$	$\overline{RD}$, $\overline{WR}$, M/$\overline{IO}$, $\overline{BHE}$	$\overline{DS}$, $\overline{R/W}$	$\overline{UDS}$, $\overline{LDS}$, $\overline{R/W}$	$\overline{DS}$, $\overline{R/W}$, SIZ0, SIZ1
External interrupt inputs	3	2	5	2	2	4	2	2	2 (3 levels)	3 (7 levels)	3 (7 levels)

489

the segment registers. Protected mode also expands addressable memory to 16 MB and allows implementation of virtual memory. The 80386/80486 followed. In the protected mode for these chips, each segment is marked to designate whether the segment is a protected-mode 16-bit 80286 code or a 32-bit protected-mode segment. This permits operating systems in protected mode to run programs in virtual 8086 mode. Protected-mode 80386/80486 operating systems can establish multiple virtual 8086 tasks.

The 80386/80486 are full 32-bit microprocessors. The cache memories and pipelines are on-chip and the 80486 has on-chip floating point.

8086 and 8088 Microprocessors

The 8086 and 8088 microprocessors were developed as extensions of Intel's earlier 8080 microprocessor series. A number of changes were made in the 8086/8088, the most obvious being the fact that computations can be performed using 16-bit data versus 8-bit data for the 8080. There are a number of other advantages, however, including multiplication and division instructions, instruction queuing to improve operation speed, the ability to address one million bytes of memory, more general registers, and more instructions and addressing modes.

The 8086 and 8088 chips are part of a series that include the clock generator and interface chips and a floating-point arithmetic chip (the 8089).

The pin-outs for the 8086 and 8088 are shown in Fig. 11.2. As explained in Chap. 8, the address and data lines are shared by using time-division multiplexing. The principal difference between the 8086 and 8088 lies in the number of data lines output to the bus. The 8086 has 16 data lines on its bus, and the 8088 has only 8. This is shown by the number of AD (address/data) lines versus A (address) lines in the pin-out for each chip. The 8086 use 16 of the address lines for data also, so that AD_0 to AD_{15} are used for address and data while the 8088 has only AD_0 to AD_7 for data and uses A_8 to A_{19} for addresses. The internal data paths on the chips are the same, however; and each can add, subtract, multiply, or divide 16-bit binary numbers.

The result of sharing output lines is that several chips are required to demultiplex the address data and control lines. One possible configuration is shown in Fig. 11.3. The output from these extra chips forms the actual bus for the 8086 or 8088. The control lines from the chips are used to strobe the data address and control signals into the bus interface chips.

An important feature of the 8086 or 8088 microprocessor is the instruction queue used. The 8086/8088 chips read instructions in order from the memory in advance of their operation, and the instructions are placed in a queue consisting of a set of flip-flop registers. This speeds up operation because the processor can continue executing a time-consuming instruction (multiplication, for example) and at the same time read instructions from the memory of the processor. Then the processor can execute fast instructions (shift or test instructions, for example) from the queue at a speed faster than memory cycle times. Logic is supplied so that if the computer branches (jumps), the instructions in the queue are discarded if necessary.

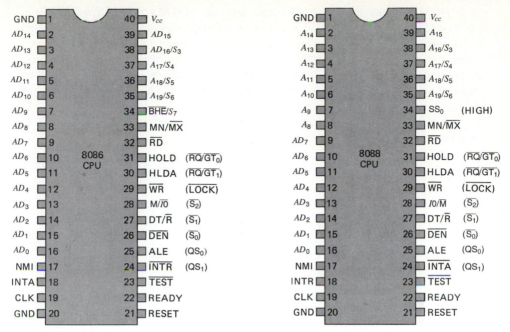

FIGURE 11.2
Pin-outs for 8086 and 8088 processors.

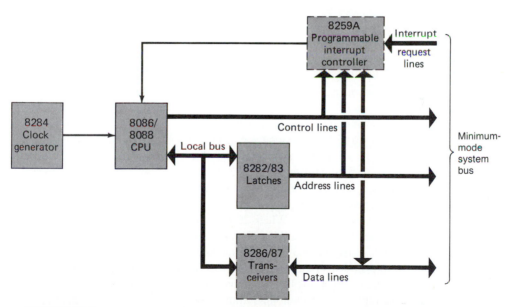

FIGURE 11.3
8086 and 8088 bus setup.

The 8086/8088 has a special output pin, the MN/$\overline{\text{MX}}$ pin. When this pin is connected to +5V, the processor is placed in minimum mode; when it is connected to 0V, the processor is placed in maximum mode. When in the minimum mode, the processor is used in single-processor systems. In the maximum mode, several processors can be used with an 8288 bus controller, which provides a special multibus architecture for multiprocessor systems. The maximum mode is for large arrays of memory, processors, and I/O devices.

A block diagram of the registers of the 8086 and 8088 is shown in Fig. 11.4. Note that there are eight general registers.

The 8086/8088 processor has a number of addressing modes. Addresses are 20 bits in length. Each address is formed in two sections, which are then added: a segment address and an offset. The segment address is a full 20 bits, and the offset address is 16 bits.

There are four segment registers, CS, DS, SS, and ES, each containing 16 bits. These registers must be loaded by the program to starting values because the contents of one of these registers are *automatically* added to each address as it is generated. The contents of the 16-bit segment registers are first shifted left four binary places, however. (This is the equivalent of multiplying the contents of the registers by 16.) Loading the segment registers with 0s would simply place the program and stacks in the first 2^{16} words in memory and would effectively remove this feature for simple programs.

When a program is executed, the contents of the program counter are automatically added to CS to form each instruction address. Data offsets are automatically added to DS (or ES in special cases), and stack offsets are automatically added to SS. Setting the CS, DS, and SS registers to addresses in different parts of a large memory would cause the instructions, data, and stacks to be in different parts of the memory. Setting the CS, SS, and DS registers to the same number would place everything in the same part of memory. Once the segment registers are set, the processor simply generates 16-bit offset addresses in a conventional manner from the instruction words, while adding the segment register to each address to form the final 20-bit address. If a program really needed 2^{20} addresses, it would be necessary to change the segment registers from time to time to utilize the entire memory.

In effect, the 8086 or 8088 generates conventional 16-bit (offset) addresses by using instruction words and then adds the contents of a 20-bit number to each of these offsets to form a 20-bit final address.

Quite a number of addressing modes are used to form the offsets in the 8086/8088 chip. Operands can be in general registers, memory, or I/O ports, and immediate addressing is provided. When 20-bit addresses are generated, the second byte in an instruction word contains information as to how the 16-bit offset or effective-address part of the address is to be calculated. (The first 3 and last 2 bits in this byte provide that information.) In general, this section of the address is formed by summing the contents of a displacement (part of the instruction word), an index register, and a base register. Any combination of these three can be used. This implements, for example, direct addressing, register indirect addressing, and based indexed addressing (summing the base register, index register, and displacement).

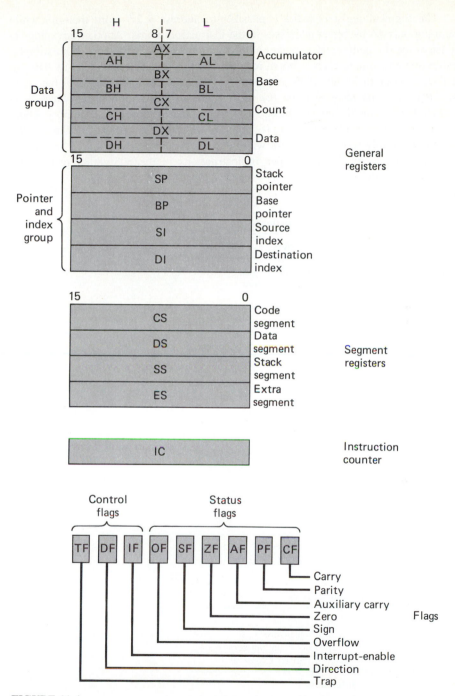

FIGURE 11.4
General-purpose registers in the 8086 and 8088.

The segment registers make it possible to address a 2^{20}-word memory while generating only 16-bit offset addresses in the instruction words. Another advantage is that use of the segment registers makes a program relocatable in memory. For example, consider the case where each segment register is set to the same number, say 0102_{16}, and then a program is run. If the segment registers are set to $FF02_{16}$ and the same program is run, the result will be the same (unless the program prints where it is located). This means that an operating system can place a program in memory where it desires. It can even place several programs in different parts of memory, while the programmer simply writes a program without concern about where it will be run.

There are many different types of instructions in the 8086/8088 processors. Figure 11.5 lists them.

Program transfer instructions

Unconditional transfers

CALL	Call procedure
RET	Return from procedure
JMP	Jump

Conditional transfers

JA/JNBE	Jump if above/not below nor equal
JAE/JNB	Jump if above or equal/not below
JB/JNAE	Jump if below/not above nor equal
JBE/JNA	Jump if below or equal not above
JC	Jump if carry
JE/JZ	Jump if equal/zero
JG/JNLE	Jump if greater/not less nor equal
JGE/JNL	Jump if greater or equal/not less
JL/JNGE	Jump if less/not greater nor equal
JLE/JNG	Jump if less or equal/not greater
JNC	Jump if not carry
JNE/JNZ	Jump if not equal/not zero
JNO	Jump if not overflow
JNP/JPO	Jump if not parity/parity odd
JNS	Jump if not sign
JO	Jump if overflow
JP/JPE	Jump if parity/parity even
JS	Jump if sign

Iteration controls

LOOP	Loop
LOOPE/LOOPZ	Loop if equal/zero
LOOPNE/LOOPNZ	Loop if not equal/not zero
JCXZ	Jump if register CX = 0

Interrupts

INT	Interrupt
INTO	Interrupt if overflow
IRET	Interrupt return

FIGURE 11.5
Instruction repertoire for the 8086 and 8088.

Data transfer instructions	
General purpose	
MOV	Move byte or word
PUSH	Push word onto stack
POP	Pop word off stack
XCHG	Exchange byte or word
XLAT	Translate byte

Input, output	
IN	Input byte or word
OUT	Output byte or word

Address object	
LEA	Load effective address
LDS	Load pointer using DS
LES	Load pointer using ES

Flag transfer	
LAHF	Load AH register from flags
SAHF	Store AH register in flags
PUSHF	Push flags onto stack
POPF	Pop flags off stack

Bit manipulation instructions	
Logicals	
NOT	"Not" byte or word
AND	"And" byte or word
OR	"Inclusive or" byte or word
XOR	"Exclusive or" byte or word
TEST	"Test" byte or word

Shifts	
SHLSAL	Shift logical arithmetic left byte or word
SHR	Shift logical right byte or word
SAR	Shift arithmetic right byte or word

Rotates	
ROL	Rotate left byte or word
ROR	Rotate right byte or word
RCL	Rotate through carry left byte or word
RCR	Rotate through carry right byte or word

Arithmetic instructions	
Addition	
ADD	Add byte or word
ADC	Add byte or word with carry
INC	Increment byte or word by 1
AAA	ASCII adjust for addition
DAA	Decimal adjust for addition

Subtraction	
SUB	Subtract byte or word
SBB	Subtract byte or word with borrow
DEC	Decrement byte or word by 1
NEG	Negate byte or word
CMP	Compare byte or word
AAS	ASCII adjust for subtraction
DAS	Decimal adjust for subtraction

Multiplication	
MUL	Multiply byte or word unsigned
IMUL	Integer multiply byte or word
AAM	ASCII adjust for multiply

Division	
DIV	Divide byte or word unsigned
IDIV	Integer divide byte or word
AAD	ASCII adjust for division
CBW	Convert byte to word
CWD	Convert word to doubleword

String instructions	
REP	Repeat
REPE/REPZ	Repeat while equal/zero
REPNE/REPNZ	Repeat while not equal/not zero
MOVS	Move word string
MOVSB/MOVSW	Move byte or word string
CMPS	Compare byte or word string
SCAS	Scan byte or word string
LODS	Load byte or word string
STOS	Store byte or word string

FIGURE 11.5
Instruction repertoire for the 8086 and 8088 (*continued*). (*Courtesy Intel Corporation.*)

In all, the 8086 and the 8088 are powerful processors with 16-bit internal operations, the ability to address a large memory, many addressing modes, and a large instruction repertoire.

11.3   6800 MICROPROCESSOR SERIES

A microcomputer series widely used as a controller and in PCs is the 6800 microprocessor series, first developed by Motorola. (Chips for this series are also available from a number of other manufacturers.)

The 6800 was the first in a series of chips including the 6801 and 6805 and the 6802, and 6809. The 68000 series evolved from the 6800 series, and the 6800 general structure continues through all later versions, although many additions and expansions have been made to the architecture. Becoming familiar with any chip in the 68XX or 68XXX group is a good step toward being able to use any chip in this series, since they are all quite similar.

A good example of how this series has evolved is the 6809. This chip follows the 6800 and 6802, having the same registers as the 6800 but with a second stack pointer and a direct-page base address register. The 6809 instructor repertoire is the most advanced in the 6800 series and includes many addressing modes and integer multiplication. Position-independent code can be generated, and features for compilers are included. The interrupt facility resembles the 6802 but has a "fast interrupt" in addition. The 6802/6809 buses are essentially the same. There is a 6809, a 68A09, and a 68B09, which run at different clock rates (B is the fastest). An interface built for the 6800 will operate with the 6809 (that is, interfaces are "upward-compatible). Fig. 11.6 shows the overall 6809 organization.

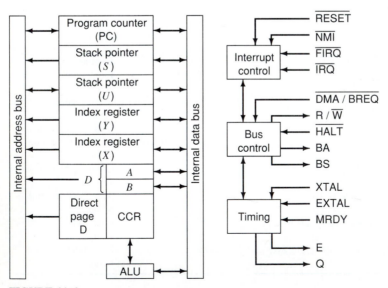

FIGURE 11.6
6809 microprocessor organization. (*Courtesy Motorola Inc.*)

The 6809 has an 8-bit data bus and a 16-bit address bus. From a programming viewpoint, the CPU chip contains the following registers (refer to Fig. 11.7):

Accumulator, *A* (an 8-bit accumulator)

Accumulator, *B* (an 8-bit accumulator)

Index register, *X* (a 16-bit index register)

Index register, *Y* (a 16-bit index register)

User stack pointer, *U* (a 16-bit register that points to a stack in memory)

Hardware stack pointer, *S* (a 16-bit register)

Program counter, PC (the instruction counter containing 16 bits)

Status register, CCR (an 8-bit register used to store the results of arithmetic and other operations as well as interrupt status bits)

Direct register, *D* (an 8-bit register used to extend addresses and form pages)

The repertoire for this CPU chip includes over 200 different instructions. The basic operation code is 8 bits, but there are several extended op codes of 16 bits. (The first 8 bits signal that the following are more op code bits.) There are several different addressing modes, which are described in Table 11.2. A list of the instructions for this microprocessor chip is shown in Tables 11.3–11.5.

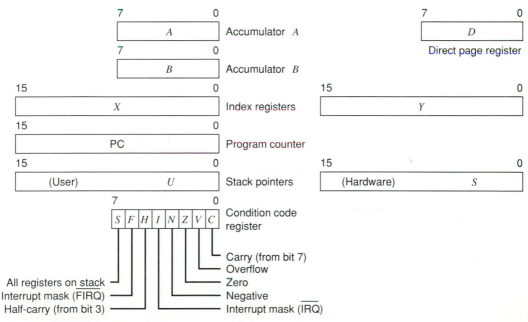

FIGURE 11.7
Basic registers used in programming the 6809. (*Courtesy Motorola Inc.*)

TABLE 11.2
6809 Addressing modes

Syntax	Mode	Addressing function
> Value Value	Direct extended	EA = Value[1]
< Value Value	Direct-short	EA = D ¦ Value[2]
# Value	Inmmediate	Operand = Value
R Value,R SValue,R ACC,R	Indexed	EA = [R] EA = Value + [R] EA = SValue + [R] EA = [ACC] + [R]
R+ R++	Autoincrement	EA = [R] R ← [R] + 1 EA = [R] R ← [R] + 2
−R −−R	Autodecrement	R ← [R] − 1 EA = [R] R ← [R] − 2 EA = [R]
Value, PCR	Relative	EA = OFF + [PC] EA = SOFF + [PC]
[Value]	Extended indirect	EA = [Value]
[R] [Value,R] [ACC,R]	Indexed indirect	EA = [EA indexed]
[R++]	Autoincrement indirect	EA = [EA autoincrement]
[−−R]	Autoindecrement indirect	EA = [EA autodecrement]
[Value, PCR]	Relative indirect	EA = [EA relative]

(Courtesy Motorola Inc.)

[1] The 16 bit address forms the effective address, EA.

[2] The 8-bit address in an instruction word is the least significant part of the 16-bit address and the 8 bits in the *D* register the most significant 8 bits.

Table 11.2 Notation

R	= *X, Y, U,* or *S* register
ACC	= *A, B,* or *D* register
EA	= Effective address
[ ]	= "Contents of." Thus, [*A*] → *B* means "the contents of *A* are moved in *B*."
Value	= 16-bit number
SValue	= 8-bit number
OFF	= 16-bit signed offset
SOFF	= 8-bit signed "short" offset
PC	= Program counter
D	= Direct page register

TABLE 11.3
6809 Instructions *(pp. 499–501)*

Operations	Mnemonic	Immediate Op	Direct Op	Index Op	Extended Op	Implied Op	Operation† (All register labels refer to contents)
Add	ADDA	8B	9B	AB	BB		$A + M \rightarrow A$
	ADDB	CB	DB	EB	FB		$B + M \rightarrow B$
Add D	ADD	C3	D3	E3	F3		$D + M \rightarrow D$
Add with carry	ADCA	89	99	A9	B9		$A + M + C \rightarrow A$
	ADCB	C9	D9	E9	F9		$B + M + C \rightarrow B$
AND	ANDA	84	94	A4	B4		$A \cdot M \rightarrow A$
	ANDB	C4	D4	E4	F4		$B \cdot M \rightarrow B$
	ANDCC	1C					$CCR \cdot M \rightarrow CCR$
	CWAI	3C					$CCR \cdot M \rightarrow CCR$ (Regs. on S stack)
Bit test	BITA	85	95	A5	B5		$A \cdot M$
	BITB	C5	D5	E5	F5		$B \cdot M$
Clear	CLR			6F	7F		$00 \rightarrow M$
	CLRA					4F	$00 \rightarrow A$
	CLRB					5F	$00 \rightarrow B$
Compare	CMPA	81	91	A1	B1		$A - M$
	CMPB	C1	D1	E1	F1		$B - M$
	CMPD	1083	1093	10A3	10B3		$D - M$
	CMPS	118C	119C	11AC	11BC		$S - M$
	CMPU	1183	1193	11A3	11B3		$U - M$
	CMPX	8C	9C	AC	BC		$X - M$
	CMPY	108C	109C	10AC	10BC		$Y - M$
1s complement	COM			63	73		$\overline{M} \rightarrow M$
	COMA					43	$\overline{A} \rightarrow A$
	COMB					53	$\overline{B} \rightarrow B$

499

TABLE 11.3
6809 Instructions (*continued*)

Operations	Mnemonic	Immediate Op	Direct Op	Index Op	Extended Op	Implied Op	Operation† (All register labels refer to contents)
2s complement (negate)	NEG			60	70		$00 - M \rightarrow M$
	NEGA					40	$00 - A \rightarrow A$
	NEGB					50	$00 - B \rightarrow B$
Decimal adjust, A	DAA					19	Changes Addition of BCD characters into BCD format
Decrement	DEC			6A	7A		$M - 1 \rightarrow M$
	DECA					4A	$A - 1 \rightarrow A$
	DECB					5A	$B - 1 \rightarrow B$
Exclusive OR	EORA	88	98	A8	B8		$A \oplus M \rightarrow A$
	EORB	C8	D8	E8	F8		$B \oplus M \rightarrow B$
Increment	INC			6C	7C		$M + 1 \rightarrow M$
	INCA					4C	$A + 1 \rightarrow A$
	INCB					5C	$B + 1 \rightarrow B$
Load accumulator	LDA	86	96	A6	B6		$M \rightarrow A$
	LDB	C6	D6	E6	F6		$M \rightarrow B$
Inclusive OR	ORAA	8A	9A	AA	BA		$A + M \rightarrow A$
	ORAB	CA	DA	EA	FA		$B + M \rightarrow B$
	ORCC	1A					$CCR + M \rightarrow CCR$
Multiply	MUL					3D	$A \cdot B \rightarrow D$ (unsigned)
Push data	PSHS					34	Push registers on stack
	PSHU					36	
Pull data	PULS					35	Pull registers from stack
	PULU					37	

Rotate left	ROL ROLA ROLB		09	69	79	49 59	$\left.\begin{array}{l}M\\A\\B\end{array}\right\}$ $\boxed{}\,\cdots\,\boxed{}$ $C\;b_7\;\leftarrow\;b_0$
Rotate right	ROR RORA RORB		06	66	76	46 56	$\left.\begin{array}{l}M\\A\\B\end{array}\right\}$ $b_7\;\rightarrow\;C\;b_0$
Shift left, arithmetic	ASL ASLA ASLB		08	68	78	48 58	$\left.\begin{array}{l}M\\A\\B\end{array}\right\}$ $C\;b_7\;\leftarrow\;b_0\leftarrow 0$
Shift right, arithmetic	ASR ASRA ASRB		07	67	77	47 57	$\left.\begin{array}{l}M\\A\\B\end{array}\right\}$ $b_7\;\rightarrow\;b_0\;C$
Shift right, logic	LSR LSRA LSRB		04	64	74	44 54	$\left.\begin{array}{l}M\\A\\B\end{array}\right\}$ $0\rightarrow\;\boxed{}\cdots\boxed{}\rightarrow\;b_7 \quad b_0\;C$
Store accumulator	STA STB		97 D7	A7 E7	B7 F7		$A\rightarrow M$ $B\rightarrow M$
Subtract	SUBA SUBB SUBD	80 C0 83	90 D0 93	A0 E0 A3	B0 F0 B3		$A-B\rightarrow A$ $B-M\rightarrow B$ $D-M\rightarrow D$
Subtract with carry	SBCA SBCB	82 C2	92 D2	A2 E2	B2 F2		$A-M-C\rightarrow A$ $B-M-C\rightarrow B$
Transfer registers	TFR TBA					1F 17	$R_1\rightarrow R_2$ $B\rightarrow A$
Test, zero, or minus	TST TSTA TSTB		0D	6D	7D	4D 5D	$M-00$ $A-00$ $B-00$

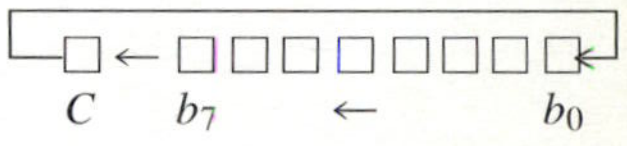

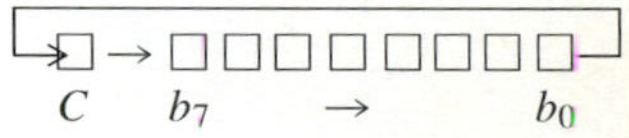

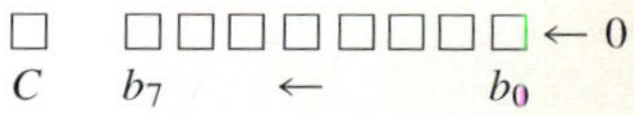

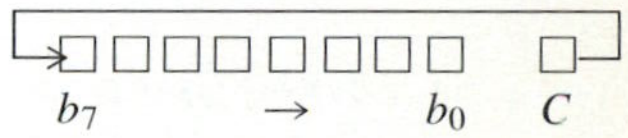

(Courtesy Motorola Inc.)

†Op code (hexadecimal)

+ Arithmetic plus   − Arithmetic minus   + Boolean inclusive OR M Complement of M 0 Bit = 0

· Boolean AND   ⊕ Boolean exclusive OR   → Transfer into   00 Byte = 0

Note: Accumulator addressing mode instructions are included in the column for implied addressing.

TABLE 11.4
6809 Index register and stack manipulation instructions

Pointer operations	Mnemonic	Immediate Op	Direct Op	Indexed Op	Extended Op	Implied Op	Operation
Load index register	LDX/LDY	8E/108E	9E/109E	AE/10AE	BE/10BE		$M \rightarrow X_H, (M+1) \rightarrow X_L$ (Y same)
Load stack pointer	LDS	10CE	10DE	10EE	10FE		$M \rightarrow SP_H, (M+1) \rightarrow SP_L$
Store index register	STX/STY		9F/109F	AF/10AF	FF/109F		$X_H \rightarrow M, X_L \rightarrow (M+1)$ (Y same)
Store stack pointer	STS		10DF	10EF	10FF		$SP_H \rightarrow M, SP_L \rightarrow (M+1)$
Store stack pointer	STU		DF	EF	FF		$M \rightarrow U_H, (M+1) \rightarrow U_L$
Load stack pointer	LDU	CE	DE	EE	FE		$U_H \rightarrow M_H, U_L \rightarrow (M+1)$
Load effective address	LEAX/Y			30/31			$X \leftarrow EA$

Addressing modes

502

TABLE 11.5
6809 Jump and branch instructions

Operations	Mnemonic	Addressing modes				Branch test
		Relative Op	Indexed Op	Extended Op	Implied Op	
Branch always	BRA/LBRA	20/16				None
Branch if carry clear	BCC/LBCC	24/1024				$C = 0$
Branch if carry set	BCS/LBCS	25/1025				$C = 1$
Branch if = 0	BEQ/LBEQ	27/1027				$Z = 1$
Branch if ≥ 0	BGE/LBGE	2C/102C				$N \oplus V = 0$
Branch if > 0	BGT/LBG	2E/102E				$Z + (N \oplus V) = 0$
Branch if higher	BHI/LBHI	22/1022				$C + Z = 0$
Branch if ≤ 0	BLE/LBLE	2F/102F				$Z + (N \oplus V) = 1$
Branch if lower or same	BLS/LBLS	23/1023				$C + Z = 1$
Branch if < 0	BLT/LBLT	2D/102D				$N \oplus V = 1$
Branch if minus	BMI/LBMI	2B/102B				$N = 1$
Branch if not equal to zero	BNE/LBNE	26/1026				$Z = 0$
Branch if overflow clear	BVC/LBVC	28/1028				$V = 0$
Branch if overflow set	BVS/LBVS	29/1029				$V = 1$
Branch to subroutine	BSR	8D				
Jump	JMP		6E	7E		Direct opcode is 0D
Jump to subroutine	JSR		AD	BD		Direct opcode is 9D
No operation	NOP				12	Advances program counter only
Return from interrupt	RTI				3B	
Return from subroutine	RTS				39	
Software interrupt	SWI/SWI2/SWI3				3F/103F/113F	
Wait for interrupt	SYNC				13	

The way in which conditional BRANCH instructions operate deserves mention. When an arithmetic or boolean operation is performed, the status bits are set according to the result of this operation. Tables 11.5 and 11.6 show the status bits and detail their function. The BRANCH instructions use the values of these bits to determine whether a branch is to be made.

For instance, let us assume accumulator A is added to accumulator B. If the sum is negative, the N bit will be set to a 1. We also assume no overflow, so V will be set to a 0. Now if a BLT (branch if less than 0) instruction follows, the computer will branch to the address given by the address part of the instruction. If the result of the addition were 0 or positive, no branch would occur, and the next instruction in sequence would be taken.

The interrupt mask bit (I) in the status register is set on when external input/output devices are allowed to interrupt the computer. A device interrupts by placing a 0 on the $\overline{IRQ}$ line of the bus. When an interrupt occurs, the computer automatically jumps to the address stored at locations FFF8 and FFF9, which is an interrupt servicing routine (program). To simplify and shorten the interrupt servicing program, this microprocessor automatically transfers the values in all the CPU registers to a stack in the memory and places the address of these stored register contents in the stack pointer. The S bit is set on to show that all registers are stored. The interrupt servicing program can then simply service the printer, reader, or whatever generated the interrupt; it will later return the contents of the CPU registers to their status at the time of interruption and restart the program where it left off, using a single RTI instruction.

Maintaining these stored registers on a stack also enables the interrupt servicing program to be interrupted, since the contents of the registers are again placed on the stack. In this way several interrupts can follow one another, and the program can service each interrupt in turn and then return to the original program.

The F status bit allows devices to use the $\overline{FIRQ}$ line on the bus to interrupt. In this case the processor jumps to the address given in location FFF6 and FFF7, but only the PC and CCR are stored, and the S bit is made a 0. When a return from the service program is made using RTI, only the PC and CCR are restored. There is also an NMI line on the bus that can be used to generate interrupts that is always operable (i.e., not maskable).

TABLE 11.6
Condition code register bits

Condition code register

The condition code register indicates the results of an ALU operation and other status information:

negative (N), zero (Z), overflow (V), carry from bit 7 (C), and half-carry from bit 3 (H).

Bits of the condition code register are used as testable conditions for the conditional branch instructions. I is the interrupt mask bit for $\overline{FIRQ}$, F is the fast interrupt bit for $\overline{FIRQ}$, and S shows if all registers are on the stack.

The interrupt lines are prioritized in the following order: $\overline{RESET}$, $\overline{NMI}$, $\overline{IRQ}$, $\overline{FIRQ}$, (so that if $\overline{IRQ}$ and $\overline{FIRQ}$ are enabled at the same time, $\overline{IRQ}$ is serviced first, for example).

Table 11.7 shows a short program for the 6809 microprocessor. Its purpose is to add a table of 8-bit bytes located in the memory starting at address 51_{16}. The number of bytes in the table is stored in location 50_{16}. The sum of the numbers is to be stored at location 0F in the memory. Carries from the addition are ignored.

The first instruction, CLRA, simply clears accumulator A. The LDB instruction gets the number of bytes in the table from location 50_{16} in the memory and stores that number in register B. Notice that in 6809 assembly language, a hexadecimal number is designated by placing a $ in front of the number. Also notice that the address 50 occurs in the second memory address of the instruction word, and the addressing mode is immediate.

LDX #$01 loads the value 1 in the index register. The symbol # tells the assembler to use this as an actual number, not as an address. This immediate-address operand requires 2 bytes since the index register contains 16 bits. Also note that the least significant byte is the last byte in the 3-byte instruction word.

ADDA $50,X is an addition instruction in *indexed* addressing mode. In the 6809 the indexed mode is indicated by the X in the statement. The $50 (for hexadecimal 50) gives the offset. The actual address used is formed by adding the offset to the contents of the index register. The first time through the loop, the address will be the offset 50_{16} plus 1, or 51_{16}. Notice that the offset is loaded in the memory following the op code and is a single byte. (A check of the op codes will indicate that AB is the op code for an indexed-mode addition.) After this instruction is executed, accumulator A will contain the number at location 51.

The LEAX 1,X adds 1 to the index register, which will now contain 2. DECB decrements register B and also sets the status bits. In particular, if B becomes 0, the Z status bit will be set to a 1, and this will indicate that the entire table has been processed.

The BNE LOOP instruction tests the Z bit and causes a branch if Z is *not* a 1. When Z becomes a 1, the program control "falls through" the BNE to the STA instruction.

TABLE 11.7
A 6809 program

Label	Op code	Operand	Comments
	CLRA		CLEAR A
	LDB	$50	GET NO. OF ENTRIES
	LDX	#$01	LOAD INDEX REGISTER
LOOP	ADDA	$50,X	
	LEAX	1,X	INCREMENT X REGISTER
	DECB		DECREMENT B
	BNE	LOOP	
	STA	$0F	

When the program control loops back the first time, the index register plus the offset now equals 52, so the number at that address will be added into accumulator *A* by the ADDA $50.X instruction. This process continues with numbers at successive locations being added into *A* until the table end is reached. Then the STA $0F instruction stores the sum at location F in the memory.

Subroutine calls for the 6809 are made by a JSR (jump subroutine) instruction, which pushes the program counter's contents (2 bytes)[1] on top of the stack (also adjusting the stack pointer). When an RTS (return from subroutine) instruction is given, the address (2 bytes) on top of the stack is placed in the program counter, causing a return to the instruction after the initial JSR.

An example of a subroutine is shown in Table 11.8. ORG $30 is an *assembler directive* telling the assembler to place the subroutine starting at location 30_{16} in the memory. The purpose of this subroutine is to find where in a table in the memory a character lies. The parameters are passed as follows: (1) the address of the end of the table must be in the index register before the subroutine is entered, (2) the number of entries in the table is placed in accumulator *B*, and (3) the character to be searched for must be in accumulator *A*.

The subroutine is entered at SRCH, where the CMPA 0,X instruction causes the byte at the memory address given by the index register (notice that the offset is 0) to be compared with accumulator *A*. If they are equal, the *Z* status bit will be set to 1, and the BEQ FINIS instruction will test this instruction and branch to FINIS. Otherwise, the index register will be decremented so that it points to the next lowest entry in the table. Accumulator *B* will then be decremented by DECB, and if this sets the *Z* flag to 1, indicating a 0 in *B*, the search will be ended. Otherwise, the return to SRCH will cause the next entry in the table to be compared with the character in accumulator *A*. This will be repeated until all table entries have been examined.

RTS will cause a return to the calling program, with accumulator *B* containing the number in the table at which the matched character lies.

---

[1] After the program counter has already been updated to point to the next instruction.

TABLE 11.8
6809 Subroutine for table lookup

Label	Op code	Operand	Comments
	ORG	$30	SET ORIGIN
SRCH	CMPA	0,X	CHAR = TABLE ENTRY?
	BEQ	FINIS	YES QUIT
	LEAX	1,X	INCREMENT X REGISTER
	DECB		DECREMENT B
	BNE	SRCH	TEST FOR END
FINIS	RTS		RETURN TO CALLER

TABLE 11.9
Calling 6809 subroutine

Op code	Operand	Comments
LDX	#ENDTA	LOAD IR WITH TABLE END
LDB	#20	LOAD B WITH NO. OF ENTRIES
LDA	CHAR	LOAD A WITH CHAR
JSR	SRCH	
STA	MABEL	

A possible calling program segment is shown in Table 11.9. LDX loads the index register with the address of the end of the table, which is assumed to be at ENDTA. The number of table entries is assumed to be 20_{10}, and LDB loads B with that value. (No $ symbol means decimal.) JSR causes a jump to the subroutine, and the jump back from the subroutine using RTS will cause the STA instruction to be executed.

When a set of chips for a microprocessor of this kind is used with a fixed program, such as in an industrial controller, the program is generally developed by using system software, which is provided by the chips' manufacturer and software vendors and placed in a ROM memory. A ROM memory can be addressed and used just like a RAM memory when it is connected to a microprocessor CPU (except, of course, that we cannot write into a ROM).

Considerable effort is made by the manufacturers of microprocessor chips to facilitate programming the microprocessor, preparing the PLDs and loading the ROMs, when required. Higher-level languages are generally provided, enabling programs to be written in FORTRAN, C, Pascal, or another compiler language, which is then translated into the program for the microcomputer.

11.4   PDP-11 SERIES

The PDP-11 series includes minicomputers and microcomputers. It has been a great success for DEC, and the VAX computers closely follow its architectural principles. The design team for the PDP-11 included Gordon Bell, who had also worked on the PDP-8 and then, as vice president, produced the VAX series. His influence is apparent everywhere. The PDP-11 computers have 16-bit words, each containing two 8-bit bytes (see Fig. 11.8). Notice, however, that each address in memory contains 1 byte. The eight general registers are 16 bits each, and a computer word has 16 bits.

The PDP-11 reads from and writes into external input/output devices in the same manner that it reads from and writes into high-speed memory. Each input/output device is simply given an address in memory. To read from an address, and in turn an input/output device, the computer uses not a special I/O instruction, but a MOVE instruction, an ADD instruction, or whatever is desired. This means that status regis-

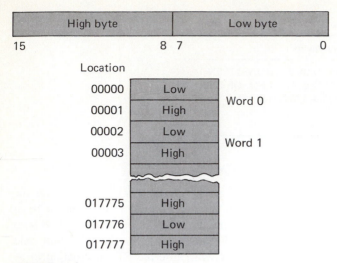

FIGURE 11.8
Memory organization of PDP-11.

ters must be used by the CPU (as in Chap. 8) to determine whether a device can be written into or has something to read.

There is a complex interrupt structure in the PDP-11. The CPU continually puts a status number on three wires of its bus. Each external device has a status number, and if that status number is greater than the CPU status number, it has the right to interrupt. Setting a CPU's status number to its maximum stops all interrupts. The CPU's status number is set under program control and can be changed as the program operates.

Interrupts are "vectored" (see Chap. 8) in that an interrupting device places data (an interrupt vector) on the bus lines, which enable the CPU to transfer control directly to a service program for the interrupting device.

The general registers of the PDP-11 are shown in Fig. 11.9(a). Notice that register R_6 is a stack pointer and R_7 is the program counter. These can be used and addressed just as the other general-purpose registers, making for interesting instruction variations.

The CPU in the PDP-11 includes a status register, as shown in Fig. 11.9(b). This status register contains the priority number just discussed, which is placed on the bus in bits 5 to 7. Bits 11 to 15 in Fig. 11.9(b) are used by the operating system to control program operations (in the larger PDP-11 models, and not discussed here).

The N, Z, V, C bits in the status word are set and reset as instructions are operated. For example, the N bit indicates when a result is negative. If an ADD instruction is performed and the result is negative, the N bit will be set to a 1; otherwise, it will be a 0. Similarly, the Z bit indicates a zero result and will be set on if an instruction's result is zero.

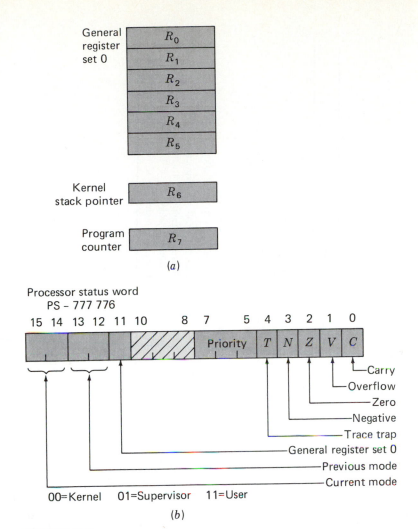

FIGURE 11.9
PDP-11 organization. (*a*) General registers. (*b*) Processor status word.

The conditional JUMP or BRANCH instructions in the PDP-11 use these bits to determine whether a jump is to be taken. For instance, BNE (branch on negative) will cause a branch only if the N bit is a 1. As another example, BEQ (branch on equal) causes a branch only if the Z bit is a 1.

Table 11.10 lists the addressing modes for the PDP-11. The addressing mode number is placed before the register number in an instruction word and indicates how the designated register is to be used. Table 11.11 gives the instructions for the computer.

TABLE 11.10
Addressing modes for PDP-11 minicomputer

Address	Mode	Name	Symbolic	Description
General register	0	Register	R	(R) is operand (e.g., $R_2 = \%2$)
Mode R	1	Register deferred	(R)	(R) is address
	2	Auto increment	(R)+	(R) is address; (R) + (1 or 2)
	3	Auto increment deferred	@(R)+	(R) is address of address; (R) + 2
	4	Auto decrement	−(R)	(R) − (1 or 2); (R) is address
	5	Auto decrement deferred	@−(R)	(R) − 2; (R) is address of address
	6	Index	X(R)	(R) + X is address
	7	Index deferred	@X(R)	(R) + X is address of address
Program counter, Reg = 7	2	Immediate	#n	Operand n follows instruction
Mode 7	3	Absolute	@#A	Address A follows instruction
	6	Relative	A	Instruction address + 4 + X is address
	7	Relative deferred	@A	Instruction address + 4 + X is address of address

510

TABLE 11.11
PDP-11 Instruction repertoire (*pp. 511–515*)

Legend

Op codes

■	0 for word/1 for byte
SS	Source field (6 bits)
DD	Destination field (6 bits)
R	General register (3 bits) 0 to 7
XXX	Offset (3 bits) +127 to −128
N	Number (3 bits)
NN	Number (6 bits)

Operations

( )	Contents of
s	Contents of source
d	Contents of destination
r	Contents of register
←	Becomes
X	Relative address
%	Register definition

Boolean

$\wedge$	= AND
$\vee$	= Inclusive OR
$\veebar$	= Exclusive OR
$\sim$	= Not

Condition codes

*	Conditionally set/cleared
–	Not affected
0	Cleared
1	Set

Single operand: OPR dst

15				6	5		0
	OP CODE					DD	

Mnemonic	Op code	Instruction	dst Result	N	Z	V	C
General							
CLR(B)	■050DD	Clear	0	0	1	0	0
COM(B)	■051DD	Complement (1s)	$\sim d$	*	*	0	1
INC(B)	■052DD	Increment	$d + 1$	*	*	*	–
DEC(B)	■053DD	Decrement	$d - 1$	*	*	*	–
NEG(B)	■054DD	Negate (2s complement)	$-d$	*	*	*	*
TST(B)	■057DD	Test	d	*	*	0	0
Rotate and Shift							
ROR(B)	■060DD	Rotate right	ROT C, d	*	*	*	*
ROL(B)	■061DD	Rotate left	C, d ROT	*	*	*	*
ASR(B)	■062DD	Arithmetic shift right	$d/2$	*	*	*	*
ASL(B)	■063DD	Arithmetic shift left	$2d$	*	*	*	*
SWAB	0003DD	Swap bytes		*	*	0	0
Multiple precision							
ADC(B)	■055DD	Add carry	$d + C$	*	*	*	*
SBC(B)	■056DD	Subtract carry	$d - C$	*	*	*	*
▲SXT*	0067DD	Sign extend	0 or − 1	–	*	*	–

TABLE 11.11
PDP-11 Instruction repertoire (*continued*)

Double operand: OPR src, dst OPR src, R or OPR R, dst

15	12	11		9	8	6	5		0
	OP CODE			SS				DD	

15	12	11		9	8	6	5		0
	OP CODE			R				SS OR DD	

Mnemonic	Op code	Instruction	Operation	N	Z	V	C
General							
MOV(B)	■1SSDD	Move	$d \leftarrow s$	*	*	0	—
CMP(B)	■2SSDD	Compare	$s - d$	*	*	*	*
ADD	06SSDD	Add	$d \leftarrow s + d$	*	*	*	*
SUB	16SSDD	Subtract	$d \leftarrow d - s$	*	*	*	*
Logical							
BIT(B)	■3SSDD	Bit test (AND)	$s \wedge d$	*	*	0	—
BIC(B)	■4SSDD	Bit clear	$d \leftarrow (\sim s) \wedge d$	*	*	0	—
BIS(B)	■5SSDD	Bit set (OR)	$d \leftarrow s \wedge d$	*	*	0	—
▲*Register*							
MUL	070RSS	Multiply	$r \leftarrow r \times s$	*	*	0	*
DIV	071RSS	Divide	$r \leftarrow r/s$	*	*	*	*
ASH	072RSS	Shift arithmetically		*	*	*	*
ASHC	073RSS	Arithmetic shift combined		*	*	*	*
XOR	074RDD	Exclusive OR	$d \leftarrow r \vee d$	*	*	0	*

TABLE 11.11
PDP-11 Instruction repertoire (*continued*)

Branch: B—location

If condition is satisfied:
Branch to location,
New PC ← updated PC + (2 × offset)

$$\underbrace{\text{address of branch instruction}}\Big|2$$

```
 15              7              0
+-------------------+-------------+
|    BASE CODE      |     XXX     |
+-------------------+-------------+
```

Mnemonic	Instruction	Base code	Branch condition
Branches			
BR	Branch (unconditional)	000400	(always)
BNE	Branch if not equal (to 0)	001000	$\neq 0$ $Z = 0$
BEQ	Branch if equal (to 0)	001400	$= 0$ $Z = 1$
BPL	Branch if plus	100000	$+$ $N = 0$
BMI	Branch if minus	100400	$-$ $N = 1$
BVC	Branch if overflow is clear	102000	$V = 0$
BVS	Branch if overflow is set	102400	$V = 1$
BCC	Branch if carry is clear	103000	$C = 0$
BCS	Branch if carry is set	103400	$C = 1$
Signed Conditional Branches			
BGE	Branch if greater than or equal (to 0)	002000	≥ 0 $N \veebar V = 0$
BLT	Branch if less than (0)	002400	< 0 $N \veebar V = 1$
BGT	Branch if greater than (0)	003000	> 0 $N \vee (N \veebar V) = 0$
BLE	Branch if less than or equal (to 0)	003400	≤ 0 $Z \vee (N \veebar V) = 1$
Unsigned Conditional Branches			
BHI	Branch if higher	101000	$>$ $C \vee Z = 0$
BLOS	Branch if lower or same	101400	$\leq$ $C \vee Z = 1$
BHIS	Branch if higher or same	103000	$\geq$ $C = 0$
BLO	Branch if lower	103400	$<$ $C = 1$

TABLE 11.11
PDP-11 Instruction repertoire (*continued*)

Jump and subroutine

Mnemonic	Op code	Instruction	Notes
JMP	0001DD	Jump	PC ← dst
JSR	004RDD	Jump to subroutine	Use same R
RTS	00020R	Return from subroutine	Aid in subroutine return
▲MARK	0064NN	Mark	
▲SOB	077RNN	Subtract 1 and branch (if ≠ 0)	(R) − 1, then if (R) ≠ 0: PC ← updated PC − (2 × NN)

Trap and interrupt

Mnemonic	Op code	Instruction	Notes
EMT	104000 to 104377	Emulator trap (not for general use)	PC at 30, PS at 32
TRAP	104400 to 104777	Trap	PC at 34, PS at 36
BPT	000003	Break-point trap	PC at 14, PS at 16
IOT	000004	Input/output trap	PC at 20, PS at 22
RTI	000002	Return from interrupt	
▲RTT	000006	Return from interrupt	Inhibit T bit trap

TABLE 11.11
PDP-11 Instruction repertoire (*continued*)

Condition code operations

15													
			OP CODE	BASE	000240								

15		7	5	4	3	2	1	0
OP CODE					H	Z	V	C

0 = Clear selected condition code bits
1 = Set selected condition code bits

Mnemonic	Op code	Instruction	N	Z	V	C
CLC	000241	Clear C	—	—	—	0
CLV	000242	Clear V	—	—	0	—
CLZ	000244	Clear Z	—	0	—	—
CLN	000250	Clear N	0	—	—	—
CCC	000257	Clear all condition code bits	0	0	0	0
SEC	000261	Set C	—	—	—	1
SEV	000262	Set V	—	—	1	—
SEZ	000264	Set Z	—	1	—	—
SEN	000270	Set N	1	—	—	—
SCC	000277	Set all condition code bits	1	1	1	1

Miscellaneous

Mnemonic	Op code	Instruction
HALT	000000	Halt
WAIT	000001	Wait for interrupt
RESET	000005	Reset external bus
NOP	000240	(No operation)
●SPL	00023N	Set priority level (to N)
▲MFPI	0065SS	Move from previous instruction space
▲MTPI	0066DD	Move to previous instruction space
●MFPD	1065SS	Move from previous data space
●MTPD	1066DD	Move to previous data space

Note: ▲ Applies to 11/35, 11/40, 11/45 computers. ● Applies to 11/45 computer.

515

Table 11.12 shows a sample section of a program for a PDP-11. This is a subroutine that reads from a teletypewriter keyboard. There is a status byte (interface register) at address 177030 in the memory that tells when the keyboard has a new character. The subprogram places characters in a table until a period is typed, at which time control is transferred to another subprogram.

The section shown in Table 11.12 is from an actual assembler listing for a PDP-11, all numbers are in octal. The programmer writes all text from the label column to the right. Semicolons indicate comments; everything to the right of a semicolon is a comment and is ignored by the assembler. The listing was prepared by the programmer who wrote the assembly-language program and fed it into the assembler program, which generated this listing.

The leftmost column lists locations in the memory, and the next column shows the contents of these locations. For instance, TSTB (test byte) has op code 105767, and the assembler has read the programmer's TSTB instruction and converted it to octal value.

The statement TSTB tests the byte at the address given. If the value there is negative, it places a 1 in the N bit; if it is zero, a 1 is placed in the Z bit. KSR designates the address in memory, 177030, where the status byte for the keyboard is located. The programmer has (in an earlier section of the program) told the assembler the value of KSR. If the keyboard has a character ready, the sign bit of the KSR byte will be a 1, causing the N bit to go on.

The next instruction, BPL READ, says branch to READ if $N = 0$. This means that if no character is available, the program goes back to READ and looks again. This continues until a character is ready and $N = 1$.

The BPL has an op code of 100. The next byte contains the displacement, or offset, for the branch in 2s complement form. The address for the branch is equal to two times the offset byte's value (375), added to the address of the next instruction. In this case the offset value is negative, and a branch would go back to location 524.

When $N = 1$, the instruction word at location 532 will be executed. This is a MOVB (move byte) instruction, which causes a byte to be moved from KSB, which is 177024 (the address of the keyboard's buffer, the value of which the program has

TABLE 11.12
A PDP-11 program segment

Memory address	Contents	Label	Op code	Address part	Comments
000524	105767	READ:	TSTB	KSR	;READY
	177030				
000530	100375		BPL	READ	;NO
000532	116710		MOVB	KSB, @R0	;MOVE IT INTO THE TABLE
	177024				
000536	005267		INC	COUNT	;INCREASE COUNT
	000200				
000542	122027		CMPB	(R0) +, #256	;IS IT A PERIOD?
	000256				
000546	001366		BNE	READ	;NO

already given to the assembler), to the value pointed to by R_0. This is an example of indirect addressing, where R_0 is used to point to the actual address. Prior to this section of the program, the programmer has loaded R_0 with the starting location of the table in the memory where the input characters are to be stored.

The program now checks to see whether the input character is a period, which has octal code 256, by comparing it with the character just loaded in the memory. Notice that indirect addressing is again used. The plus sign causes the value in R_0 to be incremented. Only if the character pointed to is equal to 256 will the Z bit be set to 1.

The BNE (branch on not equal) instruction checks this. If the character is a period, it transfers control to another program; otherwise, control is transferred back to the READ, where another character is then read from the keyboard.

The variety and complexities of the PDP-11's instruction repertoire can be appreciated only through a study of the manuals for this computer. The preceding example should point out the kind of efficient programs that can be written for this computer.

11.5   68000 MICROPROCESSOR SERIES

The 68000 microprocessor series consists of semiconductor chips that include a number of support chips, such as I/O processors, floating-point arithmetic chips, and bus handler chips. The 68000 performs 32-bit arithmetic and logic operations internally. This microprocessor series can directly address 16 megabytes to 4 gigabytes of memory, depending on the model. The I/O is memory-mapped.

Several chips offer variations and extensions of the 68000. The 68008 is an 8-bit bus version that uses 8-bit memories and peripherals but has full compatibility with 68000 software. The 68010 is like the 68000 but can continue an instruction that has been interrupted by a bus error; this facilitates virtual memory system operations. The 68012 is a 68010 with a 30-bit address bus. The 68020 is a "full" 32-bit microprocessor in a 114-pin-grid package. It has 4 gigabytes of address space and a 256-byte instruction cache. Data bus width is controlled and can be 8, 16, or 32 bits. There are also some instruction set enhancements (additional instructions). The 6881 floating-point unit can be added to provide floating-point operations, and a 68851 paged memory management unit is available as well.

The 68030 and 68040 have a cache on the chip, as well as paging. The 68040 has on-chip floating-point instructions. The basic architecture still follows the 68000, and peripheral interfaces designed for the earlier chips will still work with the newer chips.

We will describe the 68000 architecture as the generic architecture for each of the succeeding chips and also show the variations. The variations and additions are chip-dependent, and manuals for individual chips list the additions and enhancements for a specific chip. The 68000 remains the "flagship" in this series, containing the basic architectural features found in later chips.

Chapter 8 showed a drawing of the 68000 bus and the timing signals for READs and WRITEs on the bus. Chapter 10 discussed status bits and branches. The bus is asynchronous in order to accommodate both slow and fast memory and I/O devices.

The basic registers in the 68000 series are shown in Fig. 11.10. The registers are 32-bits, and there are eight data registers along with seven address registers and

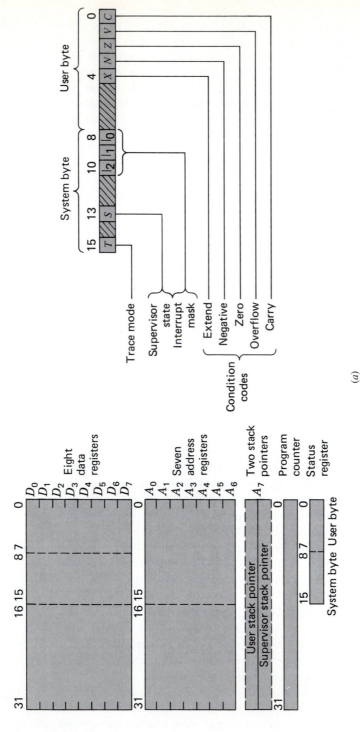

FIGURE 11.10

68000, 68020, 68030 registers. (a) 68000 basic register. (*Courtesy Motorola Inc.*)

(a)

518

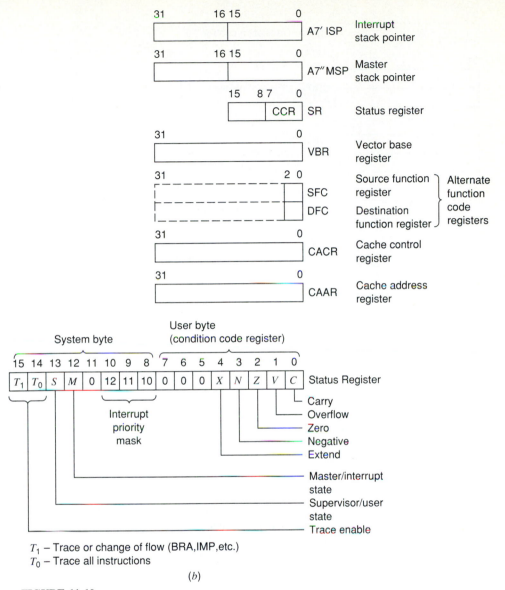

T_1 – Trace or change of flow (BRA,IMP,etc.)
T_0 – Trace all instructions

(b)

FIGURE 11.10
(b) Additional 68020 registers. (*Courtesy Motorola Inc.*)

a program counter. There are actually two stack pointers. A status bit determines whether the 68000 is in the supervisor (operating system) mode or user mode; this bit also determines which of the two stack pointers are in use. The status register is shown in Fig. 11.10 and contains 5 bits for condition codes.

The 68000 supervisor and user modes are an important feature. There are privileged instructions that can be executed in supervisor mode, but not in user mode.

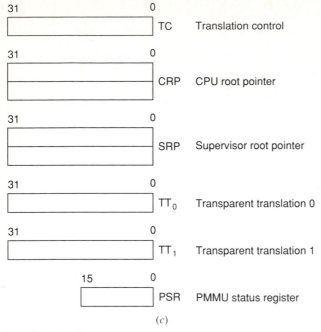

(c)

FIGURE 11.10
(c) Additional 68030 registers. *(Courtesy Motorola Inc.)*

When the supervisor/user mode select bit is a 1, the 68000 uses the supervisor stack pointer, and the privileged instructions are available. When the select bit is a 0, the user stack pointer is employed, and certain instructions will not execute.

Figure 11.11 shows that data are organized into bits, bytes, words, and long words and shows how these are placed in the memory, which has 8 bits (1 byte) at each address. Instruction words can be from one word (16 bits) to four words in length.

Stacks in the 68000 go from high memory to low memory. So the stack pointer is decremented when data are pushed into a stack and incremented when data are popped from a stack.

Let us examine a particular instruction to understand how the addressing operates. The ANDI (for AND immediate) has the following instruction word format.

15	14	13	12	11	10	9	8	7	6	5	4	3	2	1	0
0	0	0	0	0	0	1	0	Size		Mode			Address register		
Word data (16)								Byte data (8)							
Long word (32 bits)															

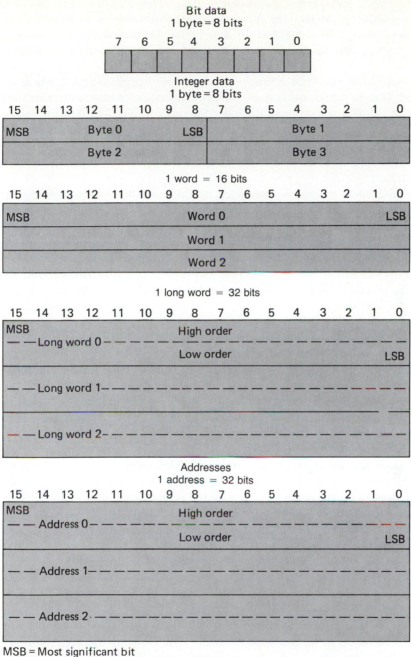

MSB = Most significant bit
LSB = Least significant bit

FIGURE 11.11
Organization of data in memory for 68000.

The op-code part of this instruction is 02_{16}. This tells the microprocessor that the instruction is ANDI. The function of this instruction is to AND the data that immediately follow the first 16 bits of the instruction (word), which is called the *source*, with the destination operand and to place the result in the destination.

The number of bits in an ANDI instruction word depends on the 2 bits in the *size* section. If these are 00, the operation is a byte operation and the instruction word is two 16-bit words in length, with the immediate data in bits 7 to 0 of the second word. If the size bits are 01, the instruction word is again 32 bits in length, but the immediate operand is the entire 16 bits in the second word. If the size bits are 10, then ANDI has a 32-bit-long word for its immediate data and the instruction word is 48 bits in length.

The destination operand is determined by the mode bits and address register bits. If the mode bits are 000, then the destination is the register given by the address register bits. If these are 010, for example, then data register 2 (refer to Fig. 11.10) will be the destination register, and the part of that register used (byte word or long word) will be determined by the size section. If, for example, the data register used is 010 and the size bits are 00, bits 7 to 0 in data register 2 will be ANDed with bits 7 to 0 in the second word in the instruction, with the result placed in bits 7 to 0 of data register 2.

If the mode bits are 010, then the address register given by the address register bits in the instruction word will contain the address of the (destination) data in memory. For example, if the mode bits are 010, the address register bits are 011; then address register 3 will contain the address of the operand. So if address register 3 contains 0143_{16}, the operand will be at that location in memory. If the size bits are 00, bits 7 to 0 of that location in memory will be used for the AND, and the result will be placed in these bits. If the size bits are 01, then the entire word beginning in location 0143_{16} will be ANDed with the 16 bits in the second word of the instruction and the result placed in memory location 0143_{16}.

The instruction repertoire is described in what Motorola calls its register transfer language (as in Chap. 9). In their system, (A_n) means, "The contents of A_n gives the location in memory of the operand." (The n in A_n is given by the address register bits. The register A_n is frequently called the *pointer* because it points to the operand.) The notation $A_n @+$ is called "address register indirect with postincrement" and $A_n - @$ is called "address register indirect with predecrement."

The notation $(A_n -)$ means, "Decrement A_n and use the result as the address of the operand." The notation $(A_n)+$ means, "Use the contents of A_n to determine the location in memory and then increment." For $(A_n)+$ and $(A_n -)$, the number in A_n is incremented or decremented by 1, 2, or 4 depending on whether the instruction is a byte, word, or long-word instruction.

The notation $A_n @$ is also used to mean, "A_n contains the address of the operand." This is the same as (A_n) but leads to the notation $(A_n) @$, which means, "Take the address in A_n, go to that address in memory, and at that address find the address of the operand." In effect, for $(A_n) @$, the number in A_n is the address of the address of the operand.

Mode	Generation
Register direct addressing	
Data register direct	EA = Dn
Address register direct	EA = An
Absolute data addressing	
Absolute short	EA = (Next Word)
Absolute long	EA = (Next Two Words)
Program counter relative addressing	
Relative with offset	EA = (PC) + d_{16}
Relative with index and offset	EA = (PC) + (Xn) + d_8
Register indirect addressing	
Register indirect	EA = (An)
Postincrement register indirect	EA = (An), An ← An + N
Predecrement register indirect	An ← An − N, EA = (An)
Register indirect with offset	EA = (An) + d_{16}
Indexed register indirect with offset	EA = (An) + (Xn) + d_6
Immediate data addressing	
Immediate	DATA = Next Word(s)
Quick immediate	Inherent Data
Implied addressing	
Implied register	EA = SR, USP, SP, PC

Notes:

EA = Effective Address

An = Address Register

Dn = Data Register

Xn = Address or Data Register used as Index Register

SR = Status Register

PC = Program Counter

d_8 = 8-bit Offset (displacement)

d_{16} = 16-bit Offset (displacement)

N = 1 for Byte, 2 for Words, and 4 for Long Words. If An is the stack pointer and the operand size byte, N = 2 to keep the stack pointer on a word boundary.

( ) = Contents of

← = Replaces

FIGURE 11.12
Addressing modes for 68000.

Figure 11.12 shows the addressing modes for the 68000. These cover most of the conventional modes for addressing and offer considerable options to the programmer.

Several selected instructions from the 68000's large instruction set are shown in Fig. 11.13. A large number of instructions are available, including most conventional instructions.

The following register transfer language definitions are used for the operation description in the details of the instruction set.

Operands

An	address register	SSP	supervisor stack pointer
Dn	data register	USP	user stack pointer
Rn	any data or address register	SP	active stack pointer (equivalent to A_7)
PC	program counter	X	extend operand (from condition codes)
SR	status register	Z	zero condition code
CCR	condition codes (low-order byte of status register)	V	overflow condition code

Immediate Data	—immediate data from the instruction		
d	—address displacement	Destination	destination location
Source	—source location	Vector	location of exception vector

Subfields and Qualifiers

<bit> OF <operand>	selects a single bit of the operand
<operand>[<bit number>:<bit number>]	selects a subfield of an operand
(<operand>)	the contents of the referenced location
<operand> 101	the operand is binary coded decimal; operations are to be performed in decimal.
<operand> @ <mode>	the register indirect operator that indicates that the operand register points to the memory location of the instruction operand. The optional mode qualifiers are −, +, (d), and (d, ix); these are explained in Chapter 2.

Operations

Operations are grouped into binary, unary, and other.

Binary	these operations are written <operand><op><operand>, where <op> is one of the following:
→	left operand is moved to the location specified by the right operand
↔	contents of the two operands are exchanged
+	operands are added
−	right operand is subtracted from the operand
.	operands are multiplied
/	first operand is divided by second operand
∧	operands are logically ANDed
∨	operands are logically ORed
⊕	operands are logically exclusively ORed
<	relation test, true if left operand is less than right operand
>	relation test, true if left operand is not equal to right operand
shifted by	the left operand is shifted or rotated by the number of positions specified
rotated by	by the right operand

Unary	
~ <operand>	operand is logically complemented
<operand>sign-extended	operand is sign-extended; all bits of the upper half are made equal to high-order bit of the lower half
<operand>tested	operand is compared to 0; the results are used to set the condition codes

FIGURE 11.13

Selected instructions for 68000 (*pp. 524–531*). (*Courtesy Motorola Inc.*)

ANDI   **AND Immediate**

Operation: Immediate Data $\wedge$ (Destination)→Destination

Assembler syntax: ANDI # <data>,<ea>

Attributes: Size = (Byte, Word, Long)

Description: AND the immediate data to the destination operand and store the result in the destination location. The size of the operation may be specified to be byte, word, or long. The size of the immediate data matches the operation size

Condition codes

X	N	Z	V	C
—	*	*	0	0

N Set if the most significant bit of the result is set. Cleared otherwise.
Z Set if the result is zero. Cleared otherwise.
V Always cleared.
C Always cleared.
X Not affected.

Instruction format

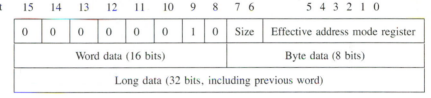

15	14	13	12	11	10	9	8	7 6	5 4 3 2 1 0
0	0	0	0	0	0	1	0	Size	Effective address mode register

Word data (16 bits)	Byte data (8 bits)

Long data (32 bits, including previous word)

Instruction fields

Size field   Specifies the size of the operation:
00   byte operation
01   word operation
10   long operation

Effective Address field: Specifies the destination operand. Only data alterable addressing modes are allowed as shown:

Addressing Mode	Mode	Register	Addressing Mode	Mode	Register
Dn	000	register number	d(An, Xi)	110	register number
An	—	—	Abs.W	111	000
(An)	010	register number	Abs.L	111	001
(An)+	011	register number	d(PC)	—	—
−(An)	100	register number	d(PC, Xi)	—	—
d(An)	101	register number	Imm	—	—

Immediate field (Data immediately following the instruction):
If size = 00, then the data is the low order byte of the immediate word.
If size = 01, then the data is the entire immediate word.
If size = 10, then the data is the next two immediate words.

FIGURE 11.13
Selected instructions for 68000.

JSR | **Jump to Subroutine**

Operation:　　PC $\rightarrow - $ (SP); Destination $\rightarrow$ PC

Assembler syntax:　JSR <ea>

Attributes:　Unsized

Description:　The long-word address of the instruction immediately following the JSR instruction is pushed onto the system stack. Program execution then continues at the address specified in the instruction.

Condition codes:　Not affected.

Instruction format

15	14	13	12	11	10	9	8	7	6	5 4 3 2 1 0
0	1	0	0	1	1	1	0	1	0	Effective address mode register

Instruction fields

Effective address field:　Specifies the address of the next instruction. Only control addressing modes are allowed as shown:

Addressing Mode	Mode	Register	Addressing Mode	Mode	Register
Dn	—	—	d(An, Xi)	110	register number
An	—	—	Abs.W	111	000
(An)	010	register number	Abs.L	111	001
(An)+	—	—	d(PC)	111	010
−(An)	—	—	d(PC, Xi)	111	011
d(An)	101	register number	Imm		

Bcc | **Branch Conditionally**

Operation:　If (condition true) then PC + d $\rightarrow$ PC

Assembler syntax:　Bcc <label>

Attributes:　Size = (Byte, Word)

Description:　If the specified condition is met, program execution continues at location (PC) + displacement. Displacement is a 2s complement integer that counts the relative distance in bytes. The value in PC is the current instruction location plus 2. If the 8-bit displacement in the instruction word is 0, then the 16-bit displacement (word immediately following the instruction) is used. "cc" may specify the following conditions:

CC	carry clear	0100	$\overline{C}$	LS	low or same	0011	$C + Z$
CC	carry set	0101	C	LT	less than	1101	$N \cdot \overline{V} + \overline{N} \cdot V$
EQ	equal	0111	Z	MI	minus	1011	N
GE	greater or equal	1100	$N \cdot V + \overline{N} \cdot \overline{V}$	NE	not equal	0110	$\overline{Z}$
GT	greater than	1110	$N \cdot V \cdot \overline{Z} + \overline{N} \cdot \overline{V} \cdot \overline{Z}$	PL	plus	1010	$\overline{N}$
HI	high	0010	$\overline{C} \cdot \overline{Z}$	VC	overflow clear	1000	$\overline{V}$
LE	less or equal	1111	$\overline{Z} + N \cdot \overline{V} + \overline{N} \cdot V$	VS	overflow set	1001	V

FIGURE 11.13
Selected instructions for 68000.

Condition codes: Not affected.

Instruction format

15	14	13	12	11 10 9 8	7 6 5 4 3 2 1 0
0	1	1	0	Condition	8-bit Displacement

16-bit Displacement if 8-bit Displacement = 0

Instruction fields
  Condition field: One of 14 conditions discussed in description.
  8-bit displacement field: 2s complement integer specifying the relative distance (in bytes) between the branch instruction and the next instruction to be executed if the condition is met.
  16-bit displacement field: Allows a larger displacement than 8 bits. Used only if the displacement is equal to 0.

Note: A short branch to the immediately following instruction cannot be done because it would result in a zero offset, which forces a word branch instruction definition.

MULS   Signed Multiply

Operation: (Source)*(Destination)→Destination

Assembler syntax: MULS<ea>, Dn

Attributes: Size = (Word)

Description: Multiply two signed 16-bit operands yielding a 32-bit signed result. The operation is performed using signed arithmetic. A register operand is taken from the low-order word; the upper word is unused. All 32 bits of the product are saved in the destination data register.

Condition codes

X	N	Z	V	C
—	*	*	0	0

N Set if the result is negative. Cleared otherwise.
Z Set if the result is zero. Cleared otherwise.
V Always cleared.
C Always cleared.
X Not affected.

Instruction format

15	14	13	12	11 10 9	8	7	6	5 4 3 2 1 0
1	1	0	0	Register	1	1	1	Effective address mode register

Instruction fields
  Register field: Specifies one of the data registers. This field always specifies the destination.
  Effective address field: Specifies the source operand. Only data addressing modes are allowed as shown:

Addressing Mode	Mode	Register	Addressing Mode	Mode	Register
Dn	000	register number	d(An, Xi)	110	register number
An	—	—	Abs.W	111	000
(An)	010	register number	Abs.L	111	001
(An)+	011	register number	d(PC)	111	010
−(An)	100	register number	d(PC, Xi)	111	011
d(An)	101	register number	Imm	111	100

FIGURE 11.13
Selected instructions for 68000.

RTS   **Return from Subroutine**

Operation: (SP) + → PC

Assembler syntax: RTS

Attributes: Unsized

Description: The program counter is pulled from the stack. The previous program counter is lost.

Condition codes: Not affected.

Instruction format

15	14	13	12	11	10	9	8	7	6	5	4	3	2	1	0
0	1	0	0	1	1	1	0	0	1	1	1	0	1	0	1

CMP   **Compare**

Operation: (Destination) − (Source)

Assembler syntax: CMP <ea>, Dn

Attributes: Size = (Byte, Word, Long)

Description: Subtract the source operand from the destination operand and set the condition codes according to the result; the destination location is not changed. The size of the operation may be specified to be byte, word, or long.

Condition codes

X	N	Z	V	C
—	*	*	*	*

N   Set if the result is negative. Cleared otherwise.
Z   Set if the result is zero. Cleared otherwise.
V   Set if an overflow is generated. Cleared otherwise.
C   Set if a borrow is generated. Cleared otherwise.
X   Not affected.

Instruction format

15	14	13	12	11 10 9	8 7 6	5 4 3 2 1 0
1	0	1	1	Register	Op-mode	Effective address mode register

Instruction fields

Register field: Specifies the destination data register.

Op-mode field:

Byte	Word	Long	Operation
000	001	010	(<Dn>)−(<ea>)

Effective address field: Specifies the source operand. All addressing modes are allowed as shown:

Addressing Mode	Mode	Register	Addressing Mode	Mode	Register
Dn	000	register number	d(An, Xi)	110	register number
An*	001	register number	Abs.W	111	000
(An)	010	register number	Abs.L	111	001
(An)+	011	register number	d(PC)	111	010
−(An)	100	register number	d(PC, Xi)	111	011
d(An)	101	register number	Imm	111	100

*Word and long only

Note: CMPA is used when the destination is an address register. CMPI is used when the source is immediate data. CMPM is used for memory to memory comparisons. Most assemblers automatically make this distinction.

FIGURE 11.13
Selected instructions for 68000.

528

DIVS   **Signed Divide**

Operation: (Destination)/(Source) $\rightarrow$ Destination

Assembler syntax: DIVS <ea>, Dn

Attributes: Size = (Word)

Description: Divide the destination operand by the source operand, and store the result in the destination. The destination operand is a long operand (32 bits) and the source operand is a word operand (16 bits). The operation is performed using signed arithmetic. The result is a 32-bit result such that:

1. The quotient is in the lower word (least significant 16 bits).
2. The remainder is in the upper word (most significant 16 bits).

The sign of the remainder is always the same as the dividend unles the remainder is equal to zero. Two special conditions may arise:

1. Division by zero causes a trap.
2. Overflow may be detected and set before completion of the instruction. If overflow is detected, the condition is flagged but the operands are unaffected.

Condition codes

X	N	Z	V	C
—	*	*	*	0

N Set if the quotient is negative. Cleared otherwise. Undefined if overflow.
Z Set if the quotient is zero. Cleared otherwise. Undefined if overflow.
V Set if division overflow is detected. Cleared otherwise.
C Always cleared.
X Not affected.

Instruction format

15	14	13	12	11 10 9	8	7	6	5 4 3 2 1 0
1	0	1	1	Register	1	1	1	Effective address mode register

Instruction fields
Register field: Specifies any of the eight data registers. This field always specifies the destination operand.
Effective address field: Specifies the source operand. Only data addressing modes are allowed as shown:

Addressing Mode	Mode	Register	Addressing Mode	Mode	Register
Dn	000	register number	d(An, Xi)	110	register number
An	—	—	Abs.W	111	000
(An)	010	register number	Abs.L	111	001
(An)+	011	register number	d(PC)	111	010
−(An)	100	register number	d(PC, Xi)	111	011
d(An)	101	register number	Imm	111	100

Note: Overflow occurs if the quotient is larger than a 16-bit signed integer.

FIGURE 11.13
Selected instructions for 68000.

Operation: (Source) + (Destination) → Destination
Assembler: ADD <ea>, Dn
Syntax: ADD Dn, <ea>
Attributes: Size = (Byte, Word, Long)
Description: Add the source operand to the destination operand, and store the result in the destination location. The size of the operation may be specified to be byte, word, or long. The mode of the instruction indicates which operand is the source and which is the destination, as well as the operand size.

Condition codes

X	N	Z	V	C
*	*	*	*	*

N Set if the result is negative. Cleared otherwise.
Z Set if the result is zero. Cleared otherwise.
V Set if an overflow is generated. Cleared otherwise.

C Set if a borrow is generated. Cleared otherwise.
X Set the same as the carry bit.

Instruction format

15	14	13	12	11 10 9	8 7 6	5 4 3 2 1 0
1	1	0	1	Register	Op-mode	Effective address mode register

Instruction fields

Register field: Specifies any of the eight destination data registers.

Op-mode field:

Byte	Word	Long	Operation
000	001	010	(<Dn>)+(<ea>)→<Dn>
100	101	110	(<ea>)+(<Dn>)→<ea>

Effective address field: Determines addressing mode:

(*a*) If the location specified is a source operand, then all addressing modes are allowed as shown:

Addressing Mode	Mode	Register	Addressing Mode	Mode	Register
Dn	000	register number	d(An, Xi)	110	register number
An*	001	register number	Abs.W	111	000
(An)	010	register number	Abs.L	111	001
(An)+	011	register number	d(PC)	111	010
−(An)	100	register number	d(PC, Xi)	111	011
d(An)	101	register number	Imm	111	100

(*b*) If the location specified is a destination operand, then only alterable memory addressing modes are allowed as shown:

Addressing Mode	Mode	Register	Addressing Mode	Mode	Register
Dn	—	—	d(An, Xi)	110	register number
An	—	—	Abs.W	111	000
(An)	010	register number	Abs.L	111	001
(An)+	011	register number	d(PC)	—	—
−(An)	100	register number	d(PC, Xi)	—	—
d(An)	101	register number	Imm	—	—

Note: 1. If the destination is a data register, then it cannot be specified by using the destination <ea> mode, but must use the destination Dn mode instead.
2. ADDA is used when the destination is an address register. ADDI and ADDQ are used when the source is immediate data. Most assemblers automatically make this distinction.
3. Word and Long only.

FIGURE 11.13
Selected instructions for 68000.

Operation: (Destination) − (Source) → Destination
Assembler: SUB <ea>, Dn
Syntax: SUB Dn, <ea>
Attributes: Size = (Byte, Word, Long)
Description: Subtract the source operand from the destination operand, and store the result in the destination. The size of the operation may be specified to be byte, word, or long. The mode of the instruction indicates which operand is the source and which is the destination, as well as the operand size.

Condition codes   X   N   Z   V   C

*	*	*	*	*

N   Set if the result is negative. Cleared otherwise.   C   Set if a borrow is generated. Cleared otherwise.
Z   Set if the result is zero. Cleared otherwise.   X   Set the same as the carry bit.
V   Set if an overflow is generated. Cleared otherwise.

Instruction format   15   14   13   12   11 10 9   8 7 6   5 4 3 2 1 0

1	0	0	1	Register	Op-mode	Effective address mode register

Instruction fields
Register field: Specifies any of the eight destination data registers.

Op-mode field:

Byte	Word	Long	Operation
000	001	010	(<Dn>)−(<ea>)→<Dn>
100	101	110	(<ea>)−(<Dn>)→<ea>

Effective address field: Determines addressing mode
(a) If the location specified is a source operand, then all addressing modes are allowed as shown:

Addressing Mode	Mode	Register	Addressing Mode	Mode	Register
Dn	000	register number	d(An, Xi)	110	register number
An*	001	register number	Abs.W	111	000
(An)	010	register number	Abs.L	111	001
(An)+	011	register number	d(PC)	111	010
−(An)	100	register number	d(PC, Xi)	111	011
d(An)	101	register number	Imm	111	100

(b) If the location specified is a destination operand, then only alterable memory addressing modes are allowed as shown:

Addressing Mode	Mode	Register	Addressing Mode	Mode	Register
Dn	—	—	d(An, Xi)	110	register number
An	—	—	Abs.W	111	000
(An)	010	register number	Abs.L	111	001
(An)+	011	register number	d(PC)	—	—
−(An)	100	register number	d(PC, Xi)	—	—
d(An)	101	register number	Imm	—	—

Note: 1. If the destination is a data register, then it cannot be specified by using the destination <ea> mode, but must use the destination Dn mode instead.
2. SUBA is used when the destination is an address register. SUBI and SUBQ are used when the source is immediate data. Most assemblers automatically make this distinction.
3. For byte-size data, register direct is not allowed.

FIGURE 11.13
Selected instructions for 68000.

Notice that addresses are generated in 32-bit registers and are complete addresses. The pin-out in Fig. 11.14 shows that all 24 address lines and 16-bit data lines are externally available. And there is no multiplexing of these lines because the 68000 has a 64-pin package, which provides for the necessary connections.

The 68000 microprocessor chip and its support chip provide a powerful instruction repertoire and high-speed operation of programs. They are widely used in everything from personal computers to communication and control systems. To give some feeling for the 68000 series assembly language, a short section of code in assembly language follows. This section of program examines two alphanumeric strings and determines if they are equal. If they are equal, the program sets D_0 to 0 and jumps (branches) to the EQUAL location in memory. If the strings are not equal, the program sets D_0 to -1 and goes to NEQUAL. The first section consists of some comments (comments are preceded by asterisks), and there are also comments on the lines. The code makes use of a DBxx instruction, which in this case is a DBNE (for not equal). This instruction examines the Z bit and makes the branch if the condition is not satisfied. This instruction also decrements any data register that is referenced (D_4, for example) and does not make the branch if that register is -1. This makes it possible to form a loop with a counter and to exit the loop if a test fails or when the counter reaches its goal.

```
* This code processes two strings of alphanumeric
* characters. Each character is 1 byte.
*
* In this subroutine A1 points to one input string.
* A2 points to the other string to be compared
*
* Branches to appropriate subroutines are included.
* D4 contains the string lengths in bytes minus 1.
*
         MOV      A1,A3          ;program begins here
COMP     CMP.B    (A1)+,(A2)+    ;indirect register addresses
         DBNE     D4,COMP
         BNE      TSTN           ;check for not equal character
         BEQ      EQU            ;characters equal
TSTN     MOVEQ.L  #-1,D0         ;set D0 to -1
         BRA      NEQUAL         ;branch to failed code
EQU      MOVEQ.L  #0,D0          ;set D0 to 0
         BRA      EQUAL          ;jumps to OK code
```

A DBcc instruction (Decrement and branch conditionally) operates as follows: if cc is *false*, then $[Dn]-1 \rightarrow Dn$; if $[Dn] \neq -1$, then $[PC] + disp \rightarrow PC$. This is very useful in forming loops. The cc can stand for NE for not equal, EQ for equal, VS for overflow set, LT for less than, GT for greater than, and so on.

As a further example of 68000 series programming, the following program searches for an alphanumeric string M in memory beginning at a location stored in A_4. M ends with an *. Another alphanumeric string Q beginning in A_1 with its length D stored in D_0 is compared with successive D characters in M to see if D occurs in M (this is like looking for a specific word in some text).

Pin Name	Description
D_0–D_{15}	Data bus
A_1–A_{23}	Address bus
$\overline{AS}$	Address strobe
$R/\overline{W}$	Read/Write control
$\overline{UDS}$, $\overline{LDS}$	Upper, lower data strobes
$\overline{DTACK}$	Data transfer acknowledge
FC_0, FC_1, FC_2	Function code (status) outputs
$\overline{IPL_0}$, $\overline{IPL_1}$, $\overline{IPL_2}$	Interrupt requests
$\overline{BERR}$	Bus error
$\overline{HALT}$	Halt processor
$\overline{RESET}$	Reset processor or reset external devices
CLK	Clock
$\overline{BR}$	Bus request
$\overline{BG}$	Bus grant
$\overline{BGACK}$	Bus grant acknowledge
E	Enable (clock) output
$\overline{VMA}$	Valid memory address
$\overline{VPA}$	Valid peripheral address
V_{cc}, GND	Power (+5 V) and Ground

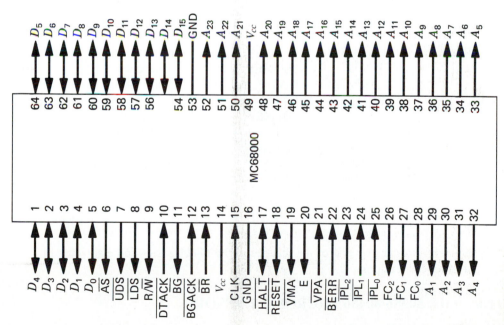

FIGURE 11.14
Pin-out for 68000.

```
* STRING SEARCH subroutine:
* M is ASCII string terminated by "*"
*
* A4 contains start of M.
* A1 contains start of pattern string Q with length in D0.
*
* Result of search is in A2. If Q is in M.
* A2 will hold starting address where Q is found; else
* A2 is returned as zero.
              ORG         $2000
FIND          MOVEM.W     D1/D3,−(SP)
              MOVEM.L     A4/A3,−(SP)
* Search M for first character of Q
              MOVE.B      (A1),D3        ; first char of Q
INIT          SUBA.L      A2,A2          ; clear A2
CHECK         CMPI.B      #'*',(A4)      ; end of M?
              BEQ.S       HOMES          ; yes — go home
              CMP.B       (A4)+,D3       ; M char equal Q char?
              BNE.S       CHECK          ; no
* First Q char has been found, compare rest of Q
              MOVE.W      D0,D1              ; D1 = length of Q
              SUBQ.W      #2,D1              ; loop for len Q−1
              MOVEA.L     A1,A3              ; A3 −− > Q
              ADDQ.L      #1,A3              ; A3 −− > second char of Q
              CMPI.B      #'*',(A6)          ; look for *
              BEQ.S       LOC                ; a match
              MOVEA.L     A4,A2              ; A2 points to M char
REPT          CMPI.B      #'*',(A2)          ; end
              BEQ.S       HOMES              ; if so, return
              CMPM.B      (A3)+,(A2)+        ; M char = Q char?
              BNE.S       INIT               ; no — resume
              DBF         D1,REPT            ; yes — continue
LOC                                          ; new label here
              SUBQ.L      #1,A4              ; Q located
              MOVEA.L     A4,A2              ; put start addr. in A2
HOMES         MOVEM.L     (SP)+,A4/A3
              MOVEM.W     (SP)+,D1/D3
              RTS
              END
```

This program illustrates several of the features in the 68000 series and also some of the assembler conventions.

11.6   THE 80386/80486 MICROPROCESSOR

The 80386 and 80486 are the latest microprocessors to be developed by Intel. They are faster and more complex, offering additional features to those of the 8080, 8086, 80286, and other Intel processors that preceded them.

Figure 11.15 shows the organization of the 80386 chip. The chip is sectioned into "units," each of which has a specific function:

The *instruction decode unit* takes bytes from the prefetch queue, determines the number of bytes needed for the next instruction, obtains the entire instruction from the prefetch queue, reformats the op code into an internal instruction format, and places the decoded instruction into the instruction queue. The instruction decode unit also tells the "bus interface unit" if the instruction decoded will cause a memory reference, allowing operands to be obtained in advance.

The *execution unit* performs shifts, additions, multiplications, and similar operations. The CPU register set is contained within the execution unit. The unit has a barrel shifter that can perform multiple-bit shifts in a single clock cycle. The execution unit uses this capability in shift instructions, to accelerate multiplication, and to generate indexed addressed.

The *bus interface unit* (BIU) is used when an instruction needs to write data to memory or to the I/O channel, the BIU is presented with the data and physical address.

The instruction decode unit takes each instruction from a 16-byte instruction queue, and the *instruction prefetch unit* instructs the BIU to fetch succeeding dwords in memory. When the prefetch unit receives a dword, it places it in the queue and (if the queue is not full) requests another dword. The prefetch unit is notified when the execution unit processes a CALL, JMP, or interrupt so that it can begin fetching

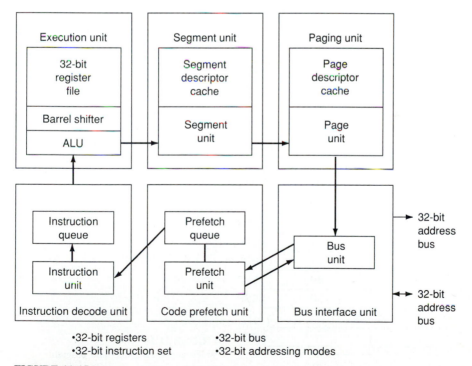

FIGURE 11.15
80386 block diagram. (*Courtesy Intel Corporation.*)

instructions from the new address. The queue is emptied whenever a CALL, JMP, or interrupt occurs, preventing the execution unit from receiving invalid instructions.

The *segmentation unit* translates segmented addresses into linear addresses. The segmentation unit contains a cache that holds descriptor table information for the six segment registers.

The *paging unit* takes the addresses generated by the segmentation unit and converts them to physical addresses (when paging is disabled, the addresses generated by the segmentation unit become physical addresses). When paging is used, the address space of the 80386 is divided into 4096-byte pages. A page table is used to translate segmented addresses to physical addresses. A cache called the *translation lookaside buffer* (refer to Chap. 6) contains entries for the 32 most recently used pages. When a page entry is not found in the translation buffer, the BIU fetches the entry from the RAM.

80386 Registers

Figures 11.16 and 11.17 show the 80386 basic registers. The general-purpose registers are as follows:

EAX is the basic accumulator.

EBX is the base (address) register, which can hold addresses for indexing and indirection.

ECX holds the number of iterations or shifts.

EDX is the data register and an extension of the accumulator (it is used to hold addresses for input and output).

ESI and EDI are the source and destination index registers.

EBP is the base pointer and is used for accessing stack data.

ESP is the stack pointer.

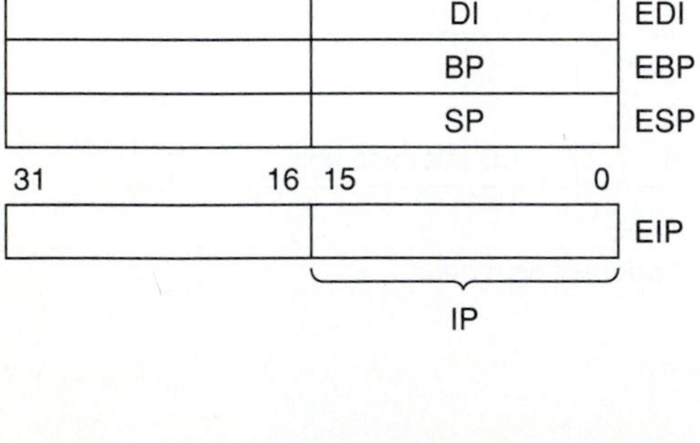

31		16 15	8 7	0	
		AH A	X AL		EAX
		BH B	X BL		EBX
		CH C	X BL		ECX
		DH D	X DL		EDX
		SI			ESI
		DI			EDI
		BP			EBP
		SP			ESP

31		16 15		0	
					EIP

IP

FIGURE 11.16
80386 general registers and program counter. (*Courtesy Intel Corporation.*)

General data and address registers

31	16 15	0		
		AX	EAX	
		BX	EBX	
		CX	ECS	
		DX	EDS	
		SI	ESI	
		DI	EDI	
		BP	EBP	
		SP	ESP	

Segment selector registers

15	0		
	CS	Code stack
	SS	
	DS	
	ES	Data
	FS	
	GS	

Instruction pointer and flag register

31	16 15	0	
	IP	EIP	
	Flags	EFLAGS	

FIGURE 11.17
Registers available to operating system. (*Courtesy Intel Corporation.*)

EIP is the program counter (the IP stands for "Instruction pointer," a synonym for program counter).

The *E* in these names indicates an *extended* or 32-bit register. Figure 11.17 shows how the lower halves of these registers (bits 0 through 15) have the same names but with no *E*.

The flags in the 80386 flag register are identified as follows:

DF indicates whether string instructions will increase (0) or decrease their pointers.

IF (interrupt enable), when a 1, enables interrupts.

TF (trap) places the process in a single-step mode.

SF (sign) indicates whether or not the result of the latest arithmetic (or logical) operation had a 1 in its most significant bit.

ZF (zero) is a 1 for zero and a 0 for nonzero.

AF (auxiliary carry) indicates whether or not the latest arithmetic operation produced a carry from bit 3.

PF (even parity), when a 1, indicates that the result of the latest arithmetic or logical operation had even parity.

CF (carry) is set or reset depending on whether or not the last arithmetic, logical, or shift instruction produced a carry.

Figure 11.17 shows the *segment registers*, which are available to the operation system only. These are:

CS is the *code selector register* and selects the segment from which the processor will obtain instructions.

SS is the *stack selector register*, which selects the stack segment.

DS, ES, FS, and GS are the *data selector registers* and select the segments that contain data.

11.31 80386 DATA TYPES

There are several data types in the 80386, as shown in Fig. 11.18. In this system, a byte is 8 bits, a word is 16 bits, a double word (dword) is 32 bits and a quad word (qword) is 64 bits. Other data types are:

Single bits, bit strings, and signed or unsigned bytes

Offsets (16- or 32-bit quantities) and pointers (which include a 16-bit segment selector and a 16- or 32-bit offset)

Characters (8-bit ASCII)

Packed BCD (two digits per byte) and unpacked BCD (one digit per byte)

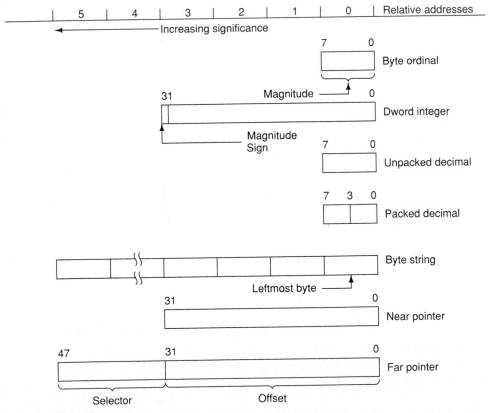

FIGURE 11.18
Data types. (*Courtesy Intel Corporation.*)

Intel makes what are called (floating-point) numerical processors, and the 80287 and 80387 chips use the IEEE format explained in Chapter 2. The floating-point 80287 or 80387 numerical coprocessor (see Chap. 8) handles 32-bit, 64-bit, and 80-bit representations of real numbers. The 80486 has a floating-point section on the chip and does not require an additional coprocessor.

We now present an overview of the 80386 instruction set. The 80386 has a great many instructions, so only certain representative instructions from each category have been chosen; these are shown in Table 11.13.

The general format for instruction encoding is shown in Fig. 11.19. Instructions consist of one or two op code bytes, possibly an address specifier (consisting of the *mod r/m* byte and *scaled index base* byte), a displacement (if required), and an immediate data field (if required). Within the op codes, smaller fields may be defined. These fields define such information as direction of the operation (right or left), size of the displacements, register encoding, and sign extension.

Instructions referring to an operand in memory generally have an addressing mode byte following the primary op code byte(s). This byte, the *mod r/m* byte, specifies the address mode to be used. Certain encodings of the *mod r/m* byte indicate that a second addressing byte, the *scaled index base* byte, follows the mod r/m byte to fully specify the addressing mode.

The addressing modes include a displacement immediately following the mod r/m byte or a scaled index byte. If a displacement is present, the possible sizes are 8, 16, and 32 bits. If the instruction specifies an immediate operand, the immediate operand follows any displacement bytes. The immediate operand, if specified, is always the last field of the instruction.

Several fields are not shown in Fig. 11.19(*a*); the complete set is shown in Fig. 11.19(*b*).

The 80386/80486 extends the 8086 address lengths to 32 bits and the data types to 32 bits. Also, whether an instruction performs operations of 16 bits or 32 bits depends on the *D* bit in the code segment descriptor or an address or operand prefix, which gives the length (either 32 bits or 16 bits) for both operands and effective addresses during the execution of that code segment. In the real address mode (or virtual 8086 mode), no code segment descriptors are used, but a *D* value of 0 is assumed internally by the 80386 when it is operating in these modes.

The *operand size prefix* and the *effective address size prefix* allow individual overriding of the default selection of operand size and effective address size. These prefixes may precede any op code bytes and affect only the instruction they precede. If necessary, one or both of the prefixes may be placed before the op code bytes. The presence of the operand size prefix and the effective address size prefix will toggle the operand size or the effective address size, respectively, to the value "opposite" the default setting. The 32-bit extensions are available in all 80386 modes, including the real address mode or the virtual 8086 mode. In these modes the default is always 16 bits, so prefixes are needed to specify 32-bit operands or addresses. Within each instruction are several fields indicating register selection and addressing mode, and the exact encodings of these fields are given. For any given instruction performing a data operation, the instruction is executed as a 32-bit operation or a 16-bit operation.

TABLE 11.13
Selected 80386/80486 instructions

ADD: Adds the contents of the source operand to the destination operand and stores the sum in the destination.

Examples:

```
ADD AX, BX      ; AX ← AX + BX
ADD EAX, ABLE ; EAX ← EAX + ABLE
ADD ABLE, EBX ; ABLE ← ABLE + EBX
ADD CL, 50      ; CL ← CL + 50
```

AND causes a logical AND to store the result in the destination operand. C and OF are cleared by this operation.

Examples:

```
AND AX, SX      ; AX ← AX·SX
AND EAX, ABLE ; EAX ← EAX·ABLE
AND ABLE, EBX ; ABLE ← ABLE·EBX
```

CALL: performs a subroutine and does the following:
Pushes offset address of following instruction on the stack;
If procedure being called is declared as FAR, pushes segment address of following instruction on the stack;
Loads IP with the offset address of the procedure called;
If procedure being called is declared as FAR, it loads CS with the segment address of the procedure being called;
Execution continues at the newly loaded CS:IP address until RET is encountered.

Examples:

```
CALL SQROOT ;
CALL [BX]      ; Subroutine is at address pointed to by BX
CALL AX        ; Address in AX
```

CMP compare: The source operand is subtracted from the destination operand and the result is used to set the following flags: OF, SF, ZF, AF, PF, and CF.

Examples:

```
CMP AX, BX     ;
CMP AX, ABLE  ; ABLE must be a word
CMP ABLE, EBX ; ABLE must be a dword
```

DIV (divide): For a byte operand, DIV divides AX by the operand, stores the result in AL and the remainder in AH. For a word DIV divides the contents of DX:AX by the contents of the operand and stores the result in AX and the remainder in DX. When the operand is a doubleword value. DIV divides the contents of EDX:EAX by the operand and stores the result in EAX and the remainder in EDX. Numbers are considered unsigned.

Examples:

```
DIV BX     ; AX ← DX:AX/BX
DIV ABLE ; AX ← DX:AX/ABLE
```

IN (input from port): Loads a byte, word, or doubleword to AL, AX, or EAX, respectively, from the port address.

JE (jump if equal): Program branches to the operand address if the zero flag is set.

Example:

```
JE HOME
```

TABLE 11.13
Selected 80386/80486 instructions (*continued*)

JG (jump if greater): Program branches to operand address if the sign flag equals the overflow flag or if the zero flag is clear.

Example:
    JG KING

JMP (jump): Causes the program to jump to the operand address.

Example:
    JMP HOME

MOV (move): transfers the contents of the source operand to the destination operand. The operands must be of the same length.

Examples:
    MOV BX, AX   ; BX ← AX
    MOV ABLE, AX ; ABLE ← AX

MUL (multiply): For a byte operand, AL is multiplied by the contents of the operand and the result stored in AX. For a word, AX is multiplied by the operand and the result stored in the combined register DX:AX. For doubleword, EAX is multiplied by the operand and the result stored in EDX:EAX. Numbers are considered unsigned integers.

Examples:
    MUL BX ; DX:AX ← AX × BX
    MUL ECX ; EDX:EAX ← EAX × ECX

OUT (output to port): OUT transfers a byte (AL), word (AX), or doubleword (EAX) to the port address.

Examples:
    OUT 24H, AL
    OUT DX, AX

POP (pop): Removes a word or double word from stack and transfers it to the destination operands address.

Examples:
    POP AX
    POP ABLE

PUSH (push): Transfers operand to top of stack.

Examples:
    PUSH BX
    PUSH ABLE

SUB (subtract): Subtracts the source operand from the destination operand and stores the result in the destination operand. The flags affected are OF, SF, ZF, AF, PF, and CF.

Examples:
    SUB BX, AX   ; BX ← BX − AX
    SUB AX, ABLE ; AX ← AX − ABLE

Courtesy Intel Corporation.

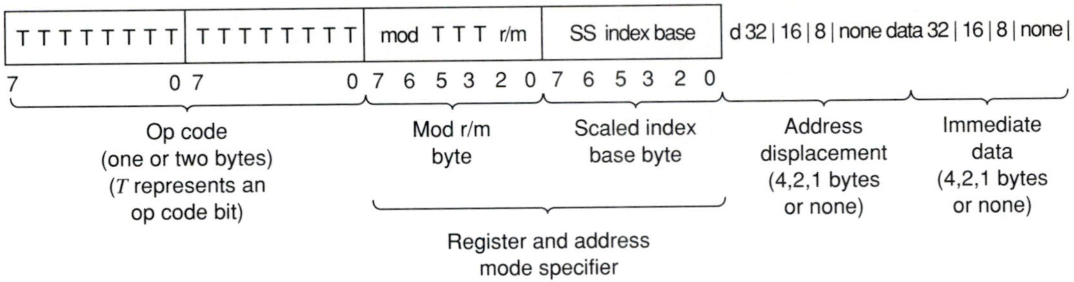

(a)

Field name	Description	Number of bits
w	Specifies if data is byte or full size (full size is either 16 or 32 bits)	1
d	Specified direction of data operation	1
s	Specifies if an immediate data field must be sign-extended	1
reg	General purpose specifier	3
mod r/m	Address mode specifier (effective address can be a general register)	2 for mod; 3 for r/m
ss	Scale factor for scaled index address mode	2
index	General register to be used as index register	3
base	General register to be used as base register	3
sreg2	Segment register specifier for CS, SS, DS, ES	2
sreg3	Segment register specifier for CS, SS, DS, ES, FS, GS	3
tttm	For conditional instructions, specifies a condition asserted or a condition negated, ttt specifies condition tested	4

(b)

FIGURE 11.19

(a) Op code layout. (b) Field name definition. (*Courtesy Intel Corporation*)

Within the constraints of the operation size, the *w* field encodes the operand size as either 1 byte or the full operation size, as shown in Fig. 11.20(*a*).

The general register is specified by the reg field, which appears in the primary op code bytes, the reg field of the mod r/m byte, or the r/m field of the mod r/m byte, as shown in Fig. 11.20(*b*) and (*c*).

The sreg field in some instructions is a 2-bit field allowing one of the four segment registers to be specified. The sreg field in other instructions is a 3-bit field allowing the 80386 FS and GS segment registers to be specified, as shown in Fig. 11.20(*d*).

Encoding of reg field when w field is not present in instruction

Reg field	Register selected during 16-bit data operations	Register selected during 32-bit data operations
000	AX	EAX
001	CX	ECX
010	DX	EDX
011	BX	EBX
100	SP	ESP
101	BP	EBP
101	SI	ESI
101	DI	EDI

(a)

Register specified by reg field during 16-bit data operations

	Function of w field	
Reg	(w = 0)	(w = 1)
000	AL	AX
001	CL	CX
010	DL	DX
011	BL	BX
100	AH	SP
101	CH	BP
110	DH	SI
111	BH	DI

(b)

Register specified by reg field during 32-bit data operation

	Function of w field	
Reg	w = 0	w = 1
000	AL	EAX
001	CL	ECX
010	DL	EDX
011	BL	EBX
100	AH	ESP
101	CH	EBP
110	DH	ESI
111	BH	EDI

(c)

2-bit sreg2 field

2-bit sreg2 field	Segment register selected
00	ES
01	CS
10	SS
11	DS

3-bit sreg3 field

3-bit sreg3 field	Segment register selected
000	ES
001	CS
010	SS
011	DS
100	FS
101	GS
110	not used
111	not used

(d)

FIGURE 11.20
Instruction field encodings. (*a*) Encoding of reg field when *w* field is not present in instruction. (*b*) Register specified by reg field during 16-bit data operation. (*c*) Register specified by reg field during 32-bit data operation. (*d*) 2-bit sreg2 field and 3-bit sreg3 field. (*Courtesy Intel Corporation.*)

The primary addressing byte in the 80386/80486 is the mod r/m byte which contains three bits [shown as TTT in Fig. 11.19(a)] used as an extension of the primary op code or as a register field (reg). A second byte of addressing information, the scaled-index-base (s.i.b.) byte, can be specified. This byte is specified when the 32-bit addressing mode is used and the mod r/m byte has r/m = 100 and mod = 00, 01, or 10. When the s.i.b. byte is present, the 32-bit addressing mode is a function of the mod, ss, index, and base fields.

To calculate an effective address, either 16-bit addressing or 32-bit addressing can be used. When 16-bit addressing is used, the mod r/m byte is interpreted as a 16-bit addressing mode specifier. When 32-bit addressing is used, the "mod r/m" byte is interpreted as a 32-bit addressing mode specifier. Figure 11.21 shows all encodings of the 16- and 32-bit addressing modes. They illustrate the rich instruction repertoire of the 80386/80486.

Mod/rm	Effective address	Mod/rm	Effective address
00 000	DS:[BX + Si]	10 000	DS:[BX + Si + d16]
00 001	DS:[BX + Di]	10 001	DS:[BS + Di + d16]
00 010	SS:[BP + Si]	10 010	SS:[BP + Si + d16]
00 011	SS:[BP + Di]	10 011	SS:[BP + Di + d16]
00 100	DS:[Si]	10 100	DS:[Si + d16]
00 101	DS:[Di]	10 101	DS:[Di + d16]
00 110	DS:d16	10 110	SS:[BP + d16]
00 111	DS:[BX]	10 111	DS:[BX + d16]
01 000	DS:[BX + Si + d8]	11 000	register
01 001	DS:[BX + Di + d8]	11 001	register
01 010	SS:[BP + Si + d8]	11 010	register
01 011	SS:[BP + Di + d8]	11 011	register
01 100	DS:[Si + d8]	11 100	register
01 101	DS:[Di + d8]	11 101	register
01 110	SS:[BP + d8]	11 110	register
01 111	DS:[BX + d8]	11 111	register

Register specified by r/m during 16-bit data operations			Register specified by r/m during 32-bit data operations		
	Function of w field			Function of w field	
Mod r/m	w = 0	w = 1	Mod r/m	w = 0	w = 1
11 000	AL	AX	11 000	AL	EAX
11 001	CL	CX	11 001	CL	ECX
11 010	DL	DX	11 010	DL	EDX
11 011	BL	BX	11 011	BL	EBX
11 100	AH	SP	11 100	AH	ESP
11 101	CH	BP	11 101	CH	EBP
11 110	DH	SI	11 110	DH	ESI
11 111	BH	DI	11 111	BH	EDI

FIGURE 11.21
Address field encodings. (a) Encoding of 16-bit address mode with mod r/m byte. (*Courtesy Intel Corporation.*)

Mod/rm	Effective address	Mod/rm	Effective address
00 000	DS:[EAX]	10 000	DS:[EAX + d32]
00 001	DS:[ECX]	10 001	DS:[ECX + d32]
00 010	DS:[EDX]	10 010	DS:[EDX + d32]
00 011	DS:[EBX]	10 011	DS:[EBX + d32]
00 100	s.i.b is present	10 100	s.i.b is present
00 101	DS:d32	10 101	SS:[EBP + d32]
00 110	DS:[ESi]	10 110	DS:[ESi + d32]
00 111	DS:[EDi]	10 111	DS:[EDi + d32]
01 000	DS:[EAX + d8]	11 000	register
01 001	DS:[ECX + d8]	11 001	register
01 010	SS:[EDX + d8]	11 010	register
01 011	SS:[EBX + d8]	11 011	register
01 100	s.i.b is present	11 100	register
01 101	SS:[EBP + d8]	11 101	register
01 110	DS:[ESi + d8]	11 110	register
01 111	DS:[EDi + d8]	11 111	register

Register specified by r/m during 32-bit data operations

Mod r/m	Function of w field	
	w = 0	w = 1
11 000	AL	EAX
11 001	CL	ECX
11 010	DL	EDX
11 011	BL	EBX
11 100	AH	ESP
11 101	CH	EBP
11 110	DH	ESI
11 111	BH	EDI

Register specified by r/m during 16-bit data operations

Mod r/m	Function of w field	
	w = 0	w = 1
11 000	AL	AX
11 001	CL	CX
11 010	DL	DX
11 011	BL	BX
11 100	AH	SP
11 101	CH	BP
11 110	DH	SI
11 111	BH	DI

Encoding of operation direction (*D*) field

In some two-operand instructions the d field indicates which operand is considered the source and which is the destination.

d	Direction of operation
0	Register/memory ← register "reg" field indicates source operand; "mod r/m" or "mod as index base" indicates destination operand
1	Register ← register/memory "reg" field indicates destination operand; "mod r/m" or "mod as index base" indicates source operand

FIGURE 11.21

(*b*) Encoding of 32-bit address mode with mod r/m byte (no s.i.b. byte). (*Courtesy Intel Corporation.*)

Mod base	Effective address	ss	Scale factor
00 000	DS:[EAX + (scaled index)]	00	x1
00 001	DS:[ECX + (scaled index)]	01	x2
00 010	DS:[EDX + (scaled index)]	10	x4
00 011	DS:[EBX + (scaled index)]	11	x8
00 100	SS:[ESP + (scaled index)]		
00 101	DS:[d32 + (scaled index)]		
00 110	DS:[ESi + (scaled index)]		
00 111	DS:[EDi + (scaled index)]		

Index	Index register

Mod base	Effective address	Index	Index register
01 000	DS:[EAX + (scaled index) + d8]	000	EAX
01 001	DS:[ECX + (scaled index) + d8]	001	ECX
01 010	DS:[EDX + (scaled index) + d8]	010	EDX
01 011	DS:[EBX + (scaled index) + d8]	011	EBX
01 100	SS:[ESP + (scaled index) + d8]	100	no index reg**
01 101	SS:[EBP + (scaled index) + d8]	101	EBP
01 110	DS:[ESi + (scaled index) + d8]	110	ESi
01 111	DS:[EDi + (scaled index) + d8]	111	EDi
10 000	DS:[EAX + (scaled index) + d32]		
10 001	DS:[ECX + (scaled index) + d32]		
10 010	DS:[EDX + (scaled index) + d32]		
10 011	DS:[EBX + (scaled index) + d32]		
10 100	SS:[ESP + (scaled index) + d32]		
10 101	SS:[EBP + (scaled index) + d32]		
10 110	DS:[ESi + (scaled index) + d32]		
10 111	DS:[EDi + (scaled index) + d32]		

Note: Mod field is mod r/m byte: ss, index, base fields in s.i.b byte

** When index field is 100, indicating "no index register," then ss field MUST equal 00. If index is 100 and ss does not equal 00, the effective address is undefined.

FIGURE 11.21
(*c*) Encoding of 32-bit address mode (mod r/m byte and s.i.b. byte present). (*Courtesy Intel Corporation.*)

QUESTIONS

11.1. Sketch, describe, and discuss the merits of one of the machine architectures that have been presented, or that of any other machine with which you are familiar (or with which you would like to be familiar—including any of your own "ideal" designs).

11.2. A real-time system for manufacturing control is to be constructed using a computer. The system is to perform two functions:
  (*a*) The computer has to automatically test cameras as they are manufactured. This involves, among other things, reading 1000 values each second from several A/D converters and checking to see if the values are within prescribed limits.
  (*b*) The computer has to service four terminals that run inquiries against the data base maintained on the cameras, and it also has to run some FORTRAN and Cobol programs.
  Give an architecture for the computer to be used.

11.3. Show how the 6809 microprocessor subroutine call will not destroy the return address in a recursive subroutine call because of the use of the stack.

11.4. Show how the 80386 jump to a subroutine will not destroy the return location in a recursive subroutine call because of the stack.

11.5. Compare PDP-11 addressing to the 68000 addressing modes.

11.6 Discuss the architecture of the 6809 versus the 8086 microprocessor.

11.7. The following is a short program for the 6809, which was written to compute $Y = 32(9 - 7)$ and store it. The programmer has converted the program into hexadecimal and is now prepared to enter it into the computer. There are several mistakes in the program. Find as many as possible and explain each.

#	Address	Op	Operand	Label	Mnemonics	Operand	Comments
01	0200	4F		START	CLRA		; CLEAR REGISTER A
02	0201	86	0E		LDA	X	; LOAD X INTO REGISTER A
03	0203	43			COMA		; COMPLEMENT X
04	0204	8B	09		ADDA(IM)	#09	; ADD 9
05	0206	CE	05		LDX(IM)	#05	; LOAD INDEX REGISTER WITH 5
06	0208	49		LOOP	ROLA		; ROTATE LEFT 1 BIT (MULTIPLY BY 2)
07	0209	09			DEX		; DECREMENT INDEX REGISTER
08	020A	26	FD		BNE	LOOP	; ROTATE AGAIN IF INDEX REGISTER $\neq 0$
09	020C	97	0F		STAA	Y	; AFTER MULTIPLYING BY $2^5 = 32$, STORE THE RESULT IN Y
10	020E	07		X	DATA	1 BYTE	
11	020F	00		Y	DATA	1 BYTE	; DATA IN THIS LOCATION WILL BE REPLACED BY VALUE OF Y

11.8. Write a short program for the 6809 that will determine the number of bytes in a table that have 1s in their sign bits. The number of elements in the table is stored at location 50, and the table begins in location 60. The number of bytes with 1 in the sign bit is to be stored in location 51.

11.9. Write a program in assembly language for the 80386 microprocessor that will multiply a number X by 32 and then subtract 14 from the result. (Ignore overflows.)

11.10. Write a program in assembly language for the 68000 microprocessor that will multiply Y by 16 and then subtract 15 from the result. (Ignore overflows.)

11.11. Write a subroutine for the 80386 microprocessor that will double the number in the accumulator and then subtract 5. (Ignore overflows.)

11.12. Write a subroutine for the 68000 that will add accumulator A to accumulator B, store the result in accumulator A, and then subtract 12 from this result, storing that in accumulator B. (Ignore overflows.)

11.13. Write a subroutine call for the 68000 that will utilize the subroutine written in Question 11.12. Before this subroutine call, place 13 in accumulator A and 23 in accumulator B.

11.14. Discuss PDP-11 addressing, where the addressing mode (or modes) is carried in the address section, versus placing that information in the op code.

11.15. Write a program for the PDP-11 that will add the number in R_1 to the number in R_3 and then store this number at location 63_8 in the memory.

11.16. Show the mode information in the two 3-bit fields in a PDP-11 instruction word that uses both source and destination registers in a direct addressing mode.

11.17. Explain why placing often-used data in the first 256 words of the memory in a 6809 will shorten some instruction words.

11.18. Explain the following sentence: The 6809 has two index registers and the PDP-11 can use any general register as an index register.

11.19. Explain how the auto-increment and auto-decrement instruction modes in the PDP-11 can be useful in processing tables.

11.20. In the 8088/8086 an interrupt is serviced as follows. The device being serviced places on the data lines of the 8086 bus an instruction word representing a special instruction, called RST. Three bits of this instruction give the address of the next instruction to be executed. The interrupting device places the correct 3 bits in the section of the RST instruction on the bus, and the 8086 then takes the next instruction from that location. (See op code description of RST.) In that location is a jump to the subroutine that actually services the device generating the interrupt. Discuss the advantages and disadvantages of this procedure.

11.21. Translate the following program into hexadecimal for the 6809:

```
        ORG       $50
        LDX       #$79
        LDA       #$20
BLKC    LEAX 1,X
        CMPA      X
        BEQ       BLKC
        STX       $55
```

11.22. The program in Question 11.21 stores the address of the first nonspace character in a string at location 55 in the memory. Analyze the program operation instruction by instruction.

11.23. Translate the following section of program into hexadecimal for the 68000, showing the contents of each memory location:

```
        ORG     $1000
TOIT    DC.B    'TOM'
        DC.B    23,$4A,$5
        DC.L    52,TOIT+20
```

11.24. Analyze the operation of the section of program given in Question 11.23 instruction by instruction, explaining what it does.

11.25. Translate the following PDP-11 program into octal. What does this short section of program do?

```
READ    TSTB    KSR         ; READY
        BPL     READ        ; NO
        INC     R5          ; INC BUFFER PTR
        MOVB    KSB; @R5    ; STORE INPUT
        MOV     @R5;R4      ; STORE LASCHR
        JSR     PC,PRINT    ; PRINT INPUT
        BR      READ        ; READ NEXT CHAR
PRINT   CMPB    R4, #212
```

Place the READ statement at location 500_8. KSB is at location 1775628.

11.26. Suppose we push *A*, *B*, *D*, and *F* on a stack, pop the stack twice, and then push *M* and *N* onto the stack. If we pop letters from the stack three times, what letters will be popped and in what order?

11.27. Explain extended addressing, implied addressing, and relative addressing in the 6809 microprocessor.

11.28. Explain how the BRANCH IF ZERO instruction works on the 6809 microprocessor.

11.29. Explain the difference between an ADD ACCUMULATOR with carry (ADCA) and an ADD (ADDA or ADDB) instruction for the 6809 microprocessor.

11.30. Explain a ROTATE RIGHT instruction on the 6809 microprocessor.

11.31. What are the differences between ROTATE and SHIFT instructions on the 68000 microprocessor? Why are both useful?

11.32. Explain the BRANCH TO SUBROUTINE and the RETURN FROM SUBROU-TINE instructions for the 68000 microprocessor. How would they be used to enter and then exit from a subroutine?

11.33. Explain the register indirect and immediate addressing modes for the 80386 microprocessor.

11.34. Explain how two of the arithmetic-type instructions for the 80386 affect the setting of the condition flags.

11.35. Explain the PUSH and POP instructions in the 80386 microprocessor.

11.36. How do conditional JUMP instructions work in the 80386 microprocessor?

11.37. Explain the CALL and RET instructions for the 80386 microprocessor. Compare these with the JSR and RTS instructions for the 68000 microprocessor.

11.38. Explain the ADI instruction for the 8086 microprocessor, and contrast it to the ADM instruction.

11.39. Explain the STA and LDA instructions for the 6809 microprocessor.

11.40. Compare the ADM instruction for the 8086 with the ADDA and ADDB instructions for the 68000.

11.41. Contrast the PUSH and POP instructions for the 80386 with the DES and INS instructions for the 68000.

11.42. Compare the BRANCH instructions for the 68000 with those for the 80386.

11.43. Write a program to service the printer interface in Chap. 8 for the 80386 microprocessor.

11.44. Explain how the BNE LOOP instruction operates in Table 11.17, calculating the value of the jump in the computer word and seeing whether it points to the right location in the memory.

11.45. Modify the program in Table 11.7 so that the number of characters in the table is passed using register *A* instead of register *B*.

11.46. Modify the programs so that Table 11.8 passes the lowest table address in memory instead of the end of the table. This will require modification to both Tables 11.7 and 11.8.

11.47. Explain how the SSR instruction operates in Table 11.9.

11.48. Convert the program in Table 11.7 into binary as an assembler would.

11.49. For the 80386 or 6809 microprocessor, explain how you would pass parameters if two tables should both be searched for an input character, and the start or end points of each table must be given to the subroutine as well as the character to be searched for and the number of characters in each table.

11.50. Explain how the bracket notation is used for the LDA instruction in the instruction repertoire table for the 6809.

11.51. Write a program like that in Table 11.9 with the aim of finding the smallest number in the table.

11.52. Explain how the index instructions in the 6809 can be used to sequence through two tables located at different positions in the memory but with the same number of elements.

11.53. The MOVE instruction in the 8086 uses register pair *HL* as a pointer to the memory. Explain how register pair *HL* can be loaded.

11.54. Find two examples of relative addressing in the sample programs given in this chapter.

11.55. Compare paging to relative addressing as an address strategy.

11.56. Compare the pin-outs for the 8086 and 68000 microprocessors with regard to economy and interfacing considerations.

11.57. Explain how programs and data can be distributed through a memory by using the 8086 segment registers.

11.58. What are the advantages of having four segment registers versus two segment registers in the 8086?

11.59. For the 68000 write in binary an ANDI instruction that will AND 01011110 with the word at location FF in memory. The value FF is in general register 3.

11.60. Write an ADD instruction in binary for the 68000 that will add two operands of your choice. Explain how the instruction works.

11.61. Explain the meaning of $(A_4)+$ in the 68000 register transfer language.

11.62. Discuss how the supervisor and user modes for the 68000 might be useful in a timeshared system.

11.63. Does a computer with I/O instructions and a bus provide all the facility of a memory-mapped system? Explain your answer.

11.64. Text is stored in the main memory starting at location 1000_{16}. The text consists of a string of ASCII characters. Each character occupies 1 byte, consisting of the 7-bit ASCII code and a parity bit in the MSB position. The character string is terminated by an all-zero *null* character. Write a 68000 program that counts the number of occurrences of the word *an* in the stored text.

11.65. Why does the Intel 80386 microprocessor require a two-step rather than a one-step page translation process?

CHAPTER 12

DIGITAL CIRCUITS

12.1 CIRCUIT PRINCIPLES

The intent of this chapter is first to explain some of the circuit principles relating to all digital circuits and then to examine, one at a time, the major circuit technologies. Basic facts about the general properties of each circuit technology are given, and some of the advantages and disadvantages of each type of circuit are pointed out.

Before we analyze logic circuits, the general characteristics of transistors and diodes are discussed. No attempt will be made to explain the physics of junction semiconductor devices. Semiconductor physics and a detailed analysis of the operating characteristics of junction devices are so interwoven with the manufacturing techniques, the geometry of the junctions, and many other considerations that the subject has grown into a highly specialized (and very fascinating) field, which is treated in detail in other books. For our purposes, and for the purposes of most users of circuit devices, it is the operational characteristics of these devices that are important, and we limit our discussion to these operational characteristics.

The characteristics of diodes are first briefly noted. A semiconductor diode is made of two pieces of semiconductor material[1] of different types joined together. One type is called *p-type* material, and the other is *n-type* material [see Fig. 12.1(a)].[2]

---

[1] A semiconductor has conductivity roughly halfway between that of metals, which are good conductors, and that of insulators, which conduct poorly.

[2] *n*-type material has an excess of negative current carriers (electrons), and *p*-type material has an excess of positive current carriers (holes). Thus, current flows readily when the *p*-type material is positive and the *n*-type material is negative. Alternatively, very little current flows when the *p*-type material is negative and the *n*-type material is positive.

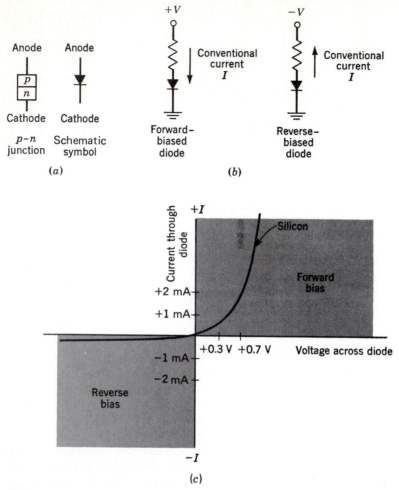

FIGURE 12.1
Diode symbol and characteristics.

When two different types of semiconductor material are joined, a *semiconductor junction* is formed; such a junction is also called a *diode*.[3] In Fig. 12.1(*a*), the *p*-type material is referred to as the *anode* of the diode, and the *n*-type material is called the *cathode* of the diode. Figure 12.1(*a*) also shows the schematic symbol for the diode.

A study of semiconductor, or solid state, devices would explain the physical internal workings of the diode. However, our sole interest is to view the diode as a component in electronic switching circuits, so we examine the diode from the

---

[3] Millions of junctions can be fabricated on a single chip in VLSI, but quantities of thousands are more frequent.

viewpoint of its electrical characteristics only. When we apply an electric voltage, possibly through a resistor as in Fig. 12.1(*b*), so that the anode of the diode is positive with respect to the cathode, the diode is said to be *forward-biased*. A diode that is forward-biased will conduct current rather freely. (*Conventional current* is used in our discussion; conventional current flows from positive to negative.)

Figure 12.1(*c*) shows a typical characteristic curve for a diode. The curve shown is for a semiconductor diode of fair size. Smaller diodes will pass less current. Notice that, when forward-biased, this diode drops on the order of 0.7 V.[4] (The forward-biased region on the graph lies to the right of the ordinate.) When the cathode of a diode is positive with respect to the anode, the diode is said to be *reverse-biased*, and it will present a very high resistance to current flow [refer to Fig. 12.1(*b*) and (*c*)]. This ranges from tens to hundreds of megohms.[5]

A diode may therefore be thought of as a kind of electronic switch that is closed (freely passes current) when forward-biased and open (passes almost no current) when reverse-biased.

There are two general types of transistors used in computer circuits: bipolar and field-effect transistors (FETs, which are covered later). A *bipolar transistor* consists of either a piece of *n* material between two pieces of *p* material or a piece of *p* material between two pieces of *n* material. The first is called a *pnp* transistor and the second an *npn* transistor. Figure 12.2 shows this. The pieces of *n* and *p* material are named; for the *pnp* transistor the "middle" piece is *n*-type and is called the *base*, and the two *p*-type pieces are called the *collector* and *emitter*. For the *npn* transistor, the *p*-type material is the base, and the two pieces of *n*-type material are the emitter and collector.

---

[4] Provided enough current flows.

[5] The part of the curve for silicon diodes that lies below the 0 current level is somewhat distorted since a diode actually passes less than a few nanoamperes when reverse-biased (1 nA = 10^{-9} A).

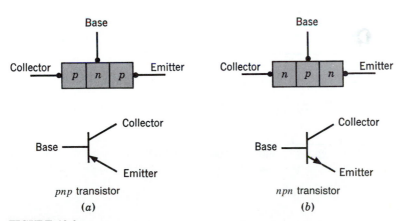

FIGURE 12.2
Transistor symbols and designations.

Figure 12.3 shows an *npn* transistor in a circuit with the emitter grounded. The currents and voltages in the circuit are identified as follows: The current *into* the base of the transistor is called I_b, the current *into* the collector is called I_c, and the current *into* the emitter is called I_e. The voltage of the collector is called V_{ce} (this is the voltage between the collector and the emitter), and the voltage at the base is called V_{be} (the voltage between base and emitter).

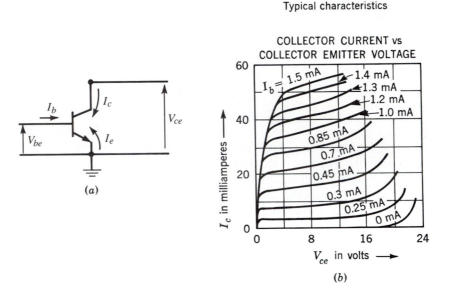

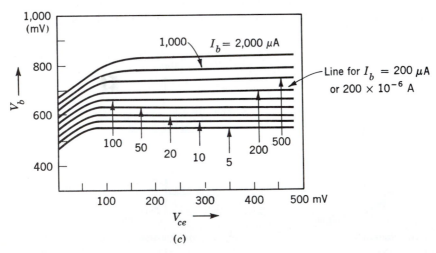

FIGURE 12.3
npn transistor common-emitter configuration and its operation.

In this configuration the transistor can be operated in three modes: (1) *active region*, (2) *saturated*, and (3) *cutoff*. First let us define these terms, and then we will examine the transistor's characteristics in each region of operation.

1. *Active*. The *npn* transistor in Fig. 12.3(*a*) is in the *active region* when current flows into the base, that is, when I_b is positive and when V_{ce} is more positive than V_{be} (the collector is more positive than the base).[6]
2. *Saturated*. The *npn* transistor in Fig. 12.3(*a*) is in the *saturated region* when positive current flows into the base (I_b is positive) and when V_{ce} is equal to or less than V_{be} (the collector is less positive than the base).
3. *Cutoff*. The *npn* transistor is said to be *cut off* when either no current flows into the base or current flows out of the base (when I_b is either 0 or negative).

Active. Transistors used in television or radio circuits are most often operated in the active region, because a small change in base current then causes a large change in collector current, thus making it possible to amplify the input. To examine this, refer to the set of transistor curves presented in Fig. 12.3(*b*).

In the active region the base-emitter junction is forward-biased, and the base-collector junction is reverse-biased. Thus, current flows easily from base to emitter, but the base-to-collector current is small. As current is increased through the base-emitter junction, however, this stimulates current flow through the base from the collector to the emitter. The fact that a small change in base current causes a large change in current from the collector to the emitter is the "secret" of the transistor's usefulness as an amplifier. The base of a transistor is made very thin, which encourages the flow of current through the base (from collector to emitter) once the base area begins to "break down" (that is, to permit current flow) owing to the current from base to emitter. Notice that this base-emitter current also controls the collector-emitter current.

Saturated. When the input current I_b is positive but V_{ce} is less than V_{be}, both the base-collector and the base-emitter junctions will be forward-biased, and the transistor will "look like" two forward-biased diodes. Current will flow freely in both the base and the base-collector junctions.[7]

Cutoff. When no current or negative current flows into the base (that is, V_{be} is negative), the transistor is cut off, and virtually no current flows in the collector ($I_c = 0$). This can be seen in Fig. 12.3(*b*), for with 0.25 mA into the base, less than 3 mA will flow in the collector; and for I_b equal to 0, virtually no current flows in the collector ($I_c = 0$).[8] If V_{be} is negative (the base is negative with respect to

---

[6] The voltage and current values in this and the diode discussions are typical of "standard" TTL circuitry (to be discussed).

[7] Some curves for a saturated transistor are shown in Fig. 12.3(*c*). Notice that the collector voltages are less than the base voltages. Also, the base voltages are very "flat" for wide ranges of collector voltage. For instance, with a base current I_b of 100 μA (microamperes) (1 μA $= 10^{-6}$ A), the base voltage will be about 0.35 V when the collector is from 0.1 to 0.5 V.

[8] The slight "turnup" in the ends of the curves in Fig. 12.3(*b*) is due to junction breakdown at higher voltages. The transistor is to be operated with collector voltage of less than $+10$ V.

the emitter), both junctions of the transistor will be reverse-biased, and virtually no current will flow in the circuit (I_c and I_b will be 0).[9]

Let us now examine the operation of the inverter circuit in Fig. 12.4(a). A load resistor of 500 Ω has been added to the collector circuit and an input resistor of 2000 Ω to the base circuit. The plot of an input/output signal for this circuit is shown in Fig. 12.4(b).

In Fig. 12.4(b) the input starts at 0 V, so that no base current flows in the transistor (it is cut off). As a result, the output is at +5 V, since no current flows in the collector and no voltage is dropped across R2.

As the input becomes positive, current begins to flow into the base, and the transistor passes into the active region. This causes current to flow in the collector circuit, and this current flows through resistor R2, so the output begins to fall. At some point the output will fall below the voltage at the base, which will be held at

---

[9] When transistor junctions are made very small, as in VLSI, the currents and voltages become quite small also. Reducing transistor dimensions, voltages, and currents is called *scaling*. This also reduces power consumption (but can also reduce speed of operation).

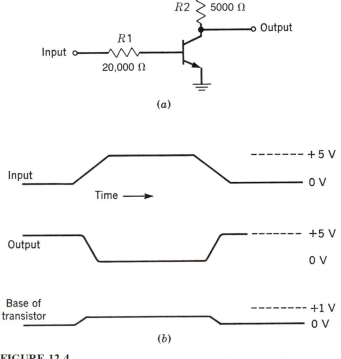

(a)

(b)

FIGURE 12.4
The transfer inverter. (a) Inverter circuit. (b) Waveforms for inverter circuit.

about 0.8 V—the base-emitter junction is well forward-biased by the current through resistor $R1$—and the transistor will be saturated.

When the voltage at the input goes back to 0 V, the process is reversed; the transistor passes from saturation through the active region and is again cut off. Notice that the output from the transistor is an "inverted" near-replica of the input; therefore, the circuit is called an *inverter*.

Note: An *npn* transistor is, strictly speaking, "cut off" when the base current is 0 or negative, which means, for our circuits, when the base voltage V_{be} is 0 or negative. In general practice, a transistor is said to be cut off when "negligible" current flows. This is, of course, not precise, nor can it be made so. What is meant is that so little current flows into the base that virtually no current flows in the collector circuit.

The operation of a *pnp* transistor is essentially the same as that of the *npn* transistor, except that all the polarities are reversed. For instance, the *pnp* transistor is cut off when I_b is positive or into the base. The voltage V_{ce} is made negative for *pnp* transistors in the common-base circuit.

12.2   DIODE GATES

The Diode AND Gate

In most systems a 0 and a 1 are represented by a positive dc signal (representing a 1) and a (approximately) 0 V dc signal (representing a 0). The function of the AND gate circuit is to produce a positive dc signal at its output when a positive dc signal is applied to all the inputs to the circuit simultaneously. If the inputs to the circuit are labeled X, Y, and Z, the circuit will produce a positive dc signal only when a positive dc signal is simultaneously applied to X and Y and Z.

Figure 12.5(*a*) illustrates a two-input diode AND gate. In this circuit, a 0 V dc level represents a binary 0 and a +3-V signal a binary 1. If both inputs are at 0 V, both diodes will be forward-biased, and the output will be held at 0 V by the diodes. The total voltage drop across the resistor will be 5 V.[10]

If the X input line goes to 3 V and the Y input remains at 0 V, the diode connected to the Y input will still be forward-biased, and the output will remain at 0 V dc. (Notice that, in this case, the X input diode will be reverse-biased, and 3 V will be dropped across the diode.) If the input at Y goes to +3 V and X remains at 0 V, the output will be at 0 V dc.

When the inputs at X and Y both go to the +3-V level, the output level will rise to +3 V, and the output will represent a 1.

The responses of the diode AND gate to several input conditions are illustrated in Fig. 12.5(*a*). The circuit could have more than two inputs, in which case a diode would be required for each input, with each additional diode connected just as the two diodes are connected in the figure. If four diodes are connected, the output will rise

---

[10] We have assumed, for simplicity of explanation, that no voltage is dropped across a forward-biased diode. In fact, for silicon diodes, the output would be at approximately +0.7 V and the drop across the resistor about 4.3 V.

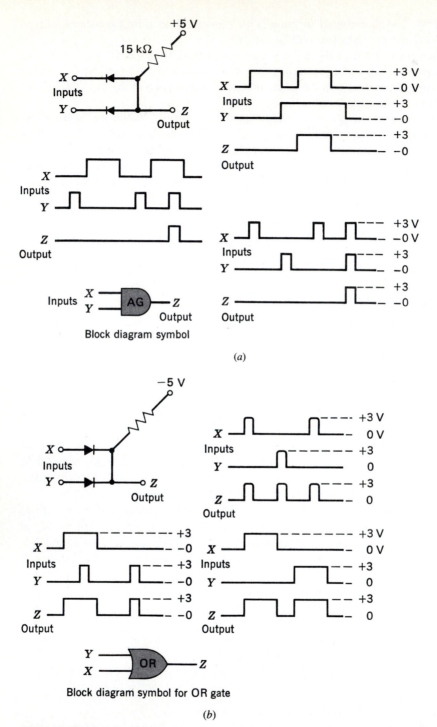

FIGURE 12.5
(a) Diode AND gate. (b) Diode OR gate.

to the +3-V signal level only when the input signals to all four diodes are positive. There is a practical limit to the number of diodes that can be connected in this manner, however, because the diodes do not actually have an infinite back resistance or zero forward resistance. With a large number of inputs, the finite forward and back resistances of the diodes will cause varying output levels, depending on the state of the inputs.

The Diode OR Gate

The OR gate has the property that a signal representing a 1 will appear at the output if any of the inputs represents a 1. Figure 12.5(*b*) illustrates a diode OR gate circuit with two inputs (*X* and *Y*) and one output. The inputs to the circuit consist of 0 V signals representing 0s and +3-V signals representing 1s. If both inputs to the circuit are at 0 V dc, both diodes will be forward-biased, and the output of the circuit will be at 0 V dc, representing a 0. If either input to the circuit rises to +3 V dc, the diode at this input will be forward-biased, and the output will rise to +3 V, representing a 1. The diode at the input remaining at 0 V will then be reverse-biased by the +3-V signal at the output. This circuit has the property that the output level will be at the level of the most positive input.

If both inputs to the circuit rise to +3 V, the output will again be at +3 V. (This circuit is sometimes referred to as an *inclusive* OR circuit because the output is a 1 when both inputs are 1s.)

More inputs may be added to the circuit illustrated in Fig. 12.5(*b*); a diode is required for each input. If any one or any combination of the inputs rises to the +3-V level, the output will be at +3 V.

As in the case of the diode AND gate, it is not practical to have too many inputs to the circuit because the forward and back resistances of the diodes are finite, and different combinations of input signals will cause different signal levels at the outputs.

12.3   TRANSISTOR-TRANSISTOR LOGIC

The line of circuits called *transistor-transistor logic* (TTL) is now the most widely used bipolar line because of its high speed. The characteristic that distinguishes TTL circuits from other circuit lines is a multiple-emitter transistor at the input circuit. The schematic diagram for this kind of transistor is shown as $T1$ in Fig. 12.6(*a*). The multiple-emitter transistor simply has a larger-than-normal collector area and several base-emitter junctions. The two-emitter transistor in Fig. 12.6(*a*) functions as a two-transistor circuit because it is effectively two transistors with a common collector and base. Figures 12.6(*b*) and (*c*) shows the TTL input circuit in separate transistor and multiple-emitter transistor form. The transistors, $T1A$, $T1B$, and $T1C$ are combined to form a single multiple-emitter transistor $T1$ in Fig. 12.6(*c*). This circuit operates as follows. If one of three inputs X, Y, and Z is at 0 V, current will flow through $R1$ and the base-emitter junction of $T1$ to the input. This will hold the base of $T1$ at about 0.5 V. The base collector of $T1$ and the base emitter of $T2$ form two junctions in series with resistor $R3$ to ground, so the base of $T2$ will not be more than 0.2 V positive, which is insufficient to turn on $T2$. Little (leakage only) current will flow in the collector circuit of $T1$, and $T2$ will be off. As a result, no current will flow

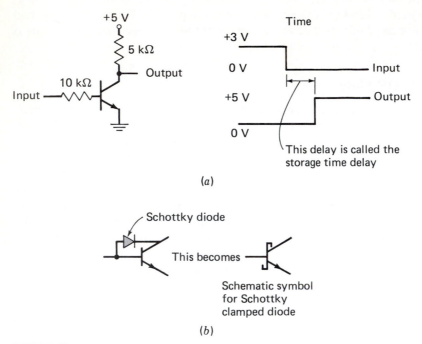

FIGURE 12.6
TTL gate circuit. (*a*) Schematic symbol and equivalent circuit. (*b*) Discrete version of TTL gate. (*c*)
Multiple-emitter TTL gate.

through resistors $R2$ and $R3$, and the emitter of $T2$ will be at ground and the collector
at +5 V.

    If all three inputs are at a level of +3.5 V (the 1 level), then current will flow
through $R1$ and the base-collector junction of $T1$ (which is forward-biased) into the
base of $T2$, turning it on. Current will flow through $R1$ and $R2$ until the transistor
$T2$ is saturated, with its emitter and collector both at about 2.5 V. At this time, the
three emitter-base junctions of the multiple-emitter transistor will be reverse-biased.

    The two outputs from the collector and emitter of $T2$ operate as "scissors,"
which close when $T2$ is on and open when $T2$ is off. That is, the emitter and
collector of $T2$ will be at about the same voltage (closed) when $T2$ is on, and the
emitter will be at ground and the collector at +5 V when $T2$ is off (open).

    Notice that $T2$ is on when the three inputs are high (1s) and off when any one
of the three inputs is low (a 0). Thus, the circuit operation is basically that of a NAND
gate. Logic levels for TTL are geared so that 0 to 0.7 V represents a 0 and +2.5 to
+5 V represents a 1.

    A complete TTL NAND gate is shown in Fig. 12.7. This is a *second-generation*
TTL circuit and is typical of the circuits offered by the major TTL manufacturers in
their medium-speed lines.

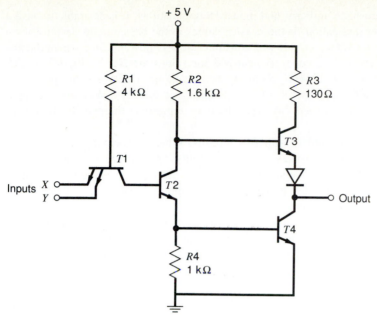

FIGURE 12.7
Classic TTL NAND gate.

Let us examine the operation of the circuit in Fig. 12.7 by assuming that input Y is at $+3.5$ V and X is at 0 V. Therefore, $T1$ has its base-emitter junction connected to Y reversed-biased, and the full current from $R1$ flows through the base-emitter junction connected to X. At this time (1) $T2$ will be off, (2) $T4$ will be off because with no current through $R4$ its base will be essentially at ground, and (3) $T3$ will be turned on by current flowing through $R2$. As a result, the output will be at $+5$ V minus the base-emitter drop for $T3$.

Let us assume that the input voltage at X is slowly raised positive. As a result, the collector of $T1$ goes positive, and $T2$ begins to conduct. As the emitter of $T2$ becomes more and more positive, $T4$ begins to conduct, and as the collector of $T2$ becomes more and more negative, $T3$ begins to turn off. Finally, $T2$ will saturate and $T4$ will be saturated and therefore will have an output of about $+0.5$ V or less.

The circuit in Fig. 12.7 will have about 4-ns turn-on delays and 7-ns turn-off delays and a power dissipation of about 10 mW.

The reason for the high speeds lies in the all-transistor construction of the TTL and in the fact that the final stage drives current in both directions. The standard transistor inverter has an output that is "driven down" by the turning on of the output transistor. When the transistor is turned off, however, the rising edge is formed by the resistor at the circuit's output supplying current to all the stray capacity in this circuit and any circuits connected to the output. Therefore, the rise time is exponential. With TTL's two-transistor output (the circuit is called a *totem pole*), the rising edge is "driven up" by the upper transistor turning on and the lower transistor turning off. This gives a sharp edge, and the falling edge is similarly sharp.

In many aerospace, military, and industrial applications, it is desirable to have a much lower power dissipation. If the resistor values in the basic circuit design shown in Fig. 12.7 are raised, the circuit will consume far less power. Circuit manufacturers offer low-power TTL circuits. Typical resistor values are $R1 = 40$, $R2 = 20$, $R3 = 500$, and $R4 = 12$ kΩ. Naturally there will be a decrease in speed, but low-power gates are still capable of 23-ns delays at only 1-mW power dissipation. These circuits are labeled 74L xx, where xx represents the specific IC designation.

There is a famous problem with TTL circuits. When TTL circuits are switched, they generate large current "spikes" on their outputs, and interconnections must be carefully watched to prevent ringing or even circuit damage. Sometimes, capacitors are even placed across the +5 V to ground power supply on each circuit container to prevent spikes in the power supply voltage.

The problem develops because it is possible for both $T3$ and $T4$ in Fig. 12.7 to be on simultaneously when the circuit is switching. For instance, if the output is switching from a 0 to a 1 level, then $T4$ must go off and $T3$ must go on. But if $T3$ goes on before $T4$ is completely off, then both transistors will be on simultaneously, almost short-circuiting the +5 V to ground.

The current spike problem has plagued the TTL family and is clearly in evidence in the circuit of Fig. 12.7. Although $T3$ and $T4$ can both be on during turn-on and turn-off, the turn-off case is usually worse since the storage time of $T4$ causes both transistors to be on for a greater time. Turn-on current spiking may be lowered by increasing the ratio of $R2$ to $R4$. In this way the collector of $T2$ reaches a lower voltage before $T4$ begins to conduct. There is a tradeoff involved, however, since increasing $R2$ decreases the "on" drive for $T4$, decreasing its turn-on time. The increased value of $R2$ also results in decreased noise immunity. So far, no perfect answer to current spiking has been found, but the diode in Fig. 12.7 between $T3$ and $T4$ is a great help.

Although the standard 7400 series TTL circuits are fast, there is always a desire to speed up circuit lines. To further increase the speeds of TTL, a basic problem must be dealt with. When a transistor is saturated and must be turned off, before it begins to go off there is a delay (caused by the minority carriers) called the *storage time delay*. This is shown in Fig. 12.8(a), where a transistor inverter is turned off from saturation. Although this delay is on the order of nanoseconds, it is still significant since several of the TTL circuit transistors become saturated at various times.[11]

To alleviate this problem, the fastest TTL circuits use a diode clamp between base and collector. This is shown in Fig. 12.8(b). The diode used is not a conventional diode, however, but a special diode (called a *Schottky diode*) formed by the junction of a metal and a semiconductor.

The Schottky diode is faster than conventional diodes because electrons that have crossed the junction and entered the metal when current is flowing are not distinguishable from the conduction electrons of the metal. Since these electrons are majority carriers, there is no delay associated with minority-carrier recombination as

---

[11] Gold doping is often used to reduce minority-carrier storage times in switching transistors.

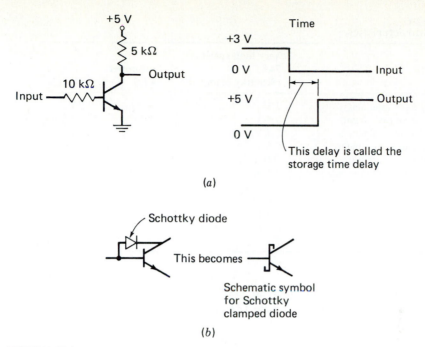

FIGURE 12.8
Schottky clamped transistor. (*a*) Storage delay. (*b*) Schottky diode and transistor.

in semiconductor diodes. As a result, reverse recovery times from Schottky diodes are generally in the low-picosecond range. Further, because of the choice of materials (aluminum or platinum silicides), the forward drop of the Schottky diode is less than for a conventional diode.

A transistor with a Schottky diode connected from base to collector will switch faster because it is not allowed to saturate. The minority-carrier storage time normally associated with the transistor's coming out of saturation is avoided, and the circuit can operate faster. This transistor–Schottky diode combination is given a special schematic diagram symbol, as shown in Fig. 12.8(*b*).

The use of Schottky clamped transistors has resulted in a series of high-speed TTL circuits with delays on the order of 1 ns (rise and fall times are on the order of 2 ns). Figure 12.9(*b*) shows a typical circuit. Notice that the transistors are Schottky clamped transistors, so storage delays are reduced. The operation of this circuit is essentially the same as that of Fig. 12.7, except that the transistors do not saturate. Circuits in this series are designated 74Sxx or 74ASxx.

The diodes connected to ground at the inputs dampen negative spikes and negative-going signals that may occur during ringing. These circuits must be carefully interconnected, however. Wire or printed-circuit connections more than 8 in. in length should be treated with respect and terminated according to the rules given by the circuits' manufacturers.

Table 12.1 gives some characteristics of several TTL lines. Notice that speed is associated with power consumption.

TABLE 12.1
TTL Characteristics

	Very high speed 74AS (Schottky clamped)	Low-power 74 LS	74 ALS
High-level input (minimum)	2 V	2 V	2 V
Low-level input (maximum)	0.8 V	0.8 V	0.7 V
High-level output (minimum)	2.7 V	2.4 V	2.4 V
Low-level output (maximum)	0.5 V	0.4 V	0.3 V
High-level noise margin (minimum)	700 mV	400 mV	400 mV
Low-level noise margin (minimum)	300 mV	400 mV	400 mV
Maximum input load current	−2 mA	−1.6 mA	−0.8 mA
Average power per gate	10 mW	2 mW	1.5 mW
Typical delay, high to low	0.9 ns	4 ns	5 ns
Typical delay, low to high	0.9 ns	6 ns	4 ns
Supply voltage	5 V	5 V	5 V

TTL circuits are also available in MSI. The MSI seven-segment decoder and BCD counters presented in Chap. 4 were TTL. A simplified TTL gate is used internally for such MSI circuits; this gate is shown in Fig. 12.9(a).

Manufacturers make a special TTL gate that can be connected in a wired-AND circuit. Figure 12.10(a) shows the basic circuit. The inputs are ANDed by the multiple-emitter input transistor and inverted by the output transistor. The output transistor has no resistor to +5V, however; thus, the circuit is not complete and an external resistor must be supplied. The advantage of the circuit is that if two or more such circuits have their outputs connected, they form a NAND-to-wired-AND configuration, as in Fig. 12.10(b).

Figure 12.10(b) also shows that a resistor must be connected to +5V from the wired-AND output, but only a single resistor is required. Generally, this resistor is not shown on block diagrams, but it is included in Fig. 12.10(b) to show how the circuit is connected. The AND function is performed at the outputs because if any output transistor is on (saturated), it will force all outputs to the 0 level at about 0.2 V.

Several open-collector NAND gates are sometimes packaged in a single IC container. These gates make for economical, reasonably fast circuitry, and they are widely used. The gates can also be used to connect to bus wires, which are normally high but are to be forced low to indicate status.

Input-Output Levels and Noise

When TTL packages are interconnected or interfaced with other circuitry, the input and output capabilities must be considered. Noise protection is also a consideration in TTL designs.

Figure 12.7 shows the standard 7400 series NAND gate. If the Y input is held at +5 V through connection to a power supply, for example, the circuit becomes an inverter with a single X input. If X is at 0 V, the output will be high. How far positive from 0 V can X be raised before the output may go low? Manufacturers' specifications

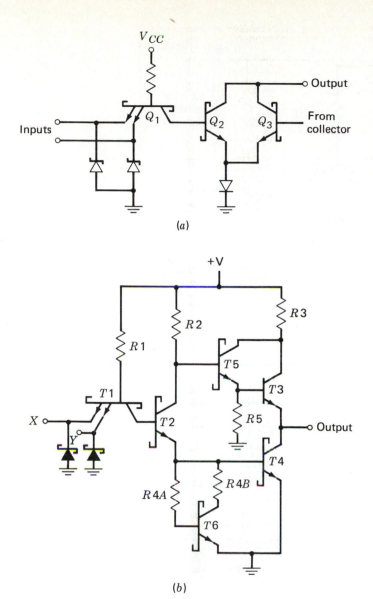

FIGURE 12.9
(a) Schottky MSI circuit. (b) Schottky clamped TTL gate.

give 0.8 V as the *worst-case low input*. This means that if X is greater than 0.8 V, the output may come down. It also means that inputs below 0.8 V are considered to be 0 (binary value) inputs.

In Fig. 12.7, suppose X is at +5 V; the output will then be low. How low can we make the X input before the output may go high? Manufacturers specify the *worst-case high input* as 2 V. This means that inputs above 2 V are considered as logic 1 inputs.

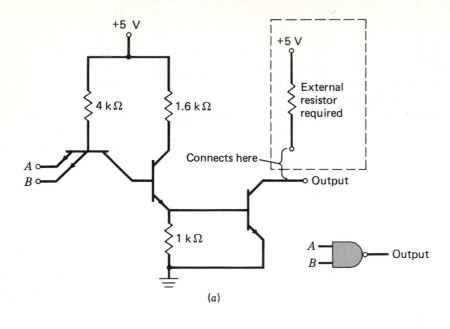

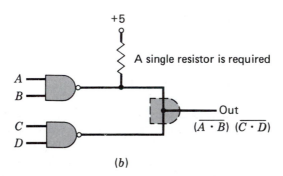

FIGURE 12.10
Open-collector TTL gate and wired-AND connection. (*a*) Open-collector TTL gate. (*b*) Open-collector TTL gates connected in wired-AND gate.

Clearly, there could be inputs between 0.8 and 2 V. This region is called a *region of ambiguity*, and manufacturers do not guarantee successful operation for inputs in this region.

The next obvious question concerns output levels. Manufacturers specify worst-case output values as 0.4 and 2.4 V. This means binary 0 outputs will always be less than 0.4 V and binary 1 outputs will always be greater than 2.4 V.

The preceding discussion shows that TTL gates will operate reliably when interconnected if loading and noise are ignored. It also shows that there is a *noise margin* of 0.4 V at both levels. If connected wires generate a noise signal of less than 0.4 V, no errors will occur. To prevent larger noise signals, connections between circuits should be not too close together, and many computer automated circuit board packages carefully isolate connections. If you build circuits, be careful not to place wires too close together for long runs.

The next consideration is how many circuits can be loaded on an output. The output of a TTL circuit can supply or source $-400\mu A$ when high, according to manufacturers' specs. TTL circuits can accept or sink 16 mA when low. A single TTL input requires 1.6 mA when low and 40 μA when held high. This means that 10 inputs can be connected to a single output; this is called the *fan-out* for the circuits. The current requirements must be considered if standard TTL circuits are connected with other circuits, and also if TTL circuits are interconnected with low-power, Schottky, or other TTL lines.

12.4 EMITTER-COUPLED LOGIC

Emitter-coupled logic (ECL) has other common names: *current-mode logic* (CML), *current-steering logic*, and *nonsaturating logic*. The last term is the key to this type of circuit. When transistors are operated in a saturated condition, they turn off slowly because of the delay caused by a charge stored in the collector and base region.[12] This delay in turn-off time can be eliminated by operating transistors only in either the active or the off region. As will be seen, in these circuits current is "steered" rather than having voltage levels passed around.

The ECL line is the fastest currently available. Manufacturers of ECL have a number of basic circuits, each with different features and drawbacks. ECL has not proved as popular as TTL, primarily because it is more expensive, harder to cool, more difficult to interconnect, and is considered to have less noise immunity (this is debatable). Also, ECL may be faster than is necessary in many applications. On the other hand, the superfast computers use ECL (Cray computers, for example) as do a number of the highest-speed special-purpose computers.

The basic ECL configuration can be best described by examining a particular inverter. Figure 12.11 shows an ECL inverter with an input X. The logic levels in this system are as follows: binary 0 is represented by -1.55 V and binary 1 by -0.75 V. Notice that this is "positive logic," since, although both levels are negative, the more positive level, -0.75, is the binary 1. Also, notice the small signal difference between 0 and 1.

The circuit's operation is based on a *differential amplifier* consisting of $T4$ and $T3$. When the input to $T3$ is at -1.55 V, $T3$ will be off and current will flow through $R3$ and $R2$. Calculation will indicate a drop of about 0.8 V across $R2$. Therefore, figuring a base-emitter drop of 0.75 V for $T1$, we see the X output will be at -1.55 V. Since $T2$ is cut off by the -1.55-V input, very little current will flow through $R1$, and the output $\overline{X}$ will be at the base-emitter drop voltage across $T2$. So the output will be at -0.75 V.

Examination will show that if the input is at -0.75 V, transistor $T3$ will be on, $T4$ will be off, the X output will be at -0.75 V, and the $\overline{X}$ output at -1.55 V. (The key to analyzing this circuit is to notice that in a differential amplifier circuit such as

---

[12] This was called the storage delay in the preceding section.

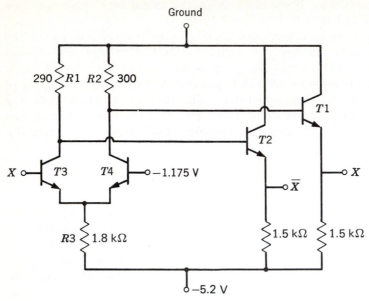

FIGURE 12.11
Basic circuit of ECL gate (*Motorola Inc.*).

the $T3$ to $T4$ form, the current through the resistor $R3$ shared by the two emitters will be almost constant.) Notice that the transistors are never saturated. They are either in their active region or off.

A three-input gate is shown in Fig. 12.12. This is a combined NOR and OR gate, as shown by the block diagram, depending on which output connection is used.

As time has passed, several generations of ECL circuits have evolved. In general the circuits have become faster and require more power with each generation. More facilities and more complicated logic per chip are also available in the new lines, including MSI chips. Notice that the circuits in Fig. 12.11 require three voltages: ground, -1.175 V, and -5.2 V. Later versions provide a circuit on each chip to generate the intermediate voltage (in this case, -1.175 V), so that only a single power supply is required.

Figure 12.13 shows the four generations Motorola has gone through with their ECL, which is called Motorola ECL, or MECL, and also Fairchild's 10,000 series. Table 12.2 outlines some of the characteristics of these circuits, and the speed versus power relation and general noise characteristics can be deduced from the table. From Fig. 12.13 it is evident which variations were employed as technology advanced. For instance, notice that the circuit to produce the third -1.175-V bias voltage for the MECL 1 line is not included on the chip, whereas all subsequent lines have this as an internal feature.

Corresponding resistor values differ among MECL lines. This is necessary to achieve the varying speed and power improvements. Of course, speed is not determined by resistor values alone; transistor geometries, although not shown on a schematic, are a major factor. The transistor geometries in conjunction with the resistor values provide the speed and power characteristics of the different families.

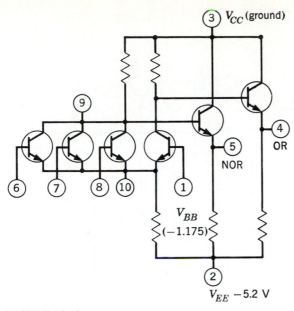

TRUTH TABLE

Inputs			Outputs	
8	7	6	5	4
0	0	0	1	0
0	0	1	0	1
0	1	0	0	1
0	1	1	0	1
1	0	0	0	1
1	0	1	0	1
1	1	0	0	1
1	1	1	0	1

FIGURE 12.12
ECL three-input gate.

Notice also that Fairchild 10,000 and MECL III gates are supplied with base pull-down resistors (50 kΩ) to each of the input transistors, whereas the other two families are not. These resistors provide a path for base leakage current to unused input bases, causing them to be well turned off.

A final significant difference between the families lies in the output circuits. MECL I circuits normally are supplied with output pull-down resistors on the chip. MECL II circuits can be obtained with or without output resistors. MECL III and Fairchild 10,000 circuits normally have open outputs. The use of on-chip output resistors has both advantages and limitations. An advantage is that fewer external components are required. However, with open outputs the designer can choose both the value and the location of the terminating resistance to meet system requirements. Finally, the use of external resistors reduces on-chip heating and power dissipation, allowing more complex LSI and increasing chip life and reliability.

12.5 METAL-OXIDE SEMICONDUCTOR CIRCUITS

The circuits described so far are all termed *bipolar circuits* and use "conventional" transistors. For large-scale integration (LSI), often another type of transistor, called a *field-effect transistor* (FET), is used. Although the characteristics of these FETs have not proved desirable for some applications (because of their slowness, delicacy, and lack of drive characteristics), their ease of manufacture, small size, and small power dissipation have offset the negative factors and have led to FETs constructed of

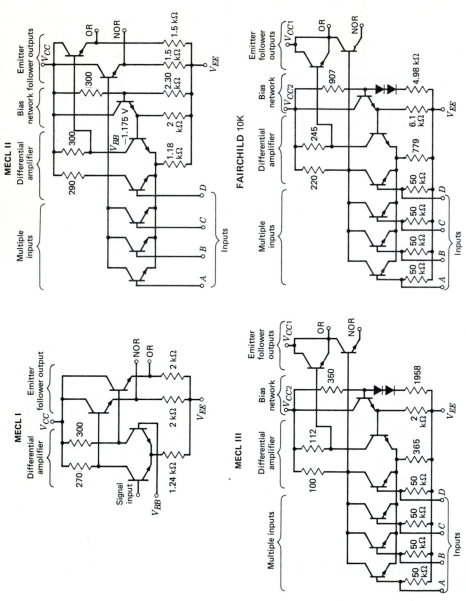

FIGURE 12.13
Several generations of ECL circuits.

TABLE 12.2
General characteristics of ECL circuits

Feature	MECL I	MECL II	Fairchild 10K series	Fairchild 100K series	MECL III
Gate propagation delay, ns	8	4	2	0.75	0.75
Gate edge speed, ns	8.5	4	3.5	1.5	0.75
Flip-flop toggle speed (minimum), MHz	30	70	125	500	500
Gate power, mW	31	22	25	65	60
Input pull-down resistors, kΩ	No	No	50	50	2, 50

metal-oxide semiconductor (MOS) as the primary technology for use in large arrays. FETs constructed of MOS are called MOSFETs.

Figure 12.14(a) shows a cross section of a FET of p-channel type. As shown in Fig. 12.14(b), a substrate of n-type (silicon) material is first formed, and two separate low-resistivity p-type regions are diffused into this substrate. Then the surface of this structure is covered with an insulating oxide layer. Holes are cut into the oxide, two metal contacts are made to the two pieces of p material, and a thin piece of metal called the *gate (G)* is placed over what is called the *channel*.

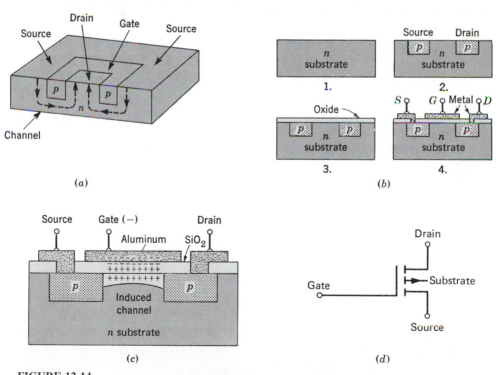

FIGURE 12.14
MOSFET structure. (a) General configuration. (b) Fabrication steps. (c) Cross section with gate biased negative. (d) Schematic symbol.

With no voltages applied, this structure (refer to Fig. 12.14) forms two diodes back to back. If we attempt to force current from source to drain, the alternate *pn* junction followed by an *np* junction will not permit current flow (in either direction).

The gate is used to cause and control current flow in the following manner. Consider the source to be grounded and the drain connected to a negative voltage through a resistor; Fig. 12.15 shows this. [The schematic symbol for the FET is shown in Fig. 12.14(*d*).] The metal area of the gate and the insulating oxide layer and semiconductor channel form a capacitor, with the metal gate as the top plate and the *n*-material substrate as the lower plate. Making the gate potential negative causes a corresponding positive charge in the *n*-type semiconductor substrate along the channel, as shown in Fig. 12.14(*c*). Given sufficient negative potential on the gate, the positive charge induced in the channel finally causes this section of material to become *p*-type, and current begins to flow from source to drain—thus the term *current-enhancement mode*.

The more negative the gate becomes, the more "*p*-type" the semiconductor channel becomes, and the more current flows. As a result, this type of MOS is also called PMOS.

As a switching circuit, a FET can be used to form an inverter. With a 0, or ground, input, the circuit shown in Fig. 12.15 will have a −5-V output; with a −2-V or more negative input, the output will go to about 0 V.

Instead of forming actual resistors for these circuits, another FET is used, thus simplifying manufacture. This is shown in Fig. 12.15. The FET resistor's gate areas are controlled so that the FET represents a high resistance (perhaps 100 to 1000 kΩ) when the gate is at the drain potential. Some manufacturers show this FET by using the regular symbol, and others use the resistor-plus-bar symbol, also seen in the figure.

When a *p*-type substrate with *n* doping for the source and drain is used, as in Fig. 12.16, the *n*-channel transistor is formed as shown. The schematic symbols for the *n*-channel transistor and an inverter circuit are shown in Fig. 12.16(*a*) and (*b*). Notice that the circuit uses a positive voltage and behaves similarly to an *npn* transistor inverter circuit. This type of MOS is called NMOS.

A NOR gate can be formed in NMOS, as shown in Fig. 12.17(*a*). The logic levels for this circuit are 0 to 1 V for a binary 0 and > +1.5 V for a binary 1. (This is positive logic.) If any of the inputs *A*, *B*, or *C* is a 1, the corresponding FET will conduct, causing the output to go to about +0.8 V or less. If all inputs are at +0.8 V or less, all the FETs will be off and the output will be at +8 V (or more).

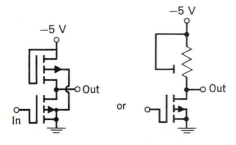

FIGURE 12.15
Alternative schematic symbols for MOSFET resistive element.

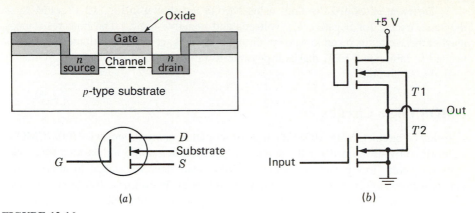

FIGURE 12.16
(a) n-channel MOSFET transistor. (b) n-channel inverter.

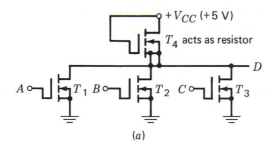

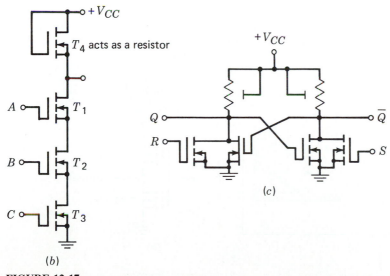

FIGURE 12.17
FET logic circuits. (a) Three-input NOR gate. (b) Three-input NAND gate. (c) RS flip-flop.

Different gates and flip-flops using NMOS are shown in Fig. 12.17. (PMOS is the same except for negative V_{cc} voltages and negative logic.) The high resistances used in these circuits mean low power dissipation. This, combined with the small areas needed to fabricate a FET, makes it possible to fabricate large numbers of circuits on a single, small chip.

CMOS Logic Circuits

A series of circuits using MOSFET transistors called *complementary MOS* (CMOS) was originally developed for the aerospace and oceanographic industries. These circuits have very low power consumption and considerable resistance to noise. They are, however, slower than the very high-speed bipolar logic lines. But large numbers of circuits can be placed on a single chip, the power supply voltage can vary over a large range, and the circuits are relatively economical to manufacture. The newest CMOS circuits have become relatively fast and are widely used for everything from electronic watches and calculators to microprocessors.

The CMOS circuits are fabricated as illustrated in Fig. 12.18(a), which shows that both n- and p-channel transistors can be fabricated on the same substrate.

The simplest form of CMOS integrated circuit consists of one n-channel and one p-channel MOS transistor, with both gate contacts tied together to form the input and both drain contacts tied together to form the output. This circuit is the basic CMOS inverter [Fig. 12.18(b)]. When the voltage at the input is near ground level, the gate-to-source voltage of the p-channel transistor approaches the value of the supply voltage $+V$, and the p-channel is turned on. A low-resistance path is created between the supply voltage and the output, while a high-resistance path exists between the output and ground because the n-channel transistor is off. The output voltage will approach that of the supply voltage, $+V$. When the input voltage is near $+V$, the p-channel turns off and the n-channel turns on, causing the output voltage to approach ground.

Notice that in either state the circuit's power consumption is extremely low because one transistor is always off and because n- and p-channel transistors exhibit

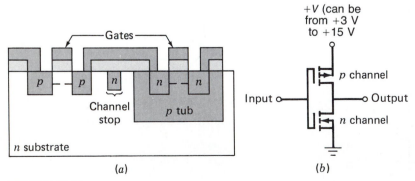

FIGURE 12.18
CMOS inverter. (a) CMOS elements. (b) Circuit that is the basic CMOS inverter.

very high resistance when off, permitting very low leakage current to flow through the transistor that is in the off condition.

When conventional metal- and silicon-gate technologies are used, protective channel stops are provided to minimize leakage current between separate transistors, as shown in Fig. 12.18(*a*). All *p*-channel devices must be surrounded by a continuous *n*-channel stop, which can also act as a conducting path for the external power supply to appropriate locations. Similarly, *p*-channel stops surround all *n*-channel devices and provide a conducting path between those *n*-channel devices that are electrically connected to the lowest potential and the external ground contact.

A two-input NOR gate can be constructed as shown in Fig. 12.19. Each additional input requires an additional *p*- and *n*-channel pair of MOS transistors.

Table 12.3 gives some details of CMOS operation versus other circuit lines. Notice the low power consumption (nanowatts, when they are not being switched), competitive speeds, and noise protection.

74C00 Series CMOS Input-Output Levels and Noise

The desirable characteristics of CMOS have made it possible for manufacturers to produce circuit lines in SSI, MSI, and VLSI. The packing density, which is the number of circuits that can be placed on a given area of silicon, is high; the power consumption is low; and the circuits interface well. The lack of very high-speed operation has been the only problem, and this is continually improving.

CMOS has been produced in a series numbered 74C00, which has the same in-line packages with gate and flip-flop structures identical to the 7400 TTL series. This includes pin-for-pin and function-for-function compatibility. These circuits have been successful, particularly for low-power applications.

Several points must be noted, however. First, the CMOS circuits can be operated with power supply voltages from +3 to +15 V; they are not limited to the +5 V TTL

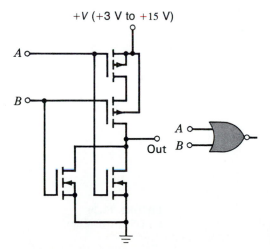

FIGURE 12.19
CMOS NOR gate.

TABLE 12.3
Circuit line characteristics

	Standard TTL 74	Low power TTL	Schottky clamped TTL	CMOS 5-V supply	CMOS 10-V supply	ECL
Quiescent power, mW	10	1	20	10^{-6}	2×10^{-6}	60
Propagation delay, ns	4	20	1.5	10	7	0.3
Flip-flop toggle frequency, MHz	45	25	100	50	60	600
Noise immunity, V	0.4	0.4	0.8	2	4	0.5
Fan-out	10	10	10	10	10	5

supply. Second, the CMOS packages can be interconnected with TTL standard, low-power, Schottky, and other lines, but adjustments must be made. Finally, all CMOS inputs must be connected, and the circuits must be more carefully handled (because of their high input impedance).

When CMOS 74C00 packages are interconnected or interfaced with other cir-circuitry, the input and output capabilities must be considered. Noise protection is also a consideration in CMOS designs. The following paragraphs examine these subjects.

Figure 12.20 shows the marginal "standard" 74C series NAND gate. If the Y input is held positive through connection to the power supply, the circuit becomes

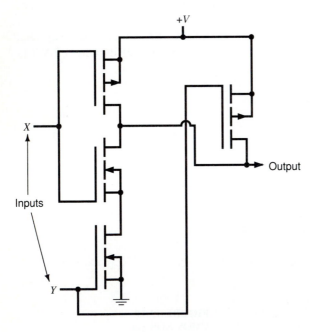

FIGURE 12.20
CMOS NAND gate.

an inverter with a single X input. If X is at 0 V, the output will be high. How far positive from 0 V can X be raised before the output may go low? The answer is not as simple as for TTL because the power supply voltage must be considered. As an example, if the power supply is +5 V, then X can be raised to 2 V before a change; if the power supply is 10 V, X can be raised to 4 V. A good rule is: Take 1/10 of the power supply voltage, and add and subtract this number from half the power supply voltage to define the region of ambiguity. For +5 V, this gives +2 V and +3 V, so voltages above +3 are 1s and voltages below +2 are 0s.

Clearly, we could connect inputs between 2 and 3 V, but this represents the region of ambiguity, for which the manufacturer does not guarantee successful operation. For CMOS outputs from gates, however, the levels are generally about 0.5 to 1 V above ground for 0s, and 0.5 to 1 V less than the power supply voltage for 1s, so there is no problem interconnecting the circuits.

As with TTL, there is a noise margin depending on the power supply voltage. In interconnecting CMOS you must be careful, particularly if other circuit lines are intermixed, because CMOS input impedances are high. Be careful not to place wires too close together for long runs.

The next consideration is loading. There are several CMOS 7400 series circuit lines, including 74HC (high speed), 74HCT (with TTL compatibility), 74AC (very high speed), and 74ACT (very high speed with TTL compatibility). As with TTL bipolar circuits, the characteristics of the particular line used must be determined. A fan-out of 10 is almost always available, but as manufacturing techniques change this number rises and falls as new lines are introduced.

It is important to note that the power required per gate increases linearly as the gate's output changes value. A gate whose output changes 100,000 times per second requires about 10 times the power of a gate being toggled 10,000 times per second. This is because CMOS gates have an output that requires almost no power in either state; but when the state changes, current is required to charge up the capacitances in the circuit, and some current passes through the transistors as they go through the active state.

12.6 DAC IMPLEMENTATION

The most straightforward digital-to-analog converter (DAC) involves the use of a resistor network. A basic type of resistor network DAC is illustrated in Fig. 12.21, which shows a network with four inputs. Each input is connected to a switch connecting a resistor to either 0 V or V_+. When a switch is in the position connecting to V_+, the binary bit represents a 1; when the switch connects to 0 V, the input bit is a binary 0. The output at E_0 will then be a dc voltage in the range of 0 to V_+ and will be proportional to the value of the binary number represented by the inputs.

For instance, if the input number is 0111 (leftmost switch down, other three up), the output voltage of E_0 will be $\frac{7}{15}V_+$; if the input is 1111, E_0 will be V_+; and if the input is 0001, E_0 will be at $\frac{1}{15}V_+$. For example, if V_+ were 15 V, then for an input of 0111 the output would be 7 V, for input 1000 the output would be 8 V, and for input 1111 (all switches up) the output would be 15 V. to achieve accuracy, all the

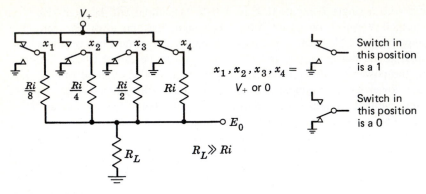

FIGURE 12.21
D/A converter network.

resistors should be of the precision type. More resolution can be added by increasing the number of inputs and adding a resistor for each input. (The resistor values are halved for each input added.)

Resistor networks of this type are manufactured by several firms. The resistors are generally laser-trimmed to the necessary accuracies. Often electronic (transistor-driven) switches are packaged in an IC container with the resistors, forming a complete DAC.

Figure 12.22 shows another type of resistor network that can be used for D/A conversion. The advantage of this network is that only two different values of resistors

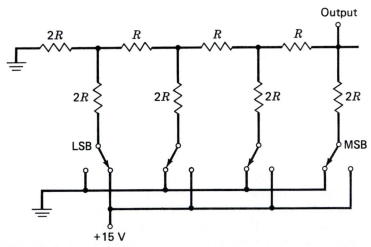

FIGURE 12.22
D/A converter with two resistor sizes.

are used. The inputs are shown as switches, but generally semiconductor switches or level-setting amplifiers are used. The disadvantage of this converter is that two resistors are required per input.

There are several other circuits for DACs, and the design and construction of these devices represent a growing area in the computing field.

QUESTIONS

12.1. For what current does the silicon diode graphed in Fig. 12.1(c) have a voltage drop of +0.6 V?

12.2. For the saturated transistor graphed in Fig. 12.3(c), what is the base voltage, which is also the base-emitter drop, when $I_b = 2000 \ \mu A$ and V_{ce} is 200 mV?

12.3. For Question 12.2, what is the difference between the base voltage and the collector voltage at that time?

12.4. Consider the following circuit (assume a silicon diode):

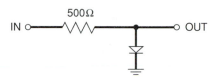

If we make IN a voltage of +5 V, the OUT point will be at about _____.

12.5. If, for Question 12.4, IN were −7 V, give the corresponding OUT voltage and resistor current.

12.6. If V_{ce} is held at +8 V and I_b is changed from 0.85 to 1 mA, what is the resultant change in I_c for the transistor in Fig. 12.3?

12.7. What is the current gain through the transistor for Question 12.6 (the ratio of the change in I_b to I_c)?

12.8. Draw the schematic for a diode AND gate with four inputs.

12.9. If the X input to the OR gate in Fig. 12.5 (b) is at +3 V and the Y input is at 0.5 V, what will the output voltage be? Assume silicon diodes with a forward drop of 0.6 V.

12.10. For the circuit described in the preceding question, what will be the output level if X is at 0.1 V and Y is at 0.8 V?

12.11. Draw the schematic for a four-input diode OR gate.

12.12. Draw the schematic for a diode AND-to-OR gate network that realizes the boolean algebra function $AB + CD$.

12.13. Analyze the output levels for the circuit you designed in the preceding question for input levels of +3 V for a logic 1 and +0.5 V for a logic 0.

12.14. In the following circuit, assume the inputs A and B are both at ground potential (0 V) and that transistor T_2 is off. If the input B is raised to +2 V and then lowered back to 0 V, describe the operation of the circuit.

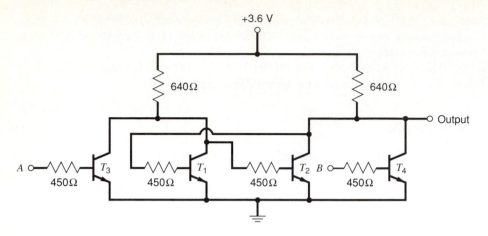

12.15. For the TTL circuit in Fig. 12.6(c), if all inputs are at +3 V, what will be the approximate voltages at the emitter and collector of $T2$?

12.16. Which transistors in the circuit in Fig. 12.7 are saturated when both inputs are low?

12.17. Which transistors in the circuit in Fig. 12.7 are saturated when both inputs are high?

12.18. Using the information gained in the preceding two questions, discuss how the use of Schottky clamped transistors might speed up the circuit in Fig. 12.7.

12.19. The following is a schematic for a TTL NAND gate. If the X input is at +3 V and the Y input at 0 V, what will the approximate voltages be at points A, B, C, and D?

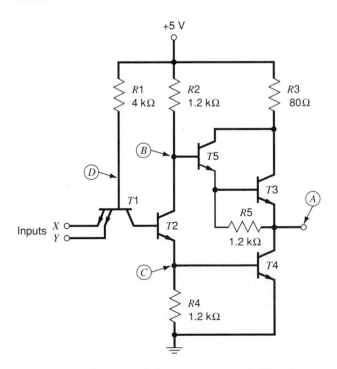

12.20. Explain the action of the two output transistors in the TTL gate in Fig. 12.7.

12.21. If $T4$ shorts in Fig. 12.7 so that the emitter and collector are both permanently connected to the base, what will be the output? Explain.

12.22. Given a single *npn* transistor, how would you connect it to make the three-input ECL gate in Fig. 12.12 a four-input gate?

12.23. Assume that the inputs X and Y to the following circuit are at ground potential and transistor T_1 is off. Explain the operation of the circuit if the input X is made $+5$ V and then returned to ground.

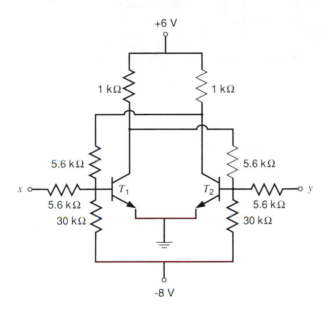

12.24. The ability of a given TTL circuit to drive other circuits is often specified in terms of what is called a *unit load*. For the 7400 series TTL, a unit load is 40 μA (to ground) when the level is in the high state, and the circuit is able to accept 1.6 mA in the low state. An input to a NAND gate in the 7400 series requires one unit load to be driven low or high. A NAND gate's output in the 7400 series can drive 20 unit loads when high and 10 unit loads when low. If a TTL NAND gate is connected to five inputs to other NAND gates and the output is high, how many amperes might the output supply to ground?

12.25. Using the data in the preceding question, how many gate inputs can be safely connected to a given gate output? (This is called the *fan-out* for the gate.)

12.26. Why is the unit load greater for the low level than for the high level? Examine the basic TTL circuit to get your answer.

12.27. Explain why TTL outputs go from low to high faster than a standard inverter when a long wire or other capacitative load must be driven.

12.28. Why do CMOS gates require so little power when they are not changing states?

12.29. What are some advantages of MOS over conventional bipolar circuits?

12.30. (*a*) Draw a block diagram showing the logical operation of the following circuit. (You can use AND gates, NAND gates, OR gates, NOR gates, etc. in your diagram.)

    (*b*) Explain some advantages and disadvantages of the circuit.

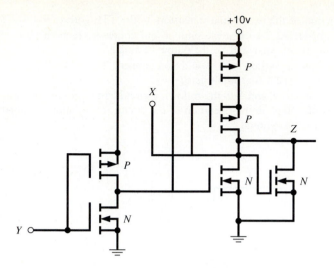

12.31. Calculate the power dissipated in resistor $R2$ for both output states of the ECL circuit in Fig. 12.11.

ANSWERS TO SELECTED ODD NUMBERED QUESTIONS

CHAPTER 1

1.1. Microprocessors are commonly used in automobile ignition systems, automobile instrumentation systems, aircraft guidance systems, home thermostat systems, oven control systems, washing machines, and many other devices. They now are used for everything from stoplights to dishwasher controls.

1.3. How is computer time that is not used to be billed? Who pays for computer maintenance? What are charges for backup tapes, and how are they maintained? Is there a class of time that costs more (at 11 A.M., for example, the computer may be very busy; but at 11 P.M. it may be unused)?

1.5. Batch processing consists of collecting jobs to be performed by the computer and then processing these jobs as they are entered. Most batch systems use a monitor program that is part of the operating system to control the sequence of operation of the programs. Insurance companies use batch systems to process their new accounts and customer claims, for example, each day. Banks also run batch jobs first thing in the morning to update customer accounts, and payroll operations generally are batched weekly or monthly.

1.7.

Address	Op code	Address part
1	CLA	40
2	ADD	41
3	ADD	42
4	STO	43
5	HLT	000
40	contains	X
41	contains	Y
42	contains	Z
43	contains	0

1.9.

Address	Operation	Operand
1	CLA	20
2	MUL	20
3	STO	40
4	CLA	21
5	MUL	21
6	ADD	40
7	STO	40
8	CLA	22
9	MUL	22
10	ADD	40
11	STO	40
12	HLT	
20	contains	X
21	contains	Y
22	contains	Z
40	contains	0

1.17.

Address	Operation	Operand
1	CLA	20
2	STO	21
3	CLA	21
4	MUL	20
5	STO	21
6	CLA	50
7	ADD	51
8	STO	50
9	BRM	3
10	CLA	21
11	ADD	20
12	STO	40
13	HLT	
20	contains	X
21	contains	0
50	contains	-5
51	contains	1

We will now store $X^5 + X$ in the address assigned by the assembler to the variable D.

Address	Operation	Operand
A	DEC	0
B	DEC	-5
C	DEC	1
D	DEC	0
	CLA	X
	STO	D
E	CLA	D
	MUL	X
	STO	D
	CLA	B
	ADD	C
	STO	B
	BRM	E
	CLA	D
	ADD	X
	STO	D
	HLT	

1.21. If we assume that two integers are used.

Address	Operation	Operand
1	CLA	30
2	SUB	31
3	BRM	5
4	HLT	
5	HLT	

The computer stops at address 4 if the numbers are in ascending order, and at 5 if the numbers are in descending order. Here we check to see whether all three numbers are in ascending or descending order.

Address	Operation	Operand
1	CLA	30
2	SUB	31
3	BRM	10
4	CLA	31
5	SUB	32
6	BRM	13
7	HLT	
10	CLA	31
11	SUB	32
12	BRM	15
13	HLT	
15	HLT	

This program stops at address 13 if the numbers are in neither ascending nor descending order, at address 7 if the numbers are ascending, and at address 15 if the numbers are descending.

1.25.

Address	Operation	Operand
1	CLA	26
2	SUB	25
3	BRM	300
4	BRA	400

1.27.

Address	Operation	Operand
P	CLA	A
	SUB	B
	BRM	M
	CLA	A
	SUB	C
	BRM	M
	CLA	A
	STO	X
	HLT	
M	CLA	B
	SUB	C
	BRM	N
	CLA	B
	STO	X
	HLT	
N	CLA	C
	STO	X
	HLT	

1.29.

Address	Operation	Operand	Address	Operation	Operand
1	CLA	300	13	CLA	6
2	BRM	5	14	ADD	400
3	STO	300	15	STO	6
4	BRA	7	16	CLA	401
5	SUB	300	17	ADD	400
6	STO	300	18	STO	401
7	CLA	3	19	BRM	1
8	ADD	400	20	HLT	
9	STO	3	300 ⎫ contains		
10	CLA	5	329 ⎭ numbers		
11	ADD	400	400 contains 1		
12	STO	5	401 contains −30		

CHAPTER 2

2.1. (*a*) 101011   (*b*) 1000000   (*c*) 100000000000
      (*d*) 0.011   (*e*) 0.11011   (*f*) 0.0111
      (*g*) 1000000000.1   (*h*) 10000011.1001   (*i*) 10000000000.0001

2.3. (*a*) 13   (*b*) 27   (*c*) 11
      (*d*) 0.6875   (*e*) 0.203125   (*f*) 0.212890625
      (*g*) 59.6875   (*h*) 91.203125   (*i*) 22.3408203125

2.5. (a) 11   (b) 36   (c) 19
       (d) 0.8125   (e) 0.5625   (f) 0.3125
       (g) 11.1875   (h) 9.5625   (i) 5.375

2.7. (a) $10100.11 = 20.75$ (b) $1001010 = 74$ (c) $1.1 = 1.5$
       (d) $10101 = 21$

2.9. (a) $\begin{array}{r} 1101.1 \\ 1011.1 \\ \hline 11001.0 \end{array}$ $\begin{array}{r} 13.5 \\ 11.5 \\ \hline 25 \end{array}$ (b) $\begin{array}{r} 101101 \\ 110110 \\ \hline 1100011 \end{array}$ $\begin{array}{r} 45 \\ 109 \\ \hline 154 \end{array}$

       (c) $\begin{array}{r} 0.0011 \\ 0.1110 \\ \hline 1.0001 \end{array}$ $\begin{array}{r} 0.1875 \\ 0.875 \\ \hline 1.0625 \end{array}$ (d) $\begin{array}{r} 1100.011 \\ 1011.011 \\ \hline 10111.110 \end{array}$ $\begin{array}{r} 12.375 \\ 11.375 \\ \hline 23.750 \end{array}$

2.11. (a) $\begin{array}{r} 1000000 \\ -100000 \\ \hline 100000 \end{array}$ (b) $\begin{array}{r} 1111111 \\ -111111 \\ \hline 1000000 \end{array}$

        (c) $\begin{array}{r} 1011101.1 \\ -101010.11 \\ \hline 110010.11 \end{array}$ (d) $\begin{array}{r} 1010100.01001 \\ -110000.01010 \\ \hline 100011.11111 \end{array}$

2.13. (a) $\begin{array}{r} 100101 \\ -100011 \\ \hline 000010 \end{array}$ (b) $\begin{array}{r} 10000000 \\ 01000000 \\ \hline 1000000 \end{array}$

        (c) $\begin{array}{r} 1011110.1 \\ 101011.11 \\ \hline 110010.11 \end{array}$ (d) $\begin{array}{r} 11111111 \\ 1111111 \\ \hline 10000000 \end{array}$

2.15. (a) 100100000   (b) 11111100   (c) 100
        (d) 1.1   (e) 10100000001.101   (f) 10.1

2.17. (a) $\begin{array}{r} 1111 \\ 1101 \\ \hline 1111 \\ 11110 \\ 1111 \\ \hline 11000011 \end{array}$ (b) $\begin{array}{r} 1111 \\ 1010 \\ \hline 11110 \\ 11110 \\ \hline 10010110 \end{array}$

        (c) $\begin{array}{r} 100 \\ 1011\overline{)101100} \\ 1011 \\ \hline 000 \end{array}$ (d) $\begin{array}{r} 11.1 \\ 1100\overline{)101010.0} \\ 1100 \\ \hline 10010 \\ 1100 \\ \hline 1100 \\ 1100 \\ \hline 0 \end{array}$

        (e) $\begin{array}{r} 111.11 \\ 10.1 \\ \hline 11111 \\ 111110 \\ \hline 10011.011 \end{array}$ (f) $\begin{array}{r} 10110.1 \\ 100.11 \\ \hline 101101 \\ 101101 \\ 10110100 \\ \hline 1101010.111 \end{array}$

2.19. 9s COMPLEMENT   10s COMPLEMENT

    (*a*) 4563   4564

    (*b*) 8067   8068

    (*c*) 54.84   54.85

    (*d*) 81.706   81.707

2.21. 9s COMPLEMENT   10s COMPLEMENT

    (*a*) 6345   6346

    (*b*) 7877   7878

    (*c*) 45.80   45.81

    (*d*) 62.736   62.737

2.23. 1s COMPLEMENT   2s COMPLEMENT

    (*a*) 0100   0101

    (*b*) 00100   00101

    (*c*) 0100.10   0100.11

    (*d*) 00100.10   00100.11

2.25. 1s COMPLEMENT   2s COMPLEMENT

    (*a*) 010000   010001

    (*b*) 011011   011100

    (*c*) 01000.01   01000.10

    (*d*) 01100.00   01100.01

2.27.   9s COMPLEMENT   10s COMPLEMENT

    (*a*)

```
        948                  948
        765                  766
      1 713                  714
       ↳ 1
        714
```

    (*b*)

```
        347                  347
        736                  737
      1 083                  084
       ↳ 1
        084
```

    (*c*)

```
        349.5                349.5
        754.6                754.7
      1 104.1                104.2
       ↳  1
        104.2
```

    (*d*)

```
        412.7                412.7
        590.7                590.8
      1 003.4                  3.5
       ↳  1
          3.5
```

2.29.   9s COMPLEMENT   10s COMPLEMENT

(a)   1024   1024
                  9086   9087
                  ‾0110‾   ‾0111‾
                    → 1
                  ‾111‾

(b)   249   249
                  862   863
                  ‾111‾   ‾112‾
                    → 1
                  ‾112‾

(c)   24.1   24.1
                  86.5   86.6
                  ‾10.6‾   ‾10.7‾
                    → 1
                  ‾10.7‾

(d)   239.3   239.3
                  880.5   880.6
                  ‾119.8‾   ‾119.9‾
                    → 1
                  ‾119.9‾

2.31.   1s COMPLEMENT   2s COMPLEMENT

(a)   1011   1011
                  1010   1011
                  ‾1 0101‾   ‾0110‾
                    → 1
                  ‾0110‾

(b)   11011   11011
                  00110   00111
                  ‾1 00001‾   ‾00010‾
                    → 1
                  ‾10‾

(c)   10111.1   10111.1
                  01100.0   01100.1
                  ‾1 00011.1‾   ‾100.0‾
                    → 1
                  ‾100.0‾

(d)   11011.00   11011.00
                  01100.00   01100.01
                  ‾1 00111.00‾   ‾111.01‾
                    → 1
                  ‾111.01‾

2.33. $2^6 = 64$

2.35. 1000 different numbers in each case (from 0 to 999, for instance)

2.37. 0, 1, 2, 3, 10, 11, 12, 13, 20, 21

2.39. 0, 1, 2, 3, 4, 5, 6, 7, 8, 9, A, 10, 11, 12, 13, 14, 15, 16, 17, 18, 19, 1A, 20, 21, 22

2.41. (a)
```
   .1001
   .1001
 ⌐ 0010
 └─→  1
   .0011
```
(b)
```
   .1110
   .1001
 ⌐ 0111
 └─→  1
   .1000
```
(c)
```
   01111
   10110
 ⌐ 00101
 └─→   1
   .00110
```
(d)
```
   11011
   00110
 ⌐ 00001
 └─→   1
   00010
```

(e)
```
     1110101
     0101101
  ⌐1 0100010
  └──→     1
     0100011
```

2.45. (a)
```
 45,056
  1,536
    192
      7
 46,791
```
(b)
```
 24,576
  1,024
    160
     12
 25,772
```
(c)
```
 40,960
  1,024
    144
      2
 42,130
```
(d)
```
  851,968
    8,192
    1,792
       96
        3
  862,051
```

2.49. (a) 55   (b) 556   (c) 267
(d) 66.3   (e) 3.554

2.53. (a) 1644   (b) 514   (c) 1041.3
(d) 1170.76051   (e) 10515.5

2.57. (a) B7   (b) 9C   (c) 4F
(d) 0.7E   (e) B7A

2.61.
(a)
```
    1
   $15_8$
 +$14_8$
   $31_8$
```
(b)
```
    1
   $24_8$
 +$36_8$
   $62_8$
```
(c)
```
    1
  $126_8$
 +$347_8$
  $475_8$
```
(d)
```
    1
   $67_8$
 +$45_8$
  $134_8$
```

(e)
```
     1
   $136_8$
 +$636_8$
  $774_8$
```

2.79. 00001   0000011

CHAPTER 3

3.1. (a)

X	Y	Z	XYZ	$\overline{X}\,\overline{Y}\,\overline{Z}$	$XYZ + \overline{X}\,\overline{Y}\,\overline{Z}$
0	0	0	0	1	1
0	0	1	0	0	0
0	1	0	0	0	0
0	1	1	0	0	0
1	0	0	0	0	0
1	0	1	0	0	0
1	1	0	0	0	0
1	1	1	1	0	1

(b)

A	B	C	ABC	$A\bar{B}\bar{C}$	$\bar{A}\bar{B}\bar{C}$	$ABC + A\bar{B}\bar{C} + \bar{A}\bar{B}\bar{C}$
0	0	0	0	0	1	1
0	0	1	0	0	0	0
0	1	0	0	0	0	0
0	1	1	0	0	0	0
1	0	0	0	1	0	1
1	0	1	0	0	0	0
1	1	0	0	0	0	0
1	1	1	1	0	0	1

(c)

A	B	C	$B\bar{C}$	$\bar{B}C$	$B\bar{C} + \bar{B}C$	$A(B\bar{C} + \bar{B}C)$
0	0	0	0	0	0	0
0	0	1	0	1	1	0
0	1	0	1	0	1	0
0	1	1	0	0	0	0
1	0	0	0	0	0	0
1	0	1	0	1	1	1
1	1	0	1	0	1	1
1	1	1	0	0	0	0

(d)

A	B	C	A + B	A + C	$\bar{A} + \bar{B}$	$(A + B)(A + C)(\bar{A} + \bar{B})$
0	0	0	0	0	1	0
0	0	1	0	1	1	0
0	1	0	1	0	1	0
0	1	1	1	1	1	1
1	0	0	1	1	1	1
1	0	1	1	1	1	1
1	1	0	1	1	0	0
1	1	1	1	1	0	0

3.3. Only the values of the expressions are listed:

(a)

A	B	$A\bar{B} + \bar{A}B$
0	0	0
0	1	1
1	0	1
1	1	0

(b)

A	B	C	$A\bar{B} + B\bar{C}$
0	0	0	0
0	0	1	0
0	1	0	1
0	1	1	0
1	0	0	1
1	0	1	1
1	1	0	1
1	1	1	0

(c)

A	C	$A\overline{C} + AC$
0	0	0
0	1	0
1	0	1
1	1	1

(d)

A	B	C	$A\overline{B}C + AB\overline{C} + \overline{A}BC$
0	0	0	0
0	0	1	0
0	1	0	0
0	1	1	1
1	0	0	0
1	0	1	1
1	1	0	1
1	1	1	0

(e)

A	B	C	$A(A\overline{B}C + \overline{A}B\overline{C} + AB\overline{C})$
0	0	0	0
0	0	1	0
0	1	0	0
0	1	1	0
1	0	0	1
1	0	1	1
1	1	0	1
1	1	1	0

3.7. (a) $\overline{B}\,\overline{C} + \overline{A}\,\overline{C} + \overline{A}\,\overline{B}$　　(b) $\overline{C} + \overline{B} + \overline{A}$　　　　(c) $A(B + C)$
(d) A is a minimal expression

3.9. (a) $ABC(A\overline{B}\,\overline{C} + A\overline{B}C + \overline{A}BC) = 0$, for no assignment of binary values will make this expression take the value 1.
(b) $AB + A\overline{B} + \overline{A}C + \overline{A}\,\overline{C} = 1$, for every assignment of values will give this expression the value 1.
(c) $XY + XY\overline{Z} + XY\overline{Z} + \overline{X}YZ = XY + YZ$
(d) $XY(\overline{X}YZ + X\overline{Y}\,\overline{Z} + \overline{X}\,\overline{Y}\,\overline{Z}) = 0$

3.11. (a) $\overline{A}(\overline{B} + \overline{C})(\overline{A} + \overline{B}) = \overline{A}\,\overline{B} + \overline{A}\,\overline{C}$ or $\overline{A}(\overline{B} + \overline{C})$
(b) $\overline{A}\,\overline{B} + \overline{B}\,\overline{C} + \overline{A}\,\overline{C}$
(c) $(\overline{A} + \overline{B})(B + \overline{C})(\overline{C} + D) = \overline{A}B\overline{C} + \overline{A}\,\overline{C} + \overline{A}BD + \overline{A}\,\overline{C}D$
$\qquad\qquad\qquad\qquad\qquad = \overline{A}\,\overline{C} + \overline{B}\,\overline{C} + \overline{A}BD$
(d) $(\overline{A} + \overline{B}) + (C + \overline{D})(B + \overline{C}) = \overline{A} + \overline{B} + BC + B\overline{D} + \overline{C}\,\overline{D} = \overline{A}\,\overline{B} + C + \overline{D}$
(e) $\overline{A} + \overline{B}\,\overline{C} + CD$

3.13. The important columns in these tables are as follows:

X	Y	Z	$(\overline{X+Y+Z})$	$\overline{X}\,\overline{Y}\,\overline{Z}$
0	0	0	1	1
0	0	1	0	0
0	1	0	0	0
0	1	1	0	0
1	0	0	0	0
1	0	1	0	0
1	1	0	0	0
1	1	1	0	0

X	Y	Z	$(\overline{XYZ})$	$\overline{X}+\overline{Y}+\overline{Z}$
0	0	0	1	1
0	0	1	1	1
0	1	0	1	1
0	1	1	1	1
1	0	0	1	1
1	0	1	1	1
1	1	0	1	1
1	1	1	0	0

3.15. (a) $\overline{A}BC + A\overline{B}C + AC + BC = AC + BC$

(b) $A\overline{B} + A\overline{C} + ABC + AB\overline{C} + \overline{A}BC + \overline{B}C$

(c) $A\overline{B} + A\overline{B}C = A\overline{B}$

3.17. Rule 13

3.19. (a) $AB + AD + BC + CD$

(b) $AB + AD + AC + BC + CD + C + BD + D + DC = C + D + AB$

(c) $AB + A\overline{D} + BC + CD$

(d) $A\overline{B} + A\overline{C}$

3.21. $\overline{X}\,\overline{Y}Z + XY\overline{Z}$

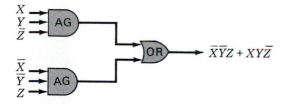

3.25. $XY + X\overline{Z}$

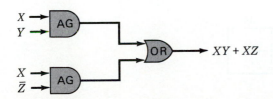

3.27.

X	Y	$X + \overline{X}Y$	$X + Y$
0	0	0	0
0	1	1	1
1	0	1	1
1	1	1	1

3.29. $Y\overline{Z} + \overline{Y}Z$ is the sum-of-products expression, and $(Y + Z)(\overline{Y} + \overline{Z})$ is the product-of-sums expression.

3.35.

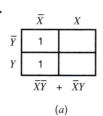

	$\overline{X}$	X
$\overline{Y}$	1	
Y	1	

$$\overline{X}\overline{Y} + \overline{X}Y$$

(a)

	$\overline{X}\,\overline{Y}$	$\overline{X}Y$	XY	$X\overline{Y}$
$\overline{Z}$	1		1	
Z				

$$\overline{X}\,\overline{Y}\overline{Z} + XY\overline{Z}$$

(b)

	$\overline{X}\,\overline{Y}$	$\overline{X}Y$	XY	$X\overline{Y}$
$\overline{Z}$	1	1		
Z	1			

$$\overline{X}\,\overline{Y}\overline{Z} + \overline{X}\,\overline{Y}$$

(c)

	$\overline{X}\,\overline{Y}$	$\overline{X}Y$	XY	$X\overline{Y}$
$\overline{Z}$	1	1		1
Z				

$$\overline{X}\,\overline{Y}\overline{Z} + \overline{X}Y\overline{Z} + X\overline{Y}\overline{Z}$$

(d)

	$\overline{X}\,\overline{Y}$	$\overline{X}Y$	XY	$X\overline{Y}$
$\overline{Z}$	1	1		1
Z				

$$\overline{X}\overline{Z} + \overline{Y}\overline{Z}$$

(e)

	$\overline{A}\,\overline{B}$	$\overline{A}B$	AB	$A\overline{B}$
$\overline{C}$				
C				

$$AB(\overline{\overline{A}\overline{B}\overline{C}} + \overline{B}C)$$

(f)

3.39.

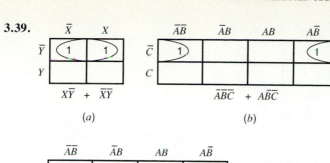

$$X\bar{Y} + \bar{X}Y$$

(a)

$$\overline{ABC} + A\bar{B}\bar{C}$$

(b)

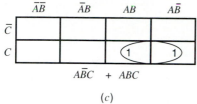

$$A\bar{B}C + ABC$$

(c)

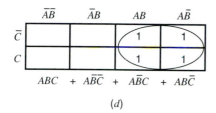

$$ABC + AB\bar{C} + A\bar{B}C + A\bar{B}\bar{C}$$

(d)

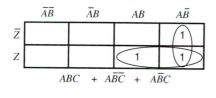

$$ABC + AB\bar{C} + A\bar{B}\bar{C}$$

(e)

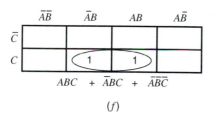

$$ABC + \bar{A}BC + \overline{ABC}$$

(f)

3.41.

	$\overline{X}\overline{Y}$	$\overline{X}Y$	XY	$X\overline{Y}$
$\overline{Z}$	1			
Z	1		1	1

$$m_0 + m_1 + m_5 + m_7$$

(a)

	$\overline{X}\overline{Y}$	$\overline{X}Y$	XY	$X\overline{Y}$
$\overline{Z}$				1
Z	1	1		1

$$m_1 + m_3 + m_4 + m_5$$

(b)

	$\overline{X}\overline{Y}$	$\overline{X}Y$	XY	$X\overline{Y}$
$\overline{Z}$		1		
Z	1	1		1

$$m_1 + m_2 + m_3 + m_5$$

(c)

	$\overline{X}\overline{Y}$	$\overline{X}Y$	XY	$X\overline{Y}$
$\overline{Z}$	1			
Z			1	1

$$m_1 + m_2 + m_3 + m_5$$

(d)

	$\overline{X}\overline{Y}$	$\overline{X}Y$	XY	$X\overline{Y}$
$\overline{Z}$	1			
Z			1	1

$$m_0 + m_5 + m_7$$

(e)

3.45. (b)

	$\overline{W}\overline{X}$	$\overline{W}X$	WX	$W\overline{X}$
$\overline{Y}\overline{Z}$	1	1	1	1
$\overline{Y}Z$			1	1
$Y Z$				1
$Y\overline{Z}$	1			1

$$m_0 = \overline{W}\,\overline{X}\,\overline{Y}\,\overline{Z} \qquad m_{10} = W\overline{X}Y\overline{Z}$$
$$m_2 = \overline{W}\,\overline{X}Y\,\overline{Z} \qquad m_{11} = W\overline{X}YZ$$
$$m_4 = \overline{W}X\overline{Y}\,\overline{Z} \qquad m_{12} = WX\overline{Y}\,\overline{Z}$$
$$m_8 = W\overline{X}\,\overline{Y}\,\overline{Z} \qquad m_{13} = WX\overline{Y}Z$$
$$m_9 = W\overline{X}\,\overline{Y}Z$$

$$m_0 + m_2 + m_4 + m_8 + m_9 + m_{10} + m_{11} + m_{12} + m_{13}$$
$$\overline{X}\,\overline{Z} + \overline{Y}\,\overline{Z} + W\overline{X} + W\overline{Y}$$
$$\overline{Z}(\overline{X} + \overline{Y}) + W(\overline{X} + \overline{Y})$$
$$(\overline{Z} + W)(\overline{X} + \overline{Y})$$

3.47. (a) $m_1 + m_3 + m_5 + m_7 + m_{12} + m_{13} + m_8 + m_9$

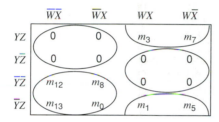

Product of sums:
$$\overline{(WY + WZ)} = (\overline{W} + \overline{Y})(W + Z)$$

Sum of products:
$$W\overline{Y} + \overline{W}Z$$

(b) $m_0 + m_5 + m_7 + m_8 + m_{11} + m_{13} + m_{15}$

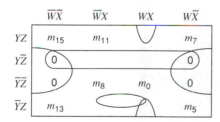

Product of sums:
$$(X\overline{Z} + Y\overline{Z} + \overline{W}\,\overline{X}Z + \overline{X}\,\overline{Y}Z)$$
$$= (X + Z)(\overline{Y} + Z)(W + X + \overline{Z})$$
$$(X + Y + \overline{Z})$$

3.49. (a) $\overline{A}\,\overline{B}\,\overline{C} + A\overline{B}\,\overline{C} + ABC + \overbrace{\overline{A}B\overline{C} + \overline{A}BC}^{\text{don't-cares}} = \overline{B}\,\overline{C}$

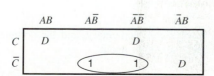

don't-cares

(b) $ABC + A\overline{B}\,\overline{C} + AB\overline{C} + A\overline{B}C = A$

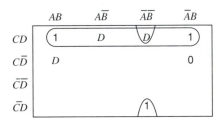

don't-cares

(c) $ABCD + \overline{A}\,\overline{B}\,CD + \overline{A}BCD + A\overline{B}CD + \overline{A}\,\overline{B}CD + ABC\overline{D}$

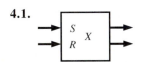

CHAPTER 4

4.1.

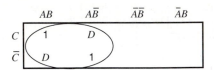

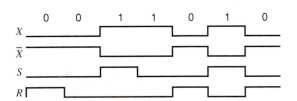

4.3. True. A flip-flop's two outputs are always complementary, and the complement of the complemented signal is, of course, the signal itself.

4.5.

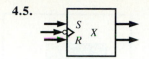

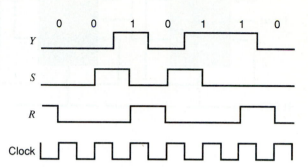

4.7. It will never have a 1 output.

4.9.

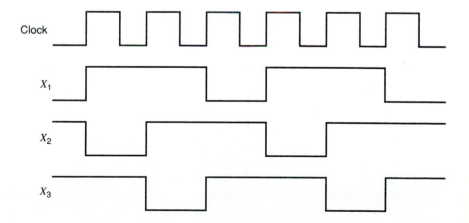

4.11. The waveforms are shown below:

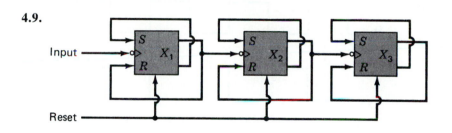

4.13.

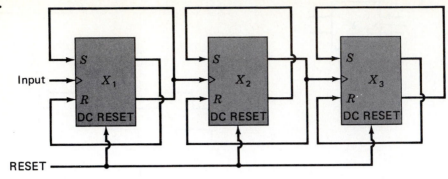

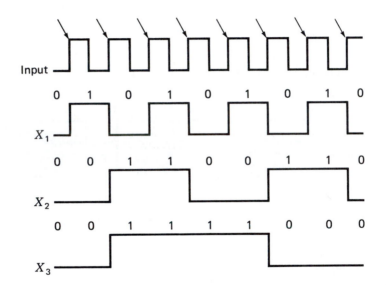

4.15.

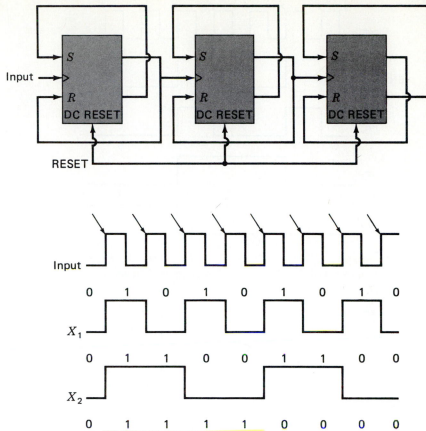

4.17.

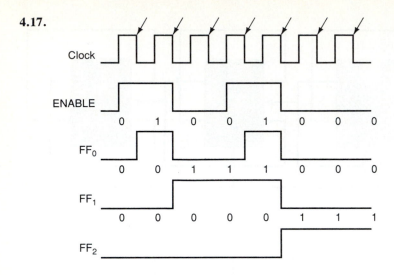

4.19. Assuming ENABLE $=1$, the waveforms are as follows.

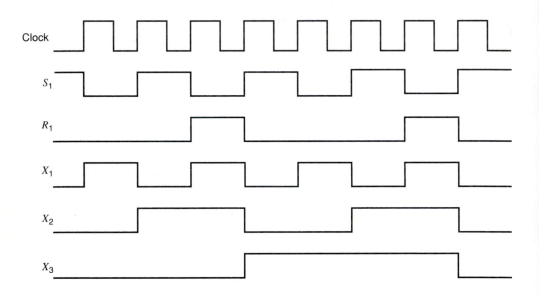

Note: We assume that the flip-flops start at 0. Observe that we may write R_2 as X_2X_1 with ENABLE equal to 1.

4.21. The sequence is (in hexadecimal): 0,1,A,B,C,D,C,D,C,D,....

4.23. (*a*) 160   (*b*) 80

4.25. There are two chips of the type shown in Fig. 4.16(*c*) and one of the type shown in Fig. 4.16(*e*). If we call these chips c_1, c_2 and e, they are connected as follows:

Clock to c_1, pin 1

c_1, pin 5 to c_1, pin 12 and c_2, pin 5

c_1, pin 7 to c_2, pin 8

c_1, pin 9 to c_2, pin 1 and e, pin 12

c_2, pin 7 to e, pin 8

c_2, pin 9 to carry-out

c_2, pin 12 to e, pin 13

Pins 9, 10, and 11 of e are connected together

4.31. Assuming negative-edge-triggered flip-flops as shown, the waveforms are sketched below. Note that:

$$S_1 = A_1 \oplus A_3, \qquad R_1 = \overline{S_1}, \qquad S_2 = A_1,$$
$$R_2 = \overline{A_1}, \qquad S_3 = A_2, \qquad \text{and } R_3 = \overline{A_2}$$

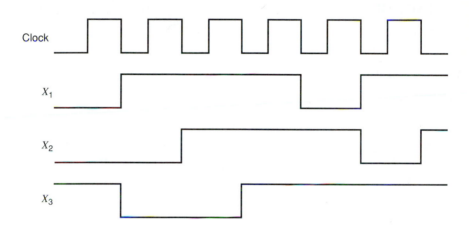

4.33.

X_1	X_2	X_3	
1	0	0	
1	1	0	
0	1	1	
1	0	1	
0	1	0	
0	0	1	
0	0	0	
1	0	0	
⋮	⋮	⋮	(repeats periodically)

4.35. $A = 0, B = 0, C = 0, D = 1, E = 1, F = 1, G = 1, H = 0$

4.37. SET

4.39. The design is shown below:

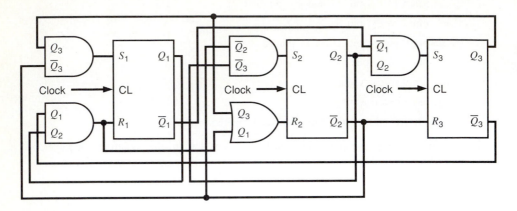

CHAPTER 5

5.1.

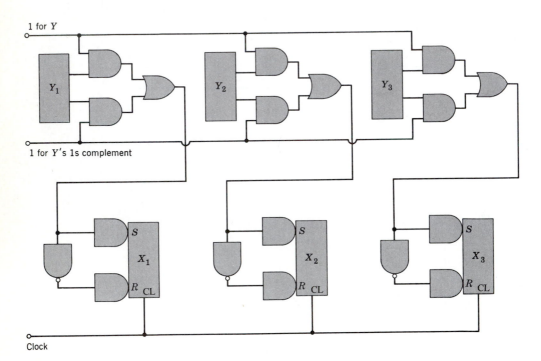

5.3. (a) $\underline{0}0110$ (b) $\underline{0}1010$
     (c) $\underline{1}1100$ (d) Not representable

5.5. -4 would be stored $\underline{1}0100$ in the magnitude system, $\underline{1}1011$ in the 1s complement system, and $\underline{1}1100$ in the 2s complement system.

5.7. $S = 1$ and $C_o = 1$

5.9. -12 in 1s complement; -13 in 2s complement

5.11. The sum will overflow the register and cause an incorrect addition. Most machines sense for this and turn on an "addition overflow" bit or indicate the overflow in some manner.

5.15.

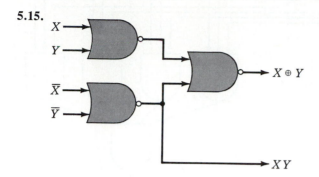

5.17. The logic diagram is shown below:

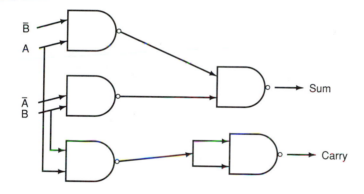

5.19. The logic diagram is shown below:

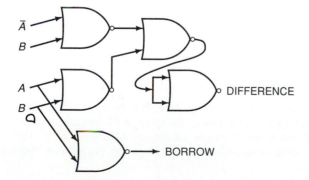

5.23. No

5.25.

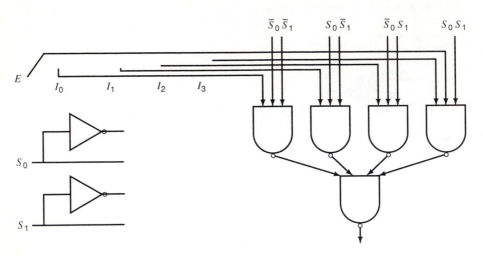

5.29. Logical addition, $\underline{0}111011$

Logical multiplication, $\underline{0}100010$

Exclusive OR, $\underline{0}011001$

5.31. The logical MULTIPLY will clear those digits of X where 0s occur in Y, and the logical ADD will add 1s into the places in X where 1s occur in Y.

5.37. None

5.53. 0101 produces 0100, and 0011 produces 0110.

5.55. The D flip-flop holds the carry for the next stage of the addition.

5.61. (*a*) 0 0000 0000 0100 0011

(*b*) 1 0000 0010 0010 0010

(*c*) 0 0001 0010 0011 0100

(*d*) 1 0001 0010 1001 0111

5.63. (*a*) 0 0000 0000 0100 0011

(*b*) 1 1001 0111 0111 0111

(*c*) 0 0001 0010 0011 0100

(*d*) 1 1000 0111 0000 0010

5.65. (*a*) 0 0000 0000 0100 0011

(*b*) 1 1001 0111 0111 1000

(*c*) 0 0001 0010 0011 0100

(*d*) 1 1000 0111 0000 0011

5.67. Add an additional AND gate to each group. One input to the AND gate would be the SHIFT LEFT control line; the output of the stage to the immediate right would be the other input. J and K inputs can be put on the AND gates at the rightmost flip-flop to allow the same versatile control of its input as the leftmost flip-flop in Fig. 5.17 experiences.

5.69. We show the procedure for 7×9. Load 00111 into B and 01001 into Y:

X	B	Y	Notes
00000	00111	01001	Examine LSB of B
01001	00111		Add $X + Y$
00100	10011		Shift X, B right
00100	10011		Examine LSB of B
01101	10011		Add $X + Y$
00110	11001		Shift X, B right
00110	11001		Examine LSB of B
01111	11001		Add $X + Y$
00111	11100		Shift X, B right
00111	11100		Examine LSB of B
00011	11110		Shift X, B right
00011	11110		Examine LSB of B
00001	11111		Shift X, B right

Answer = 63

5.71. Beginning: $X = 10111$ (23)   After: $X = 00101$ (Remainder = 5)
$\qquad\qquad\quad Y = 00110$ (6) $\qquad\quad Y = 00110$
$\qquad\qquad\quad B = 00000$ $\qquad\qquad\qquad\quad B = 00011$ (Quotient = 3)

5.73. The essential steps are:

X	B	Y	Notes
01110	00000	00011	Shift Y left twice
		01100	3 steps needed
00010	00000		$X - Y$ positive
00100	00001		Shift X, B left
			Add 1 to B
11000	00001		$X - Y$ negative
00100	00001		Add Y back
01000	00010		Shift X, B left
11100	00010		$X - Y$ negative
01000	00010		Add Y back
10000	00100		Shift X, B left
00010	00100		Shift X right 3 times

Remainder = 2, quotient = 4 (which is the case for 14/3)

CHAPTER 6

6.1. A 12-bit MAR is needed for 4096 words; we therefore need a 12×4096 decoder— 4096 AND gates are needed. If we use the two-dimensional approach, we can get by with two 6×64 decoders, each requiring 64 AND gates; that is, 128 AND gates are needed.

6.7. The following scheme is the general idea: The given chip may be viewed as realizing a 4K by 1-bit memory; thus, 16 such chips are needed. We will have a common address bus to all 16 chips; further, the D input and D output lines will be ORed together. We use a 4×16 decoder to determine which chip we want, connecting the decoder outputs to the various CHIP SELECT lines. The inputs to the decoder use 4 address lines; the other 12 go to each of the chips.

6.11.

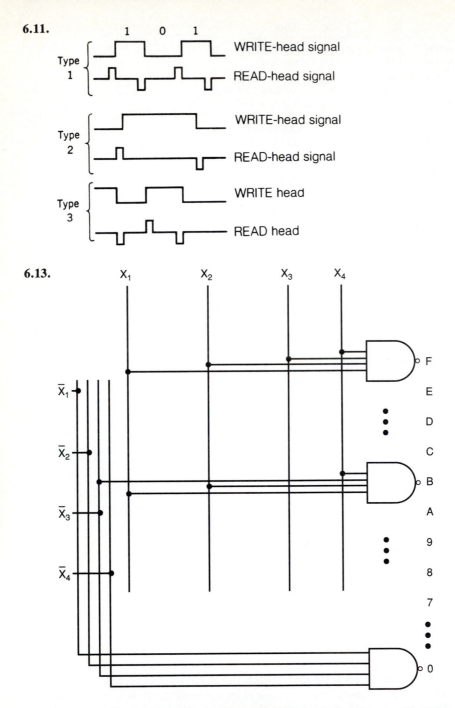

6.13.

6.21. Here is a concise explanation: When SELECT is 0, the output is 0; when SELECT is 1, we may ignore it—the output is the state of the flip-flop, and the flip-flop inputs depend just on WRITE and INPUT. When WRITE is 0, the S and R inputs to the flip-flop are both 0 and it will not change state, regardless of the value of INPUT.

The output is simply the current state of the flip-flop (i.e., a READ is performed). When WRITE is 1, the flip-flop will be set to the value of the input (i.e., a WRITE operation is performed).

6.29. If there are b bits per track and the disk revolves r times per second, we can read rb bits per second; the average access time for a bit is the one that is $b/2$ bits away. This will take $1/2r$ seconds to appear under the head.

6.33. 262,500 bits/s

CHAPTER 7

7.3.

Decimal	2,4,2,1 code	Even-parity check
0	0000	0
1	0001	1
2	0010	1
3	0011	0
4	0100	1
5	1011	1
6	1100	0
7	1101	1
8	1110	1
9	1111	0

7.7. The second and third rows have even parity and so contain errors. The parity check row on the bottom indicates 1 for an even number of 1s in a given column and 0 for an odd number. So column 4 needs an extra 1, as does column 7. The 1 in column 7 of necessity occurs in row 3; the 1 in column 4, therefore, occurs in row 2. The intended pattern (if we view the rightmost bit as a parity-check bit, the ASCII equivalents are as shown):

1010	0100	R
1001	0010	I
1000	1111	G
1001	0001	H
1010	1000	T
0111	1111	(parity check)

7.9. 10. One such code can be formed by adding a leading 0 to each of the 4-bit Gray code groups listed in Table 7.2 and then adding another 16 rows with the four rightmost binary digits the same as those in the table but with their order reversed and with a leading 1 added to each code row.

7.11.

Decimal	3	3	2	1
0	0	0	0	0
1	0	0	0	1
2	0	0	1	0
3	0	1	0	0
4	0	1	0	1
5	0	1	1	0
6	1	1	0	0
7	1	1	0	1
8	1	1	1	0
9	1	1	1	1

7.13. The ASCII code for 6, assuming odd parity, is 10110110. The transmission looks like

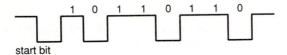

start bit

7.31. There will be seven comparators with analog reference inputs of 6.5, 5.5, ..., 0.5 and outputs $A, B, \ldots, G$. If we call the digital outputs X_0, X_1, and X_2, the desired boolean function is derived as follows:

Analog range	$A\,B\,C\,D\,E\,F\,G$	$X_0\,X_1\,X_2$
<0.5	0 0 0 0 0 0 0	0 0 0
>0.5,<1.5	0 0 0 0 0 0 1	1 0 0
>1.5,<2.5	0 0 0 0 0 1 1	0 1 0
>2.5,<3.5	0 0 0 0 1 1 1	1 1 0
>3.5,<4.5	0 0 0 1 1 1 1	0 0 1
>4.5,<5.5	0 0 1 1 1 1 1	1 0 1
>5.5,<6.5	0 1 1 1 1 1 1	0 1 1
>6.5	1 1 1 1 1 1 1	1 1 1

This yields $X_0 = A + \overline{B}C + \overline{D}E + \overline{F}G$, $X_1 = B + \overline{D}FG$, $X_2 = D$. (The drawing of the circuit is left to the reader.)

7.33. The resolution of a D/A converter is the number of bits, R. If the voltage output range is 0 to V volts, then each step in the output is equal to $V/(2^R - 1)$. The quantization error is usually defined for an A/D converter; if it maps an analog input in the 0 to V range onto R bits, then each real analog voltage is forced to a value of the form $kV/(2^R - 1)$, and the average quantization error is $\frac{1}{2}$ of the step size, or $(\frac{1}{2})V(2^R - 1)$.

7.35. The Gray to binary conversion is given by:

$g_2\,g_1\,g_0$	$b_2\,b_1\,b_0$
0 0 0	0 0 0
0 0 1	0 0 1
0 1 1	0 1 0
0 1 0	0 1 1
1 1 0	1 0 0
1 1 1	1 0 1
1 0 1	1 1 0
1 0 0	1 1 1

7.37. The weight is $10/(2^6 - 1) = \frac{10}{63}$.

CHAPTER 8

8.1. Connect the ENABLE line into an inverter, and pass the inverter output to the DISABLE line of the three-state driver. It then functions as one with an ENABLE input.

8.11. The "mask" part of the ANI instruction could be varied to 40H or 20H, for example, in order to test various other status bits. In conjunction with the JZ instruction, then, the specific status bit used could easily be found and tested.

8.15. Decimal 6 is equal to 00000110 in binary. Hence, we remove the inverters from A_2 and A_1 in Figure 8.23 and add an inverter to A_0. All else remains unchanged.

8.17. The status register number for the keyboard will be 6; for the printer it will be 8. The code is:

KEYSTAT	IN	6	PRINTSTAT	IN	8
	ANI	8OH		ANI	8OH
	JZ	KEYSTAT		JZ	PRINTSTAT
	IN	5		LDA	CHAR
	STA	CHAR		OUT	7

8.25. Direct memory access involves data transfer independent of the CPU's direct intervention. This is very fast.

8.27. One binary line can be designated for each device. Also, a simple shifting operation can indicate the device by virtue of the number of shifts needed.

CHAPTER 9

9.3. The timing table is shown in Table 9.2 with the following additions (op code 00100 = BRM):

BRM (from Table 9.3)

I and T_0	SET R	Tell memory to read instruction word
I and T_1	MB INTO OP,	Operation portion of instruction word into the operation register
	RESET R	Clear memory READ flip-flop
I and T_2 and AC_0	MB INTO IC	If sign bit of accumulator is 1 (contents are negative), use the address portion of the instruction address as the next instruction address
I and T_2 and AC_0	INCREMENT IC	If sign bit of accumulator is 0 (contents are not negative), use the next sequential address in memory as the next instruction address
I and T_3	IC INTO MA	Set up to read the next instruction from memory; leave $I = 1$ so that the next cycle will be another instruction cycle

BRA

I and T_0	SET R	Tell memory to read instruction
I and T_1	MB INTO OP,	Operation portion of instruction word into the operation register
	RESET R	Clear memory READ flip-flop
I and T_2	MB INTO IC	Use address portion of instruction word as the next instruction address
I and T_3	IC INTO MA	Set up to read the next instruction from memory; leave $I = 1$ so that the next cycle will be another instruction cycle

---

The control signal generation logic in Figs. 9.6 and 9.8 should be augmented with the following:

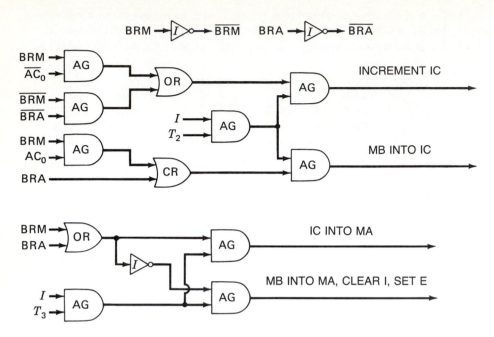

9.7. Instructions that require an execution cycle generally must access memory to obtain or to store an operand. Examples from the instruction set of Table 9.2 include ADD and STORE. Instructions that do not require an access to memory for an operand generally do not require an execution cycle. In such cases there may be no operand, or the operand may be obtained as part of the instruction and manipulated solely within the central registers of the processor. Examples are BRM, BRA, and CLR.

9.17. This question says: Provide a microprogram for the BRM branch-on-minus instruction of Table 9.3. The op code in the BRM instruction is $00100 = 4_{10}$.

Microprogram ROM location	C_0 to C_6	Microprogram C_7 to C_n
0	—	$1 \rightarrow R$; IAR $+ 1 \rightarrow$ IAR
1	—	$MB_{0-4} \rightarrow$ OP; IAR $+ 1 \rightarrow$ IAR; $0 \rightarrow R$
2	—	OP $+$ IAR $+ 1 \rightarrow$ IAR
3	20_{10}	$C_{0-6} \rightarrow$ IAR
.	.	.
.	.	.
.	.	.
7	40_{10}	$C_{0-6} \rightarrow$ IAR
.	.	.
.	.	.
.	.	.
40	42_{10}	IF ($AC_0 = 1$) THEN $C_{0-6} \rightarrow$ IAR; ELSE IAR $+1 \rightarrow$ IAR
41	43_{10}	$C_{0-6} \rightarrow$ IAR; IC $+1 \rightarrow$ IC
42	—	$MB_{0-24} \rightarrow$ IC
43	—	IC $\rightarrow$ MA; $0 \rightarrow$ IAR
.	.	.
.	.	.
.	.	.

9.29.

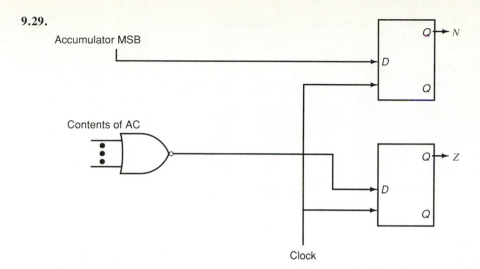

Accumulator MSB

Contents of AC

Clock

9.35. $X_0, X_2, \ldots, X_8 \rightarrow Y$

CHAPTER 10

10.1. In brief, single-accumulator structures allow somewhat simpler control logic; on the other hand, they cause rather inflexible programming relative to multiple-accumulator machines.

10.5. We need two accesses to the high-speed memory and one to the large memory; thus, $0.25(2) + 0.5 = 1.0\mu s$ are needed once the instruction is fetched.

10.7. Seven. One code says "no indexing"; the remaining seven codes are available for selecting an index register.

10.9.

Address	Index	Op code	Operand address
0	1	SIR	6
1	1	CAD	300
2	0	MUL	310
3	0	STO	310
4	1	BRI	1
5	0	HLT	0

We must initialize location 310 to 1 for this to work.

CHAPTER 11

11.5. The PDP-11, in brief, has essentially the same addressing modes as the 68000.

11.15. ADD   R1,R3

MOV   R3,63

11.19. The index registers are automatically advanced or decreased by 1, allowing forward or backward movements through fixed-size arrays to take place more easily.

11.21. Here is the machine code:

Location	Machine code		Instruction	
50	CE 00 79		LDX	#$79
53	86 20		LDAA	#$20
55	30	BLKC	LEAX	1,X
56	A1		CMPA	0,X
57	27 FC		BEQ	BLKC
59	DF 55		STX	$55

11.27. Extended addressing involves a 16-bit address anywhere in memory. Implied addressing requires no address specification; it is implied by the instruction. Relative addressing involves a signed byte displacement relative to the program counter.

11.29. The ADDA instruction adds the accumulator to a second operand, usually in memory, whereas the ADCA adds the accumulator to a second operand and also adds in the value of the c flip-flop.

11.35. Stacks in the 80786 grow to lower addresses, that is, down in memory. So a PUSH instruction places data on top of the stack and then decrements the stack pointer; a POP increments the stack pointer after removing the requested data.

11.39. LDA and STA load and store, respectively, directly to and from memory and the A register.

CHAPTER 12

12.1. About 1.5 mA

12.3. About 850 mV

12.5. OUT will be at -7 V, and almost no current will flow

12.7. About 70

12.9. $+2.4$ V

12.11.

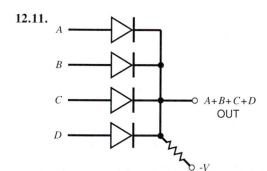

12.15. Emitter at 0.5–0.7 V, collector the same

12.17. $T2$ and $T3$

12.29. Less power consumption, greater packing density

BIBLIOGRAPHY

Alford, R. C.: *Programmable Logic Designer's Handbook*. Howard W. Sams, Indianapolis, 1989.

Andrews, M.: *Computer Organization*. Computer Science Press, Rockville, Md., 1987.

Baer, J. L.: *Computer System Architecture*. Computer Science Press, Potomac, Md., 1980.

Bic, L., and A. Shaw: *The Logical Design of Operating Systems*. Prentice-Hall, Englewood Cliffs, N.J., 1988.

"Cache Subsystems," in *80386 Hardware Reference Manual*. Intel, Santa Clara, Ca., 1987.

Desrochers, G.: *Principles of Parallel Multiprocessing*. McGraw-Hill, New York, 1987.

"8085AH-2/8085AH-1 8-Bit HMOS Microprocessor," Intel, Santa Clara, Ca., 1981.

"8087 Numeric Data Coprocessor" Intel (Data Sheet 205835), Santa Clara, Ca., October 1984.

80386 Programmer's Reference Manual. Intel, Santa Clara, Ca., 1986.

El-Ayat, K., and R. Agarwal: "The Intel 80386—Architecture and Implementation," *IEEE Micro*, December 1985.

Flynn, M., J. Johnson, and S. Wakefield: "On Instruction Sets and Their Formats," *IEEE Transactions on Computers*, March 1985.

Freer, J.: *Systems Design with Advanced Microprocessors*. Howard W. Sams, Indianapolis, 1989.

Freese, R.: "Optical Disks Become Erasable," *IEEE Spectrum*, February 1988.

Furht, B., and V. Milutinovic: "A Survey of Microprocessor Architectures for Memory Management," *IEEE Computer*, March 1987.

Hamacher, V., Z. Vranesic, and S. Zaky: *Computer Organization*. McGraw-Hill, New York, 1984.

Hayes, J.: *Computer Architecture and Organization*, 2d ed. McGraw-Hill, New York, 1988.

iAPX 86, 88, 186, 188 Hardware Reference Manual. Intel, Santa Clara, Ca.

"IEEE Standard Graphic Symbols for Logic Functions," 1984.

"IEEE Standard for Binary Floating-Point Arithmetic" (ANSI/IEEE Order 953CN), 1985.

Kane, G.: *MIPS R2000RISC Architecture*. Prentice-Hall, Englewood Cliffs, N.J., 1988.

Kelly-Bootle, S.: *68000 Programming by Example*. Howard W. Sams, Indianapolis, 1988.

Krutz, R.: *Interfacing Techniques in Digital Design with Emphasis on Microprocessors*. Wiley, New York, 1988.

Leventhal, L.: *80386 Programming Guide*. Bantam Books, New York, 1989.

Lilja, D.: "Reducing the Branch Penalty in Pipelined Processors," *IEEE Computer*, July 1988.

McCluskey, E. J.: *Logic Design Principles*, Prentice-Hall, Englewood Cliffs, N.J., 1986.

Microcomputer Programmable Logic Handbook. Intel, Santa Clara, Ca., 1989.

Microprocessor and Peripheral Handbook. Intel, Santa Clara, Ca., 1988.

Milutinovic, V. M., ed.: *Computer Architecture*. North-Holland Press, New York, 1988.

Morse, S., and D. Albert: *The 80386/387 Architecture*. Wiley, New York, 1987.

Motorola: *MC68030 Users Manual*. Prentice Hall, Englewood Cliffs, N.J., 1985.

Motorola: *MC68000 Users Manual*. Motorola Inc., 1980.

Pappas, C. H., and W. H. Murray: *80386 Microprocessor Handbook*. Osborne McGraw-Hill, Berkeley, Ca., 1989.

Pohm, A., and O. Agrawal: *High-Speed Memory Systems*. Reston Publishing Co., Reston, Va., 1983.

Slater, M.: *Microprocessor-based Design*. Prentice-Hall, Englewood Cliffs, N.J., 1989.

Stone, H.: *High-Performance Computer Architecture*. Addison-Wesley, Reading, Ma., 1987.

Tabak, D.: *RISC Architecture*. Wiley, New York, 1987.

Van de Goor, A. J.: *Computer Design and Architecture*. Addison-Wesley, Reading, Ma., 1989.

INDEX

Abacus, 21
Absolute accuracy, digital-to-analog conversion, 349
Absolute loader, 11
Access, types of (random or sequential), 245
Access arm, magnetic disk, 276
Access rights, 304
Access time:
  magnetic disk, 278
  memory, 7, 245
Accumulator(s), 12, 191, 214
Accuracy:
  analog-to-digital conversion, 347
  digital-to-analog conversion, 349
Active region mode of transistor, 555
ADD line, 197, 198
Add-and-shift algorithm, 232
Adder, 193–197, 200–205
  arithmetic, 193–206
  in binary system, 24
  in binary-coded-decimal system, 34, 206–209
  Boolean, 56
  in complement systems, 31–33
  high-speed, 229, 231–232, 233, 234
Address, 245, 383
  vs. contents, 246
  in instruction, 12–13, 421–422, 453–456
  symbolic referencing of, 17
Address line, 259
Address part, 418
Address register (see Memory address register)
Address translation, 298
ADDRESS VALID line, 388
Addressing:
  input-output device, 389–391
  register, 453, 454–455
  techniques of, 457–469
Aiken, Howard, 1
Air traffic control system, 5
Airline reservation system, 3, 5, 323
Algebra, modern (see Boolean algebra)
Algebra of sets, 55
Algebraic formula, progamming of, 56
Algorithm, arithmetic, 212, 213

Alphanumeric code (see Character code)
Alphanumeric displays, 333
ALU (see Arithmetic-logic unit)
Ambiguous output, analog-to-digital conversion, 352
American Standard Code for Information Interchange (ASCII), 45–46, 342, 345
Analog device, data collection from, 346–347, 361–366
Analog multiplexer (AMUX), 365–366
Analog quantities, 5
Analog-to-digital (A/D) conversion, 346, 350–361
Analog-to-digital converter (ADC), 5, 346, 350–351
AND gate, 57–59
  wired, 103–106
AND operation, 224
Aperture time, sample-and-hold amplifier, 365
Applications programming:
  business and scientific, 1, 8–12
  flowcharting of, 8
Arabic numerals, 21
Archival storage, 292
Arithmetic:
  fixed-point, 38
  floating-point, 40, 44–45
  high-speed, 229, 231–236
Arithmetic element, generalized, 212, 213–214
Arithmetic operations, 190–236
  algorithms for, 211, 213
  in binary system, 22–24
  controlling, 424–430
  execution of, 424–430
  with floating-point numbers, 44–45
Arithmetic register, 425
Arithmetic-logic unit (ALU), 7, 190, 343
  basic operations, 211–224
  construction of, 191
  logical operations, 224–225
Array programmer, 117n
Assembler directive, 506
Assembler program, 8, 10–11
Assembly language:
  coding example, 18

relation to machine language, 8, 16–17
Assignment problem, 175
Associative cache, 308
Associative law, 57, 63
Associative memory, 299, 300
Asynchronous bus, 385–389
Asynchronous operation, 136
Asynchronous transmission, 344–345
Audio cassette, 286
Auxiliary memory, 244

B box, 466
Babbage, Charles, 1
Baby boards, 343
Back plane, 343
Backup, Winchester disk, 286
Backup memory, 244
Balanced multiplicative decoder network,
    252, 253
Bartee, T. C., 175n, 438n
Base, transistor, 553
Base address, 295
Base in number systems, 22
Based indexed addressing, 492
BASIC, 8, 19
Batch processing, 3
Bell, Gordon, 507
Binary (*see* Flip-flop)
Binary counter, 145–150
Binary half-adder, 193
Binary operation, 59
Binary sequence detector, 166
Binary system:
    arithmetic operations in, 22–24
    bistable device and, 22
    complements in, 33–35
    conversion of: to hexadecimal system,
        37–38, 39
    to octal system, 36, 37
    division in, 25–26
    multiplication in, 24–25, 214–219
Binary up-down counter, 149
Binary-coded-decimal (BCD) adder, 202–205
Binary-coded-decimal (BCD) code, 34
Binary-coded-decimal (BCD) counter, 150–152
Binary-coded-decimal (BCD) system:
    multiplication in, 25–26
    number representation in, 33–35, 206–209
    reasons for use of, 33–34
Biphase-mark recording technique, 314
Bipolar logic, 156
Bipolar transistor, 553, 569
Birkhoff, G., 175n
Bistable device:
    and binary system, 22
    flip-flop as, 133

Bit line, 266
Bit map, 334
Bit times, 345
Bits, words composed of, 191
Black box, gate as, 57
Blank, zero, 160
Block, magnetic tape, 282
Block diagram, of gate network, 70
Block number, 307
Block set associative technique, 308
Boole, George, 55
Boolean algebra, 55–117
    basic laws of, 62–65
    derivation of an expression, 66–69
    duality of, 66
    fundamental concepts of, 56–57
    gate network design using, 70
Branch instruction:
    conditional, 14, 434, 469
    operation of, 15–16, 433–435
    in pipelining, 477–479
    unconditional, 14, 434, 469
Bridging circuit, 202
Bubble memory, 287
Burroughs 1700, 456
Burroughs 5500, 456
Bus:
    connecting keyboard to, 343–344
    connecting main memory and CPU,
        259–263, 264
    connecting printer to, 410–412
    control of, 383–385
    format and operation of, 383–389
    interface to, 373, 378–383
    standard, 399–404
    sharing lines on, 378–380
Bus interface unit (BIU), 535
Bus master, 383, 402
Business applications:
    output devices for, 322
    vs. scientific applications, 452–453
Bus-limited speed, 378
Byte:
    in computer organization, 38
    in direct mapping, 308
    represented in hexidecimal number system, 37
Byte-addressable memory, 289

Cable, connection by, 372–373
Cache memory, 292, 304–309
Calculus of propositions, 55
Caldwell, S. H., 62n
Calling program, 474
Canonical expansion, 67
Capacitor in dynamic random-access memory,
    266

Card, punched (*see* Punched card)
Carry, 193–194
  in addition, 24
  delay in, 201
  end-around, 195
CARRY line, 151
Carry propagation delay, 232
Carry-look-ahead circuit, 202
Carry-overs, 24
Carry-ripple problem, 201
Cassette drive, 286
Cathode-ray-tube (CRT) display, 3, 331–336
  refreshing, 333
  scanning, 332
Central processing unit (CPU):
  computer components controlled by, 372–373
  and main memory, connecting by bus,
    259–263, 264
Chain printer, 338
Channel:
  FET, 571
  I/O, 284
  magnetic tape, 284
  punched paper tape, 327
Channel program, 378
Character code:
  BCD and EBCDIC, 46
  error-detecting, 17, 342–343
  printer, 337
  punched card, 329
  punched paper tape, 327–329
  standardized codes, 45–46, 342
Character recognition devices, 329–331
Character-at-a-time printer, 338–339
Characteristic (exponent) in floating-point
    system, 40, 41
Charge-coupled device (CCD) as secondary
    memory, 287–288
Check bit, 342
Chip (*see* Integrated circuit)
Circuit(s):
  design of, register transfer language for,
    438–441
  principles and technology of, 551–557
  (*See also* Integrated circuit; Logic circuit)
Circuit board, connection using, 52
Circuit lines (*see* Integrated-circuit lines)
Clock:
  and memory cycle, 421
  usefulness of, 136
  waveform, 136–137
Clock pulse, 136
Clocked flip-flop, 138
  latch, 140
Cobol, 8, 19
Coding in programming process, 8

Collector, transistor, 553
Combinational network, 69, 166
  (*See also* Gate network)
Communications:
  character codes used in, 345
  serial transmission of, 344–346
  speed of, 345
  terminal in, 322–323
Commutative law, 63
Compact disk read-only memory (CD-ROM), 288
Comparator:
  in analog-to-digital converter, 354
Compiler, 8, 11
Compiler language, 18
Complement, 147
  in binary-coded-decimal system, 33–35
  forming of, in adder, 197
  to represent a negative number, 28–33
Complementary MOS (CMOS) technology,
    154, 574–577
Complementation, logical, performed by
    inverter, 59–60
Complementer in BCD adder, 207
Complex instruction set computer (CISC),
    479–480
Computer architecture, 453
Computer industry:
  growth of, 2
  history of, 1–3
Computer systems, types of, 3–5
Computer word structures, 289–290
Computer-aided design (CAD), 182
Computer-independent language, 19
Computers:
  applications for, 1, 3–6
  arithmetic operations basic to, 190
  components of, 6–8
  connection of, 372–373
  (*See also specific components*)
  control unit's function in, 7, 417
  design of, 55–56
  early, 1–3
  generations of, 2
  instructions for controlling
    (*see* Instruction(s), machine)
  large and small, compared, 375
  organization of, 375–378
Condition codes, 469–470, 504
Conditional operation, 213
Connection:
  by cable, 372–373
  of computer components, 259–263, 264
  of integrated circuit, 152–158
  of programmable array logic, 177–178
Content-addressable memory, 298
Control line, 389

Control memory, 443
Control register, 425
   sequence of operation of, 423–424
Control signal:
   microprogramming of, 441–442
   sequencing of, 428–429, 430–433
Control system, 5–6
   data collection in, 346–347
Control unit, 7, 417
Control wire, 259
Controller module (bus), 402
Conventional current, 553
Conversion:
   binary to hexadecimal, 37–38, 39
   binary to octal, 36, 37
   decimal to binary, 26–27
   decimal to octal, 36, 37
   hexadecimal to decimal, 37–38, 39
   octal to decimal, 36, 37
Copy-back cache memory, 307
Cost vs. speed compromise, 245
Counter:
   BCD, 150–152
   binary, 149
   design of, 163–166
   shift instruction controlled by, 435–438
Counter ADC, 357–359
Counter design table, 163
Counter table of sequence of states, 155
Counting in binary system, 22–23
CRAY computers, 456
Cross-coupling, gate, 140
Crosstalk, 279
Current, conventional, 553
Current enhancement mode, FET, 572
Current-mode logic (CML) (*see*
   Emitter-coupled logic)
Current-steering logic (*see* Emitter-coupled
   logic)
Custom chip, 108, 181
Cutoff mode of transistor, 555–556
Cycle stealing, 374
Cycle time (*see* Memory cycle)
Cylinder printer, 339

D flip-flop, 140, 148–150
D latch, 140, 141
Daisy wheel printer, 339
Data bus (IEEE-488 bus interface), 399
Data collection (acquisition):
   from analog device, 361–366
   in real-time control systems, 346–347
Data entry, input devices for, 322–331
DATA VALID and DATA RECEIVED lines,
   337–338
Data wire, 259

DC RESET line, 145
Debouncing, in keyboard design, 327
Decade counter (*see* Binary-coded-decimal
   counter)
Decimal system, 21–22
   complement in, for negative number, 28–33
   conversion of: to binary system, 26–27
   to octal system, 36, 37
Decoder, 248, 251–254
Decoder matrix, 251
Degree of associativity, 308
Delay time, 144n
De Morgan's theorems, 65–66, 91, 95
Demand paging, 297
Density, 286
Design of computers, 55–56
Device number, 404
Differential amplifier, 567
Digital cassette, 286
Digital recording technique, 309–315
Digital-to-analog (D/A) conversion, 347
Digital-to-analog converter (DAC), 5, 347–350,
   577–579
Dimensionality of main memory, 254–259
Diode:
   gate, 557–559
   in programmable array logic, 111
   semiconductor, 552
Direct addressing, 457–461
Direct mapped cache memory, 305–307
Direct mapping, 307, 308
Direct memory access (DMA), 374
Direct-access storage device (DASD), 245n,
   279, 293
Directed graph, 168
Disk (*see* Floppy disk; Magnetic disk)
Displacement, 295, 297
Display device, 322
Distributive law, 63, 64
Division:
   in binary system, 25–26, 220–224
   restoring technique for, 221
Don't-care outputs, 86–87
Dot matrix printer, 339
Double words, 290
Drive, magnetic disk, 280
Droop, sample-and-hold amplifier, 365
Drop-on-demand ink jet technology, 341
Dropout, 343
Drum printer, 338
Dual in-line package (DIP), 152
Dump, hexadecimal and octal, 37
Duodecimal system, 22
Dwords, 290
Dynamic random-access memory (DRAM),
   266–271

E flip-flop, 423
EBCDIC (extended binary-code-decimal interchange code), 46
Eckert, S. P., 2
Edge, square wave, 136
Edge-triggered flip-flop, 138n
Edsac, 2
Edvac, 2
Effective address size prefix, 539
8, 4, 2, 1 BCD character, 34, 208, 209
Electrically alterable ROM (EAROM), 275
Electrically erasable programmable ROM (EEPROM), 275
Electroluminescent (EL) displays, 336
Electromagnetic printer, 340
Electrostatic paper, 340
Electrostatic printer, 340, 341
Emitter, transistor, 553
Emitter-coupled logic (ECL), 567, 569, 570
Emitter-coupled logic (ECL) circuit, NOR gate in, 568
Emulation, 447n
Enabling, 147
Encoding from keyboard, 323, 325
End-around carry, 195
Eniac, 2
Equivalent circuit:
  NAND gate, 91–93
  NOR gate, 96–98
Erasable and reprogrammable ROM (EPROM), 275
Error-correcting code, 342–343
Error-detecting code, 17, 342–343
Even parity, 342
Excess-3 code, 36
Exclusive OR operation (*see* Sum modulo 2 operation)
Execution cycle, 421
Execution of instructions, 12–13, 421–433
Execution unit, 535
Exponent (characteristic) in floating-point system, 38
Expression(s):
  algebraic, 56
  high-level language, 18–19
  logical: evaluation of, 60–62
    simplification of, 65
Extended binary-coded-decimal interchange code (EBCDIC), 46
Extended direct-addressing instructions, 459
Extract masking operation, 224

Fairchild 10,000 series, 568, 569
Falling edge, 136
Fan-out, 567

Field-effect transistor (FET), 156, 553, 569, 571–574
Field-programmable gate arrays, 181
Field-programmable logic array (FPLA), 109, 111n, 181
Field-programmable logic sequencer (FPLS), 181
Field-programmable ROM (PROM), 275n
Files, 10
Finite state machine, 171n, 174
Firmware, 447
Fixed-head magnetic disk, 278
Fixed-point operation, 38
Flag bit, 470
Flag register, 473–474
Flagged copy-back, 307
Flat panel displays, 336–337
Flatbed plotters, 337
Flash converter, 354–357
Flat pack, 153
Flexible disk, 280
Flip-flop(s):
  as bistable device, 133
  characteristics of, 132–135
  clock input of, 136–138
  design of, 138–144
  gates used in, 139–140, 142
  on integrated circuit, 152–158
  in logic design, 132–135
  master-slave, 142–144
  memory constructed from, 133–135
  in shift register, 144–145
  standard conventions to describe, 133
  state of, 133, 134, 168
  in transfer circuit, 135
Floating-point operation, 40, 44–45
Floating-point routines, 40
Floating-point system, 38–45
Floppy disk, 279, 280–281
Flowchart, 8
Flying head magnetic disk, 279
Forbidden input, 140
Formula, algebraic, programming of, 56
Fortran, 8, 19, 486
Forward-biased diode, 553
4-bit arithmetic-logic unit, 227, 228
Four-stage counter, 147
Fraction:
  in binary system, 23
  decimal, conversion of, to binary, 27
  hexadecimal, conversion of, 38
Fraction (mantissa) in floating-point system, 41
Full adder, 194–195, 200–202, 232
Full-screen editors, 10
Fused connection:
  of programmable array logic, 178
  of programmable logic array, 115

Gate(s):
  cross-coupling, 140
  defined in terms of input and output signal, 57
  design using, 139–142
  diode, 557–559
  FET, 571
  flip-flops made from, 139–140, 142
  on integrated circuit, 106, 153
  interconnecting, 69–70
Gate array, 181
Gate network, 55–117
  design of, using Boolean algebra, 69–70
  (*See also* AND gate; NAND gate; NOR gate)
Gated flip-flop, 139–140, 142
Gated-clocked binary counter, 147
General interface management bus (IEEE-488 bus interface), 399
General registers, 191
General-purpose registers, 453
Generations, computer, 2
Generic array logic (GAL), 181
Graphics display, 333–334
Gray code (unit-distance code), 271, 352–353
Ground of integrated circuit, 154

Half words, 290
Half-adder, 193
Hall-effect keyboards, 327
Handshake, 388
Handwriting, optical character reading of, 330
Hard array logic (HAL), 112
Hard copy:
  in interactive systems, 4
  from keyboarded input, 327
Hard copy terminal, 4
Hard disk, 279
Harvard recording technique, 314
Head:
  floppy disk, 280
  magnetic disk, 278, 279
Header field, 11
Hexadecimal number system, 37–38, 39
  uses of, 37
Hidden 1 principle, 42
High-level language, 8, 18–19
High-speed arithmetic, 229, 231–236
High-speed memory (*see* Main memory)
Hollerith code, 329
Home computer (*see* Microcomputer)
Horizontal microprogramming, 445
Huntington, E. V., 62n

I flip-flop, 423
IBM:
  early computers, 2

floating-point operations in computers by, 41–42
360 series, 2
IEEE Standard for Binary Floating-Point Arithmetic, 42
IEEE-488 bus interface, 399
Immediate addressing, 461–463
Impact printer, 339
Inclusive OR circuit, 559
Index register, 466
Indexed addressing, 466–469, 505
Indirect addressing, 465–466
Industry standard bus, 399
Information security, 480
Ink jet printer, 340
Inner memory (*see* Main memory)
Input device:
  as computer component, 7
  for data entry, 322–332
Input signal:
  of gate, 57
  multiple, 58
Input-output (I/O):
  isolated, 389
  memory-mapped, 389, 391–394
Input-output device:
  addressing of, 389–391
  analog, 346–347, 361–366
  connecting to bus, 374
  device number, 386
  interrupt in, 395–399
  polling, 396
Input-output machine instruction, 391–392
Input-output processor, 375
Input-output statement in high-level language, 18–19
Instruction(s), machine:
  address in, 12–13, 453–455
  execution of, 12–13, 421–433
  format of, 12, 453–456
  length of, 456–457
  in memory, 453–455
  privileged, 519
  queued, 490
  representation of, 456–457
  types of, 14–16
  (*See also specific instructions*)
Instruction counter, 422–423
Instruction cycle, 421–424
Instruction decode unit, 535
Instruction prefetch unit, 535
Instruction word, 417–421
Instructions, 11
Integer part (mantissa) in floating-point system, 40
Integer representation system, 191–193

Integrated circuit (IC):
  connecting, 152–158
  container, 107, 108, 152–153
  custom chips, 108, 181
  design with, 152–166
  gate network implementation using, 106, 153
  ground of, 154
  historical introduction of, 2
  manufacture of, 158–162
  manufacturers' specifications for, 159–160
  NAND gates on, 93
  pin out of, 106
  power supply of, 154
  technology of, 152
Integrated-circuit (IC) lines, 155–157
  comparison of, table, 157
Integrated-circuit (IC) memory (*see*
    Random-access memory)
Intel 8080 chip, 389, 390, 391, 404, 487–488
  description and instructions for, 457–458,
    461, 465–466
Intel 8086/8088 chips, 301, 389, 391, 397,
    404, 488, 490–496
  description and instructions for, 495
Intel 80386/80486, description and instructions
    for, 461, 463, 466, 468–469, 534–546
Interactive systems, 3
Interblock gap, magnetic tape, 282
Interface board, keyboard, 343
Interface to bus, 372
  standard, 399–404
Interfacing:
  a keyboard, 404–410
  a printer, 410–412
Interleaving, 304–305
Interpreters, 11
Interrupt:
  generating, 396, 476
  from input-output device, 395–399
  mask, 473
  servicing, 395–396, 476
Interrupt line, 374
Interrupt service program, 476
Inverter, 557
  complementation performed by, 59–60
Inverter circuit, 59
Isolated input-output, 389

JK flip-flop, 148, 165, 167
Job in batch processing, 3
Jump instruction (*see* Branch instruction)

Karnaugh map, 78–79
Kerr rotation, 288–289
Key rollover protection, in keyboard design,
  327

Keyboard:
  connecting to bus, 343–344
  construction of, 323
  encoding from, 323, 325
  interface board, 326
  interfacing, 404–410
  of paper tape punch, 327
  program control of keyboard interface,
    409–410
  of terminal, 323–324
Keyboard status word, 406
Keyboarding:
  hard copy from, 327
  of punched paper tape, 327
Keypad, 323
Keypunch (card-punch machine), 327

Language:
  assembly, 8, 16–17, 18
  computer-independent, 19
  high-level, 8, 18–19
  in programming process, 8–12
  register transfer, 438–441
Large-scale integration (LSI), 3, 108n, 159,
  569
  design problems in, 106
Laser printer, 340–341
Latch, 140
Latency delay, 278
Leading edge, 136
Least recently used algorithm, 293, 308
Least significant bit (LSB), digital-to-analog
  conversion, 347
Lebow, I. L., 438n
Light-emitting diode (LED), 336
Lights as an output device, 336
Line editors, 10
Line printer, 337
Linear recurring sequence generator, 154n
Linear shift register, 154n
Linear virtual memories, 294
Linear-select memory, 248–251
Lines, IC (*see* Integrated-circuit lines)
Link, directed graph, 168
Linking of programs, 10
Listener, 402
Load, standard, 157
Loader, 11
Logic circuit, generalized, 57–59
  (*See also* Gate network)
Logic design:
  gates and flip-flops used in, 132–135
  integrated circuits used in, 152–158
Logic networks, 69
Logical addition, 56
Logical expressions, 60–62, 65

Logical multiplication, 57
Logical operation in arithmetic-logic unit,
    8, 16–17
Lower byte, 394

McCluskey, Ed, 175n
Machine language, relation to assembly
    language, 8, 16–17
Macintosh portable computer, 375–376
Macro, 10–11
Magnetic bubble memory, 287–288
Magnetic character reader, 330
Magnetic disk:
  changeable and fixed, 278
  construction of, 280
  as memory element, 275–279
  speed and capacity of, 276
Magnetic ink character reading (MICR), 330
Magnetic tape:
  advantages of, 282
  construction of, 282–286
  layout of, 285
  offline printing from, 337
Magnetic tape device, construction of,
    283, 284
Magneto-optic technology, 288, 290
Magnitude bit, 191
Main memory, 244
  construction of, 248–251, 263–275
  and CPU, connecting by bus, 259–263, 264
  dimensionality of, 254–259
  and number of components needed to
    construct, 254–255
  organization of, by words, 245–246
  reading and writing of, 246–247
Manchester Mark I, 2n
Manchester recording technique, 314
Mantissa in floating-point system, 38
  fraction form, 40–41
  integer part, 40
Manual procedures, mechanization of, 3–4
Many-to-one decoder, 251
Map method for simplication of gate network
    expressions, 78–81
Mark (communications), 345n
Mask, interrupt, 473
Mask in IC manufacturing process, 111
Masking operation, 224
Mask-programmable ICs, 181
Master-slave flip-flop, 138n, 142–144
Mauchly, J. W., 2
Mealy, George, 175n
Mealy machine, 174–175
Mechanization of manual procedures, 3–4
Medium-scale integration (MSI), 108n, 159
Memory:

as computer component, 7
construction of, 248–251, 263–275
flip-flop used to construct, 133–135
instruction in, 453–455
operations affecting, 263–271
organization of, 245, 254–259
speed vs. cost compromise, 245
program in, 3, 7
protection, 480
terminology to describe, 244–245
Memory address register (MAR), 247, 248,
    421, 423
Memory buffer register, 247, 421
MEMORY ENABLE (ME), 259
Memory management unit (MMU), 292
Memory module, packaged, 247
Memory-mapped input-ouput, 389, 391–394
Metal-oxide semiconductor (MOS) technology,
    156, 569, 571–574
Microcomputer:
  interactive nature of, 3
  interface layout, 343–344
  uses of, 452
Microoperations, 439, 441
Microprocessor:
  chip development, 487
  chip sets, in computers, calculators, etc.,
    343n, 452
Microprogamming, 441–448
Minicomputer, uses of, 452
Minimization, 87–91, 418
  (*See also* Simplification of expressions for
    gate networks)
Minterm of Karnaugh map, 78–81
Miss ratio, 305
Mnemonic operation codes, 16
Mod r/m byte, 539
Modem, 4, 346
Module (disk pack), 279n
Modulo 8 counter, 147
Modulo 16 counter, 147
Monolithic integrated circuitry, 158
Monotonic output, digital-to-analog conversion,
    349
Moore, Edward, 174, 175n
Moore machine, 174
MOSFET (metal-oxide semiconductor
    field-effect transistor), 571
Most significant bit (MSB), digital-to-analog
    conversion, 347
Motherboards, 343
Motorola emitter-coupled logic (MECL), 568,
    569
Motorola 6800 chip, 496
  description and instructions for, 458–459,
    462, 463–464, 467, 468

Motorola 68000 chip, 392–394, 496
  description and instructions for, 517–534
Movable-head magnetic disk, 278
Multimaster bus, 402
Multiple registers, 453
Multiplexer, 227, 229, 230, 365–366
Multiplexer channel, 375
Multiplication:
  binary, 24–25, 214–219
  Boolean, 57
  decimal, 219–220
  high-speed, 232, 235–236
  instruction, 14
  logical, 57
Multiprocessor, 375, 379, 380
Multiprogamming, 294, 375
Multitasking operating systems, 12, 294
Multiuser operating systems, 12

n-channel metal-oxide semiconductor (NMOS)
    technology, 572, 574
n-type semiconductor material, 551
NAND gate, 75–78
  design using, 91–95
  equivalent circuit for, 91–93
  multiple-input, 91
NAND-to-AND gate, design using, 100–101
National Bureau of Standards, 399
Negative bit, 470
Negative number, representation of, 27–28
  in BCD system, 33–35
  use of complements, 28–33
Negative-edge clocked flip-flop, 138
Negative-going edge, 136
Next-address control signal in
    microprogramming, 443
9s complement, 29, 206–209
NMOS (n-channel metal-oxide semiconductor)
    technology, 572, 574
Node, directed graph, 168
Noise margin, 566
Nondestructive read, 246
Nonimpact printer, 340
Nonrepresentable number, 197
Nonrestoring technique for division, 221
Nonreturn-to-zero mark (NRZI) recording
    technique, 313
Nonreturn-to-zero (NRZ) recording technique,
    310, 313–315
Nonsaturating logic (see Emitter-coupled logic)
NOR gate, 75–78
  design using, 95–99
  in emitter-coupled logic circuit, 568
  equivalent circuit for, 96–98
  multiple-input, 96–97
NOR-to-OR gate, design using, 102–103

Normalized form in floating-point system, 42
npn transistor, 159, 553–554, 557
Number-crunching computers, 453
Number representation system:
  binary-coded-decimal (BCD) systems,
    33–35, 206–209
  complement systems, 28–33
  floating-point, 40
  integer, 191–193
  signed-magnitude, 40, 192
  for very large or very small numbers, 38

Object program, 10
Octal number system, 35–36
Odd parity, 323, 329, 342
Offline printing of magnetic tape, 337
Offset, 295, 297
Offsetting a signal, 366
1s complement system, 31–32
OP code (operation code), 423
  mnemonic, 16
OP-code register, 423
Open-collector output, 104
Operand, 10
Operating systems, 10, 11–12
  protection of, 480
Operation(s):
  arithmetic (see Arithmetic operations)
  conditional, 213
  fixed-point, 38
  floating-point, 40, 44–45
  logical, 224–227
  memory-type, 263–271
  register, 244
  singular vs. binary, 59
Operation code (OP code), 423
  mnemonic, 16
Operation code (OP code) register, 244
Optical character reading (OCR), 244
Optical storage devices, 288
OR gate, 57–59
  wired, 103–106, 251
OR operation, 224
Original equipment manufacturer (OEM)
    devices, 452
Oscilloscope display, 5, 331
Output device, 8
Output signal:
  of flip-flop, 133–134
  of gate, 57
Overflow, 196, 197, 198
Overrange feature in analog-to digital converter,
    350

p-channel metal oxide semiconductor (PMOS)
    technology, 574

p-type semiconductor material, 551, 572
Package, IC, 107, 108, 152–153
Packed (packaged) field, logical multiplication to extract, 57
Page fault, 297
Page frames, 297
Page table, 297
Paging (addressing technique), 270, 295
Paging unit, 536
Pallette, 334
Paper, thermal and electrostatic, 340
Paper tape, dimensions and layout of, 328
Paper tape punch, 327
Paper tape reader, 327
Parallel adder, 197–200
Parallel binary adder, 195–197
Parallel multiplier, 232, 235–236, 237
Parallel transmission, 344
Parentheses and evaluation of an expression, 60–62
Parity, 342–343
    magnetic tape, 284
    punched paper tape, 329
Parity-check code, 342
Pascal, 8, 19
PDP-8, 418
PDP-11, 507–510
    description and instructions for, 459–460, 462–463, 464–465, 511–514
Peripheral device (*see* Input-output device)
Peripheral processing unit (PPU), 378
Personal computer (*see* Microcomputer)
Phase-encoded recording technique, 314
Pin, integrated circuit, 152
Pin out, 106
Pipelining, 476–479
Pixel, 333–334, 335
PMOS (*p*-channel metal-oxide semiconductor) technology, 574
pnp transistor, 159, 557
Pointer, stack, 445
Pointer register, 522
Polling, 396
Popping the stack, 455
Positional notation, 21
Positive logic, 134
Positive-edge clocked flip-flop, 137
Positive-going edge, 136
Power supply of integrated circuit, 154
Precision:
    in analog-to-digital conversion, 347
    in floating-point system, 40
Pressure roll, magnetic tape device, 283
Prime implicant (PI), 84, 88
Principle of localized reference, 292

Print engine, 340
Print wheel, 337–338
Printed-circuit board, connecting integrated circuits on, 152
Printer(s), 74, 337–341
    connecting to bus, 410–412
    construction of, 339, 341
Priority for interrupt, 397
Privileged instruction, 519
Problem-oriented language, 18
Procedures, mechanization of, 3–4
Process, 12
    derivation of, 71–73
    for simplification of gate network expressions, 86–91
Product term, 67, 70
Product-of-sums expression, 71
Program(s):
    calling, 474
    in memory, 3, 7
    relocatable, 295, 457
    translation of (source to object), 8, 10–11
Program card (keypunch), 327
Program control of keyboard interface, 409–410
Program listings, 17
Programmable array logic (PAL), 108
    programming of, 177–178
    state machine implemented with, 176–181
Programmable interface, 399
Programmable logic array (PLA), 108
    program table for, 114, 116
    programming of, 112–117
Programmable ROM (PROM), 272, 275
Programmer, 111n
Programming:
    flowcharting in, 8
    of PLAs and PALs, 112–117, 177–178
    of read-only memory, 271–275
    steps in, 8–9
Programming system (*see* Language)
Proof by perfect induction, 61, 63, 64–65
Propositional calculus, 55
Protected mode, 472
Punched card:
    in batch processing, 3
    layout of, 329
Punched card (unit-record) machines, 1, 2
Punched paper tape, dimensions and layout of, 328
Pushing the stack, 455

Quantizing, analog-to-digital conversion, 350
Quarter-adder, 193
Queue, instruction, 490
Quinary system, 22
Quine-McCluskey minimization technique, 87–91

R flip-flop, 423
Race problem, 144
Radix (base), 22
Radix-minus-one complement, 30
Random access, 245
Random sequence generation, 154n
Random-access memory (RAM), 244, 245–247
    access time of, 245
    connecting to bus, 259–263
    technologies of, 263–271
Random-access storage device, 245
READ line, 386
Read mode, 472
Read-only access rights, 481
Read-only memory (ROM), 247, 271–275
    manufacture of, 272–274
    programming of, 271–275
    truth table realized by, 271–272
Read-write head:
    magnetic disk, 279
    magnetic tape device, 284, 286
Read-write line, 388
Read-write memory, 247
Real addresses, 294
Real memory, 294
Real-time control systems, 5
    automatic vs. semiautomatic, 5
    data collection in, 346–347
Record, magnetic tape, 282
Recording technique, 286
Recursive subprogram, 476
Reduced instruction set computer (RISC), 455,
    479–480
Redundancy and error-detecting code, 342
Reed, I. S., 62n, 438
Refreshing:
    cathode-ray tube (CRT), 333
    memory, 266
Region of ambiguity, 566
Register(s):
    address of, 453, 454–455
    basic operations with single or multiple, 453
    flip-flops in, 135
    as memory element, 247
    types and names of, 28
    (*See also specific registers*)
Register transfer language, 438–441
Relative addressing, 463–465
Relocatable program, 295, 457
Relocating loader, 11
Representable number, 197
RESET (R) line, flip-flop, 134, 145
Resolution, digital-to-analog conversion, 347
Rest period between clock pulses, 136
Restoring technique for division, 221
Restricted input, 140

Return-to-bias (RB) recording technique, 310,
    311–312
Return-to-zero (RZ) recording technique, 310,
    311
Reverse-biased diode, 553
Ring security system, 481
Ripple counter, 147
Rising edge, 136
Roman numerals, 21
Rotational delay, 278
RS flip-flop, 133, 135, 140, 148, 149
    waveform of, 141
RS latch, 141

Sample-and-hold amplifier, 363–365
Sampling in real-time control systems,
    363
Saturated mode of transistor, 555
Scaled index base byte, 539
Scaling, 556n
    in floating-point system, 40
Scanning, cathode-ray tube (CRT), 332
Schottky diode, 562–563
Scientific applications:
    and business applications, compared,
    452–453
    output devices for, 452
Scratchpad register, 465
Secondary memory, 244
Second-generation computers, 2
Second-generation TTL circuit, 560
Sectors, magnetic disk, 276–277
Security, 480–483
Security level, 481
Seek time, 278
Segment, 301
    base address, 302
    pointer, 295
    registers, 301, 537
    selector, 301
Segmentation, 295
Segmentation unit, 536
Segmented virtual memory, 294–295, 296
Select inputs, 365
Selector channel, 375
Semiconductor diode, 552
Semiconductor junction, 552
Semiconductor memory (*see* Random-access
    memory)
Semicustom fabrication processes, 178
Semisynchronous system, 389
Sequential access, 245
Sequential machine (*see* State machine)
Sequential magnitude comparator, 171–174
Sequential-access storage device, 245
Serial transmission, eleven-bit code, 344–346

Serial-access storage device, 245n
Series-parallel BCD adder, 207–208, 210
Set associative technique, 308
SET (S) line, flip-flop, 133
Settling time, sample-and-hold amplifier, 365
Seven-segment decoder, 160, 162
Shaft encoder, 338, 351–354
Shift instruction, 435–438
    operation of, 209, 211, 212
Shift register:
    with feedback, 154
    flip-flop in, 144–145
    magnetic bubble memory as, 287–288
Sign bit, 27–28, 191
Signal:
    control, microprogramming of, 441–442
    skewing, 324
    translating a, 366
    voltage and, 134
Signal conditioning, 366
Signed magnitude:
    in BCD system, 206–209
    in binary integer system, 192
Signed number (*see* Negative number)
Signed-integer binary system, 192
Signetics PLA, 113
Simplification of expressions for gate networks,
    65
    map method for, 78–81
    minimization, 418
Simulation, 446
Simultaneous converter, 354–357
Single-address instruction, 418
Single-user operating system, 11
Singular operation, 59
Size bit, 522
Skewing, signal, 324
Skip instruction (*see* Branch instruction)
Slave (bus), 384
Small-scale integration (SSI), 106, 108n
Smart terminal, 4, 322, 323
Smoothing in keyboard design, 327
Solid-state keyboard, 327
Source program, 10
Space (communications), 345n
Speed vs. cost compromise, 245
Speed-up of arithmetic, 229, 231–236
Sperry Rand, 2
Split-frequency recording technique, 314
Square wave, 136
Stack, 455–456
Stack pointer, 455
Staircase, digital-to-analog conversion, 347
Standard load, 157
Standard-cell devices, 181
Start bit, 345

Start character, magnetic tape, 282
State:
    analysis of, 166–171
    of flip-flop, 133, 134, 168
    sequence of, 155–156
        shown by counter table, 155
State diagram, 166
    formed from directed graph, 168
State machine, 171
    PAL implementation of, 176–181
State table, 166, 169–171
Statement, high-level language, 11
Static random-access memory (SRAM), 248,
    263–266
Status bit and branch instruction, 434n
Status register, 396
Status word generator interface for keyboard,
    406
Step-counter register, 437
Stone, M. H., 62n
Stop bit, 345
Stop character, magnetic tape, 282
Storage hierarchies, 290–293
Storage time delay, 562
Stored-program concept, 2
Streaming tape drive, 282n, 286
Subcube of Karnaugh map, 81, 82
    maximal, 83–84
Subprogram (subroutine) calling, 474–476
SUBTRACT line, 197–198
Subtraction:
    in BCD system, 34, 206–209
    in binary system, 24
    by parallel adder, 197–200
Successive-approximation ADC, 357, 359–361
Sum modulo 2 operation, 224
Sum term, 57n, 70–71
Sum-of-products expression, 67, 71
    derivation of, 71–73
    of gate network input, 70
    for simplifying gate network expressions, 71
Supercomputers, uses of, 3, 453
Supervisor mode, 472, 473, 481
Surface mounting, 159
Switching algebra (*see* Boolean algebra)
Symbolic referencing of addresses, 17
Sync pulse and recording technique, 315
Synchronous bus, 385–389
Synchronous operation, 136
Synchronous transmission, 344, 345–346
Systems programs, 9

Talker, 402
Tape, magnetic (*see* Magnetic tape)
Tape cartridge, 286
Tape cassette, 286

Tape transport, 282
Telephone system in communications, 346
10s complement, 29, 30, 206–209
Tension arm, magnetic tape device, 283
Terminal:
  communications standards for, 322–323
  construction of, 331–336
  CRT, 4, 322
  in interactive systems, 4
  keyboard of, 323–324
  typewriter-like, 327
Text editors, 10
Thermal paper, 340
Thermal printer, 340
Third-generation computers, 2
Three-input-variable expression, 73–75
Three-stage counter, 147
Three-state driver, 378, 382
Timesharing in interactive systems, 4–5, 294
Timing signal for memory cycle, 427
Toggle (*see* Flip-flop)
Totem pole circuit, 561
Trace bit, 473
Track, magnetic disk, 276
Tracking ADC, 359
Transfer bus (IEEE-488 bus interface), 399
Transfer circuit, flip-flop in, 135
Transfer instruction (*see* Branch instruction)
Transfer rate, 279
Transistor(s):
  in integrated circuits, 156–157
  types of, 551–557
Transistor-transistor logic (TTL), 559–564
  input-output levels and noise, 564–567
Transistor-transistor logic (TTL) circuit, 154
  wired OR and AND gate in, 104
Translating a signal, 366
Translation look-aside buffer (TLB), 300, 356
Translation program (assembler, compiler, etc.),
  8, 10–11
Translator, magnetic tape device, 282
Transmission:
  serial, 344–346
  synchronous, 344, 345–346
Transportable languages, 8
Traps, 476
Tree-type decoding network, 252
Trial division, 222
Tristate driver, 378
True complement, 30
True magnitude (*see* Signed magnitude)
Truth table:
  for gate network design, 60
  logical expression evaluated by, 60–61
  realized by read-only memory, 271–272
Turing machine, 174

2, 4, 2, 1 code, 34–35
Two-address instruction, 453
Two-dimensional selection system, 254
Two-level network, 71
2s complement system, 30, 31, 32–33
Typewriter terminal, 327

Unary operation, 59
Unit-distance code (Gray code), 271, 352–353
U.S. Board of the Census, 2
Univac, 2
User mode, 472, 481

Vacuum column, magnetic tape device, 282–283
Vacuum tubes in computers, 2
Variable(s):
  in Boolean algebra, 63
Vectored interrupt, 396
Veitch diagram, 78n
Vertical microprogramming, 445
Very large-scale integration (VLSI), 3, 108n, 159
Video display terminal (VDT), 4, 322
Virtual addresses, 294
Virtual memory, 293–296
  example of, 302–304
  implementing segmented, 301–302
  paged, 297–301
Virtual pages, 297
Voltage:
  of analog device, 347
  and signal, 134
Von Neumann, John, 2

W flip-flop, 423
Wafer (*see* Integrated circuit)
Waveform:
  sampling, 364
  square wave, 136
Weight, digital-to-analog conversion, 347
Weighted binary code, 34
Winchester disk, 279
  backup of, 286
Wired OR and AND gate, 103–106, 251
Word length, 245
Working set, 293
Workstation, 4, 182
Worst-case high/low input, 565
WRITE line, 247
Write-through cache memory, 307

X/Y plotters, 337

Zero, floating-point representation of, 44
Zero blanking, 160
Zero-address instruction, 470
Zerobit, 470